NEW MERMAIDS

General editors:
William C. Carroll, Boston University
Brian Gibbons, University of Münster
Tiffany Stern, University of Oxford

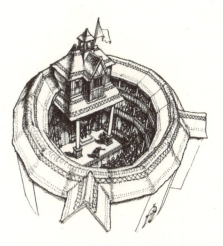

Reconstruction of an Elizabethan theatre
by C. Walter Hodges

NEW MERMAIDS

THOMAS MIDDLETON
FOUR PLAYS

THE ROARING GIRL
Edited by Elizabeth Cook

A CHASTE MAID IN CHEAPSIDE
Edited by Alan Brissenden
Adelaide University

WOMEN BEWARE WOMEN
Edited by William C. Carroll
Boston University

THE CHANGELING
Edited by Michael Neill
University of Auckland

NEW MERMAIDS

THOMAS MIDDLETON

FOUR PLAYS

THE ROARING GIRL
A CHASTE MAID IN CHEAPSIDE
WOMEN BEWARE WOMEN
THE CHANGELING

Introduction by William C. Carroll

methuen | drama

LONDON · NEW YORK · OXFORD · NEW DELHI · SYDNEY

METHUEN DRAMA
Bloomsbury Publishing Plc
50 Bedford Square, London, WC1B 3DP, UK

BLOOMSBURY, METHUEN DRAMA and the Methuen Drama logo are trademarks
of Bloomsbury Publishing Plc

First published in Great Britain 2012
Reprinted 2018

CONTENTS

ACKNOWLEDGEMENTS

This anthology, *Thomas Middleton: Four Plays*, brings together the texts and commentaries from individual plays in the current New Mermaid series, originally edited by Elizabeth Cook (*The Roaring Girl*), Alan Brissenden (*A Chaste Maid in Cheapside*), Michael Neill (*The Changeling*) and the present editor (*Women Beware Women*). Each individual edition offers a full critical and scholarly Introduction, while the Introduction to this anthology surveys the four plays and their place in Middleton's career in a more concentrated form. The 'Notes on the Texts' at the end come from each individual volume. All line numbers throughout the Introduction, textual annotations and 'Notes on the Texts' have been corrected from the original editions, where necessary, to reflect the lineation in this anthology.

Special thanks go to my fellow General Editors: Brian Gibbons, whose *Christopher Marlowe: Four Plays* (2011) was the first in this new series of anthologies, providing a strong example to follow; and Tiffany Stern, who kindly read the Introduction in draft and offered much-appreciated advice and suggestions. Simon Trussler did a superb job in preparing the proofs, Anna Brewer was efficient and understanding in shepherding the project, and Sue Gibbons was an extraordinarily meticulous and helpful copy editor. Margaret Bartley continues to be an ideal publisher, and I was very happy to be able to work with her again.

Vera Effigies
Tho: Midletoni Gent:

Portrait of Thomas Middleton, London, 1657 © Victoria and Albert Museum, London

INTRODUCTION

A full recognition of Thomas Middleton's greatness as a dramatist has been delayed for over three centuries. The other major playwrights of the period have had collected editions of their works published by themselves (Ben Jonson) or by their colleagues after their deaths (Shakespeare; Francis Beaumont and John Fletcher), or their canon is small enough to be more easily gathered together (Christopher Marlowe). But Middleton's plays were not published in a collected edition until the nineteenth century, and his birth date was not even known until 1931; the complete range of all his works, not just his plays, their dates of composition and/or performance, and the extent of his involvement in London's literary and civic life have only been finally established in the past 50 years, culminating in the publication in 2007 of the Oxford *Collected Works* and its accompanying *Companion*.[1] Many of Middleton's best-known plays have been superbly edited in previous decades,[2] but only in the past decade has it been possible to measure his entire career.

And Middleton's career is remarkable in many ways. No playwright of the period, not even Shakespeare, Scott McMillin has noted, 'had his work performed on a greater variety of London stages',[3] and Middleton wrote in a wide variety of genres, several of which – such as the civic pageant, or the prose satire – Shakespeare never undertook. And while Shakespeare and Marlowe have traditionally been associated with a particular theatre company and a single theatre,[4] Middleton wrote for at least six different companies[5] and his work was performed in many different theatres[6] – facts which suggest Middleton's professional flexibility

1 See 'Further Reading', below, for full citations. These works hereafter cited as *Works* and *Companion*.
2 Most notably in single-play editions in the Fountainwell Drama Texts series, the Regents Renaissance Drama series, the Revels Plays series and the New Mermaid series; selections of his plays – usually, the same group – have appeared from Oxford and Cambridge University Press, and Penguin.
3 Scott McMillin, 'Middleton's Theatres', *Works*, p. 77.
4 Shakespeare with the Lord Chamberlain's Men, later the King's Men, at the Theatre and later the Globe; and Marlowe with the Admiral's Men at the Rose. But see Roslyn L. Knutson, 'What's So Special about 1594?' and Holger Schott Syme, 'The Meaning of Success: Stories of 1594 and Its Aftermath', both in *Shakespeare Quarterly*, vol. 61 no. 4 (2010), for strong challenges to the traditional view.
5 The Children of Paul's, the Children of the Chapel, the King's Men, Prince Henry's Men, Lady Elizabeth's Men, and Prince Charles's Men; see McMillin, 'Middleton's Theatres', *Works*.
6 St Paul's, the Blackfriars, the Swan, the Globe, the Fortune and the Phoenix, among others, as well as (in his civic pageants) the streets of London.

and competence. Although Middleton's plays were not performed at court as often as were Shakespeare's plays and Jonson's masques, he nevertheless surpassed them in other ways: his *A Game at Chess* (1624) had the longest continuous run of *any* play in the period 1576–1642 – nine consecutive performances, before it was shut down.[7] In his own lifetime, then, Middleton was a well-known and successful literary professional, yet it was not until the twentieth century that his plays were once again professionally performed.[8]

This anthology cannot do full justice to Middleton's range as an artist, but the four plays collected here represent some of Middleton's greatest work. Earlier in his career, he became a master of the 'city comedy' genre, usually performed by boys' companies, and *A Chaste Maid in Cheapside* is probably his greatest achievement in this form,[9] while *The Roaring Girl* has increasingly been recognized for its anticipations of contemporary issues of gender identity. Both plays are set in London, one of the two key locations in Middleton's plays. *The Changeling* has frequently been termed Middleton's best play, but his other tragedies generally are also superb;[10] this play and *Women Beware Women* are set at court, the favourite site of Middleton's tragedies. This collection thus brings together two city comedies from 1611–1613, and two tragedies from 1621–1622. Although they are classified in different genres, these plays in fact have much in common, as we shall see.

One final note here: I have been referring to *The Roaring Girl* and to *The Changeling* as plays by 'Middleton', but like all playwrights of this

---

7 See Margot Heinemann, *Puritanism and Theatre: Thomas Middleton and Opposition Drama Under the Early Stuarts* (Cambridge, 1980) and Jerzy Limon, *Dangerous Matter: English Drama and Politics in 1623/4* (Cambridge, 1986) on the political context. Six manuscript texts and two printed editions of the play survive, which means that there are more contemporary copies of this play than of any other from the period; see Taylor's discussion, *Works* (pp. 1773–9, 1825–9) and *Companion* (pp. 712–911).

8 The first reported professional productions: *Roaring Girl*: Royal Shakespeare Company, 1983; *Chaste Maid*: Royal Court Theatre, 1966; *Women Beware Women*: Royal Shakespeare Company, 1962; *The Changeling*: Royal Court Theatre, 1961. There had been a few earlier amateur productions, but these productions re-established each play as worthy of public performance. Dates in each case are taken from the Introductions in the relevant New Mermaid editions. See also Annaliese Connolly, 'In the Repertoire: *Women Beware Women* on Stage', in Andrew Hiscock, ed., *Women Beware Women: A Critical Guide* (London, 2011).

9 Among the others: *The Phoenix* (1603–4); *Michaelmas Term* (1604–6); *A Trick to Catch the Old One* (1605); *A Mad World, My Masters* (1605); and *Your Five Gallants* (1607).

10 In addition to *Women Beware Women* in this volume, *The Revenger's Tragedy* (1606) and *The Lady's Tragedy* (sometimes known as *The Second Maiden's Tragedy*, 1611) are particularly powerful.

period, Middleton wrote in collaboration with others,[11] including, it seems, Shakespeare (on *Timon of Athens*); Middleton appears also to have revised *Macbeth* and *Measure for Measure* some years after they were first performed. The extent of Middleton's collaboration with Shakespeare continues to be debated,[12] but the scholarly consensus now suggests that Shakespeare is unusual in that he wrote so many plays by himself. Middleton single-authored at least twelve plays, two of which – *Chaste Maid* and *Women Beware Women* – are printed here, and he co-wrote *Roaring Girl* with Thomas Dekker and *The Changeling* with William Rowley.

In *The Roaring Girl*, Middleton and Dekker depict one of London's more notorious characters, Mary (known as 'Moll Cut-purse') Frith.[13] The real-life Frith appears in several legal documents of the period as a malefactor: for instance, she 'confessed that she had long frequented all or most of the disorderly and licentious places' in London, 'usually in the habit of a man [and] resorted to alehouses Taverns Tobacco shops and also to play houses there to see plays and prizes'; she apparently appeared onstage at 'the Fortune [theatre] in mans apparel and in her boots and with a sword by her side, she told the company there present that she thought many of them were of opinion that she was a man, but if any of them would come to her lodging they should find that she is a woman and some other immodest and lascivious speeches she also used at that time'. She is said to have sat upon the stage 'in mans apparel and played upon her lute and sang a song'.[14] The character of Moll Cutpurse appeared in and was referred to in other plays as well.[15] She was, in modern terms, a flamboyant celebrity.

A cross-dressing, quarrelling, tobacco-smoking, assertive woman character was thus placed at the centre of a rather conventional city comedy plot, in which two young lovers overcome the social and economic

---

11 Most frequently with Dekker and Rowley, but also with Michael Drayton, John Webster, Anthony Munday, John Ford, and possibly Thomas Heywood; see James P. Bednarz, 'Collaboration: The Shadow of Shakespeare', and Heather Hirschfeld, 'Collaboration: Sustained Partnerships', both in *Thomas Middleton in Context*, ed. Suzanne Gossett (Cambridge, 2011); and MacDonald P. Jackson, 'Early Modern Authorship: Canons and Chronologies', *Companion*, pp. 80–97.

12 E.g. Brian Vickers, 'Disintegrated: Did Middleton adapt *Macbeth*?', *TLS*, 28 May 2010.

13 First performed and printed in 1611; entered in the Stationers' Register 18 February 1612.

14 Quoted from Elizabeth Cook, New Mermaid edn, pp. xvii–xviii.

15 Moll was a character in Nathaniel Field's *Amends for Ladies* (1618), and in 1610 John Day entered a book title, *A Booke called the Madde Pranks of Merry Moll of the Bankside, with her walks in Man's Apparel and to what Purpose*, in the Stationers' Register (no copy survives). Her supposed autobiography appeared well after her death, *The Life and Death of Mrs. Mary Frith, commonly called Moll Cutpurse* (1662).

impediments that frustrate their desires; unseeing and unfeeling parents are tricked (with Moll's help), taught a lesson, and young romantic love triumphs in the end. What throws all of this action off-centre is the figure of Moll herself, and the extraordinary confluence of sexual and economic discourse in the play, in which women's sexuality is commodified and most marriages understood as an economic transaction between men – what has been called 'the traffic in women'.[16] Each play in this collection, in fact, offers a stinging critique of marriage, while showing surprising sympathy for women. Moll functions in *Roaring Girl* as a grotesque site of male attraction and repulsion, as her name suggests (Moll is a typical whore's name, but is also a nickname for 'Mary', so also suggesting the Virgin Mary[17]). Her sexuality seems openly to cross gender boundaries and social categories. She is, Sir Alexander says, a creature that 'nature hath brought forth / To mock the sex of woman. It is a thing / One knows not how to name . . . 'tis woman more than man, / Man more than woman, and (which to none can hap) / The sun gives her two shadows to one shape' (1.2.127–32); she 'slips from one company to another', Laxton says admiringly, and leeringly, 'like a fat eel between a Dutchman's fingers' (2.1.181–2). In modern productions, Moll has increasingly been played as a proto-feminist heroine, beginning with the first modern professional production, in which Helen Mirren performed the part 'with the swaggering heartiness of a pantomime Robin Hood', as one reviewer put it.[18]

But for all her transgressive sexuality and mannish behaviour (note that she never pretends to be a man, but merely acts and dresses as one), Moll never actually does anything particularly transgressive, resists all sexual advances, and dismantles her opponents easily (in Laxton's case – his name puns on 'lacks a stone [testicle]' – she unmans him[19]). And although she helps engineer the marriage of Sebastian Wengrave and Mary Fitz-Allard (another character called Mary/Moll), Moll speaks against marriage: 'I have no humour to marry, I love to lie o'both sides o'th'bed myself, and again o'th'other side; a wife you know ought to be obedient, but I fear me I am too headstrong to obey, therefore I'll ne'er go about it . . . I have the head now of myself, and am man enough for a woman; marriage is but a chopping and changing, where a maiden loses one head and has a

16 Gayle Rubin, 'The Traffic in Women: Notes on the "Political Economy" of Sex', in *Toward an Anthropology of Women*, ed. Rayna R. Reiter (New York, 1975), pp. 157–210.

17 Middleton's wife's name was Magdalen (and 'Maria'/Mary in one document); see 'Middleton's Life', pp. xxiv–xv below.

18 Quoted from Elizabeth Cook, New Mermaid edn, p. xxvi.

19 Cook (New Mermaid edn) observes, though, that in the 1983 RSC production, 'Jonathan Hyde's Laxton came across as a chillingly diabolical figure' (p. xxvi).

worse i'th'place' (2.2.34–42). Sir Alexander Wengrave, for his part, opposes his son's proposed marriage to Mary Fitz-Allard because, Sebastian reports to her, he 'asked what is she but a beggar's heir? / He scorned thy dowry of five thousand marks' (1.1.81–2); having 'reckoned up what gold / This marriage would draw from him ... he swore, / To lose so much blood could not grieve him more' (1.1.77–9). Sir Alexander threatened to disinherit Sebastian if he saw the marriage through. But Sir Alexander then opposes his son's pretended-marriage to Moll because she is monstrous. In the end, having been tricked into believing that his son has married Moll, Sir Alexander accepts Mary Fitz-Allard's poor economic status as better than Moll's transgressive one. In each of the plays in this collection, Middleton sets up conflicts between social status, economic power and sexual desire; in the comedies, the conflicts are often located in the parents (Sir Alexander here, the Yellowhammers in *Chaste Maid*) and are in the end resolved, set aside, or simply ignored. In the tragedies, though, these social conflicts will prove fatal. Marriage up or down the social hierarchy is a recurrent plot motif not only in Middleton but in much of Jacobean drama; Middleton brings to the issue an almost Brechtian sense that money makes the world go round, and that romantic love is invariably undermined or compromised by socio-economic forces. The 1983 Royal Shakespeare Company production emphasised this aspect of the play through its set, which was 'emblematic and included ... a set of cog-wheels to represent Tudor and Stuart capitalism', as well as a stage filled with non-speaking actors 'representing the voiceless cripples, beggars, and hangers-on who live on the leavings' of capitalism.[20]

Roaring Girl also anticipates the later plays in its extraordinary interrogation of the social semiotics of outward appearance, particularly clothing and fashion. Moll's cross-dressing, both in real-life London and in the play, reflected (and perhaps added to) early modern anxieties about gender and social status. How could one know another's social rank, even gender, if outside appearance did not conform to certain rules? There had been an elaborate system of sumptuary laws in early modern England, which had attempted to establish, in precise detail, the kind of clothing that could be worn by (and therefore designated) each level of the nobility, for both men and women.[21] Such rules – increasingly more honoured

---

20 Cook, New Mermaid edn, p. xxvi.

21 Thus, 'Cloth of gold, Sylver tissued, Silke of purple color' could only be worn by 'Earls and above that rank and Knights of the Garter in their purple mantles', while further down the chain of nobility 'Knights' eldest sons, and all above that rank. [and] Those with net income of £100' could wear 'Velvet in Jerkins Hose Doublets'. The list was equally precise for women. Quoted from Lisa Jardine, *Still Harping on Daughters: Women and Drama in the Age of Shakespeare*, New York, 1989.

in the breach than in the observance – reflected a widespread cultural anxiety about social mobility in the period, and were allowed to lapse by King James in 1604.[22] To look ahead for a moment, Middleton will show the now-estranged couple Bianca and Leantio mock each other for the pretentious finery of their clothes.[23] *Roaring Girl* reflects this concern about identity (Mary is literally '*masked*', 5.2.128 sd. in the final scene), but its deeper concern is the mutability of gender identity specifically. The play's very performance relies on the mistaking of boy actors for females, but Moll offers an even broader challenge to the ways in which 'men' and 'women' are categorized. (The historical context for such interest will be further discussed in relation to *Women Beware Women*.)

Roaring Girl's representation of London is, in literary terms, concrete and realistic: the play is peppered with allusions to streets and areas of London, to current social concerns, and above all to its economic life. The stage direction opening 2.1 offers a commercial scene: '*The three shops open in a rank: the first a pothecary's shop, the next a feather-shop, the third a sempster's shop*', each ruled over by one of the play's characters. Middleton specialised in the 'shop scene, where some sort of representation of a tradesman's stall stood on the platform stage', as McMillin has noted,[24] and so *Chaste Maid* begins: '*Enter* MAUDLINE *and* MOLL, *a shop being discovered.*' *Chaste Maid* is perhaps Middleton's masterpiece, and is certainly unique in that it is 'the only extant play certainly known to have been presented at the Swan Theatre'.[25] Its setting in London's Cheapside is essential.[26]

The title of the play is an oxymoron: there *are* no chaste women in Cheapside, where absolutely everything is for sale, especially marriage and sex.[27] The play closely represents London's new economic power, the

---

22 See Lawrence Stone, 'Social Mobility in England, 1500–1700', *Past and Present*, vol. 33 no. 1 (1966), 16–55.

23 Leantio: 'Stay, stay, let's see your cloth-of-silver slippers'; Bianca: 'I could nev'r see you in such good clothes / In my time' (*WBW* 4.1.55, 59–60).

24 McMillin, *Works*, p. 83.

25 Alan Brissenden, New Mermaid edn, p. xxvii. The play was first performed in 1613, though not printed until 1630 (according to its title page); it was entered in the Stationers' Register 8 April 1630. The title page says that it was 'neuer before printed' and 'hath beene often acted at the Swan on the Banke-side, by the Lady Elizabeth her Seruants'. The Swan was a round, outdoor theatre, located near, but built before, Shakespeare's Globe.

26 Cheapside was the site of the City's chief market, and, as Brissenden notes, from the fourteenth through the eighteenth centuries Cheapside was 'the culminating point on the main processional route through the city for royal entries to London and major civic observances, particularly the inauguration of the Lord Mayor' (New Mermaid edn., p. xi).

27 There is also likely a pun 'chaste' = 'chased' (i.e. a prostitute). Several of Middleton's titles are puns or jokes: *A Roaring Girl* is also an oxymoron, as the usual phrase was 'a roaring boy', while *The Changeling*, as we will see, has multiple meanings.

middling sort of merchants who produced so much wealth in the period, yet also were known for their lowbrow crassness and the emptiness of their values. At the end of the play, when the Yellowhammers (he is a goldsmith) believe that their daughter Moll is dead, they develop a new business plan within seconds – no time for mourning here – in which they will lay low for a time (because 'All the whole street will hate us, and the world / Point me out cruel'), then marry off their other child, the foolish Tim, to the whore that Sir Walter Whorehound has introduced as a rich Welsh woman; Maudline (another of Middleton's ironic names[28]) Yellowhammer is thrilled: 'Mass, a match! / We'll not lose all at once, somewhat we'll catch' (5.2.107–8, 114–5). Everyone's motive in the play is economic, with the possible exception of Touchwood Junior and Moll, the conventional couple moved by romantic love.

The play's construction is brilliant – an intersecting set of plots that centre on sex and money: the Yellowhammers are working to marry off their children to people they believe are wealthy suitors, and Yellowhammer is revealed to have a mistress and a bastard child somewhere; Allwit[29] has for many years accepted his wife's affair with Sir Walter Whorehound, a union that has produced many illegitimate children; Tim Yellowhammer woos the 'Welsh' gentlewoman, said to be Whorehound's wealthy niece but actually a prostitute; Touchwood Senior – whose phallic potency is so great that he impregnates any woman in a single encounter – and his wife split up because they have too many children (and of course Touchwood Senior also has had numerous illegitimate children by his mistresses); Sir Oliver Kix[30] and his wife, bereft of children and therefore unable to inherit wealth, hire Touchwood Senior to impregnate Lady Kix, thus impoverishing Whorehound. The Touchwoods are poor but fertile; the Kixes are rich but impotent. Children are on the one hand valued because they permit the transfer of wealth through inheritance or being married off, but children are also just so much litter, especially the numerous illegitimate children that are a kind of waste byproduct of each marriage. In one of the play's most startling scenes, a poor Wench abandons her child to two Promoters (informer-spies); believing that her basket contains mutton or veal, the two men discover a child underneath it all, and rather than try to raise it

---

28 The name comes from Magdalene, traditionally Mary Magdalene, the friend of Jesus, known as a reformed prostitute; also a pun on 'maudlin', or 'sentimental'. Mrs Yellowhammer is anything but sentimental, and was willing to prostitute her daughter to Sir Walter Whorehound.

29 The name is a play on 'wittol': (a) a cuckold; (b) all wit [an ironic tag]; (3) all 'wit' = penis [again, ironic].

30 'Kix' = dry, sapless, i.e. impotent.

themselves, they resolve to 'send the child to Branford' (2.2.214–15), or Brainford, a notorious haunt of prostitutes.[31] The message is iconic and clear: children are like meat, to be disposed of when unwanted.

The Wench's child is discovered because the Promoters are watching for those who try to eat meat during Lent, the time when the play takes place. The Lenten period is just one of many religious references generally mocked or undermined in the play. There has been much scholarly discussion about Middleton's own religion. He has been termed a Puritan, or a Calvinist[32] – but he is often simply cynical. No one in the play observes Lent, for example: the Wench is smuggling meat, the Promoters are intercepting and consuming or selling it, and the baby in the basket, said to be lamb, is a blasphemous confusion of the Lamb of God, and Moses in the basket. The sacrament of marriage is largely empty. Touchwood Junior and Moll both 'die' and are resurrected as Easter approaches[33] (they 'rise from their coffins', 5.4.29 s.d.), but it is all a pre-planned trick; and the Puritan women, gathered to assist the christening of Lady Allwit's latest child by Whorehound, get drunk, over-indulge in sweets, and vomit and urinate in the bedchamber, so that the wine is turned into urine in a parody of transubstantiation. 'Lady Kix is dry' (3.2.243), but these women leak everywhere.[34] The play ends not with the triumph of romantic love, in Touchwood Junior and Moll's marriage, but in the Yellowhammers' discovery that Tim has in fact married a whore who can only be proved 'honest' (chaste) through his chop-logic Latin. It's not an *un*happy ending by any means, but a sour aftertaste lingers. As with most Middleton plays, it is difficult to draw any clear morals at the conclusion. Adultery is never punished, and every child in the play is illegitimate. Behind the respectable façades of each social class lies an ethical void.

No doubt the most famous unchaste maid in Middleton's time was Frances Howard, whose marriage to and divorce from the Third Earl of

---

31 The scene echoes one of the most famous scenes in medieval drama, from *The Second Shepherds' Play*.

32 Puritan: Heinemann, op. cit.; Calvinist: Gary Taylor, *Companion*, p. 451.

33 As R.B. Parker notes, the time scheme of the play 'stretches from before Lent ... through the fasting season (it is not yet "Mid-Lent Sunday" at [2.2.207]), to the "resurrections" of Moll and Touchwood Junior which must take place at Easter if Lady Kix is to have time to find herself pregnant after her "physicking" at the end of III.iii' (Revels edn, p. xxxi).

34 See Gail Kern Paster, 'Leaky Vessels: The Incontinent Women of City Comedy', *Renaissance Drama*, vol. 18 (1987), 43–65. Male liquidity, by contrast, equals potency, from Touchwood Senior's hyperpotent semen, figured as 'a little vial of almond-milk' (3.3.103), to the name of the play's official villain, Walter = 'water' = semen. Ceri Sullivan describes the key historical context of the development of London's water supply, in 'Supplying the City', in Gossett, *Thomas Middleton in Context*, pp. 83–9.

Essex, remarriage to Robert Carr, and trial for murder was a sensation from 1613 throughout the 1620s. In his Revels edition, Parker links the Kix subplot to the Howard scandal,[35] but Middleton's interest in strong and transgressive women characters transcended even these spectacular scandals. Middleton was unusual both in presenting so many women characters in his plays (at least eighteen in *Chaste Maid*, though some productions have played the Puritan women clearly in drag[36]), and particularly strong and forceful women, like Moll in *Roaring Girl*. Many of the greatest modern actresses have been drawn to these parts, including Helen Mirren (Moll in *Roaring Girl* and Beatrice-Joanna in *The Changeling*), Diana Rigg (Bianca in *Women Beware Women*), Judi Dench (Bianca), Miranda Richardson (Beatrice-Joanna) and Harriet Walter (Livia in *Women Beware Women*). In his prefatory poem to *Women Beware Women*,[37] Nathaniel Richards remarked that Middleton 'knew the rage, / Madness of women crossed; and for the stage / Fitted their humours, hell-bred malice, strife / Acted in state, presented to the life.' In Livia, Bianca, Isabella, and the Mother, Middleton creates in *Women Beware Women* strikingly well-defined, transgressive, doomed women; no conventional story of romantic love, no Mary Fitz-Allard or Mary Yellowhammer, will rescue them.

The multiple tragedies in *Women Beware Women* turn on failed and/or enforced marriages, a topic of considerable contemporary interest; in the comedies, such proposed marriages, as we have seen, are thwarted, but not in the tragedies, and here again is a possible link to the Howard scandal.[38] As Livia points out to Fabritio, who insists that Isabella marry the doltish Ward, the law forbids enforcement: 'You may compel, out of the power of father, / Things merely harsh to a maid's flesh and blood, / But when you come to love, there the soil alters; / Y'are in another country' (1.2.133–6), and Isabella laments 'the heart-breakings /

---

35 'It seems inconceivable that the Kix situation, with its public quarrelling about impotency, talk of drugs and divorce, implication of the lady's scandalous past at court . . . and good offices of a third person who is really the lady's lover, could have failed to recall the current scandal. The very name "Kix" resembles "Essex". Moreover, when the divorce finally went through and Carr married Lady Essex, Middleton wrote a *Masque of Cupid* for them which was performed' in January 1614 (Revels edn, p. xxxiv). Parker goes on to note that the Kix plot also resembles many stories in the Italian *novella* tradition. See David Lindley, *The Trials of Frances Howard: Fact and Fiction at the Court of King James* (London, 1993).

36 Parker, Revels edn, p. xxix; the count is twenty women characters in *Works*, p. 958.

37 Probably first performed in 1621, though not printed until 1657; entered in the Stationers' Register on 9 September 1653.

38 Among contemporary plays on the subect, consider George Wilkins' *The Miseries of Enforced Marriage* (1607); and see Glenn H. Blayney, 'Enforcement of Marriage in English Drama (1600–1650)', *Philological Quarterly*, vol. 38 (1959), 459–72.

Of miserable maids, where love's enforced!' (1.2.166–7). The commodification of female sexuality surely reaches its *reductio ad absurdum* in all of Jacobean literature in 3.3 when the grotesque Ward inspects Isabella for her suitability to marriage like a horse at market: Isabella's breath, teeth, legs, gait ('a clean-treading wench') and genitals ('*She walks about while they duck down to look up her dress,*' 3.3.117s.d.) are examined. If children are like meat in *Chaste Maid*, all women are treated as such in *Women Beware Women*. Yet while Middleton produces a strong sympathy for these women early on, and an admiration for Livia's self-control and strength, they soon turn immoral or deadly. The play's somewhat ambiguous title suggests that, even in a brutal patriarchal world, in which rape is countenanced in the great, women can be as murderous as men.

The play's title probably echoes a speech by Misogynos in the anonymous play, *Swetnam the Woman-hater* (*c.* 1618, published 1620).[39] This play was part of the 'women's controversy', a vigorous debate between misogynist literature and defences of women that had been reenergised in the first two decades of the seventeenth century. The controversy over a woman's place in society became sharply focused during the Reformation, when largely Protestant ideas – of a woman's right to choose her own husband, of a woman's relative equality within marriage, of the possibility of divorce – came into conflict with more traditional beliefs.[40] In 1615, Joseph Swetnam's *The Arraignment of Lewd, Idle, Froward, and Unconstant Women*, a bilious misogynist attack, launched a pamphlet war of further attacks but also strong defences of women.[41] King James himself attacked women's style of mannish dress, of the sort Moll in *The Roaring Girl* flaunts, as one contemporary reported in 1620: 'Our pulpits ring continually of the insolence and impudence of women: and to help the matter forward, the players have likewise taken them to task, and so too the ballads and ballad-singers, so that they can come nowhere but their ears tingle. And, if all this will not serve, the King threatens to fall upon their husbands, parents, or friends, that have, or should have power over them, and make them pay for it.'[42] The women

---

39 'And Fortune, if thou be'st a deitie, / Give me but opportunities, that I / May all the follies of your Sex declare, / That henceforth Men of Women may beware' (3.2.90–3), from Coryl Crandall, ed., *Swetnam the Woman-hater* (Purdue, 1969).

40 See Anthony Fletcher, 'The Protestant Idea of Marriage in Early Modern England', in Anthony Fletcher and Peter Roberts, eds, *Religion, Culture, and Society in Early Modern Britain* (Cambridge, 1994).

41 Among the defences: Rachel Speght, *A Muzzle for Melastomus* (1617); Esther Sowernam, *Esther Hath Hanged Haman* (1617); Constantia Munda, *The Worming of a Mad Dog* (1617). See Linda Woodbridge, *Women and the English Renaissance: Literature and the Nature of Womankind, 1540–1620* (Urbana, Ill., 1984).

42 *The Letters of John Chamberlain*, ed. N.E. McClure (Philadelphia, 1939), vol. 2, p. 289.

in *Women Beware Women*, however, use their freedom not to cross-dress but to love, betray, and murder.

One of the play's most striking and famous scenes brings all these issues together. In 2.2, Livia engages the Mother in a game of chess on the stage below while the Duke surprises Bianca on the upper stage. The two 'games' are brilliantly made parallel, with the Duke's cunning in out-maneouvering Bianca made to parallel Livia's trapping of the Mother. Bianca, whose name means 'white', is linked to the Mother's playing the white pieces, while Livia is the black queen (with a pun on 'quean'=whore). As the goal of any chess game is checkmating your opponent, so the goal of the Duke's game is sexual mating; the 'death' of the white King in the chess game is simultaneous with the Duke's sexual 'death', or orgasm – his rape of Bianca – offstage.

Women Beware Women represents a striking range of social, sexual and moral transgressions, by both men and women. It is one of the few Jacobean plays which actually features rape or incest (both, here), instead of merely threatening them. At the same time, the play raises central questions of social class and economic position, with Middleton's consid-erable powers of cultural/economic analysis – as we have seen in the comedies – registering minute social distinctions that can have life or death implications. The play's logic expresses sexual transgression in terms of social displacement, and vice versa. So the rape of Bianca is as much an assertion of the Duke's status as of his desire ('I can command: / Think upon that', 2.2.362–3), and adultery is considered a lesser sin than incest (Hippolito sleeps with his niece Isabella) because it does not subvert 'natural' hierarchy, yet still involves the strong–older/weak–younger lover dynamic. Hippolito's reaction to Leantio's name as Livia's sexual partner ignores their adulterous relationship, rather it is all about his class status and age: 'He's a factor! . . . The poor old widow's son!' (4.1.162–3). At her death, Bianca – who has married 'up' to the Duke – realises that her status in the Duke's palace is artificial and false: 'What make I here? These are all strangers to me, / Not known but by their malice' (5.2.206–7). Both men and women are victims and agents of evil; beneath the glittering sur-faces of wealth and power, as Bianca discovers, is 'a leprous soul' (5.2.205). Bianca blames her own gender: 'Oh the deadly snares / That women set for women, without pity / Either to soul or honour!' (5.2.211–13), but Middleton shows that the very life and values of this court are corrupt, particularly in the final scene, with its bizarre, almost comic series of interlocking murders, suggesting the court's self-destructive collapse under its own values. The 2010 production of the play at the National Theatre, however, scrapped the text to produce a dream- and drug-tinged nightmare accompanied by a strong jazz score that attempted to convert courtly corruption into a more modern framework.

The Changeling[43] is Middleton's most famous play, and has been his most performed and anthologised text over the past century and a half. In it, he returns to several familiar interests: the representation of strong, complex female characters; the overwhelming power of desire; class conflict; the miseries of marriage; and the Frances Howard scandal. These interests are all closely related and woven together in a powerful plot that enacts, again, the corruption of the court. In seeking an annulment of her first marriage, Howard had been 'searched' to determine her (dubious) virginity[44] (reflected in the virginity test that Beatrice-Joanna evades in *The Changeling*), and in 1616 she and her second husband, Robert Carr (now the Earl of Somerset) were tried for the murder of Sir Thomas Overbury, who had opposed their marriage. Howard and Carr were found guilty, their accomplices executed, but – given their rank – they were spared death and sentenced to imprisonment in the Tower; in January 1622 they were released from the Tower, and so the scandal became fresh news again. Middleton had also glanced at the scandal in his tragicomedy, *The Witch* (c. 1616).[45] *The Changeling* should not be read as an allegory of the Howard scandal, of course, and the play equally alludes to other large political issues of the day, namely England's relation to Spain. This play is one of three – with *The Spanish Gypsy* and *A Game at Chess* – written 1622–4 that treat Spanish themes. English playwrights, from Thomas Kyd in *The Spanish Tragedy* (c. 1587–9) on, had always invoked Spain as a site of treachery and dangerous Catholicism, but the topic was particularly fresh and raw in the early 1620s, when the former enemy was being courted by James as a potential ally through the marriage of his surviving son Charles to the Spanish Infanta.[46]

The great dramatic power of *The Changeling* is not founded on its historical allusiveness, but on the stunning depiction of Beatrice-Joanna's

---

43 Probably first performed in 1622, though not printed until 1653; entered in the Stationers' Register on 19 October 1652. It was the first play licensed for performance in the new Phoenix Theatre, and was performed at court on 4 January 1624 (Neill, New Mermaid edn, p. xxxiii).

44 'The Lady hath ben visited and searcht by some auncient Ladies and midwifes expert in those matters, who both by inspection and otherwise find her upon theyre oath a pure virgin: which some Doctors thincke a straunge asseveration, and make yt more difficult then to be discerned' (*Letters of John Chamberlain*, I.461); see Lindley, *The Trials of Frances Howard*, pp. 77–122. Cf. Diaphanta: 'She will not search me? Will she? / Like the forewoman of a female jury?' (4.1.99–100).

45 See Elizabeth Schafer, ed., *The Witch* (New Mermaid, London, 1994), pp. xv–xix.

46 For a lucid summary of the historical context, see Darby, *Thomas Middleton in Context*, pp. 144–50.

descent into murder and Deflores' grotesque surrender to desire's imperative. Beatrice-Joanna, like Bianca in *Women Beware Women*, has been interpreted in radically different ways.[47] Both, with their virgin-suggestive names, have been seen as innocents corrupted by the world (Beatrice-Joanna was first seen by Alsemero in 'the temple…what omen yet / Follows of that?', 1.1.1–3); but both have also been seen as already morally corrupted as soon as they appear, with the plot leading inevitably to their self-realisation. Yet both, arguably, are also rape victims.[48] Beatrice-Joanna, in any event, quickly succumbs to her desire to be rid of her suitor Alonzo and convinces her servant Deflores to murder him. In Deflores – whose 'face is bad enough', like a 'basilisk', an 'ominous, ill-faced fellow' (2.1.37, 1.1.110, 2.1.53) – Middleton constructs a fantastic character, so hideous on the outside that Beatrice-Joanna cannot recognise that he ultimately reflects the hideousness within her.[49] On the stage, Deflores has been portrayed with a completely normal appearance, but also with a disfiguring red birthmark (Bob Hoskins, in the 1993 BBC version), or with a half-mask ('ostensibly to conceal his deformity, but also suggesting a split personality'[50]); a National Theatre production in 1988 had Deflores played by a black actor, using race rather than rank as a key to the play.

After murdering Alonzo, Deflores cuts off his finger to bring it and the ring to Beatrice-Joanna, and one of the truly great scenes in Jacobean drama follows, as Deflores comes to claim his reward of her. In pledging his 'service' to Beatrice-Joanna in 2.2, Deflores' language operates on two levels, that of chivalry but also of sexuality, while Beatrice-Joanna hears only what she wants to hear. When Deflores claims her virginity – hence, his name, which suggests 'deflowers' – in 3.3, Beatrice-Joanna simply cannot see what she has done, what Deflores is, or what her own desires have made her. To say that she is in denial is an understatement. Deflores quickly sets her straight, after she offers him literal treasure instead of the sexual treasure he seeks, in powerful words that chill the heart even as they reveal the truth:

47 The name 'Beatrice' might suggest 'blessed one', and 'Joanna' 'the Lord's grace', but Neill (New Mermaid edn) also points out that all the names derive from the play's principal source. In the 1973 BBC production, Helen Mirren seemed to be a soft, almost blank innocent at the beginning, while in the 1993 BBC production, Elizabeth McGovern was overtly erotic from the beginning.

48 See William C. Carroll, New Mermaid edn, pp. xxiii–xxvi, and Anthony Dawson, '*Women Beware Women* and the Economy of Rape', *Studies in English Literature, 1500–1900*, vol. 27 no. 2 (1987), 303–20.

49 In *Women Beware Women*, Bianca at last understands that 'A blemished face best fits a leprous soul' (5.2.205).

50 Neill, New Mermaid edn, p. xxxix.

> Look but into your conscience, read me there –
> 'Tis a true book, you'll find me there your equal.
> Push! Fly not to your birth, but settle you
> In what the act has made you, you're no more now;
> You must forget your parentage to me –
> You're the deed's creature: by that name
> You lost your first condition; and I challenge you,
> As peace and innocency has turned you out
> And made you one with me. (3.3.132–40)

After this, there can be no forgiveness, no salvation, and the play spirals down, in a grotesque parody of the final scene in *Romeo and Juliet*, into further paroxysms of delusion and murder. In becoming 'the deed's creature', Beatrice-Joanna experiences the tragic condition of action and consequence.

The play's subplot, set in the madhouse of Alibius, has at times been cut in production[51] or dismissed critically; this part of the play, it is thought, was written by Rowley, and some have therefore rejected it as unworthy of and unconnected to the main plot. Recent scholarship, however, has demonstrated that, as Michael Neill observes, 'what the two plots lack in superficial connectedness, the overall design makes up in thematic and poetic coherence'. Hence, the true madmen mirror the madness of desire that engulfs Deflores and Beatrice-Joanna, Isabella's fidelity to her wedding vows contrasts to Beatrice-Joanna's dismissal of hers, and so on.[52] Everyone in the madhouse suffers from the same kind of insatiable desire that drives Deflores, and 'love' is reconfigured, in both plots, as madness and disease. The very title of the play works on multiple levels, connecting both main plot and subplot at many points.[53]

At a key moment in the play, Middleton engineers a bed-trick, in which one sexual partner is unknowingly taken for another. Alsemero, now married to Beatrice-Joanna, actually enjoys her servant Diaphanta on the wedding night, and the now-jealous Beatrice-Joanna urges Deflores to set a fire, which destroys Diaphanta. Deflores discharges his 'piece' (a gun) 'As 'twere to cleanse the chimney' (5.1.46–7) – the play is a windfall for Freudian analysis – leading to Beatrice-Joanna's romantic and unwittingly ironic praise: 'How heartily he [Deflores] serves me! His face loathes one, / But look upon his care, who would not love him? / The east

---

51 See the useful stage history in Neill, New Mermaid edn, pp. xxxiii–xlv.

52 Ibid., pp. xiv–xv; see Neill's discussion, pp. xiv–xvii.

53 'Changeling' could mean (1) an idiot; (2) a faithless, inconstant person; (3) someone illegitimately substituting for another; (4) a stupid or deformed child left in place of one stolen by fairies.

is not more beauteous than his service' (5.1.70–2). When Deflores and Beatrice-Joanna are locked in a 'closet', or inner room, the remaining characters hear her off-stage cries and groans – 'Oh, oh, oh!' – as both 'horrid sounds' (5.3.140) and a perverse replication of the groans of sexual intercourse, but Deflores has in fact stabbed her and himself. Just before dying, Deflores taunts Alsemero: 'Yes, and the while [that Alsemero was with Diaphanta] I coupled with your mate / At barley-break[54] – now we are left in hell', to which Vermandero replies, 'We are all there, it circumscribes us here' (5.3.162–4). These lines are a clear allusion to Marlowe's *Dr Faustus*, when Mephastophilis informs Faustus of hell's location: 'Hell hath no limits, nor is circumscribed / In one self place; for where we are is hell, / And where hell is, must we ever be.'[55] Faustus at least could blame his damnation, in part, on the external temptations of Mephastophilis and Lucifer. In Middleton's cold, secular worlds – in spite of the occasional ghost or witch – the characters have only themselves to blame. They are 'the deed's creature' and, as Beatrice-Joanna gasps out, ''Tis time to die, when 'tis a shame to live' (5.3.179). In his tragedies as well as his comedies, Middleton's gaze into human folly and self-destruction is relentless.

54 As Neill annotates, '[T]he popular game known as "Barley-brake" . . . was played by couples holding hands: one couple were confined to a circle, known as "hell", and would try to catch the other couples as they ran through it; those caught would have to replace the couple in hell, and the game continued until every pair had served its term there' (3.2.160n.). This game, and the reference to hell, is one of the significant verbal and conceptual links between the main plot and the subplot (where an offstage madman refers to the game in 3.2).

55 Christopher Marlowe, *Dr Faustus*, ed. Roma Gill, rev. Ros King, New Mermaid edn, 2008, 5.120–2.

MIDDLETON'S LIFE

Thomas Middleton lived and worked in London nearly all his life.[56] Born in 1580, he was christened at St Lawrence Jewry on 18 April, and was buried on 4 July 1627 at his parish church in Newington Butts. His father, William, was a bricklayer and gentleman with his own coat of arms; he died in January 1586, and in November 1586 his widow, Anne, married Thomas Harvey, who had just returned, impoverished, from a voyage to Virginia. Within weeks of the marriage, Harvey was revealed to be an unscrupulous adventurer, almost solely interested in gaining control of his wife's estate. A protracted and ugly series of lawsuits engulfed the family over the next two decades, beginning with Harvey's attempt to take over the property that Anne had put in trust for her children before she met him. Allen Waterer, who married Middleton's sister, Avis, in 1596, immediately became a party to the lawsuits as well. By 1603, when both Anne Harvey and Allen Waterer died, Middleton had spent a good part of his time assisting his mother in the various legal battles. Even after Waterer's death, Avis and her second husband, John Empson, continued legal action over the family property.

Middleton's life was early and frequently connected to the professional theatre. A large part of the family property at question in the various lawsuits was 'the grounde called the Curteyn where now comenlye the Playes be played' – that is, the Curtain Theatre (built in 1577). After matriculating at Queen's College, Oxford in April 1598, moreover, Middleton was forced in June 1600 to convey his half-share of the Curtain property to his brother-in-law Waterer for money 'paid and disbursed for my advauncement & preferment in the university of Oxford where I am nowe a student'. Some time during the next eight months, however, he had to return to London to deal with the continuing series of lawsuits, and it was reported, as of 8 February 1601, that Middleton 'remaynethe heare in London daylie accompaninge the players'. As Middleton's brother-in-law, Thomas Marbeck, was an actor

---

56 The chief facts of Middleton's life have been set forth in two articles by Mark Eccles: 'Middleton's Birth and Education', *Review of English Studies* vol 7 (1931), 431–41, and '"Thomas Middleton A Poett"', *Studies in Philology*, vol. 54 (1957), 516–36. Virtually all the facts in this commentary derive from Eccles. I have also found useful R.C. Bald, 'Middleton's Civic Employments', *Modern Philology*, vol. 31 (1933), 65–78; Mildred G. Christian, 'A Sidelight on the Family History of Thomas Middleton', *Studies in Philology*, vol. 44 (1947), 490–6; and P.G. Phialas, 'Middleton's Early Contact with the Law', *Studies in Philology*, vol. 52 (1955), 186–94. For the most recent consideration of Middleton's life, see Gary Taylor, 'Thomas Middleton: Lives and Afterlives', *Works*, pp. 25–58.

for the Admiral's Men, Middleton may have met his wife through this association. Middleton in any event never graduated from Oxford, and was already a professional playwright at the time he would have been receiving his degree.

Since his son Edward was aged nineteen in 1623, we assume Middleton was married in about 1602. His wife, Magdalen (she is 'Maria' or Mary in one document), was the granddaughter of the famous composer and organist John Marbeck; Eccles believes she was probably the Maulyn Marbeck christened on 9 July 1575 at St Dunstan's in the West. Middleton's widow petitioned in February 1628 for a gift of money from the City of London, which suggests that his estate had been small. She died five months later, in July 1628, and was also buried at Newington.

Middleton published one book of verse, *The Wisdom of Solomon Paraphrased* (1597), before he entered Oxford, and two more, *Micro-Cynicon* (1599) and the *Ghost of Lucrece* (1600), while presumably still a student. In 1602 Henslowe recorded that Middleton was working on three plays: a collaboration with Dekker, Munday, Drayton and Webster on *Caesar's Fall* (now lost); *Randal, Earl of Chester* (also lost); and an un-named play. Two years later, in 1604, he published two satiric prose pieces, *The Black Book* and *The Ant and the Nightingale*. If the quality of these works is debatable, it is clear that, soon after he left Oxford, Middleton was both an active and a highly productive writer. His output continued unabated for many years. Beginning in 1613 and continuing until his death, he also wrote a number of civic pageants and entertainments; as early as 1604, he had written a speech given as part of Dekker's *The Magnificent Entertainment* for King James's official entry into London. Middleton was appointed City Chronologer in 1620, to record the memorable acts and occurrences of the City. From his inheritance stake in The Curtain to his pageants for the City, Middleton's whole life traces the arc of the recently invented career of the professional playwright.

FURTHER READING

Note: the reader is urged to consult *The Collected Works* and the *Companion to the Collected Works*, listed below, on each topic.

Complete Works

Thomas Middleton: The Collected Works, gen. eds. Gary Taylor and John Lavagnino, Oxford, 2007

Thomas Middleton and Early Modern Textual Culture: A Companion to the Collected Works, gen. eds. Gary Taylor and John Lavagnino, Oxford, 2007

Biography and Authorship

Jackson, MacD.P., *Studies in Attribution in Middleton and Shakespeare*, Salzburg, 1979

Lake, D.J., *The Canon of Thomas Middleton's Plays: Internal Evidence for the Major Problems of Authorship*, Cambridge, 1975

Taylor, Gary, 'Middleton, Thomas (bap. 1580, d. 1627)', *Oxford Dictionary of National Biography*, Oxford, 2004; online edn, May 2008 [www.oxforddnb.com/view/article/18682, accessed 27 Sept 2011]

Books

Chakravorty, Swapan, *Society and Politics in the Plays of Thomas Middleton*, Oxford, 1996

Friedenreich, K., ed., *'Accompaninge the Players': Essays Celebrating Thomas Middleton, 1580–1980*, New York, 1983

Gossett, Suzanne, ed., *Thomas Middleton in Context*, Cambridge, 2011

Heinemann, Margot, *Puritanism and the Theatre: Thomas Middleton and Opposition Drama under the Early Stuarts*, Cambridge, 1980

O'Callaghan, Michelle, *Thomas Middleton, Renaissance Dramatist*, Edinburgh, 2009

Steen, Sara Jayne, *Ambrosia in an Earthen Vessel: Three Centuries of Audience and Reader Response to the Works of Thomas Middleton*, New York, 1993

Taylor, Gary, and Trish Thomas Henley, eds, *The Oxford Handbook of Thomas Middleton*, Oxford, 2012

Selected Criticism on Individual Plays

THE ROARING GIRL

Cook, Elizabeth, ed., *The Roaring Girl*, London, The New Mermaids, 1997

Forman, Valerie, 'Marked Angels: Counterfeits, Commodities, and *The Roaring Girl*', *Renaissance Quarterly*, vol. 54 (2001), 1531–60

Garber, Marjorie, 'The Logic of the Transvestite: *The Roaring Girl*', in David S. Kastan and Peter Stallybrass, eds., *Staging the Renaissance: Reinterpretations of Elizabethan and Jacobean Drama*, London, 1991

Howard, Jean, 'Sex and Social Conflict: The Erotics of *The Roaring Girl*', in Susan Zimmerman, ed., *Erotic Politics: Desire on the Renaissance Stage*, London, 1992

Mulholland, Paul, ed., *The Roaring Girl*, Manchester, The Revels Plays, 1987

Orgel, Stephen, 'The Subtexts of *The Roaring Girl*', in Zimmerman, *Erotic Politics*, op. cit.

Rose, Mary Beth, 'Women in Men's Clothing: Apparel and Social Stability in *The Roaring Girl*', *English Literary Renaissance*, vol. 14 (1984), 367–91

A CHASTE MAID IN CHEAPSIDE

Brissenden, Alan, ed., *A Chaste Maid in Cheapside*, London, The New Mermaids, 2002

Howard, Jean, *Theater of a City: The Places of London Comedy, 1598–1642*, Philadelphia, 2007

Newman, Karen, '*A Chaste Maid in Cheapside* and London', in Garrett A. Sullivan et al., eds., *Early Modern English Drama: A Critical Companion*, Oxford, 2006

Parker, R.B., ed., *A Chaste Maid in Cheapside*, London, The Revels Plays, 1969

Paster, Gail Kern, 'Leaky Vessels: The Incontinent Women of City Comedy', *Renaissance Drama*, NS, vol. 18 (1987), 43–65

WOMEN BEWARE WOMEN

Carroll, William. C., ed., *Women Beware Women*, London, The New Mermaids, 1994

Christensen, Ann C., 'Settling House in Middleton's *Women Beware Women*', *Comparative Drama*, vol. 29 (1995), 493–518

Dawson, A. B., '*Women Beware Women* and the Economy of Rape', *Studies in English Literature, 1500–1900*, vol. 27 (1987), 303–20

Hiscock, Andrew, ed., *Women Beware Women: A Critical Guide*, London, 2011

Mulryne, J.R., ed., *Women Beware Women*, Manchester, The Revels Plays, 1975

Thomson, Leslie, '"Enter Above": The Staging of *Women Beware Women*', *Studies in English Literature*, vol. 26 (1986), 331–43

THE CHANGELING

Bawcutt, N.W., ed., *The Changeling*, London, The Revels Plays, 1958

Bromham, A. and Z. Bruzzi, *The Changeling and the Years of Crisis, 1619–24: A Hieroglyph of Britain*, London, 1990

Haber, Judith, '"I(t) Could Not Choose but Follow": Erotic Logic in *The Changeling*', *Representations*, vol. 81 no.1 (2003), 79–98

Malcolmson, Cristina, '"As Tame as the Ladies": Politics and Gender in *The Changeling*', *English Literary Renaissance*, vol. 20 (1990), 320–39

Neill, Michael, '"Hidden Malady": Death, Discovery, and Indistinction in *The Changeling*', in *Issues of Death: Mortality and Identity in English Renaissance Tragedy*, Oxford, 1997

————— ed., *The Changeling*, London, The New Mermaids, 2006

The Roaring Girle.

OR

Moll Cut-Purſe.

As it hath lately beene Acted on the Fortune-ſtage by
the Prince his Players.

Written by *T. Middleton* and *T. Dekkar.*

My caſe is alter'd, I muſt worke for my liuing.

Printed at *London* for *Thomas Archer*, and are to be ſold at his
ſhop in Popes head-pallace, neere the Royall
Exchange. 1611.

Facsimile of the title-page of the edition of 1611:

The Prince his Players In 1603 the Admiral's Men, who had for over twenty years been the servants of Lord Howard of Effingham, Lord High Admiral, were transferred to Prince Henry, James I's eldest son. Three years before, they had made the Fortune their permanent home under the lucrative but somewhat tyrannical overlordship of Edward Alleyn and Philip Henslowe, whose diary (up to 1603) provides copious notes of the company's activities.

Popes head-pallace The Pope's Head Tavern in Pope's Head Alley (a lane running south from Cornhill to Lombard Street) may have been originally part of King John's palace. More than one bookseller is recorded as issuing books from the 'Palace', and the alley was largely occupied by booksellers' shops from about 1600. Thomas Archer was also the printer in 1609 of the anonymous *Every Woman in Her Humour*.

My case is alter'd, I must worke for my liuing The first half of the sentence is a common proverbial expression, giving title to one of Jonson's comedies (1597, published 1609). The whole sentence may be a quotation; 'case' in this context refers to clothing. Moll (i.e. Mary Frith) is shown in the picture wearing 'the great Dutch slop' (see II.ii.77–8); she has a 'standing collar' (III.iii.26) and 'roses' on her shoes (IV.ii.7).

2

TO THE COMIC PLAY-READERS,
VENERY AND LAUGHTER

The fashion of play-making I can properly compare to nothing so naturally as the alteration in apparel: for in the time of the great crop-doublet, your huge bombasted plays, quilted with mighty words to lean purpose, was only then in fashion. And as the doublet fell, neater inventions began to set up. Now in the time of 5 spruceness, our plays follow the niceness of our garments, single plots, quaint conceits, lecherous jests, dressed up in hanging sleeves, and those are fit for the times and the termers: such a kind of light-colour summer stuff, mingled with diverse colours, you shall find this published comedy, good to keep you in an afternoon from 10 dice, at home in your chambers; and for venery you shall find enough for sixpence, but well couched and you mark it. For Venus being a woman passes through the play in doublet and breeches, a brave disguise and a safe one, if the statute untie not her codpiece point. The book I make no question but is fit for many of your 15 companies, as well as the person itself, and may be allowed both gallery room at the playhouse, and chamber room at your lodging.

Title   *Venery* good hunting, or (in this play more importantly) the pursuit of sexual pleasure. Cf. III.i.40 and *Northward Ho!*, III.i.87: 'Venery is like usury . . . it may be allowed though it be not lawful.'

  3   *crop-doublet* a short doublet, richly padded, which went out of fashion about 1580. Stubbes in his *Anatomy of Abuses* (1583) writes of 'doublets with great bellies . . . stuffed with four, five, or six pounds of bombast at the least'. Bombast was cotton wool used for stuffing, but the word was regularly in figurative use as well.

4–5   *as the doublet fell* It became longer and longer till the 1590s, but then shrank and became hollow-bellied.

6–7   *single plots* hardly characteristic of 1611, and Middleton may be writing ironically

  7   *hanging sleeves* no longer caught in at the cuff

  8   *termers* those who came to London for the terms of the Inns of Court, often just for amusement

 12   *sixpence* the ordinary price of a (printed) play
          well couched both 'richly embroidered' and 'well hidden'
          and an (= if)

14–15   *if the statute untie not her codpiece point* Though there was much legislation regulating the dress of particular trades and classes, none is known which proscribed women from wearing men's clothes. Presumably, therefore, the phrase is proleptic: 'provided no law is made to prevent her going dressed as a man'. Points were tags used to tie breeches or doublet (see III.i.56–8).

 17   *gallery room* The tiring room at the Fortune was an enclosed continuation of the upper gallery; presumably copies of plays were kept here.

Worse things I must needs confess the world has taxed her for, than has been written of her; but 'tis the excellency of a writer to leave things better than he finds 'em; though some obscene fellow (that 20
cares not what he writes against others, yet keeps a mystical bawdy-house himself, and entertains drunkards to make use of their pockets and vent his private bottle-ale at midnight) – though such a one would have ripped up the most nasty vice that ever hell belched forth, and presented it to a modest assembly, yet we rather 25
wish in such discoveries, where reputation lies bleeding, a slack-ness of truth, than a fullness of slander.

THOMAS MIDDLETON

18   *Worse things* For what had been written of Moll Cutpurse see the Introduction.
20   *obscene* loathsome
21   *mystical* secret, unavowed
23   *vent his private bottle-ale* There seems almost certainly some sexual joke here. 'Bottle-ale' appears in *2 Henry IV*, II.iv.131, where the Arden editor suggests it means small beer; and this seems to be confirmed by a remark in Nashe's *Fouleweather's Prognostications* (*Works*, ed. Wilson, III, 392): 'the predominant qualities of this [the summer] quarter is heat and dryness, whereby I do gather that, through the influence of Cancer, bottle-ale shall be in great authority, and wheat shall do knights' service unto malt. Tapsters this quarter shall be in greater credit than cobblers, and many shall drink more than they can earn.' But it could also mean simply windy rhetoric (see Marston, *Histriomastix*, III.i.202); 'vent' can mean sniff out, uncover, or emit (urine, wind, etc.), and 'bottle' was one of innumerable words for the female pudenda (cf. *Measure for Measure*, III.ii.172).
24   *ripped up* brought into the open

PROLOGUS

A play expected long makes the audience look
For wonders: – that each scene should be a book,
Composed to all perfection; each one comes
And brings a play in's head with him: up he sums
What he would of a roaring girl have writ;   5
If that he finds not here, he mews at it.
Only we entreat you think our scene
Cannot speak high (the subject being but mean);
A roaring girl, whose notes till now never were,
Shall fill with laughter our vast theatre,   10
That's all which I dare promise: tragic passion,
And such grave stuff, is this day out of fashion.
I see attention sets wide ope her gates
Of hearing, and with covetous listening waits,
To know what girl this roaring girl should be.   15
For of that tribe are many: one is she
That roars at midnight in deep tavern bowls,
That beats the watch, and constables controls;
Another roars i'th'daytime, swears, stabs, gives braves,
Yet sells her soul to the lust of fools and slaves.   20
Both these are suburb-roarers. Then there's beside
A civil city-roaring girl, whose pride,
Feasting, and riding, shakes her husband's state,
And leaves him roaring through an iron grate.
None of these roaring girls is ours: she flies   25
With wings more lofty. Thus her character lies,

---

6   *mews* jeers by mewing
10 *our vast theatre* The Fortune was a large theatre, though not excessively so.
14 *covetous* eager
18 *beats the watch* knocks the watchman about. The watch were in the charge of a con-
     stable; the forerunners of the police, they stayed awake at night to keep watch, and
     were often portrayed as comical and incompetent (as in *Much Ado About Nothing*).
19 *gives braves* offers battle
21 *suburb-roarers* lower-class, with a dig at the proverbially licentious character of
     London suburbs. Cf. V.ii.25 and note.
     beside ed. (besides Q)
24 *through an iron grate* i.e. in prison

5

Yet what need characters, when to give a guess
Is better than the person to express?
But would you know who 'tis? Would you hear her name?
She is called Mad Moll; her life our acts proclaim.   30

DRAMATIS PERSONAE

SIR ALEXANDER WENGRAVE, *and* NEATFOOT *his man*
SIR ADAM APPLETON
SIR DAVY DAPPER
SIR BEAUTEOUS GANYMEDE
[SIR THOMAS LONG]   5
LORD NOLAND
Young [SEBASTIAN] WENGRAVE
JACK DAPPER, *and* GULL *his page*
GOSHAWK
GREENWIT   10
LAXTON

TILTYARD [*a feather-seller*] ⎫
OPENWORK [*a sempster*]   ⎬ *Cives & Uxores*
GALLIPOT [*an apothecary*]   ⎭

MOLL *the Roaring Girl*   15
TRAPDOOR
[TEARCAT]

SIR GUY FITZ-ALLARD
MARY FITZ-ALLARD *his daughter*

CURTILAX *a Sergeant, and*   20
HANGER *his Yeoman*

Ministri

[*Coachman, Porter, Tailor, Gentlemen, Cutpurses, Fellow*]

1, 7   WENGRAVE ed. (Wentgraue Q)
      NEATFOOT ed. (Neats-foot Q)
  12   TILTYARD The word means a tilting or jousting ground: its aptness for a feather-seller possibly lies in the link between feathers and archery, or feathers and gallants. The sense of 'yard' as 'penis' is also played upon.
12–14   *Cives & Uxores* (Lat.) Citizens and their Wives
  13   OPENWORK Work made like lace or crochet to show a pattern of holes. His name also reflects his nature.
  14   GALLIPOT A small glazed earthenware jar, especially one used for medicines, and hence a jocular name for an apothecary. Cf. also *The Honest Whore*, part 2, I.ii.139: '[A harlot] is the Gally-pot to which these Drones flye, not for love to the pot, but for the sweet sucket within it, her money, her money.'
  22   *Ministri* (Lat.) Servants

ACT I, SCENE i

Enter MARY FITZ-ALLARD *disguised like a sempster*
with a case for bands, and NEATFOOT *a serving-man with her,*
with a napkin on his shoulder and a trencher in his hand,
as from table

NEATFOOT

The young gentleman, our young master, Sir Alexander's son, is
it into his ears, sweet damsel, emblem of fragility, you desire to
have a message transported, or to be transcendent?

MARY

A private word or two, sir, nothing else.

NEATFOOT

You shall fructify in that which you come for: your pleasure   5
shall be satisfied to your full contentation: I will, fairest tree of
generation, watch when our young master is erected, that is to
say, up, and deliver him to this your most white hand.

MARY

Thanks, sir.

NEATFOOT

And withal certify him, that I have culled out for him, now his   10
belly is replenished, a daintier bit or modicum than any lay upon
his trencher at dinner. Hath he notion of your name, I beseech
your chastity?

MARY

One, sir, of whom he bespake falling bands.

NEATFOOT

Falling bands, it shall so be given him. – If you please to venture   15
your modesty in the hall, amongst a curl-pated company of

---

0   sd 1   *sempster* The form of the word, now restricted to the masculine, was originally,
     like all *-ster* forms, feminine.
0   sd 2   *a case for bands* a box for holding collar-bands
3   *transcendent* Unless the word has an unidentified obscene meaning, Neatfoot must
     mean it to imply a private colloquy between Mary and Sebastian, but his language
     is of course deliberately affected. Cf. Osric (*Hamlet*, V.ii) and, for a closer parallel,
     Dondolo (*Revenger's Tragedy*, II.i).
14   *falling bands* bands worn falling flat round the neck (said by Evelyn to be a new
     mode in 1625)
16   *curl-pated* Curling the hair was much affected at this time: Macaulay speaks of the
     curl-pated minions of James I.

9

rude serving-men, and take such as they can set before you, you
shall be most seriously, and ingeniously welcome.

MARY
I have dined indeed already, sir.

NEATFOOT
Or will you vouchsafe to kiss the lip of a cup of rich Orleans in   20
the buttery amongst our waiting-women?

MARY
Not now in truth, sir.

NEATFOOT
Our young master shall then have a feeling of your being here:
presently it shall so be given him.   *Exit*

MARY
I humbly thank you, sir. But that my bosom   25
Is full of bitter sorrows, I could smile
To see this formal ape play antic tricks:
But in my breast a poisoned arrow sticks,
And smiles cannot become me. Love woven slightly
(Such as thy false heart makes) wears out as lightly,   30
But love being truly bred i'th'soul (like mine)
Bleeds even to death, at the least wound it takes:
The more we quench this fire, the less it slakes.
Oh me!

Enter SEBASTIAN WENGRAVE *with* NEATFOOT

SEBASTIAN
A sempster speak with me, sayest thou?   35

NEATFOOT
Yes sir, she's there, *viva voce*, to deliver her auricular confession.

SEBASTIAN
With me, sweetheart? What is't?

18   *ingeniously* ingenuously (the two words were often confused)
19   *dined* ed. (dyed Q)
20   *Orleans* wine from the Loire area, often referred to in contemporary plays
30   *thy* (stet Q). Perhaps we should read 'the', which would confirm the proverbial
     character of Mary's observations; but she may be making a direct complaint of
     Sebastian.
33   *fire* ed. (Q omits)
36   *viva voce* (Lat.) with living voice; i.e. in person
     auricular confession The phrase was normally used of confession to a priest, and
     hence implied suspicion of something treasonable. 'Confession' frequently had
     sexual overtones.

MARY
I have brought home your bands, sir.

SEBASTIAN
Bands? – Neatfoot.

NEATFOOT
Sir.   40

SEBASTIAN
Prithee look in, for all the gentlemen are upon rising.

NEATFOOT
Yes sir, a most methodical attendance shall be given.

SEBASTIAN
And dost hear? If my father call for me, say I am busy with a
sempster.

NEATFOOT
Yes sir, he shall know it that you are busied with a needlewoman.   45

SEBASTIAN
In's ear, good Neatfoot.

NEATFOOT
It shall be so given him.   *Exit*

SEBASTIAN
Bands? Y'are mistaken, sweetheart, I bespake none: when, where,
I prithee? What bands? Let me see them.

MARY
Yes sir, a bond fast sealed, with solemn oaths,   50
Subscribed unto (as I thought) with your soul,
Delivered as your deed in sight of heaven:
Is this bond cancelled, have you forgot me?

SEBASTIAN
Ha! Life of my life, Sir Guy Fitz-Allard's daughter,
What has transformed my love to this strange shape?   55
Stay: make all sure. – So: now speak and be brief,
Because the wolf's at door that lies in wait
To prey upon us both. Albeit mine eyes

---

38   *bands* neckbands i.e. ruffs or collars. At least that is what Sebastian takes the
      'sempster' to mean.

45   *needlewoman* A cant word for a harlot, 'expert with pricks': this brings to a climax
      Neatfoot's obscene punning which I take to be so broad earlier in the scene as not
      to need special identification.

50   *bond* 'Bond' and 'band' were used interchangeably in the figurative senses.

57   *the wolf's at door* 'To keep the wolf from the door' was proverbial from an early date:
      cf. Skelton, *Colin Clout*, 146ff., 'some there be . . . Like Aaron and Ure, / The wolf from
      the door / To werrin and to keep / From their ghostly sheep'.

Are blessed by thine, yet this so strange disguise
Holds me with fear and wonder.

MARY   Mine's a loathed sight,   60
  Why from it are you banished else so long?

SEBASTIAN
  I must cut short my speech: in broken language,
  Thus much: sweet Moll, I must thy company shun,
  I court another Moll, my thoughts must run
  As a horse runs that's blind, round in a mill,   65
  Out every step, yet keeping one path still.

MARY
  Hm! Must you shun my company? In one knot
  Have both our hands by th'hands of heaven been tied,
  Now to be broke? I thought me once your bride:
  Our fathers did agree on the time when: 70
  And must another bedfellow fill my room?

SEBASTIAN
  Sweet maid, let's lose no time: 'tis in heaven's book
  Set down, that I must have thee: an oath we took
  To keep our vows; but when the knight your father
  Was from mine parted, storms began to sit   75
  Upon my covetous father's brows, which fell
  From them on me: he reckoned up what gold
  This marriage would draw from him, at which he swore,
  To lose so much blood could not grieve him more.
  He then dissuades me from thee, called thee not fair,   80
  And asked what is she but a beggar's heir?
  He scorned thy dowry of five thousand marks.
  If such a sum of money could be found,
  And I would match with that, he'd not undo it,
  Provided his bags might add nothing to it,   85
  But vowed, if I took thee, nay more, did swear it,
  Save birth, from him I nothing should inherit.

---

65   *As a horse ... in a mill* The horse used to turn small millstones walked in a constant
     circle round the stone; hence (in the next line), Sebastian's thoughts are away from
     their proper place, yet always keeping to the one path. The phrase was proverbial and
     used elsewhere by Dekker: cf. *Northward Ho!*, I.iii.129: 'I that like a horse / Ran
     blindfold in a mill (all in one circle).'

76   *brows* ed. (E.C.) (brow Q)

82   *five thousand marks* This was a lot of money (£3,333) and well above the average
     marriage settlement among the gentry. See Mulholland, p. 58 n. 65.

MARY
What follows then, my shipwreck?
SEBASTIAN   Dearest, no:
Though wildly in a labyrinth I go,
My end is to meet thee: with a side wind   90
Must I now sail, else I no haven can find,
But both must sink forever. There's a wench
Called Moll, mad Moll, or merry Moll, a creature
So strange in quality, a whole city takes
Note of her name and person: all that affection   95
I owe to thee, on her in counterfeit passion
I spend to mad my father: he believes
I doat upon this roaring girl, and grieves
As it becomes a father for a son
That could be so bewitched: yet I'll go on   100
This crooked way, sigh still for her, feign dreams
In which I'll talk only of her: these streams
Shall, I hope, force my father to consent
That here I anchor, rather than be rent
Upon a rock so dangerous. Art thou pleased,   105
Because thou seest we are waylaid, that I take
A path that's safe, though it be far about?
MARY
My prayers with heaven guide thee!
SEBASTIAN   Then I will on.
My father is at hand, kiss and begone;
Hours shall be watched for meetings; I must now,   110
As men for fear, to a strange idol bow.
MARY
Farewell.
SEBASTIAN I'll guide thee forth: when next we meet,
A story of Moll shall make our mirth more sweet.

Exeunt

___

97   *to mad* a transitive verb; 'madden'

[ACT I, SCENE ii]

Enter SIR ALEXANDER WENGRAVE, SIR DAVY DAPPER,
SIR ADAM APPLETON, GOSHAWK, LAXTON, *and* GENTLEMEN

OMNES
　　Thanks, good Sir Alexander, for our bounteous cheer.
SIR ALEXANDER
　　Fie, fie, in giving thanks you pay too dear.
SIR DAVY
　　When bounty spreads the table, faith 'twere sin,
　　At going off, if thanks should not step in.
SIR ALEXANDER
　　No more of thanks, no more: ay, marry sir.　　　　　　5
　　Th'inner room was too close, how do you like
　　This parlour, gentlemen?
OMNES　　　　　　　　　Oh passing well.
SIR ADAM
　　What a sweet breath the air casts here, so cool!
GOSHAWK
　　I like the prospect best.
LAXTON　　　　　　　　See how 'tis furnished.
SIR DAVY
　　A very fair sweet room.
SIR ALEXANDER　　　　Sir Davy Dapper,　　　　　10
　　The furniture that doth adorn this room
　　Cost many a fair grey groat ere it came here,
　　But good things are most cheap, when th'are most dear.
　　Nay when you look into my galleries,

　　1　　sp OMNES (Lat.) All
11–32　　These lines may describe the Fortune.
　　12　　*grey groat* The phrase is commonly an emphatic to suggest something of little value,
　　　　　but here perhaps means of silver.
　　13　　*good things . . . dear* A version of a popular saying recorded by Tilley in several forms,
　　　　　e.g., 'Good cheap is dear' and 'The dearer it is the cheaper' (M. P. Tilley, *A Dictionary
　　　　　of Proverbs in England in the Sixteenth and Seventeenth Centuries*, Ann Arbor, 1950)
　14ff.　　Sir Alexander's collection suggests a parody of the great collections which began to
　　　　　be made in Elizabeth's reign, and of which Lord Lumley's at Nonsuch Palace, Surrey,
　　　　　was an already famous example. Pictures were sometimes fixed to the wall so close
　　　　　together as to make a mosaic covering the wall entirely. The display hints at the kind
　　　　　of spectacular stage effects which were then becoming popular in masques and is a
　　　　　kind of visual diagram of the action of the play.

How bravely they are trimmed up, you all shall swear   15
Y'are highly pleased to see what's set down there:
Stories of men and women, mixed together
Fair ones with foul, like sunshine in wet weather;
Within one square a thousand heads are laid
So close that all of heads the room seems made;   20
As many faces there, filled with blithe looks,
Show like the promising titles of new books
Writ merrily, the readers being their own eyes,
Which seem to move and to give plaudities;
And here and there, whilst with obsequious ears   25
Thronged heaps do listen, a cutpurse thrusts and leers
With hawk's eyes for his prey: I need not show him,
By a hanging villainous look yourselves may know him,
The face is drawn so rarely. Then sir, below,
The very floor, as 'twere, waves to and fro,   30
And like a floating island seems to move,
Upon a sea bound in with shores above.

> *Enter* SEBASTIAN *and* M[ASTER] GREENWIT

OMNES
These sights are excellent.
SIR ALEXANDER   I'll show you all:
Since we are met, make our parting comical.
SEBASTIAN
This gentleman, my friend, will take his leave, sir.   35
SIR ALEXANDER
Ha, take his leave, Sebastian? Who?
SEBASTIAN   This gentleman.
SIR ALEXANDER
Your love, sir, has already given me some time,
And if you please to trust my age with more,
It shall pay double interest: good sir, stay.

---

24   *plaudities* rounds of applause
31   *a floating island* A *trompe-l'oeil* effect must be in mind here, intended to draw the
     audience more completely into the spectacle. Dekker picks up the idea again in *The
     Wonder of a Kingdom* (III.i.16ff.) and takes the parody further: 'I'll pave my great hall
     with a floor of clouds, / Wherein shall move an artificial sun, / Reflecting round
     about me golden beams / Whose flames shall make the room seem all on fire ...' All
     the devices are to give an image of the world turned upside down.
34   *comical* happy, cheerful

GREENWIT
I have been too bold.
SIR ALEXANDER   Not so, sir. A merry day   40
'Mongst friends being spent, is better than gold saved.
Some wine, some wine. Where be these knaves I keep?

Enter three or four SERVING-MEN, *and* NEATFOOT

NEATFOOT
At your worshipful elbow, sir.
SIR ALEXANDER
You are kissing my maids, drinking, or fast asleep.
NEATFOOT
Your worship has given it us right.
SIR ALEXANDER   You varlets, stir: 45
Chairs, stools, and cushions: prithee Sir Davy Dapper,
Make that chair thine.
SIR DAVY   'Tis but an easy gift,
And yet I thank you for it, sir, I'll take it.
SIR ALEXANDER
A chair for old Sir Adam Appleton.
NEATFOOT
A back friend to your worship.
SIR ADAM   Marry, good Neatfoot,   50
I thank thee for it: back friends sometimes are good.
SIR ALEXANDER
Pray make that stool your perch, good Master Goshawk.
GOSHAWK
I stoop to your lure, sir.
SIR ALEXANDER   Son Sebastian,
Take Master Greenwit to you.
SEBASTIAN   Sit, dear friend.
SIR ALEXANDER
Nay Master Laxton – furnish Master Laxton   55

40–1   *A merry day . . . gold saved* This sounds proverbial, but is not recorded in Tilley's or
       Whiting's dictionaries of proverbs.
  50   *back friend* A backer (in this instance, the back of a chair), but playing on the
       alternative meaning of false friend. At this period stools were still commoner than
       chairs even in fairly elegant houses.
  52   *Master* ed. (M. Q)
  53   *stoop* submit (a technical term); *lure* falconer's apparatus for recalling a hawk. The
       terminology plays on Goshawk's name.

With what he wants, a stone – a stool I would say,
A stool.
LAXTON   I had rather stand, sir.
SIR ALEXANDER   I know you had,
Good Master Laxton. So, so.
                  Exeunt [NEATFOOT *and*] SERVANTS
Now here's a mess of friends, and, gentlemen,
Because time's glass shall not be running long,   60
I'll quicken it with a pretty tale.
SIR DAVY   Good tales do well
In these bad days, where vice does so excel.
SIR ADAM
Begin, Sir Alexander.
SIR ALEXANDER   Last day I met
An aged man upon whose head was scored
A debt of just so many years as these   65
Which I owe to my grave: the man you all know.
OMNES
His name I pray you, sir.
SIR ALEXANDER   Nay, you shall pardon me:
But when he saw me, with a sigh that brake,
Or seemed to break, his heart-strings, thus he spake:
Oh my good knight, says he (and then his eyes   70
Were richer even by that which made them poor,
They had spent so many tears they had no more),
Oh sir, says he, you know it, for you ha' seen
Blessings to rain upon mine house and me:
Fortune, who slaves men, was my slave: her wheel   75
Hath spun me golden threads, for, I thank heaven,
I ne'er had but one cause to curse my stars.
I asked him then what that one cause might be.

56–8   lineation ed. (With what ... stool / I had ... stand sir. / I know ... So, so Q)
56–7   *what he wants ... stand* A weak quibble on Laxton's name (he lacks a stone) becomes
        an insulting jibe when one remembers that 'stone' was standard English for testicle.
        (Cf. the assumed name Singlestone in *A Mad World, My Masters*, II.vi.26, which
        plainly suggests eunuch.) To 'stand' had various sexual meanings, here especially to
        have an erection; to stand to a woman is to prepare for intercourse, and a stallion is
        said to stand at stud.
58   sd here ed. (at 57 Q): *So, so* appears to be a gesture of dismissal to the servants.
59   *mess* company eating together
60   *Because ... long* so that time should not hang heavy on us

OMNES

    So, sir?

SIR ALEXANDER He paused; and as we often see

    A sea so much becalmed there can be found   80

    No wrinkle on his brow, his waves being drowned

    In their own rage: but when th'imperious winds

    Use strange invisible tyranny to shake

    Both heaven's and earth's foundation at their noise,

    The seas, swelling with wrath to part that fray,   85

    Rise up, and are more wild, more mad than they –

    Even so, this good old man was by my question

    Stirred up to roughness, you might see his gall

    Flow even in's eyes: then grew he fantastical.

SIR DAVY

    Fantastical? Ha, ha.

SIR ALEXANDER   Yes, and talked oddly.   90

SIR ADAM

    Pray sir, proceed,

    How did this old man end?

SIR ALEXANDER   Marry sir, thus.

    He left his wild fit to read o'er his cards:

    Yet then (though age cast snow on all his hairs)

    He joyed because, says he, the god of gold   95

    Has been to me no niggard: that disease

    Of which all old men sicken, avarice,

    Never infected me –

LAXTON

    [Aside] He means not himself, I'm sure.

SIR ALEXANDER   For like a lamp

    Fed with continual oil, I spend and throw   100

    My light to all that need it, yet have still

    Enough to serve myself: oh but, quoth he,

    Though heaven's dew fall thus on this aged tree,

    I have a son that's like a wedge doth cleave

    My very heart-root.

---

82   *winds* ed. (wind Q)

85   *part that fray* i.e. that caused by the winds: grammar and syntax are jumbled and inconsequent in this passage

86   *they* i.e. the winds

90   *talked* ed. (talk Q, talkt Dyce)

93   *read o'er his cards* (stet Q): reckon up his position; Bowers emends to 'cares'

98–9 The aside interrupts the complete line which is spoken aloud.

SIR DAVY   Had he such a son?   105

SEBASTIAN

[*Aside*] Now I do smell a fox strongly.

SIR ALEXANDER

Let's see: no, Master Greenwit is not yet

So mellow in years as he; but as like Sebastian,

Just like my son Sebastian, such another.

SEBASTIAN

[*Aside*] How finely, like a fencer, my father fetches his by-   110
blows to hit me, but if I beat you not at your own weapon of
subtlety –

SIR ALEXANDER

This son, saith he, that should be

The column and main arch unto my house,

The crutch unto my age, becomes a whirlwind   115

Shaking the firm foundation –

SIR ADAM   'Tis some prodigal.

SEBASTIAN

[*Aside*] Well shot, old Adam Bell.

SIR ALEXANDER

No city monster neither, no prodigal,

But sparing, wary, civil, and (though wifeless)

An excellent husband, and such a traveller,   120

He has more tongues in his head than some have teeth.

SIR DAVY

I have but two in mine.

GOSHAWK

So sparing and so wary?

What then could vex his father so?

SIR ALEXANDER   Oh, a woman.

SEBASTIAN

A flesh-fly, that can vex any man.

SIR ALEXANDER   A scurvy woman,   125

110–11   *by-blows* strokes from the side
   114   *The column ... unto my house* Cf. Tourneur, *The Atheist's Tragedy*, V.i.78f.: 'On these
          two pillars [his sons] stood the stately frame / And architecture of my lofty house.'
   117   *Adam Bell* the famous archer who figures in the ballad of *Adam Bell, Clym of the
          Clough and William of Cloudesley*
   121   *more tongues . . . teeth* This presumably alludes to Sebastian's knowledge of
          languages; but proverbial phrases about the tongue usually had another edge to
          them. 'Double-tongued' meant deceitful (see II.ii.10n.) and cf. 'The tongue walks
          where the teeth speed not', a proverb quoted by Dekker in *The Gull's Horn-Book*, v.
   125   *flesh-fly* literally, a fly which deposits its eggs in dead flesh

On whom the passionate old man swore he doated:
A creature, saith he, nature hath brought forth
To mock the sex of woman. It is a thing
One knows not how to name: her birth began
Ere she was all made: 'tis woman more than man,   130
Man more than woman, and (which to none can hap)
The sun gives her two shadows to one shape:
Nay more, let this strange thing walk, stand or sit,
No blazing star draws more eyes after it.

SIR DAVY
A monster, 'tis some monster.

SIR ALEXANDER   She's a varlet.   135

SEBASTIAN
[*Aside*] Now is my cue to bristle.

SIR ALEXANDER
A naughty pack.

SEBASTIAN   'Tis false.

SIR ALEXANDER   Ha, boy?

SEBASTIAN   'Tis false.

SIR ALEXANDER
What's false? I say she's naught.

SEBASTIAN   I say that tongue
That dares speak so, but yours, sticks in the throat
Of a rank villain: set yourself aside –   140

SIR ALEXANDER
So sir, what then?

SEBASTIAN   Any here else had lied.
(*Aside*) I think I shall fit you.

128ff. This passage was taken over by Field into the Mall Cutpurse scene in *Amends for Ladies* (II.i.33ff.).

132 *two shadows to one shape* The implication is perhaps that by witchcraft she has stolen a shadow and so would have power over another's soul. The devil was normally held to cast no shadow. Possibly Sir Alexander also suggests that she has one shadow for a man and one for a woman.

134 *blazing star* i.e. a meteor, held in Elizabethan cosmology to be of ill omen, as belonging to the sublunary world of change and decay, as opposed to stars which were considered to be pure, fixed, and eternal. Cf. *The Changeling*, V.iii.154–5 and n.; and below, III.ii.96 and n. Bald (Chronology, p. 38) suggests that the comparison may have been prompted by the presence of Halley's comet.

137 *naughty pack* person of low or worthless character (cf. the still current 'baggage')

142 sd (*Aside*) This stands in Q in roman type at the end of the line after a dash, evidently influenced by the spoken word 'aside' two lines above
     fit have something ready for

SIR ALEXANDER
  Lie?
SEBASTIAN Yes.
SIR DAVY   Doth this concern him?
SIR ALEXANDER   [*Aside*] Ah sirrah boy,
  Is your blood heated? Boils it? Are you stung?
  I'll pierce you deeper yet. – Oh my dear friends,   145
  I am that wretched father, this that son,
  That sees his ruin, yet headlong on doth run.
SIR ADAM
  Will you love such a poison?
SIR DAVY   Fie, fie.
SEBASTIAN   Y'are all mad.
SIR ALEXANDER
  Th'art sick at heart, yet feel'st it not: of all these,
  What gentleman but thou, knowing his disease   150
  Mortal, would shun the cure? Oh Master Greenwit,
  Would you to such an idol bow?
GREENWIT   Not I, sir.
SIR ALEXANDER
  Here's Master Laxton, has he mind to a woman
  As thou hast?
LAXTON   No, not I, sir.
SIR ALEXANDER   Sir, I know it.
LAXTON
  Their good parts are so rare, their bad so common,   155
  I will have nought to do with any woman.
SIR DAVY
  'Tis well done, Master Laxton.
SIR ALEXANDER   Oh thou cruel boy,
  Thou would'st with lust an old man's life destroy;
  Because thou see'st I'm half-way in my grave,
  Thou shovel'st dust upon me: would thou might'st have   160
  Thy wish, most wicked, most unnatural!
SIR DAVY
  Why sir, 'tis thought Sir Guy Fitz-Allard's daughter
  Shall wed your son Sebastian.
SIR ALEXANDER   Sir Davy Dapper,
  I have upon my knees wooed this fond boy

155   *Their ... their* ed. (There ... there Q)
156   *nought* There is a contradictory play on 'naught' (as in 'naughty').

    To take that virtuous maiden.

SEBASTIAN   Hark you a word, sir.   165
    You on your knees have cursed that virtuous maiden,
    And me for loving her, yet do you now
    Thus baffle me to my face? Wear not your knees
    In such entreats, give me Fitz-Allard's daughter.

SIR ALEXANDER
    I'll give thee rats-bane rather.

SEBASTIAN   Well then you know   170
    What dish I mean to feed upon.

SIR ALEXANDER
    Hark gentlemen, he swears
    To have this cutpurse drab, to spite my gall.

OMNES
    Master Sebastian –

SEBASTIAN   I am deaf to you all.
    I'm so bewitched, so bound to my desires,   175
    Tears, prayers, threats, nothing can quench out those fires
    That burn within me.   *Exit*

SIR ALEXANDER   [*Aside*] Her blood shall quench it then.
    – Lose him not, oh dissuade him, gentlemen.

SIR DAVY
    He shall be weaned, I warrant you.

SIR ALEXANDER   Before his eyes
    Lay down his shame, my grief, his miseries.   180

OMNES
    No more, no more, away.

                     Exeunt all but SIR ALEXANDER

SIR ALEXANDER   I wash a negro,
    Losing both pains and cost: but take thy flight,
    I'll be most near thee when I'm least in sight.
    Wild buck, I'll hunt thee breathless, thou shalt run on,
    But I will turn thee when I'm not thought upon.   185

                Enter RALPH TRAPDOOR

168   *baffle* hoodwink, contradict; perhaps with a secondary meaning of disgrace
       Wear ed. (were Q)
176   *quench out* (stet Q): perhaps we should omit 'out', for better scansion and for a more
       exact parallel with the following line.
181   *I wash a negro* 'To wash an Ethiop (or blackamoor) white' is a common proverbial
       expression first recorded in late classical times (in Lucian).
185   *turn* deflect (a technical hunting term)

Now sirrah, what are you? Leave your ape's tricks and speak.

TRAPDOOR

A letter from my captain to your worship.

SIR ALEXANDER

Oh, oh, now I remember, 'tis to prefer thee into my service.

TRAPDOOR

To be a shifter under your worship's nose of a clean trencher,
when there's a good bit upon't.   190

SIR ALEXANDER

Troth, honest fellow – [*Aside*] Hm – ha – let me see,
This knave shall be the axe to hew that down
At which I stumble, 'has a face that promiseth
Much of a villain: I will grind his wit,
And if the edge prove fine make use of it.   195
– Come hither sirrah, canst thou be secret, ha?

TRAPDOOR

As two crafty attorneys plotting the undoing of their clients.

SIR ALEXANDER

Didst never, as thou has walked about this town,
Hear of a wench called Moll, mad merry Moll?

TRAPDOOR

Moll Cutpurse, sir?

SIR ALEXANDER   The same, dost thou know her then?   200

TRAPDOOR

As well as I know 'twill rain upon Simon and Jude's day next:
I will sift all the taverns i'th'city, and drink half-pots with all the
watermen o'th'Bankside, but if you will, sir, I'll find her out.

SIR ALEXANDER

That task is easy, do't then. Hold thy hand up:

---

186   *ape's tricks* fantastic or extravagant bowing
189–90 *shifter . . . upon't* Trapdoor, posing as a trusty servant, must also be implying
        duplicity: a shifter was a cozener, who would here cunningly remove the 'good bit'
        (or morsel) from under his master's nose. A trencherman or trencher-friend was a
        parasite or toady, and there is probably a hint of this too.
193   *'has* i.e. he has
197   The same quip appears in *Michaelmas Term*, III.i.146.
201   *Simon and Jude's day* 28 October, the day on which the pageants put on by the City
        Livery companies turned out, was proverbially stormy: 'Simon and Jude all the ships
        on the sea home do they crowd' (see V. S. Lean, *Collectanea* (1902–4), I, 381).
203   *watermen o'th'Bankside* 'Taylor the water-poet asserts that at this time, between
        Windsor and Gravesend, there were not fewer than forty thousand watermen' (Reed,
        qu. Collier).

What's this? Is't burnt? 205

TRAPDOOR

No sir, no, a little singed with making fireworks.

SIR ALEXANDER

There's money, spend it: that being spent, fetch more.

TRAPDOOR

Oh sir, that all the poor soldiers in England had such a leader!
For fetching, no water-spaniel is like me.

SIR ALEXANDER

This wench we speak of strays so from her kind 210
Nature repents she made her. 'Tis a mermaid
Has tolled my son to shipwreck.

TRAPDOOR

I'll cut her comb for you.

SIR ALEXANDER

I'll tell out gold for thee then: hunt her forth,
Cast out a line hung full of silver hooks 215
To catch her to thy company: deep spendings
May draw her that's most chaste to a man's bosom.

TRAPDOOR

The jingling of golden bells, and a good fool with a hobby-
horse, will draw all the whores i'th'town to dance in a morris.

SIR ALEXANDER

Or rather (for that's best – they say sometimes 220
She goes in breeches) follow her as her man.

TRAPDOOR

And when her breeches are off, she shall follow me.

SIR ALEXANDER

Beat all thy brains to serve her.

---

205   *burnt* i.e. branded (as a convicted criminal's would be)
211   *a mermaid* Mermaids were generally regarded as sinister and often identified with the Sirens (female monsters with ravishing voices whose singing lured sailors to shipwreck).
213   *I'll cut her comb* An ancient proverbial phrase: cutting a cock's comb was a usual accompaniment of gelding. So Trapdoor will destroy Moll's masculinity. The phrase also suggests clitorectomy.
218–19 *hobby-horse* The still common children's toy was already well known and frequently appears as part of the fool's equipment. But a hobby-horse was also a pantomime horse which had an important place in the morris dance: it was formed by a man inside a frame with the head and tail of a horse (*Sh. Eng.*, II, 438). 'Morris', however, was also used loosely of any rather wild dance, and 'hobby-horse' commonly of a wanton.
223   *serve* not just as a servant but as a stallion serves a mare

TRAPDOOR
Zounds sir, as country wenches beat cream, till butter comes.
SIR ALEXANDER
Play thou the subtle spider, weave fine nets   225
To ensnare her very life.
TRAPDOOR   Her life?
SIR ALEXANDER   Yes, suck
Her heart-blood if thou canst: twist thou but cords
To catch her, I'll find law to hang her up.
TRAPDOOR
Spoke like a worshipful bencher.
SIR ALEXANDER
Trace all her steps: at this she-fox's den   230
Watch what lambs enter: let me play the shepherd
To save their throats from bleeding, and cut hers.
TRAPDOOR
This is the goll shall do't.
SIR ALEXANDER   Be firm, and gain me
Ever thine own. This done, I entertain thee:
How is thy name?   235
TRAPDOOR
My name, sir, is Ralph Trapdoor, honest Ralph.
SIR ALEXANDER
Trapdoor, be like thy name, a dangerous step
For her to venture on, but unto me –
TRAPDOOR
As fast as your sole to your boot or shoe, sir.
SIR ALEXANDER
Hence then, be little seen here as thou canst,   240
I'll still be at thine elbow.
TRAPDOOR   The trapdoor's set.
Moll, if you budge y'are gone, this me shall crown:
A roaring boy the roaring girl puts down.
SIR ALEXANDER
God-'a'-mercy, lose no time.

Exeunt

229   *bencher* magistrate
233   *goll* cant term for hand
234   *entertain thee* take thee into my service
236   *Ralph* (pronounced – and sometimes spelt – Rafe) a common name for servants in contemporary plays: cf. *A Mad World, My Masters*, III.i.5.

The three shops open in a rank: the first a pothecary's shop,
the next a feather-shop, the third a sempster's shop:
MISTRESS GALLIPOT *in the first,* MISTRESS TILTYARD
in the next, MASTER OPENWORK *and his* WIFE *in the third.*
To them enters LAXTON, GOSHAWK, *and* GREENWIT

MISTRESS OPENWORK

Gentlemen, what is't you lack? What is't you buy? See fine
bands and ruffs, fine lawns, fine cambrics. What is't you lack,
gentlemen, what is't you buy?

LAXTON

Yonder's the shop.

GOSHAWK

Is that she?   5

LAXTON

Peace.

GREENWIT

She that minces tobacco?

LAXTON

Ay: she's a gentlewoman born, I can tell you, though it be her
hard fortune now to shred Indian pot-herbs.

GOSHAWK

Oh sir, 'tis many a good woman's fortune, when her husband   10
turns bankrupt, to begin with pipes and set up again.

LAXTON

And indeed the raising of the woman is the lifting up of the
man's head at all times: if one flourish, t'other will bud as fast,
I warrant ye.

GOSHAWK

Come, th'art familiarly acquainted there, I grope that.   15

---

   0   sd *in a rank* in a row, side by side
   1   *what is't you lack?* The standard street-cry of pedlars, shopmen, apprentices, etc.,
         calling for custom.
   7   *minces* shreds; tobacco was commonly sold by apothecaries
   9   *Indian pot-herbs* Pot-herbs are simply herbs boiled in a pot; perhaps a
         misunderstanding of how tobacco is prepared.
  11   *pipes* Tobacco was good business (cf. III.iii.63n.); but 'pipe' is plainly used here as a
         cant word for penis (cf. below, 43), as at *Romeo and Juliet*, IV.v.96.

LAXTON

And you grope no better i'th'dark, you may chance lie i'th'ditch when y'are drunk.

GOSHAWK

Go, th'art a mystical lecher.

LAXTON

I will not deny but my credit may take up an ounce of pure smoke.   20

GOSHAWK

May take up an ell of pure smock. Away, go. [*Aside*] 'Tis the closest striker. Life, I think he commits venery forty foot deep, no man's aware on't. I, like a palpable smockster, go to work so openly with the tricks of art, that I'm as apparently seen as a naked boy in a vial, and were it not for a gift of treachery that I   25 have in me to betray my friend when he puts most trust in me – mass, yonder he is, too – and by his injury to make good my access to her, I should appear as defective in courting as a farmer's son the first day of his feather, that doth nothing at court but woo the hangings and glass windows for a month   30 together, and some broken waiting-woman for ever after. I find those imperfections in my venery that, were't not for flattery and falsehood, I should want discourse and impudence, and he that wants impudence among women is worthy to be kicked out at bed's feet. He shall not see me yet.   35

GREENWIT

Troth this is finely shred.

---

15   *grope* seize, apprehend; there is a common sexual use of the word which here picks up Laxton's *double entendre*.

18   *mystical* secret (cf. 'Epistle to the Comic Play-Readers', l. 21)

21   *take up an ell of pure smock* i.e. lift up a woman's under-skirt (cf. *The Taming of the Shrew*, IV.iii.158)

22   *closest striker* most secret fornicator

23   *smockster* bawd: cf. *Your Five Gallants*, V.ii.45: 'you're a hired smockster . . . we are certified that you're a bawd'

25   *naked boy in a vial* (i.e. phial). Steevens's suggestion – 'I suppose he means an abortion preserved in spirits' – seems irrelevant and incredible; the point is presumably the visibility of nakedness seen through clear glass. Naked boys is a popular name for the meadow saffron which flowers after its leaves have withered; but the phrase also occurs in *The Alchemist* (III.iv.80–1) in such a way as to suggest catamite: 'competent means to keep himself, / His punk, and naked boy, in excellent fashion'.

29   *the first day of his feather* The feather has been acquired to gentrify his appearance.

31   *broken* violated, also used of unmarried mothers

LAXTON

Oh, women are the best mincers.

MISTRESS GALLIPOT

'T had been a good phrase for a cook's wife, sir.

LAXTON

But 'twill serve generally, like the front of a new almanac, as
thus: calculated for the meridian of cook's wives, but generally   40
for all Englishwomen.

MISTRESS GALLIPOT

Nay, you shall ha't, sir, I have filled it for you.

She puts it to the fire

LAXTON

The pipe's in a good hand, and I wish mine always so.

GREENWIT

But not to be used o'that fashion.

LAXTON

Oh pardon me, sir, I understand no French. I pray be covered.   45
Jack, a pipe of rich smoke.

GOSHAWK

Rich smoke? That's sixpence a pipe, is't?

GREENWIT

To me, sweet lady.

MISTRESS GALLIPOT

[*Aside to* LAXTON] Be not forgetful; respect my credit, seem
strange: art and wit makes a fool of suspicion: pray be wary.   50

LAXTON

Push, I warrant you: – come, how is't, gallants?

GREENWIT

Pure and excellent.

LAXTON

I thought 'twas good, you were grown so silent; you are like
those that love not to talk at victuals, though they make a worse
noise i'the nose than a common fiddler's prentice, and discourse   55

---

39   *the front of a new almanac* The predictions in almanacs were calculated for a given
      meridian, but could be adapted to cover the whole country.

45   *I understand no French* i.e. he declines the innuendo; cf. V.i.155.
      be covered replace your hat (to Goshawk)

50   *art and wit makes a fool of suspicion* This sounds proverbial, but appears not to be
      otherwise recorded. There is a fairly close parallel in *A Mad World, My Masters*
      (I.ii.93–5): 'The way to daunt is to outvie suspect. / Manage these principles but
      with art and life, / Welcome all nations, thou'rt an honest wife.'

a whole supper with snuffling. – I must speak a word with you
anon.

MISTRESS GALLIPOT

Make your way wisely then.

GOSHAWK

Oh what else, sir? He's perfection itself, full of manners, but not
an acre of ground belonging to 'em.   60

GREENWIT

Ay and full of form, h'as ne'er a good stool in's chamber.

GOSHAWK

But above all religious: he preyeth daily upon elder brothers.

GREENWIT

And valiant above measure: h'as run three streets from a
sergeant.

LAXTON

Puh, puh.   65

He blows tobacco in their faces

GREENWIT[*and*] GOSHAWK

Oh, puh, ho, ho.

LAXTON

So, so.

MISTRESS GALLIPOT

What's the matter now, sir?

LAXTON

I protest I'm in extreme want of money: if you can supply me
now with any means, you do me the greatest pleasure, next to   70
the bounty of your love, as ever poor gentleman tasted.

MISTRESS GALLIPOT

What's the sum would pleasure ye, sir? Though you deserve
nothing less at my hands.

LAXTON

Why, 'tis but for want of opportunity thou know'st. [*Aside*]
I put her off with opportunity still: by this light I hate her, but   75
for means to keep me in fashion with gallants: for what I take
from her, I spend upon other wenches, bear her in hand still;

---

59   *manners* with a play on 'manors'
61   *full of form* replete with propriety, with a play on 'form' in the sense of bench
70   *pleasure* The verb doubtless has here (as currently) the secondary sense of stimulate
        sexually.
73   *nothing less at my hands* i.e. than her love
77   *bear her in hand* deceive her: cf. *Macbeth*, III.i.80; *Cymbeline*, V.v.43

she has wit enough to rob her husband, and I ways enough to consume the money. – Why, how now? What? The chincough?

GOSHAWK

Thou hast the cowardliest trick to come before a man's face and   80
strangle him ere he be aware: I could find in my heart to make
a quarrel in earnest.

LAXTON

Pox, and thou dost – thou know'st I never use to fight with my
friends – thou'll but lose thy labour in't. – Jack Dapper!

Enter J[ACK] DAPPER, *and his man* GULL

GREENWIT

Monsieur Dapper, I dive down to your ankles.   85

JACK DAPPER

Save ye gentlemen, all three in a peculiar salute.

GOSHAWK

He were ill to make a lawyer, he dispatches three at once.

LAXTON

So, well said. – But is this of the same tobacco, Mistress Gallipot?
[*She gives him money secretly*]

MISTRESS GALLIPOT

The same you had at first, sir.

LAXTON

I wish it no better: this will serve to drink at my chamber.   90

GOSHAWK

Shall we taste a pipe on't?

LAXTON

Not of this by my troth, gentlemen, I have sworn before you.

GOSHAWK

What, not Jack Dapper?

LAXTON

Pardon me, sweet Jack, I'm sorry I made such a rash oath, but
foolish oaths must stand: where art going, Jack?   95

JACK DAPPER

Faith, to buy one feather.

---

79   *chincough* whooping-cough. Laxton's smoke has made Goshawk cough.
88   *is this of the same tobacco . . .?* 'She gives him money, and he pretends that he receives
only tobacco' (Collier, qu. Bullen).
89   sp *MISTRESS GALLIPOT* ed. (M. Gal. Q)
90   *drink* smoke (a common expression)

LAXTON

[*Aside*] One feather? The fool's peculiar still.

JACK DAPPER

Gull.

GULL

Master?

JACK DAPPER

Here's three halfpence for your ordinary, boy, meet me an hour   100
hence in Paul's.

GULL

[*Aside*] How? Three single halfpence? Life, this will scarce serve
a man in sauce, a ha'p'orth of mustard, a ha'p'orth of oil and a
ha'p'orth of vinegar, what's left then for the pickle herring? This
shows like small beer i'th'morning after a great surfeit of wine   105
o'er night: he could spend his three pound last night in a supper
amongst girls and brave bawdy-house boys: I thought his pockets
cackled not for nothing, these are the eggs of three pound, I'll
go sup 'em up presently.   *Exit*

LAXTON

[*Aside*] Eight, nine, ten angels: good wench i'faith, and one that   110
loves darkness well, she puts out a candle with the best tricks of
any drugster's wife in England: but that which mads her, I rail
upon opportunity still, and take no notice on't. The other night
she would needs lead me into a room with a candle in her hand
to show me a naked picture, where no sooner entered but the   115
candle was sent of an errand: now I not intending to understand her, but like a puny at the inns of venery, called for
another light innocently: thus reward I all her cunning with
simple mistaking. I know she cozens her husband to keep me,
and I'll keep her honest as long as I can, to make the poor man   120
some part of amends: an honest mind of a whoremaster! –

***

100   *three halfpence for your ordinary* An ordinary was a public eating-house that
       provided fixed-price meals. Bullen quotes from *Father Hubburd's Tales*: 'we ... took
       our repast at thrifty Mother Walker's, where we found a whole nest of pinching
       bachelors, crowded together upon forms and benches in that most worshipful three
       halfpenny ordinary'.
101   *Paul's* i.e. St Paul's, in the nave of which masterless men set up their bills for service.
       (See *Sh. Eng.*, II, 166.)
108   *cackled* gave away secrets
115   *naked picture* pornographic image
116   *errand* ed. (arrant Q)
117   *puny* freshman   121 *whoremaster* womaniser, lecher

How think you amongst you? What, a fresh pipe? Draw in a
third, man.

GOSHAWK

No, you're a hoarder, you engross by th'ounces.

At the feather-shop now

JACK DAPPER

Puh, I like it not.

MISTRESS TILTYARD What feather is't you'd have, sir?   125
These are most worn and most in fashion
Amongst the beaver gallants, the stone riders,
The private stage's audience, the twelvepenny-stool gentlemen:
I can inform you 'tis the general feather.

JACK DAPPER

And therefore I mislike it – tell me of general!   130
Now a continual Simon and Jude's rain
Beat all your feathers as flat down as pancakes.
Show me – a – spangled feather.

MISTRESS TILTYARD   Oh, to go
A-feasting with? You'd have it for a hench-boy?
You shall.   135

At the sempster's shop now

MASTER OPENWORK

Mass, I had quite forgot.
His honour's footman was here last night, wife,
Ha' you done with my lord's shirt?

MISTRESS OPENWORK   What's that to you, sir?

124   *engross* buy up wholesale, especially for reselling at an inflated price
       by th' ed. (bith Q)
125   sp MISTRESS ed. (M. Q): Master Tiltyard is not present
127   *beaver gallants* those wearing beaver hats. Stubbes in the *Anatomy of Abuses* refers to
       beaver hats at 20, 30, and 40 shillings.
       stone riders riders of stallions or, possibly, male homosexuals
128   *The private stage's audience* 'Private' playhouses were devised to circumvent the
       regulations of the Act of Common Council which forbade houses of public
       entertainment within the liberties of the City. The performances, given by children
       (who were technically in training), were to quite small and select audiences, who
       paid high prices for admission.
       twelvepenny-stool The normal price for the use of a stool was sixpence.
131   *Simon and Jude's rain* cf. I.ii.201 and n.
132   *as flat down as pancakes* proverbial from an early period
134   *hench-boy?* page; punctuation ed. (hinch-boy, Q)

I was this morning at his honour's lodging,
Ere such a snail as you crept out of your shell.   140

MASTER OPENWORK

Oh, 'twas well done, good wife.

MISTRESS OPENWORK   I hold it better, sir,
Than if you had done't yourself.

MASTER OPENWORK   Nay, so say I:
But is the countess's smock almost done, mouse?

MISTRESS OPENWORK

Here lies the cambric, sir, but wants, I fear me.

MASTER OPENWORK

I'll resolve you of that presently.   145

MISTRESS OPENWORK

Hey-day! Oh audacious groom,
Dare you presume to noblewomen's linen?
Keep you your yard to measure shepherd's holland,
I must confine you, I see that.

At the tobacco shop now

GOSHAWK

What say you to this gear?   150

LAXTON

I dare the arrant'st critic in tobacco
To lay one fault upon't.

Enter MOLL *in a frieze jerkin and a black saveguard*

GOSHAWK   Life, yonder's Moll.

LAXTON

Moll, which Moll?

GOSHAWK

Honest Moll.

LAXTON

Prithee let's call her. – Moll.   155

---

140   *snail* ed. (snake Q)
144   *wants* i.e. wants finishing, or perhaps there isn't enough material
146   *Hey-day!* ed. (Haida Q)
148   *yard* with a play on 'penis'
      shepherd's holland linen for shepherd's smocks
150   *gear* stuff; but the (then standard English) sense of genitals may be present
151   *arrant'st* ed. (arrants Q) strictest
152   sd *frieze jerkin* a jerkin made of coarse woollen cloth
      saveguard an outer petticoat worn by women to protect their dress when riding

ALL [GALLANTS]

  Moll, Moll, pist, Moll.

MOLL

  How now, what's the matter?

GOSHAWK

  A pipe of good tobacco, Moll.

MOLL

  I cannot stay.

GOSHAWK

  Nay Moll, puh, prithee hark, but one word i'faith.   160

MOLL

  Well, what is't?

GREENWIT

  Prithee come hither, sirrah.

LAXTON

  [*Aside*] Heart, I would give but too much money to be nibbling
  with that wench: life, sh'as the spirit of four great parishes, and
  a voice that will drown all the city: methinks a brave captain   165
  might get all his soldiers upon her, and ne'er be beholding to a
  company of Mile End milksops, if he could come on, and come
  off quick enough: such a Moll were a marrow-bone before an
  Italian, he would cry bona roba till his ribs were nothing but
  bone. I'll lay hard siege to her, money is that aqua fortis that   170
  eats into many a maidenhead: where the walls are flesh and
  blood, I'll ever pierce through with a golden auger.

GOSHAWK

  Now thy judgment, Moll, is't not good?

MOLL

  Yes faith 'tis very good tobacco, how do you sell an ounce?

166   *get* i.e. beget
167   *Mile End milksops* The city trained-bands were exercised at Mile End on the green
      which is now Stepney Green; it was also a place of resort for cakes and cream.
168–9 *marrow-bone before an Italian* Marrow-bone was popularly supposed to be an
      aphrodisiac. Cf. *A Mad World, My Masters*, I.ii.46ff.: 'I have conveyed away all her
      wanton pamphlets; as *Hero and Leander, Venus and Adonis*; O, two luscious
      marrowbone pies for a young married wife!' Italians were widely believed to be
      extremely lecherous and to be fond of unorthodox coital positions (cf. *Michaelmas
      Term*, III.i.18, and *A Mad World, My Masters*, III.iii.59). Moll's 'masculinity' might
      here imply a suggestion of buggery.
169   *bona roba* wench, frequently a prostitute (the term had lately been taken over from
      Italian)
170   *aqua fortis* literally nitric acid, commonly used in dilute form as a solvent
171–2 *maidenhead . . . I'll* punctuation ed. (maidenhead, where . . . bloud. I'll . . . Q).

Farewell. God b'i'you, Mistress Gallipot.   175

GOSHAWK

Why Moll, Moll.

MOLL

I cannot stay now i'faith, I am going to buy a shag ruff, the shop
will be shut in presently.

GOSHAWK

'Tis the maddest fantasticall'st girl: – I never knew so much
flesh and so much nimbleness put together.   180

LAXTON

She slips from one company to another like a fat eel between a
Dutchman's fingers. – [*Aside*] I'll watch my time for her.

MISTRESS GALLIPOT

Some will not stick to say she's a man
And some both man and woman.

LAXTON

That were excellent, she might first cuckold the husband and   185
then make him do as much for the wife.

The feather-shop again

MOLL

Save you; how does Mistress Tiltyard?

JACK DAPPER

Moll.

MOLL

Jack Dapper.

JACK DAPPER

How dost Moll?   190

MOLL

I'll tell thee by and by, I go but to th'next shop.

JACK DAPPER

Thou shalt find me here this hour about a feather.

MOLL

Nay and a feather hold you in play a whole hour, a goose will
last you all the days of your life.

The sempster shop

Let me see a good shag ruff.   195

---

177   *shag* cloth having a velvet nap on one side, usually of worsted but sometimes of silk
178   *shut in* The counter-flap projecting from the house to form a shop would be raised.

MASTER OPENWORK

Mistress Mary, that shalt thou i'faith, and the best in the shop.

MISTRESS OPENWORK

How now, greetings, love-terms with a pox between you, have I
found out one of your haunts? I send you for hollands, and
you're i'th'low countries with a mischief. I'm served with good
ware by th'shift, that makes it lie dead so long upon my hands,   200
I were as good shut up shop, for when I open it I take nothing.

MASTER OPENWORK

Nay and you fall a-ringing once, the devil cannot stop you, I'll
out of the belfry as fast as I can. – Moll.

MISTRESS OPENWORK

Get you from my shop.

MOLL

I come to buy.   205

MISTRESS OPENWORK

I'll sell ye nothing, I warn ye my house and shop.

MOLL

You goody Openwork, you that prick out a poor living
And sews many a bawdy skin-coat together,
Thou private pandress between shirt and smock,
I wish thee for a minute but a man: 210
Thou should'st never use more shapes; but as th'art

198–201 *I send you . . . nothing* A dazzling linguistic challenge. The first pun seems to derive
in particular from the brilliant wordplay of *2 Henry IV*, II.ii.21–2: 'the rest of the
low countries have made a shift to eat up thy holland': 'low countries' (with a play
on 'cunt' in 'countries' see *Hamlet*, III.ii.116) meant both the lower parts of the body
and the stews (where Poins and supposedly Master Openwork beget bastards);
hence, similarly, 'holland', as well as, literally, linen – which prompts 'shift' in the
sense of chemise. And the seemingly innocent shopkeeping talk in the second sentence conceals a complex obscenity: 'ware' was in regular use for the genitals of either
sex, but especially of women (where it was commonly 'lady's ware') (cf. *A Chaste
Maid in Cheapside*, II.i.99). The burden, then, of Mistress Openwork's complaint is
that by a trick (a shift) she is left to make what shift she can by handling her sexual
parts (those next to her shift) herself: a barren ('dead') activity, but she may as well
stop offering herself, for when she opens up her 'shop', nothing comes in.
199 *i'th'low* ed. (ith the low Q)
202 *a-ringing* scolding
203 *Moll* Her name appears at the end of a line seemingly as the last word of Openwork's
speech. But I suspect it may be the speech prefix of a missing few words from Moll,
to which Mistress Openwork's speech is a retort.
206 *warn* deny
207 *goody* shortened form of 'goodwife', a term of civility used to married women of
humble station
208 *skin-coat* a coat made of skins, but used figuratively of a person's skin itself

I pity my revenge: now my spleen's up
I would not mock it willingly.

Enter a FELLOW *with a long rapier by his side*

                      – Ha, be thankful,
Now I forgive thee.

MISTRESS OPENWORK Marry hang thee,
I never asked forgiveness in my life.   215

MOLL

You, goodman swine's-face.

FELLOW

What, will you murder me?

MOLL

You remember, slave, how you abused me t'other night in a
tavern?

FELLOW

Not I, by this light.   220

MOLL

No, but by candlelight you did, you have tricks to save your
oaths, reservations have you? And I have reserved somewhat for
you. [*Strikes him*] As you like that, call for more, you know the
sign again.

FELLOW

Pox on't, had I brought any company along with me to have   225
borne witness on't, 'twould ne'er have grieved me, but to be
struck and nobody by, 'tis my ill fortune still: why, tread upon
a worm, they say 'twill turn tail, but indeed a gentleman should
have more manners.   *Exit*

LAXTON

Gallantly performed i'faith Moll, and manfully, I love thee for-   230
ever for't: base rogue, had he offered but the least counter-buff,
by this hand I was prepared for him.

MOLL

You prepared for him? Why should you be prepared for him,
was he any more than a man?

---

213   sd FELLOW probably in the sense of thief (cf. *A Trick to Catch the Old One*, II.i.19f.)
227–8   *tread . . . tail* i.e. even the humblest will resent extreme ill-treatment: a common
        proverbial expression

LAXTON

No, nor so much by a yard and a handful London measure.   235

MOLL

Why do you speak this then? Do you think I cannot ride a stone
horse unless one lead him by th'snaffle?

LAXTON

Yes and sit him bravely, I know thou canst Moll, 'twas but an
honest mistake through love, and I'll make amends for't any
way: prithee sweet plump Moll, when shall thou and I go out   240
o'town together?

MOLL

Whither? To Tyburn, prithee?

LAXTON

Mass that's out o'town indeed, thou hang'st so many jests upon
thy friends still. I mean honestly to Brainford, Staines, or Ware.

MOLL

What to do there?   245

LAXTON

Nothing but be merry and lie together, I'll hire a coach with
four horses.

MOLL

I thought 'twould be a beastly journey: you may leave out one
well, three horses will serve if I play the jade myself.

LAXTON

Nay push, th'art such another kicking wench, prithee be kind   250
and let's meet.

MOLL

'Tis hard but we shall meet, sir.

LAXTON

Nay but appoint the place then, there's ten angels in fair gold,
Moll, you see I do not trifle with you, do but say thou wilt meet
me, and I'll have a coach ready for thee.   255

235   *London measure* a former practice of London drapers of allowing a little more than
        the standard yard. For the obscene pun on 'yard' cf. II.ii.80n.
236–7 *ride a stone horse* A stone horse is a stallion, likely to be a horse of some spirit; but
        there is likely to be in Laxton's answer a hint of Moll's assumed sexual prowess,
        though 'to ride a horse' was normally used of a man, meaning to mount a woman.
242   *Tyburn* a place of execution
244   *Brainford* a common spelling of Brentford, then a popular place for assignations (as
        were Staines and Ware), and one of the most frequently alluded to
248   *beastly* obscene; sexually bestial
249   *play the jade* act the whore: the word was used contemptuously of both horses and
        women

38

MOLL

Why, here's my hand I'll meet you sir.

LAXTON

[*Aside*] Oh good gold. – The place, sweet Moll?

MOLL

It shall be your appointment.

LAXTON

Somewhat near Holborn, Moll.

MOLL

In Gray's Inn Fields then.   260

LAXTON

A match.

MOLL

I'll meet you there.

LAXTON

The hour?

MOLL

Three.

LAXTON

That will be time enough to sup at Brainford.   265

Fall from them to the other

MASTER OPENWORK

I am of such a nature, sir, I cannot endure the house when she
scolds, sh'has a tongue will be heard further in a still morning
than Saint Antling's bell, she rails upon me for foreign wenching,
that I being a freeman must needs keep a whore i'th'suburbs,
and seek to impoverish the liberties: when we fall out, I trouble   270
you still to make all whole with my wife.

GOSHAWK

No trouble at all, 'tis a pleasure to me to join things together.

260 *Gray's Inn Fields* open fields to the north of Gray's Inn, used as an archery ground,
     but afterwards frequented by footpads
265 sd *Fall from them to the other* i.e. the other group on the stage come forward or take
     over the dialogue
267 *heard* ed. (hard Q)
268 *Saint Antling's bell* St Antholin's Church, which stood in Watling Street, near St
     Paul's, was much frequented by Puritans. In 1599 a number of clergymen of Puritan
     views established a morning lecture here, the bell for which began to ring at 5 a.m.
     and was a great nuisance to the neighbourhood (Sugden). The church, rebuilt after
     the Great Fire of 1666, was pulled down in 1874.
269 *suburbs* those, that is, beyond the liberties of the City which extended the City's
     control beyond its bounds. 'Liberties' meant also rights or privileges, and Master
     Openwork must be hinting at those of his wife.

MASTER OPENWORK

[*Aside*] Go thy ways, I do this but to try thy honesty, Goshawk.

The feather-shop

JACK DAPPER

How lik'st thou this, Moll?

MOLL

Oh singularly, you're fitted now for a bunch. [*Aside*] He looks   275
for all the world with those spangled feathers like a nobleman's
bedpost. The purity of your wench would I fain try, she seems,
like Kent, unconquered, and I believe as many wiles are in her
– oh, the gallants of these times are shallow lechers, they put
not their courtship home enough to a wench, 'tis impossible to   280
know what woman is thoroughly honest, because she's ne'er
thoroughly tried: I am of that certain belief there are more
queans in this town of their own making than of any man's
provoking; where lies the slackness then? Many a poor soul
would down, and there's nobody will push 'em: 285
Women are courted but ne'er soundly tried,
As many walk in spurs that never ride.

The sempster's shop

MISTRESS OPENWORK

Oh abominable.

GOSHAWK

Nay more, I tell you in private, he keeps a whore i'th'suburbs.

276–7   *a nobleman's bedpost* The beds of the wealthy were festooned with rich hangings.
   277   *The purity of your wench would I fain try* i.e. of Mistress Tiltyard. 'Try' is used
         frequently by Middleton in a sexual sense. So De Flores misinterprets Beatrice in
         The Changeling (II.ii.97ff.). Moll's intention is not acted upon; since the Tiltyards
         play so small a part, it may be that an episode has been cancelled.
   278   *like Kent, unconquered* It was a boast of Kentishmen that Kent had never
         been conquered. At Swanscombe (near Northfleet) in 1066, when William I
         marched round the country to secure the coast and the Channel ports, he
         is traditionally said to have met the men of Kent and confirmed their possession of
         all their laws and privileges. The phrase seems likely to be a direct theft from
         Drayton, *The Barons' Wars*, I, 323–4:
            Then those of Kent, unconquered of the rest,
            That to this day maintain their ancient right.
         There is also an apposite play on Kent/cunt.
   283   *queans* whores

MISTRESS OPENWORK

    Oh spital dealing, I came to him a gentlewoman born. I'll show   290
you mine arms when you please, sir.

GOSHAWK

    [*Aside*] I had rather see your legs, and begin that way.

MISTRESS OPENWORK

    'Tis well known he took me from a lady's service, where I was
well beloved of the steward, I had my Latin tongue, and a spice
of the French before I came to him, and now doth he keep a   295
suburbian whore under my nostrils.

GOSHAWK

    There's ways enough to cry quit with him: hark in thine ear.

MISTRESS OPENWORK

    There's a friend worth a million.

MOLL

    [*Aside*] I'll try one spear against your chastity, Mistress Tiltyard,
though it prove too short by the burr.   300

            Enter RALPH TRAPDOOR

TRAPDOOR

    [*Aside*] Mass, here she is. I'm bound already to serve her, though
it be but a sluttish trick. – Bless my hopeful young mistress with
long life and great limbs, send her the upper hand of all bailiffs
and their hungry adherents.

MOLL

    How now, what art thou?   305

TRAPDOOR

    A poor ebbing gentleman, that would gladly wait for the young
flood of your service.

---

290   *spital dealing* Spitals were originally lazar houses, but came to be used for maimed
        whores.

294   *my Latin tongue* These phrases might suggest that Mistress Openwork had herself
        been loose before marriage, especially if 'French' is taken to hint at syphilis. 'Latin
        tongue' may be another gesture towards Italian sexual habits.

296   *suburbian* obsolete spelling, commonly used where the reference was to licentious
        life there

297   *quit* ed. (quite Q: an obsolete form)

300   *burr* (burgh Q) a broad iron ring on a tilting lance, just behind the place for the hand

306–7   *young flood* the flow of tide up-river

307   *service* The word, as Christopher Ricks points out (*E in C*, 10 (1960), 296), means
        copulation as well as the duty of a servant. Together with 'stand' (cf. I.ii.56–7n.) it
        makes Trapdoor's farmyard intentions plain. 'Use' also has commonly a sexual
        meaning of course: so, he will have an erection when she needs it.

MOLL

My service! What should move you to offer your service to me,
sir?

TRAPDOOR

The love I bear to your heroic spirit and masculine womanhood.   310

MOLL

So sir, put case we should retain you to us, what parts are there
in you for a gentlewoman's service?

TRAPDOOR

Of two kinds, right worshipful: movable and immovable:
movable to run of errands, and immovable to stand when you
have occasion to use me.   315

MOLL

What strength have you?

TRAPDOOR

Strength, Mistress Moll? I have gone up into a steeple, and
stayed the great bell as't has been ringing; stopped a windmill
going.

MOLL

And never struck down yourself?   320

TRAPDOOR

Stood as upright as I do at this present.

> MOLL *trips up his heels, he falls*

MOLL

Come, I pardon you for this, it shall be no disgrace to you: I
have struck up the heels of the high German's size ere now.
What, not stand?

TRAPDOOR

I am of that nature, where I love I'll be at my mistress' foot to   325
do her service.

MOLL

Why well said, but say your mistress should receive injury, have
you the spirit of fighting in you, durst you second her?

---

321   sd here ed. (*at l. 310* Q)

323   *the high German* There are a number of allusions to the high German, who was
evidently a fencer of great size who seems to have spent some considerable time in
London. In *The Owl's Almanac*, 7, Dekker says that he 'cudgelled most of our English
fencers now about a month past'; in Shirley's *The Opportunity* he has 'beaten all the
fencers in Europe'; but he was at one time, it seems, imprisoned, for 'those escape
very hardly, like the German out of Wood-street' (*The Curtain Drawer of the World*
(1612, qu. Collier), 27).

TRAPDOOR

Life, I have kept a bridge myself, and drove seven at a time
before me.   330

MOLL

Ay?

TRAPDOOR

(*Aside*) But they were all Lincolnshire bullocks by my troth.

MOLL

Well, meet me in Gray's Inn Fields, between three and four this
afternoon, and upon better consideration we'll retain you.

TRAPDOOR

I humbly thank your good mistress-ship. [*Aside*] I'll crack your   335
neck for this kindness.   *Exit*

MOLL *meets* LAXTON

LAXTON

Remember three.

MOLL

Nay if I fail you, hang me.

LAXTON

Good wench i'faith.

then OPENWORK

MOLL

Who's this?   340

MASTER OPENWORK

'Tis I, Moll.

MOLL

Prithee tend thy shop and prevent bastards.

MASTER OPENWORK

We'll have a pint of the same wine i'faith, Moll.

[*Exeunt* MOLL *and* MASTER OPENWORK]
The bell rings

GOSHAWK

Hark the bell rings, come gentlemen.
Jack Dapper, where shall's all munch?   345

JACK DAPPER

I am for Parker's ordinary.

343   *a pint of the same wine* Bastard was a sweet Spanish wine resembling Muscadel.
       sd 2 *The bell rings* i.e. a clock strikes
346   *Parker's* unidentified

43

LAXTON

    He's a good guest to'm, he deserves his board,

    He draws all the gentlemen in a term-time thither:

    We'll be your followers, Jack, lead the way:

    Look you by my faith the fool has feathered his nest well.   350

Exeunt GALLANTS

Enter MASTER GALLIPOT, MASTER TILTYARD,
and SERVANTS *with water-spaniels and a duck*

MASTER TILTYARD

    Come shut up your shops: where's Master Openwork?

MISTRESS GALLIPOT

    Nay ask not me, Master Tiltyard.

MASTER TILTYARD

    Where's his water-dog? Puh – pist – hur – hur – pist.

MASTER GALLIPOT

    Come wenches come, we're going all to Hogsden.

MISTRESS GALLIPOT

    To Hogsden, husband?   355

MASTER GALLIPOT

    Ay, to Hogsden, pigsney.

MISTRESS GALLIPOT

    I'm not ready, husband.

MASTER GALLIPOT

    Faith that's well – hum – pist – pist.

Spits in the dog's mouth

    Come Mistress Openwork, you are so long.

MISTRESS OPENWORK

    I have no joy of my life, Master Gallipot.   360

347   *to'm* (*stet* Q); meaning 'to him' not 'to them'

351   sd 2 *water-spaniels and a duck* They are going duck-hunting – a sport in which ducks were pursued over a pond.

352   sp *MISTRESS GALLIPOT* Perhaps this speech should be given to Mistress Openwork, to whom the question would be more appropriately put, and from whom the reply would be more pointed.

353   *Puh – pist...* cf. l. 358

354   *Hogsden* i.e. Hoxton, then much resorted to for excursions by citizens and apprentices

356   *pigsney* (i.e. pig's eye) darling, pet

358   sd *Spits in the dog's mouth* Mulholland quotes William Fennor: 'When a poore man comes nigh a churlish mastiffe he must not spurne at him if he meane to go quietly by him, but flatter and stroake him on the backe, and spit in his mouth' (*Compters Commonwealth*, 1617, p. 73).

MASTER GALLIPOT

Push, let your boy lead his water-spaniel along, and we'll show
you the bravest sport at Parlous Pond. Hey Trug, hey Trug, hey
Trug, here's the best duck in England, except my wife;
Hey, hey, hey, fetch, fetch, fetch, come let's away.
Of all the year this is the sportfull'st day.   365

[*Exeunt*]

[ACT II, SCENE ii]

Enter SEBASTIAN *solus*

SEBASTIAN

If a man have a free will, where should the use
More perfect shine than in his will to love?
All creatures have their liberty in that,

Enter SIR ALEXANDER *and listens to him*

Though else kept under servile yoke and fear,
The very bondslave has his freedom there.   5
Amongst a world of creatures voiced and silent
Must my desires wear fetters? – Yea, are you
So near? Then I must break with my heart's truth,
Meet grief at a back way. – Well: why, suppose
The two-leaved tongues of slander or of truth   10

---

362   *Parlous Pond* Parlous or Perilous Pool (so called because it was the scene of many
      accidents) was a large pond lying behind St Luke's Hospital on the edge of Hoxton;
      it was a favourite place for duck-hunting and later for bathing. Though both 'pond'
      and 'sport' make sexual openings, it seems to be literal wildfowl that the citizens are
      going after.

  0   sd *solus* (Lat.) alone
  1   *free will* a key but problematic Christian tenet under pressure from Calvinist notions
      of predestination. A character called Freevill appears in Marston's *The Dutch
      Courtesan* (1605).
  5   *there.* ed. (there, Q)
  6   *silent* ed. (silent. Q)
  7   *fetters?* ed. (fetters – Q)
  9   *why, suppose* ed. (why suppose. Q)
 10   *two-leaved* ed. (two leaud Q) After some hesitation I follow Dyce and later editors.
      Collier suggested 'lewd', for which 'leaud' is a recorded contemporary spelling

Pronounce Moll loathsome: if before my love
She appear fair, what injury have I?
I have the thing I like: in all things else
Mine own eye guides me, and I find 'em prosper:
Life, what should ail it now? I know that man   15
Ne'er truly loves – if he gainsay't he lies –
That winks and marries with his father's eyes.
I'll keep mine own wide open.

Enter MOLL *and a* PORTER *with a viol on his back*

SIR ALEXANDER   Here's brave wilfulness,
A made match, here she comes, they met o'purpose.

PORTER

Must I carry this great fiddle to your chamber, Mistress Mary?   20

MOLL

Fiddle, goodman hog-rubber? Some of these porters bear so
much for others, they have no time to carry wit for themselves.

PORTER

To your own chamber, Mistress Mary?

MOLL

Who'll hear an ass speak? Whither else, goodman pageant-
bearer? They're people of the worst memories.   25

Exit PORTER

SEBASTIAN

Why, 'twere too great a burthen, love, to have them carry things
in their minds and o'their backs together.

(Holland's *Pliny*, 1601, I, 31), and we should presumably then understand it in the
sense of unlearned or ignorant. Bowers explains 'two-leaved' as a 'comparison of
the tongue to the two hinged parts of a door or gate [i.e. equivalent to the Latin
valvae; cf. Isaiah 45, 1], each of which can move independently and thus pronounce
either slander or truth', and he gives 'double-tongued' as a modern equivalent. The
aptness of the comparison is uncompelling, though the singular 'tongue' would
improve matters. But this reading may be preferred.

21   *Fiddle* There is evidently some joke here which I haven't been able to uncover. By the
eighteenth century, 'fiddle' had become one of many words for the female sexual
organs, and it could also mean a writ to arrest; but neither seems to have much
appropriateness here. Cf., however, *Henry VIII*, I.iii.39–41: 'The sly whoresons / Have
got a speeding trick to lay down ladies; / A French song and a fiddle has no fellow.'
hog-rubber used as a term of contempt, probably not clearly distinguished from
'hog-grubber', a mean or sneaking fellow

24–5   *pageant-bearer* A pageant was a portable stage, consisting of boards resting on a
framework of trestles, which could be set up in the street for the acting of plays or
other spectacles. I do not know why pageant-bearers should have been noted for
forgetfulness.

MOLL

Pardon me sir, I thought not you so near.

SIR ALEXANDER

So, so, so.

SEBASTIAN

I would be nearer to thee, and in that fashion 30
That makes the best part of all creatures honest.
No otherwise I wish it.

MOLL

Sir, I am so poor to requite you, you must look for nothing but
thanks of me: I have no humour to marry, I love to lie o'both
sides o'th'bed myself, and again o'th'other side; a wife you know 35
ought to be obedient, but I fear me I am too headstrong to
obey, therefore I'll ne'er go about it. I love you so well, sir, for
your good will I'd be loath you should repent your bargain
after, and therefore we'll ne'er come together at first. I have
the head now of myself, and am man enough for a woman; 40
marriage is but a chopping and changing, where a maiden loses
one head and has a worse i'th'place.

SIR ALEXANDER

The most comfortablest answer for a roaring girl
That ever mine ears drunk in.

SEBASTIAN   This were enough
Now to affright a fool forever from thee, 45
When 'tis the music that I love thee for.

SIR ALEXANDER

There's a boy spoils all again.

MOLL

Believe it, sir, I am not of that disdainful temper, but I could
love you faithfully.

SIR ALEXANDER

A pox on you for that word. I like you not now, 50
Y'are a cunning roarer. I see that already.

MOLL

But sleep upon this once more, sir, you may chance shift a mind
tomorrow: be not too hasty to wrong yourself, never while you
live, sir, take a wife running, many have run out at heels that
have done't: you see, sir, I speak against myself, and if every 55
woman would deal with their suitor so honestly, poor younger

39   *at first* in the first place

47

brothers would not be so often gulled with old cozening widows, that turn o'er all their wealth in trust to some kinsman, and make the poor gentleman work hard for a pension. Fare you well sir.   60

SEBASTIAN

Nay prithee one word more.

SIR ALEXANDER

How do I wrong this girl, she puts him off still.

MOLL

Think upon this in cold blood, sir, you make as much haste as if you were going upon a sturgeon voyage, take deliberation, sir, never choose a wife as if you were going to Virginia.   65

SEBASTIAN

And so we parted, my too cursed fate.

SIR ALEXANDER

She is but cunning, gives him longer time in't.

Enter a TAILOR

TAILOR

Mistress Moll, Mistress Moll: so ho ho so ho.

MOLL

There boy, there boy, what, dost thou go a-hawking after me with a red clout on thy finger?   70

TAILOR

I forgot to take measure on you for your new breeches.

---

64 *sturgeon voyage OED* can only suggest a voyage for sturgeon, which scarcely explains what Moll means; probably, like the reference to Virginia, the allusion is to a voyage of long duration for which any wife would be better than none. But sturgeons were found in the Thames, and the Lord Mayor had the right to all caught above London Bridge.

65 *as if you were going to Virginia* Presumably because there would be no chance of finding a wife once there, one must take one from home; but there may be an obscure play on the name of the colony.

66 Dyce suggests a quotation here, but none has been located.

68 *so ho ho so ho* This is a customary falconer's cry, encouraging the bird to stoop to the lure. Hence 'hawking' in the next line, and perhaps the 'red clout'. The lure was a bunch of feathers sewn on to cloth, sometimes with a piece of red meat in the middle; in the tailor's case the 'clout' seems likely to have been a pincushion worn strapped to the wrist or finger. 'There boy' was a huntsman's cry to his dogs: cf. *The Tempest*, IV.i.257.

70 *clout* strip of cloth used as a pin-cushion

SIR ALEXANDER

> Hoyda, breeches? What, will he marry a monster with two
> trinkets? What age is this? If the wife go in breeches, the man
> must wear long coats like a fool.

MOLL

> What fiddling's here? Would not the old pattern have served   75
> your turn?

TAILOR

> You change the fashion, you say you'll have the great Dutch
> slop, Mistress Mary.

MOLL

> Why sir, I say so still.

TAILOR

> Your breeches then will take up a yard more.   80

MOLL

> Well, pray look it be put in then.

TAILOR

> It shall stand round and full, I warrant you.

MOLL

> Pray make 'em easy enough.

TAILOR

> I know my fault now, t'other was somewhat stiff between the
> legs, I'll make these open enough, I warrant you.   85

SIR ALEXANDER

> Here's good gear towards, I have brought up my son to marry a
> Dutch slop and a French doublet, a codpiece-daughter.

TAILOR

> So, I have gone as far as I can go.

MOLL

> Why then, farewell.

72–3   *two trinkets* No slang or cant use is recorded. 'Trinkets' may mean testicles or (taking
        account of 'monster') suggest that he thinks her hermaphrodite with the organs of
        both sexes.

74   *coats* i.e. petticoats

75   *fiddling* fidgeting, playing about

77–8   *great Dutch slop* wide baggy breeches, then newly in fashion

80   This and the tailor's next three speeches have an obscene pun on 'yard' (penis, as at
        Love's Labour's Lost, V.ii.669). Cf. *The Honest Whore*, part 1, V.ii.259ff.: 'This was her
        tailor – you cut out her loose-bodied gown, and put in a yard more than I allowed
        her.'

86   *gear* clothing, with a secondary sense of business at hand

TAILOR

    If you go presently to your chamber, Mistress Mary, pray send   90
    me the measure of your thigh by some honest body.

MOLL

    Well, sir, I'll send it by a porter presently.   *Exit*

TAILOR

    So you had need, it is a lusty one, both of them would make any
    porter's back ache in England.   *Exit*

SEBASTIAN

    I have examined the best part of man,   95
    Reason and judgment, and in love they tell me
    They leave me uncontrolled: he that is swayed
    By an unfeeling blood past heat of love,
    His springtime must needs err, his watch ne'er goes right
    That sets his dial by a rusty clock.   100

SIR ALEXANDER

    So, and which is that rusty clock, sir, you?

SEBASTIAN

    The clock at Ludgate, sir, it ne'er goes true.

SIR ALEXANDER

    But thou goest falser: not thy father's cares
    Can keep thee right. When that insensible work
    Obeys the workman's art, lets off the hour   105
    And stops again when time is satisfied:
    But thou run'st on, and judgment, thy main wheel,
    Beats by all stops, as if the work would break,
    Begun with long pains for a minute's ruin:
    Much like a suffering man brought up with care,   110

---

    93   *a lusty one* Thighs are an obvious incitement to sexual adventure. Cf. *Romeo and Juliet* II.i.19f.: Rosaline's 'quivering thigh, / And the demesnes that there adjacent lie'.

97–100   *he that is swayed . . . rusty clock* This seems to be a rather laboured attempt to combine a sardonic comment on the old man's incapacity – once he is old and impotent he cannot hope for sexual success, his spring is no longer taut, his action is rusty, his rhythm erratic and weak – with a warning that the young (those in their springtime) be not ruled by the dicta of the elderly.

  102   *The clock at Ludgate* perhaps the clock on St Martin's Church. Old engravings show no clock on the gate itself, which (a replacement of the original) was rebuilt in 1586.

104–6   *When that insensible work . . . satisfied* When the invisible movement (of the clock) obeys the workman's art, the hour strikes and stops again after the correct number of strokes. (Lets off = removes the stop from the strike.)

  108   *Beats by all stops* See 104–6n.; but a stop is also a device to prevent overwinding.

At last bequeathed to shame and a short prayer.

SEBASTIAN

I taste you bitterer than I can deserve, sir.

SIR ALEXANDER

Who has bewitched thee, son? What devil or drug
Hath wrought upon the weakness of thy blood,
And betrayed all her hopes to ruinous folly?   115
Oh wake from drowsy and enchanted shame,
Wherein thy soul sits with a golden dream
Flattered and poisoned. I am old, my son,
Oh let me prevail quickly,
For I have weightier business of mine own   120
Than to chide thee: I must not to my grave
As a drunkard to his bed, whereon he lies
Only to sleep, and never cares to rise.
Let me dispatch in time, come no more near her.

SEBASTIAN

Not honestly? Not in the way of marriage?   125

SIR ALEXANDER

What sayst thou, marriage? In what place? The sessions house?
And who shall give the bride, prithee? An indictment?

SEBASTIAN

Sir, now ye take part with the world to wrong her.

SIR ALEXANDER

Why, wouldst thou fain marry to be pointed at?
Alas the number's great, do not o'erburden't: 130
Why, as good marry a beacon on a hill,
Which all the country fix their eyes upon,
As her thy folly doats on. If thou long'st
To have the story of thy infamous fortunes
Serve for discourse in ordinaries and taverns,   135
Th'art in the way: or to confound thy name,
Keep on, thou canst not miss it: or to strike
Thy wretched father to untimely coldness,
Keep the left hand still, it will bring thee to't.

111   *short prayer* i.e. before execution: cf. III.i.115–16
113   *bewitched* ed. (bewitch Q)
115   *all her hopes* Blood may be thought of as feminine by analogy with soul; or possibly
      we should read 'my' or 'thy'.
126   *sessions house* legislative court
139   *Keep the left hand still* act perversely, or perhaps in feigned friendship only: the date
      seems too early for an allusion to left-handed or morganatic marriage

Yet if no tears wrung from thy father's eyes, 140
Nor sighs that fly in sparkles from his sorrows,
Had power to alter what is wilful in thee,
Methinks her very name should fright thee from her,
And never trouble me.

SEBASTIAN

Why is the name of Moll so fatal, sir? 145

SIR ALEXANDER

Many one, sir, where suspect is entered,
Forseek all London from one end to t'other,
More whores of that name than of any ten other.

SEBASTIAN

What's that to her? Let those blush for themselves.
Can any guilt in others condemn her? 150
I've vowed to love her: let all storms oppose me,
That ever beat against the breast of man,
Nothing but death's black tempest shall divide us.

SIR ALEXANDER

Oh folly that can doat on nought but shame!

SEBASTIAN

Put case a wanton itch runs through one name 155
More than another, is that name the worse,
Where honesty sits possessed in't? It should rather
Appear more excellent, and deserve more praise,
When through foul mists a brightness it can raise.
Why, there are of the devil's, honest gentlemen, 160
And well descended, keep an open house,
And some o'th'good man's that are arrant knaves.
He hates unworthily that by rote contemns,
For the name neither saves, nor yet condemns:
And for her honesty, I have made such proof on't, 165
In several forms, so nearly watched her ways,
I will maintain that strict against an army,
Excepting you my father: here's her worst,
Sh'has a bold spirit that mingles with mankind,

---

146 *Many one* many a one (presumably constables)
147 *Forseek* search thoroughly, ransack
155 *Put case* suppose, perhaps with a pun on 'case' meaning vagina (as in *A Chaste Maid in Cheapside*, II.i.200)
160 *of the devil's* among those who appear to be of the devil's party
162 *o'th'good man's* an allusion to the proverb 'God is a good man'. Cf. *Much Ado*, III.v.36.

But nothing else comes near it: and oftentimes   170
Through her apparel somewhat shames her birth,
But she is loose in nothing but in mirth:
Would all Molls were no worse.

SIR ALEXANDER
This way I toil in vain and give but aim
To infamy and ruin: he will fall,   175
My blessing cannot stay him: all my joys
Stand at the brink of a devouring flood
And will be wilfully swallowed: wilfully.
But why so vain let all these tears be lost?
I'll pursue her to shame, and so all's crossed.   *Exit*   180

SEBASTIAN
He is gone with some strange purpose, whose effect
Will hurt me little if he shoot so wide,
To think I love so blindly: I but feed
His heart to this match, to draw on th'other,
Wherein my joy sits with a full wish crowned,   185
Only his mood excepted, which must change
By opposite policies, courses indirect:
Plain dealing in this world takes no effect.
This mad girl I'll acquaint with my intent,
Get her assistance, make my fortunes known: 190
'Twixt lovers' hearts she's a fit instrument,
And has the art to help them to their own:
By her advice, for in that craft she's wise,
My love and I may meet, spite of all spies.   *Exit*

174   *give but aim* The man who gave aim stood near the butt and showed how far the arrow fell from the mark.
186   *change* ed. (change. Q)

53

[ACT III, SCENE i]

Enter LAXTON *in Gray's Inn Fields with the* COACHMAN

LAXTON

Coachman.

COACHMAN

Here sir.

LAXTON

There's a tester more, prithee drive thy coach to the hither end
of Marybone Park, a fit place for Moll to get in.

COACHMAN

Marybone Park, sir.   5

LAXTON

Ay, it's in our way thou know'st.

COACHMAN

It shall be done, sir.

LAXTON

Coachman.

COACHMAN

Anon, sir.

LAXTON

Are we fitted with good frampold jades?   10

COACHMAN

The best in Smithfield, I warrant you, sir.

---

3   *tester* sixpence (from the teston of Henry VIII, originally worth a shilling, and so
     called because it carried an image of the king's head: *teste* is the old spelling of French
     tête head)
4   *Marybone Park* Until 1611 Marylebone Manor was crown property: the gardens
     (ultimately incorporated into Regent's Park) were said in *A Fair Quarrel* (IV.iv.217ff.)
     to be suitable as a burial ground for whores and panders because it was near Tyburn.
     The point of Laxton's quip, however, is enriched by the linking of a pun on
     Marybone (marrow-bone; cf. II.i.168–9n.) and 'park' in the sense of 'the female body
     as a domain where the lover may freely roam' (Eric Partridge, *Shakespeare's Bawdy*
     (1956), p. 163; cf. *Venus and Adonis*, 231ff.).
10   *frampold* mettlesome, spirited (phrampell Q) *jades* contemptuous term for horses
11   *Smithfield* The worst jades came from Smithfield Market, east of Holborn. Cf. *2
     Henry IV*, I.ii.53ff., and the proverbial 'Who goes to Westminster for a wife, to Paul's
     for a man, and to Smithfield for a horse, may meet with a whore, a knave, and a
     jade.'
     you ed. (your Q)

LAXTON

> May we safely take the upper hand of any coached velvet cap or
> tufftaffety jacket? For they keep a vild swaggering in coaches
> nowadays, the highways are stopped with them.

COACHMAN

> My life for yours, and baffle 'em too sir: – why, they are the same   15
> jades, believe it, sir, that have drawn all your famous whores to
> Ware.

LAXTON

> Nay, then they know their business, they need no more
> instructions.

COACHMAN

> They're so used to such journeys, sir, I never use whip to 'em;   20
> for if they catch but the scent of a wench once, they run like
> devils.   *Exit* COACHMAN *with his whip*

LAXTON

> Fine Cerberus, that rogue will have the start of a thousand
> ones, for whilst others trot afoot, he'll ride prancing to hell
> upon a coach-horse.   25
>
> Stay, 'tis now about the hour of her appointment, but yet I
> see her not. (*The clock strikes three*) Hark what's this? One, two,
> three, three by the clock at Savoy: this is the hour, and Gray's
> Inn Fields the place, she swore she'd meet me: ha, yonder's two
> Inns o' Court men with one wench, but that's not she, they walk   30
> toward Islington out of my way: I see none yet dressed like her,
> I must look for a shag ruff, a frieze jerkin, a short sword, and a
> saveguard, or I get none: why, Moll, prithee make haste, or the
> coachman will curse us anon.

---

12 *coached* couched; embroidered with gold. The spelling plays on the coaches that
    follow.
13 *tufftaffety* a kind of taffeta with pile or nap arranged in tufts
    vild vile
14 *nowadays* since the repeal of sumptuary law in 1603 which allowed the newly wealthy
    middle classes to dress more finely than before. These people also need coaches –
    hitherto luxury items – creating traffic jams.
15 *baffle* pass contemptuously
23 *Cerberus* watchdog of the underworld
28 *Savoy* The great palace, built originally by Simon de Montfort in 1245 and
    reconstructed as a hospital in 1509, was by 1580 the subject of complaints that it
    was used as a nursery by 'great numbers of idle wicked persons, cutpurses, cozeners
    and such other thieves': see G. L. Gomme, *London* (1914), p. 225.
31 *Islington* a suburb to the north of London and a popular resort
33 *saveguard* See II.i.152 sd n.

Enter MOLL *like a man*

MOLL

[*Aside*] Oh here's my gentleman: if they would keep their days   35
as well with their mercers as their hours with their harlots, no
bankrupt would give seven score pound for a sergeant's place,
for would you know a catchpoll rightly derived, the corruption
of a citizen is the generation of a sergeant. How his eye hawks
for venery! – Come, you are ready sir?   40

LAXTON

Ready? For what sir?

MOLL

Do you ask that now, sir? Why was this meeting 'pointed?

LAXTON

I thought you mistook me sir.
You seem to be some young barrister:
I have no suit in law – all my land's sold,   45
I praise heaven for't; 't has rid me of much trouble.

MOLL

Then I must wake you, sir, where stands the coach?

LAXTON

Who's this? Moll, honest Moll?

MOLL

So young, and purblind? You're an old wanton in your eyes, I
see that.   50

LAXTON

Th'art admirably suited for the Three Pigeons at Brainford, I'll
swear I knew thee not.

MOLL

I'll swear you did not: but you shall know me now.

LAXTON

No, not here, we shall be spied i'faith, the coach is better, come.

35–7   The construction is somewhat obscure, though the general meaning is clear: if men
were as prompt in paying their mercers' bills as in keeping assignments with harlots,
it would be worth no-one's while to buy a sergeant's place at an inflated price, for
there would no longer be the bankruptcies to provide him a living.
38   *catchpoll* sheriff's officer, especially a bum-bailiff
corruption decomposition, ceasing to exist
45   *all my land's sold* another indication of Laxton's lack
51   *Three Pigeons* a well-known inn at Brentford, at one time kept by the famous actor
John Lowin. It is mentioned in *The Alchemist*, V.iv.89, and in other plays.
54   *No, not here* Laxton mistakes Moll's use of 'know'. Coaches were used then as the
back seats of cars are now.

MOLL

    Stay. 55

LAXTON

    What, wilt thou untruss a point, Moll?

She puts off her cloak and draws

MOLL

    Yes, here's the point that I untruss, 't has but one tag, 'twill
    serve, though, to tie up a rogue's tongue.

LAXTON

    How?

MOLL

    There's the gold 60
    With which you hired your hackney, here's her pace,
    She racks hard, and perhaps your bones will feel it:
    Ten angels of mine own I've put to thine,
    Win 'em and wear 'em.

LAXTON   Hold Moll, Mistress Mary.

MOLL

    Draw, or I'll serve an execution on thee 65
    Shall lay thee up till doomsday.

LAXTON

    Draw upon a woman? Why, what dost mean, Moll?

MOLL

    To teach thy base thoughts manners: th'art one of those
    That thinks each woman thy fond flexible whore,
    If she but cast a liberal eye upon thee; 70
    Turn back her head, she's thine: or, amongst company,

---

56   *untruss a point* unfasten a tag of doublet or breeches (as for sexual intercourse: see
      Measure for Measure, III.ii.179f.)
      sd *draws* i.e. her sword

61   *hackney* horse kept for hire, figuratively a prostitute: cf. *The Honest Whore*, part 1,
      II.i.225f.   *pace* her training as a whore (cf. *Pericles*, IV.vi.63)

62   *racks* moves with the gait called a rack 'in which the two feet on each side are lifted
      almost simultaneously, and the body is left entirely without support between the
      lifting of one pair and the landing of the other' (*OED*)

64   *Win 'em and wear 'em* a popular proverbial expression, often taking the form 'Win
      her and wear her' (i.e. as a bride)

65   *Draw . . . execution on thee* To serve an execution is to make formal delivery of a
      process at law. But in addition to her obvious threat of punishing him capitally,
      Moll's words punningly mock the frustration of Laxton's lecherous intentions; for
      to 'draw' meant also to expose the penis (as a sword from a scabbard), and an
      'execution' a performance of the sexual act (see *Troilus and Cressida*, III.ii.82). Her
      threat therefore is that she will geld him.

By chance drink first to thee, then she's quite gone,
There's no means to help her: nay for a need,
Wilt swear unto thy credulous fellow lechers
That thou art more in favour with a lady   75
At first sight than her monkey all her lifetime.
How many of our sex, by such as thou
Have their good thoughts paid with a blasted name
That never deserved loosely or did trip
In path of whoredom beyond cup and lip?   80
But for the stain of conscience and of soul,
Better had women fall into the hands
Of an act silent than a bragging nothing,
There's no mercy in't. – What durst move you, sir,
To think me whorish? – A name which I'd tear out   85
From the high German's throat if it lay ledger there
To dispatch privy slanders against me.
In thee I defy all men, their worst hates,
And their best flatteries, all their golden witchcrafts,
With which they entangle the poor spirits of fools.   90
Distressed needlewomen and trade-fallen wives,
Fish that must needs bite or themselves be bitten,
Such hungry things as these may soon be took
With a worm fastened on a golden hook:

75   *thou art* ed. (th'art Q)
75–6 lineation ed. (That th'art . . . first sight / Then her . . . Q)
76   *her monkey* Monkeys were popular as pets (and proverbially lascivious); but perhaps
      the word is here used to mean favourite, though this sense seems not to be otherwise
      recorded. See, however, the apparently rather nasty quip in *Michaelmas Term*, I.i.299,
      'As an old lady delights in a page or monkey'.
80   *beyond cup and lip* beyond sharing a loving-cup and kissing
82–3 Cf. Shakespeare, Sonnet 121:
          'Tis better to be vile than vile esteemed,
          When not to be receives reproach of being;
          And the just pleasure lost, which is so deemed
          Not by our feeling, but by others' seeing.
      'Act' here refers to the act of procreation (as, e.g., at *Merchant of Venice*, I.iii.83).
86   *high German's throat* Cf. II.i.323n.
      lay ledger rested permanent, as a fixture
90   *entangle the poor spirits of fools* i.e. endanger their souls by tempting them to sin
      fools. ed. (fooles, Q)
91   *wives,* ed. (wiues. Q)
94   To angle with a golden hook is an ancient proverbial expression; cf. *A Fair Quarrel*,
      III.ii.123: 'Thou'st fished with silver hooks and golden baits.' 'Fish' was common
      contemptuous slang for women.

Those are the lecher's food, his prey, he watches   95
For quarrelling wedlocks, and poor shifting sisters,
'Tis the best fish he takes: but why, good fisherman,
Am I thought meat for you, that never yet
Had angling rod cast towards me? 'Cause, you'll say,
I'm given to sport, I'm often merry, jest: 100
Had mirth no kindred in the world but lust?
Oh shame take all her friends then: but howe'er
Thou and the baser world censure my life,
I'll send 'em word by thee, and write so much
Upon thy breast, 'cause thou shalt bear't in mind: 105
Tell them 'twere base to yield, where I have conquered.
I scorn to prostitute myself to a man,
I that can prostitute a man to me,
And so I greet thee.

LAXTON   Hear me.
MOLL   Would the spirits
Of all my slanderers were clasped in thine,   110
That I might vex an army at one time.

LAXTON

I do repent me, hold.

                                                   They fight

MOLL

You'll die the better Christian then.

LAXTON

I do confess I have wronged thee, Moll.

---

96 *wedlocks* Anthony B. Dawson suggests that 'wedlocks' here means 'marriages' and
  not, as others have glossed, 'wives'. 'Mistress Hic and Haec: Representations of Moll
  Frith', *SEL*, 33 (1993), 404 n. 24.
  poor shifting sisters perhaps frustrated spinsters, those (not necessarily literal sisters)
  who are neglected and make what shift they can; but 'shifting' may suggest those
  who 'shift beds', i.e. are promiscuous: cf. *A Trick to Catch the Old One*, V.ii.167

100–2 Cf. *The Merry Wives of Windsor*, IV.ii.105–6: 'Wives may be merry, and yet honest
  too: / We do not act that often jest and laugh.'

101 *Had* Perhaps we should read 'Hath' (unless the clause is subordinate to what
  follows): 'Had' may have been attracted by the same word two lines above. The line
  might, however, be a hypothetical, subordinate to the following clause.

105 *'cause* so that

106 *them* i.e. lechers' future victims

110 *slanderers* ed. (slanders Q)

MOLL

    Confession is but poor amends for wrong,   115

    Unless a rope would follow.

LAXTON   I ask thee pardon.

MOLL

    I'm your hired whore, sir.

LAXTON

    I yield both purse and body.

MOLL   Both are mine,

    And now at my disposing.

LAXTON   Spare my life.

MOLL

    I scorn to strike thee basely.   120

LAXTON

    Spoke like a noble girl, i'faith. [*Aside*] Heart, I think I fight with
    a familiar, or the ghost of a fencer, sh'has wounded me gal-
    lantly: call you this a lecherous voyage? Here's blood would
    have served me this seven year in broken heads and cut fingers,
    and it now runs all out together. Pox o'the Three Pigeons, I would   125
    the coach were here now to carry me to the chirurgeons.

                                                     Exit

MOLL

    If I could meet my enemies one by one thus,
    I might make pretty shift with 'em in time,
    And make 'em know, she that has wit and spirit
    May scorn to live beholding to her body for meat,   130
    Or for apparel, like your common dame
    That makes shame get her clothes to cover shame.
    Base is that mind that kneels unto her body,
    As if a husband stood in awe on's wife;
    My spirit shall be mistress of this house,   135
    As long as I have time in't. – Oh,

Enter TRAPDOOR

Here comes my man that would be: 'tis his hour.

---

115 *Confession* Moll picks up the word in the sense of auricular confession (cf. I.i.36n.),
     which would precede the shriving of a condemned man immediately before
     execution, cf. II.ii.111.

122 *familiar* familiar spirit

123 *voyage* ed. (viage Q: *an obsolete form*)

126 *chirurgeons* rhymes loosely with 'Three Pigeons'

131 *common* i.e. to the whole town

Faith, a good well-set fellow, if his spirit
Be answerable to his umbles; he walks stiff,
But whether he will stand to't stiffly, there's the point; 140
Has a good calf for't, and ye shall have many a woman
Choose him she means to make her head by his calf;
I do not know their tricks in't. Faith, he seems
A man without; I'll try what he is within.

TRAPDOOR

She told me Gray's Inn Fields 'twixt three and four, 145
I'll fit her mistress-ship with a piece of service, I'm hired to rid
the town of one mad girl.

She jostles him

What a pox ails you, sir?

MOLL

He begins like a gentleman.

TRAPDOOR

Heart, is the field so narrow, or your eyesight? 150
Life, he comes back again.

She comes towards him

MOLL

Was this spoke to me, sir?

TRAPDOOR

I cannot tell, sir.

MOLL

Go, y'are a coxcomb.

TRAPDOOR

Coxcomb? 155

MOLL

Y'are a slave.

TRAPDOOR

I hope there's law for you, sir.

MOLL

Yea, do you see, sir?

Turn[s] his hat

TRAPDOOR

Heart, this is no good dealing, pray let me know what house
you're of. 160

---

139   *answerable to his umbles* in accord with his insides, or rather, here, the figure he
        makes (umbles are the edible inward parts of an animal, especially deer)
142   *make* ed. (meke Q)
143   *their tricks in't* how they do it
158   *Yea* ed. (Ye Q)

MOLL

One of the Temple, sir.

Fillips him

TRAPDOOR

Mass, so methinks.

MOLL

And yet sometime I lie about Chick Lane.

TRAPDOOR

I like you the worse because you shift your lodging so often: I'll
not meddle with you for that trick, sir.   165

MOLL

A good shift, but it shall not serve your turn.

TRAPDOOR

You'll give me leave to pass about my business, sir.

MOLL

Your business? I'll make you wait on me before I ha' done, and
glad to serve me too.

TRAPDOOR

How sir? Serve you? Not if there were no more men in England.   170

MOLL

But if there were no more women in England, I hope you'd wait
upon your mistress then.

TRAPDOOR

Mistress!

MOLL

Oh you're a tried spirit at a push, sir.

TRAPDOOR

What would your worship have me do?   175

MOLL

You a fighter?

TRAPDOOR

No, I praise heaven, I had better grace and more manners.

MOLL

As how, I pray, sir?

TRAPDOOR

Life, 't had been a beastly part of me to have drawn my weapons

---

161   sd *Fillips him* flicks him with her finger
163   *Chick Lane* later called West Street: a particularly infamous lurking-place of thieves
       in the notorious area around Turnmill Street between Clerkenwell Green and
       Smithfield

upon my mistress; all the world would'a' cried shame of me for 180
that.

MOLL

Why, but you knew me not.

TRAPDOOR

Do not say so, mistress. I knew you by your wide straddle, as
well as if I had been in your belly.

MOLL

Well, we shall try you further, i'th'meantime we give you enter- 185
tainment.

TRAPDOOR

Thank your good mistress-ship.

MOLL

How many suits have you?

TRAPDOOR

No more suits than backs, mistress.

MOLL

Well, if you deserve, I cast off this next week, 190
And you may creep into't.

TRAPDOOR   Thank your good worship.

MOLL

Come follow me to St Thomas Apostle's,
I'll put a livery cloak upon your back
The first thing I do.

TRAPDOOR   I follow my dear mistress.

Exeunt

---

183   *your wide straddle* apparently simply a characteristic of Moll's (a habit of standing
       with her feet wide astride)
184   *in your belly* suggests sexual intercourse, which might demand a wide straddle
185–6 *give you entertainment* take you into our service
189   *backs* Bullen prints 'blacks' – presumably a misprint.
190   *this* i.e. this suit that she is wearing
192   *St Thomas Apostle's* The church was east of St Paul's, near College Hill: it was not
       rebuilt after the fire. The street in which it stood was the resort of fishermen and
       famous for fish dinners; clothiers' shops were in the neighbourhood.

[ACT III, SCENE ii]

Enter MISTRESS GALLIPOT *as from supper, her husband after her*

MASTER GALLIPOT
What Pru, nay sweet Prudence.

MISTRESS GALLIPOT
What a pruing keep you, I think the baby would have a teat it kyes so: pray be not so fond of me, leave your city humours, I'm vexed at you to see how like a calf you come bleating after me.

MASTER GALLIPOT
Nay, honey Pru: how does your rising up before all the table   5
show? And flinging from my friends so uncivilly? Fie Pru, fie, come.

MISTRESS GALLIPOT
Then up and ride, i'faith.

MASTER GALLIPOT
Up and ride? Nay, my pretty Pru, that's far from my thought, duck: why, mouse, thy mind is nibbling at something, what is't?   10
What lies upon thy stomach?

MISTRESS GALLIPOT
Such an ass as you: hoyda, y'are best turn midwife, or physician: y'are a pothecary already, but I'm none of your drugs.

MASTER GALLIPOT
Thou art a sweet drug, sweetest Pru, and the more thou art pounded, the more precious.   15

MISTRESS GALLIPOT
Must you be prying into a woman's secrets: say ye?

MASTER GALLIPOT
Woman's secrets?

---

2   *pruing* There is conceivably a play on the dialect word 'proo', which means to call an animal to a stand.
3   *kyes* i.e. cries; (baby-talk)
8   *ride* Is Mistress Gallipot picking up a sexual suggestion in her husband's last word and possibly in 'honey' as well? Certainly it seems there in her next speech. 'Ride' was Standard English for sexual intercourse (cf. below, l. 175).
10   *what is't* ed. (whats ist Q)
13   *drugs* The word was still in use as a form of 'drudges' which it puns on.

MISTRESS GALLIPOT

What? I cannot have a qualm come upon me but your teeth
waters till your nose hang over it.

MASTER GALLIPOT

It is my love, dear wife.   20

MISTRESS GALLIPOT

Your love? Your love is all words; give me deeds, I cannot abide
a man that's too fond over me, so cookish; thou dost not know
how to handle a woman in her kind.

MASTER GALLIPOT

No, Pru? Why, I hope I have handled –

MISTRESS GALLIPOT

Handle a fool's head of your own, – fie – fie.   25

MASTER GALLIPOT

Ha, ha, 'tis such a wasp; it does me good now to have her sting
me, little rogue.

MISTRESS GALLIPOT

Now fie how you vex me, I cannot abide these apron husbands:
such cotqueans, you overdo your things, they become you
scurvily.   30

MASTER GALLIPOT

[Aside] Upon my life she breeds, heaven knows how I have
strained myself to please her, night and day: I wonder why we
citizens should get children so fretful and untoward in the
breeding, their fathers being for the most part as gentle as milch
kine. – Shall I leave thee, my Pru?   35

MISTRESS GALLIPOT

Fie, fie, fie.

18–19   *teeth waters* a variant form of 'mouth waters'
   22   *cookish* like a cook, perhaps a nonce word
   23   *in her kind* as she deserves, as is proper
   25   *fool's head* head empty of sense, perhaps again with a sexual *double entendre*
   26   *sting* ed. (sing Q); arouse sexually (and cf. *The Taming of the Shrew*, II.i.213f.)
   28   *apron husbands* (aperne Q) husbands who follow their wives as if tied to their apron
        strings (Collier)
   29   *cotqueans* used contemptuously of men who act the housewife and meddle in the
        women's province; Bullen's view that the work is a variant form of 'cock-quean' or
        'cuckquean' (a female cuckold) seems unacceptable, and, unusually, no sexual
        quibble seems intended
   31   *breeds* Gallipot takes his wife's capricious irritability as a sign of pregnancy.
31–5   Gallipot inadvertently hints at the kind of class miscegenation by which the gentry
        impregnate female citizens.

MASTER GALLIPOT

Thou shalt not be vexed no more, pretty kind rogue, take no
cold, sweet Pru.   *Exit*

MISTRESS GALLIPOT

As your wit has done. Now Master Laxton, show your head,
what news from you? Would any husband suspect that a woman   40
crying 'Buy any scurvy-grass' should bring love letters amongst
her herbs to his wife? Pretty trick, fine conveyance: had jealousy a
thousand eyes, a silly woman with scurvy-grass blinds them all;
Laxton, with bays
Crown I thy wit for this, it deserves praise.   45
This makes me affect thee more, this proves thee wise,
'Lack, what poor shift is love forced to devise!
– To th' point.

She reads the letter

'Oh sweet creature –' (a sweet beginning) 'pardon my long
absence, for thou shalt shortly be possessed with my presence;   50
though Demophon was false to Phyllis, I will be to thee as Pan-
da-rus was to Cres-sida: though Aeneas made an ass of Dido, I
will die to thee ere I do so; oh sweetest creature, make much of
me, for no man beneath the silver moon shall make more of a
woman than I do of thee: furnish me therefore with thirty   55
pounds, you must do it of necessity for me; I languish till I see
some comfort come from thee; protesting not to die in thy
debt, but rather to live so, as hitherto I have and will,

                                        Thy true Laxton ever'.

Alas poor gentleman, troth I pity him,   60
How shall I raise this money? Thirty pound?
'Tis thirty sure, a 3 before an 0,
I know his threes too well. My childbed linen?
Shall I pawn that for him? Then if my mark
Be known I am undone; it may be thought   65

---

41 *scurvy-grass coclearia officinalis*, thought to be anti-scorbutic
51 *Demophon* son of Theseus: Phyllis, a princess of Thrace, hanged herself when he
    failed to keep his promise to return to her; she was turned into an almond tree which
    bore leaves when Demophon came at last and embraced it
51–2 *Pan-da-rus . . . Cres-sida* so in Q, 'to mark the difficulty with which such hard names
    were read by Mistress Gallipot' (Dyce)
53 *die to thee* punning on the sense of 'spend sexually'
62 *a 3 before an 0* Does she construe his 'three-piece suite' (penis and testicles) before
    a vagina?
64 *mark* laundry mark for identification

My husband's bankrupt: which way shall I turn?
Laxton, what with my own fears, and thy wants,
I'm like a needle 'twixt two adamants.

Enter MASTER GALLIPOT *hastily*

MASTER GALLIPOT
Nay, nay, wife, the women are all up. [*Aside*] Ha, how, reading
o' letters? I smell a goose, a couple of capons, and a gammon of   70
bacon from her mother out of the country, I hold my life. –
Steal, steal –
MISTRESS GALLIPOT Oh beshrew your heart.
MASTER GALLIPOT   What letter's that?
I'll see't.

                                        She tears the letter

MISTRESS GALLIPOT
Oh would thou hadst no eyes to see
The downfall of me and thyself: I'm forever,   75
Forever I'm undone.
MASTER GALLIPOT   What ails my Pru?
What paper's that thou tear'st?
MISTRESS GALLIPOT   Would I could tear
My very heart in pieces: for my soul
Lies on the rack of shame, that tortures me
Beyond a woman's suffering.
MASTER GALLIPOT   What means this?   80
MISTRESS GALLIPOT
Had you no other vengeance to throw down,
But even in height of all my joys –
MASTER GALLIPOT   Dear woman –
MISTRESS GALLIPOT
When the full sea of pleasure and content
Seemed to flow over me –
MASTER GALLIPOT   As thou desirest
To keep me out of bedlam, tell what troubles thee,   85
Is not thy child at nurse fallen sick, or dead?

68   *adamants* loadstones or magnets
71   *I hold my life* by my life, I'm sure of it
72   lineation ed. (*prose* Q)
85   *bedlam* Bethlehem hospital for the insane
86   *at nurse* lodged away from home with a wet-nurse

MISTRESS GALLIPOT
Oh no.

MASTER GALLIPOT Heavens bless me, are my barns and houses
Yonder at Hockley Hole consumed with fire?
I can build more, sweet Pru.

MISTRESS GALLIPOT   'Tis worse, 'tis worse.

MASTER GALLIPOT
My factor broke? Or is the Jonas sunk?   90

MISTRESS GALLIPOT
Would all we had were swallowed in the waves,
Rather than both should be the scorn of slaves.

MASTER GALLIPOT
I'm at my wits' end.

MISTRESS GALLIPOT   Oh my dear husband,
Where once I thought myself a fixed star,
Placed only in the heaven of thine arms,   95
I fear now I shall prove a wanderer;
Oh Laxton, Laxton, is it then my fate
To be by thee o'erthrown?

MASTER GALLIPOT   Defend me, wisdom,
From falling into frenzy. On my knees,
Sweet Pru, speak, what's that Laxton who so heavy   100
Lies on thy bosom?

MISTRESS GALLIPOT   I shall sure run mad.

MASTER GALLIPOT
I shall run mad for company then: speak to me,
I'm Gallipot thy husband, – Pru, – why Pru,
Art sick in conscience for some villainous deed
Thou wert about to act? Didst mean to rob me?   105
Tush I forgive thee; hast thou on my bed
Thrust my soft pillow under another's head?

88   *Hockley Hole* Hockley-in-the-Hole was later infamous as the resort of thieves and
     highwaymen, but also a place of amusement: it lay at the centre of what is now
     Clerkenwell. So notorious was it that in 1774 it was thought fitting formally to
     remove its name from the map, and it became Ray Street. Until the late eighteenth
     century Cold Bath Fields were immediately adjacent to the west.

90   *broke* absconded (or possibly bankrupt)

94   *a fixed star* See note to I.ii.134, and cf. Shakespeare, Sonnet 116: 'love ... is an ever-
     fixed mark, ... the star to every wand'ring bark'. 'Wanderer' here only loosely suggests
     the movement of a meteor, and rather refers to Mistress Gallipot's simulated fear that
     she may prove loose.

I'll wink at all faults, Pru, 'las, that's no more
Than what some neighbours near thee have done before:
Sweet honey Pru, what's that Laxton?

MISTRESS GALLIPOT   Oh.   110

MASTER GALLIPOT
Out with him.

MISTRESS GALLIPOT   Oh he's born to be my undoer.
This hand which thou call'st thine, to him was given,
To him was I made sure i'th'sight of heaven.

MASTER GALLIPOT
I never heard this thunder.

MISTRESS GALLIPOT   Yes, yes, before
I was to thee contracted, to him I swore: 115
Since last I saw him, twelve months three times told
The moon hath drawn through her light silver bow,
For o'er the seas he went, and it was said
(But rumour lies) that he in France was dead.
But he's alive, oh he's alive, he sent   120
That letter to me, which in rage I rent,
Swearing with oaths most damnably to have me,
Or tear me from this bosom: oh heavens save me.

MASTER GALLIPOT
My heart will break, – shamed and undone forever.

MISTRESS GALLIPOT
So black a day, poor wretch, went o'er thee never.   125

MASTER GALLIPOT
If thou should'st wrestle with him at the law,
Th'art sure to fall, no odd sleight, no prevention.
I'll tell him th'art with child.

MISTRESS GALLIPOT   Hm.

---

113   *made sure* contracted, betrothed: she is inventing a contract *de praesenti*, sworn
      before witnesses and a canonical impediment to any future marriage to another.
      Such a contract may exist between Sebastian and Mary Fitz-Allard; cf. *A Chaste
      Maid*, IV.i.223, and *A Trick to Catch the Old One*, IV.iv.92, in which play there is a
      scene closely similar to this one.

114   *thunder* menace

116–19 Mistress Gallipot sees herself momentarily as the Empress of Babylon, whose speech
        about the Fairy Queen in *The Whore of Babylon* (I.i.46ff.) she half-remembers: 'Five
        summers have scarce drawn their glimmering nights / Through the moon's silver
        bow...'

127   *no odd sleight* (slight Q – *a frequent spelling*) no cunning device to prevent her being
      overcome

MASTER GALLIPOT   Or give out
  One of my men was ta'en abed with thee.
MISTRESS GALLIPOT
  Hm, hm.
MASTER GALLIPOT Before I lose thee, my dear Pru,   130
  I'll drive it to that push.
MISTRESS GALLIPOT   Worse, and worse still,
  You embrace a mischief, to prevent an ill.
MASTER GALLIPOT
  I'll buy thee of him, stop his mouth with gold,
  Think'st thou 'twill do?
MISTRESS GALLIPOT   Oh me, heavens grant it would;
  Yet now my senses are set more in tune,   135
  He writ, as I remember in his letter,
  That he in riding up and down had spent,
  Ere he could find me, thirty pounds. Send that,
  Stand not on thirty with him.
MASTER GALLIPOT   Forty, Pru,
  Say thou the word, 'tis done: we venture lives   140
  For wealth, but must do more to keep our wives:
  Thirty or forty, Pru?
MISTRESS GALLIPOT Thirty, good sweet;
  Of an ill bargain let's save what we can,
  I'll pay it him with my tears, he was a man
  When first I knew him of a meek spirit,   145
  All goodness is not yet dried up I hope.
MASTER GALLIPOT
  He shall have thirty pound, let that stop all:
  Love's sweets taste best, when we have drunk down gall.

Enter MASTER TILTYARD *and his wife,* MASTER GOSHAWK,
and MISTRESS OPENWORK

  God-so, our friends; come, come, smooth your cheek;
  After a storm the face of heaven looks sleek.   150
MASTER TILTYARD
  Did I not tell you these turtles were together?
MISTRESS TILTYARD
  How dost thou, sirrah? Why, sister Gallipot!

149   *God-so* a variant form of 'catso', an exclamation of surprise or alarm
152   *sirrah* frequently feminine

MISTRESS OPENWORK

 Lord, how she's changed!

GOSHAWK

 Is your wife ill, sir?

MASTER GALLIPOT

 Yes indeed, la sir, very ill, very ill, never worse.   155

MISTRESS TILTYARD

 How her head burns, feel how her pulses work.

MISTRESS OPENWORK

 Sister, lie down a little, that always does me good.

MISTRESS TILTYARD

 In good sadness, I find best ease in that too;

 Has she laid some hot thing to her stomach?

MISTRESS GALLIPOT

 No, but I will lay something anon.   160

MASTER TILTYARD

 Come, come fools, you trouble her, shall's go, Master Goshawk?

GOSHAWK

 Yes, sweet Master Tiltyard. – Sirrah Rosamond, I hold my life
 Gallipot hath vexed his wife.

MISTRESS OPENWORK

 She has a horrible high colour indeed.

GOSHAWK

 We shall have your face painted with the same red soon at night, 165
 when your husband comes from his rubbers in a false alley;
 thou wilt not believe me that his bowls run with a wrong bias.

MISTRESS OPENWORK

 It cannot sink into me, that he feeds upon stale mutton abroad,

---

158 *sadness* seriousness
166 *his rubbers in a false alley* Bowls was an exceedingly popular game at this period: the
   alleys were often the scene of gambling and dissipation which numerous acts of
   Parliament failed to curb. Cf. Stephen Gosson, *School of Abuse* (1579): 'common
   bowling alleys are privy moths, that eat up the credit of many idle citizens, whose
   gains at home are not able to weigh down their losses abroad, whose shops are so far
   from maintaining their play, that wives and children cry out for bread, and go to
   bed supperless oft in the year' (*Sh. Eng.*, II, 465). 'Rubbers' was often a singular form.
   To bowl out the rubbers 'is to bowl a third game for the bets, when the players have
   gotten one apiece' (Randle Holme, *Academy of Armoury*, 1688). Rubbing has also a
   sexual meaning: cf. *Love's Labour's Lost*, IV.i.138–39, where Costard says 'She's too
   hard for you at pricks sir, challenge her to bowl' and Boyet replies 'I fear too much
   rubbing.'
168 *feeds . . . abroad* a common phrase for marital unfaithfulness
   mutton food for lust, hence prostitutes

having better and fresher at home.

GOSHAWK

What if I bring thee where thou shalt see him stand at rack and   170
manger?

MISTRESS OPENWORK

I'll saddle him in's kind, and spur him till he kick again.

GOSHAWK

Shall thou and I ride our journey then?

MISTRESS OPENWORK

Here's my hand.

GOSHAWK

No more; come, Master Tiltyard, shall we leap into the stirrups   175
with our women, and amble home?

MASTER TILTYARD

Yes, yes, come wife.

MISTRESS TILTYARD

In troth sister, I hope you will do well for all this.

MISTRESS GALLIPOT

I hope I shall: farewell good sister: sweet Master Goshawk.

MASTER GALLIPOT

Welcome brother, most kindly welcome sir.   180

OMNES

Thanks, sir, for our good cheer.

Exeunt all but GALLIPOT *and his wife*

MASTER GALLIPOT

It shall be so; because a crafty knave

Shall not outreach me, nor walk by my door

With my wife arm in arm, as 'twere his whore,

I'll give him a golden coxcomb; thirty pound,   185

Tush Pru, what's thirty pound? Sweet duck, look cheerly.

MISTRESS GALLIPOT

Thou art worthy of my heart, thou buy'st it dearly.

Enter LAXTON *muffled*

170–1   *at rack and manger* i.e. at his 'food'. To live at rack and manger was to live in reckless
abundance. Cf. Wyclif, *Works*, 435 (qu. *Oxf. Dict. English Proverbs*, 661): 'it is yuel to
kepe a wast hors in stable ... but it is worse to have a woman at racke and at manger'.

172   *saddle him in's kind* use him according to the man he is, do by him as he does by me
(picking up Goshawk's submerged metaphor)

173   *ride our journey* enjoy our sexual pleasure

176   *amble* originally used only of horses; the whole sentence continues the sexual punning

182   *because* to the end that

LAXTON

    Uds light, the tide's against me, a pox of your pothecaryship: oh
    for some glister to set him going; 'tis one of Hercules' labours
    to tread one of these city hens, because their cocks are still   190
    crowing over them; there's no turning tail here, I must on.

MISTRESS GALLIPOT

    Oh husband see, he comes.

MASTER GALLIPOT

    Let me deal with him.

LAXTON

    Bless you, sir.

MASTER GALLIPOT

    Be you blest too, sir, if you come in peace.   195

LAXTON

    Have you any good pudding tobacco, sir?

MISTRESS GALLIPOT

    Oh pick no quarrels, gentle sir, my husband
    Is not a man of weapon, as you are,
    He knows all, I have opened all before him
    Concerning you.

LAXTON [*Aside*]   Zounds, has she shown my letters?   200

MISTRESS GALLIPOT

    Suppose my case were yours, what would you do
    At such a pinch, such batteries, such assaults,
    Of father, mother, kindred, to dissolve
    The knot you tied, and to be bound to him?
    How could you shift this storm off?

LAXTON   If I know, hang me.   205

MISTRESS GALLIPOT

    Besides, a story of your death was read
    Each minute to me.

LAXTON [*Aside*]   What a pox means this riddling?

MASTER GALLIPOT

    Be wise, sir, let not you and I be tossed
    On lawyers' pens; they have sharp nibs and draw

---

189   *glister* an old form of 'clyster', an enema. The word was used contemptuously of
     doctors and apothecaries (as in the character name of the quack in *A Family of Love*).

190   *still* always

196   *pudding tobacco* compressed tobacco made into rolls resembling a pudding or
     sausage; but the threat in Laxton's words which Mistress Gallipot recognises
     probably comes from the suggestion that he is after Gallipot's pudding or guts

208   *tossed* bandied, made the subject of talk

Men's very heart-blood from them; what need you, sir, 210
To beat the drum of my wife's infamy,
And call your friends together, sir, to prove
Your precontract, when sh'has confessed it?

LAXTON   Hm sir,
Has she confessed it?

MASTER GALLIPOT   Sh'has, faith, to me, sir,
Upon your letter sending.

MISTRESS GALLIPOT   I have, I have. 215

LAXTON
[*Aside*] If I let this iron cool, call me slave. –
Do you hear, you dame Prudence? Think'st thou, vile woman,
I'll take these blows and wink?

MISTRESS GALLIPOT   Upon my knees –

LAXTON
Out, impudence.

MASTER GALLIPOT Good sir –

LAXTON   You goatish slaves,
No wild fowl to cut up but mine?

MASTER GALLIPOT   Alas sir, 220
You make her flesh to tremble: fright her not,
She shall do reason, and what's fit.

LAXTON   I'll have thee,
Wert thou more common than an hospital,
And more diseased.

MASTER GALLIPOT   But one word, good sir.

LAXTON   So, sir.

MASTER GALLIPOT
I married her, have lien with her, and got 225
Two children on her body, think but on that;
Have you so beggarly an appetite
When I upon a dainty dish have fed
To dine upon my scraps, my leavings? Ha, sir?

---

213   *precontract* ed. (precontact Q) cf. above, l. 113n.
220   ' "To cut up wild fowl" was a cant expression, the meaning of which is sufficiently
      obvious' (Bullen). It seems, however, not to be recorded in *OED* or in contemporary
      canting dictionaries. But cf. Webster, *The White Devil*, II.i.90–2: 'We fear /
      When Tiber to each prowling passenger / Discovers flocks of wild ducks . . .' and *Cymbeline*,
      I.iv.89: 'strange fowl light upon neighboring ponds'.
223   *common* open to all comers; cf. III.i.131
228   *a dainty dish* Cf. the modern slang 'dish' for an attractive girl.

Do I come near you now, sir?

LAXTON   Be-Lady, you touch me.   230

MASTER GALLIPOT

Would not you scorn to wear my clothes, sir?

LAXTON   Right, sir.

MASTER GALLIPOT

Then pray, sir, wear not her, for she's a garment
So fitting for my body, I'm loath
Another should put it on, you will undo both.
Your letter (as she said) complained you had spent   235
In quest of her some thirty pound, I'll pay it;
Shall that, sir, stop this gap up 'twixt you two?

LAXTON

Well, if I swallow this wrong, let her thank you:
The money being paid, sir, I am gone;
Farewell: oh women! Happy's he trusts none.   240

MISTRESS GALLIPOT

Dispatch him hence, sweet husband.

MASTER GALLIPOT   Yes, dear wife:
Pray sir, come in: ere Master Laxton part
Thou shalt in wine drink to him.

MISTRESS GALLIPOT   With all my heart.

                                        Exit MASTER GALLIPOT

– How dost thou like my wit?

LAXTON   Rarely: that wile
By which the serpent did the first woman beguile   245
Did ever since all women's bosoms fill;
Y'are apple-eaters all, deceivers still.

                                                [*Exeunt*]

230   *now* ed. (uow Q)
        Be-Lady a corruption of 'By our Lady'
243   sd *Exit* MASTER GALLIPOT ed. (Exit Maister Gallipot and his wife Q)
247   sd *Exeunt* ed. (Exit Laxton Q)

[ACT III, SCENE iii]

Enter SIR ALEXANDER WENGRAVE, SIR DAVY DAPPER,
SIR ADAM APPLETON *at one door, and* TRAPDOOR *at another door*

SIR ALEXANDER
Out with your tale, Sir Davy, to Sir Adam:
A knave is in mine eye deep in my debt.

SIR DAVY
Nay: if he be a knave, sir, hold him fast.
                              [SIR DAVY *and* SIR ADAM *talk apart*]

SIR ALEXANDER
Speak softly, what egg is there hatching now?

TRAPDOOR
A duck's egg, sir, a duck that has eaten a frog. I have cracked the   5
shell, and some villainy or other will peep out presently; the
duck that sits is the bouncing ramp, that roaring girl my mistress,
the drake that must tread is your son Sebastian.

SIR ALEXANDER
Be quick.

TRAPDOOR
As the tongue of an oyster-wench.   10

SIR ALEXANDER
And see thy news be true.

TRAPDOOR
As a barber's every Saturday night. Mad Moll –

SIR ALEXANDER
Ah.

TRAPDOOR
Must be let in without knocking at your back gate.

SIR ALEXANDER
So.   15

TRAPDOOR
Your chamber will be made bawdy.

---

0   sd 2–3 *at one door . . . at another door* i.e. of the stage: the setting is in fact a street
2   *A knave . . . debt* i.e. I have caught sight of a knave who is in my debt
5   *a duck that has eaten a frog* The phrase seems to have no more specific meaning than
     an allusion to the villainy that Trapdoor goes on to speak about.
7   *bouncing ramp* rampant, wanton creature
12   *As a barber's* Barbers are well placed to hear gossip.

SIR ALEXANDER

Good.

TRAPDOOR

She comes in a shirt of male.

SIR ALEXANDER

How, shirt of mail?

TRAPDOOR

Yes sir, or a male shirt, that's to say in man's apparel.   20

SIR ALEXANDER

To my son?

TRAPDOOR

Close to your son: your son and her moon will be in conjunction, if all almanacs lie not: her black saveguard is turned into
a deep slop, the holes of her upper body to button-holes, her
waistcoat to a doublet, her placket to the ancient seat of a cod-   25
piece, and you shall take 'em both with standing collars.

SIR ALEXANDER

Art sure of this?

TRAPDOOR

As every throng is sure of a pickpocket, as sure as a whore is of
the clients all Michaelmas Term, and of the pox after the term.

SIR ALEXANDER

The time of their tilting?   30

22–3   *in conjunction* Two planets were said to be in conjunction when they were in the
       same sign of the zodiac (their influences were then thought to reinforce one
       another); the moon is in conjunction with the sun at new moon. But 'conjunction'
       was also commonly used for copulation.

23   *saveguard* See II.i.152 sd and n.

24   *slop* See II.ii.77–8 and n.
       holes of her upper body 'Hole' has various low sexual uses and here possibly suggests
       nipples. But 'body' (of which 'bodice' is a variant form of the plural) was regularly
       used for the part of a woman's dress above the waist, which would commonly be
       laced through a series of holes. Cf. *A Mad World, My Masters*, III.iii.100.

25   *waistcoat* In the sixteenth and early seventeenth centuries elaborate waistcoats were
       fashionable. They were worn beneath an outer gown, but so as to be seen.
       placket the opening or slit at the top of a skirt or petticoat (constantly, like 'codpiece',
       with sexual associations)

26   *standing collars* Upstanding collars became fashionable for men in the early
       seventeenth century: see the illustration on the title-page. There is probably a play
       on 'stand' in the sense of an erection (cf. I.ii.56–7n.) and conceivably a hint of some
       contraceptive device.

29   *Michaelmas Term* the first term of the legal year, when the termers will have plenty
       of money

TRAPDOOR
  Three.
SIR ALEXANDER
  The day?
TRAPDOOR
  This.
SIR ALEXANDER
  Away, ply it, watch her.
TRAPDOOR
  As the devil doth for the death of a bawd, I'll watch her, do you   35
  catch her.
SIR ALEXANDER
  She's fast: here weave thou the nets, hark.
TRAPDOOR
  They are made.
SIR ALEXANDER
  I told them thou didst owe me money; hold it up: maintain't.
TRAPDOOR
  Stiffly, as a puritan does contention; – Fox, I owe thee not the   40
  value of a halfpenny halter.   [*Angrily, as in a quarrel*]
SIR ALEXANDER
  Thou shalt be hanged in't ere thou scape so. Varlet, I'll make
  thee look through a grate.
TRAPDOOR
  I'll do't presently, through a tavern grate. Drawer! Pish.   *Exit*
SIR ADAM
  Has the knave vexed you, sir?
SIR ALEXANDER   Asked him my money,   45
  He swears my son received it: oh that boy
  Will ne'er leave heaping sorrows on my heart,
  Till he has broke it quite.
SIR ADAM   Is he still wild?
SIR ALEXANDER
  As is a Russian bear.
SIR ADAM   But he has left
  His old haunt with that baggage?

39   *them* i.e. the other knights
      hold it up i.e. the pretence
43   *grate* prison grating
44   *Drawer!* He calls offstage as to a drawer in the tavern.
49   *Russian bear* Cf. *Macbeth*, III.iv.99 ('the rugged Russian bear'). Bears were imported
      from Russia for baiting, and their fierceness became proverbial.

SIR ALEXANDER   Worse still and worse,   50
   He lays on me his shame, I on him my curse.
SIR DAVY
   My son Jack Dapper then shall run with him,
   All in one pasture.
SIR ADAM   Proves your son bad too, sir?
SIR DAVY
   As villainy can make him: your Sebastian
   Doats but on one drab, mine on a thousand,   55
   A noise of fiddlers, tobacco, wine, and a whore,
   A mercer that will let him take up more,
   Dice, and a water-spaniel with a duck: oh,
   Bring him abed with these, when his purse jingles,
   Roaring boys follow at's tail, fencers and ningles   60
   (Beasts Adam ne'er gave name to), these horse-leeches suck
   My son: he being drawn dry, they all live on smoke.
SIR ALEXANDER
   Tobacco?
SIR DAVY   Right: but I have in my brain
   A windmill going that shall grind to dust
   The follies of my son, and make him wise,   65
   Or a stark fool; pray lend me your advice.
BOTH
   That shall you, good Sir Davy.
SIR DAVY   Here's the springe
   I ha' set to catch this woodcock in: an action
   In a false name (unknown to him) is entered
   I'th'counter to arrest Jack Dapper.
BOTH   Ha, ha, he.   70

56   *noise* band of musicians (not necessarily contemptuously)
57   *take up* i.e. on credit
60   *fencers* swordsmen
     ningles (or ingles) boy-favourites, catamites
61   *horse-leeches* farriers (alternatively a large variety of leech), widely used as a
     contemptuous term for rapacious parasites: cf. *A Fair Quarrel*, III.ii.170
63   *Tobacco* The popularity of smoking by the early years of James I's reign is evidenced
     by Barnabe Riche's estimate that there were then at least seven thousand tobacco
     shops in London: annual takings were said to be over £300,000.
64   *windmill* picking up the implied image of a tobacco-mill
66   *advice* ed. (advise Q). Q spelling gives a perfect rhyme.
67–8   *the springe . . . to catch this woodcock* Probably a direct theft from *Hamlet*, I.iv.115,
     which seems to be the first recorded instance of the figurative use of this phrase,
     though 'woodcock' was in common use for simpleton. Cf. also *Twelfth Night*, II.v.84.

SIR DAVY
  Think you the counter cannot break him?
SIR ADAM   Break him?
  Yes and break's heart too if he lie there long.
SIR DAVY
  I'll make him sing a counter-tenor sure.
SIR ADAM
  No way to tame him like it, there he shall learn
  What money is indeed, and how to spend it.   75
SIR DAVY
  He's bridled there.
SIR ALEXANDER   Ay, yet knows not how to mend it:
  Bedlam cures not more madmen in a year
  Than one of the counters does: men pay more dear
  There for their wit than anywhere; a counter,
  Why 'tis a university, who not sees?   80
  As scholars there, so here men take degrees,
  And follow the same studies all alike.
  Scholars learn first logic and rhetoric,
  So does a prisoner; with fine honey'd speech
  At's first coming in he doth persuade, beseech   85
  He may be lodged with one that is not itchy,
  To lie in a clean chamber, in sheets not lousy;
  But when he has no money, then does he try
  By subtle logic and quaint sophistry
  To make the keeper trust him.
SIR ADAM   Say they do?   90

71 *counter* the mayor's court or hall of justice, to which a debtor's prison was attached;
    also written 'compter'
73 *counter-tenor* a high male alto. Sir Davy suggests that he would like to geld his son
    as well as have him locked away.
76 *bridled* with a quibble on Bridewell, already a common term for a house of
    correction
80 *a university* Middleton was fond of this joke. Cf. *The Phoenix*, IV.iii.19 and *Michael-
    mas Term*, III.iv.83ff.: 'H'as at least sixteen at this instant proceeded in both the
    Counters: some bach'lors, some masters, some doctors of captivity.' Sir Thomas
    Overbury in 1613 called a prison 'an university of poor scholars, in which three arts
    are chiefly studied; to pray, to curse, and to write letters'. The joke survived until the
    nineteenth century when the Marshalsea was still known as the college, as in *Little
    Dorrit*. Dekker had personal experience of the counter.
83 *logic and rhetoric* From the foundation of the universities logic was regarded as the
    science of sciences, and both these subjects held a principal place in the curricula of
    the English universities until the middle of the seventeenth century.

SIR ALEXANDER
  Then he's a graduate.
SIR DAVY   Say they trust him not?
SIR ALEXANDER
  Then is he held a freshman and a sot,
  And never shall commence, but, being still barred,
  Be expulsed from the master's side, to th' twopenny ward,
  Or else i'th'Hole be placed.
SIR ADAM   When then, I pray,   95
  Proceeds a prisoner?
SIR ALEXANDER   When, money being the theme,
  He can dispute with his hard creditors' hearts,
  And get out clear, he's then a Master of Arts.
  Sir Davy, send your son to Wood Street College,
  A gentleman can nowhere get more knowledge.   100
SIR DAVY
  There gallants study hard.
SIR ALEXANDER   True: to get money.
SIR DAVY
  'Lies by th' heels i'faith: thanks, thanks, I ha' sent
  For a couple of bears shall paw him.

              Enter SERGEANT CURTILAX *and* YEOMAN HANGER

SIR ADAM   Who comes yonder?

93   *commence* be admitted to a degree
94   *the master's side* The governor of a prison was allowed to let certain rooms for his
      own profit; these were, of course, the best in the prison. The twopenny ward (cf.
      Chapman, et al., *Eastward Ho!*, V.ii.61) may be the mistress's side referred to in *The
      Phoenix* (IV.iii.22). The poorest prisoners were confined in the 'Hole', a name
      specially given to the worst dungeon in the Wood Street Counter.
95   *be placed* ed. (E.C.) (beg plac'd Q; beg place *Gomme*)
96   *Proceeds* advances from B.A. to a higher degree
97   *dispute* One proved one's right to proceed by engaging in a *disputatio*, in which
      parties formally sustain, attack, or defend a given question or thesis. There is a brief
      parody of a disputation in *A Chaste Maid in Cheapside*, IV.i.
99   *Wood Street College* Cf. above, l. 80 and n. Conditions in Wood Street Counter, which
      stood on the east side of the street near the junction with Gresham Street, seem to
      have been particularly bad even by the standards of the early seventeenth century (cf.
      Sh. Eng., II, 508).
102   *'Lies by th' heels* (i.e. he lies) he is being arrested (or put in irons)
103   *bears* rough fellows; cf. 'boys more tough than bears' (*The Honest Whore*, part 1,
      IV.iii.99)

SIR DAVY

They look like puttocks, these should be they.

SIR ALEXANDER   I know 'em,

They are officers: sir, we'll leave you.

SIR DAVY   My good knights,   105

Leave me, you see I'm haunted now with spirits.

BOTH

Fare you well, sir.

Exeunt [SIR] ALEX[ANDER] *and* [SIR] ADAM

CURTILAX

This old muzzle-chops should be he by the fellow's description:
– save you, sir.

SIR DAVY

Come hither, you mad varlets, did not my man tell you I watched   110
here for you?

CURTILAX

One in a blue coat, sir, told us, that in this place an old gentleman would watch for us, a thing contrary to our oath, for we
are to watch for every wicked member in a city.

SIR DAVY

You'll watch then for ten thousand, what's thy name honesty?   115

CURTILAX

Sergeant Curtilax I, sir.

SIR DAVY

An excellent name for a sergeant, Curtilax.

Sergeants indeed are weapons of the law:

When prodigal ruffians far in debt are grown,

Should not you cut them, citizens were o'erthrown.   120

Thou dwell'st hereby in Holborn, Curtilax?

CURTILAX

That's my circuit, sir, I conjure most in that circle.

SIR DAVY

And what young toward whelp is this?

104   *puttocks* kites, applied opprobriously to catchpolls
106   *spirits* kidnappers or abductors, with of course a play on the common sense
112   *One in a blue coat* This was the traditional dress of a servant until the early
      seventeenth century.
115   *honesty* i.e. honest fellow
116   *Curtilax* a much perverted form of 'cutlass', which became so distinct that it acquired
      a kind of permanent standing, the identification of the final part with 'ax' being
      favoured by the use of the weapon in delivering slashing blows (*OED*)
123   *toward* promising, hopeful

82

HANGER

Of the same litter, his yeoman, sir, my name's Hanger.

SIR DAVY

Yeoman Hanger: 125
One pair of shears sure cut out both your coats,
You have two names most dangerous to men's throats,
You two are villainous loads on gentlemen's backs,
Dear ware, this Hanger and this Curtilax.

CURTILAX

We are as other men are, sir, I cannot see but he who makes a   130
show of honesty and religion, if his claws can fasten to his liking,
he draws blood; all that live in the world are but great fish and
little fish, and feed upon one another, some eat up whole men,
a sergeant cares but for the shoulder of a man; they call us
knaves and curs, but many times he that sets us on worries more   135
lambs one year than we do in seven.

SIR DAVY

Spoke like a noble Cerberus: is the action entered?

HANGER

His name is entered in the book of unbelievers.

SIR DAVY

What book's that?

CURTILAX

The book where all prisoners' names stand, and not one amongst   140
forty, when he comes in, believes to come out in haste.

SIR DAVY

Be as dogged to him as your office allows you to be.

BOTH

Oh sir.

SIR DAVY

You know the unthrift Jack Dapper?

124   *yeoman* an assistant to an official, but also a servant subordinate to a sergeant
126   *One pair of shears ... both your coats* i.e. you are two of a kind. 'There went but a pair
       of shears between them' was a common proverbial expression: cf. *Measure for
       Measure*, I.ii.27.
129   *ware* The word was sometimes used for textiles; the image is hardly precise.
132–3 *great fish and little fish* 'The great fish eat up the small' was a bitter proverbial jest of
       constant application. Cf. *Pericles*, II.i.26–9: 'Master, I marvel how the fishes live in the
       sea. / Why, as men do a-land; the great ones eat up the little ones.'
134   *for the shoulder of a man* because he apprehends men by catching hold of their
       shoulders
137   *Cerberus* Cf. III.i.23 n.; *dogged* in l. 142 plays on this.

CURTILAX

Ay, ay, sir, that gull? As well as I know my yeoman.   145

SIR DAVY

And you know his father too, Sir Davy Dapper?

CURTILAX

As damned a usurer as ever was among Jews; if he were sure his father's skin would yield him any money, he would when he dies flay it off, and sell it to cover drums for children at Bartholomew Fair.   150

SIR DAVY

[*Aside*] What toads are these to spit poison on a man to his face! – Do you see, my honest rascals? Yonder greyhound is the dog he hunts with, out of that tavern Jack Dapper will sally: sa, sa; give the counter, on, set upon him.

BOTH

We'll charge him upo'th'back, sir.   155

SIR DAVY

Take no bail, put mace enough into his caudle, double your files, traverse your ground.

BOTH

Brave, sir.

SIR DAVY

Cry arm, arm, arm.

BOTH

Thus, sir.   160

SIR DAVY

There boy, there boy, away: look to your prey, my true English wolves, and – and so I vanish.   *Exit*

---

149   *flay* ed. (flea Q)

149–50   *Bartholomew Fair* had by this time grown to enormous size, incorporating four parishes and lasting for a fortnight from 23 August (St Bartholomew's Eve), when it was opened by the Lord Mayor. It was the Londoner's great annual jamboree, and amongst other things, the chief national cloth sale.

153   *sa, sa* in hunting, a call to attention

154   *give the counter* To hunt counter is to run a false scent, or follow it in reverse direction; so here, turn him back. There is doubtless a play on counter in the sense of prison (cf. above, ll. 71ff.).

156   *mace* Sergeants carried maces; *caudle* is gruel mixed with spiced ale, for which mace would be a regular ingredient. The same jest appears in *A Mad World, My Masters*, III.ii.69.

156–7   *double your files, traverse your ground* literally, make the ranks smaller by putting two files in one, move from side to side; but Sir Davy is presumably just being briskly military, using at random the terms he knows

CURTILAX

Some warden of the sergeants begat this old fellow, upon my
life: stand close.

HANGER

Shall the ambuscado lie in one place? 165

CURTILAX

No, nook thou yonder.

Enter MOLL *and* TRAPDOOR

MOLL

Ralph.

TRAPDOOR

What says my brave captain male and female?

MOLL

This Holborn is such a wrangling street.

TRAPDOOR

That's because lawyers walks to and fro in't. 170

MOLL

Here's such jostling, as if everyone we met were drunk and reeled.

TRAPDOOR

Stand, mistress, do you not smell carrion?

MOLL

Carrion? No, yet I spy ravens.

TRAPDOOR

Some poor wind-shaken gallant will anon fall into sore labour,
and these men-midwives must bring him to bed i'the counter, 175

163 *Some warden of the sergeants* one, that is, crabbed enough to be in charge of sergeants
165 *ambuscado* ambush, a common seventeenth-century form used especially of the
force employed
166 *nook thou yonder* ed. (uooke Q) hide in that nook
169 *wrangling* noisy, disputatious
170 Several Inns of Court stood in Holborn, then as now the principal east–west street
in the northern part of the City.
172 *carrion* A carrion or carren doe was one which was pregnant (cf. Gascoigne,
Woodmanship, p. 5); hence the quibbles in Trapdoor's next speech. Ravens are
carrion-eaters (in the more familiar sense), but 'raven' or 'ravin' also means robbery
or rapine. The complex joke is now irrecoverable without much labour.
174 *wind-shaken* weakened or flawed at heart as timber supposed cracked by force of
the wind
175 *men-midwives* another well-used joke; cf. *The Whore of Babylon*, II.i.61ff.: 'Do you
not know (mistress) what Sergeants are? . . . why they are certain men-midwives,
that never bring people to bed, but when they are sore in labour, that nobody else
can deliver them.' And see Jonson, *The Staple of News*, ind. 43ff. and Field, *Amends
for Ladies*, IV.i.164f.

there all those that are great with child with debts lie in.

MOLL

Stand up.

TRAPDOOR

Like your new maypole.

HANGER

Whist, whew.

CURTILAX

Hump, no.   180

MOLL

Peeping? It shall go hard, huntsmen, but I'll spoil your game:
they look for all the world like two infected maltmen coming
muffled up in their cloaks in a frosty morning to London.

TRAPDOOR

A course, captain; a bear comes to the stake.

Enter JACK DAPPER *and* GULL

MOLL

It should be so, for the dogs struggle to be let loose.   185

HANGER

Whew.

CURTILAX

Hemp.

MOLL

Hark Trapdoor, follow your leader.

JACK DAPPER

Gull.

GULL

Master.   190

JACK DAPPER

Didst ever see such an ass as I am, boy?

GULL

No by my troth, sir, to lose all your money, yet have false dice of
your own, why 'tis as I saw a great fellow used t'other day, he

179 *Whist* Hanger whistles questioningly to Curtilax; *whew* is likewise a whistle, but also
a verb meaning to move sharply.
182 *two infected maltmen* Mulholland (p. 171) quotes F. P. Wilson, *The Plague in
Shakespeare's London*, Oxford, 1963, p. 36: 'In 1630 it came to the notice of the Privy
Council that those who carried malt into the City were accustomed to return home
with rags "for manuring of the soiling of the ground" and the practice was forbidden.' This practice would have made maltmen particularly susceptible to infection.
184 *course* the animal pursued (*OED* 7b)

had a fair sword and buckler, and yet a butcher dry-beat him
with a cudgel.   195

MOLL *and* TRAPDOOR

Honest servant, fly; fly, Master Dapper, you'll be arrested else.

JACK DAPPER

Run, Gull, and draw.

GULL

Run, master, Gull follows you.

> *Exeunt* [JACK] DAPPER *and* GULL

CURTILAX

I know you well enough, you're but a whore to hang upon any
man.   200

MOLL

Whores then are like sergeants, so now hang you; – draw, rogue,
but strike not: for a broken pate they'll keep their beds, and
recover twenty marks damages.

CURTILAX

You shall pay for this rescue; – run down Shoe Lane and meet
him.   205

TRAPDOOR

Shoo, is this a rescue, gentlemen, or no?

MOLL

Rescue? A pox on 'em, Trapdoor, let's away,
I'm glad I have done perfect one good work today;
If any gentleman be in scrivener's bands,
Send but for Moll, she'll bail him by these hands.   210

> *Exeunt*

194   *dry-beat* beat soundly (with 'dry blows', i.e. those not drawing blood)
196   sp MOLL *and* TRAPDOOR ed. (Both Q): perhaps the speech should be divided between the two.
    servant ed. (Serieant Q corr.: Seriant Q uncorr.) I follow Dyce and Bullen. Bowers reads 'Sir' on the grounds that Gull would not be referred to before his master, and thinks the compositor may have mistakenly expanded the abbreviation 'S^r'. That would be an odd mistake; and who would call Jack Dapper 'Honest Sir'? Mulholland retains 'Sergeant' on the grounds that 'stage business of some sort could clear up the difficulty'.
198   Bullen suggests that Moll holds Curtilax at this point.
201   *rogue* i.e. Trapdoor
203   *twenty marks* The mark was worth two-thirds of a pound.
204   *rescue* the forcible taking of a person or goods out of custody – a very serious offence. Cf. *Coriolanus*, III.i.275, and *The Honest Whore*, part 1, IV.iii.141: 'A rescue, prentices, my master's catchpolled'.   *Shoe Lane* (now bridged by Holborn Viaduct) ran down from Holborn towards Fleet Street and the Bridewell.
209   *scrivener* in the general sense of notary

[ACT IV, SCENE i]

Enter SIR ALEXANDER WENGRAVE *solus*

SIR ALEXANDER

Unhappy in the follies of a son
Led against judgment, sense, obedience,
And all the powers of nobleness and wit;

Enter TRAPDOOR

Oh wretched father. – Now Trapdoor, will she come?

TRAPDOOR

In man's apparel, sir, I am in her heart now,   5
And share in all her secrets.

SIR ALEXANDER   Peace, peace, peace.
Here, take my German watch, hang't up in sight,
That I may see her hang in English for't.

TRAPDOOR

I warrant you for that now, next sessions rids her, sir, this watch
will bring her in better than a hundred constables.   10

SIR ALEXANDER

Good Trapdoor, sayst thou so? Thou cheer'st my heart
After a storm of sorrow, – my gold chain, too,
Here, take a hundred marks in yellow links.

TRAPDOOR

That will do well to bring the watch to light, sir:
And worth a thousand of your headborough's lanthorns.   15

SIR ALEXANDER

Place that o'the court cupboard, let it lie
Full in the view of her thief-whorish eye.

---

7   *my German watch* Allusions to German watches and clocks are frequent in plays of
     this period. Cf., e.g., *Love's Labour's Lost*, III.i.190, and *A Mad World, My Masters*,
     IV.i.21. They were renowned for their complexity and ingenuity.
9   *sessions* i.e. of court
13   *a hundred marks in yellow links* i.e. his chain of office as magistrate. Sir Bounteous
     Progress is cheated of an identical one in *A Mad World, My Masters* (V.i.122 and
     V.ii.170), where Follywit (disguised as a player) asks for a chain to serve for a justice's
     hat.
15   *headborough* constable
16   *court cupboard* a form of sideboard consisting normally of three shelves supported
     on elaborately carved legs

TRAPDOOR

>She cannot miss it, sir, I see't so plain
>That I could steal't myself.

SIR ALEXANDER   Perhaps thou shalt too,

>That or something as weighty; what she leaves,   20
>Thou shalt come closely in, and filch away,
>And all the weight upon her back I'll lay.

TRAPDOOR

>You cannot assure that, sir.

SIR ALEXANDER   No? What lets it?

TRAPDOOR

>Being a stout girl, perhaps she'll desire pressing,
>Then all the weight must lie upon her belly.   25

SIR ALEXANDER

>Belly or back I care not so I've one.

TRAPDOOR

>You're of my mind for that, sir.

SIR ALEXANDER

>Hang up my ruff-band with the diamond at it,
>It may be she'll like that best.

TRAPDOOR

>[Aside] It's well for her that she must have her choice, he thinks   30
>nothing too good for her. – If you hold on this mind a little
>longer, it shall be the first work I do to turn thief myself; would
>do a man good to be hanged when he is so well provided for.

SIR ALEXANDER

>So, well said; all hangs well, would she hung so too,
>The sight would please me more than all their glisterings: 35
>Oh that my mysteries to such straits should run,
>That I must rob myself to bless my son.

>>>>*Exeunt*

Enter SEBASTIAN, *with* MARY FITZ-ALLARD *like a page,*
and MOLL [*in man's clothes*]

SEBASTIAN

>Thou hast done me a kind office, without touch
>Either of sin or shame, our loves are honest.

21 *closely* secretly
23 *lets* prevents
35 *glisterings* ed. (gilsterings Q)
36 *mysteries* cunning

MOLL

    I'd scorn to make such shift to bring you together else.   40

SEBASTIAN

    Now have I time and opportunity

    Without all fear to bid thee welcome, love.   *Kiss*

MARY

    Never with more desire and harder venture.

MOLL

    How strange this shows, one man to kiss another.

SEBASTIAN

    I'd kiss such men to choose, Moll,   45

    Methinks a woman's lip tastes well in a doublet.

MOLL

    Many an old madam has the better fortune then,

    Whose breaths grew stale before the fashion came:

    If that will help 'em, as you think 'twill do,

    They'll learn in time to pluck on the hose too.   50

SEBASTIAN

    The older they wax, Moll – troth I speak seriously,

    As some have a conceit their drink tastes better

    In an outlandish cup than in our own,

    So methinks every kiss she gives me now

    In this strange form, is worth a pair of two.   55

    Here we are safe, and furthest from the eye

    Of all suspicion, this is my father's chamber,

    Upon which floor he never steps till night.

    Here he mistrusts me not, nor I his coming;

    At mine own chamber he still pries unto me,   60

    My freedom is not there at mine own finding,

    Still checked and curbed; here he shall miss his purpose.

MOLL

    And what's your business, now you have your mind, sir?

---

45   *to choose* for choice

47   *Many an old madam* Doublets were occasionally worn by women (without the pretence of being dressed as men), but whether especially by bawds seems unrecorded.

55   *pair of two* This has sometimes been amended to 'pair or two'; but 'pair' could mean a set of indeterminate number, and I have occasionally heard 'pair of two' in colloquial speech quite recently. The amendment somewhat weakens Sebastian's gesture.

57   *father's* ed. (fathets Q)

60   *still* always

63   *business, now* ed. (business now, Q)

At your great suit I promised you to come,
I pitied her for name's sake, that a Moll   65
Should be so crossed in love when there's so many
That owes nine lays apiece, and not so little:
My tailor fitted her, how like you his work?

SEBASTIAN

So well, no art can mend it for this purpose;
But to thy wit and help we're chief in debt,   70
And must live still beholding.

MOLL   Any honest pity
I'm willing to bestow upon poor ring-doves.

SEBASTIAN

I'll offer no worse play.

MOLL   Nay, and you should, sir,
I should draw first and prove the quicker man.

SEBASTIAN

Hold, there shall need no weapon at this meeting,   75
But 'cause thou shalt not loose thy fury idle,
Here take this viol, run upon the guts,
And end thy quarrel singing.

MOLL   Like a swan above bridge,
For look you here's the bridge, and here am I.

SEBASTIAN

Hold on, sweet Moll.   80

MARY

I've heard her much commended, sir, for one that was ne'er
taught.

MOLL

I'm much beholding to 'em: well since you'll needs put us
together, sir, I'll play my part as well as I can: it shall ne'er be
said I came into a gentleman's chamber and let his instrument   85
hang by the walls.

SEBASTIAN

Why well said, Moll, i'faith, it had been a shame for that gentle-

---

67 *lays* Bullen glosses 'wagers', but a sexual meaning seems more likely.
76 *'cause thou shalt not loose thy fury idle* There is probably a play here on 'fury' in the
    sense of (musical) inspiration. Cf. Morley, *Introduction to Music* (1597), p. 35: 'This
    hath been a mighty musical fury, which hath caused him to show such diversity in
    so small bounds.' Thus, 'so that your passion is not wasted'.
78 *a swan above bridge* Swans were plentiful in the London reaches of the Thames.
79 *bridge* i.e. of the musical instrument

man then, that would have let it hung still and ne'er offered
thee it.

MOLL

There it should have been still then for Moll, for though the 90
world judge impudently of me, I ne'er came into that chamber
yet where I took down the instrument myself.

SEBASTIAN

Pish, let 'em prate abroad, th'art here where thou art known
and loved: there be a thousand close dames that will call the
viol an unmannerly instrument for a woman, and therefore 95
talk broadly of thee, when you shall have them sit wider to a
worse quality.

MOLL

Push, I ever fall asleep and think not of 'em, sir, and thus I
dream.

SEBASTIAN

Prithee let's hear thy dream, Moll. 100

MOLL

      I dream there is a mistress,   *The song*
         And she lays out the money,
      She goes unto her sisters,
         She never comes at any.

      Enter SIR ALEXANDER *behind them*

      She says she went to the Burse for patterns,   105
      You shall find her at Saint Kathern's,
         And comes home with never a penny.

SEBASTIAN

That's a free mistress, faith.

SIR ALEXANDER

[*Aside*] Ay, ay, ay, like her that sings it, one of thine own choosing.

---

96 *when you shall have them sit wider* The instrument is a gamba, played at this period
    with the body of the viol gripped between the player's thighs or knees (cf. *A Trick to
    Catch the Old One*, I.i.133); the sexual punning on 'instrument' reaches its home in
    this line.

105 *the Burse* probably an allusion to the Royal Exchange, built (on the site in Cornhill)
    by Sir Thomas Gresham in 1567. See *A Chaste Maid*, I.ii.35: 'As if she lay with all the
    gaudy shops / In Gresham's Burse about her'.

106 *Saint Kathern's* perhaps St Katherine's Fair, which, until the late sixteenth century,
    had been held to provide funds for St Katherine's Hospital on Tower Hill. The
    hospital precinct had a prison called St Katherine's Hole. The whole area had by the
    seventeenth century a generally bad reputation. In *The Alchemist* (V.iii.55f.) St
    Kathern's is said to be 'where they use to keep / The better sort of mad folks'.

MOLL

But shall I dream again?   110

       Here comes a wench will brave ye,
          Her courage was so great,
       She lay with one o' the navy,
          Her husband lying i'the Fleet.
       Yet oft with him she cavilled,   115
          I wonder what she ails,
       Her husband's ship lay gravelled,
          When hers could hoise up sails,
       Yet she began like all my foes
       To call whore first: for so do those,   120
          A pox of all false tails.

SEBASTIAN

Marry, amen say I.

SIR ALEXANDER

So say I too.

MOLL

Hang up the viol now, sir: all this while I was in a dream, one
shall lie rudely then; but being awake, I keep my legs together.   125
A watch, what's o'clock here?

SIR ALEXANDER

Now, now she's trapped.

MOLL

Between one and two: nay then I care not: a watch and a musician
are cousin-germans in one thing, they must both keep time
well, or there's no goodness in 'em; the one else deserves to be   130
dashed against a wall, and t'other to have his brains knocked
out with a fiddle case. What, a loose chain and a dangling
diamond? Here were a brave booty for an evening-thief now,
there's many a younger brother would be glad to look twice in
at a window for't, and wriggle in and out like an eel in a sandbag.   135

---

114   *i'the Fleet* i.e. in the prison
121   *tails* cant term for sexual organs and so extended to their owners; here with a play
       on 'tales'
129   *cousin-germans* first cousins. The watch is German.
132–7 prose ed. (*arranged as rough verse* Q).
135   *like an eel in a sandbag* a proverbial phrase used of things languishing for want of
       proper sustenance. Cf. Jonson, *Cynthia's Revels*, II.v.18ff.: 'all the ladies and gallants
       lie languishing upon the rushes . . . and without we return quickly, they are all, as a
       youth would say, no better than a few trouts cast ashore, or a dish of eels in a sandbag'.

Oh, if men's secret youthful faults should judge 'em, 'twould be
the general'st execution that ere was seen in England; there
would be but few left to sing the ballets, there would be so
much work: most of our brokers would be chosen for hang-
men, a good day for them: they might renew their wardropes of   140
free cost then.

SEBASTIAN

This is the roaring wench must do us good.

MARY

No poison, sir, but serves us for some use,
Which is confirmed in her.

SEBASTIAN   Peace, peace.
Foot, I did hear him sure, where'er he be.   145

MOLL

Who did you hear?

SEBASTIAN   My father.
'Twas like a sight of his, I must be wary.

SIR ALEXANDER

No, wilt not be. Am I alone so wretched
That nothing takes? I'll put him to his plunge for't.

SEBASTIAN

Life, here he comes. – Sir, I beseech you take it,   150
Your way of teaching does so much content me,
I'll make it four pound, here's forty shillings, sir:
I think I name it right (help me, good Moll),
Forty in hand.

MOLL   Sir, you shall pardon me,
I have more of the meanest scholar I can teach,   155
This pays me more than you have offered yet.

SEBASTIAN

At the next quarter
When I receive the means my father 'lows me,

---

138   *ballets* ballads commemorating the deceased
139   *brokers* pawnbrokers or jobbers, but also pimps
140   *wardropes* a variant form of 'wardrobe'; but *OED* gives independently 'a rope for
        some mechanical purpose', and the intended quibble is evident
145   *Foot* i.e. 's foot (for 'God's foot')
147   *sight* sigh
149   *to his plunge* into a dilemma
152   *forty shillings* There were twenty shillings to a pound.
156   *This* i.e the meanest scholar

You shall have t'other forty.

SIR ALEXANDER   This were well now,
    Were't to a man whose sorrows had blind eyes,   160
    But mine behold his follies and untruths
    With two clear glasses. – How now?   [*Comes forward*]

SEBASTIAN   Sir.

SIR ALEXANDER   What's he there?

SEBASTIAN
    You're come in good time, sir, I've a suit to you,
    I'd crave your present kindness.

SIR ALEXANDER   What is he there?

SEBASTIAN
    A gentleman, a musician, sir, one of excellent fingering.   165

SIR ALEXANDER
    [*Aside*] Ay, I think so, I wonder how they scaped her.

SEBASTIAN
    Has the most delicate stroke, sir.

SIR ALEXANDER
    A stroke indeed, I feel it at my heart.

SEBASTIAN
    Puts down all your famous musicians.

SIR ALEXANDER
    Ay, a whore may put down a hundred of 'em.   170

SEBASTIAN
    Forty shillings is the agreement, sir, between us:
    Now sir, my present means mounts but to half on't.

SIR ALEXANDER
    And he stands upon the whole.

SEBASTIAN   Ay indeed does he, sir.

SIR ALEXANDER
    And will do still, he'll ne'er be in other tale.

159–60 Cf. *The Honest Whore*, part 1, II.i.277: 'This were well now, to one but newly fledged.'
    166 *how they scaped her* i.e. how she, supposed light-fingered, managed not to pick up
          the jewels etc., laid out to trap her
    169 *Puts down* (1) surpasses, (2) overthrows, with a hint of the sexual disease she may
          give them
    171 *Forty shillings is the agreement* This seems not to square with the trick thought up
          earlier (ll. 152ff.).
    174 *And will . . . tale* i.e. he'll not be paid: he will always be in that position, there will be
          no other reckoning

SEBASTIAN

    Therefore I'd stop his mouth, sir, and I could.   175

SIR ALEXANDER

    Hum, true, there is no other way indeed; –

    [*Aside*] His folly hardens, shame must needs succeed. –

    Now sir, I understand you profess music.

MOLL

    I am a poor servant to that liberal science, sir.

SIR ALEXANDER

    Where is it you teach?

MOLL   Right against Clifford's Inn.   180

SIR ALEXANDER

    Hum, that's a fit place for it: you have many scholars?

MOLL

    And some of worth, whom I may call my masters.

SIR ALEXANDER

    [*Aside*] Ay true, a company of whoremasters. –

    You teach to sing too?

MOLL   Marry do I sir.

SIR ALEXANDER

    I think you'll find an apt scholar of my son, especially for prick-   185

    song.

MOLL

    I have much hope of him.

SIR ALEXANDER

    [*Aside*] I am sorry for't, I have the less for that. – You can play

    any lesson?

MOLL

    At first sight, sir.   190

SIR ALEXANDER

    There's a thing called the witch, can you play that?

---

175   *and* chiefly in the sense of 'if', but a play on the other sense is pleasant

180   *Clifford's Inn*, next to the church of St Dunstan in the West, Fleet Street, was the oldest Inn in Chancery: it was the seat of all six attorneys of the Palace Court, and it was said that more misery emanated from this small spot than from any one of the most populous counties in England (*Old and New London*, I, 92).

184   *You teach to sing too* i.e. in the low sense, to copulate (see Eric Partridge, *Shakespeare's Bawdy* (1956), p. 187). Cf. *A Chaste Maid*, II.i.52, and *Troilus and Cressida*, V.ii.9ff.

185–6   *prick-song* Music sung from notes written or 'pricked', as distinguished from that learnt by ear. Sexual quibbles on this word are legion in contemporary plays.

189   *lesson* a musical exercise or composition specially written for teaching

191   *the witch* This seems to have been the name of several popular pieces.

MOLL

    I would be sorry anyone should mend me in't.

SIR ALEXANDER

    [*Aside*] Ay, I believe thee, thou hast so bewitched my son,

    No care will mend the work that thou hast done:

    I have bethought myself, since my art fails,   195

    I'll make her policy the art to trap her.

    Here are four angels marked with holes in them

    Fit for his cracked companions, gold he will give her,

    These will I make induction to her ruin,

    And rid shame from my house, grief from my heart.   200

    – Here, son, in what you take content and pleasure,

    Want shall not curb you; pay the gentleman

    His latter half in gold.

SEBASTIAN   I thank you, sir.

SIR ALEXANDER

    [*Aside*] Oh may the operation on't end three:

    In her, life; shame in him; and grief in me.   *Exit*   205

SEBASTIAN

    Faith thou shalt have 'em, 'tis my father's gift,

    Never was man beguiled with better shift.

MOLL

    He that can take me for a male musician,

    I cannot choose but make him my instrument

    And play upon him.   210

                       Exeunt omnes

192   *mend* probably in the sense of 'surpass', though 'improve' is possible
197   *angels marked with holes in them* The holes are evidently punched through the middle (see V.ii.240). The trick seems to be to land Moll either with spoiled coins, the possession of which would be an offence, or with marked ones which could later be sworn to be stolen. Angels were at this time worth 10 shillings.
209–10   *make him my instrument / And play upon him* another reminiscence of *Hamlet* (cf. III.ii.364f.)

[ACT IV, SCENE ii]

Enter MISTRESS GALLIPOT *and* MISTRESS OPENWORK

MISTRESS GALLIPOT
Is then that bird of yours, Master Goshawk, so wild?

MISTRESS OPENWORK
A goshawk, a puttock; all for prey: he angles for fish, but he
loves flesh better.

MISTRESS GALLIPOT
Is't possible his smooth face should have wrinkles in't, and we
not see them? 5

MISTRESS OPENWORK
Possible? Why, have not many handsome legs in silk stockings
villainous splay feet for all their great roses?

MISTRESS GALLIPOT
Troth sirrah, thou sayst true.

MISTRESS OPENWORK
Didst never see an archer, as thou'st walked by Bunhill, look a-
squint when he drew his bow? 10

MISTRESS GALLIPOT
Yes, when his arrows have fline toward Islington, his eyes have

---

2 *puttock* kite or buzzard, but applied generally to birds of prey. Goshawks (which
were once commoner in England than now) are not fish-eaters, but could well have
been confused with ospreys or even, by such as Mistress Openwork, with herons.
'Fish' has long been cant for loose women or female genitals.

4 *his smooth face* Cf. Dekker's *Seven Deadly Sins of London* (1606), V, 36: 'They knew
how smooth soever his looks were, there was a devil in his bosom.'

6 *silk stockings* Stubbes and other puritans were particularly severe on the extravagance
of silk stockings 'curiously knit with open seam down the leg, with quirks and clocks
about the ankles, and sometime (haply) interlaced with gold or silver threads . . .
The time hath been, when one might have clothed all his body well, from top to toe,
for less than a pair of these nether stocks will cost' (*Anatomy of Abuses*, p. 31).

7 *roses* knots of ribbons worn on the shoe (still, or again, fashionable in Jane Austen's
time): see the illustration on the title-page

9 *thou'st* ed. (tho'ast Q)
Bunhill The old artillery ground, next to the famous cemetery, just west of the site
of Finsbury Square, was regularly used for archery matches. Bullen quotes from the
Remembrancia that, in September 1623, Middleton received 20 marks 'for his
services at the shooting on Bunhill, and at the Conduit Head before the Lord Mayor
and Aldermen'.

11 *fline* flown.

shot clean contrary towards Pimlico.

MISTRESS OPENWORK

For all the world, so does Master Goshawk double with me.

MISTRESS GALLIPOT

Oh fie upon him, if he double once he's not for me.

MISTRESS OPENWORK

Because Goshawk goes in a shag-ruff band, with a face sticking   15
up in't which shows like an agate set in a cramp ring, he thinks
I'm in love with him.

MISTRESS GALLIPOT

'Las, I think he takes his mark amiss in thee.

MISTRESS OPENWORK

He has by often beating into me made me believe that my
husband kept a whore.   20

MISTRESS GALLIPOT

Very good.

MISTRESS OPENWORK

Swore to me that my husband this very morning went in a boat
with a tilt over it, to the Three Pigeons at Brainford, and his
punk with him under his tilt.

MISTRESS GALLIPOT

That were wholesome.   25

MISTRESS OPENWORK

I believed it, fell a-swearing at him, cursing of harlots, made me
ready to hoise up sail and be there as soon as he.

MISTRESS GALLIPOT

So, so.

MISTRESS OPENWORK

And for that voyage Goshawk comes hither incontinently: but

---

12   *Pimlico* not the familiar one near Victoria, but a part of Hoxton between New North
     Road and Hoxton Street. It was much frequented 'for the sake of the fresh air and
     the cakes and ale for which it was famous' (Sugden). Cf. Jonson, *The Alchemist*,
     V.ii.17ff.: 'Gallants, men, and women, / And of all sorts, tag-rag, been seen to flock
     here / In threaves, these ten weeks, as to a second Hogsden, / In days of Pimlico.'
     There are many contemporary references. The name may originally have been that
     of the owner of an alehouse.
13   *double* use duplicity, act deceitfully
16   *an agate set in a cramp-ring* Cramp-rings were worn on the finger as a protection
     against cramp and falling-sickness: in pre-Reformation times they were hallowed
     each Good Friday by the king or queen. For the slang use, see V.i.193 n.
23   *tilt* an awning over a boat
24   *punk* whore
29   *incontinently* straightaway, punning on the sense of unable to resist sexual appetite

sirrah, this water-spaniel dives after no duck but me, his hope   30
is having me at Brainford to make me cry quack.

MISTRESS GALLIPOT

Art sure of it?

MISTRESS OPENWORK

Sure of it? My poor innocent Openwork came in as I was
poking my ruff, presently hit I him i'the teeth with the Three
Pigeons: he forswore all, I up and opened all, and now stands   35
he in a shop hard by, like a musket on a rest, to hit Goshawk
i'the eye, when he comes to fetch me to the boat.

MISTRESS GALLIPOT

Such another lame gelding offered to carry me through thick
and thin – Laxton, sirrah – but I am rid of him now.

MISTRESS OPENWORK

Happy is the woman can be rid of 'em all; 'las, what are your   40
whisking gallants to our husbands, weigh 'em rightly man for
man?

MISTRESS GALLIPOT

Troth, mere shallow things.

MISTRESS OPENWORK

Idle simple things, running heads, and yet let 'em run over us
never so fast, we shopkeepers, when all's done, are sure to have   45
'em in our purse-nets at length, and when they are in, Lord,
what simple animals they are.

[MISTRESS GALLIPOT   ]

34   *poking my ruff* crimping the folds of the ruff with a poking-stick, a rod made of
     horn, bone, or latterly of steel so that it could be applied hot
36   *like a musket on a rest* The old matchlock musket was very heavy and needed a rest
     to support the barrel to ensure accuracy of aim; it consisted of a wooden pole with
     an iron fork at the upper end to rest the musket in, and a spike at the bottom to fix
     it in the ground. The soldier carried it by a lanyard over his shoulder.
41   *whisking* smart or lively
44   *running* flighty, perhaps with a secondary sense of fluent or plausible
46   *purse-nets* Bag-shaped nets of which the mouth could be drawn together with a
     string: they were used especially for catching rabbits. 'Rabbit' or 'coney' was also
     thieves' cant for a dupe and the purse-net a device by which he was caught (see
     Greene's *Notable Discovery of Cozenage* (1591) in A. V. Judges, *The Elizabethan
     Underworld* (1930), p. 136). Cf. also *The Gull's Horn-Book*, I: 'a rich man's son shall
     no sooner be out of the shell of his minority but he shall straightways be . . . ta'en
     in his own purse-nets by fencers and coney-catchers'.
48   Something is at fault in Q here, for Mistress Openwork is given two consecutive
     speeches. The second, 'Then they hang the head', is at the top of a page, and the
     catchword on the previous page is, accordingly, the speech heading. I agree with
     George R. Price ('The Manuscript and Quarto of *The Roaring Girl* ', *The Library*,

MISTRESS OPENWORK
Then they hang the head.

MISTRESS GALLIPOT
Then they droop.   50

MISTRESS OPENWORK
Then they write letters.

MISTRESS GALLIPOT
Then they cog.

MISTRESS OPENWORK
Then deal they underhand with us, and we must ingle with our
husbands abed, and we must swear they are our cousins, and
able to do us a pleasure at court.   55

MISTRESS GALLIPOT
And yet when we have done our best, all's but put into a riven
dish, we are but frumped at and libelled upon.

MISTRESS OPENWORK
Oh if it were the good Lord's will, there were a law made no
citizen should trust any of 'em all.

Enter GOSHAWK

MISTRESS GALLIPOT
Hush sirrah, Goshawk flutters.   60

GOSHAWK
How now, are you ready?

MISTRESS OPENWORK
Nay are you ready? A little thing you see makes us ready.

---

fifth series, 11 (1956), 182–3) in thinking that some short speech by Mistress Gallipot
– which might give the dialogue a more obvious sequence at this point – has
accidentally been omitted, though at what stage cannot be ascertained. Three copies
of Q have been reset at this point (see Bowers, pp. 106–7) and read, among other
accidentals, 'Then they hang head' (l. 49) and 'Then they deal' (l. 53). Perhaps
someone spotted the inconsequence of the uncorrected text, found after all that it
couldn't be easily corrected, but in unlocking the forme allowed the type to loosen
and pie, and reset it carelessly: the 'corrected' phrases have no authority.

49–50 *Then they hang the head. Then they droop* The sexual innuendoes in this passage are
        made plain here: even now the intentions of the two ladies cannot be taken at face
        value.

52   *cog* fawn, wheedle
53   *ingle* coax, cajole
54   *swear they are our cousins* Such a trick is performed on Candido in *The Honest*
     Whore, part 2.
56   *riven* split (the dish of the image would be a wooden trencher)
57   *frumped at* mocked, insulted, browbeaten

GOSHAWK

Us? Why, must she make one i'the voyage?

MISTRESS OPENWORK

Oh by any means: do I know how my husband will handle me?

GOSHAWK

[*Aside*] Foot, how shall I find water to keep these two mills go- 65
ing? – Well, since you'll needs be clapped under hatches, if I sail
not with you both till all split, hang me up at the mainyard and
duck me. – It's but liquoring them both soundly, and then
you shall see their cork heels fly up high, like two swans when
their tails are above water, and their long necks under water, 70
diving to catch gudgeons. – Come, come, oars stand ready, the
tide's with us, on with those false faces; blow winds and thou
shalt take thy husband casting out his net to catch fresh salmon
at Brainford.

MISTRESS GALLIPOT

I believe you'll eat of a cod's head of your own dressing before 75
you reach half way thither.

[*They mask themselves*]

GOSHAWK

So, so, follow close, pin as you go.

Enter LAXTON *muffled*

LAXTON

Do you hear?

MISTRESS GALLIPOT

Yes, I thank my ears.

---

66   *clapped under hatches* kept down or in silence; but 'clap' was used catachrestically
     for 'clip' (embrace)
67   *till all split* till all suffer shipwreck, or go to pieces: originally, as here, a sailors' phrase,
     though soon made over into common use. Cf. *A Midsummer Night's Dream*, I.ii.32,
     and *A Chaste Maid*, IV.ii.95.
69   *cork heels* Chopines had cork soles and high cork heels; they were worn outdoors as
     a fashionable alternative to clogs.
71   *gudgeons* doubtless with a play on the sense of (easily caught) simpletons (cf. *A
     Chaste Maid*, IV.ii.53)
72   *false faces* masks
75   *you'll eat of a cod's head of your own dressing* you'll make a fool of yourself, caught
     in your own net: a cod's head is a stupid fellow, but Mistress Gallipot must want
     him to be tricked into picking up the sexual suggestion
77   *pin* fasten

LAXTON

    I must have a bout with your pothecaryship.   80

MISTRESS GALLIPOT

    At what weapon?

LAXTON

    I must speak with you.

MISTRESS GALLIPOT

    No.

LAXTON

    No? You shall.

MISTRESS GALLIPOT

    Shall? Away, soused sturgeon, half fish, half flesh.   85

LAXTON

    'Faith, gib, are you spitting? I'll cut your tail, puss-cat, for this.

MISTRESS GALLIPOT

    'Las poor Laxton, I think thy tail's cut already: you're worsed.

LAXTON

    If I do not –   *Exit*

GOSHAWK

    Come, ha' you done?

Enter MASTER OPENWORK

        'Sfoot Rosamond, your husband.

MASTER OPENWORK

    How now? Sweet Master Goshawk, none more welcome,   90
    I have wanted your embracements: when friends meet,
    The music of the spheres sounds not more sweet
    Than does their conference; who is this? Rosamond?
    Wife? How now, sister?

GOSHAWK   Silence if you love me.

---

80   *bout* would normally imply a sexual encounter, but we know this is not Laxton's way
    with Mistress Gallipot.

86   *gib* cat, hence a term of reproach for a scold

87   *you're worsed* ed. (your worst Q). You're blemished or worsted. The Q reading could
    be understood as an abbreviated challenge – 'do your worst' – but 'worst' is a regular
    form of the past participle of the old verb 'to worse', and this seems to fit best with
    the remainder of the line.

91   *wanted your embracements* missed your company

92   *music of the spheres* the music the heavenly bodies were believed to make as they
    moved. The congruity between the ratios of their orbits with musical intervals
    confirmed a concept of divine harmony.

MASTER OPENWORK
　Why masked?
MISTRESS OPENWORK Does a mask grieve you, sir?
MASTER OPENWORK　　　　　　　　　　It does.　　　95
MISTRESS OPENWORK
　Then y'are best get you a-mumming.
GOSHAWK　　　　　　　　　　'Sfoot, you'll spoil all.
MISTRESS GALLIPOT
　May not we cover our bare faces with masks
　As well as you cover your bald heads with hats?
MASTER OPENWORK
　No masks; why, th'are thieves to beauty, that rob eyes
　Of admiration in which true love lies.　　　100
　Why are masks worn? Why good? Or why desired?
　Unless by their gay covers wits are fired
　To read the vildest looks; many bad faces
　(Because rich gems are treasured up in cases)
　Pass by their privilege current: but as caves　　　105
　Dam misers' gold, so masks are beauty's graves;
　Men ne'er meet women with such muffled eyes,
　But they curse her that first did masks devise,
　And swear it was some beldam. Come, off with't.
MISTRESS OPENWORK
　I will not.　　　110
MASTER OPENWORK
　Good faces masked are jewels kept by sprites:
　Hide none but bad ones, for they poison men's sights,
　Show them as shopkeepers do their broidered stuff,

96　*get you a-mumming* The phrase 'to go a-mumming' means to disguise oneself,
　　especially for a mumming play, which was acted with masks in dumb-show: perhaps,
　　therefore, 'you'd best keep silence'. (To play or keep mum meant, as now, to be silent.)
105　*Pass by their privilege current* i.e. are received as genuine or honest, because of the
　　privilege conferred by masks. Masks were widely used by prostitutes to spread their
　　business, but they did not always enable them to pass current: see *Northward Ho!*,
　　I.ii.83: 'we [whores] are not current till we pass from one man to another'; and *The
　　Honest Whore*, part 2, IV.i.397f.: 'She (crowned with reverend praises) passed by
　　them, I (though with face masked) could not scape the hem.'
106　*Dam* The Q reading is 'dambe', which *OED* records only as an erroneous form of
　　'dam', though 'damb' is found for 'damn'. Doubtless there is a *double entendre*, but the
　　primary sense seems best served by 'dam': misers' gold is blocked up, obscured, in
　　caves.
109　*beldam* witch
111　*sprites* ed. (spirits Q), i.e. evil spirits

By owl-light; fine wares cannot be open enough:
Prithee, sweet Rose, come strike this sail.

MISTRESS OPENWORK   Sail?

MASTER OPENWORK   Ha!   115
  Yes, wife, strike sail, for storms are in thine eyes.

MISTRESS OPENWORK
  Th'are here, sir, in my brows if any rise.

MASTER OPENWORK
  Ha, brows? What says she, friend? Pray tell me why
  Your two flags were advanced; the comedy,
  Come, what's the comedy?

MISTRESS GALLIPOT   *Westward Ho.*

MASTER OPENWORK   How?   120

MISTRESS OPENWORK
  'Tis *Westward Ho* she says.

GOSHAWK   Are you both mad?

MISTRESS OPENWORK
  Is't market day at Brainford, and your ware
  Not sent up yet?

MASTER OPENWORK What market day? What ware?

MISTRESS OPENWORK
  A pie with three pigeons in't, 'tis drawn and stays your cutting up.

GOSHAWK
  As you regard my credit –   125

MASTER OPENWORK
  Art mad?

MISTRESS OPENWORK
  Yes, lecherous goat; baboon.

direction; so here, turn him back. There is doubtless a play on counter in the sense of prison (cf. above, ll. 71ff.).

156   *mace* Sergeants carried maces; *caudle* is gruel mixed with spiced ale, for which mace would be a regular ingredient. The same jest appears in *A Mad World, My Masters*, III.ii.69.

156–7   *double your files, traverse your ground* literally, make the ranks smaller by putting two files in one, move from side to side; but Sir Davy is presumably just being briskly military, using at random the terms he knows

MASTER OPENWORK
  Baboon? Then toss me in a blanket.
MISTRESS OPENWORK
  Do I it well?
MISTRESS GALLIPOT
  Rarely.   130
GOSHAWK
  Belike, sir, she's not well; best leave her.
MASTER OPENWORK   No,
  I'll stand the storm now how fierce so e'er it blow.
MISTRESS OPENWORK
  Did I for this lose all my friends? Refuse
  Rich hopes and golden fortunes, to be made
  A stale to a common whore?
MASTER OPENWORK   This does amaze me.   135
MISTRESS OPENWORK
  Oh God, oh God, feed at reversion now?
  A strumpet's leaving?
MASTER OPENWORK   Rosamond.
GOSHAWK
  I sweat, would I lay in Cold Harbour.
MISTRESS OPENWORK
  Thou hast struck ten thousand daggers through my heart.
MASTER OPENWORK
  Not I, by heaven, sweet wife.
MISTRESS OPENWORK   Go, devil, go;   140
  That which thou swear'st by damns thee.
GOSHAWK
  'S heart, will you undo me?

128   *toss me in a blanket* Tossing in a blanket was a 'rough, irregular form of punishment'
      (*OED*), the offender being thrown repeatedly in the air from a blanket held slackly
      from the corners. There is probably a play on blanket-love, meaning illicit amours.
135   *stale* a mistress turned to ridicule for the amusement of a rival; but the whole phrase
      telescopes this with the sense of 'common stale', a prostitute used by thieves as a
      decoy
136   *at reversion* (in legal terms) in succession, conditionally on the expiry of a grant or
      at death; but reversions are also the left-overs of a dish or meal
138   *Cold Harbour* The name of a former mansion in Upper Thames Street, which passed
      through the hands of a remarkable number of noble owners and was replaced in
      the mid-sixteenth century by a collection of tenements which quickly became a
      haunt of poverty and an ad-hoc sanctuary for those wanting to disappear, as
      undoubtedly Goshawk wants at this moment (the alternative spelling 'Cole' can
      mean a cheat); but he is of course playing on the literal meaning of the name.

MISTRESS OPENWORK

    Why stay you here? The star by which you sail

    Shines yonder above Chelsea; you lose your shore;

    If this moon light you, seek out your light whore.   145

MASTER OPENWORK

    Ha?

MISTRESS OPENWORK   Push, your western pug –

GOSHAWK   Zounds, now hell roars.

MISTRESS OPENWORK

    With whom you tilted in a pair of oars,

    This very morning.

MASTER OPENWORK   Oars?

MISTRESS OPENWORK   At Brainford, sir.

MASTER OPENWORK

    Rack not my patience: Master Goshawk,

    Some slave has buzzed this into her, has he not?   150

    I run a tilt in Brainford with a woman?

    'Tis a lie:

    What old bawd tells thee this? 'Sdeath, 'tis a lie.

MISTRESS OPENWORK

    'Tis one to thy face shall justify all that I speak.

MASTER OPENWORK

    Ud'soul, do but name that rascal.   155

MISTRESS OPENWORK

    No sir, I will not.

GOSHAWK   Keep thee there, girl: – then!

MASTER OPENWORK

    Sister, know you this varlet?

143ff.   For thirty lines (143–74) Q prints a medley of verse and prose: the rhymes, some
evident pentameters, an occasional median capital, and the fact that some is printed
as verse suggest that it should all be, though the result is undoubtedly rough.

143–5   *The star . . . whore* Punctuation ed. (star, . . . sail, . . . Chelsea; . . . light you: . . . whore.
Q) I take it that this means 'you are missing your landing by not attending to the star
in the west; if that's the way you want to go, now is the time'.

  146   sp MISTRESS OPENWORK ed. (Mist. Gal. Q)
      western pug (png Q) a pug is a harlot, but western pugs were bargees who navigated
down the Thames to London, as from Brentford among other places

  148   *tilted* jousted, but also (of a boat) pitched in the waves; and cf. above l. 23 and n., and
1 Henry IV, II.iii.92, 'to tilt with lips'

  151   *run a tilt* (or run a-tilt) engage in a tilt or joust

  154   *'Tis one to thy face* (*stet* Q). Bullen suggests ' 'Tis one who to thy face . . .'

  155   *Ud'soul* God's soul.

  157   sp MASTER OPENWORK ed. (Mis. Open. Q)

MISTRESS GALLIPOT   Yes.
MASTER OPENWORK   Swear true.
　　Is there a rogue so low damned? A second Judas?
　　A common hangman? Cutting a man's throat?
　　Does it to his face? Bite me behind my back?   160
　　A cur dog? Swear if you know this hell-hound.
MISTRESS GALLIPOT
　　In truth I do.
MASTER OPENWORK His name?
MISTRESS GALLIPOT   Not for the world,
　　To have you to stab him.
GOSHAWK   Oh brave girls, worth gold.
MASTER OPENWORK
　　A word, honest Master Goshawk.   *Draw[s] out his sword*
GOSHAWK   What do you mean, sir?
MASTER OPENWORK
　　Keep off, and if the devil can give a name   165
　　To this new fury, holla it through my ear,
　　Or wrap it up in some hid character:
　　I'll ride to Oxford and watch out mine eyes
　　But I'll hear the brazen head speak: or else
　　Show me but one hair of his head or beard,   170
　　That I may sample it; if the fiend I meet
　　In mine own house, I'll kill him: – the street,
　　Or at the church door: – there ('cause he seeks to untie
　　The knot God fastens) he deserves most to die.
MISTRESS OPENWORK
　　My husband titles him.
MASTER OPENWORK   Master Goshawk, pray sir,   175
　　Swear to me that you know him or know him not,
　　Who makes me at Brainford to take up a petticoat
　　Besides my wife's.

163　*worth gold* Proverbial: cf. Munday, *Fedele and Fortunio* (1585), l. 1703: 'such a girl is
　　worth gold in a dear year'; and the subtitle of Heywood's *Fair Maid of the West* – 'A
　　girl worth gold'.
167　*hid character* code
168–72　*I'll ride to Oxford*... Friar Bacon and Friar Bungay spent seven years making a brass
　　head, so that they could ask it whether it were possible to build a wall of brass round
　　Britain. Unfortunately they neglected to note the time at which the head was to
　　speak and so received no distinct answer. Cf. *The Famous Historie of Fryer Bacon*
　　and Greene's *Honourable History of Friar Bacon and Friar Bungay* (to which
　　Middleton had in 1602 written a prologue and epilogue), esp. sc. xi.

GOSHAWK   By heaven that man I know not.
MISTRESS OPENWORK
  Come, come, you lie.
GOSHAWK   Will you not have all out?
  By heaven, I know no man beneath the moon   180
  Should do you wrong, but if I had his name,
  I'd print it in text letters.
MISTRESS OPENWORK   Print thine own then,
  Didst not thou swear to me he kept his whore?
MISTRESS GALLIPOT
  And that in sinful Brainford they would commit
  That which our lips did water at, sir, – ha?   185
MISTRESS OPENWORK
  Thou spider, that hast woven thy cunning web
  In mine own house t'insnare me: hast not thou
  Sucked nourishment even underneath this roof,
  And turned it all to poison, spitting it
  On thy friend's face (my husband), he as 'twere sleeping?   190
  Only to leave him ugly to mine eyes,
  That they might glance on thee?
MISTRESS GALLIPOT   Speak, are these lies?
GOSHAWK
  Mine own shame me confounds.
MASTER OPENWORK   No more, he's stung;
  Who'd think that in one body there could dwell   195
  Deformity and beauty, heaven and hell?
  Goodness I see is but outside: we all set,
  In rings of gold, stones that be counterfeit:
  I thought you none.
GOSHAWK   Pardon me.
MASTER OPENWORK   Truth I do.
  This blemish grows in nature, not in you,   200
  For man's creation stick even moles in scorn
  On fairest cheeks: wife, nothing is perfect born.

---

182   *text letters* large or capital letters in handwriting
185   *our lips did water at* Cf. III.ii.18–19.
189   *turned it all to poison* Spiders were commonly supposed to be poisonous, though,
      according to one view, only if known to be there. Cf. *The Winter's Tale*, II.i.40, and
      No Wit, No Help, like a Woman's, II.i.392–3.
193   sp *MASTER OPENWORK* ed. (Mist. Open. Q)
197   *counterfeit* Q has the spelling 'counterfet', which gives a perfect rhyme.

MISTRESS OPENWORK
    I thought you had been born perfect.
MASTER OPENWORK
    What's this whole world but a gilt rotten pill?
    For at the heart lies the old chore still.
    I'll tell you, Master Goshawk, – Ay, in your eye   205
    I have seen wanton fire, and then to try
    The soundness of my judgment, I told you
    I kept a whore, made you believe 'twas true,
    Only to feel how your pulse beat, but find
    The world can hardly yield a perfect friend.   210
    Come, come, a trick of youth, and 'tis forgiven.
    This rub put by, our love shall run more even.
MISTRESS OPENWORK
    You'll deal upon men's wives no more?
GOSHAWK   No: you teach me
    A trick for that.
MISTRESS OPENWORK Troth do not, they'll o'erreach thee.
MASTER OPENWORK
    Make my house yours, sir, still.
GOSHAWK   No.
MASTER OPENWORK   I say you shall: 215
    Seeing, thus besieged, it holds out, 'twill never fall.

Enter MASTER GALLIPOT, *and* GREENWIT *like a sumner,*
LAXTON *muffled aloof off*

OMNES
    How now?
MASTER GALLIPOT
    With me, sir?

---

204   *chore* i.e. core, alluding here to Adam's apple
205   *Ay* ed. (E.C.) I Q (*in* Gomme)
212   *rub* impediment: the image in the rest of the line suggests the physical rubs or roughnesses in a bowling alley, by which the bowls were deflected from their true course. Cf. III.ii.168 and n.
213   *deal upon* set to work on, but to deal with a woman also means to have sexual intercourse with her
214   *A trick for that* perhaps as in the proverbial phrase 'a trick worth two of that'. (But cf. *A Trick to Catch the Old One,* IV.iv.208.)
217   sd 1 *sumner* an official employed to summon persons to appear in court

GREENWIT

You, sir. I have gone snaffling up and down by your door this
hour to watch for you.   220

MISTRESS GALLIPOT

What's the matter, husband?

GREENWIT

I have caught a cold in my head, sir, by sitting up late in the
Rose tavern, but I hope you understand my speech.

MASTER GALLIPOT

So sir.

GREENWIT

I cite you by the name of Hippocrates Gallipot, and you by the   225
name of Prudence Gallipot, to appear upon Crastino, do you
see, Crastino sancti Dunstani, this Easter term, in Bow Church.

MASTER GALLIPOT

Where, sir? What says he?

GREENWIT

Bow: Bow Church, to answer to a libel of precontract on the
part and behalf of the said Prudence and another: y'are best, sir,   230
take a copy of the citation; 'tis but twelvepence.

OMNES

A citation?

MASTER GALLIPOT

You pocky-nosed rascal, what slave fees you to this?

LAXTON

Slave? I ha' nothing to do with you, do you hear, sir?

219　*snaffling* OED gives 'saunter' virtually on the strength of this line alone. But, as the
reference to his cold three lines later shows, the word is simply a variant form of
'snuffling' – and one which is well represented in *OED*.

223　*Rose* a fairly common name for inns and taverns: one stood on Holborn Hill, from
which coaches departed for Brentford; Greenwit's may rather have been that near
Temple Bar, frequented by lawyers

225　*Hippocrates* The name of the great Greek physician would be a suitable, if grandiose,
one for an apothecary.

227　*Crastino sancti Dunstani* on the morrow of St Dunstan (i.e. 19 May)
Bow Church The famous church on the south side of Cheapside near the corner of
Bread Street was formerly the seat of the Court of Arches, which, according to one
tradition, was (like the church – St Mary-le-Bow or St Mary de Arcubus) named
after the arched buttresses or bows which have always held up the steeple. But it may
have sat in the early medieval crypt, the massive arches of which alone survived the
Great Fire and were incorporated into Wren's rebuilding. (The crypt survived the
blitz of 1940–4 also.) To this court came all appeals in ecclesiastical matters within
the province of Canterbury.

229　*libel* in ecclesiastical law, the plaintiff's written declaration of charges in a cause

GOSHAWK

    Laxton, is't not? – what vagary is this?   235

MASTER GALLIPOT

    Trust me, I thought, sir, this storm long ago

    Had been full laid, when (if you be remembered)

    I paid you the last fifteen pound, besides

    The thirty you had first; for then you swore –

LAXTON

    Tush, tush sir, oaths;   240

    Truth, yet I'm loath to vex you, – tell you what:

    Make up the money I had a hundred pound,

    And take your bellyful of her.

MASTER GALLIPOT   A hundred pound?

MISTRESS GALLIPOT

    What, a hundred pound? He gets none: what, a hundred pound?

MASTER GALLIPOT

    Sweet Pru, be calm, the gentleman offers thus,   245

    If I will make the moneys that are past

    A hundred pound, he will discharge all courts,

    And give his bond never to vex us more.

MISTRESS GALLIPOT

    A hundred pound? 'Las, take, sir, but threescore,

    Do you seek my undoing?

LAXTON   I'll not bate one sixpence, –   250

    I'll maul you, puss, for spitting.

MISTRESS GALLIPOT   Do thy worst, –

    Will fourscore stop thy mouth?

LAXTON   No.

MISTRESS GALLIPOT   Y'are a slave,

    Thou cheat, I'll now tear money from thy throat:

    Husband, lay hold on yonder tawny-coat.

GREENWIT

    Nay, gentlemen, seeing your women are so hot, I must lose my   255

    hair in their company, I see.   [*Takes off his wig*]

---

  254   *tawny-coat* Ecclesiastical apparitors (servants of the court) wore tawny-coloured
        livery. Greenwit is so disguised.

255–6   *lose my hair* alluding to the most frequent and obvious effect of syphilis. Q has 'loose',
        and the two words were indeed often not clearly distinguished: a light pun is
        possible.

MISTRESS OPENWORK

His hair sheds off, and yet he speaks not so much in the nose as
he did before.

GOSHAWK

He has had the better chirurgeon. – Master Greenwit, is your
wit so raw as to play no better a part than a sumner's?   260

MASTER GALLIPOT

I pray, who plays a knack to know an honest man in this
company?

MISTRESS GALLIPOT

Dear husband, pardon me, I did dissemble,
Told thee I was his precontracted wife,
When letters came from him for thirty pound,   265
I had no shift but that.

MASTER GALLIPOT   A very clean shift:
But able to make me lousy. On.

MISTRESS GALLIPOT   Husband, I plucked –
When he had tempted me to think well of him –
Got feathers from thy wings, to make him fly
More lofty.

MASTER GALLIPOT A' the top of you, wife: on.   270

MISTRESS GALLIPOT

He having wasted them, comes now for more,
Using me as a ruffian doth his whore,
Whose sin keeps him in breath: by heaven I vow
Thy bed he never wronged, more than he does now.

MASTER GALLIPOT

My bed? Ha, ha, like enough, a shop-board will serve   275
To have a cuckold's coat cut out upon:
Of that we'll talk hereafter – y'are a villain.

257   *in the nose* Cf. above, l. 222; another effect of syphilis is to make the nose swollen and
        pustular.
260   *no better a part than a sumner's* Greene in his *Notable Discovery of Cozenage* gives
        instances of coney-catchers learning a smattering of law and going dressed as
        sumners or apparitors.
262   *A Knack to Know an Honest Man* is the title of an early anonymous comedy; and the
        phrase and its complement, 'a knack to know a knave', were in common proverbial
        use.
266–8 lineation ed. (*prose* Q)
266   *shift* Gallipot's answer plays on the sense of petticoat.
269   *Got* ed. (E.C.) (Get Q) Gomme and Mulholland give *Gelt*. In my reading 'plucked'
        is intransitive and its meaning is reiterated in 'Got feathers'.

LAXTON

Hear me but speak, sir, you shall find me none.

OMNES

Pray sir, be patient and hear him.

MASTER GALLIPOT

I am muzzled for biting, sir, use me how you will. 280

LAXTON

The first hour that your wife was in my eye,
Myself with other gentlemen sitting by
In your shop tasting smoke, and speech being used
That men who have fairest wives are most abused
And hardly scaped the horn, your wife maintained 285
That only such spots in city dames were stained
Justly but by men's slanders: for her own part,
She vowed that you had so much of her heart,
No man by all his wit, by any wile
Never so fine spun, should yourself beguile 290
Of what in her was yours.

MASTER GALLIPOT Yet, Pru, 'tis well:
Play out your game at Irish, sir: who wins?

MISTRESS OPENWORK

The trial is when she comes to bearing.

LAXTON

I scorned one woman thus should brave all men,
And (which more vexed me) a she-citizen. 295
Therefore I laid siege to her, out she held,
Gave many a brave repulse, and me compelled
With shame to sound retreat to my hot lust;
Then seeing all base desires raked up in dust,
And that to tempt her modest ears I swore 300
Ne'er to presume again, she said her eye
Would ever give me welcome honestly,
And, since I was a gentleman, if it run low,
She would my state relieve, not to o'erthrow

285–7 *your wife maintained. . .* perhaps this means that she maintained that such stains on
        city dames came in truth only by slanders (cf. III.i.77ff.)
285 *horn* the sign of the cuckold
292 *Irish* a game resembling backgammon (fully described in Cotton's *Compleat
        Gamester* of 1674)
293 *when she comes to bearing* To bear at backgammon is to remove a piece at the end of
        a game: cf. *Northward Ho!*, IV.i.267: 'she'd win any game when she came to bearing'.
        There is, of course, a quibble on bearing a child.

114

Your own and hers: did so; then seeing I wrought 305
Upon her meekness, me she set at nought;
And yet to try if I could turn that tide,
You see what stream I strove with, but, sir, I swear
By heaven, and by those hopes men lay up there,
I neither have nor had a base intent 310
To wrong your bed; what's done is merriment:
Your gold I pay back with this interest,
When I had most power to do't I wronged you least.

MASTER GALLIPOT
If this no gullery be sir –
OMNES   No, no, on my life.
MASTER GALLIPOT
Then, sir, I am beholden – not to you, wife – 315
But Master Laxton, to your want of doing ill,
Which it seems you have not. Gentlemen,
Tarry and dine here all.
MASTER OPENWORK   Brother, we have a jest
As good as yours to furnish out a feast.
MASTER GALLIPOT
We'll crown our table with it: wife, brag no more 320
Of holding out: who most brags is most whore.

                                        Exeunt

312   *this interest* i.e. the substance of the following line
317–18 The invitation to dine is a traditional comic resolution. Cf. the end of *Bartholomew Fair.*

[ACT V, SCENE i]

Enter JACK DAPPER, MOLL, SIR BEAUTEOUS GANYMEDE,
and SIR THOMAS LONG

JACK DAPPER

But prithee Master Captain Jack, be plain and perspicuous with
me: was it your Meg of Westminster's courage that rescued me
from the Poultry puttocks indeed?

MOLL

The valour of my wit, I ensure you, sir, fetched you off bravely,
when you were i'the forlorn hope among those desperates; Sir   5
Beauteous Ganymede here and Sir Thomas Long heard that
cuckoo, my man Trapdoor, sing the note of your ransom from
captivity.

SIR BEAUTEOUS

Uds so, Moll, where's that Trapdoor?

MOLL

Hanged I think by this time; a justice in this town, that speaks   10
nothing but 'Make a mittimus, away with him to Newgate', used
that rogue like a firework to run upon a line betwixt him and me.

OMNES

How, how?

---

1 *perspicuous* clear in statement
2 *Meg of Westminster* The exploits of this Meg (a heroine of somewhat the same stamp
   as the Roaring Girl) are told in *The Life and Pranks of Long Meg of Westminster*, 1582.
   A play about her was acted in 1594–5, and she appears in the anti-masque of
   Jonson's *The Fortunate Isles*.
3 *Poultry puttocks* The two kites were presumably attached to the Poultry counter, in
   which Dekker was once imprisoned.
5 *the forlorn hope* (Dutch *verloren hoop*) was originally a picked body of men detached
   to the front to lead an attack, and hence any group of men in a desperate state
9 *Uds so* The phrase has no specific meaning: 'Ud' as a form of the name of God was
   attached to many other words and syllables in seventeenth-century oaths, as Udsbud,
   Udshash, Udzooks. Uds so is probably a transformation, ultimately, of catso: cf.
   III.ii.149.
11 *mittimus* (Lat. 'we send') a warrant under the hand of a J.P. ordering the person
   named to be kept in custody until delivered to a court of law
12 *a firework to run upon a line* The expression, as Bullen notes, is not uncommon.
   Dyce quotes from *The Whore of Babylon* (III.i.89f.): 'Let us behold these fireworks
   that must run / Upon short lines of life.' The line is a train or fuse of gunpowder (see
   l. 14–15) which combusts along its length from one end to the other.

116

MOLL

Marry, to lay trains of villainy to blow up my life; I smelt the
powder, spied what linstock gave fire to shoot against the poor   15
captain of the galley-foist, and away slid I my man like a shovel-
board shilling. He struts up and down the suburbs I think, and
eats up whores, feeds upon a bawd's garbage.

SIR THOMAS

Sirrah Jack Dapper.

JACK DAPPER

What sayst, Tom Long?   20

SIR THOMAS

Thou hadst a sweet-faced boy, hail-fellow with thee, to your
little Gull: how is he spent?

JACK DAPPER

Troth I whistled the poor little buzzard off o' my fist, because
when he waited upon me at the ordinaries, the gallants hit me
i'the teeth still, and said I looked like a painted alderman's tomb,   25
and the boy at my elbow like a death's head. – Sirrah Jack, Moll.

MOLL

What says my little Dapper?

SIR BEAUTEOUS

Come, come, walk and talk, walk and talk.

JACK DAPPER

Moll and I'll be i'the midst.

---

15 *linstock* a staff, very like a musket rest, which held a gunner's match or lunt
16 *galley-foist* a state barge, especially that of the Lord Mayor of London. Mulholland
    notes that 'Dekker seems to have been fond of using the term for large women.'
16–17 *shovel-board shilling* Shovel-board, or shuffleboard, a game resembling shove-
    halfpenny in which silver pieces were knocked along a very long highly polished
    table into compartments marked out at the end, was widely popular. The coins most
    commonly used were Edward VI shillings (see *Merry Wives of Windsor*, I.i.156),
    specially polished so that they were proverbially slippery. Cf. Jonson, *Every Man in
    His Humour* (English version), III.v.16–17: 'They . . . made it run as smooth off the
    tongue as a shove-groat shilling.'
21 *hail-fellow* intimate
23 *whistled . . . off* a technical term in falconry, meaning to dismiss by whistling (cf.
    Othello, III.iii.262)
24–5 *hit me i'the teeth* reproached or mocked me (cf. to throw it in one's teeth): cf. *A Fair
    Quarrel*, II.ii.109
25 *a painted alderman's tomb* The Elizabethan and early Stuart period was the great
    time for half-acre tombs, which were showily painted. A death's head is a common
    accompaniment of the effigies.

MOLL

These knights shall have squires' places, belike then: well Dapper, 30
what say you?

JACK DAPPER

Sirrah Captain Mad Mary, the gull my own father, Dapper Sir
Davy, laid these London boot-halers, the catchpolls, in ambush
to set upon me.

OMNES

Your father? Away, Jack. 35

JACK DAPPER

By the tassels of this handkercher 'tis true, and what was his
warlike stratagem, think you? He thought because a wicker cage
tames a nightingale, a lousy prison could make an ass of me.

OMNES

A nasty plot.

JACK DAPPER

Ay: as though a counter, which is a park in which all the wild 40
beasts of the city run head by head, could tame me.

Enter the LORD NOLAND

MOLL

Yonder comes my Lord Noland.

OMNES

Save you, my Lord.

LORD NOLAND

Well met, gentlemen all, good Sir Beauteous Ganymede, Sir
Thomas Long. And how does Master Dapper? 45

JACK DAPPER

Thanks, my Lord.

---

30   *These knights . . . places* Squires, as the knights' armour-bearers, would take their
     positions outside those whom they served.
32–3 *Dapper Sir Davy* ((Dapper) Sir Dauy Q). Perhaps we should read 'Sir Davy Dapper',
     but Jack may be making a joke on his father's name.
33   *boot-halers* freebooters or highwaymen; Dekker uses the word several times
     catchpolls Cf. III.i.38.
36   *handkercher* the customary spoken form of the word, particularly in Midland and
     southern dialect, until the eighteenth century, but common also in literary use (cf.
     All's Well that Ends Well, V.iii.321). They were often extravagantly fringed and
     tasselled.
37–8 The analogy between the caged bird and imprisoned man was a commonplace. Cf.
     A Trick to Catch the Old One, IV.iii.48f. and Jonson, 'To the World', 29ff.
40   *counter* Cf. III.iii.71 and n.

MOLL

No tobacco, my Lord?

LORD NOLAND

No 'faith, Jack.

JACK DAPPER

My Lord Noland, will you go to Pimlico with us? We are making
a boon voyage to that nappy land of spice-cakes.   50

LORD NOLAND

Here's such a merry ging, I could find in my heart to sail to the
world's end with such company; come, gentlemen, let's on.

JACK DAPPER

Here's most amorous weather, my Lord.

OMNES

Amorous weather?

They walk

JACK DAPPER

Is not amorous a good word?   55

Enter TRAPDOOR *like a poor soldier with a patch o'er one eye,
and* TEARCAT *with him, all tatters*

TRAPDOOR

Shall we set upon the infantry, these troops of foot? Zounds,
yonder comes Moll, my whorish master and mistress; would I
had her kidneys between my teeth.

TEARCAT

I had rather have a cow-heel.

TRAPDOOR

Zounds, I am so patched up, she cannot discover me: we'll on.   60

TEARCAT

Alla corago then.

TRAPDOOR

Good your honours and worships, enlarge the ears of commis-
eration, and let the sound of a hoarse military organpipe

---

49   *Pimlico* Cf. IV.ii.12 and n.
50   *boon voyage* 'bon voyage' (Fr.). The phrase, like others, was commonly anglicised.
      nappy heady, intoxicated
      spice-cakes In Glapthorne's *Lady Mother* of 1635, III.ii (qu. Sugden under Pimlico),
      a character speaks of walking to Pimlico 'to eat plumcakes and cream'.
51   *ging* company
51–2 *the world's end* There was more than one tavern of this name then at some
      considerable distance from London.
59   *cow-heel* the foot of a cow or ox stewed to form a jelly
61   *Alla corago* a corruption of the Italian *coraggio* (courage)

penetrate your pitiful bowels to extract out of them so many
small drops of silver as may give a hard straw-bed lodging to a   65
couple of maimed soldiers.

JACK DAPPER

Where are you maimed?

TEARCAT

In both our nether limbs.

MOLL

Come, come, Dapper, let's give 'em something: 'las poor men,
what money have you? By my troth I love a soldier with my soul.   70

SIR BEAUTEOUS

Stay, stay, where have you served?

SIR THOMAS

In any part of the Low Countries?

TRAPDOOR

Not in the Low Countries, if it please your manhood, but in
Hungary against the Turk at the siege of Belgrade.

LORD NOLAND

Who served there with you, sirrah?   75

TRAPDOOR

Many Hungarians, Moldavians, Walachians, and Transylvanians,
with some Sclavonians, and retiring home, sir, the Venetian
galleys took us prisoners, yet freed us, and suffered us to beg up
and down the country.

JACK DAPPER

You have ambled all over Italy then?   80

TRAPDOOR

Oh sir, from Venice to Roma, Vecchio, Bononia, Romania,
Bolonia, Modena, Piacenza, and Tuscana with all her cities, as

---

74   *the siege of Belgrade* Belgrade has had numerous sieges, the most famous of which,
     that of 1455–6, raised by the great János Hunyadi, seems to have been the last before
     1611; from 1521 to 1688 the city remained in the hands of the Turks. There was,
     however, constant warfare in Hungary throughout this time, and perhaps Trapdoor
     has muddled memories of the so-called 'Long War' (1593–1606), a confused, and
     often bitter, partly religious struggle involving, as well as the Emperor's native
     Hungarians and the Turks, all the nationalities mentioned in the next speech. (In *A
     Fair Quarrel*, IV.i.33, we hear of roaring in Sclavonian, along with other more
     obviously Londonian dialects.)

81–4 An amble indeed: Vecchio is presumably Civitavecchia, Bononia and Bolonia are
     one and the same, the modern Bologna, Romania is Romagna, Valteria Volterra,
     Mountepulchena Montepulciano. Moll recognises that this is no proper journey but
     a string of names picked up at hearsay.

Pistoia, Valteria, Mountepulchena, Arezzo, with the Siennois,
and diverse others.

MOLL

Mere rogues, put spurs to 'em once more.   85

JACK DAPPER

Thou look'st like a strange creature, a fat butter-box, yet speak'st
English. – What art thou?

TEARCAT

Ick, mine Here? Ick bin den ruffling Tearcat, den brave Soldado,
ick bin dorick all Dutchlant gueresen: der Shellum das meere ine
Beasa ine Woert gaeb. Ick slaag um stroakes on tom Cop: dastick   90
den hundred touzun Divell halle, frollick mine Here.

SIR BEAUTEOUS

Here, here, let's be rid of their jobbering.

MOLL

Not a cross, Sir Beauteous. You base rogues, I have taken measure
of you better than a tailor can, and I'll fit you as you, monster
with one eye, have fitted me.   95

TRAPDOOR

Your worship will not abuse a soldier.

MOLL

Soldier? Thou deservest to be hanged up by that tongue which

---

86   *butter-box* contemptuous term for a Dutchman

88–91 This piece of bastard Dutch is spelt here exactly as in Q (where it is printed in black letter), though the punctuation has been regularised. A 'translation' must be a matter partly of guesswork, but it isn't entirely gibberish, though some words are hard to identify. (I have supposed that, since Tearcat goes once into Spanish, he may also include an attempt at a French word: it looks as if *Beasa* may be *baiser*.) 'I, sir? I am the ruffling Tearcat, the brave soldier, I have travelled through all Holland: the rascal who gave more [than] a kiss and a word. I beat him with blows on the head; pulled out thence a hundred thousand devils, cheerfully, sir.' To ruffle is to swagger, also to handle a woman with rude familiarity; for the cant use, see below, l. 135 and Appendix.

92   *jobbering* jabbering

93   *Not a cross* From the 14th century at the latest coins were frequently stamped with a cross on the reverse side: Sir Beauteous has made to get rid of them by offering money.

94   *fit* in the sense of 'provide for', as well as literally

94–5 *monster with one eye* a reference to Trapdoor's patch. Mulholland notes that in *Women Beware Women* a stage trap-door is referred to as 'a devil with one eye' (V.i.8).

98   *skeldering* sponging: the term seems to have been used especially of vagabonds begging under the guise of old soldiers: cf. Jonson, *Every Man Out Of His Humour*, the Characters (description of Shift): 'A threadbare shark; one that never was a soldier, yet lives upon lendings. His profession is skeldering and odling.' See *Lanthorn and Candlelight*, p. xxiv, for a description of their methods of begging.

dishonours so noble a profession: soldier, you skeldering varlet?
Hold, stand, there should be a trapdoor hereabouts.

Pull[s] off his patch

TRAPDOOR

The balls of these glaziers of mine, mine eyes, shall be shot up   100
and down in any hot piece of service for my invincible mistress.

JACK DAPPER

I did not think there had been such knavery in black patches as
now I see.

MOLL

Oh sir, he hath been brought up in the Isle of Dogs, and can
both fawn like a spaniel and bite like a mastiff, as he finds   105
occasion.

LORD NOLAND

What are you, sirrah? A bird of this feather too?

TEARCAT

A man beaten from the wars, sir.

SIR THOMAS

I think so, for you never stood to fight.

JACK DAPPER

What's thy name, fellow soldier?   110

TEARCAT

I am called by those that have seen my valour, Tearcat.

OMNES

Tearcat?

MOLL

A mere whip-jack, and that is, in the commonwealth of rogues,
a slave that can talk of sea-fight, name all your chief pirates,
discover more countries to you than either the Dutch, Spanish,   115
French, or English ever found out, yet indeed all his service is by
land, and that is to rob a fair, or some such venturous exploit;

---

100   *glaziers* cant term for eyes
102   *black patches* They were worn as ornaments by ladies and fops.
104   *the Isle of Dogs* the peninsula on the north bank of the Thames opposite Greenwich:
      according to Sugden it took its name from hunting dogs being kennelled there when
      Greenwich was a royal palace. It had become a place of refuge for debtors and
      criminals; the name gave rise to frequent jokes of this kind. In 1598 the performance
      of a now lost play by Nashe and Jonson called *The Isle of Dogs* led to the theatres
      being closed for two months. In *The Return from Parnassus*, part 2, one of the
      students retires to the Isle of Dogs to become a professional satirist.
113   *whip-jack* a vagabond who pretends to be a distressed sailor: there is a similar
      description in Dekker's *Bellman of London*

Tearcat, foot sirrah, I have your name, now I remember me, in
my book of horners – horns for the thumb, you know how.

TEARCAT

No indeed, Captain Moll (for I know you by sight), I am no   120
such nipping Christian, but a maunderer upon the pad, I confess; and meeting with honest Trapdoor here, whom you had
cashiered from bearing arms, out at elbows under your colours,
I instructed him in the rudiments of roguery, and by my map
made him sail over any country you can name so that now he   125
can maunder better than myself.

JACK DAPPER

So then, Trapdoor, thou art turned soldier now.

TRAPDOOR

Alas sir, now there's no wars, 'tis the safest course of life I could
take.

MOLL

I hope then you can cant, for by your cudgels, you, sirrah, are   130
an upright man.

TRAPDOOR

As any walks the highway, I assure you.

MOLL

And Tearcat, what are you? A wild rogue, an angler, or a ruffler?

TEARCAT

Brother to this upright man, flesh and blood, ruffling Tearcat is
my name, and a ruffler is my style, my title, my profession.   135

MOLL

Sirrah, where's your doxy? Halt not with me.

OMNES

Doxy, Moll, what's that?

MOLL

His wench.

---

119 *horns for the thumb* A horn-thumb was a thimble of horn used by cutpurses for
  protecting the thumb against the edge of the knife used in cutting the pursestrings;
  hence, by synecdoche, used of pickpockets themselves.

121 *nipping* thieving
  maunderer upon the pad beggar on the highway; so *maunder* beg

130 *you can cant* you have learnt all the appropriate specialist slang. For an explanation
  of the cant terms used in this scene, see the glossary given in the Appendix, and,
  generally, the various early authorities there cited.

136 *Halt not* don't limp, i.e. don't be roundabout or devious

TRAPDOOR

My doxy? I have by the solomon a doxy, that carries a kinchin
mort in her slate at her back, besides my dell and my dainty   140
wild dell, with all whom I'll tumble this next darkmans in the
strommel, and drink ben booze, and eat a fat gruntling cheat, a
cackling cheat, and a quacking cheat.

JACK DAPPER

Here's old cheating.

TRAPDOOR

My doxy stays for me in a boozing ken, brave captain.   145

MOLL

He says his wench stays for him in an alehouse: you are no pure
rogues.

TEARCAT

Pure rogues? No, we scorn to be pure rogues, but if you come
to our lib ken, or our stalling ken, you shall find neither him
nor me a queer cuffin.   150

MOLL

So sir, no churl of you?

TEARCAT

No, but a ben cove, a brave cove, a gentry cuffin.

LORD NOLAND

Call you this canting?

JACK DAPPER

Zounds, I'll give a schoolmaster half a crown a week, and teach
me this pedlar's French.   155

TRAPDOOR

Do but stroll, sir, half a harvest with us, sir, and you shall gabble
your bellyfull.

MOLL

Come you rogue, cant with me.

---

140   *slate* See Appendix.
141–3   i.e. I'll tumble this next night in the straw, and drink good booze, and eat a fat pig,
a capon, and a duck. For *booze* Q has *baufe*, which is evidently a misprint for *bouse*
or *bowse*. See further in the Appendix.
144   *old* fine, rare
146–7   *you are no pure rogues* Bullen takes this to be ironical; but Moll may mean pure in
the sense of sexually pure or chaste, and that is certainly the sense in which Tearcat
picks up the word.
155   *pedlar's French* 'canting language to be found among none but beggars' (*Bellman of
London*); also applied generally to unintelligible jargon. Pedlars were widely regarded
as inescapably dishonest.

SIR THOMAS

Well said, Moll, cant with her, sirrah, and you shall have money,
else not a penny.   160

TRAPDOOR

I'll have a bout if she please.

MOLL

Come on sirrah.

TRAPDOOR

Ben mort, shall you and I heave a booth, mill a ken, or nip a
bung? And then we'll coach a hogshead under the ruffmans,
and there you shall wap with me, and I'll niggle with you.   165

MOLL

Out, you damned impudent rascal.

TRAPDOOR

Cut benar whids, and hold your fambles and your stamps.

LORD NOLAND

Nay, nay, Moll, why art thou angry? What was his gibberish?

MOLL

Marry, this, my Lord, says he: Ben mort (good wench), shall
you and I heave a booth, mill a ken, or nip a bung? Shall you   170
and I rob a house, or cut a purse?

OMNES

Very good.

MOLL

And then we'll couch a hogshead under the ruffmans: and then
we'll lie under a hedge.

TRAPDOOR

That was my desire, captain, as 'tis fit a soldier should lie.   175

MOLL

And there you shall wap with me, and I'll niggle with you, and
that's all.

SIR BEAUTEOUS

Nay, nay, Moll, what's that wap?

JACK DAPPER

Nay teach me what niggling is, I'd fain be niggling.

MOLL

Wapping and niggling is all one, the rogue my man can tell you.   180

167   *Cut benar whids, and hold your fambles and your stamps* speak better words, and
hold your hands and your feet

TRAPDOOR

'Tis fadoodling, if it please you.

SIR BEAUTEOUS

This is excellent, one fit more, good Moll.

MOLL

Come you rogue, sing with me.

The song

	A gage of ben rom-booze	
	In a boozing ken of Rom-ville	185
TEARCAT	Is benar than a caster,	
	Peck, pennam, lap or popler,	
	Which we mill in deuse a vill.	
BOTH	Oh I would lib all the lightmans,	
	Oh I would lib all the darkmans,	190
	By the solomon, under the ruffmans,	
	By the solomon, in the hartmans.	
TEARCAT	And scour the queer cramp-ring,	
	And couch till a palliard docked my dell,	
	So my boozy nab might skew rom-booze well.	195

181 *fadoodling OED* has nothing earlier than 1670 for 'fadoodle', when it meant something
        ridiculous; but as Reed remarks, the explanation is evident from Trapdoor's use of it.

182 *fit* strain or bout.

183–97 sp ed. In Q there is no speech prefix following Moll's invitation until the third line
        of the song, where *T.Cat* is prefixed. At the sixth line *The song* appears in the
        right-hand margin, where a chorus is strongly suggested. *T.Cat* is again prefixed to
        the tenth line; the last two lines seem again to be a chorus. The song, translated
        with the help of *Lanthorn and Candlelight*, means:

> A quart of good wine
> In an alehouse of London
> Is better than a cloak,
> Meat, bread, whey, or pottage,
> Which we steal in the country.
> Oh I would lie all the day,
> Oh I would lie all the night,
> By the mass, under the bushes,
> By the mass, in the stocks.
> And wear bolts (or fetters)
> And sleep till a tramp lay with my wench,
> So my boozy head might drink wine well.
> Away to the highway, let us go.
> Away to the highway, let us go.

See Appendix for Dekker's definitions, and Moll's paraphrase at l. 222 ff.

187 *lap* ed. (lay Q)

188 *vill* ed. (vile Q)

193 *cramp-ring* handcuffs, a cant adaptation of the standard word (cf. IV.ii.16 and n.)

126

BOTH   Avast to the pad, let us bing,
                Avast to the pad, let us bing.

OMNES

Fine knaves i'faith.

JACK DAPPER

The grating of ten new cartwheels, and the gruntling of five
hundred hogs coming from Romford market, cannot make a   200
worse noise than this canting language does in my ears; pray,
my Lord Noland, let's give these soldiers their pay.

SIR BEAUTEOUS

Agreed, and let them march.

LORD NOLAND

Here, Moll.

MOLL

Now I see that you are stalled to the rogue, and are not ashamed   205
of your professions, look you: my Lord Noland here and these
gentlemen bestows upon you two, two bordes and a half, that's
two shillings sixpence.

TRAPDOOR

Thanks to your lordship.

TEARCAT

Thanks, heroical captain.   210

MOLL

Away.

TRAPDOOR

We shall cut ben whids of your masters and mistress-ship,
wheresoever we come.

MOLL

You'll maintain, sirrah, the old justice's plot to his face?

TRAPDOOR

Else trine me on the cheats: hang me.   215

MOLL

Be sure you meet me there.

TRAPDOOR

Without any more maundering I'll do't: follow, brave Tearcat.

200   *Romford market* Romford had an important market, and allusions to Romford hogs
        are frequent. Cf., e.g., *A Chaste Maid*, IV.i.95.
207   *bordes* shillings
212   *cut ben whids* speak well
215   *trine me on the cheats* hang me on the gallows; but cf. Appendix
217   *maundering* probably chattering; i.e. without more ado. The word is apparently
        distinct from that used above at l. 121; but cf. Appendix.

TEARCAT

    I prae, sequor; let us go, mouse.

                            Exeunt they two, manet the rest

LORD NOLAND

    Moll, what was in that canting song?

MOLL

    Troth my Lord, only a praise of good drink, the only milk   220
    which these wild beasts love to suck, and thus it was:

              A rich cup of wine,
              Oh it is juice divine,
              More wholesome for the head
              Than meat, drink, or bread;   225
              To fill my drunken pate
              With that, I'd sit up late,
              By the heels would I lie,
              Under a lousy hedge die,
              Let a slave have a pull   230
              At my whore, so I be full
              Of that precious liquor

   – and a parcel of such stuff, my Lord, not worth the opening.

        Enter a CUTPURSE *very gallant, with four or five men*
                after him, one with a wand

LORD NOLAND

    What gallant comes yonder?

SIR THOMAS

    Mass, I think I know him, 'tis one of Cumberland.   235

1 CUTPURSE

    Shall we venture to shuffle in amongst yon heap of gallants and
    strike?

2 CUTPURSE

    'Tis a question whether there be any silver shells amongst them
    for all their satin outsides.

OMNES [CUTPURSES]

    Let's try.   240

---

    218   *I prae, sequor* (Lat.) go before, I follow.
           sd *manet* (Lat.) remains
    233   sd *gallant* finely dressed
    237   *strike* steal; to strike a hand is to do a job (*Lanthorn and Candlelight*, p. xxiv)
    238   *shells* money

MOLL

Pox on him, a gallant? Shadow me, I know him: 'tis one that cumbers the land indeed; if he swim near to the shore of any of your pockets, look to your purses.

OMNES

Is't possible?

MOLL

This brave fellow is no better than a foist.   245

OMNES

Foist, what's that?

MOLL

A diver with two fingers, a pickpocket; all his train study the figging-law, that's to say cutting of purses and foisting; one of them is a nip, I took him once i'the twopenny gallery at the Fortune; then there's a cloyer, or snap, that dogs any new   250 brother in that trade, and snaps will have half in any booty; he with the wand is both a stale, whose office is to face a man i'the streets, whilst shells are drawn by another, and then with his black conjuring rod in his hand, he, by the nimbleness of his eye and juggling-stick, will, in cheaping a piece of plate at a   255 goldsmith's stall, make four or five rings mount from the top of his caduceus, and as if it were at leap-frog, they skip into his hand presently.

2 CUTPURSE

Zounds, we are smoked.

OMNES [CUTPURSES]

Ha?   260

2 CUTPURSE

We are boiled, pox on her; see, Moll, the roaring drab.

1 CUTPURSE

All the diseases of sixteen hospitals boil her! Away.

---

241   *Shadow me* follow me closely
244   sp OMNES i.e. Moll's companions
245   *foist* etc. See Appendix.
249–50   *the twopenny gallery at the Fortune* not quite the cheapest place, for one could get in for a penny. The Fortune was the theatre in which *The Roaring Girl* was then being performed.
255   *cheaping* bargaining for
257   *caduceus* strictly a herald's wand: I am not sure whether Moll is referring again to the cutpurse's stick used like a curb, or to a baton on which the goldsmith might keep rings for sale. Mercury, the nimble god of thieves, carried a caduceus; hence 'mercury': a dexterous thief.

MOLL

Bless you, sir.

1 CUTPURSE

And you, good sir.

MOLL

Dost not ken me, man?   265

1 CUTPURSE

No, trust me, sir.

MOLL

Heart, there's a knight to whom I'm bound for many favours
lost his purse at the last new play i'the Swan, seven angels in't:
make it good, you're best; do you see? No more.

1 CUTPURSE

A synagogue shall be called, Mistress Mary, disgrace me not;   270
pacus palabros, I will conjure for you, farewell.

[*Exeunt* CUTPURSES]

MOLL

Did not I tell you, my Lord?

LORD NOLAND

I wonder how thou camest to the knowledge of these nasty
villains.

SIR THOMAS

And why do the foul mouths of the world call thee Moll Cut-   275
purse? A name, methinks, damned and odious.

MOLL

Dare any step forth to my face and say,
'I have ta'en thee doing so, Moll'? I must confess,
In younger days, when I was apt to stray,
I have sat amongst such adders; seen their stings,   280
As any here might, and in full playhouses
Watched their quick-diving hands, to bring to shame
Such rogues, and in that stream met an ill name:
When next, my Lord, you spy any one of those,

---

266   *trust* ed. (rrust Q)
267ff. This episode seems to be based on an established custom of Mary Frith's.
268   *Swan* the theatre on Bankside near the Globe
270   *synagogue* presumably an assembly of thieves to get the money together. Mulholland
      notes that Dekker refers to an underworld gathering as a 'satanical synagogue' in an
      allusion to Revelation 2, 9 in *Lanthorn and Candlelight.*
271   *pacus palabros* a corruption of Spanish *pocas palabras,* few words. Cf. *The Taming of
      the Shrew,* Ind. i.5

So he be in his art a scholar, question him, 285
Tempt him with gold to open the large book
Of his close villainies: and you yourself shall cant
Better than poor Moll can, and know more laws
Of cheators, lifters, nips, foists, puggards, curbers,
With all the devil's black guard, than it is fit 290
Should be discovered to a noble wit.
I know they have their orders, offices,
Circuits and circles, unto which they are bound,
To raise their own damnation in.

JACK DAPPER   How dost thou know it?

MOLL

As you do, I show it you, they to me show it. 295
Suppose, my Lord, you were in Venice.

LORD NOLAND   Well.

MOLL

If some Italian pander there would tell
All the close tricks of courtesans, would not you
Hearken to such a fellow?

LORD NOLAND   Yes.

MOLL   And here,

Being come from Venice, to a friend most dear 300
That were to travel thither, you would proclaim
Your knowledge in those villainies, to save
Your friend from their quick danger: must you have
A black ill name, because ill things you know?
Good troth my Lord, I am made Moll Cutpurse so. 305
How many are whores in small ruffs and still looks!
How many chaste, whose names fill slander's books!
Were all men cuckolds, whom gallants in their scorns

---

289   *cheators* or fingerers, those who win money by false dice: see Appendix
        lifters thieves (an old usage revived in 'shop-lifters')
        nips etc. See Appendix.
        puggards thieves: seemingly a unique occurrence, though cf. *The Winter's Tale*,
        IV.iii.7, for *pugging*. It is possible that we should read 'priggard', a word which in
        one form or another often occurs for thief.
290   *black guard* a guard of attendants, black in person, dress, or character: cf. *Lanthorn
        and Candlelight*, p. ii: 'The great Lord of Limbo did therefore command all his Black
        Guard . . . to bestir them'
294   *raise . . . in* make more complete (literally to fatten)
303   *quick* lively

Call so, we should not walk for goring horns.
Perhaps for my mad going some reprove me, 310
I please myself, and care not else who loves me.

OMNES

A brave mind, Moll, i'faith.

SIR THOMAS

Come my Lord, shall's to the ordinary?

LORD NOLAND

Ay, 'tis noon sure.

MOLL

Good my Lord, let not my name condemn me to you or to the 315
world: a fencer I hope may be called a coward, is he so for that?
If all that have ill names in London were to be whipped, and to
pay but twelve-pence apiece to the beadle, I would rather have
his office than a constable's.

JACK DAPPER

So would I, Captain Moll: 'twere a sweet tickling office i'faith. 320

Exeunt

[ACT V, SCENE ii]

Enter SIR ALEXANDER WENGRAVE, GOSHAWK
and GREENWIT, *and others*

SIR ALEXANDER

My son marry a thief, that impudent girl,
Whom all the world stick their worst eyes upon?

GREENWIT

How will your care prevent it?

GOSHAWK   'Tis impossible.

They marry close, they're gone, but none knows whither.

SIR ALEXANDER

Oh gentlemen, when has a father's heart-strings 5
Held out so long from breaking?

---

320   *tickling* diverting, but 'tickler' was also slang for a whip

4   *close* secretly

Enter a SERVANT

Now what news, sir?

SERVANT

They were met upo'th'water an hour since, sir,
Putting in towards the Sluice.

SIR ALEXANDER   The Sluice? Come gentlemen,

[*Exit* SERVANT]

'Tis Lambeth works against us.

GREENWIT   And that Lambeth

Joins more mad matches than your six wet towns,   10
'Twixt that and Windsor Bridge, where fares lie soaking.

SIR ALEXANDER

Delay no time, sweet gentlemen: to Blackfriars,
We'll take a pair of oars and make after 'em.

Enter TRAPDOOR

TRAPDOOR

Your son, and that bold masculine ramp
My mistress, are landed now at Tower.

SIR ALEXANDER   Hoyda, at Tower?   15

TRAPDOOR

I heard it now reported.   [*Exit*]

SIR ALEXANDER   Which way, gentlemen,

Shall I bestow my care? I'm drawn in pieces
Betwixt deceit and shame.

Enter SIR [GUY] FITZ-ALLARD

SIR GUY   Sir Alexander,

You're well met, and most rightly served:

8   *the Sluice* The Sluice was an embankment built to protect the low-lying area of
     Lambeth Marsh from inundations; it was used as a landing-place. Perhaps we are
     meant also to think of the verb to sluice (to copulate with).
9   *Lambeth* was also renowned as the haunt of thieves, etc.; but there is perhaps an
     allusion to the boat-building works there; additionally Lambeth was the place from
     which (after crossing the river by boat) one would set out towards the south-west.
10   *your six wet* (i.e. riverside) *towns* A note in Reed's edition of Dodsley suggests that
     the six are Fulham, Richmond, Kingston, Hampton, Chertsey, and Staines.
11   *where fares lie soaking* In more recent centuries, to 'soak' can mean to linger over
     sexual intercourse; and the whole phrase suggests the use of the riverside towns for
     sexual excursions.
12   *to Blackfriars* i.e. they will take a boat from Blackfriars Stairs and cross to Lambeth
14   *ramp* Cf. III.iii.7.

My daughter was a scorn to you.

SIR ALEXANDER   Say not so, sir.   20

SIR GUY

A very abject she, poor gentlewoman.
Your house has been dishonoured: give you joy, sir,
Of your son's gaskin-bride, you'll be a grandfather shortly
To a fine crew of roaring sons and daughters,
'Twill help to stock the suburbs passing well, sir.   25

SIR ALEXANDER

Oh play not with the miseries of my heart.
Wounds should be dressed and healed, not vexed, or left
Wide open, to the anguish of the patient,
And scornful air let in: rather let pity
And advice charitably help to refresh 'em.   30

SIR GUY

Who'd place his charity so unworthily,
Like one that gives alms to a cursing beggar?
Had I but found one spark of goodness in you
Toward my deserving child, which then grew fond
Of your son's virtues, I had eased you now.   35
But I perceive both fire of youth and goodness
Are raked up in the ashes of your age,
Else no such shame should have come near your house,
Nor such ignoble sorrow touch your heart.

SIR ALEXANDER

If not for worth, for pity's sake assist me.   40

GREENWIT

You urge a thing past sense, how can he help you?
All his assistance is as frail as ours,
Full as uncertain where's the place that holds 'em.
One brings us water-news; then comes another

---

21   *abject* here, a noun meaning 'outcast'
22   *has* ed. (had Q)
23   *gaskin-bride* one, that is, wearing gaskins or loose breeches: the Q spelling is
     Gaskoyne, which indicates a popular and possibly correct etymology (i.e. from
     Gascony)
25   *the suburbs* were notoriously corrupt, licentious, and full of brothels. Cf. Nashe,
     Christ's Tears over Jerusalem (Works [1904], II, 148): 'London, what are thy suburbs
     but licensed stews?' But those living in the suburbs would be penniless too: cf.
     Lanthorn and Candlelight, p. ix: 'these suburb sinners have no land to live upon but
     their legs'. A suburb-sinner was a prostitute. And see the Prologus to this play, l. 21.
37   *raked up* smothered

With a full-charged mouth, like a culverin's voice,   45
And he reports the Tower: whose sounds are truest?

GOSHAWK

In vain you flatter him, Sir Alexander.

SIR ALEXANDER

I flatter him? Gentlemen, you wrong me grossly.

GREENWIT

He does it well i'faith.

SIR GUY   Both news are false,
Of Tower or water: they took no such way yet.   50

SIR ALEXANDER

Oh strange: hear you this, gentlemen, yet more plunges?

SIR GUY

They're nearer than you think for, yet more close
Than if they were further off.

SIR ALEXANDER   How am I lost
In these distractions?

SIR GUY   For your speeches, gentlemen,
In taxing me for rashness, 'fore you all   55
I will engage my state to half his wealth,
Nay to his son's revenues, which are less,
And yet nothing at all till they come from him,
That I could (if my will stuck to my power)
Prevent this marriage yet, nay banish her   60
Forever from his thoughts, much more his arms.

SIR ALEXANDER

Slack not this goodness, though you heap upon me
Mountains of malice and revenge hereafter:

---

45   *culverin* a large cannon

48   sp *SIR ALEXANDER* ed. (Fitz-All. Q) I take it that Goshawk means flatter in the sense
      of coax or wheedle, but Sir Alexander mistakes this for the common use. If Q is
      correct, presumably Goshawk is being ironic: one must then, with previous editors,
      punctuate his speech '... flatter him. Sir Alexander –', as if he were going to explain
      why 'flattery' will get him nowhere; but there seems no reason why such a speech
      should come at this point.

49   Does this mean that Goshawk and Greenwit are in the Fitz-Allard plot? Cf. l. 92.

51   *plunges* dilemmas; cf. IV.i.149

52   *think for* suppose   *close* secret, hidden

54–5 'Though I foresee that you will tax me with rashness.'

56   *engage* wager
      his i.e. Sir Alexander's

59   *if my will stuck to my power* if I would do what I could

I'd willingly resign up half my state to him,
So he would marry the meanest drudge I hire. 65
GREENWIT
He talks impossibilities, and you believe 'em.
SIR GUY
I talk no more than I know how to finish,
My fortunes else are his that dares stake with me.
The poor young gentleman I love and pity,
And to keep shame from him (because the spring 70
Of his affection was my daughter's first,
Till his frown blasted all), do but estate him
In those possessions which your love and care
Once pointed out for him, that he may have room
To entertain fortunes of noble birth, 75
Where now his desperate wants casts him upon her:
And if I do not, for his own sake chiefly,
Rid him of this disease that now grows on him,
I'll forfeit my whole state, before these gentlemen.
GREENWIT
Troth but you shall not undertake such matches, 80
We'll persuade so much with you.
SIR ALEXANDER   Here's my ring,
He will believe this token: 'fore these gentlemen
I will confirm it fully: all those lands
My first love 'lotted him, he shall straight possess
In that refusal.
SIR GUY   If I change it not, 85
Change me into a beggar.
GREENWIT   Are you mad, sir?
SIR GUY
'Tis done.
GOSHAWK   Will you undo yourself by doing,
And show a prodigal trick in your old days?
SIR ALEXANDER
'Tis a match, gentlemen.
SIR GUY   Ay, ay, sir, ay.

70–1   'Because the fountain of his love belonged first to my daughter'
72   *his* i.e. Sir Alexander's
76   *her* i.e. Moll
80   *matches* wagers
85   *In that refusal* i.e. in refusing Moll

I ask no favour; trust to you for none,   90
My hope rests in the goodness of your son.   *Exit*

GREENWIT
He holds it up well yet.

GOSHAWK   Of an old knight i'faith.

SIR ALEXANDER
Cursed be the time I laid his first love barren,
Wilfully barren, that before this hour
Had sprung forth fruits of comfort and of honour;   95
He loved a virtuous gentlewoman.

Enter MOLL *[in male dress]*

GOSHAWK   Life,
Here's Moll.

GREENWIT   Jack?

GOSHAWK   How dost thou, Jack?

MOLL   How dost thou, gallant?

SIR ALEXANDER
Impudence, where's my son?

MOLL   Weakness, go look him.

SIR ALEXANDER
Is this your wedding gown?

MOLL   The man talks monthly:
Hot broth and a dark chamber for the knight,   100
I see he'll be stark mad at our next meeting.   *Exit*

GOSHAWK
Why sir, take comfort now, there's no such matter.
No priest will marry her, sir, for a woman
Whiles that shape's on, and it was never known
Two men were married and conjoined in one: 105
Your son hath made some shift to love another.

SIR ALEXANDER
Whate'er she be, she has my blessing with her,

92   *Of* in the true manner of
99   *The man talks monthly* i.e. madly (as if under the influence of the moon). Cf. *Lant-*
      horn and Candlelight, viii: 'A moon-man signifies in English a "madman" because the
      moon hath greatest domination above any other planet over the bodies of frantic
      persons.'
100   *Hot broth and a dark chamber* treatments for insanity. The darkness was to rest the
      overstimulated imagination.
103   *No priest will marry her . . . for a woman* 'Marriages' between two men crop up in
      several plays, e.g. Fletcher's *Wild Goose Chase* and *Monsieur Thomas*.

May they be rich, and fruitful, and receive
Like comfort to their issue as I take
In them. Has pleased me now: marrying not this,   110
Through a whole world he could not choose amiss.

GREENWIT

Glad y'are so penitent for your former sin, sir.

GOSHAWK

Say he should take a wench with her smock-dowry,
No portion with her but her lips and arms?

SIR ALEXANDER

Why, who thrive better, sir? They have most blessing,   115
Though other have more wealth, and least repent:
Many that want most know the most content.

GREENWIT

Say he should marry a kind youthful sinner?

SIR ALEXANDER

Age will quench that,
Any offence but theft and drunkenness,   120
Nothing but death can wipe away:
Their sins are green even when their heads are grey.
Nay I despair not now, my heart's cheered, gentlemen,
No face can come unfortunately to me.

Enter a SERVANT

Now, sir, your news?

SERVANT   Your son with his fair bride   125
Is near at hand.

SIR ALEXANDER   Fair may their fortunes be.

GREENWIT

Now you're resolved, sir, it was never she?

SIR ALEXANDER

I find it in the music of my heart.

---

113   *with her smock-dowry* i.e. with no dowry but her smock: apparently a unique
      occurrence, but cf. *A Chaste Maid*, III.iii.76: 'I took her with one smock', and *A Trick
      to Catch the Old One*, IV.iv.8: 'She's worth four hundred a year in her very smock.'
118   *kind* winsome
119–21 *stet* Q (except for lineation, Q making a single line from *Age* to *drunkenness*). The
      sense is obscure as the sentence stands, and faulty lineation suggests that there may
      be corruption. Possibly we should read (l. 121) 'And these nothing but death can
      wipe away' – or some such phrase.
127   *resolved* persuaded

Enter MOLL *masked, in* SEBASTIAN's *hand,*
and FITZ-ALLARD

See where they come.

GOSHAWK   A proper lusty presence, sir.

SIR ALEXANDER

Now has he pleased me right, I always counselled him   130
To choose a goodly personable creature,
Just of her pitch was my first wife his mother.

SEBASTIAN

Before I dare discover my offence,
I kneel for pardon.

SIR ALEXANDER   My heart gave it thee
Before thy tongue could ask it: 135
Rise, thou hast raised my joy to greater height
Than to that seat where grief dejected it:
Both welcome to my love and care for ever.
Hide not my happiness too long, all's pardoned,
Here are our friends, salute her, gentlemen.   140

They unmask her

OMNES

Heart, who's this? Moll!

SIR ALEXANDER

Oh my reviving shame, is't I must live
To be struck blind? Be it the work of sorrow,
Before age take't in hand.

SIR GUY   Darkness and death.
Have you deceived me thus? Did I engage   145
My whole estate for this?

SIR ALEXANDER   You asked no favour,
And you shall find as little; since my comforts
Play false with me, I'll be as cruel to thee
As grief to fathers' hearts.

MOLL   Why, what's the matter with you,
'Less too much joy should make your age forgetful?   150
Are you too well, too happy?

SIR ALEXANDER   With a vengeance.

MOLL

Methinks you should be proud of such a daughter,

132   *pitch* height
141   *who's this? Moll!* ed. (who this *Moll?* Q)
150   *'Less* unless

As good a man as your son.

SIR ALEXANDER   Oh monstrous impudence.

MOLL

You had no note before, an unmarked knight;
Now all the town will take regard on you,   155
And all your enemies fear you for my sake:
You may pass where you list, through crowds most thick,
And come off bravely with your purse unpicked.
You do not know the benefits I bring with me:
No cheat dares work upon you with thumb or knife,   160
While y'ave a roaring girl to your son's wife.

SIR ALEXANDER

A devil rampant.

SIR GUY   Have you so much charity
Yet to release me of my last rash bargain,
And I'll give in your pledge?

SIR ALEXANDER   No sir, I stand to't,
I'll work upon advantage, as all mischiefs   165
Do upon me.

SIR GUY   Content: bear witness all then,
His are the lands, and so contention ends.
Here comes your son's bride, 'twixt two noble friends.

Enter the LORD NOLAND *and* SIR BEAUTEOUS GANYMEDE
with MARY FITZ-ALLARD *between them, the* CITIZENS
and their WIVES *with them*

MOLL

Now are you gulled as you would be: thank me for't,
I'd a forefinger in't.

SEBASTIAN   Forgive me, father: 170
Though there before your eyes my sorrow feigned,
This still was she for whom true love complained.

SIR ALEXANDER

Blessings eternal and the joys of angels
Begin your peace here, to be signed in heaven!
How short my sleep of sorrow seems now to me,   175

---

154   *unmarked* unnoticed, of no account
160   *cheat* in the general sense of pickpocket or cutpurse
       thumb Cf. V.i.119 and n.
165   *work upon advantage* take advantage of my position (unscrupulously): cf. *A Fair Quarrel*, III.iii.151

To this eternity of boundless comforts,
That finds no want but utterance and expression.
My Lord, your office here appears so honourably,
So full of ancient goodness, grace, and worthiness,
I never took more joy in sight of man   180
Than in your comfortable presence now.

LORD NOLAND
Nor I more delight in doing grace to virtue,
Than in this worthy gentlewoman, your son's bride,
Noble Fitz-Allard's daughter, to whose honour
And modest fame I am a servant vowed,   185
So is this knight.

SIR ALEXANDER   Your loves make my joys proud.
Bring forth those deeds of land my care laid ready,
And which, old knight, thy nobleness may challenge,
Joined with thy daughter's virtues, whom I prize now
As dearly as that flesh I call mine own.   190
Forgive me, worthy gentlewoman, 'twas my blindness
When I rejected thee; I saw thee not,
Sorrow and wilful rashness grew like films
Over the eyes of judgment, now so clear
I see the brightness of thy worth appear.   195

MARY
Duty and love may I deserve in those,
And all my wishes have a perfect close.

SIR ALEXANDER
That tongue can never err, the sound's so sweet.
Here, honest son, receive into thy hands
The keys of wealth, possession of those lands   200
Which my first care provided, they're thine own:
Heaven give thee a blessing with 'em; the best joys
That can in worldly shapes to man betide
Are fertile lands and a fair fruitful bride,
Of which I hope thou'rt sped.

SEBASTIAN   I hope so too sir.   205

MOLL
Father and son, I ha' done you simple service here.

188   *challenge* claim
196   *those* i.e. the eyes of judgment
205   *sped* provided; but (cf. previous line) to speed is to be sexually potent

141

SEBASTIAN

    For which thou shalt not part, Moll, unrequited.

SIR ALEXANDER

    Thou art a mad girl, and yet I cannot now

    Condemn thee.

MOLL   Condemn me? Troth and you should, sir,

    I'd make you seek out one to hang in my room,   210

    I'd give you the slip at gallows, and cozen the people.

    Heard you this jest, my Lord?

LORD NOLAND   What is it, Jack?

MOLL

    He was in fear his son would marry me,

    But never dreamt that I would ne'er agree.

LORD NOLAND

    Why? Thou hadst a suitor once, Jack, when wilt marry?   215

MOLL

    Who, I, my Lord? I'll tell you when i'faith:

          When you shall hear

          Gallants void from sergeants' fear,

          Honesty and truth unslandered,

          Woman manned but never pandered,   220

          Cheats booted but not coached,

          Vessels older ere they're broached.

          If my mind be then not varied,

          Next day following I'll be married.

LORD NOLAND

    This sounds like doomsday.

MOLL   Then were marriage best,   225

    For if I should repent, I were soon at rest.

SIR ALEXANDER

    In troth thou'rt a good wench, I'm sorry now

    The opinion was so hard I conceived of thee.

    Some wrongs I've done thee.

Enter TRAPDOOR

TRAPDOOR   Is the wind there now?

---

206   *simple* pure, disinterested

209   *and* if

221   *not coached* so unsuccessful in their cheating that they cannot afford to travel by
      coach

222   *Vessels* i.e. maidenheads

'Tis time for me to kneel and confess first,   230
For fear it come too late and my brains feel it.
Upon my paws I ask you pardon, mistress.

MOLL
Pardon? For what, sir? What has your rogueship done now?

TRAPDOOR
I have been from time to time hired to confound you
By this old gentleman.

MOLL   How?

TRAPDOOR   Pray forgive him,   235
But may I counsel you, you should never do't.
Many a snare to entrap your worship's life
Have I laid privily, chains, watches, jewels,
And when he saw nothing could mount you up,
Four hollow-hearted angels he then gave you,   240
By which he meant to trap you, I to save you.

SIR ALEXANDER
To all which shame and grief in me cry guilty:
Forgive me, now I cast the world's eyes from me,
And look upon thee freely with mine own,
I see the most of many wrongs before thee   245
Cast from the jaws of envy and her people,
And nothing foul but that. I'll never more
Condemn by common voice, for that's the whore
That deceives man's opinion, mocks his trust,
Cozens his love, and makes his heart unjust.   250

MOLL
Here be the angels, gentlemen, they were given me
As a musician. I pursue no pity:
Follow the law: and you can cuck me, spare not:
Hang up my viol by me, and I care not.

SIR ALEXANDER
So far I'm sorry, I'll thrice double 'em   255
To make thy wrongs amends.

---

236   *may I counsel you* if you take my advice
240   *hollow-hearted angels* i.e. with holes through the middle; cf. IV.i.197
245   *thee* ed. (hee Q)
        before thee done to thee
246   *Cast* i.e. are cast, thrown at you
252   *pursue* seek
253   *and you can cuck me* if you can get me into a cucking stool

Come, worthy friends, my honourable Lord,
Sir Beauteous Ganymede, and noble Fitz-Allard,
And you kind gentlewomen, whose sparkling presence
Are glories set in marriage, beams of society,   260
For all your loves give lustre to my joys:
The happiness of this day shall be remembered
At the return of every smiling spring:
In my time now 'tis born, and may no sadness
Sit on the brows of men upon that day,   265
But as I am so all go pleased away.

                                                        [*Exeunt*]

---

259   *gentlewomen* ed. (gentlewoman Q): addressed to the citizens' wives; *Are* in the
       following line is influenced by this plural
260   *beams* sunbeams
264   *In my time* Bowers amends to 'May time'; but Q is perfectly intelligible – Sir
       Alexander hopes the happiness will be remembered beyond his own time.

EPILOGUS

A painter having drawn with curious art
The picture of a woman (every part
Limned to the life) hung out the piece to sell:
People who passed along, viewing it well,
Gave several verdicts on it: some dispraised   5
The hair, some said the brows too high were raised,
Some hit her o'er the lips, misliked their colour,
Some wished her nose were shorter, some the eyes fuller;
Others said roses on her cheeks should grow,
Swearing they looked too pale, others cried no.   10
The workman, still as fault was found, did mend it
In hope to please all; but, this work being ended
And hung open at stall, it was so vile,
So monstrous and so ugly all men did smile
At the poor painter's folly. Such we doubt   15
Is this our comedy: some perhaps do flout
The plot, saying 'tis too thin, too weak, too mean;
Some for the person will revile the scene,
And wonder that a creature of her being
Should be the subject of a poet, seeing   20
In the world's eye none weighs so light: others look
For all those base tricks published in a book
(Foul as his brains they flowed from) of cutpurses,
Of nips and foists, nasty, obscene discourses,
As full of lies, as empty of worth or wit,   25
For any honest ear, or eye, unfit. And thus,
If we to every brain that's humorous
Should fashion scenes, we (with the painter) shall
In striving to please all, please none at all.
Yet for such faults, as either the writers' wit   30
Or negligence of the actors do commit,
Both crave your pardons: if what both have done

    Epilogus Probably delivered by Moll
  7   *hit . . . o'er* directed their criticism toward
 11   *still as* each time
 22   *a book* See Introduction, p. xi, n. 15.
 23   *cutpurses* ed. (cutpurse Q)
 27   *humorous* whimsical, full of humours or fancies

Cannot full pay your expectation,
The Roaring Girl herself, some few days hence,
Shall on this stage give larger recompense.   35
Which mirth that you may share in, herself does woo you,
And craves this sign, your hands to beckon her to you.

FINIS

34–5   There has been much discussion about what these lines refer to. Though the assump-
       tion has been commonly made that Mary Frith herself is the subject of them, it is
       possible that the allusion is to the actor playing the part, who presumably would
       shortly act again in another comedy on the same stage. See Mulholland, 'The Date
       of *The Roaring Girl*', *RES*, new series 28 (1977), 19–20.

APPENDIX

Cant and Canting

This word *canting* seems to be derived from the Latin verb *canto*, which signifies in English 'to sing' or 'to make a sound with words', that's to say 'to speak'. And very aptly may *canting* take his derivation *a cantando* 'from singing' because amongst these beggarly consorts, that can play upon no better instruments, the language of *canting* is a kind of music and he that in such assemblies can *cant* best is counted the best musician. (Dekker, *English Villainies Discovered by Lanthorn and Candlelight*, p.i).

Dekker got most of his knowledge of underworld cant at second hand. His three tracts on roguery – *The Seven Deadly Sins of London* (1606), *The Bellman of London,* and *Lanthorn and Candlelight* (both 1608) – were late-comers in a tradition of 'manifest detections' which began perhaps with Robert Copland's *Highway to the Spitalhouse* (1535) and has its more modern derivatives in extensive dictionaries of cant and slang. Dekker depended heavily on his predecessors, in particular on Thomas Harman's *A Caveat for Common Cursitors* (1566), a book which, according to S. R. (probably Samuel Rid), the somewhat peppery author of *Martin Mark-All* (1610), was out of date and inaccurate by the early seventeenth century. The third edition of *Lanthorn and Candlelight* (1612) consequently included a supplement called 'O per se O' – probably, but not certainly, by Dekker – expanding and occasionally silently correcting earlier inform-ation. Most of these tracts contain brief 'canter's dictionaries', which by and large confirm one another's definitions: the following glossary of cant words in *The Roaring Girl* is compiled, wherever possible, from Dekker's, with substantive variants noted from other sources. The sigla used are as follows:

- B: *The Bellman of London* (Dekker, 1608)
- C: *Caveat for Common Cursitors* (Thomas Harman, 1566)
- F: *The Fraternity of Vagabonds* (John Awdeley, 1561)
- L: *Lanthorn and Candlelight* (Dekker, 1608)
- M: *Martin Mark-All, Beadle of Bridewell* (Stationers' Register, 1610)
- N: *A Notable Discovery of Cozenage* (Robert Greene, 1591)
- O: *O per se O* (Dekker?, 1612)

Angler: 'a limb of an upright-man . . . in the day time, they beg from house to house, not so much for relief, as to spy what lies fit for their nets, which in the night following they fish for. The rod they angle with is a staff of five or six foot in length, in which within one inch of the top is a little hole bored quite through, into which hole they put an iron hook, and with the same do they angle at windows about midnight, the draught they pluck up being apparel, sheets, coverlets, or whatsoever their iron hooks can lay hold of ' (B)

Ben, benar: good, better (L)

Ben cove: see under *Cove*

Bing: come, go (L)

Bing awast (or *avast*): get you hence (L); steal away (O)

Boil: see under *Smoke*

Booze (or *bouse*): drink (L)

Boozing ken: alehouse (L, O)

Borde: shilling (L)

Bung: purse (L); 'now used for a pocket, heretofore for a purse' (M)

Cackling cheat: cock or capon: see *Cheat*

Caster: cloak (L)

Cheat: thing. 'By joining of two simples do they make almost all their compounds. As for example, *nab* in the canting tongue is a head, and *nab cheat* is a hat or a cap. Which word *cheat*, being coupled to other words, stands in very good stead and does excellent service . . . a *muffling cheat* signifies a napkin, a *belly cheat* an apron, a *grunting cheat* a pig, a *cackling cheat* a cock or capon, a *quacking cheat* a duck . . . and so may that word be married to many others besides' (L). The word is of course also used in the play in its standard sense.

Cheator: 'The Cheating Law, or the art of winning money by false dice: those that practise this study call themselves *cheators*, the dice *cheaters*, and the money which they purchase *cheats*' (B). For a more detailed explanation, see F.

Cheats (*chats, chates*): the gallows (L, C). 'Here he [the Bellman] mistakes both the simple word, because he found it so printed, not knowing the true original thereof, and also in the compound. As for *chates* it should be *cheats*, which word is used generally for things . . . so that if you will make a word for gallows, you must put thereto this word, *trining*, which signifies hanging; and so *trining-cheat* is as much as to say "hanging-things", or the gallows, and not *chates*' (M).

Cloyer: see under *Figging-Law*; 'priggers, filchers and cloyers (being all in English stealers)' (O)

Couch a hogshead: lie down asleep (L). 'This phrase is like an almanac that is out of date: now the Dutch word *slope* is with them used, "to sleep", and *liggen*, "to lie down" ' (M).

148

Cove, Cuffin: 'The word *cove* or *cofe* or *cuffin* signifies a man, a fellow, etc., but differs something in his property according as it meets with other words, for a gentleman is called a *gentry cove* or *cofe*, a good fellow is a *ben cofe*, a churl is called a *queer cuffin* (*queer* signifies naught and *cuffin*, as I said before, a man) and in canting they term a Justice of the Peace (because he punisheth them, belike) by no other name than by *queer cuffin*, that's to say a churl or a naughty man' (L).

Cramp-ring: hand-cuff; and see under *Scour*

Curber: 'The Curbing Law [teaches] how to hook goods out of a window... He that hooks is called the *curber*... The hook is the *curb*' (B) cf. *Angler*.

Cut ben (benar) whids: speak good (better) words (L); tell the truth (M)

Darkmans: the night (L)

Dell: 'A dell is a young wench ... but as yet not spoiled of her maidenhead ["able for generation, and not yet known or broken" (C)]. These dells are reserved as dishes for the upright-men, for none but they must have the first taste of them' (B)

Deuse a vill (or *deuceville*)*:* the country (L)

Dock: lie with, copulate, by analogy with a ship coming into dock

Doxy: whore (O); 'his woman ... which he calleth his altham, if she be his wife, and if she be his harlot, she is called his doxy' (F); 'these doxies be broken and spoiled of their maidenhead by the upright-men, and then they have their name of doxies, and not afore' (C)

Fadoodling: copulating; a fadoodle is 'something foolish' (*OED*), so fadoodling is 'playing around'

Fambles: hands (L)

Figging-Law: 'Cutting of purses and picking of pockets' (N): 'In making of which law, two persons have the chief voices, that is to say, the cutpurse and the pickpocket, and all the branches of this law reach to none but them and such as are made free denizens of their incorporation... He that cuts the purse is called the *nip*, he that is half with him is the *snap* or the *cloyer*... He that picks the pocket is called a *foist*, he that faceth the man is the *stale*' (B).

Foist: see under *Figging-Law*

Gage: a quart pot (L)

Gentry cuffin: see under *Cove*

Ging: company, gang (Dekker, *Penny-Wise, Pound-Foolish*)

Glaziers: eyes (L)

Goll: hand (Dekker, *The Wonderful Year*)

Grunt(l)ing cheat: pig; see *Cheat*

Hartmans (or *harmans*): the stocks (L)

Heave a booth (or *bough*): rob a booth (L)

Ken: house (L)

Kinchin mort: 'Kinchin-morts are girls of a year or two old, which the *morts* (their mothers) carry at their backs in their slates (which in the canting-tongue are sheets)' (B).

Lap: buttermilk or whey (L)

Lib: sleep (L)

Libken: a house to lie in (L); a house to lodge people (M)

Lifter: 'The Lifting Law . . . teacheth a kind of lifting of goods clean away' (B).

Lightmans: the day

Maund: to ask (F, L); to beg (M, O)

Maunder, maunderer: beggar (O)

Mill: to steal or rob (L)

Mort: woman (esp. one who has fallen from a better state) (L)

Mutton: food for lust (*OED*), hence a prostitute

Nab: head (L)

Niggle: to company with a woman (L). 'This word is not now used, but *wapping*, and thereof comes the name *wapping-morts*, whores' (M).

Nip (noun): see under *Figging-Law*

Nip a bung: to cut a purse (L)

Pad: a way, highway (L)

Palliard: 'he that goeth in a patched cloak' (F); some are 'natural' (born to the trade), some 'artificial': the latter 'carrieth about him the great *cleyme* [an artificially induced sore] to stir compassion up in people's hearts' (O)

Pannun (*pannam* or *pennam*): bread (L)

Peck: meat (L). '*Peck* is not meat, but *peckage*. *Peck* is taken to eat or bite' (M).

Pedlar's French: 'that canting language which is to be found among none but beggars' (B), 'invented to th'intent that, albeit any spies should secretly steal into their companies to discover them, they might freely utter their minds one to another, yet avoid that danger' (L)

Poplars (or *popler*): porridge (C), pottage (L)

Priggard (*prigger* or *prigman*): a stealer generally (O), but applied especially to *priggers of prancers* (horse-thieves) (N). But 'a prigman goeth with a stick . . . to steal clothes off the hedge' (F).

Quacking-cheat: duck; see under *Cheat*

Queer: naught, naughty (L)

Queer cuffin: see under *Cove*

Rom-booze (or *rom-bouse*): wine (L). 'This word [*rom* or *room*] is always taken in the best sense, to show a thing extraordinary or excellent' (M).

Rom-ville: London (L), or more generally a great town (M)

Ruffler: 'a ruffler goeth with a weapon to seek service, saying he hath been a servitor in the wars, and beggeth for his relief' (F). 'The ruffler and the upright-man are so like in conditions, that you would swear them brothers: they walk with cudgels alike; they profess arms alike . . . These commonly are fellows that have stood aloof in the wars, and whilst others fought, they took their heels and ran away from their captain, or else they would have been serving-men, whom for their behaviour no man would trust with a livery' (B).

Ruffmans: hedges, woods, or bushes (L). 'Not the hedge or bushes as heretofore; but now the eavesing of houses or roofs. *Cragmans* is now used for the hedge' (M).

Solomon: the Mass (L), used chiefly in oaths

Scour the (queer) cramp-ring: to wear bolts or fetters (C)

Shells: money (B)

Shifter: cozener (F)

Skelder: to live by begging, especially by passing oneself off as a wounded or disbanded soldier

Skew: all authorities agree that this means a cup (C, L, M); but in *The Roaring Girl* it is used as a verb, meaning to drink

Slate: sheet; see under *Kinchin mort*

Smoke: 'The spying of this villainy is called smoking or boiling' (B).

Snap: 'he that is half with him [the nip]' (N): see under *Figging-Law* and *Upright-man*

Stale: see under *Figging-Law*

Stall: to make or ordain (L)

Stalled to the rogue: 'I do stall thee to the rogue by virtue of this sovereign English liquor, so that henceforth it shall be lawful for thee to cant, that is to say to be a vagabond and to beg' (B).

Stalling- (or *stuling-*) *ken:* house for receiving stolen goods (L)

Stamps: legs (L)

Strike: 'the act doing' (in figging-law) (N)

Strommel (or *strummel*): straw (L)

Synagogue: an assembly of thieves (?)

Trine: hang (L); see also under *Cheats*

Upright-man: 'a sturdy big-boned knave, that never walks but (like a commander) with a short truncheon in his hand, which he calls his filchman. At markets, fairs, and other meetings his voice among beggars is of the same sound that a constable's is of, it is not to be controlled' (B). 'This man is of so much authority that, meeting with any of his profession, he may call them to account, and command a share or snap unto himself of all that they have gained by their trade in one month' (F).

Wap: see under *Niggle*

Whip-jack: 'Another sort of knaves . . . are called whip-jacks, who talk of nothing but fights at sea, piracies, drownings and ship-wrecks' (B). 'These fresh-water mariners, their ships were drowned in the plain of Salisbury' (C).

Wild dell: a dell born to the position: 'those such as are born or begotten under a hedge' (B)

Wild rogue: 'one that is born a rogue . . . begotten in barn or bushes, and from his infancy traded up in treachery'; 'a rogue is neither so stout or hardy as the upright-man' (C). He 'is a spirit that cares not in what circle he rises, nor into the company of what devils he falls: in his swaddling clouts is he marked to be a villain, and in his breeding is instructed to be so . . . These wild rogues (like wild geese) keep in flocks, and all the day loiter in fields, if the weather be warm, and at brick-kilns, or else disperse themselves in cold weather, to rich men's doors, and at night have their meetings in barns or other out-places' (B).

A selection of these various tracts (not all printed complete) was compiled by A.V. Judges and published in 1930 as *The Elizabethan Underworld*; some have been reprinted by the Early English Text Society (1869) and the New Shakespeare Society (1880). Dekker's (without *O per se O*) were included in Grosart's edition of the non-dramatic works (1884–6) and in an edition by O. Smeaton (1904). *Lanthorn and Candlelight* is reprinted complete, with *O per se O*, in a collection of Dekker's tales and tracts edited by E. D. Pendry (1967).

A
CHAST MAYD
in
CHEAPE-SIDE.

A
Pleaſant conceited Comedy
neuer before printed.

As it hath beene often acted at the
Swan on the Banke-ſide, by the
Lady ELIZABETH her
Seruants.

By THOMAS MIDELTON Gent.

LONDON,
Printed for *Francis Constable* dwelling at the
ſigne of the *Crane* in *Pauls*
Church-yard.
1630.

Title page of the quarto edition, reproduced by permission of the Huntington Library, San Marino, California.

The title is paradoxical, and perhaps proverbial: 'A chaste maid in Cheapside? Not likely!'

conceited ingenious, clever

the Swan theatre stood in Paris Garden on the Bankside; built probably in 1596, used irregularly for plays and other entertainments until 1620 and still standing, though ruinous, in 1632. The inside was sketched by a Dutch visitor, Johannes de Witt, about 1596; a copy of this sketch, made by Aernout (or Arend) van Buchell, was found in the Utrecht University Library and published in 1888; it is the only known contemporary representation of an Elizabethan public playhouse interior.

Lady Elizabeth her Servants were a company of adult players active 1611–16 in London, 1612–22 in the provinces, 1622–5 in London. Revived in 1628 as the Queen of Bohemia's Players, they continued until about 1641. The Lady Elizabeth, the eldest daughter of James I, was born in 1596, married Frederick V, Elector Palatine, in 1613, became Queen of Bohemia in 1619, and died in 1662.

Paul's Churchyard was the centre of the London book trade. There were two classes of business premises around the cathedral church, houses which bordered the churchyards, and less substantial booths (or lock-up shops) and stalls clustered round the walls and at the doors of the building itself.

The Names of the Principal Persons

1   MR contraction for 'Master'; the modern 'Mister' came into general use later in the 17th century

    YELLOWHAMMER (a) referring to his goldsmith's trade (b) a bird (c) slang for 'a gold coin' (d) a term of contempt, a fool

2   MAUDLINE pronounced and also spelt 'Maudlin' (a) Magdalene; traditionally Mary Magdalene, the friend of Jesus, was a reformed prostitute, but there is no evidence for this in the Bible (b) mawkish, sentimental

3   TIM Used by Jonson as a term of contempt: 'you are an otter, and a shad, a whit, / A very tim' (*The Alchemist* IV.vii.45–6); as an otter is 'neither fish nor flesh' (*1 Henry IV*, III.iii.127), a shad is a fish of the herring family, and a whit is the least part of something, 'Tim' also implies 'small'. See IV.i.117–19.

4   MOLL (a) diminutive of 'Mary' (b) slang for 'whore'; a prime example of Middleton's ambiguous use of names

6   WALTER WHOREHOUND The name both describes the character's pursuit of sex and signifies his fecundity, as Walter was pronounced 'water' and 'water' was slang for semen (cf. II.i.188); moreover, the water horehound plant grows in moist, low places and medicine made from it induces childbirth.

7   OLIVER KIX While 'Oliver' = fruitful, 'Kix' = dry, hollow plant stem, figuratively a sapless person. Middleton had already used this name in *A Trick to Catch the Old One* (*c.* 1605).

THE NAMES
OF THE PRINCIPAL PERSONS

MR YELLOWHAMMER, *a goldsmith*
MAUDLINE, *his wife*
TIM, *their son*
MOLL, *their daughter*
TUTOR *to Tim*   5
SIR WALTER WHOREHOUND, *a suitor to Moll*
SIR OLIVER KIX, *and his* WIFE, *kin to Sir Walter*
MR ALLWIT, *and his* WIFE, *whom Sir Walter keeps*
WELSH GENTLEWOMAN, *Sir Walter's whore*
WAT *and* NICK, *his bastards* [*by Mrs Allwit*]   10
DAVY DAHUMMA, *his man*
TOUCHWOOD SENIOR, *and his* WIFE, *a decayed gentleman*
TOUCHWOOD JUNIOR, *another suitor to Moll*
2 PROMOTERS
SERVANTS   15
WATERMEN
[PORTER
GENTLEMAN
COUNTRY WENCH, *with a child*
JUGG, *maid to Lady Kix*   20
DRY NURSE
WET NURSE
2 MEN, *with baskets*
MISTRESS UNDERMAN, *a Puritan*
PURITANS *and* GOSSIPS   25
MIDWIFE
PARSON
SUSAN, *maid to Moll*]

8   ALLWIT a pun on 'Wittol' = a complaisant cuckold, but also (a) all cleverness (b) all
    penis
11 DAHUMMA 'Come hither' in Welsh (*dewch yma*)
12 TOUCHWOOD easily inflammable tinder, particularly that used to light a musket's
    touchhole; figuratively a passionate person (especially suitable when applied to
    Touchwood Junior)
14 PROMOTERS Originally a promoter was a lawyer, but by 1600 an informer; in Lent
    the authorities had promoters spying for butchers who sold meat without a licence.
16 WATERMEN Thames boatmen, the water taximen of the time

ACT I, [SCENE i]

Enter MAUDLINE *and* MOLL, *a shop being discovered*

MAUDLINE *strict mother.*

Have you played over all your old lessons o'the virginals?

MOLL

Yes.

MAUDLINE

Yes, you are a dull maid a-late, methinks you had need have
somewhat to quicken your green sickness; do you weep? A husband! Had not such a piece of flesh been ordained, what had us 5
wives been good for? To make salads, or else cried up and down
for samphire. To see the difference of these seasons! When I was
of your youth, I was lightsome, and quick, two years before I was
married. You fit for a knight's bed – drowsy browed, dull eyed,
drossy sprited – I hold my life you have forgot your dancing: 10
when was the dancer with you? *she wants Moll*
to be more girlish

MOLL

The last week.

MAUDLINE

Last week? When I was of your bord, he missed me not a night,

---

Act I Q divides the play into acts only: scene numbers were added by Dyce

0 s.d. *discovered* Current scholarship increasingly tends to the view that a central
entrance, in which such a discovery could be made, was usual in Elizabethan
theatres; none is shown on the de Witt sketch. This direction, then, is possible
evidence for a structure being built on the stage when needed, and/or a drawable
curtain being hung from the overhang of the first gallery. See V.iv.O s.d. and note.

1 *virginals* small, legless keyboard instrument with plucked strings; playing it was a
lady-like art which could easily give rise to sexual innuendo, as here

4 *green sickness* chlorosis; anaemic disease mostly affecting young women in puberty,
giving them a pale or greenish complexion

6 *make salads* become salads (which, as they were highly seasoned, were related to
lechery)

6–7 *cried . . . samphire* sold in the streets like samphire, a name given to two unrelated
plants, one used in salads, the other pickled and eaten with meat, particularly good
with marsh mutton (cf. note to I.i.132)

8 *quick* (1) high spirited (2) pregnant

10 *sprited* spirited

10 *dancing* was popular with all classes, and London dancing schools were a sight for
visitors; the sexual innuendo in Maudline's reminiscences is plain

13 *bord* bore of a gun; 'when I was like you', with a pun on vaginal size

I was kept at it; I took delight to learn, and he to teach me; pretty
brown gentleman, he took pleasure in my company; but you   15
are dull, nothing comes nimbly from you, you dance like a
plumber's daughter, and deserve two thousand pound in lead to
your marriage, and not in goldsmith's ware.

Enter YELLOWHAMMER

YELLOWHAMMER

Now what's the din betwixt mother and daughter, ha?

MAUDLINE

Faith small, telling your daughter Mary of her errors.   20

YELLOWHAMMER

'Errors'! Nay, the city cannot hold you wife, but you must needs
fetch words from Westminster; I ha' done i'faith. Has no attorney's clerk been here a-late and changed his half-crown-piece his
mother sent him, or rather cozened you with a gilded twopence,
to bring the word in fashion for her faults or cracks in duty and   25
obedience? Term 'em e'en so, sweet wife. As there is no woman
made without a flaw, your purest lawns have frays, and cambrics
bracks.

MAUDLINE

But 'tis a husband solders up all cracks.

MOLL

What, is he come sir?

YELLOWHAMMER   Sir Walter's come.   30

He was met at Holborn Bridge, and in his company
A proper fair young gentlewoman, which I guess

---

22 *Westminster* where justice was dispensed; Henry III ordered that the great hall at
    Westminster should be 'the usual place of pleadings, and ministration of justice'
    (*Survey*, II, 117). Yellowhammer is saying, 'Has no attorney's clerk from West-
    minster been here lately to bribe you into using a highfalutin word (*errors*) for your
    daughter's faults? Isn't the ordinary language of the city good enough for you?'

23 *half-crown-piece* made of 22 carat gold, struck only in the last coinage of Henry
    VIII and one coinage of Elizabeth

24 *cozened* tricked   *gilded twopence* Twopenny pieces were of silver like all coins worth
    a shilling or less. If this one were treated to look like gold it would be counterfeit.

27 *lawns* fine linen or clothing made from it; so called because it was bleached on a
    lawn instead of the ordinary bleaching grounds
    cambrics a kind of white fine linen, originally made at Cambrai in France, or cloth-
    ing made from it

28 *bracks* flaws, faults, openings. This whole passage is innuendo.

31 *Holborn Bridge* ancient bridge over the Fleet Ditch carrying the main road from the
    west to enter London at Newgate

158

By her red hair, and other rank descriptions,
To be his landed niece brought out of Wales,
Which Tim our son (the Cambridge boy) must marry.   35
'Tis a match of Sir Walter's own making
To bind us to him, and our heirs for ever.

MAUDLINE

We are honoured then, if this baggage would be humble,
And kiss him with devotion when he enters.
I cannot get her for my life   40
To instruct her hand thus, before and after,
Which a knight will look for, before and after.
I have told her still, 'tis the waving of a woman
Does often move a man, and prevails strongly.
But sweet, ha' you sent to Cambridge,   45
Has Tim word on't?

YELLOWHAMMER

Had word just the day after when you sent him the silver spoon
to eat his broth in the hall, amongst the gentlemen commoners.

MAUDLINE

O, 'twas timely.

Enter PORTER

YELLOWHAMMER

How now?   50

PORTER

A letter from a gentleman in Cambridge.

YELLOWHAMMER

O, one of Hobson's porters: thou art welcome. I told thee Maud

---

33   *rank* (1) abundant (2) lecherous (3) covered with coarse grass; red hair was linked
     with lustfulness
41   *her hand* probably a fashionable way of carrying the hand before and behind the
     body, but here with a sexual innuendo in 'before and after'
43   *still* constantly   *waving* (a) hand movement (b) body movement up and down
48   *hall* dining hall shared by students and members of a college
     gentlemen commoners a privileged class of undergraduates at Oxford and Cambridge,
     who wore a special gown and velvet cap, dined at a separate table and paid higher fees
52   *Hobson* (1544?–1631) the famous carrier of Cambridge who gave no alternative
     choice to those hiring his horses and so gave rise to the phrase 'Hobson's choice'
     (though this has been held to be a Cambridge hoax); from 1570 to 1630 his large
     six- and eight-horse wagons carried goods and mail between Cambridge and
     London; he died very rich and Milton wrote two epitaphs on him.
     thou Yellowhammer addresses the porter as an inferior.
     thee the familiar, affectionate use

159

we should hear from Tim. [*Reads*] *Amantissimis charissimisque ambobus parentibus patri et matri.*

MAUDLINE

What's the matter?   55

YELLOWHAMMER

Nay by my troth, I know not, ask not me, he's grown too verbal; this learning is a great witch.

MAUDLINE

Pray let me see it, I was wont to understand him. *Amantissimus charissimus*, he has sent the carrier's man, he says: *ambobus parentibus*, for a pair of boots: *patri et matri*, pay the porter, or   60
it makes no matter.

PORTER

Yes by my faith mistress, there's no true construction in that; I have took a great deal of pains, and come from the Bell sweating. Let me come to't, for I was a scholar forty years ago; 'tis thus I warrant you: *Matri*, it makes no matter: *ambobus parentibus*, for   65
a pair of boots: *patri* pay the porter: *amantissimis charissimis*, he's the carrier's man, and his name is Sims, and there he says true, forsooth my name is Sims indeed; I have not forgot all my learning. A money matter, I thought I should hit on't.

YELLOWHAMMER

Go thou art an old fox, there's a tester for thee.   70

PORTER

If I see your worship at Goose Fair, I have a dish of birds for you.

YELLOWHAMMER

Why, dost dwell at Bow?

53–4   'To my most loving and dearest parents, both father and mother'. Dyce and Bullen correct the Latin throughout the play, but as in some places the grammatical mistakes indicate a greater foolishness the original has been retained in this edition, with modernized spelling.

55   *matter* content; but perhaps also 'What's the matter with you that you speak nonsense?'

62   *no true construction* inaccurate construing, translation; the porter's is just as comically bad

63   *Bell* Almost certainly a misprint for 'Bull', the inn on the western side of Bishopsgate which was Hobson's place of call.

70   *tester* sixpence (slang). First applied to the shilling of Henry VII but this became debased and the value fell.

71   *Goose Fair* held annually on the Thursday after Whitsunday at Stratford le Bow, four miles northeast of St Paul's, where young (green) roast geese were sold; 'goose' was also slang for a prostitute, so *a dish of birds* is probably said with a leer

PORTER

    All my lifetime sir I could ever say Bo, to a goose.

    Farewell to your worship. *Exit* PORTER

YELLOWHAMMER

    A merry porter. 75

MAUDLINE

    How can he choose but be so, coming with Cambridge letters

    from our son Tim?

YELLOWHAMMER

    What's here? *Maximus diligo.* Faith I must to my learned counsel

    with this gear – 'twill ne'er be discerned else.

MAUDLINE

    Go to my cousin then, at Inns of Court. 80

YELLOWHAMMER

    Fie, they are all for French, they speak no Latin.

MAUDLINE

    The parson then will do it.

Enter a GENTLEMAN *with chain*

YELLOWHAMMER

    Nay, he disclaims it, calls Latin Papistry; he will not deal with it.

    What is't you lack, gentleman?

GENTLEMAN

    Pray weigh this chain. 85

Enter SIR WALTER WHOREHOUND, WELSH GENTLEWOMAN
and DAVY DAHUMMA

SIR WALTER

    Now wench thou art welcome to the heart of the city of London.

---

73   *Bo, to a goose* proverbial. In Hollar's panorama of London (1647) Bow Church in
     the city is labelled 'Boo'. As 'bow' = cunt and 'goose' = whore, the porter is also
     making a bawdy joke.

78   Tim presumably means 'I esteem you most highly'; his Latin is more like 'I love you
     and I am the greatest'.

79   *gear* matter, stuff

80   *Inns of Court* Houses of law students, 'a whole university, as it were, of students,
     practisers or pleaders and Judges of the laws' (*Survey,* I, 76); Lincoln's Inn, Gray's
     Inn, the Inner Temple and the Middle Temple were the most important of the
     fourteen in 1603.

81   *French* The mongrel language known as 'Law French' continued in use for centuries
     in England; finally abolished by an act of Parliament in 1731.

WELSH GENTLEWOMAN
Dugat a whee.

SIR WALTER
You can thank me in English if you list.

WELSH GENTLEWOMAN
I can sir, simply.

SIR WALTER
'Twill serve to pass wench; 'twas strange that I should lie with   90
thee so often, to leave thee without English – that were
unnatural. I bring thee up to turn thee into gold, wench, and
make thy fortune shine like your bright trade. A goldsmith's shop
sets out a city maid. Davy Dahumma, not a word.

DAVY
Mum, mum sir.   95

SIR WALTER
Here you must pass for a pure virgin.

DAVY
[*Aside*] Pure Welsh virgin! She lost her maidenhead in Brecknockshire.

SIR WALTER
I hear you mumble Davy.

DAVY
I have teeth sir, I need not mumble yet this forty years.   100

SIR WALTER
The knave bites plaguily.

YELLOWHAMMER
What's your price sir?

GENTLEMAN
A hundred pound sir.

YELLOWHAMMER
A hundred marks the utmost, 'tis not for me else.

[*Exit* GENTLEMAN]

What, Sir Walter Whorehound?   105

87 'God preserve you' – a phonetic rendering of *'Duw cadw chwi'*
90 *'twas strange that* it would be strange if
91 *thee* affectionate use
93 *your* impersonal 'one's', *bright trade* referring to goldsmith's trade, but possibly
    personal, and referring to prostitution
95 *Mum* cant term, sign of silence and secrecy
97–8 *Brecknockshire* Welsh county; 'nock' was one of the many slang words for the
      female genitals
104 *marks* 1 mark was worth 13 shillings and 4 pence

MOLL

O death.   *Exit* MOLL

MAUDLINE

Why daughter;

Faith, the baggage,

[*Exit* YELLOWHAMMER *after* MOLL]

A bashful girl sir; these young things are shamefast, (modest)

Besides, you have a presence, sweet Sir Walter,   110

Able to daunt a maid brought up i'the city;

Enter MOLL [*brought back by* YELLOWHAMMER]

A brave Court spirit makes our virgins quiver,

And kiss with trembling thighs. Yet see she comes sir.

SIR WALTER

Why how now pretty mistress, now I have caught you. What, can

you injure so your time to stray thus from your faithful servant?   115

YELLOWHAMMER

Pish, stop your words good knight, 'twill make her blush else,

which wound too high for the daughters of the freedom.

'Honour', and 'faithful servant', they are compliments for the

worthies of Whitehall, or Greenwich. E'en plain, sufficient sub-

sidy words serves us sir. And is this gentlewoman your worthy   120

niece?

SIR WALTER

You may be bold with her on these terms, 'tis she sir, heir to some

nineteen mountains.

YELLOWHAMMER

Bless us all, you overwhelm me sir with love and riches.

want their kids
to be with rich
people

109   *shamefast* bashful, modest
111   s.d. *MOLL* ed. (Mary Q). Unlikely to return voluntarily, perhaps Moll is brought
        back by her father.
113   *trembling thighs* A plain reference to the lasciviousness of the court; a 'knee-
        trembler' was coitus in a standing position. Romeo's Rosaline had a 'quivering
        thigh' (*Romeo and Juliet*, II.i.19).
117   *wound* past tense of 'wind' = go, but possibly a misprint for 'sound'
        daughters of the freedom of the city of London as opposed to the court
119   *Whitehall* a royal palace from 1529 when Henry VIII took it from Cardinal Wolsey;
        it lay east of Westminster
        Greenwich ancient royal palace on the south bank of the Thames below London;
        birthplace of Henry VIII, Mary I and Elizabeth I
119–20 *subsidy* business, in this case commercial as opposed to courtly

SIR WALTER

And all as high as Paul's.   125

DAVY

Here's work i'faith.

SIR WALTER

How sayst thou Davy?

DAVY

Higher sir by far, you cannot see the top of 'em.

YELLOWHAMMER

What, man? Maudline salute this gentlewoman, our daughter if
things hit right.   130

Enter TOUCHWOOD JUNIOR

TOUCHWOOD JUNIOR

My knight with a brace of footmen
Is come and brought up his ewe mutton
To find a ram at London; I must hasten it,
Or else pick a famine; her blood's mine,
And that's the surest. Well knight, that choice spoil   135
Is only kept for me.

MOLL

Sir?

TOUCHWOOD JUNIOR

Turn not to me till thou mayst lawfully, it but whets my stomach,
which is too sharp set already. Read that note carefully, keep me
from suspicion still, nor know my zeal but in thy heart: read and   140
send but thy liking in three words, I'll be at hand to take it.

---

125   *as high as Paul's* proverbial. The cathedral tower was 245 feet (74 m) high; the
        steeple which surmounted it for another 205 feet (64 m) was destroyed by fire in
        1561.
127   *thou* Allwit consistently addresses Davy as a servant.
129   *salute* kiss
132   *ewe mutton* strumpet
134   *pick a famine* choose to starve. Some eds incorrectly emend 'peak a'famine', i.e.
        'dwindle from starvation'.
        blood passion (but also with a hunting connotation); 'She desires me sexually, and
        that ensures she'll be mine'
135   *spoil* ed. (spoy Q) prey. Another hunting image cf. IV.ii.104.
138   *thou* intimate, affectionate use
139   *sharp set* eager, keen
141   *liking* (1) consent, approval (2) sexual desire

YELLOWHAMMER
      O turn sir, turn.
      A poor plain boy, an university man
      Proceeds next Lent to a Bachelor of Art;
      He will be called Sir Yellowhammer then   145
      Over all Cambridge, and that's half a knight.
MAUDLINE
      Please you draw near, and taste the welcome of the city sir?
YELLOWHAMMER
      Come good Sir Walter, and your virtuous niece here.
SIR WALTER
      'Tis manners to take kindness.   *They welcome Sir Walter and his "niece" warmly*
YELLOWHAMMER
      Lead 'em in wife.   150
SIR WALTER
      Your company sir.
YELLOWHAMMER
      I'll give't you instantly.

            [*Exeunt* SIR WALTER, WELSH GENTLEWOMAN,
                        DAVY *and* MAUDLINE]

TOUCHWOOD JUNIOR
      How strangely busy is the devil and riches;
      Poor soul kept in too hard, her mother's eye
      Is cruel toward her, being to him.   155
      'Twere a good mirth now to set him a-work
      To make her wedding ring. I must about it.
      Rather than the game should fall to a stranger,
      'Twas honesty in me to enrich my father.   *Moll's father doesn't*
YELLOWHAMMER   *want Moll to*
      The girl is wondrous peevish; I fear nothing   *marry Junior* 160
      But that she's taken with some other love;
      Then all's quite dashed: that must be narrowly looked to;

---

142   *turn* Some eds emend 'Tim', but Yellowhammer is trying to persuade Sir Walter to
       enter his house, while telling him about Tim; Maudline adds her invitation at l. 147.
144   *Proceeds* Graduates (strictly, to a degree higher than Bachelor)
       Art could signify Yellowhammer's ignorance, but Dekker uses 'Bachelor of Art'
       without humorous intent in *The Gull's Hornbook* (1609, p. 9)
148   *Sir* was a rendering of Latin *dominus*. Used with the surname only it indicated an
       Oxford or Cambridge graduate, considered a member of the gentry; so, only *half a
       knight.*
155   *being to him* Turned to Whorehound, supporting Yellowhammer in arranging for
       Moll to marry the knight.

We cannot be too wary in our children.
What is't you lack?

TOUCHWOOD JUNIOR

O nothing now, all that I wish is present. I would have a wedding   165
ring made for a gentlewoman, with all speed that may be.

YELLOWHAMMER

Of what weight sir?

TOUCHWOOD JUNIOR

Of some half ounce, stand fair and comely, with the spark of a
diamond. Sir 'twere pity to lose the least grace.

YELLOWHAMMER

Pray let's see it; indeed sir 'tis a pure one.   170

TOUCHWOOD JUNIOR

So is the mistress.

YELLOWHAMMER

Have you the wideness of her finger sir?

TOUCHWOOD JUNIOR

Yes sure I think I have her measure about me –
Good faith 'tis down, I cannot show't you,
I must pull too many things out to be certain.   175
Let me see, long, and slender, and neatly jointed,
Just such another gentlewoman that's your daughter sir.

YELLOWHAMMER

And therefore sir no gentlewoman.

TOUCHWOOD JUNIOR

I protest I never saw two maids handed more alike;
I'll ne'er seek farther, if you'll give me leave sir.   180

YELLOWHAMMER

If you dare venture by her finger sir.

TOUCHWOOD JUNIOR

Ay, and I'll bide all loss sir.

YELLOWHAMMER

Say you so sir, let's see hither girl.

---

169 *diamond* Wedding rings were often in the form of two hands clasping a heart made
     of a jewel, or a hoop, sometimes enamelled, with small gems, and a motto engraved
     inside.
173 *measure* (1) her finger's size (2) his penis, which can measure her. Middleton uses
     the sexual imagery of fingers and rings in several plays, most potently in *The
     Changeling*.
174 *down* (1) too deep in his pocket (2) detumescent
177 *that's* as is
182 *I'll bide all loss* 'I'll still pay if I've made any mistake'

TOUCHWOOD JUNIOR
  Shall I make bold with your finger gentlewoman?

MOLL
  Your pleasure sir.   185

TOUCHWOOD JUNIOR
  That fits her to a hair sir.

YELLOWHAMMER
  What's your posy now sir?

TOUCHWOOD JUNIOR
  Mass that's true, posy i'faith, e'en thus sir:
  'Love that's wise, blinds parents' eyes'.

YELLOWHAMMER
  How, how? If I may speak without offence sir,   190
  I hold my life –

TOUCHWOOD JUNIOR
  What sir?

YELLOWHAMMER
  Go to, you'll pardon me?

TOUCHWOOD JUNIOR
  Pardon you? Ay sir.

YELLOWHAMMER
  Will you i'faith?   195

TOUCHWOOD JUNIOR
  Yes faith I will.

YELLOWHAMMER
  You'll steal away some man's daughter, am I near you?
  Do you turn aside? You gentlemen are mad wags;
  I wonder things can be so warily carried,
  And parents blinded so, but they're served right   200
  That have two eyes, and wear so dull a sight.

TOUCHWOOD JUNIOR
  [Aside] Thy doom take hold of thee.

YELLOWHAMMER
  Tomorrow noon shall show your ring well done.

---

186   *to a hair* to perfection, with a pun on 'pubic hair', continuing on from *Your pleasure*
187   *posy* a motto, originally a line of verse or 'poesie', often inscribed inside a ring
188   *Mass* 'by the Mass', an oath
197   *am I near you?* 'do I guess your aim?' said with unconscious irony
201   *wear* (were Q); some editors emend 'were so dull a'sight, but cf. IV.ii.36 for a similar
       use of this spelling in Q

TOUCHWOOD JUNIOR

Being so 'tis soon; thanks, and your leave sweet gentlewoman.

Exit

MOLL

Sir you are welcome. 205

[*Aside*] O were I made of wishes, I went with thee.

YELLOWHAMMER

Come now we'll see how the rules go within.

MOLL

That robs my joy, there I lose all I win.

Ex[eunt]

[ACT I, SCENE ii]

Enter DAVY *and* ALLWIT *severally*

DAVY

Honesty wash my eyes, I have spied a wittol.

ALLWIT

What, Davy Dahumma? Welcome from North Wales
I'faith, and is Sir Walter come?

DAVY

New come to town sir.

ALLWIT

Into the maids sweet Davy, and give order his chamber be made 5
ready instantly; my wife's as great as she can wallow Davy, and
longs for nothing but pickled cucumbers, and his coming, and
now she shall ha't boy.

DAVY

She's sure of them sir.

ALLWIT

Thy very sight will hold my wife in pleasure, till the knight come 10
himself. Go in, in, in Davy.

207 *rules* revels; 'Tumultuous frolicsome conduct' (J. O. Halliwell, *Dictionary of Archaic and Provincial Words* (1874))

0 s.d. *severally* separately
7 *pickled cucumbers* made with verjuice, the sharp, slightly fermented juice of sour grapes or crab apples – pregnancy produces strange cravings; and this is a hidden irony, as 'pickled' = poxed and cucumbers are phallic

Exit [DAVY]

The founder's come to town! I am like a man
Finding a table furnished to his hand,
As mine is still to me, prays for the founder;
Bless the right worshipful, the good founder's life.   15
I thank him, h'as maintained my house this ten years,
Not only keeps my wife, but a keeps me,
And all my family; I am at his table,
He gets me all my children, and pays the nurse,
Monthly, or weekly, puts me to nothing,   20
Rent, nor church duties, not so much as the scavenger:
The happiest state that ever man was born to.
I walk out in a morning, come to breakfast,
Find excellent cheer, a good fire in winter.
Look in my coal house about midsummer eve,   25
That's full, five or six chaldron, new laid up;
Look in my back yard, I shall find a steeple
Made up with Kentish faggots, which o'erlooks
The waterhouse and the windmills; I say nothing
But smile, and pin the door. When she lies in,   30
As now she's even upon the point of grunting,
A lady lies not in like her; there's her embossings,
Embroiderings, spanglings, and I know not what,
As if she lay with all the gaudy shops

[handwritten margin notes: – Sir Walter sleeps his wife, but he pays for Allwit's luxury life. – Sir Walter is the father to all the children]

---

13   *table* Cf. Psalm 78:19 'Can God furnish a table?' and Proverbs 9:2 'Wisdom ... hath mingled her wine; she hath also furnished her table' (*The Holy Bible*, 1611); blasphemy continues with *prays* and *bless*.

17   *a* he

18   *family* includes servants as well as children

21   *church ... scavenger* Parish dues (*duties*) could be paid in cash or service. The *scavenger* was a town officer who employed the poor to sweep the streets and chimneys; Stow says Bread Street ward, which contained part of Cheapside, had eight.

26   *chaldron* a dry measure of 36 bushels of coal; the coal trade between Newcastle and London grew tenfold between 1545 and 1625 and while Shakespeare was in London the price per chaldron rose from four shillings to nine

28   *Kentish faggots* bundles of brushwood, about eight feet long (2.44 m) and a foot (30.5 cm) through; much London firewood came from Kent

29   *waterhouse and the windmills* either the house near Broken Wharf in which Bevis Bulmer in 1594 built an 'engine' 'to convey Thames water into men's houses of West Cheap, about Paul's, Fleet Street, &c' (*Survey*, I, 8) or Sir Hugh Middleton's recently completed reservoir in Islington; windmills could be seen to both north and south of Cheapside

30   *pin* bolt

In Gresham's Burse about her; then her restoratives,   35
Able to set up a young 'pothecary,
And richly stock the foreman of a drug shop;
Her sugar by whole loaves, her wines by rundlets.
I see these things, but like a happy man,
I pay for none at all, yet fools think's mine;   40
I have the name, and in his gold I shine.
And where some merchants would in soul kiss hell,
To buy a paradise for their wives, and dye
Their conscience in the bloods of prodigal heirs,
To deck their night-piece, yet all this being done,   45
Eaten with jealousy to the inmost bone –
As what affliction nature more constrains,
Than feed the wife plump for another's veins?
These torments stand I freed of, I am as clear
From jealousy of a wife as from the charge.   50
O two miraculous blessings; 'tis the knight
Hath took that labour all out of my hands;
I may sit still and play; he's jealous for me –
Watches her steps, sets spies – I live at ease;
He has both the cost and torment; when the strings   55
Of his heart frets, I feed, laugh, or sing,
La dildo, dildo la dildo, la dildo dildo de dildo.

Enter TWO SERVANTS

1 SERVANT

What has he got a-singing in his head now?

35   *Gresham's Burse* the Royal Exchange, 'whose founder was Sir Thomas Gresham
      Knight, agent to her Majesty, built 1556–8 for the confluence and commerce of
      merchants' (John Speed, *The Theatre of . . . Great Britain* (1611), fol. 852)
38   *rundlets* barrels; large rundlets held between 12 and 18½ gallons (54.6–84.2 litres),
      small between a pint and four gallons (0.57–18.2 litres)
40   *think's* think it's
43–4 *dye . . . heirs* 'wickedly extort money from spendthrift sons of the gentry to buy
      clothing and jewellery for their whores'. Gulling 'prodigal heirs' is a major theme in
      Middleton's *Michaelmas Term* (*c.* 1606).
45   *night-piece* mistress, bedfellow
47   *nature more constrains* restricts nature more
55–6 *strings . . . frets* The heart was supposed to be braced with strings, which frayed and
      broke under emotional stress; the fret of a musical instrument was a ring of gut,
      now wood or metal, on the fingerboard to regulate fingering.
57   *dildo* This chorus has ironic overtones; a dildo is a substitute phallus.
58   *a-singing . . . head* reference to horns, the common insignia of the cuckold, a man
      with an adulterous wife

2 SERVANT

    Now he's out of work he falls to making dildoes.

ALLWIT

    Now sirs, Sir Walter's come.   60

1 SERVANT

    Is our master come?

ALLWIT

    Your master? What am I?

SERVANT

    Do not you know sir?

ALLWIT

    Pray am not I your master?

1 SERVANT

    O you are but our mistress's husband.   65

Enter SIR WALTER *and* DAVY

ALLWIT

    Ergo knave, your master. [*Therefore*]

1 SERVANT

    Negatur argumentum. [Your argument is denied.] Here comes Sir Walter, now a stands bare
    as well as we; make the most of him he's but one peep above a
    servingman, and so much his horns make him.

SIR WALTER

    How dost Jack?   [He looks down upon Allwit?]   70

ALLWIT

    Proud of your worship's health sir.

SIR WALTER

    How does your wife?

ALLWIT

    E'en after your own making sir,
    She's a tumbler i'faith, the nose and belly meets.

SIR WALTER

    They'll part in time again.   75

---

59   *work* sexual activity (slang)

66   *Ergo* 'Therefore'

67   *Negatur argumentum* 'Your argument is denied'

68   *peep* pip, degree; from a card game 'one-and-thirty' in which thirty-two was 'a pip
     out', the pips being the spots on the cards

70   *Jack* This may well be Allwit's name, but it is also a generic name for (a) a low bred,
     common fellow (Sir Walter is asserting his authority immediately) (b) a penis.

74   *She's a tumbler . . . meets* 'She's a copulator, and she's pregnant'

ALLWIT

At the good hour, they will, and please your worship.

SIR WALTER

Here sirrah, pull off my boots. Put on, put on Jack.

ALLWIT

I thank your kind worship sir.

SIR WALTER

Slippers! Heart, you are sleepy.

ALLWIT

The game begins already.   80

SIR WALTER

Pish, put on, Jack.

ALLWIT

Now I must do it, or he'll be as angry now as if I had put it on at
first bidding; 'tis but observing, 'tis but observing a man's
humour once, and he may ha' him by the nose all his life.

SIR WALTER

What entertainment has lain open here?   85
No strangers in my absence?

1 SERVANT

Sure sir not any.

ALLWIT

His jealousy begins; am not I happy now
That can laugh inward whilst his marrow melts?

SIR WALTER

How do you satisfy me?   90

1 SERVANT

Good sir be patient.

SIR WALTER

For two months' absence I'll be satisfied.

1 SERVANT

No living creature entered –

SIR WALTER

Entered? Come swear –

1 SERVANT

You will not hear me out sir –   95

---

77   *Put on* Hats were normally worn indoors; Allwit has removed his out of deference.
84   *humour* disposition
      he one, you
89   *marrow melts* with the heat generated by his jealousy

SIR WALTER
    Yes I'll hear't out sir.
1 SERVANT
    Sir he can tell himself.
SIR WALTER   Heart he can tell!
    Do you think I'll trust him? As a usurer
    With forfeited lordships. Him, O monstrous injury!
    Believe him? Can the devil speak ill of darkness?   100
    What can you say sir?
ALLWIT
    Of my soul and conscience sir, she's a wife as honest of her body
    to me as any lord's proud lady can be.
SIR WALTER
    Yet, by your leave, I heard you were once offering to go to bed
    to her.   105
ALLWIT
    No, I protest sir.
SIR WALTER
    Heart if you do, you shall take all – I'll marry.
ALLWIT
    O I beseech you sir –
SIR WALTER
    That wakes the slave, and keeps his flesh in awe.
ALLWIT
    I'll stop that gap   110
    Where e'er I find it open; I have poisoned
    His hopes in marriage already –
    Some old rich widows, and some landed virgins –

Enter two CHILDREN

    And I'll fall to work still before I'll lose him,
    He's yet too sweet to part from.   115
1 BOY
    God-den father.
ALLWIT
    Ha villain, peace.
2 BOY
    God-den father.

---

99   *forfeited lordships* Mortgaged properties claimed by moneylenders for repayment
      of loans. A jibe at the low value of knighthood. Cf. note 43–4 above.
116   *God-den* 'Good evening', but used any time after noon

173

ALLWIT

    Peace bastard; should he hear 'em! These are two foolish child-
    ren, they do not know the gentleman that sits there.   120

SIR WALTER

    Oh Wat, how dost Nick? Go to school,
    Ply your books boys, ha?

ALLWIT

    Where's your legs whoresons? They should kneel indeed if they
    could say their prayers.

SIR WALTER

    Let me see, stay,   125
    How shall I dispose of these two brats now
    When I am married? For they must not mingle
    Amongst my children that I get in wedlock –
    'Twill make foul work that, and raise many storms.
    I'll bind Wat prentice to a goldsmith, my father Yellowhammer;   130
    As fit as can be. Nick with some vintner; good, goldsmith
    And vintner; there will be wine in bowls, i'faith.

Enter ALLWIT'S WIFE

MISTRESS ALLWIT

    Sweet knight
    Welcome; I have all my longings now in town,
    Now well-come the good hour.   135

SIR WALTER

    How cheers my mistress?

MISTRESS ALLWIT

    Made lightsome, e'en by him that made me heavy.

SIR WALTER

    Methinks she shows gallantly, like a moon at full sir.

ALLWIT

    True, and if she bear a male child, there's the man in the moon
    sir.   140

SIR WALTER

    'Tis but the boy in the moon yet, goodman calf.

ALLWIT

    There was a man, the boy had never been there else.

---

123   *legs* a bow
137   *heavy* pregnant
141   *calf* blockhead. Another small but subtle irony, since a 'mooncalf' is also a false
        pregnancy.

SIR WALTER

    It shall be yours sir.

               [*Exeunt* MISTRESS ALLWIT *and* SIR WALTER]

ALLWIT

    No by my troth, I'll swear it's none of mine, let him that got it
    keep it. Thus do I rid myself of fear,   145
    Lie soft, sleep hard, drink wine, and eat good cheer.   [*Exit*]

Enter TOUCHWOOD SENIOR *and his* WIFE

MISTRESS TOUCHWOOD

'Twill be so tedious sir to live from you,
But that necessity must be obeyed.

TOUCHWOOD SENIOR

I would it might not wife, the tediousness
Will be the most part mine, that understand
The blessings I have in thee; so to part,   5
That drives the torment to a knowing heart;
But as thou sayst, we must give way to need
And live awhile asunder; our desires
Are both too fruitful for our barren fortunes.
How adverse runs the destiny of some creatures –   10
Some only can get riches and no children,
We only can get children and no riches;
Then 'tis the prudent'st part to check our wills,
And till our state rise, make our bloods lie still.
[*Aside*] Life every year a child, and some years two,   15
Besides drinkings abroad, that's never reckoned;
This gear will not hold out.

MISTRESS TOUCHWOOD

Sir, for a time, I'll take the courtesy of my uncle's house
If you be pleased to like on't, till prosperity
Look with a friendly eye upon our states.   20

TOUCHWOOD SENIOR

Honest wife I thank thee; I ne'er knew
The perfect treasure thou brought'st with thee more
Than at this instant minute. A man's happy

---

  5   *blessings* (a) happiness (b) children. Cf. Shakespeare, 'bairns [i.e. children] are
       blessings', *All's Well* I.iii.25.
  7   *thou* Touchwood Senior uses the affectionate form to his wife, who, like most wives
       to their husbands, addresses him with 'you'.
 13   *wills* sexual desires
 14   *bloods* passions
 15   *Life* 'By God's life'. An Act for the 'preventing . . . of the great abuse of the Holy
       Name of God in Stage plays, interludes . . . and such like' was passed in May 1606;
       offenders were liable for a fine of £10 for each lapse.
 16   *drinkings abroad* sexual adventures away from home
 17   *gear* (a) business (b) genitals

When he's at poorest that has matched his soul
As rightly as his body. Had I married   25
A sensual fool now, as 'tis hard to 'scape it
'Mongst gentlewomen of our time, she would ha' hanged
About my neck, and never left her hold
Till she had kissed me into wanton businesses,
Which at the waking of my better judgement   30
I should have cursed most bitterly,
And laid a thicker vengeance on my act
Than misery of the birth, which were enough
If it were born to greatness, whereas mine
Is sure of beggary, though it were got in wine.   35
Fullness of joy showeth the goodness in thee –
Thou art a matchless wife; farewell my joy.

MISTRESS TOUCHWOOD
   I shall not want your sight?

TOUCHWOOD SENIOR   I'll see thee often,
   Talk in mirth, and play at kisses with thee,
   Anything wench but what may beget beggars;   40
   There I give o'er the set, throw down the cards,
   And dare not take them up.

MISTRESS TOUCHWOOD   Your will be mine sir.   *Exit*

TOUCHWOOD SENIOR
   This does not only make her honesty perfect,
   But her discretion, and approves her judgement.
   Had her desires been wanton, they'd been blameless 45
   In being lawful ever, but of all creatures
   I hold that wife a most unmatched treasure
   That can unto her fortunes fix her pleasure,
   And not unto her blood – this is like wedlock;
   The feast of marriage is not lust but love,   50
   And care of the estate. When I please blood,
   Merely I sing, and suck out others'; then,
   'Tis many a wise man's fault; but of all men

---

41   *give o'er the set* abandon the game, as in dice, cards or tennis
44   *approves* confirms, attests
45   *desires* ed. (desire Q)
52   *sing* fuck; Parker suggests a misprint for 'sting', symbolizing lust as a flesh-fly, which
     links with *suck out others'* blood
     Merely . . . others' My slightest sexual activity always hurts somebody

I am the most unfortunate in that game
That ever pleased both genders: I ne'er played yet   55
Under a bastard. The poor wenches curse me
To the pit where e'er I come; they were ne'er served so,
But used to have more words than one to a bargain.
I have such a fatal finger in such business
I must forth with't, chiefly for country wenches,   60
For every harvest I shall hinder hay-making;

Enter a WENCH *with a child*

I had no less than seven lay in last Progress,
Within three weeks of one another's time.

WENCH

O Snaphance, have I found you?

TOUCHWOOD SENIOR   How Snaphance?

WENCH

Do you see your workmanship?   65
Nay turn not from it, nor offer to escape, for if you do,
I'll cry it through the streets, and follow you.
Your name may well be called Touchwood, a pox on you,
You do but touch and take; thou hast undone me;
I was a maid before, I can bring a certificate for it,   70
From both the churchwardens.

TOUCHWOOD SENIOR

I'll have the parson's hand too, or I'll not yield to't.

55–6   *I . . . bastard* 'At the very least there's always a bastard'. A 'bastard card' is a single card left in a hand and which counts against the player.

58   *used to have more words than one to a bargain* assume they'd not get pregnant on the first encounter. 'More words . . . bargain' is proverbial for being unwilling to agree easily.

62   *Progress* Annual royal visit to various parts of the country, usually in July and August; expensive festivities and a holiday atmosphere were expected by the sovereign.

64   *Snaphance* Flintlock on guns or, more appropriately here, a musket or gun fitted with a flintlock. The flintlock ignited touchwood in a gun's touchhole – the sexual imagery is obvious.

69   *touch and take* proverbial
      thou The Wench is growing more angry with Touchwood Senior, and does not return to 'you' until l. 101.

71   *churchwardens* lay honorary officers who helped the incumbent of a parish; they could issue the character reference needed by everyone moving out of their own parish, though these were famously unreliable (cf. 'a certificate (such as rogues have) from the head men of the Parish', Thomas Nashe, *Strange News* (1592), sig. C4)

WENCH

    Thou shalt have more, thou villain. Nothing grieves me, but
    Ellen my poor cousin in Derbyshire, thou hast cracked her
    marriage quite; she'll have a bout with thee.   75

TOUCHWOOD SENIOR

    Faith when she will I'll have a bout with her.

WENCH

    A law bout sir I mean.

TOUCHWOOD SENIOR

    True, lawyers use such bouts as other men do,
    And if that be all thy grief, I'll tender her a husband;
    I keep of purpose two or three gulls in pickle   80
    To eat such mutton with, and she shall choose one.
    Do but in courtesy, faith, wench, excuse me
    Of this half yard of flesh, in which I think it wants
    A nail or two.

WENCH   No, thou shalt find villain

    It hath right shape, and all the nails it should have.   85

TOUCHWOOD SENIOR

    Faith I am poor; do a charitable deed wench,
    I am a younger brother, and have nothing.

WENCH

    Nothing! Thou hast too much thou lying villain
    Unless thou wert more thankful.

TOUCHWOOD SENIOR   I have no dwelling,

    I brake up house but this morning; pray thee pity me,   90
    I am a good fellow, faith have been too kind
    To people of your gender; if I ha't
    Without my belly, none of your sex shall want it;
    [*Aside*] That word has been of force to move a woman.
    There's tricks enough to rid thy hand on't wench,   95

75   *bout* quarrel; taken up by Touchwood Senior in the sexual sense and used again in
        the legal sense
80   *in pickle* (a) in reserve (like preserved fruit or vegetables) (b) poxy, as the sweating
        vats used for curing venereal disease were known as 'pickling tubs'
80–1   *gulls . . . one* 'I keep a few fools for such whores and she can have one for a husband'
84   *nail* a measure of cloth, one sixteenth of a yard; here with a pun, as syphilitics'
        children sometimes lack fingernails
87   *younger brother* The custom of primogeniture, by which property and title
        descended to the first born, meant that younger sons often had to live by their wits.
        Touchwood Senior has an older brother, or else he's lying.
92–3   *if I . . . belly* (a) 'if I have uneaten food' (b) 'while I have a phallus'

Some rich man's porch, tomorrow before day,
Or else anon i'the evening – twenty devices;
Here's all I have, i'faith, take purse and all,
[*Aside*] And would I were rid of all the ware i'the shop so.

WENCH
Where I find manly dealings I am pitiful;   100
This shall not trouble you.

TOUCHWOOD SENIOR
And I protest wench, the next I'll keep myself.

WENCH
Soft, let it be got first.
[*Aside*] This is the fifth; if e'er I venture more
Where I now go for a maid, may I ride for a whore.   *Exit*   105

TOUCHWOOD SENIOR
What shift she'll make now with this piece of flesh
In this strict time of Lent, I cannot imagine;
Flesh dare not peep abroad now; I have known
This city now above this seven years,
But I protest in better state of government   110
I never knew it yet, nor ever heard of;
There has been more religious wholesome laws
In the half circle of a year erected
For common good, than memory ever knew of,

Enter SIR OLIVER KIX *and his* LADY

Setting apart corruption of promoters,   115
And other poisonous officers that infect
And with a venomous breath taint every goodness.

LADY KIX
O that e'er I was begot, or bred, or born.

SIR OLIVER
Be content sweet wife.

TOUCHWOOD SENIOR   What's here to do now?
I hold my life she's in deep passion   120
For the imprisonment of veal and mutton

---

97   *anon* straight away
99   *ware i'the shop* (a) all my other bastards (b) other whores
105   *ride* Being paraded in a cart was a punishment for whores; there is also a pun on
      straddling as a position in sexual intercourse.
107   *Lent* the period in the Christian church from Ash Wednesday to Easter Eve, of
      which the 40 week-days are devoted to fasting and penitence in commemoration
      of Christ's 40 days in the Wilderness.

a fool

Now kept in garrets, weeps for some calf's head now;
Methinks her husband's head might serve with bacon.

Enter TOUCHWOOD JUNIOR

LADY KIX
  Hist.
SIR OLIVER
  Patience sweet wife.   125
TOUCHWOOD JUNIOR
  Brother I have sought you strangely.
TOUCHWOOD SENIOR
  Why, what's the business?
TOUCHWOOD JUNIOR
  With all speed thou canst, procure a licence for me.
TOUCHWOOD SENIOR
  How, a licence?
TOUCHWOOD JUNIOR
  Cud's foot she's lost else, I shall miss her ever.   130
TOUCHWOOD SENIOR
  Nay sure thou shalt not miss so fair a mark
  For thirteen shillings fourpence.
TOUCHWOOD JUNIOR   Thanks by hundreds.   *Exit*
SIR OLIVER
  Nay pray thee cease, I'll be at more cost yet,
  Thou know'st we are rich enough.
LADY KIX   All but in blessings,
  And there the beggar goes beyond us. O, O, O,   135
  To be seven years a wife and not a child, O not a child!

mostly because no one of their own will heirit their fortune

SIR OLIVER
  Sweet wife have patience.

122   *calf's head* also means a fool
124   *Hist* Some editors give this to Touchwood Junior but as it means 'Be quiet!' it is
      appropriate for Lady Kix, as in Q.
126   *you* Here a formal use by a younger brother before the familial *thou* of ll. 128 and
      131.
      strangely extremely; 'I've been looking hard for you'
128   *licence* Only the Archbishop of Canterbury could issue a licence for a marriage in
      a place other than a church or chapel; a licence was also necessary for a marriage
      for which banns had not been called.
130   *Cud's foot* a defanged oath, 'By God's foot'
131   *mark* target
132   *thirteen shillings fourpence* value of a mark, the cost of a special marriage licence
133   *thee* Both Sir Oliver and Lady Kix use *thee* and *thou* denoting anger.

LADY KIX
    Can any woman have a greater cut?
SIR OLIVER
    I know 'tis great, but what of that wife?
    I cannot do withal; there's things making   140
    By thine own doctor's advice at 'pothecary's;
    I spare for nothing wife, no, if the price
    Were forty marks a spoonful,
    I'd give a thousand pound to purchase fruitfulness;
    'Tis but bating so many good works   145
    In the erecting of Bridewells and spital-houses,
    And so fetch it up again – for having none
    I mean to make good deeds my children.
LADY KIX
    Give me but those good deeds, and I'll find children.
SIR OLIVER
    Hang thee, thou hast had too many!   150
LADY KIX
    Thou lie'st, brevity!
SIR OLIVER
    O horrible, dar'st thou call me 'brevity'?
    Dar'st thou be so short with me?
LADY KIX
    Thou deservest worse.
    Think but upon the goodly lands and livings   155
    That's kept back through want on't.
SIR OLIVER
    Talk not on't pray thee,
    Thou'lt make me play the woman and weep too.
LADY KIX
    'Tis our dry barrenness puffs up Sir Walter –
    None gets by your not-getting, but that knight;   160

---

138 *cut* (a) misfortune (b) cunt
140 *do withal* (a) help it (b) fuck
145 *bating* diminishing
146 *Bridewells and spital-houses* Bridewell, originally a royal palace, was given to
     London by Edward VI 'to be a house of correction for lewd and dissolute livers'
     (Speed, *The Theatre of . . . Great Britain* (1611), fol. 814); here used for prisons in
     general. Spitals were hospitals, especially for leprosy and venereal disease.
147 *fetch it up again* (a) 'if I can't buy fruitfulness I'll save the money and be a
     philanthropist' (b) 'I'll recover from sexual impotence'

He's made by th'means, and fats his fortunes shortly
In a great dowry with a goldsmith's daughter.

                      [*Exit* TOUCHWOOD SENIOR]

SIR OLIVER
  They may all be deceived,
  Be but you patient wife.

LADY KIX
  I have suffered a long time.   165

SIR OLIVER
  Suffer thy heart out; a pox suffer thee!

LADY KIX
  Nay thee, thou desertless slave!

SIR OLIVER
  Come, come, I ha' done;
  You'll to the gossiping of Master Allwit's child?

LADY KIX
  Yes, to my much joy;   170
  Everyone gets before me – there's my sister
  Was married but at Bartholomew eve last,
  And she can have two children at a birth;
  O one of them, one of them would ha' served my turn.

SIR OLIVER
  Sorrow consume thee, thou art still crossing me,   175
  And know'st my nature.

                Enter a MAID

MAID
  O mistress, weeping or railing,
  That's our house harmony.

LADY KIX
  What sayst Jugg?

MAID
  The sweetest news.   180

---

162   s.d. Q has no exit for Touchwood Senior, but this would be an appropriate place for
        him to leave, having overheard the cause of the Kixes' quarrel and being reminded
        of his brother's marriage plans.

169   *gossiping* christening
        Master ed. (Q Mr). Parker reads 'Mistress' but the masculine is more appropriately
        ironic, given the recent argument.

172   *Bartholomew eve* 23 August; as it is not yet mid-Lent (II.ii.206–7), the children were
        conceived before marriage

179   *Jugg* familiar form of 'Joan', often applied to servants

LADY KIX

    What is't wench?

MAID

    Throw down your doctor's drugs,

    They're all but heretics; I bring certain remedy

    That has been taught, and proved, and never failed.

SIR OLIVER

    O that, that, that or nothing.   185

MAID

    There's a gentleman,

    I haply have his name, too, that has got

    Nine children by one water that he useth;

    It never misses, they come so fast upon him,

    He was fain to give it over.

LADY KIX   His name sweet Jugg?   190

MAID

    One Master Touchwood, a fine gentleman,

    But run behind hand much with getting children.

SIR OLIVER

    Is't possible?

MAID   Why sir, he'll undertake,

    Using that water, within fifteen year,

    For all your wealth, to make you a poor man,   195

    You shall so swarm with children.

SIR OLIVER

    I'll venture that i'faith.

LADY KIX   That shall you husband.

MAID

    But I must tell you first, he's very dear.

SIR OLIVER

    No matter, what serves wealth for?

LADY KIX   True, sweet husband.

[SIR OLIVER]

    There's land to come; put case his water stands me   200

---

183   *heretics* Physicians were suspected of using magic.

187   *haply* by chance

188   *water* (a) medicine (b) semen

200   *put case* suppose, with a pun on *case* = vagina

200–4   Q gives all these lines to Lady Kix, reversing the last two. The present arrangement follows Parker.

In some five hundred pound a pint,
  'Twill fetch a thousand, and a kersten soul.
[LADY KIX]
  And that's worth all, sweet husband.
[SIR OLIVER]
  I'll about it.

                                            Ex[*eunt*]

[ACT II, SCENE ii]

Enter ALLWIT

ALLWIT
  I'll go bid gossips presently myself;
  That's all the work I'll do, nor need I stir,
  But that it is my pleasure to walk forth
  And air myself a little; I am tied to nothing
  In this business, what I do is merely recreation,   5
  Not constraint.
  Here's running to and fro, nurse upon nurse,
  Three charwomen, besides maids and neighbours' children.
  Fie, what a trouble have I rid my hands on;
  It makes me sweat to think on't.

Enter SIR WALTER WHOREHOUND

SIR WALTER   How now Jack?   10
ALLWIT
  I am going to bid gossips for your worship's child sir;—
  A goodly girl i'faith, give you joy on her,
  She looks as if she had two thousand pound to her portion
  And run away with a tailor; a fine plump black eyed slut;
  Under correction sir,   15
  I take delight to see her: Nurse!

202   *kersten* Christian

1   *gossips* godparents, but also women friends
14 *run away with a tailor* i.e. because she has such fine clothes, but as well, tailors were
    traditionally lecherous; cf. Dekker and Webster, *Northward Ho!*: 'Tailors will be saucy
    and lickerish' (II.i.177)
16 *Nurse* The dry nurse usually looked after the child, the wet nurse suckled it.

Enter DRY NURSE

DRY NURSE   Do you call sir?

ALLWIT

I call not you, I call the wet nurse hither,

                           Exit [DRY NURSE]

Give me the wet nurse,

      Enter WET NURSE [*carrying baby*]

                ay, 'tis thou,

Come hither, come hither,

Let's see her once again; I cannot choose   20

But buss her thrice an hour.

WET NURSE

You may be proud on't sir,

'Tis the best piece of work that e'er you did.

ALLWIT

Think'st thou so Nurse? What sayst to Wat and Nick?

WET NURSE

They're pretty children both, but here's a wench   25

Will be a knocker.

ALLWIT

Pup – sayst thou me so? Pup, little countess;

Faith sir I thank your worship for this girl,

Ten thousand times, and upward.

SIR WALTER

I am glad I have her for you sir.   30

ALLWIT

Here, take her in Nurse, wipe her, and give her spoon-meat.

WET NURSE

[*Aside*] Wipe your mouth sir.   *Exit*

ALLWIT

And now about these gossips.

SIR WALTER

Get but two, I'll stand for one myself.

---

21   *buss* kiss

26   *knocker* (a) good-looker (b) notable copulator

27   *countess* A bawdy pun, following 'knocker', but see also note to III.ii.99.

31   *spoon-meat* puréed food for infants

32   *Wipe your mouth* Make a fool of yourself; but this may also refer to 'Such is the way of an adulterous woman; she eateth, and wipeth her mouth, and saith, I have done no wickedness' (Proverbs 30:20).

ALLWIT

To your own child sir? 35

SIR WALTER

The better policy, it prevents suspicion,
'Tis good to play with rumour at all weapons.

ALLWIT

Troth, I commend your care sir, 'tis a thing
That I should ne'er have thought on.

SIR WALTER [*Aside*]   The more slave;
When man turns base, out goes his soul's pure flame, 40
The fat of ease o'er-throws the eyes of shame.

ALLWIT

I am studying who to get for godmother
Suitable to your worship: now I ha' thought on't.

SIR WALTER

I'll ease you of that care, and please myself in't.
[*Aside*] My love the goldsmith's daughter, if I send, 45
Her father will command her. Davy Dahumma!

Enter DAVY

ALLWIT

I'll fit your worship then with a male partner.

SIR WALTER

What is he?

ALLWIT

A kind proper gentleman, brother to Master Touchwood.

SIR WALTER

I know Touchwood, has he a brother living? 50

ALLWIT

A neat bachelor.

SIR WALTER

Now we know him we'll make shift with him.
Dispatch, the time draws near. Come hither Davy.

Exit [*with* DAVY]

ALLWIT

In troth I pity him, he ne'er stands still.
Poor knight, what pains he takes – sends this way one, 55
That way another, has not an hour's leisure –

51   *neat* elegant
52   *make shift with* be content with

187

I would not have thy toil, for all thy pleasure.

Enter TWO PROMOTERS

Ha, how now, what are these that stand so close
At the street corner, pricking up their ears,
And snuffing up their noses, like rich men's dogs   60
When the first course goes in? By the mass, promoters,
'Tis so I hold my life, and planted there
To arrest the dead corps of poor calves and sheep,
Like ravenous creditors that will not suffer
The bodies of their poor departed debtors   65
To go to th' grave, but e'en in death to vex
And stay the corps, with bills of Middlesex.
This Lent will fat the whoresons up with sweetbreads
And lard their whores with lamb-stones; what their golls
Can clutch goes presently to their Molls and Dolls.   70
The bawds will be so fat with what they earn
Their chins will hang like udders by Easter eve,
And being stroked, will give the milk of witches.
How did the mongrels hear my wife lies in?
Well, I may baffle 'em gallantly. By your favour gentlemen,   75
I am a stranger both unto the city
And to her carnal strictness.
I PROMOTER   Good; your will sir?
ALLWIT
Pray tell me where one dwells that kills this Lent.
1 PROMOTER
How, kills? Come hither Dick,
A bird, a bird.   80

63, 67 *corps* Q has 'corps', an old plural form, but 'corpses' is unmetrical
   67   *bills of Middlesex* writs allowing arrests on bogus charges within Middlesex, which
        contained London north of the Thames, so that defendants could be tried for crimes
        committed outside the county
   69   *lard . . . lamb-stones* fatten with lambs' testicles, like sweetbreads believed to
        be   aphrodisiac
        golls hands (slang)
   70   *Molls and Dolls* names used for whores and criminals' girlfriends
 72–3   *chins . . . witches* Bawds were believed to be characterized by double chins; witches
        were believed to give suck to the devil, and their familiars, from a third nipple
        somewhere on the body. Middleton also uses this image in *The Black Book* (1604).
        (See Bullen, VIII, 12.)
   75   *baffle* insult, treat with indignity   80 *bird* victim

188

2 PROMOTER

  What is't that you would have?

ALLWIT   Faith any flesh,

  But I long especially for veal and green sauce. *cheated*

1 PROMOTER

  [*Aside*] Green goose, you shall be sauced.

ALLWIT

  I have half a scornful stomach, no fish will be admitted.

1 PROMOTER

  Not this Lent sir?   85

ALLWIT

  Lent, what cares colon here for Lent?

1 PROMOTER

  You say well sir;

  Good reason that the colon of a gentleman,

  As you were lately pleased to term your worship sir,

  Should be fulfilled with answerable food,   90

  To sharpen blood, delight health, and tickle nature.

  Were you directed hither to this street sir?

ALLWIT

  That I was, ay marry.

2 PROMOTER   And the butcher belike

  Should kill and sell close in some upper room? *secret*

ALLWIT

  Some apple loft as I take it, or a coal house,   95

  I know not which i'faith.

2 PROMOTER

  Either will serve.

  [*Aside*] This butcher shall kiss Newgate, 'less he turn up the

  bottom of the pocket of his apron;

  You go to seek him?

ALLWIT   Where you shall not find him;   100

---

  82   *green sauce* made with vinegar or verjuice with spices but without garlic; both 'veal'
        and 'green' imply gullibility and to eat 'veal and green sauce' = to be cheated

  83   *Green goose* (a) young goose made into pies for the goose fair at Bow (b) cant term
        for a cuckold

  86   *colon* belly

  90   *answerable* suitable

  94   *close* secret

  98   *kiss Newgate* go to prison; one of the gates of ancient London, Newgate was used as
        a prison for the worst class of criminals from at least 1190; it was demolished 1902–3

98–9   *turn . . . apron* offer a bribe

I'll buy, walk by your noses with my flesh,
Sheep-biting mongrels, hand basket freebooters!
My wife lies in; a foutra for promoters!   *Exit*

1 PROMOTER
That shall not serve your turn – what a rogue's this; how cunningly he came over us !   105

Enter a MAN *with meat in a basket*

2 PROMOTER
Husht, stand close.

MAN
I have 'scaped well thus far; they say the knaves are wondrous
hot and busy.

1 PROMOTER
By your leave sir,
We must see what you have under your cloak there.   110

MAN
Have? I have nothing.

1 PROMOTER
No, do you tell us that? What makes this lump stick out then;
we must see sir.

MAN
What will you see sir – a pair of sheets, and two of my wife's foul
smocks, going to the washers?   115

2 PROMOTER
O we love that sight well, you cannot please us better: what, do
you gull us? Call you these shirts and smocks?

MAN
Now a pox choke you!
You have cozened me and five of my wife's kindred
Of a good dinner; we must make it up now   120
With herrings and milk pottage.   *Exit*

1 PROMOTER
'Tis all veal.

102   *sheep-biting* whoring
      freebooters pirates, here raiding the baskets of passers-by; perhaps with a pun on
      basket = whore
103   *foutra* vulgarism for the sexual act; from the French 'foutre'
104   *serve your turn* (a) 'Your wife's pregnancy can't be used as an excuse'; under the
      stricter laws of 1613 it was illegal even for invalids and pregnant women to eat meat in
      Lent (b) continuing the sense of 'foutra', since one turns the body to be served sexually
121   *pottage* broth

190

2 PROMOTER

    All veal? Pox the worse luck; I promised faithfully to send this
    morning a fat quarter of lamb to a kind gentlewoman in Turn-
    bull street that longs, and how I'm crossed.   125

1 PROMOTER

    Let's share this, and see what hap comes next then.

Enter another [MAN] *with a basket*

2 PROMOTER

    Agreed, stand close again; another booty.
    What's he?

1 PROMOTER

    Sir, by your favour.

2 MAN

    Meaning me sir?   130

1 PROMOTER

    Good Master Oliver, cry thee mercy, i'faith.
    What hast thou there?

2 MAN

    A rack of mutton sir, and half a lamb;
    You know my mistress's diet.

1 PROMOTER

    Go, go, we see thee not; away, keep close.   135
    Heart, let him pass, thou'lt never have the wit
    To know our benefactors.

                                           [*Exit* MAN]

2 PROMOTER

    I have forgot him.

1 PROMOTER

    'Tis Master Beggarland's man, the wealthy merchant
    That is in fee with us.   140

2 PROMOTER

    Now I have a feeling of him.

1 PROMOTER

    You know he purchased the whole Lent together,

  124–5   *Turnbull Street* (corrupted form of Turnmill) ran between Clerkenwell Green and
           Cowcross Street, and was the most notorious street in London for its thieves and
           whores, one of whom *longs* because she is pregnant
    133   *rack* neck
    142   *purchased the whole Lent together* paid them for immunity over the 40 days of Lent,
           which began on Ash Wednesday

Gave us ten groats apiece on Ash Wednesday.

2 PROMOTER

True, true.

Enter a WENCH *with a basket, and a child in it*
under a loin of mutton

1 PROMOTER

A wench. 145

2 PROMOTER

Why then stand close indeed.

WENCH

[*Aside*] Women had need of wit, if they'll shift here,
And she that hath wit may shift anywhere.

1 PROMOTER

Look, look, poor fool,
She has left the rump uncovered too, 150
More to betray her; this is like a murderer
That will outface the deed with a bloody band.

2 PROMOTER

What time of the year is't sister?

WENCH

O sweet gentlemen, I am a poor servant,
Let me go. 155

1 PROMOTER

You shall wench, but this must stay with us.

WENCH

O you undo me sir;
'Tis for a wealthy gentlewoman that takes physic sir,
The doctor does allow my mistress mutton,
O as you tender the dear life of a gentlewoman, 160
I'll bring my master to you, he shall show you

---

143 *groats* first coined 1351–2, made equal to fourpence; by 1600 used for any small sum
144 s.d. The trick played by the country wench is also found in some ballads, e.g. 'The Country Girl's Policy, or the Cockney Outwitted' and 'A Tryall of Skill, performed by a poor decay'd Gentlewoman' (*Roxburghe Ballads*, ed. J. W. Ebsworth (1880–1890), VII, 286 and IX, 556).
147 *wit* (a) cleverness (b) cunt. Cf. Middleton, *More Dissemblers Besides Women* IV.ii.230–5; Shakespeare, *As You Like It* IV.i.155.
 shift (a) succeed (b) live by fraud (c) palm off something on someone
152 *band* collar; standing collars were popular 1605–30. Possibly a wristband.

A true authority from the higher powers,
And I'll run every foot.

2 PROMOTER
Well, leave your basket then,
And run and spare not.   165

WENCH
Will you swear then to me
To keep it till I come.

1 PROMOTER
Now by this light I will.

WENCH
What say you, gentleman?

2 PROMOTER
What a strange wench 'tis.   170
Would we might perish else.

WENCH
Nay then I run sir.   *Exit*

1 PROMOTER
And ne'er return I hope.

2 PROMOTER
A politic baggage,
She makes us swear to keep it;   175
I prithee look what market she hath made.

1 PROMOTER
Imprimis sir, a good fat loin of mutton;
What comes next under this cloth?
Now for a quarter of lamb.

2 PROMOTER
Now for a shoulder of mutton.   180

1 PROMOTER
Done.

2 PROMOTER
Why done sir?

1 PROMOTER
By the mass I feel I have lost,
'Tis of more weight i'faith.

---

162   *true authority* The sick, and some foreign ambassadors, were permitted by the city
        authorities to have meat during Lent.
174   *politic* cunning
177   *Imprimis* 'In the first place'
180   *Now* ed. (not Q)

2 PROMOTER

   Some loin of veal? 185

1 PROMOTER

   No faith, here's a lamb's head,

   I feel that plainly, why yet I'll win my wager.

2 PROMOTER

   Ha?

1 PROMOTER

   Swounds what's here?

2 PROMOTER

   A child. 190

1 PROMOTER

   A pox of all dissembling cunning whores.

2 PROMOTER

   Here's an unlucky breakfast.

1 PROMOTER

   What shall's do?

2 PROMOTER

   The quean made us swear to keep it too.

1 PROMOTER

   We might leave it else. 195

2 PROMOTER

   Villainous strange;

   Life, had she none to gull but poor promoters

   That watch hard for a living?

1 PROMOTER

   Half our gettings must run in sugar-sops

   And nurses' wages now, besides many a pound of soap, 200

   And tallow; we have need to get loins of mutton still,

   To save suet to change for candles.

2 PROMOTER

   Nothing mads me but this was a lamb's head with you, you felt it;

   she has made calves' heads of us.

1 PROMOTER

   Prithee no more on't, 205

---

187   *I'll* ed. (Q omits)
189   *Swounds* 'God's wounds'
194   *quean* whore
199   *sugar-sops* bread soaked in sugar water
201   *tallow* used for candles and also perhaps for babies' bottoms
203–4   *Nothing . . . us* 'Nothing makes me so annoyed as to think that you, who felt the baby, said it was a lamb's head; she's made fools of us'

There's time to get it up; it is not come
To mid-Lent Sunday yet.

2 PROMOTER

I am so angry, I'll watch no more today.

1 PROMOTER

Faith nor I neither.

2 PROMOTER

Why then I'll make a motion. 210

1 PROMOTER

Well, what is't?

2 PROMOTER

Let's e'en go to the Checker at Queen-hive and roast the loin of
mutton, till young flood; then send the child to Branford.

[*Exeunt*]

[ACT II, SCENE iii]

Enter ALLWIT *in one of Sir Walter's suits,*
and DAVY *trussing him*

ALLWIT

'Tis a busy day at our house Davy.

DAVY

Always the kursning day sir.

ALLWIT

Truss, truss me Davy.

DAVY

[*Aside*] No matter and you were hanged sir.

---

206   *get it up* make up the money we've lost
212   *Checker* an inn, with a chess-board as its sign, which gave its name to the lane where
      it stood (cf. *Survey*, I, 231)
      Queen-hive Queenhithe, 'the very chief and principal water-gate of this city' (*Survey*,
      I, 41), a quay on the north bank of the Thames
213   *young flood* the beginning of the rising tide
      Branford Brentford, eight miles upstream from London and a resort of whores as
      well as other citizens, usually spelt 'Brainford', as at V.iv.97

  0   s.d. *trussing* tying the points of his hose to his doublet; 'to truss' also means 'to hang'
  2   *kursning day* christening day
  4   *No matter and* It wouldn't matter if

ALLWIT

How does this suit fit me Davy?   5

DAVY

Excellent neatly; my master's things were ever fit for you sir, e'en
to a hair you know.

ALLWIT

Thou has hit it right Davy,
We ever jumped in one, this ten years Davy.

Enter a SERVANT *with a box*

So, well said. What art thou?   10

SERVANT

Your comfit-maker's man sir.

ALLWIT

O sweet youth, in to the nurse quick,
Quick, 'tis time i'faith;
Your mistress will be here?

SERVANT

She was setting forth sir.   15

Enter TWO PURITANS

ALLWIT

Here comes our gossips now, O I shall have such kissing work
today; sweet Mistress Underman welcome i'faith.

1 PURITAN

Give you joy of your fine girl sir,
Grant that her education may be pure,
And become one of the faithful.   20

ALLWIT

Thanks to your sisterly wishes Mistress Underman.

2 PURITAN

Are any of the brethren's wives yet come?

ALLWIT

There are some wives within, and some at home.

1 PURITAN

Verily thanks sir.

---

  6   *things* (a) clothes (b) sexual organs (in this case Mrs Allwit's)

6–7 *e'en to a hair* (a) exactly (b) right up to the pubic hair (c) even to begetting an heir

  9   *jumped in one* (a) agreed (b) copulated with the same woman. Either Allwit has been
       deceiving Sir Walter, despite his protestation at I.ii.106, or he's joking. Cf. V.i.167.

10 *well said* well done. This expression occurs several times in the play.

11 *comfit* sweet made by mixing the pulp of cooked fruit with sugar

Ex[eunt PURITANS]

ALLWIT

    Verily you are an ass forsooth;   25
    I must fit all these times, or there's no music.

Enter TWO GOSSIPS

    Here comes a friendly and familiar pair –
    Now I like these wenches well.

1 GOSSIP

    How dost sirrah?

ALLWIT

    Faith well I thank you neighbour, and how dost thou?   30

2 GOSSIP

    Want nothing, but such getting sir as thine.

ALLWIT

    My gettings wench, they are poor.

1 GOSSIP

    Fie that thou'lt say so,
    Th'ast as fine children as a man can get.

DAVY

    [*Aside*] Ay, as a man can get,   35
    And that's my master.

ALLWIT

    They are pretty foolish things,
    Put to making in minutes;
    I ne'er stand long about 'em,
    Will you walk in wenches?   40

[Exeunt GOSSIPS]

Enter TOUCHWOOD JUNIOR and MOLL

TOUCHWOOD JUNIOR

    The happiest meeting that our souls could wish for. Here's the
    ring ready; I am beholding unto your father's haste, h'as kept his
    hour.

---

26 'I have to be agreeable with all these people or else there'll be no kissing'; cf. Dekker and Webster, *Westward Ho!* V.iv.283, 'Every husband play music upon the lips of his wife'. Allwit is out to enjoy himself.
    times rhythms

32 *gettings* (a) begettings (b) earnings

42 *beholding* beholden

MOLL

He never kept it better.

Enter SIR WALTER WHOREHOUND [*with a goblet*]

TOUCHWOOD JUNIOR

Back, be silent.   45

SIR WALTER

Mistress and partner, I will put you both into one cup.

                                                              [*Drinks*]

DAVY

Into one cup, most proper,

A fitting compliment for a goldsmith's daughter.

ALLWIT

Yes sir, that's he must be your worship's partner

In this day's business, Master Touchwood's brother.   50

SIR WALTER

I embrace your acquaintance sir.

TOUCHWOOD JUNIOR

It vows your service sir.

SIR WALTER

It's near high time, come Master Allwit.

ALLWIT

Ready sir.

SIR WALTER

Will't please you walk?   55

TOUCHWOOD JUNIOR

Sir I obey your time.

                                                              Ex[*eunt*]

Enter MIDWIFE *with the child,* [MAUDLINE]
and the GOSSIPS *to the kursning*

1 GOSSIP

Good Mistress Yellowhammer.

MAUDLINE

In faith I will not.

---

47   *into one cup* pledge them both in one drink – a nice irony, since at a betrothal
      ceremony the betrothed couple would drink from the same loving cup
53   *near high time* nearly noon. Cf. 'this morning' II.ii.123–4.
56   *time* beat (continuing the musical imagery of l. 26)
      s.d. During this progress across the stage, the women are squabbling over precedence
      in following the child into the room.

1 GOSSIP

    Indeed it shall be yours.

MAUDLINE   60

    I have sworn i'faith.

1 GOSSIP

    I'll stand still then.

MAUDLINE

    So will you let the child go without company
    And make me forsworn.

1 GOSSIP

    You are such another creature.

                 [*Exeunt* 1 GOSSIP *and* MAUDLINE]

2 GOSSIP   65

    Before me? I pray come down a little.

3 GOSSIP

    Not a whit; I hope I know my place.

2 GOSSIP

    Your place? Great wonder sure! Are you any better than a comfit-
    maker's wife?

3 GOSSIP

    And that's as good at all times as a 'pothecary's.

2 GOSSIP   70

    Ye lie, yet I forbear you too.

                   [*Exeunt* 2 *and* 3 GOSSIPS]

1 PURITAN

    Come sweet sister, we go in unity, and show the fruits of peace
    like children of the spirit.

1 PURITAN

    I love lowliness.

4 GOSSIP

    True, so say I, though they strive more,
    There comes as proud behind, as goes before.   75

5 GOSSIP

    Every inch, i'faith.

                         Ex[*eunt*]

---

75   *There comes as proud . . .* Proverbial, but the meaning of 'proud' as sexually excited
     is taken up in the next line.

ACT III, [SCENE i]

Enter TOUCHWOOD JUNIOR *and a* PARSON

TOUCHWOOD JUNIOR
  O sir, if ever you felt the force of love, pity it in me.

PARSON
  Yes, though I ne'er was married sir,
  I have felt the force of love from good men's daughters,
  And some that will be maids yet three years hence.
  Have you got a licence?   5

TOUCHWOOD JUNIOR
  Here 'tis ready sir.

PARSON
  That's well.

TOUCHWOOD JUNIOR
  The ring and all things perfect; she'll steal hither.

PARSON
  She shall be welcome sir; I'll not be long
  A-clapping you together.

Enter MOLL *and* TOUCHWOOD SENIOR

TOUCHWOOD JUNIOR   O here she's come sir.   10

PARSON
  What's he?

TOUCHWOOD JUNIOR My honest brother.

TOUCHWOOD SENIOR   Quick, make haste sirs.

MOLL
  You must dispatch with all the speed you can,
  For I shall be missed straight; I made hard shift
  For this small time I have.

PARSON   Then I'll not linger:
  Place that ring upon her finger,   15
  This the finger plays the part,
  Whose master vein shoots from the heart;

2–5 The parson implies a sexual past. Cf. II.i.70–72.

  5 *licence* See note to II.i.128.

17 *heart* Popular superstition had it that a vein or nerve ran from the third finger of the
     left hand to the heart; cf. note to I.ii.55–6

Now join hands.

Enter YELLOWHAMMER *and* SIR WALTER

YELLOWHAMMER Which I will sever;
   And so ne'er again meet never.

MOLL
   O we are betrayed.

TOUCHWOOD JUNIOR Hard fate.

SIR WALTER   I am struck with wonder.   20

YELLOWHAMMER
   Was this the politic fetch, thou mystical baggage,
   Thou disobedient strumpet?
   And were so wise to send for her to such an end?

SIR WALTER
   Now I disclaim the end, you'll make me mad.

YELLOWHAMMER
   And what are you sir?   25

TOUCHWOOD JUNIOR
   And you cannot see with those two glasses, put on a pair more.

YELLOWHAMMER
   I dreamt of anger still – here take your ring sir;
   Ha this? Life 'tis the same: abominable!
   Did not I sell this ring?

TOUCHWOOD JUNIOR
   I think you did, you received money for it.   30

YELLOWHAMMER
   Heart, hark you knight,
   Here's no inconscionable villainy –
   Set me a-work to make the wedding ring,
   And come with an intent to steal my daughter;
   Did ever runaway match it?   35

SIR WALTER
   This your brother sir?

---

18 *join hands* A marriage contract was made legal by 'handfasting', the joining of hands.
     Cf. Polixenes' similar intervention preventing the marriage of his son Florizel to
     Perdita in *The Winter's Tale* IV.iv.417.

21 *politic fetch* cunning trick, stratagem
     thou used instead of 'you' to indicate Yellowhammer's anger and contempt for his
     daughter
     mystical secret

26 *glasses* his eyes, or perhaps spectacles

27 *still* always; 'I always only dreamed of being angry, now I am'

TOUCHWOOD SENIOR
    He can tell that as well as I.

YELLOWHAMMER
    The very posy mocks me to my face:
    'Love that's wise, blinds parents' eyes.'
    I thank your wisdom sir for blinding of us; 40
    We have good hope to recover our sight shortly;
    In the meantime I will lock up this baggage
    As carefully as my gold; she shall see as little sun,
    If a close room or so can keep her from the light on't.

MOLL
    O sweet father, for love's sake pity me. 45

YELLOWHAMMER
    Away!

MOLL
    Farewell sir, all content bless thee,
    And take this for comfort,
    Though violence keep me, thou canst lose me never,
    I am ever thine although we part for ever. 50

YELLOWHAMMER
    Ay, we shall part you minx.

                       Exit [YELLOWHAMMER *with* MOLL]

SIR WALTER
    Your acquaintance sir came very lately,
    Yet it came too soon;
    I must hereafter know you for no friend,
    But one that I must shun like pestilence, 55
    Or the disease of lust.

TOUCHWOOD JUNIOR
    Like enough sir, you ha' ta'en me at the worst time for words that
    e'er ye picked out; faith do not wrong me sir.   *Exit*

TOUCHWOOD SENIOR
    Look after him and spare not; there he walks
    That never yet received baffling; you're blessed 60
    More than e'er I knew. Go take your rest.   *Exit*

SIR WALTER
    I pardon you, you are both losers.   *Exit*

42–4   Cf. Corvino's treatment of his wife Celia in Jonson's *Volpone* II.v.
59   *Look after him* Beware of him
60   *baffling* insult, public humiliation

[ACT III, SCENE ii]

A bed thrust out upon the stage, ALLWIT'S WIFE *in it.*
Enter all the GOSSIPS [*including* MAUDLINE *and* LADY KIX]

1 GOSSIP

How is't woman? We have brought you home
A kursen soul.

MISTRESS ALLWIT

Ay, I thank your pains.

1 PURITAN

And verily well kursened, i'the right way,
Without idolatry or superstition,   5
After the pure manner of Amsterdam.

MISTRESS ALLWIT

Sit down good neighbours; Nurse!

NURSE

At hand forsooth.

MISTRESS ALLWIT

Look they have all low stools.

NURSE

They have forsooth.   10

2 GOSSIP

Bring the child hither Nurse; how say you now
Gossip, is't not a chopping girl, so like the father?

3 GOSSIP

As if it had been spit out of his mouth,
Eyed, nosed and browed as like a girl can be,

---

  0   s.d. *A bed* Cf. R. Brome and T. Heywood, *The Late Lancashire Witches* (1634), Act V,
      'A *Bed thrust out, Mrs Gener*[*ous*] *in't*'. Richard Hosley found 23 instances of staging
      a bed in Chamberlain's / King's Men plays 1595–1642; in 8 it is stated, and in 8 others
      implied, that the bed was brought on stage (see *Shakespeare Quarterly* 14 (1963),
      57–63). This could have been done by stage attendants, but in the Adelaide Theatre
      Group production (1971) Mrs Allwit's bed was pushed on, very rapidly, by other
      cast members.
  2   *kursen* Christian, but with a pun on 'cursed', as the christening was 'After the pure
      manner of Amsterdam', and therefore thoroughly Puritan
  6   *Amsterdam* meeting place and refuge for European dissenters, symbolic of
      Puritanism
 12   *chopping* vigorous, strapping
 13   *spit out of bis mouth* proverbial

Only indeed it has the mother's mouth. 15

2 GOSSIP

The mother's mouth up and down, up and down.

3 GOSSIP

'Tis a large child, she's but a little woman.

1 PURITAN

No believe me, a very spiny creature, but all heart,
Well mettled, like the faithful to endure
Her tribulation here, and raise up seed. 20

2 GOSSIP

She had a sore labour on't I warrant you, you can tell neighbour.

3 GOSSIP

O she had great speed;
We were afraid once,
But she made us all have joyful hearts again; 25
'Tis a good soul i'faith;
The midwife found her a most cheerful daughter.

1 PURITAN

'Tis the spirit, the sisters are all like her.

Enter SIR WALTER *with two spoons and plate,*
and ALLWIT

2 GOSSIP

O here comes the chief gossip neighbours.

SIR WALTER

The fatness of your wishes to you all ladies. 30

3 GOSSIP

O dear sweet gentleman, what fine words he has –
'The fatness of our wishes'!

2 GOSSIP

Calls us all 'ladies'!

4 GOSSIP

I promise you, a fine gentleman, and a courteous.

2 GOSSIP

Methinks her husband shows like a clown to him. 35

16   *up and down* (a) exactly (b) oral and vaginal; cf. the song, IV.i.182
18   *spiny* thin, spare
19   *mettled* courageous, with a pun on the meaning 'amorous'
28   s.d. *plate* gold or silver ware
35   *clown* country bumpkin

204

3 GOSSIP

I would not care what clown my husband were too, so I had such
fine children.

2 GOSSIP

She's all fine children gossip.

3 GOSSIP

Ay, and see how fast they come.

1 PURITAN

Children are blessings, if they be got with zeal   40
By the brethren, as I have five at home.

SIR WALTER

The worst is past, I hope now gossip.

MISTRESS ALLWIT

So I hope too good sir.

ALLWIT

Why then so hope I too for company,
I have nothing to do else.   45

SIR WALTER

A poor remembrance lady,
To the love of the babe; I pray accept of it.

MISTRESS ALLWIT

O you are at too much charge sir.

2 GOSSIP

Look, look, what has he given her, what is't gossip?

3 GOSSIP

Now by my faith a fair high standing cup, and two great 'postle   50
spoons, one of them gilt.

1 PURITAN

Sure that was Judas then with the red beard.

2 PURITAN

I would not feed my daughter with that spoon for all the world,

---

38 *She's* She has
40 *zeal* religious zeal, but also sexual enthusiasm (cf. I.i.140)
50 *high standing cup* stemmed goblet
51 *'postle spoons* usually silver, the handles ending in the figure of an apostle, often given
    by sponsors at christenings
    gilt silver covered with gold
52 *Judas . . . red beard* Ancient belief; Judas wore a red beard in medieval religious drama.
    The supposition that red hair denoted lechery (cf. the Welsh Gentlewoman) as well
    as evil generally persisted in the theatre into the late nineteenth century, so that
    villains sometimes wore red wigs.

for fear of colouring her hair; red hair the brethren like not, it
consumes them much, 'tis not the sisters' colour.   55

Enter NURSE *with comfits and wine*

ALLWIT

Well said Nurse;
About, about with them amongst the gossips:
Now out comes all the tasseled handkerchers,
They are spread abroad between their knees already;
Now in goes the long fingers that are washed   60
Some thrice a day in urine – my wife uses it –
Now we shall have such pocketing;
See how they lurch at the lower end.

1 PURITAN

Come hither Nurse.

ALLWIT

Again! She has taken twice already.   65

1 PURITAN

I had forgot a sister's child that's sick.

ALLWIT

A pox, it seems your purity loves sweet things well that puts in
thrice together. Had this been all my cost now I had been beg-
gared. These women have no consciences at sweetmeats, where
e'er they come; see and they have not culled out all the long   70
plums too – they have left nothing here but short wriggle-tail
comfits, not worth mouthing; no mar'l I heard a citizen com-
plain once that his wife's belly only broke his back: mine had
been all in fitters seven years since, but for this worthy knight
that with a prop upholds my wife and me, and all my estate   75
buried in Bucklersbury.

55 *consumes* (a) burns (in anger) (b) consummates sexually
58 *tasseled* Handkerchiefs were fashionably large, ornamental and had tassels at the
    corners.
61 *urine* was used as a cosmetic lotion, including as a dentifrice
63 *lurch at the lower end* eat up the food as quickly as possible to prevent those at the
    other end of the room from getting much (or any); but with a possible bawdy pun
    on *lower end*
71 *plums* sugar plums
    wriggle-tail tiny
73 *belly only broke his back* (a) her greed alone made him overwork and (b) her lust left
    him exhausted
74 *fitters* fragments
76 *Bucklersbury* runs south from the corner of Cheapside and the Poultry to Walbrook;

206

MISTRESS ALLWIT

    Here Mistress Yellowhammer, and neighbours,
    To you all that have taken pains with me,
    All the good wives at once.

1 PURITAN

    I'll answer for them;   80
    They wish all health and strength,
    And that you may courageously go forward,
    To perform the like and many such,
    Like a true sister with motherly bearing.

ALLWIT

    Now the cups troll about to wet the gossips' whistles;   85
    It pours down i'faith: they never think of payment.

1 PURITAN

    Fill again Nurse.

ALLWIT

    Now bless thee, two at once; I'll stay no longer;
    It would kill me and if I paid for't.
    Will it please you to walk down and leave the women?   90

SIR WALTER

    With all my heart Jack.

ALLWIT

    Troth I cannot blame you.

SIR WALTER

    Sit you all merry ladies.

ALL GOSSIPS

    Thank your worship sir.

1 PURITAN

    Thank your worship sir.   95

ALLWIT

    A pox twice tipple ye, you are last and lowest.

                            Exit [ALLWIT *with* SIR WALTER]

1 PURITAN

    Bring hither that same cup Nurse, I would fain drive away this –
    hup! – antichristian grief.

    'on both the sides throughout [it was] possessed of grocers and apothecaries'
    (*Survey,* I, 260); Allwit is saying the catering for all the christenings of his wife's
    children over the years would have ruined him
  85 *troll* pass about
  93 *merry* (a) happy (b) tipsy
  96 *tipple* tumble

[NURSE *refills goblet, then exits*]

3 GOSSIP

See gossip and she lies not in like a countess;
Would I had such a husband for my daughter.   100

4 GOSSIP

Is not she toward marriage?

3 GOSSIP

O no sweet gossip.

4 GOSSIP

Why, she's nineteen?

3 GOSSIP

Ay that she was last Lammas,
But she has a fault gossip, a secret fault.   105

4 GOSSIP

A fault, what is't?

3 GOSSIP

I'll tell you when I have drunk.

4 GOSSIP

Wine can do that, I see, that friendship cannot.

3 GOSSIP

And now I'll tell you gossip – she's too free.

4 GOSSIP

Too free?   110

3 GOSSIP

O ay, she cannot lie dry in her bed.

4 GOSSIP

What, and nineteen?

3 GOSSIP

'Tis as I tell you gossip.

[*Enter* NURSE *and speaks to* MAUDLINE]

MAUDLINE

Speak with me Nurse? Who is't?

NURSE

A gentleman from Cambridge,   115

99   *countess* At the end of January 1613 it was reported that 'the Countess of Salisbury
     was brought abed of a daughter, and lies in very richly, for the hanging of her
     chamber, being white satin, embroidered with gold (or silver) and pearl is valued at
     fourteen thousand pounds' (John Chamberlain, *Letters*, ed. N. E. McLure (Phila-
     delphia, 1939), I, 415–16).
104 *Lammas* 1 August; harvest festival of the early English church

I think it be your son forsooth.

MAUDLINE
'Tis my son Tim i'faith,
Prithee call him up among the women,

[*Exit* NURSE]

'Twill embolden him well,
For he wants nothing but audacity;   120
Would the Welsh gentlewoman at home were here now.

LADY KIX
Is your son come forsooth?

MAUDLINE
Yes from the university forsooth.

LADY KIX
'Tis a great joy on ye.

MAUDLINE
There's a great marriage towards for him.   125

LADY KIX
A marriage?

MAUDLINE
Yes sure, a huge heir in Wales,
At least to nineteen mountains,
Besides her goods and cattle.

Enter TIM [*and* NURSE]

TIM
O, I'm betrayed.   *Exit*   130

MAUDLINE
What gone again? Run after him good Nurse;

[*Exit* NURSE]

He's so bashful, that's the spoil of youth;
In the university they're kept still to men,
And ne'er trained up to women's company.

LADY KIX
'Tis a great spoil of youth, indeed.   135

Enter NURSE *and* TIM

NURSE
Your mother will have it so.

---

129 *cattle* property (as in 'chattels', another form of the word), including in this case the
      Welshwoman's 'Two thousand runts' (IV.i.90)
133 *still* always

MAUDLINE

Why son, why Tim; what, must I rise and fetch you? For shame
son.

TIM

Mother you do intreat like a freshwoman;
'Tis against the laws of the university   140
For any that has answered under bachelor
To thrust 'mongst married wives.

MAUDLINE

Come we'll excuse you here.

TIM

Call up my tutor mother, and I care not.

MAUDLINE

What, is your tutor come? Have you brought him up?   145

TIM

I ha' not brought him up, he stands at door,
Negatur, there's logic to begin with you mother.

MAUDLINE

Run call the gentleman Nurse, he's my son's tutor;
Here eat some plums.

[Exit NURSE]

TIM

Come I from Cambridge, and offer me six plums?   150

MAUDLINE

Why how now Tim,
Will not your old tricks yet be left?

TIM

Served like a child,
When I have answered under bachelor?

MAUDLINE

You'll never lin till I make your tutor whip you; you know   155

---

139   *freshwoman* Tim's nonce word from 'freshman', a first-year university student.
      Cambridge University did not admit women to full membership, awarding them
      degrees, until 1947, though the first women's college, Girton, had been founded in
      1869.

141   *answered under bachelor* satisfied the requirements for a Bachelor's degree

147   *Negatur* 'It is denied'; standard Latin phrase in academic disputation

155   *lin* cease

      whip To be whipped as a disciplinary measure was a great disgrace.

how I served you once at the free school in Paul's church-
yard?

TIM

O monstrous absurdity!
Ne'er was the like in Cambridge since my time;
Life, whip a bachelor? You'd be laughed at soundly;   160
Let not my tutor hear you,
'Twould be a jest through the whole university;
No more words mother.

Enter TUTOR

MAUDLINE

Is this your tutor Tim?

TUTOR

Yes surely lady, I am the man that brought him in league with   165
logic, and read the Dunces to him.

TIM

That did he mother, but now I have 'em all in my own pate, and
can as well read 'em to others.

TUTOR

That can he mistress, for they flow naturally from him.

MAUDLINE

I'm the more beholding to your pains sir.   170

TUTOR

Non ideo sane.

MAUDLINE   True, he was an idiot indeed
When he went out of London, but now he's well mended;
Did you receive the two goose pies I sent you?

TUTOR

And eat them heartily, thanks to your worship.

MAUDLINE

'Tis my son Tim, I pray bid him welcome gentlewomen.   175

156   *free school* St Paul's school was rebuilt and largely endowed in 1512 by John Colet,
       Dean of Paul's, for 153 poor scholars; William Lily was the first high master, but
       Tim may have been there under the illustrious Richard Mulcaster (1596–1608).
166   *Dunces* (a) writings of Duns Scotus (1265?–1308?) and supporters of his theological
       views, which were attacked by the humanists and reformers of the 16th century (b)
       fools
169   *naturally* (a) spontaneously (b) foolishly
171   *Non ideo sane* 'Not indeed on that account'
173   *goose pies* made with a jointed goose, spices, ale, fried onions and wine, baked in
       pastry; here the word accentuates Tim's foolishness

TIM

'Tim'? Hark you, 'Timothius' mother, 'Timothius'!

MAUDLINE

How, shall I deny your name? 'Timothius', quoth he?
Faith there's a name, 'tis my son Tim forsooth.

LADY KIX

You're welcome Master Tim.   *Kiss*

TIM

O this is horrible, she wets as she kisses;   180
Your handkercher sweet tutor, to wipe them off, as fast as they
come on.

2 GOSSIP

Welcome from Cambridge.   *Kiss*

TIM

This is intolerable! This woman has a villainous sweet breath,
did she not stink of comfits; help me sweet tutor, or I shall rub   185
my lips off.

TUTOR

I'll go kiss the lower end the whilst.

TIM

Perhaps that's the sweeter, and we shall dispatch the sooner.

1 PURITAN

Let me come next. Welcome from the wellspring of discipline,
that waters all the brethren.   *Reels and falls*   190

TIM

Hoist, I beseech thee.

3 GOSSIP

O bless the woman – Mistress Underman!

1 PURITAN

'Tis but the common affliction of the faithful,
We must embrace our falls.

TIM

I'm glad I 'scaped it, it was some rotten kiss sure,   195

---

176   *Timothius* The correct Latin is *Timotheus* = 'Honouring God'.
179   s.d. *Kiss* The English were at this time notorious for the freedom with which they
       kissed in greeting.
185   *comfits* 'kissing-comfits' were intended to sweeten the breath
189–90 *Welcome . . . brethren* Cambridge was the intellectual centre of Puritanism and its
       closeness to the Continent made it more accessible than Oxford to Calvinist
       influence.
194   *embrace our falls* An opportunistic and over-literal interpretation of Calvin's doctrine
       that humankind's fallen state must be humbly accepted.

It dropped down before it came at me.

Enter ALLWIT *and* DAVY

ALLWIT

Here's a noise! Not parted yet?
Hyda, a looking glass; they have drunk so hard in plate,
That some of them had need of other vessels.
Yonder's the bravest show.   200

ALL GOSSIPS

Where? Where sir?

ALLWIT

Come along presently by the Pissing-conduit,
With two brave drums and a standard bearer.

ALL GOSSIPS

O brave.

TIM

Come tutor.   205

Ex[eunt TIM *and* TUTOR]

ALL GOSSIPS

Farewell sweet gossip.

Ex[eunt GOSSIPS]

MISTRESS ALLWIT

I thank you all for your pains.

1 PURITAN

Feed and grow strong.   *Exit*

ALLWIT

You had more need to sleep than eat;

---

197   *parted* departed
198   *looking glass* (a) Mistress Underman is still on the floor and the sarcastic Allwit calls
       for a looking glass to see if she is still breathing; cf. *King Lear* V.iii.262–5 (b) a
       chamber pot
200   *show* procession
202   *Pissing-conduit* Possibly the conduit at the western end of Cheapside, near Paul's
       Gate and Bladder Street, named here from the slenderness of its stream of water.
       The name could be both generic and specific. The 'little Conduit, called the pissing
       Conduit' by Stow (I, 183) was by the Stocks Market, beyond Poultry, and so not in
       Cheapside itself, though Parker and Barber both prefer this to the Paul's Gate
       conduit. See E. H. Sugden, A *Topographical Dictionary to the Works of Shakespeare
       and his Fellow Dramatists* (Manchester, 1925), p. 127.
203   *two . . . drums and a standard hearer* The phallic symbolism, which so excites the
       gossips, is obvious.

Go take a nap with some of the brethren, go,　　　　　　210
And rise up a well edified, boldified sister;
O here's a day of toil well passed o'er,
Able to make a citizen hare-mad;
How hot they have made the room with their thick bums;
Dost not feel it Davy?　　　　　　215

DAVY

Monstrous strong sir.

ALLWIT

What's here under the stools?

DAVY

Nothing but wet sir, some wine spilt here belike.

ALLWIT

Is't no worse thinkst thou?
Fair needlework stools cost nothing with them Davy.　　　　　　220

DAVY

[*Aside*] Nor you neither i'faith.

ALLWIT

Look how they have laid them,
E'en as they lie themselves, with their heels up;
How they have shuffled up the rushes too Davy,
With their short figging little shittle-cork heels;　　　　　　225
These women can let nothing stand as they find it;
But what's the secret thou'st about to tell me
My honest Davy?

DAVY

If you should disclose it sir –

ALLWIT

Life, rip my belly up to the throat then Davy.　　　　　　230

210　*nap* Anabaptists held that a man and a woman could lie together without moral taint provided they were asleep.
213　*hare-mad* Hares grow wilder in the breeding season, around March.
214　*bums* (a) padded rolls worn on the hips beneath the skirt (b) backsides
217　*stools* Padded furniture was becoming fashionable, large sums being spent on embroidered coverings.
224　*rushes* An indication that rushes were strewn on the public theatre stage, as well as on the floors of houses.
225　*figging* fucking, but a generally derisive term used here in a line of concentrated bawdiness
　　short . . . heels 'short-heeled' = wanton; cf. *Revenger's Tragedy* I.ii.184, 'Their tongues as short and nimble as their heels'
　　shittle-cork wedge heels (and soles) of cork, fashionable 1595–1620; 'shittle' = shuttle as in 'shuttle-cock' (which was slang for 'whore')　　230　*Life* 'God's life'

DAVY

My master's upon marriage.

ALLWIT

Marriage Davy? Send me to hanging rather.

DAVY

[*Aside*] I have stung him.

ALLWIT

When, where? What is she Davy?

DAVY

E'en the same was gossip, and gave the spoon.   235

ALLWIT

I have no time to stay, nor scarce can speak,

I'll stop those wheels, or all the work will break.   *Exit*

DAVY

I knew 'twould prick. Thus do I fashion still

All mine own ends by him and his rank toil;

'Tis my desire to keep him still from marriage;   240

Being his poor nearest kinsman, I may fare

The better at his death; there my hopes build

Since my Lady Kix is dry, and hath no child.   *Exit*

[ACT III, SCENE iii]

Enter both the TOUCHWOODS

TOUCHWOOD JUNIOR

Y'are in the happiest way to enrich yourself,

And pleasure me brother, as man's feet can tread in,

For though she be locked up, her vow is fixed only to me;

Then time shall never grieve me, for by that vow,

E'en absent I enjoy her, assuredly confirmed that none   5

Else shall, which will make tedious years seem gameful

236–7 *speak . . . break* A common rhyme ('ea' = 'a' sound in 'bake'); cf. Thomas Morley's
lyric, 'Now is the month of Maying'.

242–3 *build . . . child* Shakespeare rhymes 'child . . . spilled', *Romeo and Juliet* III.i.146–7.

243 *dry* barren

5 *I* ed. (Q omits)

6 *gameful* joyful

To me. In the mean space lose you no time sweet brother;
You have the means to strike at this knight's fortunes
And lay him level with his bankrupt merit;
Get but his wife with child, perch at tree top,   10
And shake the golden fruit into her lap.
About it before she weep herself to a dry ground,
And whine out all her goodness.

TOUCHWOOD SENIOR
Prithee cease, I find a too much aptness in my blood
For such a business without provocation;   15
You might'well spared this banquet of eringoes,
Artichokes, potatoes, and your buttered crab;
They were fitter kept for your own wedding dinner.

TOUCHWOOD JUNIOR
Nay and you'll follow my suit, and save my purse too,
Fortune dotes on me; he's in happy case   20
Finds such an honest friend i'the common place.

TOUCHWOOD SENIOR
Life what makes thee so merry? Thou hast no cause
That I could hear of lately since thy crosses,
Unless there be news come, with new additions.

TOUCHWOOD JUNIOR
Why there thou hast it right: 25
I look for her this evening brother.

TOUCHWOOD SENIOR
How's that, look for her?

TOUCHWOOD JUNIOR
I will deliver you of the wonder straight brother:
By the firm secrecy and kind assistance
Of a good wench i'the house, who, made of pity,   30
Weighing the case her own, she's led through gutters,

10–11   *perch . . . lap* Plucking the golden apples borne by a tree in the Garden of the Hesperides, the daughters of Hesperus, was a common sexual metaphor; here the image is of a harvester shaking the fruit down while up the tree. Cf. *The Changeling* III.ii.168–9.

12   *weep . . . ground* before she loses her fertility

16   *might'well spared* might as well have spared

16–17   *eringoes . . . crab* All thought to be aphrodisiacs; 'eringo' was the candied fruit of sea holly, 'potato' was probably the sweet potato or yam. Cf. John Marston, *The Scourge of Villainy*, Satire III, ll. 67–74.

21   *friend i'the common place* a friend at the right time, 'a friend at court'; literally, the court of common pleas at Westminster

31   *gutters* roof gutters between houses. See IV.i.281.

Strange hidden ways, which none but love could find,
Or ha' the heart to venture; I expect her
Where you would little think.

TOUCHWOOD SENIOR   I care not where,
So she be safe, and yours.

TOUCHWOOD JUNIOR   Hope tells me so,   35
But from your love and time my peace must grow.   *Exit*

TOUCHWOOD SENIOR
You know the worst then brother. Now to my Kix,
The barren he and she; they're i'the next room,
But to say which of their two humours hold them
Now at this instant, I cannot say truly.   40

SIR OLIVER
Thou liest barrenness.   KIX *to his* LADY *within*

TOUCHWOOD SENIOR
O is't that time of day? Give you joy of your tongue,
There's nothing else good in you; this their life
The whole day from eyes open to eyes shut,
Kissing or scolding, and then must be made friends,   45
Then rail the second part of the first fit out,
And then be pleased again, no man knows which way,
Fall out like giants, and fall in like children –
Their fruit can witness as much.

    Enter SIR OLIVER KIX *and his* LADY

SIR OLIVER
'Tis thy fault.   50

LADY KIX
Mine, drouth and coldness?

SIR OLIVER
Thine, 'tis thou art barren.

LADY KIX
I barren! O life that I durst but speak now
In mine own justice, in mine own right – I barren!
'Twas otherways with me when I was at court;   55

37 *worst* i.e. 'Things can only get better from now on.'
39 *humours* moods, dispositions
46 *fit* (a) struggle (b) section of song or poem
48 *fall in* (a) make up after a quarrel (b) have sex
51 *drouth* drought
55 *court* Another reference to loose living in high places; cf. V. C. Gildersleeve, *Government Regulation of Elizabethan Drama* (1908), p. 109.

I was ne'er called so till I was married.

SIR OLIVER
I'll be divorced.

LADY KIX   Be hanged! I need not wish it,
That will come too soon to thee: I may say,
'Marriage and hanging goes by destiny',
For all the goodness I can find in't yet.   60

SIR OLIVER
I'll give up house, and keep some fruitful whore,
Like an old bachelor in a tradesman's chamber;
She and her children shall have all.

LADY KIX
Where be they?

TOUCHWOOD SENIOR
[*Coming forward*] Pray cease;   65
When there are friendlier courses took for you
To get and multiply within your house,
At your own proper costs in spite of censure,
Methinks an honest peace might be established.

SIR OLIVER
What, with her? Never!   70

TOUCHWOOD SENIOR
Sweet sir.

SIR OLIVER
You work all in vain.

LADY KIX
Then he doth all like thee.

TOUCHWOOD SENIOR
Let me intreat sir.

SIR OLIVER
Singleness confound her,   75
I took her with one smock.

LADY KIX
But indeed you came not so single,
When you came from shipboard.

57   *divorced* Sir Oliver would have found it difficult, as legislation was necessary for
     divorce; ecclesiastical courts could grant a separation for adultery or cruelty or
     annulment for an illegally contracted marriage but remarriage was forbidden.
59   *Marriage . . . destiny* proverbial
68   *At . . . censure* 'At your own cost despite any social criticism'
76   *one smock* i.e. very little property
77   *single* celibate; possibly 'lousy'

218

SIR OLIVER
  Heart she bit sore there;
  Prithee make's friends.   80
TOUCHWOOD SENIOR
  Is't come to that? The peal begins to cease.
SIR OLIVER
  I'll sell all at an outcry.
LADY KIX
  Do thy worst, slave!
  Good sweet sir, bring us into love again.
TOUCHWOOD SENIOR
  Some would think this impossible to compass;   85
  Pray let this storm fly over.
SIR OLIVER
  Good sir pardon me, I'm master of this house,
  Which I'll sell presently; I'll clap up bills this evening.
TOUCHWOOD SENIOR
  Lady, friends – come?
LADY KIX
  If e'er ye loved woman, talk not on't sir;   90
  What, friends with him? Good faith do you think I'm mad?
  With one that's scarce the hinder quarter of a man?
SIR OLIVER
  Thou art nothing of a woman.
LADY KIX
  Would I were less than nothing.   *Weeps*
SIR OLIVER
  Nay prithee what dost mean?   95
LADY KIX
  I cannot please you.
SIR OLIVER
  I'faith thou art a good soul, he lies that says it;
  Buss, buss, pretty rogue.
LADY KIX
  You care not for me.
TOUCHWOOD SENIOR
  Can any man tell now which way they came in?   100
  By this light I'll be hanged then.

82 *outcry* auction, proclaimed by the common crier
88 *presently* at once
    clap up bills put up posters

SIR OLIVER
　Is the drink come?

TOUCHWOOD SENIOR
　Here's a little vial of almond-milk　　　　　　　　　*Aside*
　That stood me in some three pence.

SIR OLIVER
　I hope to see thee, wench, within these few years,　　　　105
　Circled with children, pranking up a girl,
　And putting jewels in their little ears;
　Fine sport i'faith.

LADY KIX
　Ay had you been aught, husband,
　It had been done ere this time.　　　　　　　　　　　110

SIR OLIVER
　Had I been aught? Hang thee, hadst thou been aught;
　But a cross thing I ever found thee.

LADY KIX
　Thou art a grub to say so.

SIR OLIVER
　A pox on thee.

TOUCHWOOD SENIOR
　By this light they are out again at the same door,　　　115
　And no man can tell which way;
　Come, here's your drink sir.

SIR OLIVER
　I will not take it now sir,
　And I were sure to get three boys ere midnight.

LADY KIX
　Why there thou show'st now of what breed thou com'st;　120
　To hinder generation! O thou villain,
　That knows how crookedly the world goes with us
　For want of heirs, yet put by all good fortune.

SIR OLIVER
　Hang, strumpet, I will take it now in spite.

103　*almond-milk* made from sweet almonds, pounded, with water, stirred into thick
　　　barley water, sweetened and boiled; used in milk puddings
104　*stood me in* cost me
106　*pranking up* dressing smartly
107　*their* Dyce and Bullen emend to 'her', but both sexes wore earrings until about 1660.
109　*aught* anything

TOUCHWOOD SENIOR
  Then you must ride upon't five hours.   125
SIR OLIVER
  I mean so. Within there?

                    Enter a SERVANT

SERVANT
  Sir?
SIR OLIVER
  Saddle the white mare,
                                      [*Exit* SERVANT]
  I'll take a whore along, and ride to Ware.
LADY KIX
  Ride to the devil.   130
SIR OLIVER
  I'll plague you every way;
  Look ye, do you see, 'tis gone.   *Drinks*
LADY KIX
  A pox go with it.
SIR OLIVER
  Ay, curse and spare not now.
TOUCHWOOD SENIOR
  Stir up and down sir, you must not stand.   135
SIR OLIVER
  Nay I'm not given to standing.
TOUCHWOOD SENIOR
  So much the better sir for the ———
SIR OLIVER
  I never could stand long in one place yet,
  I learnt it of my father, ever figient;
  How if I crossed this sir?   *Capers*   140
TOUCHWOOD SENIOR
  O passing good sir, and would show well a-horseback; when you

---

129   *Ware* twenty miles north of London, like Brentford a trysting place for lovers legal
       and illicit; the Saracen's Head inn contained the Great Bed of Ware, 10 ft 9 in (3.3 m)
       square, now in the Victoria and Albert Museum, London
136   *standing* (a) being still (b) keeping an erection
137   The lacuna here and others elsewhere in the play may indicate that the actor is to *ad
       lib*, or whisper to his listener; alternatively, that the Master of the Revels may have
       deleted a perceived obscenity.
139   *figient* restless, fidgety
140   *crossed* jumped across a table or chair

come to your inn, if you leapt over a joint-stool or two 'twere
not amiss – although you brake your neck sir.   *Aside*

SIR OLIVER

What say you to a table thus high sir?

TOUCHWOOD SENIOR

Nothing better sir, if it be furnished with good victuals.   145
You remember how the bargain runs about this business?

SIR OLIVER

Or else I had a bad head: you must receive sir four hundred
pounds of me at four several payments: one hundred pound
now in hand.

TOUCHWOOD SENIOR

Right, that I have sir.   150

SIR OLIVER

Another hundred when my wife is quick: the third when she's
brought to bed: and the last hundred when the child cries; for if
it should be stillborn, it doth no good sir.

TOUCHWOOD SENIOR

All this is even still; a little faster sir.

SIR OLIVER

Not a whit sir,   155
I'm in an excellent pace for any physic.

Enter a SERVANT

SERVANT

Your white mare's ready.

SIR OLIVER

I shall up presently: one kiss, and farewell.

LADY KIX

Thou shalt have two love.

SIR OLIVER

Expect me about three.   160

Exit [*with* SERVANT]

142   *joint-stool* solidly constructed of pieces fitted together, often carved, about 2 ft (60 cm)
         high; very common. Stool-leaping was a fashionable game.
147   *bad head* ironic reference to cuckold's horns
151   *wife* ed. (wifes Q)
         quick pregnant
154   *even* exact
         faster Sir Oliver has been capering all this while.
156   *physic* medicine

LADY KIX

    With all my heart sweet.

TOUCHWOOD SENIOR

    By this light they have forgot their anger since,
    And are as far in again as e'er they were;
    Which way the devil came they? Heart I saw 'em not,
    Their ways are beyond finding out. Come sweet lady.   165

LADY KIX

    How must I take mine sir?

TOUCHWOOD SENIOR

    Clean contrary; yours must be taken lying.

LADY KIX

    Abed sir?

TOUCHWOOD SENIOR

    Abed, or where you will for your own ease;
    Your coach will serve.   170

LADY KIX

    The physic must needs please.

Ex[*eunt*]

---

162   *since* now
170   *coach* First introduced in 1564, coaches were popular by the early 17th century and
       Dekker remarks, 'close caroaches were made running bawdy-houses' (*The Owl's*
       Almanac (1618), p. 8).

ACT IV, [SCENE i]

Enter TIM *and* TUTOR

TIM

   Negatur argumentum, tutor.

TUTOR

   Probo tibi, pupil, *stultus non est animal rationale.*

TIM

   Falleris sane.

TUTOR

   Quæso ut taceas, probo tibi –

TIM

   Quomodo probas domine?   5

TUTOR

   Stultus non habet rationem, ergo non est animal rationale.

TIM

   Sic argumentaris domine, stultus non habet rationem, ergo non est
   animal rationale, negatur argutmentum again tutor.

TUTOR

   Argutmentum iterum probo tibi domine, qui non participat de
   ratione nullo modo potest vocari rationalibus, but *stultus non*   10
   participat de ratione, ergo stultus nullo modo potest dicere.

TIM

   Participat.

TUTOR

   Sic disputus, qui participat quomodo participat?

TIM

   Ut homo, probabo tibi in syllogismo.

TUTOR

   Hunc proba.   15

1–17   *Tim.* Your argument is denied, tutor. *Tut.* I am proving to you, pupil, that a fool is
      not a rational animal. *Tim.* Indeed you will be wrong. *Tut.* I ask you to be silent, I
      am showing you. *Tim.* How will you prove it, master? *Tut.* A fool has no reason,
      therefore he is not a rational animal. *Tim.* Thus you argue, master, a fool does not
      have reason, therefore he is not a reasonable animal; your argument is denied again,
      tutor. *Tut.* I will demonstrate the argument to you again, sir: he who doesn't partake
      of reason can in no way be called rational, but a fool does not partake of reason,
      therefore a fool can in no way be called rational. *Tim.* He does partake. *Tut.* So you
      hold; how does the partaker partake? *Tim.* As a man; I will prove it to you in a
      syllogism. *Tut.* Prove it. *Tim.* I prove it thus, master: a fool is a man just as you and
      I are, man is a rational animal, just so a fool is a rational animal.

TIM

Sic probo domine, stultus est homo sicut tu et ego sum, homo est
animal rationale, sicut stultus est animal rationale.

Enter MAUDLINE

MAUDLINE

Here's nothing but disputing all the day long with 'em.

TUTOR

Sic disputus, stultus est homo sicut tu et ego sum homo est animal
rationale, sicut stultus est animal rationale.   20

MAUDLINE

Your reasons are both good what e'er they be;
Pray give them o'er, faith you'll tire yourselves,
What's the matter between you?

TIM

Nothing but reasoning about a fool, mother.

MAUDLINE

About a fool, son? Alas what need you trouble your heads about   25
that, none of us all but knows what a fool is.

TIM

Why what's a fool, mother?
I come to you now.

MAUDLINE

Why one that's married before he has wit.

TIM

'Tis pretty i'faith, and well guessed of a woman never brought up   30
at the university: but bring forth what fool you will mother, I'll
prove him to be as reasonable a creature as myself or my tutor
here.

MAUDLINE

Fie 'tis impossible.

TUTOR

Nay he shall do't forsooth.   35

TIM

'Tis the easiest thing to prove a fool by logic,
By logic I'll prove anything.

11   *de* (*ac* Folger Q)
19–20 *Tut.* So you contend: a fool is a man just as you and I are, man is a rational animal,
       just as a fool is a rational animal.
28   *I come to you* a term in academic disputation for 'I put the question to you'
29   *wit* (a) intelligence (b) penis
31   *bring forth* ironic, as Maudline brought forth Tim at his birth

225

MAUDLINE

What thou wilt not?

TIM

I'll prove a whore to be an honest woman.

MAUDLINE

Nay by my faith, she must prove that herself, or logic will never   40
do't.

TIM

'Twill do't I tell you.

MAUDLINE

Some in this street would give a thousand pounds that you could
prove their wives so.

TIM

Faith I can, and all their daughters too, though they had three   45
bastards. When comes your tailor hither?

MAUDLINE

Why, what of him?

TIM

By logic I'll prove him to be a man,
Let him come when he will.

MAUDLINE

How hard at first was learning to him? Truly sir I thought he   50
would never a took the Latin tongue. How many Accidences do
you think he wore out ere he came to his Grammar?

TUTOR

Some three or four?

MAUDLINE

Believe me sir, some four and thirty.

TIM

Pish, I made haberdines of 'em in church porches.   55

---

46   *tailor* Tailors, especially women's, were considered unmanly; cf. nursery rhyme, 'Four
and twenty tailors / Went to kill a snail', and note to II.ii.14.

51   *Accidences* books of the rudiments of Latin grammar; Tim was, not surprisingly,
a slow learner it seems

55   *haberdines* salt dried codfish. Dyce suggests, 'Perhaps Tim alludes to some childish
sport'. Frost suggests a game where cut-out fish shapes are blown over a line on the
floor; Parker cites a Christmas game, 'Selling of fish', and 'the foolscap decorated with
paper emblems of red herring worn by Jack-of-Lent'. As 'cod' = scrotum, however,
this is the first of a series of *doubles entendres* concluded when Maudline invites the
tutor to 'withdraw a little into my husband's chamber'.

MAUDLINE

He was eight years in his Grammar, and stuck horribly at a foolish place there called *as in presenti.*

TIM

Pox I have it here now.

MAUDLINE

He so shamed me once before an honest gentleman that knew me when I was a maid.   60

TIM

These women must have all out.

MAUDLINE

'*Quid est grammatica?*' Says the gentleman to him (I shall remember by a sweet, sweet token), but nothing could he answer.

TUTOR

How now pupil, ha, *quid est grammatica?*   65

TIM

Grammatica? Ha, ha, ha!

MAUDLINE

Nay do not laugh son, but let me hear you say it now: there was one word went so prettily off the gentleman's tongue, I shall remember it the longest day of my life

TUTOR

Come, *quid est grammatica?*   70

TIM

Are you not ashamed tutor? *Grammatica?* Why, *recte scribendi atque loquendi ars*, sir-reverence of my mother.

MAUDLINE

That was it i'faith: why now son I see you are a deep scholar; and master tutor a word I pray, let us withdraw a little into my husband's chamber; I'll send in the North Wales gentlewoman to him,   75
she looks for wooing: I'll put together both, and lock the door.

---

57   *as in presenti* Introductory phrase in the part of Lily and Colet's *A Short Introduction to Grammar* (1549) dealing with inflections of verbs; several writers make puns on it, e.g. Marston, *What You Will,* II.i. Here the pun is on both 'arse' (see l. 72) and 'cunt' (see l. 75).

61   *must have all out* must tell all, but with a sexual suggestion

62   *Quid est grammatica?* 'What is grammar?'

71–2 'The art of speaking and writing correctly'; (see J. D. Reeves, 'Middleton and Lily's Grammar', *N&Q,* 197 (1952), 75–6).

72   *sir-reverence* (i) with apologies to (ii) excrement (continuing the pun on *ars*)

76   *lock the door* Cf. Allwit's 'pin the door' I.ii.30.

TUTOR

    I give great approbation to your conclusion.

                             Exit [*with* MAUDLINE]

TIM

    I mar'l what this gentlewoman should be

    That I should have in marriage, she's a stranger to me:

    I wonder what my parents mean i'faith,   80

    To match me with a stranger so:

    A maid that's neither kiff nor kin to me:

    Life, do they think I have no more care of my body

    Than to lie with one that I ne'er knew,

    A mere stranger,   85

    One that ne'er went to school with me neither,

    Nor ever playfellows together?

    They're mightily o'erseen in't methinks;

    They say she has mountains to her marriage,

    She's full of cattle, some two thousand runts;   90

    Now what the meaning of these runts should be,

    My tutor cannot tell me;

    I have looked in Rider's Dictionary for the letter R,

    And there I can hear no tidings of these runts neither;

    Unless they should be Rumford hogs,   95

    I know them not,

                Enter WELSH GENTLEWOMAN

    And here she comes.

    If I know what to say to her now

    In the way of marriage, I'm no graduate;

    Methinks i'faith 'tis boldly done of her   100

    To come into my chamber being but a stranger;

    She shall not say I'm so proud yet, but I'll speak to her:

    Marry as I will order it,

    She shall take no hold of my words I'll warrant her;

    She looks and makes a curtsey –   105

---

79   *stranger* foreigner

82   *kiff* kith, neighbour (as in 'kith and kin')

88   *o'erseen* mistaken

90   *runts* small breed of Welsh and Highland cattle

93   *Rider's Dictionary* English-Latin and Latin-English dictionary compiled by the Bishop of Killaloe, John Rider, first published at Oxford in 1589.

95   *Rumford* (Romford) in Essex 12 miles (20 km) north-east of London, held hog markets on Tuesdays and grain and cattle markets on Wednesdays

Salve tu quoque puella pulcherrima,
Quid vis nescio nec sane curo –
Tully's own phrase to a heart.

WELSH GENTLEWOMAN

    I know not what he means;
    A suitor quotha?   110
    I hold my life he understands no English.

TIM

    Fertur me hercule tu virgo,
    Wallia ut opibus abundis maximis.

WELSH GENTLEWOMAN

    What's this *fertur* and *abundundis*?
    He mocks me sure, and calls me a bundle of farts.   115

TIM

    I have no Latin word now for their runts; I'll make some shift or
    other: *Iterum dico opibus abundat maximis montibus et fontibus*
    et ut ita dicam rontibus, attamen vero homanculus ego sum natura
    simule arte bachalarius lecto profecto non parata.

WELSH GENTLEWOMAN

    This is most strange; may be he can speak Welsh –   120
    Avedera whee comrage, derdue cog foginis?

TIM

    Cog foggin? I scorn to cog with her, I'll tell her so too, in a word
    near her own language: *Ego non cogo.*

WELSH GENTLEWOMAN

    Rhegosin a whiggin harle ron corid ambre.

106–7   'Hail to you too, most beautiful maiden; what you want I don't know and certainly
       don't care.'
  108   *Tully's* Cicero's
  110   *quotha?* said he? indeed?
112–13   'It's said, by Hercules, young lady, that Wales has the greatest abundance of riches.'
       Fertur prounced 'Fartur'
117–19   'Again I say that you abound in resources, in the greatest mountains and fountains
       and, as I could say, runts; however I am truly but a little chap by nature and by art
       a bachelor, not actually ready for bed'. The Latin is by no means clear. The reference to
       Tim's size indicates that the part was probably played by one of the Queen's Revels boys.
  121   'Can you speak Welsh, for God's sake are you pretending with me?' A phonetic
       rendering for '*A fedrwch chwi Cymraeg, er Duw cog fo gennyf?*' (The final 's' may be
       due to a misreading of the copytext.)
  122   *Cog* Probably a pun on 'cog' = lie (deceive).
  123   'I won't come together [with you].'
  124   The first part could mean 'Some cheese and whey after a walk', a phonetic rendering
       of '*Rhyn gosyn a chwig gin ar ôl bod yn cerdedd am dro*'. The Welsh were popularly
       thought to delight in cheese.

TIM

By my faith she's a good scholar, I see that already;   125
She has the tongues plain, I hold my life she has travelled;
What will folks say? 'There goes the learned couple'!
Faith if the truth were known, she hath proceeded.

Enter MAUDLINE

MAUDLINE

How now, how speeds your business?

TIM

I'm glad my mother's come to part us.   130

MAUDLINE

How do you agree forsooth?

WELSH GENTLEWOMAN

As well as e'er we did before we met.

MAUDLINE

How's that?

WELSH GENTLEWOMAN

You put me to a man I understand not;
Your son's no English man methinks.   135

MAUDLINE

No English man! Bless my boy,
And born i'the heart of London?

WELSH GENTLEWOMAN

I ha' been long enough in the chamber with him,
And I find neither Welsh nor English in him.

MAUDLINE

Why Tim, how have you used the gentlewoman?   140

TIM

As well as a man might do, mother, in modest Latin.

MAUDLINE

Latin, fool?

TIM

And she recoiled in Hebrew.

MAUDLINE

In Hebrew, fool? 'Tis Welsh.

TIM

All comes to one, mother.   145

128   *proceeded* (a) graduated (b) gone past virginity
143   *recoiled* answered

MAUDLINE
> She can speak English too.

TIM
> Who told me so much?
> Heart, and she can speak English, I'll clap to her,
> I thought you'd marry me to a stranger.

MAUDLINE
> You must forgive him, he's so inured to Latin,   150
> He and his tutor, that he hath quite forgot
> To use the Protestant tongue.

WELSH GENTLEWOMAN
> 'Tis quickly pardoned forsooth.

MAUDLINE
> Tim make amends and kiss her,
> He makes towards you forsooth.   155

TIM
> O delicious, one may discover her country by her kissing. 'Tis a
> true saying, there's nothing tastes so sweet as your Welsh mutton.
> It was reported you could sing.

MAUDLINE
> O rarely Tim, the sweetest British songs.

TIM
> And 'tis my mind, I swear, before I marry   160
> I would see all my wife's good parts at once,
> To view how rich I were.

MAUDLINE
> Thou shalt hear sweet music Tim.
> Pray, forsooth.   *Music and Welsh song*

[WELSH GENTLEWOMAN *sings*]
>   *The Song*
>   Cupid is Venus' only joy,   165
>   But he is a wanton boy,
>   A very, very wanton boy,
>   He shoots at ladies' naked breasts,

---

148   *clap* clasp, stick closely to, with a hidden irony as 'clap' also = pox
152   *Protestant tongue* English
156   *country* a familiar pun (cf. *Hamlet*, III.ii.121)
157   *Welsh mutton* was famous, but Tim's speech is all unconscious *double entendre*: cf.
       I.i.132
158   *sing* used again with a sexual sense; cf. II.i.52
165–90 The first nine lines of this song, with two additional lines, occur in Middleton's *More
       Dissemblers Besides Women*, I.iv.

He is the cause of most men's crests,
I mean upon the forehead,   170
Invisible but horrid;
'Twas he first taught upon the way
To keep a lady's lips in play.

Why should not Venus chide her son,
For the pranks that he hath done,   175
The wanton pranks that he hath done?
He shoots his fiery darts so thick,
They hurt poor ladies to the quick,
Ah me, with cruel wounding;
His darts are so confounding,   180
That life and sense would soon decay,
But that he keeps their lips in play.

Can there be any part of bliss,
In a quickly fleeting kiss,
A quickly fleeting kiss?   185
To one's pleasure, leisures are but waste,
The slowest kiss makes too much haste,
And lose it ere we find it,
The pleasing sport they only know,
That close above and close below.   190

TIM
I would not change my wife for a kingdom;
I can do somewhat too in my own lodging.

Enter YELLOWHAMMER *and* ALLWIT

YELLOWHAMMER
Why well said Tim, the bells go merrily,
I love such peals a-life; wife lead them in a while,
Here's a strange gentleman desires private conference.   195
[*Exeunt* MAUDLINE, TIM *and* WELSH GENTLEWOMAN]

---

169   *crests* cuckolds' horns
178   *quick* tenderest part, but with a bawdy implication
182   *lips* those above and below
189   Frost adds a line here to equalize the stanzas.
192   *lodging* 'on my own account', but with a bawdy pun; Bullen unnecessarily adds s.d.
       Sings.
194   *a-life* as my life; extremely

You're welcome sir, the more for your name's sake.
Good Master Yellowhammer, I love my name well;
And which o'the Yellowhammers take you descent from,
If I may be so bold with you, which, I pray?

ALLWIT

The Yellowhammers in Oxfordshire,   200
Near Abbington.

YELLOWHAMMER

And those are the best Yellowhammers, and truest bred: I came
from thence myself, though now a citizen: I'll be bold with you:
you are most welcome.

ALLWIT

I hope the zeal I bring with me shall deserve it.   205

YELLOWHAMMER

I hope no less; what is your will sir?

ALLWIT

I understand by rumours, you have a daughter,
Which my bold love shall henceforth title 'cousin'.

YELLOWHAMMER

I thank you for her sir.

ALLWIT

I heard of her virtues, and other confirmed graces.   210

YELLOWHAMMER

A plaguy girl sir.

ALLWIT

Fame sets her out with richer ornaments
Than you are pleased to boast of; 'tis done modestly.
I hear she's towards marriage.

YELLOWHAMMER

You hear truth sir.   215

ALLWIT

And with a knight in town, Sir Walter Whorehound.

YELLOWHAMMER

The very same sir.

ALLWIT

I am the sorrier for't.

YELLOWHAMMER

The sorrier? Why cousin?

---

201   *Abbington* (Abingdon), in Berkshire, on the Thames 56 miles (90 km) north-west of
       London; six miles (10 km) south of Oxford

ALLWIT

'Tis not too far past is't? It may be yet recalled?   220

YELLOWHAMMER

Recalled, why good sir?

ALLWIT

Resolve me in that point, ye shall hear from me.

YELLOWHAMMER

There's no contract passed.

ALLWIT

I am very joyful sir.

YELLOWHAMMER

But he's the man must bed her.   225

ALLWIT

By no means coz, she's quite undone then,

And you'll curse the time that e'er you made the match;

He's an arrant whoremaster, consumes his time and state,

—— whom in my knowledge he hath kept this seven years,

Nay coz, another man's wife too.   230

YELLOWHAMMER

O abominable!

ALLWIT

Maintains the whole house, apparels the husband,

Pays servants' wages, not so much, but ——

YELLOWHAMMER

Worse and worse, and doth the husband know this?

ALLWIT

Knows? Ay and glad he may too: 'tis his living;   235

As other trades thrive, butchers by selling flesh,

Poulters by venting conies, or the like, coz.

YELLOWHAMMER

What an incomparable wittol's this?

ALLWIT

Tush, what cares he for that?

Believe me coz, no more than I do.   240

222   *Resolve . . . point* Satisfy me
223   *contract* A *de praesenti* contract of marriage was made by two people agreeing before
        witnesses to take each other as man and wife and was held to be binding (cf. Webster,
        The Duchess of Malfi, II.i.392); a contract *de futuro* was an agreement to marry in the
        future and could be broken.   *passed* (past Q)
229   The lacunae here and four lines further on are in Q; see note to III.iii.137.
237   *Poulters* (a) Sellers of birds (b) Bawds
        venting conies selling (a) rabbits (b) prostitutes

YELLOWHAMMER
What a base slave is that?

ALLWIT
All's one to him; he feeds and takes his ease,
Was ne'er the man that ever broke his sleep
To get a child yet by his own confession,
And yet his wife has seven.   245

YELLOWHAMMER
What, by Sir Walter?

ALLWIT
Sir Walter's like to keep 'em, and maintain 'em,
In excellent fashion, he dares do no less sir.

YELLOWHAMMER
Life has he children too?

ALLWIT
Children? Boys thus high,   250
In their Cato and Cordelius.

YELLOWHAMMER
What, you jest sir!

ALLWIT
Why, one can make a verse,
And is now at Eton College.

YELLOWHAMMER
O this news has cut into my heart coz.   255

ALLWIT
It had eaten nearer if it had not been prevented.
One Allwit's wife.

YELLOWHAMMER
Allwit? Foot, I have heard of him;
He had a girl kursened lately?

ALLWIT
Ay, that work did cost the knight above a hundred mark.   260

YELLOWHAMMER
I'll mark him for a knave and villain for't!
A thousand thanks and blessings, I have done with him.

251 *Cato and Cordelius* Dionysius Cato's *Disticha de Moribus,* written in the 3rd or 4th
century, and Marthurin Cordier's *Colloquia scholastica* (1564) were famous
textbooks, approved by Puritans.
254 *Eton College* founded by Henry VI in 1440, in Buckinghamshire some 23 miles (38 km)
west of London on the Thames opposite Windsor
256 *prevented* anticipated
258 *Foot* God's foot

ALLWIT

    [*Aside*] Ha, ha, ha, this knight will stick by my ribs still,
    I shall not lose him yet, no wife will come;
    Where'er he woos, I find him still at home, ha, ha!   *Exit*   265

YELLOWHAMMER

    Well grant all this, say now his deeds are black,
    Pray what serves marriage, but to call him back;
    I have kept a whore myself, and had a bastard,
    By Mistress Anne, in Anno —
    I care not who knows it; he's now a jolly fellow,   270
    H'as been twice warden, so may his fruit be,
    They were but base begot, and so was he;
    The knight is rich, he shall be my son-in-law
    No matter so the whore he keeps be wholesome,
    My daughter takes no hurt then; so let them wed,   275
    I'll have him sweat well e'er they go to bed.

Enter MAUDLINE

MAUDLINE

    O husband! Husband!

YELLOWHAMMER

    How now Maudline?

MAUDLINE

    We are all undone, she's gone, she's gone.

YELLOWHAMMER

    Again? Death which way?   280

MAUDLINE

    Over the houses:
    Lay the waterside, she's gone forever else.

YELLOWHAMMER

    O venturous baggage!

                                      Exit [*with* MAUDLINE]

Enter TIM *and* TUTOR

---

267   *call him back* reform him
269   *in Anno* 'in the year', punning on the mother's name
271   *warden* (a) see note II.i.71 (b) a pear, taken up punningly in *fruit*. Pears were sexually
        symbolic; cf. *Romeo and Juliet* II.i.37.   *his* Sir Walter's
272   *They* Sir Walter's children by Mrs Allwit
274   *wholesome* free of the pox
276   *sweat well* in a steam tub to cure any venereal disease
282   *Lay* Set watch on

TIM

    Thieves, thieves, my sister's stol'n!
    Some thief hath got her: 285
    O how miraculously did my father's plate 'scape!
    'Twas all left out, tutor.

TUTOR

    Is't possible?

TIM

    Besides three chains of pearl and a box of coral.
    My sister's gone, let's look at Trig stairs for her;   290
    My mother's gone to lay the Common stairs
    At Puddle wharf, and at the dock below
    Stands my poor silly father. Run sweet tutor, run.

                                  Exit [with TUTOR]

[ACT IV, SCENE ii]

Enter both the TOUCHWOODS

TOUCHWOOD SENIOR

    I had been taken brother by eight sergeants,
    But for the honest watermen; I am bound to them,
    They are the most requiteful'st people living,
    For as they get their means by gentlemen.
    They are still the forwardest to help gentlemen.   5

---

290   *Trig stairs* a landing place on the Thames at the bottom of Trig Lane; appropriate for
       Tim, as *trig* was slang for a coxcomb, a dandified fool

291–2 *Common stairs at Puddle wharf* about two hundred yards upstream from Trig stairs;
       appropriate for Maudline. The 'dock' is presumably Dung wharf, downstream, where
       the garbage was dumped on to barges. The reference continues the cloacan stream
       of scatological references in the play.

293   *silly* pitiable, helpless

  1 *sergeants* sheriff's officers

  2 *watermen* the taxicab men of the time. John Taylor, the 'water-poet', reckoned that
     by 1614 2,000 small boats plied the river about London and between Windsor and
     Gravesend; 40,000 lives were maintained by their labour. Queenhithe was their
     headquarters and they were renowned for strong language.

  3 *most requiteful'st* most willing to return favours

You heard how one 'scaped out of the Blackfriars,
But a while since from two or three varlets
Came into the house with all their rapiers drawn,
As if they'd dance the sword dance on the stage,
With candles in their hands like chandlers' ghosts,   10
Whilst the poor gentleman so pursued and bandied
Was by an honest pair of oars safely landed.

TOUCHWOOD JUNIOR
I love them with my heart for't.

Enter three or four WATERMEN

1 WATERMAN
Your first man sir.

2 WATERMAN
Shall I carry you gentlemen with a pair of oars?   15

TOUCHWOOD SENIOR
These be the honest fellows;
Take one pair, and leave the rest for her.

TOUCHWOOD JUNIOR
Barn Elms.

TOUCHWOOD SENIOR
No more brother.   [*Exit*]

1 WATERMAN
Your first man.   20

2 WATERMAN
Shall I carry your worship?

TOUCHWOOD JUNIOR
Go, and you honest watermen that stay,
Here's a French crown for you;
There comes a maid with all speed to take water,
Row her lustily to Barn Elms after me.   25

6   *Blackfriars* theatre, the second known 'private' theatre, indoors and lit by candles; used by boys' companies 1600–08 and by the King's Men 1608–42.
9   *sword dance* Among the different kinds of sword dances included in plays of the time were adaptations of folk dances and choreographed mock fights.
10 *candles* Ghosts carried symbolic objects so that they could be recognized; the ruffians needed candles to find their victim in the indoors Blackfriars theatre.
11 *bandied* hit at, struck to and fro
14 *your first man* the watermen's trade cry
18 *Barn Elms* a park and manor house upstream opposite Hammersmith, well-known for assignations and duels
23 *French crown* French *ecu*, worth about the same as the English crown (5 shillings)
24 *take water* A bawdy pun; cf. Touchwood Senior's 'water' at II.i.188.

2 WATERMAN

    To Barn Elms, good sir: make ready the boat Sam,

    We'll wait below.

Ex[eunt WATERMEN]

Enter MOLL

TOUCHWOOD JUNIOR

    What made you stay so long?

MOLL

    I found the way more dangerous than I looked for.

TOUCHWOOD JUNIOR

    Away quick, there's a boat waits for you,   30

    And I'll take water at Paul's wharf, and overtake you.

MOLL

    Good sir do, we cannot be too safe.

[*Exeunt*]

Enter SIR WALTER, YELLOWHAMMER, TIM *and* TUTOR

SIR WALTER

    Life, call you this close keeping?

YELLOWHAMMER

    She was kept under a double lock.

SIR WALTER

    A double devil.   35

TIM

    That's a buff sergeant, tutor, he'll ne'er wear out.

YELLOWHAMMER

    How would you have women locked?

TIM

    With padlocks father, the Venetian uses it,

    My tutor reads it.

SIR WALTER

    Heart, if she were so locked up, how got she out?   40

---

31   *Paul's wharf* was between Puddle wharf and Trig stairs

36   *buff* tough, whitish oxhide leather usually worn by sergeants

38   *Venetian* women were believed lascivious and weak and the men cruel and oppres-
      sive, using *padlocks* on doors and chastity belts.

39   *reads* advises, or in the normal sense; cf. 'The sly Venetian locked his lady's ware, /
      Yet through her wit Actaeon's badge he bare' (*Ariosto's Satires,* [Tr.] G. Markham
      (1608), sig. K2r); Actaeon was transformed into a horned stag for watching the
      goddess Artemis bathing.

YELLOWHAMMER

There was a little hole looked into the gutter,
But who would have dreamt of that?

SIR WALTER

A wiser man would.

TIM

He says true, father, a wise man for love will seek every hole: my
tutor knows it.   45

TUTOR

Verum poeta dicit.

TIM

Dicit Virgilius, father.

YELLOWHAMMER

Prithee talk of thy gills somewhere else, she's played the gill with
me: where's your wise mother now?

TIM

Run mad I think, I thought she would have drowned herself; she   50
would not stay for oars, but took a smelt boat: sure I think she
be gone a-fishing for her.

YELLOWHAMMER

She'll catch a goodly dish of gudgeons now,
Will serve us all to supper.

> *Enter* MAUDLINE *drawing* MOLL *by the hair,*
> *and* WATERMEN

MAUDLINE

I'll tug thee home by the hair.   55

WATERMEN

Good mistress, spare her.

MAUDLINE

Tend your own business.

WATERMEN

You are a cruel mother.

> *Ex[eunt* WATERMEN]

---

41 *looked* opened
45 *knows* Ironic; as the tutor has cuckolded Yellowhammer.
46–7 'The poet speaks truth'; 'Virgil says it'. Tim is confusing the very moral Virgil with
the more erotic Ovid.
48 *gill* wench
51 *smelt* any small and easily caught fish, therefore applied, like *gudgeon,* to a simpleton
53–4 'She'll make us all look fools'

MOLL

O my heart dies!

MAUDLINE

I'll make thee an example for all the neighbours' daughters.   60

MOLL

Farewell life.

MAUDLINE

You that have tricks can counterfeit.

YELLOWHAMMER

Hold, hold Maudline!

MAUDLINE

I have brought your jewel by the hair.

YELLOWHAMMER

She's here knight.   65

SIR WALTER

Forbear or I'll grow worse.

TIM

Look on her, tutor, she hath brought her from the water like a
mermaid; she's but half my sister now, as far as the flesh goes, the
rest may be sold to fishwives.

MAUDLINE

Dissembling cunning baggage!   70

YELLOWHAMMER

Impudent strumpet!

SIR WALTER

Either give over both, or I'll give over:
Why have you used me thus unkind mistress?
Wherein have I deserved?

YELLOWHAMMER

You talk too fondly sir. We'll take another course and prevent all;   75
we might have done't long since; we'll lose no time now, nor
trust to't any longer: tomorrow morn as early as sunrise we'll
have you joined.

MOLL

O bring me death tonight, love pitying fates,
Let me not see tomorrow up upon the world.   80

YELLOWHAMMER

Are you content sir, till then she shall be watched?

68–9   *mermaid . . . fishwives* More unconscious irony; *mermaid* could mean 'whore', and
fishwife, 'bawd'.

MAUDLINE
> Baggage you shall.

Exit [with MOLL *and* YELLOWHAMMER]

TIM
> Why father, my tutor and I will both watch in armour.

TUTOR
> How shall we do for weapons?

TIM
> Take you no care for that, if need be I can send for con- 85
> quering metal tutor, ne'er lost day yet; 'tis but at Westminster –
> I am acquainted with him that keeps the monuments; I can
> borrow Harry the Fifth's sword, 'twill serve us both to watch
> with.

Exit [with TUTOR]

SIR WALTER
> I never was so near my wish, as this chance 90
> Makes me; ere tomorrow noon,
> I shall receive two thousand pound in gold,
> And a sweet maidenhead
> Worth forty.

Enter TOUCHWOOD JUNIOR *with a* WATERMAN

TOUCHWOOD JUNIOR
> O thy news splits me. 95

WATERMAN
> Half drowned, she cruelly tugged her by the hair,
> Forced her disgracefully, not like a mother.

TOUCHWOOD JUNIOR
> Enough, leave me like my joys.

Exit WATERMAN

> Sir, saw you not a wretched maid pass this way?
> Heart villain, is it thou?

Both draw and fight

SIR WALTER   Yes slave, 'tis I. 100

TOUCHWOOD JUNIOR
> I must break through thee then, there is no stop

---

86   *Westminster* The Abbey monuments could be viewed for a penny. Tim's foolishness
is exposed again, since Henry V's armour had been stolen, with his head of silver,
though Edward III's sword was still there.

94   *forty* Later in the 17th century 150 gold *ecus* (about £37) and a year's keep were
quoted as the price of a virgin in Venice. (See F. Henriques, *Prostitution and Society*
(1963) II, p. 89).

That checks my tongue and all my hopeful fortunes,
That breast excepted, and I must have way.

SIR WALTER
Sir, I believe 'twill hold your life in play.
                              [*Wounds* TOUCHWOOD JUNIOR]

TOUCHWOOD JUNIOR
Sir, you'll gain the heart in my breast at first?   105

SIR WALTER
There is no dealing then? Think on the dowry for two thousand
pounds.

TOUCHWOOD JUNIOR   [*Wounds* SIR WALTER]
O now 'tis quit sir.

SIR WALTER
Being of even hand, I'll play no longer.

TOUCHWOOD JUNIOR
No longer, slave?   110

SIR WALTER
I have certain things to think on,
Before I dare go further.

TOUCHWOOD JUNIOR
But one bout?
I'll follow thee to death, but ha't out.

                                              Ex[eunt]

---

102 *checks my tongue* stops me speaking; Touchwood Junior is also likening himself to a
     dog following a scent, 'giving tongue', and playing on his adversary's name; cf. I.i.135.
104 *in play* at risk. This begins a series of gaming images. Middleton later used such
     imagery with great effect in *Women Beware Women* II.ii, when the conversation
     during a chess game forms an ironic commentary on a seduction.
105 *Sir ... first?* (first Q) 'You think you're going to stab me through the heart straight
     off?'
106–7 Sir Walter is offering Touchwood Junior a compromise deal allowing him to share
       in the dowry.

ACT V, [SCENE i]

Enter ALLWIT, *his* WIFE, *and* DAVY DAHUMMA

MISTRESS ALLWIT
  A misery of a house.
ALLWIT
  What shall become of us?
DAVY
  I think his wound be mortal.
ALLWIT
  Think'st thou so Davy?
  Then am I mortal too, but a dead man Davy;   5
  This is no world for me, when e'er he goes,
  I must e'en truss up all, and after him Davy,
  A sheet with two knots, and away.

Enter SIR WALTER *led in hurt*

DAVY   O see sir,
  How faint he goes, two of my fellows lead him.
MISTRESS ALLWIT
  O me!   [*Swoons*]   10
ALLWIT
  Hyday, my wife's laid down too, here's like to be
  A good house kept, when we are altogether down;
  Take pains with her good Davy, cheer her up there,
  Let me come to his worship, let me come.
SIR WALTER
  Touch me not villain, my wound aches at thee,   15
  Thou poison to my heart.
ALLWIT   He raves already,
  His senses are quite gone, he knows me not;
  Look up an't like your worship, heave those eyes,
  Call me to mind, is your remembrance left?
  Look in my face, who am I an't like your worship?   20
SIR WALTER
  If any thing be worse than slave or villain.

---

  7 *truss up all* pack up everything
  8 *sheet* a shroud, with knots at the head and feet
18, 20 *an't like* if it pleases

Thou art the man.
ALLWIT   Alas his poor worship's weakness,
He will begin to know me by little and little.
SIR WALTER
No devil can be like thee.
ALLWIT   Ah poor gentleman,
Methinks the pain that thou endurest –   25
SIR WALTER
Thou know'st me to be wicked, for thy baseness
Kept the eyes open still on all my sins,
None knew the dear account my soul stood charged with
So well as thou, yet like Hell's flattering angel
Would'st never tell me on't, let'st me go on,   30
And join with death in sleep, that if I had not waked
Now by chance, even by a stranger's pity,
I had everlastingly slept out all hope
Of grace and mercy.
ALLWIT   Now he is worse and worse,
Wife, to him wife, thou wast wont to do good on him.   35
MISTRESS ALLWIT
How is't with you sir?
SIR WALTER   Not as with you,
Thou loathsome strumpet! Some good pitying man
Remove my sins out of my sight a little;
I tremble to behold her, she keeps back
All comfort while she stays; is this a time,   40
Unconscionable woman, to see thee?
Art thou so cruel to the peace of man,
Not to give liberty now? The devil himself
Shows a far fairer reverence and respect
To goodness than thyself; he dares not do this,   45
But parts in time of penitence, hides his face;
When man withdraws from him, he leaves the place;
Hast thou less manners, and more impudence,
Than thy instructor? Prithee show thy modesty,
If the least grain be left, and get thee from me.   50

25   *Methinks* I think. Dyce added 'mads thee' to complete the line, Q has 'endurest',
     Parker emends 'endurest – ', which makes good sense, with Sir Walter interrupting
     Allwit.
35   *do good* with a pun on 'do' = copulate
46   *parts* (part Q) departs

Thou should'st be rather locked many rooms hence,
From the poor miserable sight of me,
If either love or grace had part in thee.
MISTRESS ALLWIT
    He is lost for ever.
ALLWIT   Run sweet Davy quickly,
    And fetch the children hither – sight of them   55
    Will make him cheerful straight.

                                        [*Exit* DAVY]
SIR WALTER   O death! Is this
    A place for you to weep? What tears are those?
    Get you away with them, I shall fare the worse
    As long as they are a-weeping; they work against me;
    There's nothing but thy appetite in that sorrow,   60
    Thou weep'st for lust, I feel it in the slackness
    Of comforts coming towards me;
    I was well till thou began'st to undo me;
    This shows like the fruitless sorrow of a careless mother
    That brings her son with dalliance to the gallows,   65
    And then stands by, and weeps to see him suffer.

                Enter DAVY *with the* CHILDREN

DAVY
    There are the children sir, an't like your worship;
    Your last fine girl, in troth she smiles,
    Look, look, in faith sir.
SIR WALTER   O my vengeance!
    Let me for ever hide my cursed face   70
    From sight of those, that darkens all my hopes,
    And stands between me and the sight of Heaven;
    Who sees me now, he too and those so near me,
    May rightly say, I am o'er-grown with sin;
    O how my offences wrestle with my repentance;   75
    It hath scarce breath –
    Still my adulterous guilt hovers aloft,
    And with her black wings beats down all my prayers
    Ere they be half way up; what's he knows now

---

65   *dalliance* over-indulgence
69   *vengeance* God's vengeance, as represented in the children before him
73   *he* (ho Q); Dyce emends 'O too', Bullen 'O, O', George 'go to', Parker 'her too', but 'he'
     is acceptable, referring to (a) God, who 'sees [Sir Walter] now' or (b) 'who(ever)'

How long I have to live? O what comes then? 80
My taste grows bitter, the round world, all gall now,
Her pleasing pleasures now hath poisoned me,
Which I exchanged my soul for:
Make way a hundred sighs at once for me.

ALLWIT
Speak to him Nick.

NICK   I dare not, I am afraid. 85

ALLWIT
Tell him he hurts his wounds Wat, with making moan.

SIR WALTER
Wretched, death of seven.

ALLWIT
Come let's be talking somewhat to keep him alive.
Ah sirrah Wat, and did my lord bestow that jewel on thee,
For an epistle thou mad'st in Latin? 90
Thou art a good forward boy, there's great joy on thee.

SIR WALTER
O sorrow!

ALLWIT   Heart, will nothing comfort him?
If he be so far gone, 'tis time to moan;
Here's pen, and ink, and paper, and all things ready,
Will't please your worship for to make your will? 95

SIR WALTER
My will? Yes, yes, what else? Who writes apace now?

ALLWIT
That can your man Davy an't like your worship,
A fair, fast, legible hand.

SIR WALTER
Set it down then:
Imprimis, I bequeath to yonder wittol, 100
Three times his weight in curses.

ALLWIT
How?

SIR WALTER
All plagues of body and of mind –

ALLWIT
Write them not down Davy.

---

84   'Let a hundred sighs of repentance make a way (to heaven) for me'.
87   *seven* Mrs Allwit's children by Sir Walter
100 *Imprimis* In the first place

DAVY

It is his will, I must.   105

SIR WALTER

Together also,

With such a sickness, ten days ere his death.

ALLWIT

[*Aside*] There's a sweet legacy,

I am almost choked with't.

SIR WALTER

Next I bequeath to that foul whore his wife,   110

All barrenness of joy, a drouth of virtue,

And dearth of all repentance: for her end,

The common misery of an English strumpet,

In French and Dutch, beholding ere she dies

Confusion of her brats before her eyes,   115

And never shed a tear for it.

Enter a SERVANT

SERVANT   Where's the knight?

O sir, the gentleman you wounded is newly departed.

SIR WALTER

Dead? Lift, lift, who helps me?

ALLWIT

Let the law lift you now, that must have all,

I have done lifting on you, and my wife too.   120

SERVANT

You were best lock yourself close.

ALLWIT   Not in my house sir,

I'll harbour no such persons as men-slayers,

Lock yourself where you will –

SIR WALTER   What's this?

MISTRESS ALLWIT   Why husband!

ALLWIT

I know what I do wife.

---

114   *French* The 'French disease' was syphilis.

Dutch probably sexually transmitted disease also, as a 'Dutch widow' was a harlot
(see Middleton's *A Trick to Catch the Old One* III.iii.15–17), but it could refer to
drunkenness

115   *Confusion* Shaming. Cf. Psalm 109:29 'Let mine adversaries be clothed with shame,
and let them cover themselves with their own confusion . . .'

120   *lifting* (a) assisting (b) stealing (c) fucking

MISTRESS ALLWIT   You cannot tell yet;
    For having killed the man in his defence,   125
    Neither his life, nor estate will be touched, husband.

ALLWIT
    Away wife! Hear a fool! His lands will hang him.

SIR WALTER
    Am I denied a chamber?
    What say you forsooth?

MISTRESS ALLWIT
    Alas sir, I am one that would have all well,   130
    But must obey my husband. Prithee love
    Let the poor gentleman stay, being so sore wounded;
    There's a close chamber at one end of the garret
    We never use, let him have that I prithee.

ALLWIT
    We never use? You forget sickness then,   135
    And physic times: is't not a place of easement?

Enter a SERVANT

SIR WALTER
    O death ! Do I hear this with part
    Of former life in me? What's the news now?

SERVANT
    Troth worse and worse, you're like to lose your land
    If the law save your life sir, or the surgeon.   140

ALLWIT
    Hark you there wife.

SIR WALTER
    Why how sir?

SERVANT
    Sir Oliver Kix's wife is new quickened;
    That child undoes you sir.

SIR WALTER   All ill at once.

ALLWIT
    I wonder what he makes here with his consorts?   145
    Cannot our house be private to ourselves,

---

127   *Hear a fool* Listen to the silly woman!
      lands His lands will be forfeited to the Crown, since he's a murderer, so he is more
      likely to hang.
133   *close chamber* secluded room, here the *place of easement,* the lavatory
145   *consorts* companions (i.e. his two servants)

But we must have such guests? I pray depart sirs.
And take your murderer along with you –
Good he were apprehended ere he go,
He's killed some honest gentleman. Send for officers!   150

SIR WALTER

I'll soon save you that labour.

ALLWIT   I must tell you sir,
You have been somewhat bolder in my house
Than I could well like of; I suffered you
Till it stuck here at my heart; I tell you truly
I thought you had been familiar with my wife once.   155

MISTRESS ALLWIT

With me? I'll see him hanged first; I defy him,
And all such gentlemen in the like extremity.

SIR WALTER

If ever eyes were open, these are they;
Gamesters farewell, I have nothing left to play.

Exit [*with* SERVANTS]

ALLWIT

And therefore get you gone sir.

DAVY   Of all wittols,   160
Be thou the head. Thou the grand whore of spitals.   *Exit*

ALLWIT

So since he's like now to be rid of all,
I am right glad I am so well rid of him.

MISTRESS ALLWIT

I knew he durst not stay, when you named officers.

ALLWIT

That stopped his spirits straight.   165
What shall we do now wife?

MISTRESS ALLWIT

As we were wont to do.

ALLWIT

We are richly furnished, wife, with household stuff.

MISTRESS ALLWIT

Let's let out lodgings then,

---

150   *officers* of the watch could arrest offenders and take them before the constable or
justice of the peace

159   *Gamesters* (a) Gamblers (b) Lechers

161   *spitals* places for the indigent and foully diseased (cf. note to II.i.146). 'To rob the
spital' = to make gain or profit in a particularly mean or dastardly manner.

And take a house in the Strand.

ALLWIT   In troth a match wench: 170
     We are simply stocked with cloth of tissue cushions,
     To furnish out bay windows: push, what not that's quaint
     And costly, from the top to the bottom.
     Life, for furniture, we may lodge a countess:
     There's a close-stool of tawny velvet too,   175
     Now I think on't wife.

MISTRESS ALLWIT   There's that should be sir;
     Your nose must be in every thing.

ALLWIT   I have done wench;
     And let this stand in every gallant's chamber:
     There's no gamester like a politic sinner,
     For who e'er games, the box is sure a winner.   180

                Exit [*with* MISTRESS ALLWIT]

[ACT V, SCENE ii]

         Enter YELLOWHAMMER *and his* WIFE

MAUDLINE
     O husband, husband, she will die, she will die,
     There is no sign but death.

YELLOWHAMMER   'Twill be our shame then.

MAUDLINE
     O how she's changed in compass of an hour.

---

170   *Strand* the most fashionable part of London, running from Temple Bar to Charing
       Cross; a resort of high class whores

171   *simply* absolutely

172   *bay windows* were used by whores to display themselves (cf. Middleton, *Hengist,*
       King of Kent III.i.143); Allwit's use of 'quaint' (= cunt) indicates an intention of
       setting up a brothel.

175   *close-stool* a chamber pot in a stool or box

176   *There's that. . .* There's everything there ought to be

180   *box* the box into which money was placed by gamesters as a kind of cover charge;
       'every player, at the first hand he draweth, payeth a crown to the box, by the way of
       relief towards the house charges' (G. Walker, *A Manifest Detection of the Most Vile*
       and Detestable Use of Diceplay, ed. J. O. Halliwell (1850), p. 12) Allwit is comparing
       himself to the box, which no matter what happens, contains the money. There may
       also be a pun on box = coffin.

YELLOWHAMMER

    Ah my poor girl! Good faith thou wert too cruel

    To drag her by the hair.   5

MAUDLINE

    You would have done as much sir,

    To curb her of her humour.

YELLOWHAMMER

    'Tis curbed sweetly, she catched her bane o'th' water.

Enter TIM

MAUDLINE

    How now Tim?

TIM

    Faith busy, mother, about an epitaph   10

    Upon my sister's death.

MAUDLINE

    Death! She is not dead I hope?

TIM

    No: but she means to be, and that's as good,

    And when a thing's done, 'tis done –

    You taught me that, mother.   15

YELLOWHAMMER

    What is your tutor doing?

TIM

    Making one too, in principal pure Latin,

    Culled out of Ovid *de Tristibus.*

YELLOWHAMMER

    How does your sister look, is she not changed?

TIM

    Changed? Gold into white money was never so changed,   20

    As is my sister's colour into paleness.

Enter MOLL

YELLOWHAMMER

    O here she's brought, see how she looks like death.

---

  8   *water* pun on 'Walter'

14   *when a thing's done* Proverbial, with an allusion to a game called 'A thing done' cf.
      Jonson's *Cynthia's Revels* IV.3.160–70. where the context is bawdy.

17   *principal* excellent

18   Ovid's *Tristia* (melancholy poems) was a commonly used Latin text book.

20   *white money* silver

TIM

    Looks she like death, and ne'er a word made yet?
    I must go beat my brains against a bed post,
    And get before my tutor.   [*Exit*]

YELLOWHAMMER   Speak, how dost thou?   25

MOLL

    I hope I shall be well, for I am as sick at heart
    As I can be.

YELLOWHAMMER   'Las my poor girl,

    The doctor's making a most sovereign drink for thee,
    The worst ingredients, dissolved pearl and amber;
    We spare no cost girl.

MOLL   Your love comes too late,   30

    Yet timely thanks reward it. What is comfort,
    When the poor patient's heart is past relief?
    It is no doctor's art can cure my grief.

YELLOWHAMMER

    All is cast away then;
    Prithee look upon me cheerfully.   35

MAUDLINE

    Sing but a strain or two, thou wilt not think
    How 'twill revive thy spirits: strive with thy fit,
    Prithee sweet Moll.

MOLL

    You shall have my good will, mother.

MAUDLINE

    Why, well said, wench.   40

[MOLL *sings*]

The Song

    Weep eyes, break heart,
    My love and I must part;
    Cruel fates true love do soonest sever,

---

25   *get* beget [a poem]

     thou Yellowhammer and Maudline, all solicitous, now use the affectionate 'thou' for
     their daughter.

29   *ingredients* (ingredience Q)

     pearl and amber were believed to have great medicinal properties; Robert Boyle says
     that the 'reducing of pearls to a fine powder affords a rich medicine' (*Works* (1772)
     p. 133), and a solution of amber with spirit of wine is 'a friend to the stomach, the
     entrails, the nervous parts, and even the head' (p. 329).

37   *strive . . . fit* (a) struggle with your condition, which betokens death (b) put up a
     fight by singing a strain

O I shall see thee, never, never, never.
O happy is the maid whose life takes end,   45
Ere it knows parent's frown, or loss of friend.
Weep eyes, break heart,
My love and I must part.

Enter TOUCHWOOD SENIOR *with a letter*

MAUDLINE
O, I could die with music: well sung girl!
MOLL
If you call it so, it was.   50
YELLOWHAMMER
She plays the swan, and sings herself to death.
TOUCHWOOD SENIOR
By your leave sir.
YELLOWHAMMER
What are you sir? Or what's your business pray?
TOUCHWOOD SENIOR
I may be now admitted, though the brother
Of him your hate pursued, it spreads no further;   55
Your malice sets in death, does it not sir?
YELLOWHAMMER
In death?
TOUCHWOOD SENIOR He's dead: 'twas a dear love to him,
It cost him but his life, that was all sir:
He paid enough, poor gentleman, for his love.
YELLOWHAMMER
[*Aside*] There's all our ill removed, if she were well now.   60
Impute not, sir, his end to any hate
That sprung from us; he had a fair wound brought that.
TOUCHWOOD SENIOR
That helped him forward, I must needs confess:
But the restraint of love, and your unkindness,
Those were the wounds that from his heart drew blood;   65
But being past help, let words forget it too:
Scarcely three minutes ere his eyelids closed
And took eternal leave of this world's light,
He wrote this letter, which by oath he bound me,

51 *swan* Swans were proverbially believed to sing only before they died; cf. Orlando
Gibbons' madrigal, 'The Silver Swan'.
56 *sets* declines, wanes

254

To give to her own hands; that's all my business.   70
YELLOWHAMMER
    You may perform it then, there she sits.
TOUCHWOOD SENIOR
    O with a following look.
YELLOWHAMMER
    Ay, trust me sir, I think she'll follow him quickly.
TOUCHWOOD SENIOR
    Here's some gold
    He willed me to distribute faithfully amongst your servants.   75
YELLOWHAMMER
    'Las what doth he mean sir?
TOUCHWOOD SENIOR
    How cheer you mistress?
MOLL
    I must learn of you sir.
TOUCHWOOD SENIOR
    Here's a letter from a friend of yours,
    And where that fails, in satisfaction   80
    I have a sad tongue ready to supply.
MOLL
    How does he, ere I look on't?
TOUCHWOOD SENIOR
    Seldom better, h'as a contented health now.
MOLL
    I am most glad on't.
MAUDLINE
    Dead sir?   85
YELLOWHAMMER
    He is. Now wife let's but get the girl
    Upon her legs again, and to church roundly with her.
MOLL
    O sick to death he tells me:
    How does he after this?
TOUCHWOOD SENIOR
    Faith, feels no pain at all, he's dead sweet mistress.   90
MOLL
    Peace close mine eyes.   [*Swoons*]

---

72 *following* as though she were about to follow Touchwood Junior in death
87 *roundly* smartly, without delay

YELLOWHAMMER

   The girl, look to the girl, wife.

MAUDLINE

   Moll, daughter, sweet girl speak;

   Look but once up, thou shalt have all the wishes of thy heart

   That wealth can purchase.   95

YELLOWHAMMER

   O she's gone for ever, that letter broke her heart.

TOUCHWOOD SENIOR

   As good now, then, as let her lie in torment,

   And then break it.

Enter SUSAN

MAUDLINE

   O Susan, she thou lovedst so dear is gone.

SUSAN

   O sweet maid!   100

TOUCHWOOD SENIOR

   This is she that helped her still,

   I've a reward here for thee.

YELLOWHAMMER

   Take her in,

   Remove her from our sight, our shame, and sorrow.

TOUCHWOOD SENIOR

   Stay, let me help thee, 'tis the last cold kindness   105

   I can perform for my sweet brother's sake.

[Exeunt TOUCHWOOD SENIOR and SUSAN,
carrying MOLL]

YELLOWHAMMER

   All the whole street will hate us, and the world

   Point me out cruel: it is our best course wife,

   After we have given order for the funeral,

   To absent ourselves, till she be laid in ground.   110

MAUDLINE

   Where shall we spend that time?

YELLOWHAMMER

   I'll tell thee where wench, go to some private church,

   And marry Tim to the rich Brecknock gentlewoman.

---

  96   *heart* See note to I.ii.55–6.

112   *private* secret

ere was no want of any thing of life,
make these virtuous precedents man and wife.   20

IT

eat pity of their deaths.
                              Ne'er more pity.

KIX

makes a hundred weeping eyes, sweet gossip.

HWOOD SENIOR

annot think, there's any one amongst you,
this full fair assembly, maid, man, or wife,
hose heart would not have sprung with joy and gladness   25
have seen their marriage day?

would have made a thousand joyful hearts.

CHWOOD SENIOR

then apace, and take your fortunes,
ake these joyful hearts, here's none but friends.
        [MOLL *and* TOUCHWOOD JUNIOR *rise from their coffins*]

ive sir? O sweet dear couple.   30

CHWOOD SENIOR

ay, do not hinder 'em now, stand from about 'em;
she be caught again, and have this time,
ne'er plot further for 'em, nor this honest chambermaid
hat helped all at a push.

CHWOOD JUNIOR

ood sir, apace.   35

ON

ands join now, but hearts for ever,
hich no parent's mood shall sever.
u shall forsake all widows, wives, and maids:
u, lords, knights, gentlemen, and men of trades:
nd if in haste, any article misses,   40
o interline it with a brace of kisses.

---

0 *precedents* examples worthy to be followed
4 *at a push* in an emergency
5 s.p. TOUCHWOOD JUNIOR ed. (TOUCHWOOD SENIOR Q)
6 The parson takes up his doggerel wedding service where he left off at III.i.18, over-
   lapping half a line.
7 *mood* specifically, anger
0 *article* part of the ceremony; legal term, as is *interline*
1 *brace* pair, and also a clasp or support

MAUDLINE
    Mass, a match!
    We'll not lose all at once, somewhat we'll catch.   115
                    Exit [*with* YELLOWHAMMER]

[ACT V, SCENE iii]

                Enter SIR OLIVER *and* SERVANTS

SIR OLIVER
    Ho, my wife's quickened, I am a man for ever!
    I think I have bestirred my stumps i'faith:
    Run, get your fellows all together instantly,
    Then to the parish church, and ring the bells.

1 SERVANT
    It shall be done sir.   [*Exit*]   5

SIR OLIVER
    Upon my love I charge you villain, that you make a bonfire before
    the door at night.

2 SERVANT
    A bonfire sir?

SIR OLIVER
    A thwacking one I charge you.

2 SERVANT
    [*Aside*] This is monstrous.   [*Exit*]   10

SIR OLIVER
    Run, tell a hundred pound out for the gentleman
    That gave my wife the drink, the first thing you do.

3 SERVANT
    A hundred pounds sir?

SIR OLIVER
    A bargain, as our joys grows,
    We must remember still from whence it flows,   15
    Or else we prove ungrateful multipliers:
    The child is coming, and the land comes after;

---

114 *a match* (a) agreed (b) a marriage

2 *bestirred my stumps* been (a) busy (b) sexually active
4, 6 *bells, bonfire* Church bells were rung and bonfires lit to announce important
      happenings.

The news of this will make a poor Sir Walter.
I have struck it home i'faith.

3 SERVANT
That you have, marry, sir.   20
But will not your worship go to the funeral
Of both these lovers?

SIR OLIVER
Both, go both together?

3 SERVANT
Ay sir, the gentleman's brother will have it so,
'Twill be the pitifullest sight; there's such running,   25
Such rumours, and such throngs, a pair of lovers
Had never more spectators, more men's pities,
Or women's wet eyes.

SIR OLIVER
My wife helps the number then?

3 SERVANT
There's such a drawing out of handkerchers,   30
And those that have no handkerchers, lift up aprons.

SIR OLIVER
Her parents may have joyful hearts at this,
I would not have my cruelty so talked on,
To any child of mine, for a monopoly.

3 SERVANT
I believe you sir.   35
'Tis cast so too, that both their coffins meet,
Which will be lamentable.

SIR OLIVER
Come, we'll see't.

                                              Ex[eunt]

---

19   *struck it home* hit the target in (a) sport (b) sex
29   *helps the number* adds to the number of mourners
34   *monopoly* (a) both Queen Elizabeth and King James were notorious for granting
      exclusive commercial rights in commodity dealing (b) ironic reference to Sir Oliver's
      having unawares surrendered his marital 'monopoly'
36   *cast* arranged

[ACT V, SCENE iv]

*Recorders dolefully playing. Enter at one door
of the gentleman, solemnly decked, his sword
attended by many in black, his brother being
mourner. At the other door, the coffin of the vi
a garland of flowers, with epitaphs pinned on it
by maids and women. Then set them down one
against the other, while all the company seem to
mourn; there is a sad song in the music ro*

[*The company includes* SIR OLIVER *and* LAD
MR *and* MRS ALLWIT, SUSAN *and a* PARS

TOUCHWOOD SENIOR
Never could death boast of a richer prize
From the first parent, let the world bring forth
A pair of truer hearts; to speak but truth
Of this departed gentleman, in a brother,
Might by hard censure be called flattery,
Which makes me rather silent in his right
Than so to be delivered to the thoughts
Of any envious hearer starved in virtue,
And therefore pining to hear others thrive.
But for this maid, whom envy cannot hurt
With all her poisons, having left to ages
The true, chaste monument of her living name,
Which no time can deface, I say of her
The full truth freely, without fear of censure;
What nature could there shine, that might redeem
Perfection home to woman, but in her
Was fully glorious; beauty set in goodness
Speaks what she was, that jewel so infixed;

---

0   s.d. *Recorders* were the most common wind instruments of the
        mentioned in plays (e.g., *Hamlet* III.ii.367–96). The stage directi
        the evidence of the de Witt sketch that the Swan had two do
        mentioned here may be the gallery above the stage shown in the
        mime is discussed in D. Mehl, *The Elizabethan Dumb Show* (19
2   *From the first parent* Since the time of Adam
15–16   *redeem . . . woman* returning to women the perfection that Eve l
16   *but* only

TOUCHWOOD SENIOR
    Here's a thing trolled nimbly. Give you joy brother,
    Were't not better thou should'st have her,
    Than the maid should die?

MISTRESS ALLWIT
    To you sweet mistress bride.   45

ALL
    Joy, joy to you both.

TOUCHWOOD SENIOR
    Here be your wedding sheets you brought along with you; you
    may both go to bed when you please to.

TOUCHWOOD JUNIOR
    My joy wants utterance.

TOUCHWOOD SENIOR
    Utter all at night then brother.   50

MOLL
    I am silent with delight.

TOUCHWOOD SENIOR
    Sister, delight will silence any woman,
    But you'll find your tongue again, among maidservants,
    Now you keep house, sister.

ALL
    Never was hour so filled with joy and wonder.   55

TOUCHWOOD SENIOR
    To tell you the full story of this chambermaid,
    And of her kindness in this business to us,
    'Twould ask an hour's discourse. In brief 'twas she
    That wrought it to this purpose cunningly.

ALL
    We shall all love her for't.   60

Enter YELLOWHAMMER *and his* WIFE

ALLWIT
    See who comes here now.

TOUCHWOOD SENIOR
    A storm, a storm, but we are sheltered for it.

YELLOWHAMMER
    I will prevent you all, and mock you thus,

42   *trolled nimbly* spoken quickly   47 *wedding sheets* the shrouds
50   *Utter* (a) Say (b) Ejaculate
63   *prevent* get in before

You, and your expectations; I stand happy,
Both in your lives, and your hearts' combination. 65
TOUCHWOOD SENIOR
Here's a strange day again.
YELLOWHAMMER The knight's proved villain,
All's come out now, his niece an arrant baggage;
My poor boy Tim is cast away this morning,
Even before breakfast: married a whore
Next to his heart.
ALL A whore?
YELLOWHAMMER His niece forsooth. 70
ALLWIT
I think we rid our hands in good time of him.
MISTRESS ALLWIT
I knew he was past the best, when I gave him over.
What is become of him pray sir?
YELLOWHAMMER
Who, the knight? He lies i'th' knight's ward now.
[*To* LADY KIX]
Your belly, lady, begins to blossom, there's no peace for him, 75
His creditors are so greedy.
SIR OLIVER
Master Touchwood, hear'st thou this news?
I am so endeared to thee for my wife's fruitfulness,
That I charge you both, your wife and thee,
To live no more asunder for the world's frowns; 80
I have purse, and bed, and board for you:
Be not afraid to go to your business roundly,
Get children, and I'll keep them.
TOUCHWOOD SENIOR Say you so sir?
SIR OLIVER
Prove me, with three at a birth, and thou dar'st now.
TOUCHWOOD SENIOR
Take heed how you dare a man, while you live sir, 85
That has good skill at his weapon.

---

70 *Next to his heart* (a) Nearest in affection (b) On an empty stomach
74 *knight's ward* There were four grades of accommodation in the two Counters (debtors' prisons), and the Fleet Prison: the master's side, the knight's ward, the twopenny ward and the hole, for those who could pay nothing; cf. Chapman, Jonson and Marston, *Eastward Ho!* V.ii.42.
77, 79 *thou, thee* show affectionate respect
82 *roundly* with gusto, but with a pun on 'round' = pregnant

Enter TIM *and* WELSH GENTLEWOMAN

SIR OLIVER

Foot, I dare you sir.

YELLOWHAMMER

Look gentlemen, if ever you saw the picture
Of the unfortunate marriage, yonder 'tis.

WELSH GENTLEWOMAN

Nay, good sweet Tim.   90

TIM

Come from the university,
To marry a whore in London, with my tutor too?
O tempora! O mors!

TUTOR

Prithee Tim be patient.

TIM

I bought a jade at Cambridge,   95
I'll let her out to execution tutor,
For eighteen pence a day, or Brainford horse races;
She'll serve to carry seven miles out of town well.
Where be these mountains? I was promised mountains,
But there's such a mist, I can see none of 'em.   100
What are become of those two thousand runts?
Let's have a bout with them in the meantime.
A vengeance runt thee!

MAUDLINE   Good sweet Tim, have patience.

TIM

Flectere si nequeo superos Acheronta movebo, mother.

MAUDLINE

I think you have married her in logic Tim.   105
You told me once, by logic you would prove

88   *saw* ed. (say Q, obsolete past tense of 'see')
93   'O time! O death!' Tim's version of 'O *tempora! O mores*' 'Oh, the times! Oh, the
      manners!' (Cicero, *In Catilinam* I.i.I).
95   *jade* (a) worn-out horse (b) whore
96   *execution* performance, in this case, sexual. Tim is saying that as he already has a
      horse in Cambridge, he'll hire out his wife as a prostitute.
97   *Brainford* Brentford (see note II.ii.213); horseracing was one of the entertainments
      for visitors; Tim's speech is *double entendre*.
102   *have a bout* have an argument (Q *about*)
103   *runt* reprove, admonish (though the meaning is stronger here)
104   'Since I cannot prevail upon the powers above, I shall work on the lower regions'
      (Virgil, *Aeneid*, VII, 312).

A whore an honest woman; prove her so Tim
And take her for thy labour.

TIM   Troth I thank you.
I grant you I may prove another man's wife so,
But not mine own.   110

MAUDLINE
There's no remedy now Tim,
You must prove her so as well as you may.

TIM
Why then my tutor and I will about her,
As well as we can.
Uxor non est meretrix, ergo falacis.   115

WELSH GENTLEWOMAN
Sir if your logic cannot prove me honest,
There's a thing called marriage, and that makes me honest.

MAUDLINE
O there's a trick beyond your logic Tim.

TIM
I perceive then a woman may be honest according to the English
print, when she is a whore in the Latin. So much for marriage   120
and logic. I'll love her for her wit, I'll pick out my runts there:
and for my mountains, I'll mount upon ———

YELLOWHAMMER
So fortune seldom deals two marriages
With one hand, and both lucky. The best is,
One feast will serve them both: marry, for room   125
I'll have the dinner kept in Goldsmiths' Hall,
To which kind gallants, I invite you all.

[*Exeunt*]

FINIS

---

108   *for thy labour* (a) hard work in argument (b) for your sexual efforts
113   *about* deal with (with a sexual innuendo)
115   'A wife is not a whore, therefore you are wrong'
118   *trick* a common play on the Latin *meretrix* = 'whore' and merry 'trick'
121   *I'll love ... there* (a) I'll love her for her cleverness and get my rewards there (b) I'll
       love her for her sexual organ and work away there for my children
122   *mount upon* in the sexual sense; the lacuna is in Q
126   *Goldsmiths' Hall* the hall of the Goldsmiths' Company, in Foster Lane off Cheapside,
       'a proper house, but not large' (*Survey*, I, 305).

WOMEN
BEWARE
WOMEN

A
TRAGEDY,
BY
Tho. Middleton, Gent.

LONDON:
Printed for *Humphrey Mosel*

TO THE READER

When these amongst others of Mr. Thomas Middleton's excellent poems came to my hands, I was not a little confident but that his name would prove as great an inducement for thee to read, as me to print them, since those issues of his brain that have already seen the sun have by their worth gained themselves a free entertainment amongst all that are ingenious; and I am most certain that these will no way lessen his reputation, nor hinder his admission to any noble and recreative spirits. All that I require at thy hands is to continue the author in his deserved esteem, and to accept of my endeavours which have ever been to please thee.

5

10

Farewell

---

1 *these Women Beware Women* (*c.* 1621) was printed together with *More Dissemblers Besides Women* (*c.* 1615–19) as *Two New Playes* by Humphrey Moseley in 1657. Moseley also published *No Wit, No Help Like a Woman's* (*c.* 1611) in a separate octavo in 1657.

Upon The Tragedy of
My Familiar Acquaintance,
Thomas Middleton

Women beware Women: 'tis a true text
Never to be forgot. Drabs of state vexed
Have plots, poisons, mischiefs that seldom miss
To murder virtue with a venom kiss.
Witness this worthy tragedy, expressed   5
By him that well deserved among the best
Of poets in his time. He knew the rage,
Madness of women crossed; and for the stage
Fitted their humours, hell-bred malice, strife
Acted in state, presented to the life.   10
I that have seen't can say, having just cause,
Never came tragedy off with more applause.

Nathaniel Richards

2   *Drabs of state* whores of great men
10 *in state* with great pomp and ceremony
13 A dramatist and poet, known especially for his play *The Tragedy of Messalina* (pr. 1640), Richards may have been responsible for delivering a copy of Middleton's play to the printer, Moseley. Richards could have seen the play at any time between *c.* 1621 and 1642, the closing of the theatres; no other record of performance exists.

DRAMATIS PERSONAE

DUKE OF FLORENCE
LORD CARDINAL, *brother to the* DUKE
TWO CARDINALS *more*
A LORD
FABRITIO, *father to* ISABELLA [*and brother to* LIVIA *and* HIPPOLITO] 5
HIPPOLITO, *brother to* FABRITIO [*and* LIVIA, *uncle to* ISABELLA]
GUARDIANO, *uncle to the foolish* WARD
THE WARD, *a rich young heir*
LEANTIO, *a factor, husband to* BIANCA
SORDIDO, *the* WARD'*s man* 10

LIVIA, *sister to* FABRITIO [*and* HIPPOLITO, *aunt to* ISABELLA]
ISABELLA, *niece to* LIVIA [*and* HIPPOLITO, *daughter of* FABRITIO]
BIANCA, LEANTIO'*s wife*
WIDOW, *his* [LEANTIO'*s*] *mother*

STATES *of* FLORENCE 15
CITIZENS
A 'PRENTICE
BOYS
MESSENGER
SERVANTS 20
[*Two* LADIES, LORDS, PAGES, GUARD]
[*Figures in the Masque:*
HYMEN, GANYMEDE, HEBE, NYMPHS, CUPIDS]

The Scene:
FLORENCE

---

9 *factor* commercial agent
13 BIANCA ed. (Brancha O) The octavo spells her name 'Brancha' throughout – a mis-reading of Middleton's 'e' ('Beancha') or, less likely, his 'i' ('Biancha'). Middleton's source, Malespini's *Ducenta Novelle,* spells the name 'Bianca'; in several places in the play, moreover, the metre requires a tri-syllabic pronunciation – hence, 'Bianca'.
15 STATES nobility
17 A 'PRENTICE an apprentice

ACT I, SCENE i

Enter LEANTIO *with* BIANCA *and* MOTHER
[*Bianca stands apart*]

MOTHER
Thy sight was never yet more precious to me;
Welcome with all the affection of a mother,
That comfort can express from natural love.
Since thy birth-joy – a mother's chiefest gladness,
After sh'as undergone her curse of sorrows –   5
Thou wast not more dear to me than this hour
Presents thee to my heart. Welcome again.

LEANTIO
[*Aside*] 'Las poor affectionate soul, how her joys speak to me!
I have observed it often, and I know it is
The fortune commonly of knavish children   10
To have the loving'st mothers.

MOTHER   What's this gentlewoman?

LEANTIO
Oh you have named the most unvalued'st purchase
That youth of man had ever knowledge of.
As often as I look upon that treasure
And know it to be mine – there lies the blessing –   15
It joys me that I ever was ordained
To have a being, and to live 'mongst men;
Which is a fearful living, and a poor one,
Let a man truly think on't.
To have the toil and griefs of fourscore years   20
Put up in a white sheet, tied with two knots –
Methinks it should strike earthquakes in adulterers,
When ev'n the very sheets they commit sin in
May prove, for aught they know, all their last garments.

---

   3   *express* distil, press out
   5   *curse of sorrows* pain of childbirth (cf. Genesis 3:16)
  12   *unvalued'st* invaluable, inestimable
12–14 *purchase . . . treasure* The expression of personal relations in the language of com-
       merce begins here.
  21   *white sheet . . . two knots* funeral shroud, fastened by knot at head and feet

Oh what a mark were there for women then! 25
But beauty able to content a conqueror,
Whom earth could scarce content, keeps me in compass;
I find no wish in me bent sinfully
To this man's sister, or to that man's wife:
In love's name let 'em keep their honesties, 30
And cleave to their own husbands, 'tis their duties.
Now when I go to church, I can pray handsomely;
Not come like gallants only to see faces,
As if lust went to market still on Sundays.
I must confess I am guilty of one sin, Mother, 35
More than I brought into the world with me,
But that I glory in: 'tis theft, but noble
As ever greatness yet shot up withal.

MOTHER
How's that?

LEANTIO   Never to be repented, Mother,
Though sin be death; I had died, if I had not sinned, 40
And here's my masterpiece: do you now behold her!
Look on her well, she's mine, look on her better –
Now say, if't be not the best piece of theft
That ever was committed; and I have my pardon for't:
'Tis sealed from Heaven by marriage.

MOTHER   Married to her! 45

LEANTIO
You must keep counsel, Mother, I am undone else;
If it be known, I have lost her; do but think now
What that loss is – life's but a trifle to't.
From Venice, her consent and I have brought her
From parents great in wealth, more now in rage; 50

25   *mark* example
26   *conqueror* Alexander the Great is said to have wept because there were no more
      worlds to conquer.
27   *in compass* within limits
30   *honesties* chastities
32–4 *Now . . . Sundays* Many writers of the time complained that church-going had
      become merely a social event.
35–6 *sin . . . with me* original sin
37–8 *'tis theft . . . withal* a theft as noble as any that ever helped a great man rise in the
      world
40   *sin be death* allusion to Romans 6:23: 'the wages of sin is death'
46   *keep counsel* keep it secret

272

But let storms spend their furies. Now we have got
A shelter o'er our quiet innocent loves,
We are contented. Little money sh'as brought me.
View but her face, you may see all her dowry,
Save that which lies locked up in hidden virtues,　　　　　55
Like jewels kept in cabinets.

MOTHER　　　　　　　　　Y'are to blame,
If your obedience will give way to a check,
To wrong such a perfection.

LEANTIO　　　　　　　　How?

MOTHER　　　　　　　　　　　Such a creature,
To draw her from her fortune, which no doubt,
At the full time, might have proved rich and noble:　　　60
You know not what you have done. My life can give you
But little helps, and my death lesser hopes;
And hitherto your own means has but made shift
To keep you single, and that hardly too.
What ableness have you to do her right, then,　　　　　65
In maintenance fitting her birth and virtues?
Which ev'ry woman of necessity looks for,
And most to go above it, not confined
By their conditions, virtues, bloods, or births,
But flowing to affections, wills, and humours.　　　　　70

LEANTIO

Speak low, sweet Mother; you are able to spoil as many
As come within the hearing; if it be not
Your fortune to mar all, I have much marvel.
I pray do not you teach her to rebel,
When she's in a good way to obedience,　　　　　　　75
To rise with other women in commotion
Against their husbands, for six gowns a year,

56　*to blame* ed. (too blame O). Middleton frequently uses 'blame' as an adjective and
　　'to' as the adverb 'too', i.e. too blameworthy; this edition modernizes the seven
　　occurrences in the play to the more familiar 'to blame'.
57　*check* a rebuke, but also a term in chess, anticipating the chess game in II.ii
63　*but made shift* barely managed
64　*keep you single* maintain you as a bachelor
　　hardly in hard circumstances; with difficulty
69–70　*conditions … humours* i.e. most women seek to go beyond 'necessity' – the social and
　　biological limitations of their births – to satisfy the less stable demands of desire
　　('affections' = passions; 'wills' = sexual desire; 'humours' = whims of personality)
76　*commotion* disorder, insurrection

And so maintain their cause, when they're once up,
In all things else that require cost enough.
They are all of 'em a kind of spirits soon raised,   80
But not so soon laid, Mother. As for example,
A woman's belly is got up in a trice –
A simple charge ere it be laid down again;
So ever in all their quarrels, and their courses.
And I'm a proud man, I hear nothing of 'em,   85
They're very still, I thank my happiness,
And sound asleep; pray let not your tongue wake 'em.
If you can but rest quiet, she's contented
With all conditions that my fortunes bring her to:
To keep close as a wife that loves her husband;   90
To go after the rate of my ability,
Not the licentious swinge of her own will,
Like some of her old schoolfellows. She intends
To take out other works in a new sampler,
And frame the fashion of an honest love,   95
Which knows no wants but, mocking poverty,
Brings forth more children, to make rich men wonder
At divine Providence, that feeds mouths of infants,
And sends them none to feed, but stuffs their rooms
With fruitful bags, their beds with barren wombs.   100
Good Mother, make not you things worse than they are,
Out of your too much openness – pray take heed on't –
Nor imitate the envy of old people,
That strive to mar good sport, because they are perfect.
I would have you more pitiful to youth,   105
Especially to your own flesh and blood.
I'll prove an excellent husband, here's my hand;

80–1   *spirits . . . laid* like demons or ghosts called up ('raised') or sent down ('laid'); but
       also sexual connotations of arousal and orgasm, as in ll. 82–3
  83   *simple charge* ironic: actually, a difficult or expensive business
  90   *keep close* live a secluded life
91–2   *rate . . . will* i.e. to live according to my means, rather than the unchecked
       inclinations of her own desires; but also with suggestion of her loose sexual desires
  92   *swinge* freedom of action; impulse
  94   *take . . . sampler* i.e. unlike other women, she will copy other forms (of behaviour)
       in a new model. The metaphor of embroidery continues in 'frame', l. 95.
 100   *bags* money bags
 104   *perfect* completed, contented

Lay in provision, follow my business roundly,
And make you a grandmother in forty weeks.
Go, pray salute her, bid her welcome cheerfully. 110
MOTHER
Gentlewoman, thus much is a debt of courtesy
Which fashionable strangers pay each other
At a kind meeting [*Kisses* BIANCA]; then there's more than one,
Due to the knowledge I have of your nearness.
I am bold to come again, [*Kisses her again*] and now salute you 115
By th'name of daughter, which may challenge more
Than ordinary respect. [*Kisses her again*]
LEANTIO [*Aside*]   Why, this is well now,
And I think few mothers of threescore will mend it.
MOTHER
What I can bid you welcome to, is mean;
But make it all your own; we are full of wants, 120
And cannot welcome worth.
LEANTIO [*Aside*]   Now this is scurvy,
And spake as if a woman lacked her teeth.
These old folks talk of nothing but defects,
Because they grow so full of 'em themselves.
BIANCA
Kind Mother, there is nothing can be wanting 125
To her that does enjoy all her desires.
Heaven send a quiet peace with this man's love,
And I am as rich as virtue can be poor;
Which were enough after the rate of mind,
To erect temples for content placed here. 130
I have forsook friends, fortunes, and my country,
And hourly I rejoice in't. Here's my friends,
And few is the good number. [*To* LEANTIO] Thy successes,
Howe'er they look, I will still name my fortunes;
Hopeful or spiteful, they shall all be welcome. 135
Who invites many guests has of all sorts,

108   *business roundly* 'Business' frequently has a sexual connotation in the play; 'roundly'
      = energetically. The phrase anticipates the wife's pregnancy, referred to in l. 109.
118   *mend it* do it better
120   *wants* deficiencies
121   *scurvy* irritating; also, the disease
122   *lacked her teeth* one symptom of scurvy
129   i.e. as measured by the standard of the contented mind

As he that traffics much drinks of all fortunes;
Yet they must all be welcome, and used well.
I'll call this place the place of my birth now,
And rightly too, for here my love was born,   140
And that's the birthday of a woman's joys.
You have not bid me welcome since I came.

LEANTIO
That I did questionless.

BIANCA   No sure, how was't?
I have quite forgot it.

LEANTIO   Thus. [*Kisses her*]

BIANCA   Oh sir, 'tis true,
Now I remember well. I have done thee wrong,
Pray tak't again, sir. [*Kisses him*]   145

LEANTIO   How many of these wrongs
Could I put up in an hour, and turn up the glass
For twice as many more!

MOTHER
Will't please you to walk in, daughter?

BIANCA   Thanks, sweet Mother;
The voice of her that bare me, is not more pleasing.

                                Exeunt [MOTHER *and* BIANCA]   150

LEANTIO
Though my own care and my rich master's trust
Lay their commands both on my factorship,
This day and night I'll know no other business
But her and her dear welcome. 'Tis a bitterness
To think upon tomorrow, that I must leave her
Still to the sweet hopes of the week's end.   155
That pleasure should be so restrained and curbed
After the course of a rich workmaster,
That never pays till Saturday night!
Marry, it comes together in a round sum then,
And does more good, you'll say. Oh fair-eyed Florence!   160
Didst thou but know what a most matchless jewel
Thou now art mistress of, a pride would take thee,

---

137   *traffics* trades
147   *turn up the glass* turn over an hour-glass
152   *factorship* Leantio is a clerk or agent for a merchant.
158   *After* dependent on
163   *pride* a sense of pride; but also with strong sexual overtone

Able to shoot destruction through the bloods
Of all thy youthful sons! But 'tis great policy
To keep choice treasures in obscurest places: 165
Should we show thieves our wealth, 'twould make 'em bolder.
Temptation is a devil will not stick
To fasten upon a saint; take heed of that.
The jewel is cased up from all men's eyes;
Who could imagine now a gem were kept,   170
Of that great value, under this plain roof?
But how in times of absence? What assurance
Of this restraint then? Yes, yes – there's one with her.
Old mothers know the world; and such as these,
When sons lock chests, are good to look to keys.   *Exit*   175

ACT I, SCENE ii

Enter GUARDIANO, FABRITIO, *and* LIVIA
[*and* SERVANT]

GUARDIANO
    What, has your daughter seen him yet? Know you that?
FABRITIO
    No matter, she shall love him.
GUARDIANO   Nay, let's have fair play,
    He has been now my ward some fifteen year,
    And 'tis my purpose – as time calls upon me –
    By custom seconded, and such moral virtues,
    To tender him a wife. Now, sir, this wife   5
    I'd fain elect out of a daughter of yours.

---

165   *policy* cunning
168   *stick* hesitate

  3   *ward* The guardian of a ward would want to marry off his charge before he
     reached the age of majority (21), in order to secure a payment from the father of
     the bride or, if his ward refused the match, a fine from the estate. This relationship
     led to extensive corruption on the part of guardians at the time. If the bride refused
     the match, however, no fine could be levied.
  4   *as time calls upon me* The Ward is 'almost twenty' (l. 78), hence almost at the age
     of majority.

You see my meaning's fair; if now this daughter
So tendered – let me come to your own phrase, sir –
Should offer to refuse him, I were hanselled.
[*Aside*] Thus am I fain to calculate all my words 10
For the meridian of a foolish old man,
To take his understanding! [*To him*] What do you answer, sir?

FABRITIO

I say still she shall love him.

GUARDIANO   Yet again?
And shall she have no reason for this love?

FABRITIO   15

Why, do you think that women love with reason?

GUARDIANO

[*Aside*] I perceive fools are not at all hours foolish,
No more than wise men wise.

FABRITIO   I had a wife,
She ran mad for me; she had no reason for't,
For aught I could perceive. What think you,
Lady sister?   20

GUARDIANO [*Aside*] 'Twas a fit match that,
Being both out of their wits. [*To him*] A loving wife, it seemed,
She strove to come as near you as she could.

FABRITIO

And if her daughter prove not mad for love too,
She takes not after her; nor after me,
If she prefer reason before my pleasure.   25
[*To* LIVIA] You're an experienced widow, lady sister,
I pray let your opinion come amongst us.

LIVIA

I must offend you then, if truth will do't,
And take my niece's part, and call't injustice
To force her love to one she never saw.   30

---

10   *hanselled* A 'hansel' is a gift given at the beginning of the New Year or a new
     venture; Guardiano's allusion is thus ironic – i.e. he would be left with little.
12   *meridian* point of highest development (in this case, intellectual)
13   *take* measure; catch
17   *fools . . . foolish* proverbial
20–1 *you, / Lady* ed. (you Lady O)
30–3 *injustice . . . well* Jacobean discourse frequently debated the legal and moral rights
     of a father to marry off his daughter to whomever he chose; technically, the
     daughter had to consent to the marriage. Plays such as George Wilkins's *The
     Miseries of Enforced Marriage* (1607) dramatized real-life cases.

Maids should both see, and like – all little enough;
If they love truly after that, 'tis well.
Counting the time, she takes one man till death,
That's a hard task, I tell you; but one may
Enquire at three years' end amongst young wives,   35
And mark how the game goes.

FABRITIO   Why, is not man
Tied to the same observance, lady sister,
And in one woman?

LIVIA   'Tis enough for him;
Besides, he tastes of many sundry dishes
That we poor wretches never lay our lips to –   40
As obedience, forsooth, subjection, duty, and such kickshaws,
All of our making, but served in to them.
And if we lick a finger then sometimes
We are not to blame: your best cooks use it.

FABRITIO   45
Th'art a sweet lady, sister, and a witty –

LIVIA
A witty! Oh the bud of commendation
Fit for a girl of sixteen! I am blown, man,
I should be wise by this time – and for instance,
I have buried my two husbands in good fashion,
And never mean more to marry.   50

GUARDIANO   No, why so, lady?

LIVIA
Because the third shall never bury me.
I think I am more than witty; how think you, sir?

FABRITIO
I have paid often fees to a counsellor
Has had a weaker brain.

LIVIA   Then I must tell you,
Your money was soon parted.   55

---

34   *Counting* considering
37   *game* with sexual connotation
42   *kickshaws* fancy dishes (i.e. trifles)
44–5 *lick a finger . . . best cooks* i.e. women should have some of the same rights to 'taste'
      as men. Livia's egalitarian point, however, is made through an obscene sexual meta-
      phor which foreshadows the sexual transgressions to come.
48   *blown* fully blossomed, no longer a 'bud' (l. 47)
56   *Your . . . parted* 'A fool and his money are soon parted' (Tilley, F 452).

GUARDIANO [*To* FABRITIO]   Light her now, brother!

LIVIA

Where is my niece? Let her be sent for straight.

                        [*Exit* SERVANT]

If you have any hope 'twill prove a wedding,
'Tis fit i'faith she should have one sight of him,
And stop upon't, and not be joined in haste,
As if they went to stock a new-found land.   60

FABRITIO

Look out her uncle, and y'are sure of her,
Those two are nev'r asunder: they've been heard
In argument at midnight, moonshine nights
Are noondays with them; they walk out their sleeps,
Or rather at those hours appear like those   65
That walk in 'em, for so they did to me.
Look you, I told you truth; they're like a chain,
Draw but one link, all follows.

        Enter HIPPOLITO *and* ISABELLA *the niece*

GUARDIANO   Oh affinity,

What piece of excellent workmanship art thou!
'Tis work clean wrought, for there's no lust, but love in't,   70
And that abundantly; when in stranger things
There is no love at all, but what lust brings.

FABRITIO

[*To* ISABELLA] On with your mask, for 'tis your part to see now,
And not be seen. Go to, make use of your time;
See what you mean to like; nay, and I charge you,   75
Like what you see. Do you hear me? There's no dallying.
The gentleman's almost twenty, and 'tis time

---

56   *Light . . . brother!* O's line has seemed obscure to many editors, leading to such emendations as 'like enow', with 'Brother' given to Livia, and 'Plight her now', again giving 'Brother' to Livia. Gill suggests, reasonably, that 'perhaps Guardiano is inciting Fabritio to answer Livia, to bring her down, now she is in full, witty flight?' The term 'brother' could be used very loosely.

61   *stock a new-found land* Middleton refers to the hastily-arranged marriages – in some cases, the couples had not previously met – designed to populate one of the New World colonies, probably Virginia: 'Take deliberation, sir, never choose a wife as if you were going to Virginia' (*The Roaring Girl* II.ii.66–7).

65   *walk . . . sleeps* walk together rather than sleep

71   *clean* competent; morally pure

72   *stranger things* men and women not related, hence strangers

He were getting lawful heirs, and you a-breeding on 'em.

ISABELLA

Good father!

FABRITIO   Tell not me of tongues and rumours!

You'll say the gentleman is somewhat simple –   80

The better for a husband, were you wise,

For those that marry fools, live ladies' lives.

On with the mask, I'll hear no more, he's rich;

The fool's hid under bushels.

>   [ISABELLA *puts on mask*]

LIVIA   Not so hid neither,

But here's a foul great piece of him, methinks;   85

What will he be, when he comes altogether?

Enter the WARD *with a trap-stick, and* SORDIDO *his man*

WARD

Beat him?

I beat him out o'th'field with his own cat-stick,

Yet gave him the first hand.

SORDIDO   Oh strange!

WARD   I did it,

Then he set jacks on me.   90

SORDIDO   What, my lady's tailor?

WARD

Ay, and I beat him too.

SORDIDO   Nay, that's no wonder,

He's used to beating.

WARD   Nay, I tickled him

When I came once to my tippings.

SORDIDO   Now you talk on 'em,

There was a poulterer's wife made a great complaint of you last

---

80   *tongues* gossip
85   *bushels* large quantities (of money, in his case)
87   s.d. *trap-stick* also 'cat-stick' (l. 89). A cat-stick was used in the country game of Tip-Cat (or Cat-and-Trap) to strike a wooden 'cat' (a short piece of wood tapered outward at both ends) so that it flies into the air, where it can be struck again.
90   *first hand* the first strike in the game
91   *jacks* common fellows
        tailor Tailors were proverbially cowards (and thieves).
93   *beating* used to being beaten; used to 'beaten' or embroidered cloth
94   *tippings* presumably a term in the Tip-Cat game

night to your guardianer, that you struck a bump in her child's   95
head, as big as an egg.

WARD

An egg may prove a chicken then, in time; the poulterer's wife
will get by't. When I am in game, I am furious; came my
mother's eyes in my way, I would not lose a fair end. No, were
she alive, but with one tooth in her head, I should venture the   100
striking out of that. I think of nobody when I am in play, I am
so earnest. Coads-me, my guardianer! Prithee lay up my cat
and cat-stick safe.

SORDIDO

Where, sir, i'th'chimney-corner?

WARD   Chimney-corner!

SORDIDO   105

Yes, sir, your cats are always safe i'th'chimney-corner,
Unless they burn their coats.

WARD   Marry, that I am afraid on.

SORDIDO

Why, then I will bestow your cat i'th'gutter,
And there she's safe, I am sure.

WARD   If I but live
To keep a house, I'll make thee a great man,
If meat and drink can do't. I can stoop gallantly,   110
And pitch out when I list; I'm dog at a hole.
I mar'l my guardianer does not seek a wife for me;
I protest I'll have a bout with the maids else,
Or contract my self at midnight to the larder-woman,

95–104   A prose passage suddenly intrudes into the verse – a common occurrence in this
          play. The alternation of prose and verse helps characterize the Ward throughout, a
          country bumpkin whose efforts at higher social discourse continually collapse back
          into such colloquial prose.
    96   *guardianer* guardian
    99   *get* gain
          in game playing Tip-Cat; having sex
   100   *fair end* good result
   103   *Coads-me* i.e. 'egad' – a mild oath
106–7   *cats . . . chimney . . . burn* sexual innuendo: 'cats' = whores; 'chimney' = female
          genitals; 'burn' = symptom of venereal disease
111–12   *stoop gallantly . . . pitch out . . . dog at a hole* All three are terms from a game, perhaps
          Tip-Cat, but all are also sexual puns: 'stoop gallantly', according to Mulryne, alludes
          to 'stoop-gallant', a term for venereal disease; 'pitch out' = ejaculation; 'hole' =
          female genitals.
   113   *mar'l* abbreviation for 'marvel'

In presence of a fool or a sack-posset.   115

GUARDIANO
    Ward!

WARD   I feel myself after any exercise
    Horribly prone. Let me but ride, I'm lusty,
    A cock-horse straight, i'faith.

GUARDIANO   Why, ward, I say!

WARD
    I'll forswear eating eggs in moonshine nights;
    There's nev'r a one I eat, but turns into a cock   120
    In four and twenty hours; if my hot blood
    Be not took down in time, sure 'twill crow shortly.

GUARDIANO
    Do you hear, sir? Follow me, I must new school you.

WARD
    School me? I scorn that now, I am past schooling.
    I am not so base to learn to write and read;   125
    I was born to better fortunes in my cradle.

                    Exit [WARD, GUARDIANO, *and* SORDIDO]

FABRITIO
    [*To* Isabella] How do you like him, girl? This is your husband.
    Like him or like him not, wench, you shall have him,
    And you shall love him.

LIVIA   130
    Oh soft there, brother! Though you be a Justice,
    Your warrant cannot be served out of your liberty.
    You may compel, out of the power of father,
    Things merely harsh to a maid's flesh and blood,

116   *fool* A verbal 'contract' for marriage was enacted if the proper words of declaration
        were spoken in the presence of a witness; but since this witness would be a 'fool',
        the contract would not be binding. Touchstone seeks a similarly flawed contract
        when he engages Sir Oliver Martext to marry him in *As You Like It* (III.ii).
        fool . . . sack-posset 'Fool' is a dish of fruit mixed with cream, a kind of trifle; 'sack-
        posset' was a drink made with sack, sugar, eggs and spices.

118   *prone* i.e. to lechery

118–19   *ride . . . cock-horse* a child's hobby-horse; also with strong sexual connotation of a
        loose woman

120   *eggs . . . nights* Eggs were thought to be an aphrodisiac; 'moonshine nights' were
        traditionally times of sexual festivity and release. Mulryne also suggests 'eggs-in-
        moonshine', a dish resembling poached eggs.

121–3   *cock . . . took down . . . crow* i.e. the cock will crow, but also the Ward's phallus will
        ejaculate ('crow') if it is not detumesced ('took down')

131   *Justice* a Justice of the Peace

132   *liberty* area of his legal jurisdiction

But when you come to love, there the soil alters;
Y'are in another country, where your laws   135
Are no more set by, than the cacklings of geese
In Rome's great Capitol.

FABRITIO   Marry him she shall, then,
Let her agree upon love afterwards.   *Exit*

LIVIA
You speak now, brother, like an honest mortal
That walks upon th'earth with a staff;   140
You were up i'th'clouds before. You'd command love –
And so do most old folks that go without it.
[*To* HIPPOLITO] My best and dearest brother, I could
    dwell here;
There is not such another seat on earth,
Where all good parts better express themselves.   145

HIPPOLITO
You'll make me blush anon.

LIVIA
'Tis but like saying grace before a feast, then,
And that's most comely; thou art all a feast,
And she that has thee, a most happy guest.
Prithee cheer up thy niece with special counsel.   [*Exit*]   150

HIPPOLITO
[*Aside*] I would 'twere fit to speak to her what I would; but
'Twas not a thing ordained, Heaven has forbid it;
And 'tis most meet that I should rather perish
Than the decree divine receive least blemish.
Feed inward, you my sorrows, make no noise,   155
Consume me silent, let me be stark dead
Ere the world know I'm sick. You see my honesty;
If you befriend me, so.

ISABELLA [*Aside*]   Marry a fool!
Can there be greater misery to a woman
That means to keep her days true to her husband,   160
And know no other man! So virtue wills it.
Why, how can I obey and honour him,

137–8 *geese . . . Capitol* Juno's sacred geese were kept on the Capitoline Hill. Their cackling
       once awoke the Romans to a surprise attack by the Gauls, but Livia's analogy seems
       to dismiss their effectiveness here.
146   *parts* qualities of mind and body
151   *thy* ed. (that O)
158   *You* presumably a reference to 'you my sorrows' (l. 156)

But I must needs commit idolatry?
A fool is but the image of a man,
And that but ill made neither. Oh the heart-breakings   165
Of miserable maids, where love's enforced!
The best condition is but bad enough:
When women have their choices, commonly
They do but buy their thraldoms, and bring great portions
To men to keep 'em in subjection –   170
As if a fearful prisoner should bribe
The keeper to be good to him, yet lies in still,
And glad of a good usage, a good look
Sometimes. By'r Lady, no misery surmounts a woman's!
Men buy their slaves, but women buy their masters;   175
Yet honesty and love makes all this happy
And, next to angels', the most blest estate.
That Providence, that has made ev'ry poison
Good for some use, and sets four warring elements
At peace in man, can make a harmony   180
In things that are most strange to human reason.
Oh but this marriage! [*To him*] What, are you sad too, uncle?
'Faith, then there's a whole household down together.
Where shall I go to seek my comfort now
When my best friend's distressed? What is't afflicts you, sir?   185

HIPPOLITO
'Faith, nothing but one grief that will not leave me,
And now tis welcome; ev'ry man has something
To bring him to his end, and this will serve,
Joined with your father's cruelty to you –
That helps it forward.   190

ISABELLA   Oh be cheered, sweet uncle!

164–5 *idolatry ... image* She doubly commits idolatry, because a fool is only an 'image' of
a man, and man is the image of God.
170 *portions* marriage dowries
175 *Sometimes. By'r* ed. (Sometimes by'r O)
178 *estate* condition
180 *four warring elements* Earth, air, fire and water, combined in equal portions, form
an ideal balance of nature or psychological state. Perhaps an echo of *I Tamburlaine*:
'Nature that framed us of four elements / Warring within our breasts for regiment, /
Doth teach us all to have aspiring minds' (II.vii.18–20). In saying that 'Providence'
'sets four warring elements / At peace', Isabella is inverting Tamburlaine's much
different view that 'Nature' sets these elements at war; her naivety will soon vanish.

How long has't been upon you? I nev'r spied it;
What a dull sight have I! How long, I pray, sir?

HIPPOLITO

Since I first saw you, niece, and left Bologna.

ISABELLA

And could you deal so unkindly with my heart,
To keep it up so long hid from my pity?   195
Alas, how shall I trust your love hereafter?
Have we passed through so many arguments,
And missed of that still, the most needful one?
Walked out whole nights together in discourses,
And the main point forgot? We are to blame both;   200
This is an obstinate, wilful forgetfulness,
And faulty on both parts. Let's lose no time now.
Begin, good uncle, you that feel't; what is it?

HIPPOLITO

You of all creatures, niece, must never hear on't,
'Tis not a thing ordained for you to know.   205

ISABELLA

Not I, sir! All my joys that word cuts off;
You made profession once you loved me best –
'Twas but profession!

HIPPOLITO   Yes, I do't too truly,
And fear I shall be chid for't. Know the worst, then:
I love thee dearlier than an uncle can.   210

ISABELLA

Why, so you ever said, and I believed it.

HIPPOLITO

[*Aside*] So simple is the goodness of her thoughts,
They understand not yet th'unhallowed language
Of a near sinner. I must yet be forced –
Though blushes be my venture – to come nearer.   215
[*To her*] As a man loves his wife, so love I thee.

ISABELLA   What's that?

Methought I heard ill news come toward me,
Which commonly we understand too soon,

196   *keep* shut
198   *arguments* topics, discussions
216   *nearer* become more explicit; get even closer
218–25 Somewhat obscure passage. The first hint of bad news, she implies, will be
       understood immediately, even sooner than merely hearing it; rather than welcome
       it, she will forestall ever hearing it by forswearing all discourse.

Than over-quick at hearing. I'll prevent it,
Though my joys fare the harder. Welcome it?   220
It shall nev'r come so near mine ear again.
Farewell all friendly solaces and discourses,
I'll learn to live without ye, for your dangers
Are greater than your comforts. What's become
Of truth in love, if such we cannot trust,   225
When blood that should be love is mixed with lust?   *Exit*

HIPPOLITO
The worst can be but death, and let it come;
He that lives joyless, ev'ry day's his doom.   *Exit*

ACT I, SCENE iii

Enter LEANTIO *alone*

LEANTIO
Methinks I'm ev'n as dull now at departure
As men observe great gallants the next day
After a revels; you shall see 'em look
Much of my fashion, if you mark 'em well.
'Tis ev'n a second Hell to part from pleasure
When man has got a smack on't. As many holidays   5
Coming together makes your poor heads idle
A great while after, and are said to stick
Fast in their fingers' ends, ev'n so does game
In a new-married couple for the time;

---

220   *Than* ed. (Then O). This seems a comparative, but O may also be correct, as
      Holdsworth (p. 89) notes.
      prevent anticipate
227   *blood* Isabella means 'natural relation', but the word also suggests, contrary to her
      intention, 'sexual desire'. The word 'blood' appears frequently in the play; its
      meaning may range from 'birth' or 'natural relations', to 'inclination', 'arousal',
      'desire' and 'sexual appetite'. Several quite different meanings may be invoked
      simultaneously, as here.

6   *smack* taste
8–9   *stick . . . ends* Frost suggests their 'aching head in hand', but it seems more likely to
      refer to a physical inability (parallel to the intellectual one, 'poor heads idle') after
      'many holidays'.
9   *game* sexual pleasure

It spoils all thrift, and indeed lies a-bed   10
To invent all the new ways for great expenses.

       [*Enter*] BIANCA *and* MOTHER *above*

See, and she be not got on purpose now
Into the window to look after me.
I have no power to go now, and I should be hanged.
Farewell all business, I desire no more   15
Than I see yonder. Let the goods at quay
Look to themselves; why should I toil my youth out?
It is but begging two or three year sooner,
And stay with her continually – is't a match?
Oh fie, what a religion have I leaped into!   20
Get out again, for shame! The man loves best
When his care's most, that shows his zeal to love.
Fondness is but the idiot to affection,
That plays at hot-cockles with rich merchants' wives –
Good to make sport withal when the chest's full,   25
And the long warehouse cracks. 'Tis time of day
For us to be more wise; 'tis early with us,
And if they lose the morning of their affairs,
They commonly lose the best part of the day.
Those that are wealthy, and have got enough,   30
'Tis after sunset with 'em; they may rest,
Grow fat with ease, banquet, and toy and play,
When such as I enter the heat o'th'day,
And I'll do't cheerfully.

BIANCA   I perceive, sir,
Y'are not gone yet; I have good hope you'll stay now.   35

LEANTIO
    Farewell, I must not.

BIANCA   Come, come, pray return.
Tomorrow, adding but a little care more,

    12   *expenses* Like much of the economic language in the play, 'expense' carries both a
           financial and a sexual meaning.
13, 15   *and* if
    20   *match* bargain
    24   *Fondness . . . affection* Foolish infatuation ('fondness') is a mockery of real passion
           ('affection'); 'idiot' is personified, hence infatuation is like a fool or court jester
           to the monarch Affection.
    25   *hot–cockles* a game like blindman's buff; also with insinuation of sexual fondling
    27   *cracks* i.e. because it is so full
    37   *return.* ed. (return O)

Will dispatch all as well. Believe me, 'twill, sir.

LEANTIO

    I could well wish myself where you would have me;
    But love that's wanton must be ruled awhile   40
    By that that's careful, or all goes to ruin.
    As fitting is a government in love,
    As in a kingdom; where 'tis all mere lust
    'Tis like an insurrection in the people
    That, raised in self-will, wars against all reason.   45
    But love that is respective for increase
    Is like a good king, that keeps all in peace.
    Once more, farewell.

BIANCA   But this one night, I prithee.

LEANTIO

    Alas, I'm in for twenty, if I stay,
    And then for forty more, I have such luck to flesh.   50
    I never bought a horse but he bore double.
    If I stay any longer, I shall turn
    An everlasting spendthrift; as you love
    To be maintained well, do not call me again,
    For then I shall not care which end goes forward.   55
    Again, farewell to thee.   *Exit*

BIANCA   Since it must, farewell too.

MOTHER

    'Faith daughter, y'are to blame, you take the course
    To make him an ill husband, troth you do,
    And that disease is catching, I can tell you –
    Ay, and soon taken by a young man's blood,   60
    And that with little urging. Nay, fie, see now,
    What cause have you to weep? Would I had no more,
    That have lived threescore years; there were a cause
    And 'twere well thought on. Trust me, y'are to blame,
    His absence cannot last five days at utmost.   65
    Why should those tears be fetched forth? Cannot love

---

47   *respective for increase* concerned to make a profit. 'Increase' also has an implication
     of natural procreation, as opposed to 'mere lust' (l. 44).

48   *good king* a conventional compliment to King James

52   *bore double* i.e. was strong or large enough to carry two riders. Leantio refers to
     what he claims is his habitual good fortune in sex, but unwittingly also anticipates
     Bianca's infidelity with the Duke – she will then bear 'double' riders.

56   *which end goes forward* i.e. I won't care what happens (cf. Tilley, E 130); also a
     sexual connotation

Be ev'n as well expressed in a good look,
But it must see her face still in a fountain?
It shows like a country maid dressing her head
By a dish of water. Come, 'tis an old custom   70
To weep for love.

Enter two or three BOYS, *and a* CITIZEN *or two,*
with an APPRENTICE

BOYS
Now they come, now they come!
2 BOY   The Duke!
3 BOY   The State!
CITIZEN
How near, boy?
1 BOY   I'th'next street, sir, hard at hand.
CITIZEN
You sirrah, get a standing for your mistress,
The best in all the city.   75
APPRENTICE   I have't for her, sir,
'Twas a thing I provided for her overnight,
'Tis ready at her pleasure.
CITIZEN
Fetch her to't then, away sir!

                                            [*Exit* APPRENTICE]
BIANCA
What's the meaning of this hurry,
Can you tell, Mother?   80
MOTHER   What a memory
Have I! I see by that years come upon me.
Why, 'tis a yearly custom and solemnity,
Religiously observed by th'Duke and State
To St Mark's Temple, the fifteenth of April.
See if my dull brains had not quite forgot it!   85

69   *still* always
      fountain i.e. reflected in the waters of a fountain; but also reflected in 'tears' (l. 67)
73   *State* the nobles of the city, next to the Duke in rank
75   *standing* a place to stand and see
78   *pleasure* The apprentice jokes on 'standing' (l. 75), or an erection, ready for her
      'pleasure'.
83   *solemnity* festival
85   The Feast of St Mark's was April 25 on the Gregorian calendar; Middleton may
      have converted it to the 15th, as England was then still on the Julian calendar.

'Twas happily questioned of thee, I had gone down else,
Sat like a drone below, and never thought on't.
I would not to be ten years younger again,
That you had lost the sight; now you shall see
Our Duke, a goodly gentleman of his years.   90

BIANCA

Is he old, then?

MOTHER   About some fifty-five.

BIANCA

That's no great age in man, he's then at best
For wisdom and for judgement.

MOTHER   The Lord Cardinal
His noble brother, there's a comely gentleman,
And greater in devotion than in blood.   95

BIANCA

He's worthy to be marked.

MOTHER   You shall behold
All our chief States of Florence; you came fortunately
Against this solemn day.

BIANCA   I hope so always.

                                                    Music

MOTHER

I hear 'em near us now; do you stand easily?

BIANCA   100

Exceeding well, good Mother.

MOTHER   Take this stool.

BIANCA

I need it not, I thank you.

MOTHER   Use your will, then.

        Enter in great solemnity six KNIGHTS *bare-headed,*
        then two CARDINALS, *and then the* LORD CARDINAL,
        then the DUKE; *after him the* STATES *of* FLORENCE
        by two and two, with variety of music and song

                Exit [all but MOTHER *and* BIANCA]

92   *fifty-five* King James I was fifty-five years old on 19 June 1621; if the following lines
      are more compliment to James, the allegory would soon have to end, considering
      the Duke's subsequent actions.
95   *comely* handsome
96   *blood* birth
99   *Against* in time for

MOTHER
　　How like you, daughter?
BIANCA　　　　　　　　　　'Tis a noble State.
　　Methinks my soul could dwell upon the reverence
　　Of such a solemn and most worthy custom.
　　Did not the Duke look up? Methought he saw us.　　　　　　105
MOTHER
　　That's ev'ryone's conceit that sees a duke:
　　If he look steadfastly, he looks straight at them,
　　When he perhaps, good careful gentleman,
　　Never minds any; but the look he casts
　　Is at his own intentions, and his object　　　　　　　　　　110
　　Only the public good.
BIANCA　　　　　　　　　Most likely so.
MOTHER
　　Come, come, we'll end this argument below.

　　　　　　　　　　　　　　　　　　　　　　　Exeunt

107　*conceit* idea, opinion
109　*careful* full of cares, responsibility
113　*argument* topic

ACT II, SCENE i

Enter HIPPOLITO, *and Lady* LIVIA *the widow*

LIVIA
A strange affection, brother, when I think on't!
I wonder how thou cam'st by't.

HIPPOLITO   Ev'n as easily
As man comes by destruction, which oft-times
He wears in his own bosom.

LIVIA   Is the world
So populous in women, and creation   5
So prodigal in beauty and so various?
Yet does love turn thy point to thine own blood?
'Tis somewhat too unkindly. Must thy eye
Dwell evilly on the fairness of thy kindred,
And seek not where it should? It is confined   10
Now in a narrower prison than was made for't.
It is allowed a stranger; and where bounty
Is made the great man's honour, 'tis ill husbandry
To spare, and servants shall have small thanks for't.
So he Heaven's bounty seems to scorn and mock,   15
That spares free means and spends of his own stock.

HIPPOLITO
Never was man's misery so soon sewed up,
Counting how truly.

LIVIA   Nay, I love you so,
That I shall venture much to keep a change from you
So fearful as this grief will bring upon you.   20
'Faith, it even kills me, when I see you faint
Under a reprehension, and I'll leave it,

---

7   *thy point* the point of a compass needle; also a sexual connotation ('point' = phallus)
     blood relations, kin
8   *unkindly* unnatural ('kind' = kin or family)
12 *bounty* liberality, generosity
14 *To spare* to be frugal
16 *free means . . . stock* i.e. ignores the rest of womankind for his own family ('stock' = goods; family); 'spends' also = ejaculate
17 *sewed* ed. (sow'd O). Some editors emend to 'summed'.
22 *reprehension* reprimand

Though I know nothing can be better for you.
Prithee, sweet brother, let not passion waste
The goodness of thy time, and of thy fortune.   25
Thou keep'st the treasure of that life I love
As dearly as mine own; and if you think
My former words too bitter, which were ministered
By truth and zeal, 'tis but a hazarding
Of grace and virtue, and I can bring forth   30
As pleasant fruits as sensuality wishes
In all her teeming longings. This I can do.

HIPPOLITO
Oh nothing that can make my wishes perfect!

LIVIA
I would that love of yours were pawned to't, brother,
And as soon lost that way as I could win.   35
Sir, I could give as shrewd a lift to chastity
As any she that wears a tongue in Florence.
Sh'ad need be a good horsewoman, and sit fast,
Whom my strong argument could not fling at last.
Prithee take courage, man; though I should counsel   40
Another to despair, yet I am pitiful
To thy afflictions, and will venture hard –
I will not name for what, 'tis not handsome;
Find you the proof, and praise me.

HIPPOLITO   Then I fear me,
I shall not praise you in haste.

LIVIA   This is the comfort,   45
You are not the first, brother, has attempted
Things more forbidden than this seems to be.
I'll minister all cordials now to you.
Because I'll cheer you up, sir.

HIPPOLITO   I am past hope.

24   *passion* suffering
26   *Thou keep'st* i.e. you must keep
32   *teeming* fertile, ever-increasing
33   *perfect* completed
34   *pawned to't* pledged to guarantee Livia's success
36   *give . . . lift* i.e. attack
       shrewd sharp, cunning
37   *wears a tongue* i.e. women who gossip also attack the chastity of others
43   *handsome* decent
48   *cordials* medicines which stimulate the heart

LIVIA

Love, thou shalt see me do a strange cure then,   50
As e'er was wrought on a disease so mortal,
And near akin to shame. When shall you see her?

HIPPOLITO

Never in comfort more.

LIVIA   Y'are so impatient too.

HIPPOLITO

Will you believe? Death, sh'as forsworn my company,
And sealed it with a blush.

LIVIA   So, I perceive   55
All lies upon my hands then; well, the more glory
When the work's finished.

Enter SERVANT

How now, sir, the news!

SERVANT

Madam, your niece, the virtuous Isabella,
Is 'lighted now to see you.

LIVIA   That's great fortune.
Sir, your stars bless. You simple, lead her in.   60

Exit SERVANT

HIPPOLITO

What's this to me?

LIVIA   Your absence, gentle brother;
I must bestir my wits for you.

HIPPOLITO   Ay, to great purpose.

Exit HIPPOLITO

LIVIA

Beshrew you, would I loved you not so well!
I'll go to bed, and leave this deed undone.
I am the fondest where I once affect,   65
The carefull'st of their healths, and of their ease, forsooth,
That I look still but slenderly to mine own.
I take a course to pity him so much now

---

54 *believe? Death* ed. (believe death O). 'Death' is a contraction of the expletive 'by
    God's death'.
59 *'lighted* arrived
60 *simple* fool, blockhead. Some editions emend to 'bless you simply'.
65 *fondest* most foolish
    affect love

That I have none left for modesty and myself.
This 'tis to grow so liberal; y'have few sisters   70
That love their brother's ease 'bove their own honesties.
But if you question my affections,
That will be found my fault.

Enter ISABELLA *the niece*

                              Niece, your love's welcome.
Alas, what draws that paleness to thy cheeks?
This enforced marriage towards?
ISABELLA   It helps, good aunt,   75
Amongst some other griefs; but those I'll keep
Locked up in modest silence, for they're sorrows
Would shame the tongue more than they grieve the thought.

LIVIA

Indeed, the Ward is simple.
ISABELLA   Simple! That were well;
Why, one might make good shift with such a husband.   80
But he's a fool entailed, he halts downright in't.

LIVIA

And knowing this, I hope 'tis at your choice
To take or refuse, niece.
ISABELLA   You see it is not.
I loathe him more than beauty can hate death
Or age, her spiteful neighbour.
LIVIA   Let't appear, then.   85

ISABELLA

How can I, being born with that obedience
That must submit unto a father's will?
If he command, I must of force consent.

LIVIA

Alas, poor soul! Be not offended, prithee,
If I set by the name of niece awhile,   90
And bring in pity in a stranger fashion.

70 *liberal* over-generous; also a connotation of 'licentious'
73 s.d. This entrance is placed after 'This enforced marriage towards' in O.
75 *towards* approaching, imminent
80 *make good shift* succeed
81 *entailed* i.e. he has hereditary qualities which make him a fool
     halts downright stops completely at 'fool'
88 *of force* of necessity
90 *set by* set aside

It lies here in this breast, would cross this match.

ISABELLA

How, cross it, aunt?

LIVIA   Ay, and give thee more liberty
Than thou hast reason yet to apprehend.

ISABELLA

Sweet aunt, in goodness keep not hid from me   95
What may befriend my life.

LIVIA   Yes, yes, I must,
When I return to reputation,
And think upon the solemn vow I made
To your dead mother, my most loving sister –
As long as I have her memory 'twixt mine eyelids,   100
Look for no pity now.

ISABELLA   Kind, sweet, dear aunt –

LIVIA

No, 'twas a secret I have took special care of,
Delivered by your mother on her deathbed –
That's nine years now – and I'll not part from't yet,
Though nev'r was fitter time, nor greater cause for't.   105

ISABELLA

As you desire the praises of a virgin –

LIVIA

Good sorrow! I would do thee any kindness,
Not wronging secrecy or reputation.

ISABELLA

Neither of which, as I have hope of fruitfulness,
Shall receive wrong from me.

LIVIA   Nay, 'twould be your own wrong, 110
As much as any's, should it come to that once.

ISABELLA

I need no better means to work persuasion, then.

LIVIA

Let it suffice, you may refuse this fool,
Or you may take him, as you see occasion
For your advantage; the best wits will do't.   115

---

92 *cross* thwart
93 *liberty* Cf. II.i.70n.
99 *sister* i.e. sister-in-law
100 *'twixt mine eyelids* in my mind's eye
109 *fruitfulness* ed. (fruit- / ness O)

Y'have liberty enough in your own will,
You cannot be enforced; there grows the flower,
If you could pick it out, makes whole life sweet to you.
That which you call your father's command's nothing;
Then your obedience must needs be as little. 120
If you can make shift here to taste your happiness,
Or pick out aught that likes you, much good do you.
You see your cheer, I'll make you no set dinner.

ISABELLA
And trust me, I may starve for all the good
I can find yet in this. Sweet aunt, deal plainlier. 125

LIVIA
Say I should trust you now upon an oath,
And give you in a secret that would start you,
How am I sure of you, in faith and silence?

ISABELLA
Equal assurance may I find in mercy,
As you for that in me.

LIVIA   It shall suffice. 130
Then know, however custom has made good,
For reputation's sake, the names of niece
And aunt 'twixt you and I, w'are nothing less.

ISABELLA
How's that?

LIVIA   I told you I should start your blood.
You are no more allied to any of us, 135
Save what the courtesy of opinion casts
Upon your mother's memory, and your name,
Than the merest stranger is, or one begot
At Naples when the husband lies at Rome;
There's so much odds betwixt us. Since your knowledge 140

---

121   *make shift* make an effort, bestir yourself
       taste your happiness This carries a general sexual innuendo.
122   *likes* pleases
       do you may it do you
123   *cheer . . . dinner* 'cheer' = meal, food; i.e. you see what there is, I won't describe
       it further
127   *start* startle
129   *mercy* i.e. God's divine mercy on the Day of Judgement
133   *w'are nothing less* i.e. we are not actually related
134   *start your blood* startle; sexually arouse
140   *There's . . . us* i.e. there is so much distance in our relationship

Wished more instruction, and I have your oath
In pledge for silence, it makes me talk the freelier.
Did never the report of that famed Spaniard,
Marquis of Coria, since your time was ripe
For understanding, fill your ear with wonder?   145

ISABELLA

Yes, what of him? I have heard his deeds of honour
Often related when we lived in Naples.

LIVIA

You heard the praises of your father then.

ISABELLA

My father!

LIVIA   That was he. But all the business
So carefully and so discreetly carried,   150
That fame received no spot by't, not a blemish.
Your mother was so wary to her end,
None knew it but her conscience, and her friend,
Till penitent confession made it mine,
And now my pity, yours. It had been long else,   155
And I hope care and love alike in you,
Made good by oath, will see it take no wrong now.
How weak his commands now, whom you call father?
How vain all his enforcements, your obedience?
And what a largeness in your will and liberty,   160
To take, or to reject, or to do both?
For fools will serve to father wise men's children.
All this y'have time to think on. Oh my wench!
Nothing o'erthrows our sex but indiscretion;
We might do well else of a brittle people   165
As any under the great canopy.
I pray forget not but to call me aunt still;

---

144   *Marquis of Coria* The name is given in Middleton's source; Coria is a town in Spain.
149   *business* affair; with a sexual connotation
151   *fame* reputation
152   *end* death
153   *friend* euphemism for 'lover'
160   *will and liberty* self-determination and freedom. Both words also have strong sexual overtones.
165   *brittle* fickle or frail
166   *great canopy* the sky; perhaps the theatre structure itself (cf. *Hamlet* II.ii.300–1: 'the most excellent canopy, the air'). The 'canopy' was the underside of the roof covering part of the stage.

Take heed of that, it may be marked in time else.
But keep your thoughts to yourself, from all the world,
Kindred, or dearest friend, nay, I entreat you,   170
From him that all this while you have called uncle;
And though you love him dearly, as I know
His deserts claim as much ev'n from a stranger,
Yet let not him know this, I prithee do not –
As ever thou hast hope of second pity,   175
If thou shouldst stand in need on't, do not do't.

ISABELLA
Believe my oath, I will not.

LIVIA   Why, well said.
[*Aside*] Who shows more craft t'undo a maidenhead,
I'll resign my part to her.

Enter HIPPOLITO

[*To him*]   She's thine own, go.   *Exit* [LIVIA]

HIPPOLITO
[*Aside*] Alas, fair flattery cannot cure my sorrows!   180

ISABELLA
[*Aside*] Have I passed so much time in ignorance,
And never had the means to know myself
Till this blest hour? Thanks to her virtuous pity
That brought it now to light; would I had known it
But one day sooner! He had then received   185
In favours, what, poor gentleman, he took
In bitter words: a slight and harsh reward
For one of his deserts.

HIPPOLITO [*Aside*]   There seems to me now
More anger and distraction in her looks.
I'm gone, I'll not endure a second storm;   190
The memory of the first is not past yet.

ISABELLA
[*Aside*] Are you returned, you comforts of my life,
In this man's presence? I will keep you fast now,
And sooner part eternally from the world
Than my good joys in you. [*To him*] Prithee, forgive me,   195
I did but chide in jest; the best loves use it

175   *second pity* i.e. more assistance from Livia
179–80   s.d. *Enter* HIPPOLITO . . . *Exit* ed. (*Exit. / Enter* HIPPOLITO O)

300

Sometimes, it sets an edge upon affection.
When we invite our best friends to a feast
'Tis not all sweetmeats that we set before them,
There's somewhat sharp and salt, both to whet appetite,   200
And make 'em taste their wine well. So, methinks,
After a friendly, sharp and savoury chiding,
A kiss tastes wondrous well, and full o'th'grape.

                                       [*She kisses him*]

How think'st thou, does't not?
HIPPOLITO   'Tis so excellent,
I know not how to praise it, what to say to't.   205
ISABELLA
This marriage shall go forward.
HIPPOLITO   With the Ward!
Are you in earnest?
ISABELLA   'Twould be ill for us else.
HIPPOLITO
[*Aside*] For us? How means she that?
ISABELLA [*Aside*]   Troth, I begin
To be so well, methinks, within this hour,
For all this match able to kill one's heart,   210
Nothing can pull me down now. Should my father
Provide a worse fool yet – which I should think
Were a hard thing to compass – I'd have him either:
The worse the better, none can come amiss now,
If he want wit enough. So discretion love me,   215
Desert and judgement, I have content sufficient.
[*To him*] She that comes once to be a housekeeper
Must not look every day to fare well, sir,
Like a young waiting-gentlewoman in service;
For she feeds commonly as her lady does,   220
No good bit passes her, but she gets a taste on't.

197–203 *set an edge . . . o'th'grape* 'Edge' suggests sexual arousal. This passage equates sexual
           appetite with an appetite for food, in a string of double entendres, ending in a kiss.
213 *compass* achieve
      either i.e. I'd have him just as willingly
215 *want* lack
215–16 *discretion . . . Desert and judgement* Hippolito's qualities
217–24 *housekeeper . . . get 'em* Another extended conflation of the language of food,
           commerce and sexuality: the 'house-keeper' is the married housewife, and the
           'young waiting-gentlewoman' is an unmarried girl.

But when she comes to keep house for herself,
She's glad of some choice cates then once a week,
Or twice at most, ánd glad if she can get 'em:
So must affection learn to fare with thankfulness.   225
Pray make your love no stranger, sir, that's all.
[*Aside*] Though you be one yourself, and know not on't,
And I have sworn you must not.   *Exit*
HIPPOLITO   This is beyond me!
Never came joys so unexpectedly
To meet desires in man. How came she thus?   230
What has she done to her, can any tell?
'Tis beyond sorcery, this, drugs, or love-powders;
Some art that has no name, sure, strange to me
Of all the wonders I e'er met withal
Throughout my ten years' travels; but I'm thankful for't.   235
This marriage now must of necessity forward;
It is the only veil wit can devise
To keep our acts hid from sin-piercing eyes.   *Exit*

ACT II, SCENE ii

Enter GUARDIANO *and* LIVIA

LIVIA

How, sir, a gentlewoman so young, so fair
As you set forth, spied from the widow's window!
GUARDIANO
She!
LIVIA   Our Sunday-dinner woman?
GUARDIANO
And Thursday-supper woman, the same still.

---

223   *cates* delicacies, as opposed to simple food
231   *she* refers to Livia

2   *spied from* she looked out from; she was seen at. The ambiguous grammar suggests
    that she did the spying, *and* that she was the object spied.
3–4   *Sunday-dinner . . . Thursday-supper* The Mother was probably entertained twice a
    week as an act of charity.

I know not how she came by her, but I'll swear 5
She's the prime gallant for a face in Florence;
And no doubt other parts follow their leader.
The Duke himself first spied her at the window;
Then in a rapture, as if admiration
Were poor when it were single, beckoned me, 10
And pointed to the wonder warily,
As one that feared she would draw in her splendour
Too soon, if too much gazed at. I nev'r knew him
So infinitely taken with a woman,
Nor can I blame his appetite, or tax 15
His raptures of slight folly; she's a creature
Able to draw a State from serious business,
And make it their best piece to do her service.
What course shall we devise? H'as spoke twice now.

LIVIA
    Twice?

GUARDIANO   'Tis beyond your apprehension 20
    How strangely that one look has catched his heart!
    'Twould prove but too much worth in wealth and favour
    To those should work his peace.

LIVIA   And if I do't not,
    Or at least come as near it – if your art
    Will take a little pains and second me – 25
    As any wench in Florence of my standing,
    I'll quite give o'er, and shut up shop in cunning.

GUARDIANO
    'Tis for the Duke, and if I fail your purpose,
    All means to come, by riches or advancement,
    Miss me and skip me over!

LIVIA   Let the old woman then 30
    Be sent for with all speed, then I'll begin.

---

  6   *prime* top, best
      gallant male or female fashionable person
  7   *leader* i.e. her 'face'
 10 *single* unshared
15–16 *tax . . . folly* criticize his passion as trivial folly
 18 *piece* work, accomplishment
 20 *apprehension* ed. (apprehension. O)
 21 *strangely* ed. (strangly O)
 23 *work his peace* satisfy his desires

GUARDIANO

A good conclusion follow, and a sweet one,
After this stale beginning with old ware.
Within there!

Enter SERVANT

SERVANT   Sir, do you call?
GUARDIANO   Come near, list hither.
                    [*Talks aside with servant*]
LIVIA

I long myself to see this absolute creature,   35
That wins the heart of love and praise so much.
GUARDIANO

Go, sir, make haste.
LIVIA   Say I entreat her company;
Do you hear, sir?
SERVANT   Yes, madam.   *Exit*
LIVIA   That brings her quickly.
GUARDIANO

I would 'twere done; the Duke waits the good hour,
And I wait the good fortune that may spring from't.   40
I have had a lucky hand these fifteen year
At such court-passage with three dice in a dish.
Signor Fabritio!

Enter FABRITIO

FABRITIO

Oh sir, I bring an alteration in my mouth now.
GUARDIANO

[*Aside*] An alteration! No wise speech, I hope;   45
He means not to talk wisely, does he trow?
[*To him*] Good! What's the change, I pray, sir?
FABRITIO   A new change.

---

33 *stale . . . ware* old goods, i.e. the Mother
35 *absolute* complete, perfect
42 *court-passage* 'Passage is a Game at Dice to be play'd at but by two, and it is
    performed with three Dice. The *Caster* throws continually till he hath thrown
    Doubles under ten, and then he is out and loseth; or doublets above ten, and then
    he *passeth* and wins' (Charles Cotton, *Compleat Gamester* [1674], p. 167; quoted in
    Gill). 'Court passage' also suggests sexual encounters at Court; 'three dice in a dish'
    also carries a sexual insinuation.
47 *new change* a comical redundancy; perhaps also a reference to the so-called 'New

GUARDIANO

    [*Aside*] Another yet! 'Faith, there's enough already.

FABRITIO

    My daughter loves him now.

GUARDIANO   What, does she, sir?

FABRITIO

    Affects him beyond thought, who but the Ward, forsooth!   50

    No talk but of the Ward; she would have him

    To choose 'bove all the men she ever saw.

    My will goes not so fast as her consent now;

    Her duty gets before my command still.

GUARDIANO

    Why then, sir, if you'll have me speak my thoughts,   55

    I smell 'twill be a match.

FABRITIO   Ay, and a sweet young couple,

    If I have any judgement.

GUARDIANO [*Aside*]   'Faith, that's little.

    [*To him*] Let her be sent tomorrow before noon,

    And handsomely tricked up; for 'bout that time

    I mean to bring her in and tender her to him.   60

FABRITIO

    I warrant you for handsome; I will see

    Her things laid ready, every one in order,

    And have some part of her tricked up tonight.

GUARDIANO

    Why, well said.

FABRITIO   'Twas a use her mother had,

    When she was invited to an early wedding;   65

    She'd dress her head o'ernight, sponge up herself,

    And give her neck three lathers.

GUARDIANO [*Aside*]   Ne'er a halter?

FABRITIO

    On with her chain of pearl, her ruby bracelets,

    Lay ready all her tricks and jiggam-bobs.

        Change' (an addition to the Royal Exchange), a meeting-place for merchants,
        opened in the Strand in 1609, which some thought unnecessary

    59   *tricked up* dressed up

    64   *use* custom

    67   *halter* A halter would be made of leather (thus the pun on 'lather'); halters are for
        horses, cows and people going to be hanged.

    69   *tricks and jiggam-bobs* ornaments and knick-knacks. 'Tricks' also has a sexual
        connotation. Cf. also 'tricked' (l. 59) and 'tricks' (l. 188).

GUARDIANO
  So must your daughter.

FABRITIO   I'll about it straight, sir.   *Exit*   70

LIVIA
  How he sweats in the foolish zeal of fatherhood
  After six ounces an hour, and seems
  To toil as much as if his cares were wise ones!

GUARDIANO
  Y'have let his folly blood in the right vein, lady.

LIVIA
  And here comes his sweet son-in-law that shall be.   75
  They're both allied in wit before the marriage;
  What will they be hereafter, when they are nearer?
  Yet they can go no further than the fool:
  There's the world's end in both of 'em.

          Enter WARD *and* SORDIDO, *one with a shuttlecock,*
                   the other a battledore

GUARDIANO   Now, young heir!

WARD
  What's the next business after shittlecock now?   80

GUARDIANO
  Tomorrow you shall see the gentlewoman
  Must be your wife.

WARD   There's ev'n another thing too
  Must be kept up with a pair of battledores.
  My wife! What can she do?

GUARDIANO
  Nay, that's a question you should ask yourself, Ward,   85
  When y'are alone together.

                         [LIVIA *and* GUARDIANO *talk apart*]

72 *After* at the rate of
74 *let . . . blood* reference to blood-letting as a medical cure; used here figuratively, as
    Livia has precisely described Fabritio's 'foolish zeal'
79 *world's end* i.e. as far as one can go
    s.d. *shuttlecock* ed. (shittlecock O). This edition retains the Ward's mis-
    pronunciations; the excretory pun is explicitly invoked in 'stool-ball' at III.iii.83.
    shuttlecock . . . battledore The 'shuttlecock' is struck back and forth by a racquet, or
    'battledore', in this precursor game to modern badminton. The Ward, at ll. 82–4,
    will make the equation women = shuttlecocks = whores, because women
    supposedly 'shuttle' back and forth between 'cocks', to 'do', and are 'kept up' by
    phallic 'battledores'.
82 *thing* i.e. phallus

WARD   That's as I list.
    A wife's to be asked anywhere, I hope;
    I'll ask her in a congregation, if I have a mind to't,
    and so save a licence. My guardianer has no more wit than
    an herb-woman that sells away all her sweet herbs and   90
    nosegays, and keeps a stinking breath for her own
    pottage.

SORDIDO
    Let me be at the choosing of your beloved,
    If you desire a woman of good parts.

WARD
    Thou shalt, sweet Sordido.   95

SORDIDO
    I have a plaguey guess: let me alone to see what she is. If I but
    look upon her – 'way, I know all the faults to a hair that you
    may refuse her for.

WARD
    Dost thou? I prithee let me hear 'em, Sordido.

SORDIDO
    Well, mark 'em then; I have 'em all in rhyme.   100
    The wife your guardianer ought to tender
    Should be pretty, straight and slender;
    Her hair not short, her foot not long,
    Her hand not huge, nor too too loud her tongue;
    No pearl in eye, nor ruby in her nose,   105
    No burn or cut, but what the catalogue shows.
    She must have teeth, and that no black ones,
    And kiss most sweet when she does smack once;
    Her skin must be both white and plumped,
    Her body straight, not hopper-rumped,   110

---

87   *asked* ed. (ask O)
88–9 *ask . . . licence* He will proclaim the banns of marriage publicly, and so save the
    expense of a special licence.
91–2 *breath . . . pottage* blowing on soup to cool it
96   *plaguey guess* shrewd or sharp judgement
97   *'way* straightaway, immediately
105 *pearl in eye* whitish spot in eye, the result of a cataract or a disease like smallpox
    ruby i.e. pimple
106 *burn or cut* To 'burn' is a symptom of venereal disease; 'cut' = slang for female
    genitals (cf. Malvolio in *Twelfth Night* II.v.86–8).
109 *plumped* ed. (plump O)
110 *hopper-rumped* 'The hopper of a mill is shaped like an inverted pyramid and has a
    hopping or shaking movement' (Gill) – i.e. with large buttocks.

Or wriggle sideways like a crab;
She must be neither slut nor drab,
Nor go too splay-foot with her shoes,
To make her smock lick up the dews.
And two things more, which I forgot to tell ye: 115
She neither must have bump in back, nor belly.
These are the faults that will not make her pass.

WARD

And if I spy not these, I am a rank ass.

SORDIDO

Nay more; by right, sir, you should see her naked,
For that's the ancient order.

WARD   See her naked?   120
That were good sport, i'faith. I'll have the books turned over;
And if I find her naked on record,
She shall not have a rag on. But stay, stay,
How if she should desire to see me so, too?
I were in a sweet case then, such a foul skin.   125

SORDIDO

But y'have a clean shirt, and that makes amends, sir.

WARD

I will not see her naked for that trick, though.   *Exit*

SORDIDO

Then take her with all faults, with her clothes on!
And they may hide a number with a bum-roll.
'Faith, choosing of a wench in a huge farthingale   130
Is like the buying of ware under a great penthouse:
What with the deceit of one,
And the false light of th'other, mark my speeches,
He may have a diseased wench in's bed,
And rotten stuff in's breeches.   *Exit* 135

---

112   *drab* whore
116   *have bump ... belly* be neither hunchbacked nor pregnant
119–25 *naked ... skin* This custom is described in Thomas More's *Utopia,* but the passage
       also says the male wooer should appear naked to the woman, as the Ward fears.
125   *case* situation; clothing
129   *bum-roll* a cushion worn to hold out the skirt
130   *farthingale* a framework of hoops, worn about the waist, which extended a
       woman's dress
131   *penthouse* a sloping roof over a door or window. It would block the light from a
       merchant's shop, hence make it more difficult to judge the quality of his goods in
       such a 'false light' (l. 133).
135   *rotten stuff* poor quality cloth; venereal disease

GUARDIANO
    It may take handsomely.
LIVIA   I see small hindrance.
    How now, so soon returned?

                Enter MOTHER

GUARDIANO   She's come.
LIVIA   That's well.
    Widow, come, come, I have a great quarrel to you,
    'Faith, I must chide you, that you must be sent for!
    You make yourself so strange, never come at us;   140
    And yet so near a neighbour, and so unkind!
    Troth, y'are to blame, you cannot be more welcome
    To any house in Florence, that I'll tell you.
MOTHER
    My thanks must needs acknowledge so much, madam.
LIVIA
    How can you be so strange then? I sit here   145
    Sometime whole days together without company,
    When business draws this gentleman from home,
    And should be happy in society,
    Which I so well affect as that of yours.
    I know y'are alone, too; why should not we,   150
    Like two kind neighbours, then supply the wants
    Of one another, having tongue-discourse,
    Experience in the world, and such kind helps
    To laugh down time, and meet age merrily?
MOTHER
    Age, madam! You speak mirth; 'tis at my door,   155
    But a long journey from your ladyship yet.
LIVIA
    My faith, I'm nine and thirty, ev'ry stroke, wench,
    And 'tis a general observation
    'Mongst knights' wives or widows, we accompt
    Ourselves then old, when young men's eyes leave looking at's.   160
    'Tis a true rule amongst us, and ne'er failed yet
    In any but in one, that I remember;

136   *take* work, succeed
140   *so strange* so much a stranger
152   *tongue-discourse* facility in conversation
154   *merrily* ed. (merely O)

Indeed, she had a friend at nine and forty;
Marry, she paid well for him, and in th'end
He kept a quean or two with her own money,   165
That robbed her of her plate and cut her throat.

MOTHER

She had her punishment in this world, madam,
And a fair warning to all other women
That they live chaste at fifty.

LIVIA   Ay, or never, wench.
Come, now I have thy company I'll not part with't   170
Till after supper.

MOTHER   Yes, I must crave pardon, madam.

LIVIA

I swear you shall stay supper. We have no strangers, woman,
None but my sojourners and I, this gentleman
And the young heir his ward; you know our company.

MOTHER

Some other time I will make bold with you, madam.   175

GUARDIANO

Nay, pray stay, widow.

LIVIA   'Faith, she shall not go;
Do you think I'll be forsworn?

Table and chess [are prepared]

MOTHER   'Tis a great while
Till supper time; I'll take my leave then, now, madam,
And come again i'th'evening, since your ladyship
Will have it so.

LIVIA   I'th'evening! By my troth, wench,   180
I'll keep you while I have you; you have great business, sure,
To sit alone at home; I wonder strangely
What pleasure you take in't! Were't to me now,
I should be ever at one neighbour's house
Or other all day long. Having no charge,   185
Or none to chide you, if you go, or stay,

163   *friend* lover. See II.i.153n.
165   *quean* whore
166   *plate* silver dishes and cutlery
168   *fair . . . women* perhaps an allusion to the anonymous play *A Warning for Fair
       Women* (1599)
173   *sojourners* house guests staying with her
182   *strangely* greatly
185   *charge* responsibility, duty

310

Who may live merrier, ay, or more at heart's ease?
Come, we'll to chess, or draughts; there are an hundred tricks
To drive out time till supper, never fear't, wench.

MOTHER

I'll but make one step home, and return straight, madam.   190

LIVIA

Come, I'll not trust you; you use more excuses
To your kind friends than ever I knew any.
What business can you have, if you be sure
Y'have locked the doors? And that being all you have,
I know y'are careful on't. One afternoon   195
So much to spend here! Say I should entreat you now
To lie a night or two, or a week with me,
Or leave your own house for a month together –
It were a kindness that long neighbourhood
And friendship might well hope to prevail in.   200
Would you deny such a request? I'faith,
Speak truth, and freely.

MOTHER   I were then uncivil, madam.

LIVIA

Go to then, set your men; we'll have whole nights
Of mirth together ere we be much older, wench.

MOTHER

[*Aside*] As good now tell her, then, for she will know't;   205
I have always found her a most friendly lady.

LIVIA

Why, widow, where's your mind?

MOTHER   Troth, ev'n at home, madam.

To tell you truth, I left a gentlewoman
Ev'n sitting all alone, which is uncomfortable,
Especially to young bloods.

LIVIA   Another excuse!   210

MOTHER

No, as I hope for health, madam, that's a truth;
Please you to send and see.

LIVIA   What gentlewoman? Pish!

---

188   *chess* Middleton was technically knowledgeable about chess; his play *A Game At
      Chess* (1624), an allegory of English/Spanish foreign relations, would become the
      most popular play of the period.
203   *men* chessmen

MOTHER
    Wife to my son, indeed, but not known, madam,
    To any but yourself.
LIVIA   Now I beshrew you,
    Could you be so unkind to her and me,   215
    To come and not bring her? 'Faith, 'tis not friendly.
MOTHER
    I feared to be too bold.
LIVIA   Too bold? Oh what's become
    Of the true hearty love was wont to be
    'Mongst neighbours in old time?
MOTHER   And she's a stranger, madam.
LIVIA
    The more should be her welcome. When is courtesy   220
    In better practice, than when 'tis employed
    In entertaining strangers? I could chide, i'faith.
    Leave her behind, poor gentlewoman, alone too!
    Make some amends, and send for her betimes, go.
MOTHER
    Please you command one of your servants, madam.   225
LIVIA
    Within there.

Enter SERVANT

SERVANT   Madam.
LIVIA   Attend the gentlewoman.
MOTHER
    [*Aside*] It must be carried wondrous privately
    From my son's knowledge, he'll break out in storms else.
    [*To* SERVANT] Hark you, sir.
                  [*They talk privately; exit* SERVANT]
LIVIA [*Aside to* GUARDIANO]Now comes in the heat of your part.
GUARDIANO
    [*Aside to* LIVIA] True, I know it, lady, and if I be out,   230
    May the Duke banish me from all employments,
    Wanton, or serious.
LIVIA   So, have you sent, widow?

---

224   *betimes* at once
229–30   *part . . . out a* theatrical metaphor: to 'be out' is to forget the lines of a 'part'

MOTHER

    Yes, madam, he's almost at home by this.

LIVIA

    And 'faith, let me entreat you, that henceforward
    All such unkind faults may be swept from friendship,   235
    Which does but dim the lustre. And think thus much,
    It is a wrong to me, that have ability
    To bid friends welcome, when you keep 'em from me;
    You cannot set greater dishonour near me,
    For bounty is the credit and the glory   240
    Of those that have enough. I see y'are sorry,
    And the good 'mends is made by't.

MOTHER   Here she's, madam.

    Enter BIANCA, *and* SERVANT [*who shows her in, then exits*]

BIANCA

    [*Aside*] I wonder how she comes to send for me now?

LIVIA

    Gentlewoman, y'are most welcome, trust me y'are,
    As courtesy can make one, or respect   245
    Due to the presence of you.

BIANCA   I give you thanks, lady.

LIVIA

    I heard you were alone, and 't had appeared
    An ill condition in me, though I knew you not,
    Nor ever saw you – yet humanity
    Thinks ev'ry case her own – to have kept your company   250
    Here from you, and left you all solitary.
    I rather ventured upon boldness then
    As the least fault, and wished your presence here –
    A thing most happily motioned of that gentleman,
    Whom I request you, for his care and pity,   255
    To honour and reward with your acquaintance;
    A gentleman that ladies' rights stands for,
    That's his profession.

242   *'mends* amends
248   *ill condition* bad manners
249   *humanity* humaneness
254   *motioned of* proposed by
257   *stands for* professes or defends; has an erection
258   *profession* an ironic reference to Guardiano's 'profession' as guardian, as well as his
        assertion. See note at I.ii.3.

BIANCA   'Tis a noble one,
  And honours my acquaintance.
GUARDIANO   All my intentions
  Are servants to such mistresses.
BIANCA   'Tis your modesty   260
  It seems, that makes your deserts speak so low, sir.
LIVIA
  Come, widow. [*To* BIANCA] Look you, lady, here's our business;
  Are we not well employed, think you?   [*Points to chess table*]
                            An old quarrel
  Between us, that will never be at an end.
BIANCA   No,
  And methinks there's men enough to part you, lady.   265
LIVIA
  Ho! But they set us on, let us come off
  As well as we can, poor souls, men care no farther.
  I pray sit down, forsooth, if you have the patience
  To look upon two weak and tedious gamesters.
GUARDIANO
  'Faith, madam, set these by till evening,   270
  You'll have enough on't then; the gentlewoman,
  Being a stranger, would take more delight
  To see your rooms and pictures.
LIVIA   Marry, good sir,
  And well remembered! I beseech you show 'em her;
  That will beguile time well. Pray heartily do, sir,   275
  I'll do as much for you; here, take these keys,
  Show her the monument too – and that's a thing
  Everyone sees not; you can witness that, widow.
MOTHER
  And that's worth sight indeed, madam.
BIANCA   Kind lady,
  I fear I came to be a trouble to you.   280

258–9   *one, / And* ed. (one, and O)
259–60 *intentions / Are* ed. (intentions are O)
264–5 *No, / And* ed. (No, and O)
  265 *men* chessmen
  266 *set us on* encourage or incite; sexually arouse
       come off come through, get free; achieve sexual orgasm
  277 *monument* a carved figure in wood or stone

LIVIA
Oh nothing less, forsooth.
BIANCA   And to this courteous gentleman,
That wears a kindness in his breast so noble
And bounteous to the welcome of a stranger.
GUARDIANO
If you but give acceptance to my service,
You do the greatest grace and honour to me   285
That courtesy can merit.
BIANCA   I were to blame else,
And out of fashion much. I pray you lead, sir.
LIVIA
After a game or two w'are for you, gentlefolks.
GUARDIANO
We wish no better seconds in society
Than your discourses, madam, and your partner's there.   290
MOTHER
I thank your praise. I listened to you, sir,
Though when you spoke there came a paltry rook
Full in my way, and chokes up all my game.
                                        Exit GUARDIANO *and* BIANCA
LIVIA
Alas, poor widow, I shall be too hard for thee.
MOTHER
Y'are cunning at the game, I'll be sworn, madam.   295
LIVIA
It will be found so, ere I give you over.
She that can place her man well –
MOTHER   As you do, madam.
LIVIA
– As I shall, wench, can never lose her game.
Nay, nay, the black king's mine.

281   *nothing less* i.e. not at all
292   *rook* the chesspiece, now also known as the castle. In Middleton's time, it was also
      called the 'duke' (see l. 300).
295   *game* the chessgame, but here – as throughout this scene – with an obvious sexual
      connotation as well
296   *ere . . . over* before I am finished with you
297   *man* the chesspiece; the duke offstage
299   *black king* the chesspiece, here associated with evil, in contrast to the 'saintish'
      'white king' at l. 305

MOTHER   Cry you mercy, madam.

LIVIA

And this my queen.

MOTHER   I see't now.

LIVIA   Here's a duke   300

Will strike a sure stroke for the game anon;

Your pawn cannot come back to relieve itself.

MOTHER

I know that, madam.

LIVIA   You play well the whilst;

How she belies her skill! I hold two ducats

I give you check and mate to your white king,   305

Simplicity itself, your saintish king there.

MOTHER

Well, ere now, lady,

I have seen the fall of subtlety. Jest on.

LIVIA

Ay, but simplicity receives two for one.

MOTHER

What remedy but patience!

Enter above GUARDIANO *and* BIANCA

BIANCA   Trust me, sir,   310

Mine eye nev'r met with fairer ornaments.

GUARDIANO

Nay, livelier, I'm persuaded, neither Florence

Nor Venice can produce.

BIANCA   Sir, my opinion

Takes your part highly.

GUARDIANO   There's a better piece

Yet than all these.

[Enter] DUKE *above*

---

299 *Cry you mercy* The rules of modern chess require a similar phrase if a player accid-
     entally touches the wrong piece.

301 *stroke* blow; also a sexual connotation

302 *pawn . . . back* A pawn can move only forward; thus Bianca cannot escape or go
     back.

304 *hold* wager

309 *simplicity . . . one* Livia, playing black, seems to have taken 'two' of the white
     ('simplicity') pieces for 'one' of her black ones.

314 *Takes your part* supports your argument

BIANCA	Not possible, sir!	
GUARDIANO	Believe it;	315

    You'll say so when you see't. Turn but your eye now,

    Y'are upon't presently.   *Exit*

BIANCA [*Sees* DUKE]   Oh sir!

DUKE   He's gone, beauty!

    Pish, look not after him! He's but a vapour

    That when the sun appears is seen no more.

BIANCA

    Oh treachery to honour!

DUKE   Prithee, tremble not;   320

    I feel thy breast shake like a turtle panting

    Under a loving hand that makes much on't.

    Why art so fearful? As I'm friend to brightness,

    There's nothing but respect and honour near thee.

    You know me, you have seen me; here's a heart   325

    Can witness I have seen thee.

BIANCA   The more's my danger.

DUKE

    The more's thy happiness. Pish, strive not, sweet!

    This strength were excellent employed in love, now,

    But here 'tis spent amiss. Strive not to seek

    Thy liberty and keep me still in prison.   330

    I'faith, you shall not out till I'm released now;

    We'll be both freed together, or stay still by't;

    So is captivity pleasant.

BIANCA   Oh my lord!

DUKE

    I am not here in vain; have but the leisure

    To think on that, and thou'lt be soon resolved.   335

    The lifting of thy voice is but like one

    That does exalt his enemy, who, proving high,

    Lays all the plots to confound him that raised him.

    Take warning, I beseech thee; thou seem'st to me

    A creature so composed of gentleness   340

    And delicate meekness, such as bless the faces

    Of figures that are drawn for goddesses,

317   *presently* immediately
321   *turtle* turtle-dove
323   *brightness* beauty
327   *happiness* personal well-being; good fortune
337   *exalt* raise; sexually arouse (continued in 'raised', l. 338)

And makes art proud to look upon her work;
I should be sorry the least force should lay
An unkind touch upon thee.

BIANCA   Oh my extremity!   345
My lord, what seek you?

DUKE   Love.

BIANCA   'Tis gone already,
I have a husband.

DUKE   That's a single comfort;
Take a friend to him.

BIANCA   That's a double mischief,
Or else there's no religion.

DUKE   Do not tremble
At fears of thine own making.

BIANCA   Nor, great lord,   350
Make me not bold with death and deeds of ruin
Because they fear not you; me they must fright,
Then am I best in health. Should thunder speak
And none regard it, it had lost the name
And were as good be still. I'm not like those   355
That take their soundest sleeps in greatest tempests;
Then wake I most, the weather fearfullest,
And call for strength to virtue.

DUKE   Sure I think
Thou know'st the way to please me. I affect
A passionate pleading 'bove an easy yielding,   360
But never pitied any; they deserve none
That will not pity me. I can command:
Think upon that. Yet if thou truly knewest
The infinite pleasure my affection takes
In gentle, fair entreatings, when love's businesses   365
Are carried courteously 'twixt heart and heart,
You'd make more haste to please me.

BIANCA   Why should you seek, sir,
To take away that you can never give?

348   *friend* lover. See II.i.153n.
      to in addition to
351   *bold with* be presumptuous of; take liberties with
353–8 She is in best (moral) health when she pays attention to, or feels 'fright' at, the
      'thunder' (l. 353) and 'greatest tempests' (l. 356) of moral prohibition. She will 'wake'
      (l. 357) most when the greatest ('fearfullest') temptations – as now – are present.

DUKE

But I give better in exchange: wealth, honour.
She that is fortunate in a duke's favour   370
Lights on a tree that bears all women's wishes;
If your own mother saw you pluck fruit there,
She would commend your wit and praise the time
Of your nativity. Take hold of glory.
Do not I know y'have cast away your life   375
Upon necessities, means merely doubtful
To keep you in indifferent health and fashion –
A thing I heard too lately, and soon pitied –
And can you be so much your beauty's enemy
To kiss away a month or two in wedlock,   380
And weep whole years in wants for ever after?
Come, play the wise wench, and provide for ever;
Let storms come when they list, they find thee sheltered.
Should any doubt arise, let nothing trouble thee;
Put trust in our love for the managing   385
Of all to thy heart's peace. We'll talk together,
And show a thankful joy for both our fortunes.

Exit [both] above

LIVIA

Did not I say my duke would fetch you over, widow?

MOTHER

I think you spoke in earnest when you said it, madam.

LIVIA

And my black king makes all the haste he can, too.   390

MOTHER

Well, madam, we may meet with him in time yet.

LIVIA

I have given thee blind mate twice.

MOTHER   You may see, madam,

My eyes begin to fail.

LIVIA   I'll swear they do, wench.

371–2   *tree . . . fruit* an allusion to the Fall, described in Genesis 3, when Eve ate of the fruit
          of the tree against God's command
376   *merely* completely
382   *wise* ed. (wife O)
388   *fetch you over* i.e. get the better of you
392   *blind mate* when your opponent places you in checkmate but does not see it, calling
          out only 'check' (Livia is the one who has blinded her opponent, of course); also a
          reference to the sexual mating offstage

319

Enter GUARDIANO

GUARDIANO

[*Aside*] I can but smile as often as I think on't,
How prettily the poor fool was beguiled, 395
How unexpectedly! It's a witty age.
Never were finer snares for women's honesties
Than are devised in these days; no spider's web
Made of a daintier thread than are now practised
To catch love's flesh-fly by the silver wing. 400
Yet to prepare her stomach by degrees
To Cupid's feast, because I saw 'twas queasy,
I showed her naked pictures by the way –
A bit to stay the appetite. Well, advancement!
I venture hard to find thee; if thou com'st 405
With a greater title set upon thy crest,
I'll take that first cross patiently, and wait
Until some other comes greater than that.
I'll endure all.

LIVIA

The game's ev'n at the best now; you may see, widow, 410
How all things draw to an end.

MOTHER   Ev'n so do I, madam.

LIVIA

I pray take some of your neighbours along with you.

MOTHER

They must be those are almost twice your years, then,
If they be chose fit matches for my time, madam.

LIVIA

Has not my duke bestirred himself?

MOTHER   Yes, 'faith, madam; 415
H'as done me all the mischief in this game.

---

400 *flesh-fly* the blow-fly, which deposits its eggs in flesh; also a sexual connotation
401 *stomach* sexual appetite
404 *stay* settle; enhance
406–8 *greater . . . that* i.e. if reward comes to one more elevated (with 'greater title'), he will endure such a disappointment ('cross') in the hope of an even 'greater' reward later
411 *to an end* the end of the chessgame; the sexual climax off–stage. The mother also understands Livia to refer to the end of life.
414 *time* age
415–16 *madam; / H'as* ed. (Madam; h'as O)

LIVIA
H'as showed himself in's kind.
MOTHER   In's kind, call you it?
I may swear that.
LIVIA   Yes 'faith, and keep your oath.
GUARDIANO
[*Aside*] Hark, list! There's somebody coming down; 'tis she.

Enter BIANCA

BIANCA
[*Aside*] Now bless me from a blasting! I saw that now   420
Fearful for any woman's eye to look on.
Infectious mists and mildews hang at's eyes,
The weather of a doomsday dwells upon him.
Yet since mine honour's leprous, why should I
Preserve that fair that caused the leprosy?   425
Come, poison all at once!
[*Aside to* GUARDIANO]   Thou in whose baseness
The bane of virtue broods, I'm bound in soul
Eternally to curse thy smooth-browed treachery,
That wore the fair veil of a friendly welcome,
And I a stranger; think upon't, 'tis worth it.   430
Murders piled up upon a guilty spirit
At his last breath will not lie heavier
Than this betraying act upon thy conscience.
Beware of off'ring the first-fruits to sin:
His weight is deadly who commits with strumpets   435
After they have been abased and made for use;
If they offend to th'death, as wise men know,
How much more they, then, that first make 'em so?
I give thee that to feed on. I'm made bold now,
I thank thy treachery; sin and I'm acquainted,   440

417   *in's kind* in his own nature
420   *blasting* infection; withering under a pernicious influence
422   *Infectious . . . mildews* Mists and fog were thought to cause disease.
424   *why* ed. (who O)
425   *that fair* her beauty
427   *broods* hatches
428   *smooth-browed* i.e. hypocritical
435   *His weight is deadly* i.e. his soul is mortally guilty   *commits* fornicates
437   *they* those who 'commit'
438   *'em* them (the strumpets)

No couple greater; and I'm like that great one
Who, making politic use of a base villain,
He likes the treason well, but hates the traitor,
So I hate thee, slave.

GUARDIANO [*Aside*]   Well, so the Duke loves me,
I fare not much amiss then; two great feasts   445
Do seldom come together in one day,
We must not look for 'em.

BIANCA   What, at it still, Mother?

MOTHER
You see we sit by't; are you so soon returned?

LIVIA
[*Aside*] So lively and so cheerful? A good sign, that.

MOTHER
You have not seen all since, sure?

BIANCA   That have I, Mother,   450
The monument and all. I'm so beholding
To this kind, honest, courteous gentleman,
You'd little think it, Mother, showed me all,
Had me from place to place, so fashionably;
The kindness of some people, how't exceeds!   455
'Faith, I have seen that I little thought to see
I'th'morning when I rose.

MOTHER   Nay, so I told you
Before you saw't, it would prove worth your sight.
I give you great thanks for my daughter, sir,
And all your kindness towards her.

GUARDIANO   Oh good widow!   460
Much good may 't do her – [*Aside*] forty weeks hence, i'faith.

Enter SERVANT

LIVIA
Now, sir?

SERVANT   May't please you, madam, to walk in?
Supper's upon the table.

LIVIA   Yes, we come;
Will't please you, gentlewoman?

---

443   Italics indicate a proverbial saying; see Tilley, K 64.
454   *Had me* brought me; had me sexually
461   *may 't* ed. (may O)

BIANCA   Thanks, virtuous lady –
  [*Aside to* LIVIA] Y'are a damned bawd!
  [*Aloud to others*]   I'll follow you forsooth,   465
  Pray take my mother in. [*Aside*] An old ass go with you!
  [*Aloud*] This gentleman and I vow not to part.
LIVIA
  Then get you both before.
BIANCA [*Aside*]   There lies his art.
              Exeunt [BIANCA, GUARDIANO, *and* SERVANT]
LIVIA
  Widow, I'll follow you.
                                   [*Exit* MOTHER]
              Is't so, 'damned bawd'?
  Are you so bitter? 'Tis but want of use;   470
  Her tender modesty is sea-sick a little,
  Being not accustomed to the breaking billow
  Of woman's wavering faith, blown with temptations.
  'Tis but a qualm of honour, 'twill away;
  A little bitter for the time, but lasts not.   475
  Sin tastes at the first draught like wormwood water,
  But drunk again, 'tis nectar ever after.   *Exit*

---

468   *There lies his art* As a pander, Guardiano goes 'before' the Duke.
471–2   *sea-sick . . . breaking billow* The implied voyage is a metaphor of the first sexual
      encounter.
476   *wormwood water* a drink prepared from the herb wormwood, known for its
      bitterness

ACT III, SCENE i

Enter MOTHER

MOTHER
    I would my son would either keep at home,
    Or I were in my grave!
    She was but one day abroad, but ever since
    She's grown so cutted, there's no speaking to her.
    Whether the sight of great cheer at my lady's   5
    And such mean fare at home work discontent in her,
    I know not, but I'm sure she's strangely altered.
    I'll nev'r keep daughter-in-law i'th'house with me
    Again, if I had an hundred. When read I of any
    That agreed long together, but she and her mother   10
    Fell out in the first quarter? Nay, sometime
    A grudging of a scolding the first week, by'r Lady.
    So takes the new disease methinks in my house.
    I'm weary of my part, there's nothing likes her;
    I know not how to please her here a-late.   15
    And here she comes.

Enter BIANCA

BIANCA   This is the strangest house
    For all defects, as ever gentlewoman
    Made shift withal to pass away her love in.
    Why is there not a cushion-cloth of drawn work,
    Or some fair cut-work pinned up in my bedchamber,   20
    A silver-and-gilt casting-bottle hung by't?
    Nay, since I am content to be so kind to you
    To spare you for a silver basin and ewer,

  2–3   *grave! / She* ed. (grave; she O)
    4   *cutted* curt, snappish
   12   *grudging* a small portion
   13   *new disease* a fashionable phrase for any undiagnosed disease marked by fever
   14   *likes* pleases
   19   *drawn work* ornamental work made by drawing out some of the threads of warp
         and woof to form patterns
   20   *cut-work* embroidery or lace, the pattern being 'cut' out rather than woven in
   21   *casting-bottle* bottle for sprinkling perfume

Which one of my fashion looks for of duty –
She's never offered under, where she sleeps –   25
MOTHER
   [*Aside*] She talks of things here my whole state's not worth.
BIANCA
   Never a green silk quilt is there i'th'house, Mother,
   To cast upon my bed?
MOTHER   No, by troth, is there,
   Nor orange tawny neither.
BIANCA   Here's a house
   For a young gentlewoman to be got with child in!   30
MOTHER
   Yes, simple though you make it, there has been three
   Got in a year in't – since you move me to't –
   And all as sweet-faced children and as lovely
   As you'll be mother of; I will not spare you.
   What, cannot children be begot, think you,   35
   Without gilt casting-bottles? Yes, and as sweet ones.
   The miller's daughter brings forth as white boys
   As she that bathes her self with milk and bean-flour.
   'Tis an old saying, 'one may keep good cheer
   In a mean house'; so may true love affect   40
   After the rate of princes, in a cottage.
BIANCA
   Troth, you speak wondrous well for your old house here;
   'Twill shortly fall down at your feet to thank you,
   Or stoop when you go to bed, like a good child,
   To ask you blessing. Must I live in want,   45
   Because my fortune matched me with your son?
   Wives do not give away themselves to husbands,
   To the end to be quite cast away; they look

---

23   *To spare you for* not to demand of you   *ewer* a water pitcher
25   *under* less
26   *state* estate
29   *orange tawny* considered a courtier's colour
37   *white boys* a term of endearment: 'darlings'
38   *bathes . . . bean-flour* a sign of extreme extravagance. Cf. Middleton's *The Revenger's Tragedy* (III.v.84–5): the proud woman 'grieve[s] her maker / In sinful baths of milk, when many an infant starves'.
39   *good* ed. (gook O)
40   *affect* have its effect
48   *To the end* with the intention

To be the better used, and tendered rather,
Highlier respected, and maintained the richer; 50
They're well rewarded else for the free gift
Of their whole life to a husband. I ask less now
Than what I had at home when I was a maid
And at my father's house, kept short of that
Which a wife knows she must have – nay, and will, 55
Will, Mother, if she be not a fool born;
And report went of me that I could wrangle
For what I wanted when I was two hours old,
And by that copy, this land still I hold.
You hear me, Mother. *Exit*

MOTHER   Ay, too plain methinks; 60
And were I somewhat deafer when you spake
'Twere nev'r a whit the worse for my quietness.
'Tis the most suddenest, strangest alteration,
And the most subtlest that ev'r wit at threescore
Was puzzled to find out. I know no cause for't; but 65
She's no more like the gentlewoman at first
Than I am like her that nev'r lay with man yet,
And she's a very young thing where'er she be.
When she first lighted here, I told her then
How mean she should find all things; she was pleased, forsooth, 70
None better. I laid open all defects to her,
She was contented still. But the devil's in her,
Nothing contents her now. Tonight my son
Promised to be at home; would he were come once,
For I'm weary of my charge, and life too. 75
She'd be served all in silver, by her good will,
By night and day; she hates the name of pewterer,
More than sick men the noise, or diseased bones
That quake at fall o'th'hammer, seeming to have

---

49 *tendered* cherished
59 *copy* copyhold (the right of ownership established by custom, i.e. by her childhood behaviour)
69 *lighted* arrived. See II.i.59n.
74 *once* at once
77 *pewterer* Pewter is a metal of inferior quality; the making of pewter objects – plates, tankards – involves hammering.
78 *noise* The very 'sick' and 'diseased' are extremely sensitive to noise; there is possibly also a reference to 'sounds supposed to have been heard before the death of any person' (*English Dialect Dictionary*).

A fellow-feeling with't at every blow.   80
What course shall I think on? She frets me so.
                    [*She withdraws to back of the stage*]

                    Enter LEANTIO

LEANTIO
How near am I now to a happiness
That earth exceeds not! Not another like it!
The treasures of the deep are not so precious
As are the concealed comforts of a man,   85
Locked up in woman's love. I scent the air
Of blessings when I come but near the house.
What a delicious breath marriage sends forth!
The violet-bed's not sweeter. Honest wedlock
Is like a banqueting-house built in a garden,   90
On which the spring's chaste flowers take delight
To cast their modest odours; when base lust
With all her powders, paintings, and best pride,
Is but a fair house built by a ditch side.
When I behold a glorious dangerous strumpet,   95
Sparkling in beauty and destruction too,
Both at a twinkling, I do liken straight
Her beautified body to a goodly temple
That's built on vaults where carcasses lie rotting;
And so by little and little I shrink back again,   100
And quench desire with a cool meditation;
And I'm as well methinks. Now for a welcome
Able to draw men's envies upon man:
A kiss now that will hang upon my lip,
As sweet as morning dew upon a rose,   105
And full as long. After a five days' fast

86–9   *I scent . . . sweeter* perhaps an echo of Duncan's ironic description of Macbeth's
         castle: 'This castle hath a pleasant seat. The air / Nimbly and sweetly recommends
         itself / Unto our gentle senses' (*Macbeth* I.vi.1–3)
  90   *banqueting-house* a favourite feature of Jacobean gardens; known as sites of secret
         sexual encounters
  93   *pride* finery
  94   *ditch side* Moorditch and the City Ditch were essentially open sewers at this time.
98–9   *goodly . . . rotting* allusion to Matthew 23:27: 'Woe unto you, scribes and Pharisees,
         hypocrites! for ye are like unto whited sepulchres, which indeed appear beautiful
         outward, but are within full of dead men's bones, and of all uncleanness'.
 100   *shrink back* lose the thought; lose an erection

She'll be so greedy now, and cling about me,
I take care how I shall be rid of her;
And here't begins.

[*Enter* BIANCA; MOTHER *comes forward*]

BIANCA   Oh sir, y'are welcome home.
MOTHER
  Oh is he come? I am glad on't.
LEANTIO   Is that all?   110
  [*Aside*] Why this? As dreadful now as sudden death
  To some rich man, that flatters all his sins
  With promise of repentance when he's old,
  And dies in the midway before he comes to't.
  [*To her*] Sure y'are not well, Bianca! How dost, prithee?   115
BIANCA
  I have been better than I am at this time.
LEANTIO
  Alas, I thought so.
BIANCA   Nay, I have been worse too
  Than now you see me, sir.
LEANTIO   I'm glad thou mend'st yet,
  I feel my heart mend too. How came it to thee?
  Has any thing disliked thee in my absence?   120
BIANCA
  No, certain, I have had the best content
  That Florence can afford.
LEANTIO   Thou makest the best on't.
  Speak, Mother, what's the cause? You must needs know.
MOTHER
  Troth, I know none, son, let her speak herself
  [*Aside*] Unless it be the same gave Lucifer   125
  A tumbling cast: that's pride.
BIANCA
  Methinks this house stands nothing to my mind;

---

111   *this?* i.e. her lack of affection
120   *disliked* displeased
121–2 *best . . . afford* the greatest pleasure the city of Florence has to offer; the greatest
       sexual pleasure the Duke of Florence has to offer
125–6 *Lucifer / A* ed. (Lucifer a O)
126   *tumbling cast* wrestling throw
127   *stands nothing to my mind* is not situated as I would prefer

I'd have some pleasant lodging i'th'high street, sir,
Or if 'twere near the court, sir, that were much better;
'Tis a sweet recreation for a gentlewoman,   130
To stand in a bay-window and see gallants.

LEANTIO

Now I have another temper, a mere stranger
To that of yours, it seems; I should delight
To see none but yourself.

BIANCA   I praise not that:

Too fond is as unseemly as too churlish;   135
I would not have a husband of that proneness
To kiss me before company, for a world.
Beside, 'tis tedious to see one thing still, sir,
Be it the best that ever heart affected;
Nay, were't yourself, whose love had power, you know,   140
To bring me from my friends, I would not stand thus
And gaze upon you always. Troth, I could not, sir;
As good be blind and have no use of sight
As look on one thing still. What's the eye's treasure,
But change of objects? You are learned, sir,   145
And know I speak not ill; 'tis full as virtuous
For woman's eye to look on several men,
As for her heart, sir, to be fixed on one.

LEANTIO

Now thou com'st home to me; a kiss for that word.

BIANCA

No matter for a kiss, sir, let it pass;   150
'Tis but a toy, we'll not so much as mind it;
Let's talk of other business and forget it.
What news now of the pirates, any stirring?
Prithee discourse a little.

---

131   *stand in a bay-window* typical of whores, offering themselves to view in windows
132   *temper* disposition
135   *fond* foolishly infatuated
136   *proneness* tendency, inclination; also with sexual connotation (cf. I.ii.118)
144–5   *What's . . . objects* proverbial wisdom
146   *'tis* ed. ('till O)
150   *matter* occasion
151   *toy* trifle
153   *pirates* The reference to pirates is in one of Middleton's sources, but it is also highly topical, as an English fleet sailed on 12 October 1620 to disperse pirates who were attacking English shipping routes.

MOTHER [*Aside*]   I am glad he's here yet
  To see her tricks himself; I had lied monstrously   155
  If I had told 'em first.
LEANTIO   Speak, what's the humour, sweet,
  You make your lip so strange? This was not wont.
BIANCA
  Is there no kindness betwixt man and wife
  Unless they make a pigeon-house of friendship,
  And be still billing? 'Tis the idlest fondness   160
  That ever was invented, and 'tis pity
  It's grown a fashion for poor gentlewomen;
  There's many a disease kissed in a year by't,
  And a French curtsy made to't. Alas, sir,
  Think of the world, how we shall live; grow serious –   165
  We have been married a whole fortnight now.
LEANTIO
  How? A whole fortnight! Why, is that so long?
BIANCA
  'Tis time to leave off dalliance; 'tis a doctrine
  Of your own teaching, if you be remembered.
  And I was bound to obey it.
MOTHER [*Aside*]   Here's one fits him;   170
  This was well catched, i'faith, son, like a fellow
  That rids another country of a plague
  And brings it home with him to his own house.

                                        Knock within
  Who knocks?
LEANTIO   Who's there now? Withdraw you, Bianca,
  Thou art a gem no stranger's eye must see,   175
  Howev'r thou please now to look dull on me.

                                        Exit [BIANCA]

                    Enter MESSENGER

  Y'are welcome, sir; to whom your business, pray?
MESSENGER
  To one I see not here now.

157 *wont* customary
160 *fondness* foolishness
164 *French curtsy* i.e. an excessive courtesy; but also a reference to the so-called 'French disease', syphilis (cf. l. 163)
170 *fits him* punishes him in kind
176 *please* ed. (pleas'd O)

LEANTIO	Who should that be, sir?

MESSENGER

    A young gentlewoman I was sent to.

LEANTIO   A young gentlewoman?

MESSENGER

    Ay, sir, about sixteen. Why look you wildly, sir?   180

LEANTIO

    At your strange error. Y'have mistook the house, sir.

    There's none such here, I assure you.

MESSENGER   I assure you too,

    The man that sent me, cannot be mistook.

LEANTIO

    Why, who is't sent you, sir?

MESSENGER   The Duke.

LEANTIO   The Duke?

MESSENGER

    Yes, he entreats her company at a banquet   185

    At Lady Livia's house.

LEANTIO   Troth, shall I tell you, sir,

    It is the most erroneous business

    That e'er your honest pains was abused with.

    I pray forgive me, if I smile a little;

    I cannot choose, i'faith, sir, at an error   190

    So comical as this –I mean no harm though.

    His grace has been most wondrous ill informed;

    Pray so return it, sir. What should her name be?

MESSENGER

    That I shall tell you straight too: Bianca Capella.

LEANTIO

    How, sir, Bianca? What do you call th'other?   195

MESSENGER

    Capella. Sir, it seems you know no such, then?

LEANTIO

    Who should this be? I never heard o'th'name.

MESSENGER

    Then 'tis a sure mistake.

LEANTIO   What if you enquired

    In the next street, sir? I saw gallants there

    In the new houses that are built of late.   200

    Ten to one, there you find her.

193   *return it* take the message back

MESSENGER   Nay, no matter,
I will return the mistake, and seek no further.

LEANTIO
Use your own will and pleasure, sir, y'are welcome.

                                                Exit MESSENGER
What shall I think of first? Come forth, Bianca.
Thou art betrayed, I fear me.

                        Enter BIANCA

BIANCA   Betrayed? How, sir?   205

LEANTIO
The Duke knows thee.

BIANCA   Knows me! How know you that, sir?

LEANTIO
H'as got thy name.

BIANCA [*Aside*]   Ay, and my good name too,
That's worse o'th'twain.

LEANTIO   How comes this work about?

BIANCA
How should the Duke know me? Can you guess, Mother?

MOTHER
Not I with all my wits; sure, we kept house close.   210

LEANTIO
Kept close! Not all the locks in Italy
Can keep you women so. You have been gadding,
And ventured out at twilight to th'court-green yonder,
And met the gallant bowlers coming home;
Without your masks too, both of you, I'll be hanged else!   215
Thou hast been seen, Bianca, by some stranger;
Never excuse it.

BIANCA   I'll not seek the way, sir.
Do you think y'have married me to mew me up
Not to be seen? What would you make of me?

---

206   *Knows me* is acquainted with me; has carnal knowledge of me
212   *gadding* term frequently used to describe idle, roving women
213–14   *court-green . . . bowlers* Lawn-bowling, a popular game among the nobility, was
         played on a bowling-green; here, perhaps, one near to a 'court'.
215   *masks* Italian women were expected to wear masks or veils out of doors; some
         aristocratic women in England occasionally wore masks, especially to balls and
         dances.
218   *mew* imprison, lock up

LEANTIO
A good wife, nothing else.
BIANCA   Why, so are some   220
That are seen ev'ry day, else the devil take 'em.
LEANTIO
No more then, I believe all virtuous in thee,
Without an argument; 'twas but thy hard chance
To be seen somewhere, there lies all the mischief.
But I have devised a riddance.
MOTHER   Now I can tell you, son,   225
The time and place.
LEANTIO   When, where?
MOTHER   What wits have I?
When you last took your leave, if you remember,
You left us both at window.
LEANTIO   Right, I know that.
MOTHER
And not the third part of an hour after,
The Duke passed by in a great solemnity   230
To St Mark's Temple, and to my apprehension
He looked up twice to th'window.
LEANTIO   Oh there quickened
The mischief of this hour!
BIANCA [*Aside*]   If you call't mischief,
It is a thing I fear I am conceived with.
LEANTIO
Looked he up twice, and could you take no warning!   235
MOTHER
Why, once may do as much harm, son, as a thousand;
Do not you know one spark has fired an house
As well as a whole furnace?
LEANTIO   My heart flames for't!
Yet let's be wise, and keep all smothered closely;
I have bethought a means. Is the door fast?   240
MOTHER
I locked it myself after him.
LEANTIO   You know, Mother,
At the end of the dark parlour there's a place

231   *apprehension* knowledge
232   *quickened* began; became pregnant. The double meaning leads to Bianca's 'con-
       ceived' (l. 234).

333

So artificially contrived for a conveyance,
No search could ever find it. When my father
Kept in for manslaughter, it was his sanctuary; 245
There will I lock my life's best treasure up.
Bianca!

BIANCA   Would you keep me closer yet?
Have you the conscience? Y'are best ev'n choke me up, sir!
You make me fearful of your health and wits,
You cleave to such wild courses. What's the matter? 250

LEANTIO
Why, are you so insensible of your danger
To ask that now? The Duke himself has sent for you
To Lady Livia's, to a banquet forsooth.

BIANCA
Now I beshrew you heartily, has he so!
And you the man would never yet vouchsafe 255
To tell me on't till now. You show your loyalty
And honesty at once; and so farewell, sir.

LEANTIO
Bianca, whither now?

BIANCA   Why, to the Duke, sir.
You say he sent for me.

LEANTIO   But thou dost not mean
To go, I hope!

BIANCA   No? I shall prove unmannerly, 260
Rude and uncivil, mad, and imitate you.
Come, Mother, come, follow his humour no longer.
We shall be all executed for treason shortly.

MOTHER
Not I, i'faith; I'll first obey the Duke,
And taste of a good banquet, I'm of thy mind. 265
I'll step but up, and fetch two handkerchiefs
To pocket up some sweetmeats, and o'ertake thee.   *Exit*

BIANCA
[*Aside*] Why, here's an old wench would trot into a bawd now,

---

243   *artificially* artfully
      conveyance secret passage
245   *Kept . . . manslaughter* stayed indoors after he had committed manslaughter
254   *beshrew* curse
266   *handkerchiefs* used for carrying small objects
268   *trot into* turn into

For some dry sucket or a colt in marchpane.   *Exit*

LEANTIO

Oh thou the ripe time of man's misery, wedlock,   270
When all his thoughts, like over-laden trees,
Crack with the fruits they bear, in cares, in jealousies!
Oh that's a fruit that ripens hastily,
After 'tis knit to marriage; it begins
As soon as the sun shines upon the bride   275
A little to show colour. Blessed powers!
Whence comes this alteration? The distractions,
The fears and doubts it brings are numberless,
And yet the cause I know not. What a peace
Has he that never marries! If he knew   280
The benefit he enjoyed, or had the fortune
To come and speak with me, he should know then
The infinite wealth he had, and discern rightly
The greatness of his treasure by my loss.
Nay, what a quietness has he 'bove mine,   285
That wears his youth out in a strumpet's arms,
And never spends more care upon a woman
Than at the time of lust; but walks away,
And if he find her dead at his return,
His pity is soon done: he breaks a sigh   290
In many parts, and gives her but a piece on't!
But all the fears, shames, jealousies, costs and troubles,
And still renewed cares of a marriage bed
Live in the issue, when the wife is dead.

Enter MESSENGER

MESSENGER

A good perfection to your thoughts.

LEANTIO   The news, sir?   295

MESSENGER

Though you were pleased of late to pin an error on me,
You must not shift another in your stead too:
The Duke has sent me for you.

269   *sucket* crystallized fruit
       colt in marchpane the figure of a young horse made out of marchpane (marzipan)
287   *spends* expends; slang term for ejaculation
294   *issue* children
295   *good perfection* a successful conclusion
297   *shift another in your stead* try another cunning trick in your own case

LEANTIO   How, for me, sir?
  [*Aside*] I see then 'tis my theft; w'are both betrayed.
  Well, I'm not the first has stolen away a maid: 300
  My countrymen have used it. [*To him*] I'll along with you, sir.
                                        Exeunt

ACT III, SCENE ii

A Banquet prepared. Enter GUARDIANO *and* WARD

GUARDIANO
  Take you especial note of such a gentlewoman,
  She's here on purpose; I have invited her,
  Her father, and her uncle to this banquet.
  Mark her behaviour well, it does concern you;
  And what her good parts are, as far as time   5
  And place can modestly require a knowledge of,
  Shall be laid open to your understanding.
  You know I'm both your guardian and your uncle;
  My care of you is double, ward and nephew,
  And I'll express it here.
WARD   'Faith, I should know her   10
  Now, by her mark, among a thousand women:
  A little, pretty, deft and tidy thing, you say?
GUARDIANO
  Right.
WARD   With a lusty sprouting sprig in her hair?
GUARDIANO
  Thou goest the right way still; take one mark more:
  Thou shalt nev'r find her hand out of her uncle's,   15
  Or else his out of hers, if she be near him.
  The love of kindred never yet stuck closer

---

301   *used* practised

11   *mark* distinctive characteristic; and with sexual connotation
12   *deft* dainty
13   *lusty* large
       sprig an ornament made from a sprig of a plant; or perhaps an ornament made in
       the shape of a sprig; and with sexual connotation

Than theirs to one another; he that weds her
Marries her uncle's heart too.

Cornets [sound]

WARD   Say you so, sir,
Then I'll be asked i'th'church to both of them.   20

GUARDIANO
Fall back, here comes the Duke.

WARD   He brings a gentlewoman,
I should fall forward rather.

Enter DUKE, BIANCA, FABRITIO, HIPPOLITO, LIVIA,
MOTHER, ISABELLA, *and* ATTENDANTS

DUKE   Come, Bianca,
Of purpose sent into the world to show
Perfection once in woman; I'll believe
Henceforward they have ev'ry one a soul too,   25
'Gainst all the uncourteous opinions
That man's uncivil rudeness ever held of 'em.
Glory of Florence, light into mine arms!

Enter LEANTIO

BIANCA
Yon comes a grudging man will chide you, sir.
The storm is now in's heart and would get nearer,   30
And fall here if it durst; it pours down yonder.

DUKE
If that be he, the weather shall soon clear.
List, and I'll tell thee how.   [*Whispers to* BIANCA]

LEANTIO [*Aside*]   A-kissing too?
I see 'tis plain lust now, adultery boldened;
What will it prove anon, when 'tis stuffed full   35
Of wine and sweetmeats, being so impudent fasting?

DUKE [*To* LEANTIO]
We have heard of your good parts, sir, which we honour

22   *fall forward* i.e. have sex
25   *soul* There is no mention in Genesis 2:7 of God breathing a soul into Eve, as He did
      for Adam; hence, the alleged absence of a soul in woman became a stock
      misogynist insult. The question was hotly debated in the pamphlets concerned
      with the controversy over women.
28   *light* arrive (a verb). Cf. I.ii.56.
36   *impudent* immodest
37   *parts* qualities

337

With our embrace and love.
[*To* GENTLEMAN]   Is not the captainship
Of Rouans' citadel, since the late deceased,
Supplied by any yet?
GENTLEMAN   By none, my lord.   40
DUKE [*To* LEANTIO]
    Take it, the place is yours then, and as faithfulness
    And desert grows, our favour shall grow with't:
                              [LEANTIO *kneels*]
    Rise now the captain of our fort at Rouans.
LEANTIO
    The service of whole life give your grace thanks.
DUKE
    Come sit, Bianca.
LEANTIO [*Aside*]   This is some good yet,   45
    And more than ev'r I looked for; a fine bit
    To stay a cuckold's stomach. All preferment
    That springs from sin and lust, it shoots up quickly,
    As gardeners' crops do in the rotten'st grounds;
    So is all means raised from base prostitution,   50
    Ev'n like a sallet growing upon a dunghill.
    I'm like a thing that never was yet heard of,
    Half merry and half mad – much like a fellow
    That eats his meat with a good appetite,
    And wears a plague-sore that would fright a country;   55
    Or rather like the barren, hardened ass,
    That feeds on thistles till he bleeds again.
    And such is the condition of my misery.
LIVIA
    Is that your son, widow?
MOTHER   Yes, did your ladyship
    Never know that till now?
LIVIA   No, trust me, did I.   60

39, 43 *Rouans* Middleton may have meant Rouens; but in his *Itinerary* (I, Book 2, p. 148),
        Fynes Moryson refers to one of the forts at Florence as being in an area where 'there
        is a place vulgarly called *le Ruinate*, that is, the ruinous', and the (ironic) name may
        have been intended as appropriate for Leantio.
    47 *stay* settle; enhance
    50 *means* resources
    51 *sallet* any green vegetable used in a salad
    56 *barren* stupid
59–60 *ladyship / Never* ed. (Ladiship never O)

[*Aside*] Nor ever truly felt the power of love
And pity to a man, till now I knew him.
I have enough to buy me my desires,
And yet to spare; that's one good comfort,
[*To* LEANTIO]   Hark you.
Pray let me speak with you, sir, before you go.   65

LEANTIO
With me, lady? You shall, I am at your service.
[*Aside*] What will she say now, trow, more goodness yet?

WARD
I see her now, I'm sure; the ape's so little,
I shall scarce feel her; I have seen almost
As tall as she sold in the fair for ten pence.   70
See how she simpers it, as if marmalade
Would not melt in her mouth! She might have the kindness,
    i'faith,
To send me a gilded bull from her own trencher,
A ram, a goat, or somewhat to be nibbling.
These women when they come to sweet things once,   75
They forget all their friends, they grow so greedy;
Nay, oftentimes their husbands.

DUKE   Here's a health now, gallants,
To the best beauty at this day in Florence.

BIANCA
Whoe'er she be, she shall not go unpledged, sir.

DUKE
Nay, you're excused for this.

BIANCA   Who, I my lord?   80

DUKE
Yes, by the law of Bacchus; plead your benefit,
You are not bound to pledge your own health, lady.

68   *ape* a term of endearment
70   *for ten pence* i.e. not worth much at all
71–2   *marmalade . . . mouth* Proverbial: 'He looks as if butter would not melt in his
       mouth' (Tilley, B 774).
73   *trencher* platter
73–4   *gilded bull . . . ram . . . goat* more animal figures in marzipan; cf. the 'colt' at III.i.269.
       All these animals were standard emblems of lechery; they also all wore horns, thus
       suggesting that the Ward will be a cuckold.
77   *health* a toast
81   *Bacchus* god of wine
       plead your benefit claim your exemption from this 'law' (through 'benefit of clergy',
       literate people could claim exemption from the law)

339

BIANCA

That's a good way, my lord, to keep me dry.

DUKE

Nay, then I will not offend Venus so much,

Let Bacchus seek his 'mends in another court.   85

Here's to thyself, Bianca.   [*He drinks*]

BIANCA   Nothing comes

More welcome to that name than your grace.   [*She drinks*]

LEANTIO [*Aside*]   So, so;

Here stands the poor thief now that stole the treasure,

And he's not thought on. Ours is near kin now

To a twin misery born into the world: 90

First the hard-conscienced worldling, he hoards wealth up;

Then comes the next, and he feasts all upon't;

One's damned for getting, th'other for spending on't.

Oh equal justice, thou hast met my sin

With a full weight; I'm rightly now oppressed,   95

All her friends' heavy hearts lie in my breast.

DUKE

Methinks there is no spirit amongst us, gallants,

But what divinely sparkles from the eyes

Of bright Bianca; we sat all in darkness,

But for that splendour. Who was't told us lately   100

Of a match-making rite, a marriage-tender?

GUARDIANO

'Twas I, my lord.

DUKE   'Twas you indeed. Where is she?

GUARDIANO

This is the gentlewoman.

FABRITIO   My lord, my daughter.

DUKE

Why, here's some stirring yet.

FABRITIO   She's a dear child to me.

DUKE

That must needs be; you say she is your daughter.   105

---

83   *dry* thirsty; lacking sexual moistness (continued in the reference to 'Venus' in the
       next line)
85   *'mends* legal remedies
96   i.e. I am now suffering as much as her friends from whom I 'stole' (l. 88) her
101   *marriage-tender* formal offer of marriage
104   *some stirring yet* i.e. here's some excitement; also with sexual connotation (cf. 'stir',
       l. 110)

FABRITIO

    Nay, my good lord, dear to my purse, I mean,

    Beside my person; I nev'r reckoned that.

    She has the full qualities of a gentlewoman;

    I have brought her up to music, dancing, what not,

    That may commend her sex and stir her husband.   110

DUKE

    And which is he now?

GUARDIANO   This young heir, my lord.

DUKE

    What is he brought up to?

HIPPOLITO [*Aside*]   To cat and trap.

GUARDIANO

    My lord, he's a great ward, wealthy, but simple;

    His parts consist in acres.

DUKE   Oh, wise-acres!

GUARDIANO

    Y'have spoke him in a word, sir.

BIANCA   'Las, poor gentlewoman,   115

    She's ill bestead, unless sh'as dealt the wiselier

    And laid in more provision for her youth:

    Fools will not keep in summer.

LEANTIO [*Aside*]   No, nor such wives

    From whores in winter.

DUKE   Yea, the voice too, sir?

FABRITIO

    Ay, and a sweet breast too, my lord, I hope,   120

    Or I have cast away my money wisely;

    She took her pricksong earlier, my lord,

    Than any of her kindred ever did.

    A rare child, though I say't, but I'd not have

---

112   *cat and trap* Cf. I.ii.87 s.d.n.

114   *parts* qualities

116   *bestead* situated

118–19   *Fools . . . winter* 'Fools' (= delicacy, trifle; cf. I.ii.116n.) will go bad in the heat of the summer, while wives will go bad in winter (i.e. turn into a whore = hoar, or hoarfrost).

120   *breast* singing voice; bosom. Fabritio unwittingly praises Isabella's musical talents in sexual double meanings (see next two notes).

122   *pricksong* written music, 'pricked' into the paper. The obvious sexual pun on 'prick' leads to 'swell' (l. 125) and 'puffed up' (l. 126) = proud; pregnant.

The baggage hear so much; 'twould make her swell straight,   125
And maids of all things must not be puffed up.

DUKE

Let's turn us to a better banquet, then,
For music bids the soul of man to a feast,
And that's indeed a noble entertainment,
Worthy Bianca's self. [*To her*] You shall perceive, beauty,   130
Our Florentine damsels are not brought up idly.

BIANCA

They are wiser of themselves, it seems, my lord,
And can take gifts when goodness offers 'em.

Music

LEANTIO

[*Aside*] True, and damnation has taught you that wisdom,
You can take gifts, too. Oh that music mocks me!   135

LIVIA

[*Aside*] I am as dumb to any language now
But love's, as one that never learned to speak.
I am not yet so old but he may think of me;
My own fault, I have been idle a long time;
But I'll begin the week and paint tomorrow,   140
So follow my true labour day by day.
I never thrived so well as when I used it.

[ISABELLA *sings*]

Song

What harder chance can fall to woman,
Who was born to cleave to some man,
Than to bestow her time, youth, beauty,   145
Life's observance, honour, duty,
On a thing for no use good,
But to make physic work, or blood
Force fresh in an old lady's cheek?

---

125 *baggage* a demeaning term for a young woman. Cf. Juliet's father: 'Out, you
     baggage!' *{Romeo and Juliet* III.v.156).
128 *of man* ed. (of a man O)
140 *paint* use cosmetics, a practice invariably condemned on moral grounds. Cf.
     Hamlet's 'let her paint an inch thick' *{Hamlet* V.i. 193).
143–55 The Ward's commentary may be spoken simultaneously with the song, as O prints
     them side by side.
148 *make physic work* make a medicine work through mild excitement – an ironic
     comment on the Ward's power to stimulate sexually. 'Physic' may also = laxative.
148–9 *blood / Force* ed. (blood force O)   149 *fresh in* ed. (fresh / In O)

> *She that would be* 150
> *Mother of fools, let her compound with me.*

WARD

Here's a tune indeed! Pish, I had rather hear one ballad sung
i'th'nose now, of the lamentable drowning of fat sheep and oxen,
than all these simpering tunes played upon cats' guts and sung
by little kitlings. 155

FABRITIO

How like you her breast now, my lord?

BIANCA [*Aside to* DUKE]   Her breast?
He talks as if his daughter had given suck
Before she were married, as her betters have;
The next he praises, sure, will be her nipples.

DUKE

[*Aside to her*] Methinks now, such a voice to such a husband 160
Is like a jewel of unvalued worth
Hung at a fool's ear.

FABRITIO   May it please your grace
To give her leave to show another quality?

DUKE

Marry, as many good ones as you will, sir,
The more the better welcome.

LEANTIO [*Aside*]   But the less 165
The better practised. That soul's black indeed
That cannot commend virtue; but who keeps it?
The extortioner will say to a sick beggar,
Heaven comfort thee, though he give none himself.
This good is common.

FABRITIO   Will it please you now, sir, 170
To entreat your ward to take her by the hand,
And lead her in a dance before the Duke?

GUARDIANO

That will I, sir, 'tis needful. Hark you, nephew.

149–50 *cheek? / She* ed. (cheek, she O)
   151 *compound with* join or agree with
   155 *kitlings* little cats; whores
   156 *Her breast?* Bianca's reaction suggests the term 'breast' for 'voice' was an odd,
         affected usage.
   160 *to* compared to
   161 *unvalued* priceless
172–99 A dance was a traditional emblem of harmony, and often associated with wed-
         dings, but below the surface harmony here is a complex sexual intrigue.

FABRITIO

    Nay, you shall see, young heir, what y'have for your money,

    Without fraud or imposture.

WARD   Dance with her!   175

    Not I, sweet guardianer, do not urge my heart to't,

    'Tis clean against my blood; dance with a stranger!

    Let whoso will do't, I'll not begin first with her.

HIPPOLITO

    [*Aside*] No, fear't not, fool, sh'as took a better order.

GUARDIANO

    Why, who shall take her then?

WARD   Some other gentleman.   180

    Look, there's her uncle, a fine-timbered reveller –

    Perhaps he knows the manner of her dancing, too;

    I'll have him do't before me. I have sworn, guardianer;

    Then may I learn the better.

GUARDIANO   Thou'lt be an ass still.

WARD

    Ay, all that, uncle, shall not fool me out.   185

    Pish, I stick closer to myself than so.

GUARDIANO

    [*To* HIPPOLITO] I must entreat you, sir, to take your niece

    And dance with her; my ward's a little wilful,

    He would have you show him the way.

HIPPOLITO   Me, sir?

    He shall command it at all hours, pray tell him so.   190

GUARDIANO

    I thank you for him, he has not wit himself, sir.

HIPPOLITO

    [*To* ISABELLA] Come, my life's peace.

    [*Aside*]   I have a strange office on't here.

    'Tis some man's luck to keep the joys he likes

    Concealed for his own bosom, but my fortune

---

177   *blood* inclination

178   *whoso* ed. (who's O)

179   *a better order* i.e. she has made a better arrangement, by taking Hippolito before the Ward

180   *take her* take for the dance; take sexually

181   *fine-timbered* well-built

185   *fool me out* i.e. make me change my mind

192   *office* duty

To set 'em out now, for another's liking –   195
Like the mad misery of necessitous man,
That parts from his good horse with many praises,
And goes on foot himself. Need must be obeyed
In ev'ry action, it mars man and maid.

Music. A dance [by HIPPOLITO *and* ISABELLA], *making honours
to the* DUKE *and curtsy to themselves, both before and after*

DUKE

Signor Fabritio, y'are a happy father,   200
Your cares and pains are fortunate; you see
Your cost bears noble fruits. Hippolito, thanks.

FABRITIO

Here's some amends for all my charges yet:
She wins both prick and praise where'er she comes.

DUKE

How lik'st, Bianca?

BIANCA   All things well, my lord,   205
But this poor gentlewoman's fortune, that's the worst.

DUKE

There is no doubt, Bianca, she'll find leisure
To make that good enough; he's rich and simple.

BIANCA

She has the better hope o'th'upper hand, indeed,
Which women strive for most.

GUARDIANO [*To* WARD]   Do't when I bid you, sir.   210

WARD

I'll venture but a hornpipe with her, guardianer,
Or some such married man's dance.

GUARDIANO   Well, venture something, sir.

WARD

I have rhyme for what I do.

GUARDIANO [*Aside*]   But little reason, I think.

---

198   *Need* necessity
199   s.d.1 *honours* bows
204   *prick and praise* i.e. highest praise. The 'prick' was the mark in the centre of an
      archery target; there is also an obvious sexual connotation, to which Fabritio may
      be oblivious.
211   *hornpipe* a vigorous dance; 'horn' = cuckold and 'pipe' = phallus, hence the
      suitability of this dance for a 'married man' (l. 212)
212   *Well* ed. (we'll O)

WARD

Plain men dance the measures, the cinquepace the gay;
Cuckolds dance the hornpipe, and farmers dance the hay;   215
Your soldiers dance the round, and maidens that grow big;
Your drunkards, the canaries; your whore and bawd, the jig.
Here's your eight kind of dancers, he that finds the ninth, let
him pay the minstrels.

DUKE

Oh here he appears once in his own person!   220
I thought he would have married her by attorney,
And lain with her so too.

BIANCA   Nay, my kind lord,
There's very seldom any found so foolish
To give away his part there.

LEANTIO [*Aside*]   Bitter scoff!
Yet I must do't; with what a cruel pride   225
The glory of her sin strikes by my afflictions!

Music. [*The*] WARD *and* ISABELLA *dance;*
he ridiculously imitates HIPPOLITO

DUKE

This thing will make shift, sirs, to make a husband,
For aught I see in him; how thinks't, Bianca?

BIANCA

'Faith, an ill-favoured shift, my lord. Methinks
If he would take some voyage when he's married,   230
Dangerous, or long enough, and scarce be seen
Once in nine year together, a wife then
Might make indifferent shift to be content with him.

DUKE

A kiss! [*Kisses* BIANCA] That wit deserves to be made much on.

214   *measures* a stately dance
       cinquepace galliard (a lively French dance)
215   *hay* country dance
216   *round* circling dance; also, the watch kept by soldiers
217   *Your . . . your* ed. (you . . . you O)
       canaries lively dance thought to have come from the Canary Islands; also a sweet
       wine from the Canary Islands
       jig lively, rapid dance; associated with lewdness
221   *by attorney* by proxy
226   *glory* boastfulness
       strikes by thrusts aside
229   *shift* attempt

Come, our caroche.

GUARDIANO   Stands ready for your grace.   235

DUKE

My thanks to all your loves. Come, fair Bianca,
We have took special care of you, and provided
Your lodging near us now.

BIANCA   Your love is great, my lord.

DUKE

Once more our thanks to all.

OMNES   All blest honours guard you.

                               Cornets flourish

            Exe[unt] all but LEANTIO *and* LIVIA

LEANTIO

[*Aside*] Oh hast thou left me then, Bianca, utterly!   240
Bianca! Now I miss thee. Oh return,
And save the faith of woman! I nev'r felt
The loss of thee till now; 'tis an affliction
Of greater weight than youth was made to bear.
As if a punishment of after-life   245
Were fall'n upon man here; so new it is
To flesh and blood, so strange, so insupportable
A torment, ev'n mistook, as if a body
Whose death were drowning must needs therefore suffer it
In scalding oil.

LIVIA   Sweet sir!

LEANTIO [*Aside*]   As long as mine eye saw thee,   250
I half enjoyed thee.

LIVIA   Sir?

LEANTIO [*Aside*]   Canst thou forget
The dear pains my love took, how it has watched
Whole nights together in all weathers for thee,
Yet stood in heart more merry than the tempests
That sung about mine ears, like dangerous flatterers   255
That can set all their mischief to sweet tunes;
And then received thee from thy father's window
Into these arms at midnight, when we embraced
As if we had been statues only made for't,

---

235   *caroche* a stately coach
248   *A torment, ev'n mistook* mistaken torment
259   *only made for't* only made for embracing

To show art's life, so silent were our comforts,   260
And kissed as if our lips had grown together!
LIVIA
[*Aside*] This makes me madder to enjoy him now.
LEANTIO
[*Aside*] Canst thou forget all this? And better joys
That we met after this, which then new kisses
Took pride to praise?
LIVIA [*Aside*]   I shall grow madder yet. [*To him*] Sir!   265
LEANTIO
[*Aside*] This cannot be but of some close bawd's working.
[*To her*] Cry mercy, lady. What would you say to me?
My sorrow makes me so unmannerly,
So comfort bless me, I had quite forgot you.
LIVIA
Nothing but, ev'n in pity to that passion,   270
Would give your grief good counsel.
LEANTIO   Marry, and welcome, lady;
It never could come better.
LIVIA   Then first, sir,
To make away all your good thoughts at once of her,
Know most assuredly she is a strumpet.
LEANTIO
Ha! 'Most assuredly'! Speak not a thing   275
So vilde so certainly, leave it more doubtful.
LIVIA
Then I must leave all truth, and spare my knowledge,
A sin which I too lately found and wept for.
LEANTIO
Found you it?
LIVIA   Ay, with wet eyes.
LEANTIO   Oh perjurious friendship!
LIVIA
You missed your fortunes when you met with her, sir.   280
Young gentlemen that only love for beauty,
They love not wisely; such a marriage rather
Proves the destruction of affection –
It brings on want, and want's the key of whoredom.

260   *show art's life* to show how lifelike the artwork is
266   *close* secret
276   *vilde* vile

I think y'had small means with her.
LEANTIO   Oh not any, lady.   285
LIVIA
    Alas, poor gentleman, what meant'st thou, sir,
    Quite to undo thyself with thine own kind heart?
    Thou art too good and pitiful to woman.
    Marry, sir, thank thy stars for this blest fortune
    That rids the summer of thy youth so well   290
    From many beggars that had lain a-sunning
    In thy beams only else, till thou hadst wasted
    The whole days of thy life in heat and labour.
    What would you say now to a creature found
    As pitiful to you, and as it were   295
    Ev'n sent on purpose from the whole sex general,
    To requite all that kindness you have shown to't?
LEANTIO
    What's that, madam?
LIVIA   Nay, a gentlewoman, and one able
    To reward good things, ay, and bears a conscience to't.
    Could'st thou love such a one, that – blow all fortunes –   300
    Would never see thee want?
    Nay more, maintain thee to thine enemy's envy?
    And shalt not spend a care for't, stir a thought,
    Nor break a sleep, unless love's music waked thee;
    No storm of fortune should. Look upon me,   305
    And know that woman.
LEANTIO   Oh my life's wealth, Bianca!
LIVIA
    Still with her name? Will nothing wear it out?
    That deep sigh went but for a strumpet, sir.
LEANTIO
    It can go for no other that loves me.
LIVIA
    [*Aside*] He's vexed in mind; I came too soon to him;   310
    Where's my discretion now, my skill, my judgement?
    I'm cunning in all arts but my own love.
    'Tis as unseasonable to tempt him now

285   *small means* i.e. she had no real dowry
296   *sex general* all women
300   *blow all fortunes* i.e. come what may
303   *And shalt* and you shall

So soon, as a widow to be courted
Following her husband's corse, or to make bargain   315
By the grave-side, and take a young man there:
Her strange departure stands like a hearse yet
Before his eyes, which time will take down shortly.   *Exit*

LEANTIO

Is she my wife till death, yet no more mine?
That's a hard measure. Then what's marriage good for?   320
Methinks by right I should not now be living,
And then 'twere all well. What a happiness
Had I been made of, had I never seen her;
For nothing makes man's loss grievous to him
But knowledge of the worth of what he loses;   325
For what he never had, he never misses.
She's gone for ever, utterly; there is
As much redemption of a soul from Hell,
As a fair woman's body from his palace.
Why should my love last longer than her truth?   330
What is there good in woman to be loved
When only that which makes her so has left her?
I cannot love her now, but I must like
Her sin, and my own shame too, and be guilty
Of law's breach with her, and mine own abusing;   335
All which were monstrous. Then my safest course,
For health of mind and body, is to turn
My heart, and hate her, most extremely hate her;
I have no other way. Those virtuous powers
Which were chaste witnesses of both our troths,   340
Can witness she breaks first – and I'm rewarded
With captainship o'th'fort! A place of credit,
I must confess, but poor; my factorship
Shall not exchange means with't. He that died last in't,

314–15   *widow ... corse* As Richard courted Lady Anne in the presence of her father-in-law's corpse in *Richard III*.

317   *strange* like a stranger; not yet familiar
   hearse a wooden structure erected over the coffin for a certain period of time

327–8   *there ... Hell* Proverbial: There is no Redemption from hell' (Tilley, R 60).

330   *truth* faithfulness

333   *but* unless

335   *law's breach* i.e. adultery

342–4   *place ... with't* i.e. the captainship is an honour, but it does not even pay as much as his factorship

He was no drunkard, yet he died a beggar   345
For all his thrift. Besides, the place not fits me:
It suits my resolution, not my breeding.

Enter LIVIA

LIVIA
  [*Aside*] I have tried all ways I can, and have not power
  To keep from sight of him. [*To him*] How are you now, sir?
LEANTIO
  I feel a better ease, madam.
LIVIA   Thanks to blessedness!   350
  You will do well, I warrant you, fear it not, sir.
  Join but your own good will to't; he's not wise
  That loves his pain or sickness, or grows fond
  Of a disease whose property is to vex him
  And spitefully drink his blood up. Out upon't, sir,   355
  Youth knows no greater loss. I pray let's walk, sir.
  You never saw the beauty of my house yet,
  Nor how abundantly fortune has blessed me
  In worldly treasure; trust me, I have enough, sir,
  To make my friend a rich man in my life,   360
  A great man at my death; yourself will say so.
  If you want anything and spare to speak,
  Troth, I'll condemn you for a wilful man, sir.
LEANTIO
  Why sure, this can be but the flattery of some dream.
LIVIA
  Now by this kiss, my love, my soul and riches,   365
  'Tis all true substance. [*Kisses him*]
  Come, you shall see my wealth, take what you list;
  The gallanter you go, the more you please me.
  I will allow you, too, your page and footman,
  Your race-horses, or any various pleasure   370
  Exercised youth delights in. But to me
  Only, sir, wear your heart of constant stuff;
  Do but you love enough, I'll give enough.

347   *my resolution, not my breeding* my courage, not my low birth
355   *drink his blood up* Unrequited love was widely believed to dry up the blood.
360   *friend* lover. See II.i.153n.
372   *constant stuff i.e.* of one colour; figuratively, to be faithful

351

LEANTIO

Troth then, I'll love enough and take enough.

LIVIA

Then we are both pleased enough.   375

Exeunt

ACT III, SCENE iii

Enter GUARDIANO *and* ISABELLA *at one door,*
and the WARD *and* SORDIDO *at another*

GUARDIANO

Now, nephew, here's the gentlewoman again.

WARD

Mass, here she's come again; mark her now, Sordido.

GUARDIANO

This is the maid my love and care has chose
Out for your wife, and so I tender her to you;
Yourself has been eye-witness of some qualities   5
That speak a courtly breeding, and are costly.
I bring you both to talk together now,
'Tis time you grew familiar in your tongues;
Tomorrow you join hands, and one ring ties you,
And one bed holds you – if you like the choice.   10
Her father and her friends are i'th'next room,
And stay to see the contract ere they part;
Therefore dispatch, good Ward, be sweet and short.
Like her or like her not, there's but two ways;
And one your body, th'other your purse pays.   15

WARD

I warrant you, guardianer, I'll not stand all day thrumming,
But quickly shoot my bolt at your next coming.

---

12   *contract* marriage contract
14–15 *two . . . pays* The Ward has two choices, both of which require him to 'pay': either
       marry (giving his body), or pay a fine to his guardian (cf. I.ii.3n.)
16   *thrumming* playing a musical instrument idly; copulating
17   *shoot my bolt* give my decision; ejaculate. Proverbial: 'A Fool's bolt is soon shot'
       (Tilley, F 515); the 'bolt' or bird-bolt was an arrow used for fowling (cf. 'birding', l.
       18), and was also frequently associated with Cupid.

GUARDIANO

Well said! Good fortune to your birding then.   *[Exit]*

WARD

I never missed mark yet.

SORDIDO

Troth, I think, master, if the truth were known,   20

You never shot at any but the kitchen-wench,

And that was a she-woodcock, a mere innocent,

That was oft lost, and cried at eight and twenty.

WARD

No more of that meat, Sordido, here's eggs o'th'spit now,

We must turn gingerly. Draw out the catalogue   25

Of all the faults of women.

SORDIDO

How, all the faults! Have you so little reason to think so much

paper will lie in my breeches? Why, ten carts will not carry it, if

you set down but the bawds. All the faults? Pray let's be content

with a few of 'em; and if they were less, you would find 'em   30

enough, I warrant you. Look you, sir.

ISABELLA

[Aside] But that I have th'advantage of the fool

As much as woman's heart can wish and joy at,

What an infernal torment 'twere to be

Thus bought and sold, and turned and pried into; when, alas,   35

The worst bit is too good for him! And the comfort is,

H'as but a cater's place on't, and provides

All for another's table; yet how curious

The ass is, like some nice professor on't,

That buys up all the daintiest food i'th'markets,   40

And seldom licks his lips after a taste on't!

---

18   *birding* fowling; wenching

19   *mark* archery target; figuratively, female genitals

22   *she-woodcock* a simpleton ('innocent' = half-wit). The woodcock was proverbially
an easy bird to capture.

23   *cried* i.e. like a lost child announced by the town-crier

24   *eggs o'th'spit* i.e. delicate business

28   *carts* Carting, or carrying criminals (especially women) through the streets in a
cart, was a common legal punishment.

37   *cater's* the person who buys the 'cates', or provisions, for a household

38   *curious* fastidious

39   *nice professor* pedantic expert (one who 'professes' knowledge)

SORDIDO

Now to her, now y'have scanned all her parts over.

WARD

But at what end shall I begin now, Sordido?

SORDIDO

Oh ever at a woman's lip, while you live, sir; do you ask that
question?   45

WARD

Methinks, Sordido, sh'as but a crabbed face to begin with.

SORDIDO

A crabbed face? That will save money.

WARD

How! Save money, Sordido?

SORDIDO

Ay, sir, for having a crabbed face of her own, she'll eat the less
verjuice with her mutton; 'twill save verjuice at year's end, sir.   50

WARD

Nay, and your jests begin to be saucy once, I'll make you eat
your meat without mustard.

SORDIDO

And that in some kind is a punishment.

WARD

Gentlewoman, they say 'tis your pleasure to be my wife, and
you shall know shortly whether it be mine or no, to be your hus-   55
band; and thereupon thus I first enter upon you. [*Kisses her*]
Oh most delicious scent! Methinks it tasted as if a man had
stepped into a comfit-maker's shop to let a cart go by, all the
while I kissed her. It is reported, gentlewoman, you'll run mad
for me, if you have me not.   60

ISABELLA

I should be in great danger of my wits, sir,

For being so forward, [*Aside*] should this ass kick backward now!

WARD

Alas, poor soul! And is that hair your own?

---

43   *what* ed. (*not in* O)
49   *crabbed* punning on 'crab' = crab-apple
50   *verjuice* sour juice or puree made from crab-apples, used as a condiment
51   *and* if
58   *comfit-maker's shop* i.e. a sweet-smelling place; a comfit-maker = confectioner
63   *hair your own?* Loss of hair was one symptom of venereal disease; wearing an
      elaborate wig was also a sign of vanity and affectation in women. The boy-actor
      playing Isabella, in a final irony, was of course wearing a wig.

ISABELLA

Mine own? Yes sure, sir, I owe nothing for't.

WARD

'Tis a good hearing; I shall have the less to pay when I have   65
married you. [*To* SORDIDO] Look, does her eyes stand well?

SORDIDO

They cannot stand better than in her head, I think; where
would you have them? And for her nose, 'tis of a very good
last.

WARD

I have known as good as that has not lasted a year, though.   70

SORDIDO

That's in the using of a thing; will not any strong bridge fall
down in time, if we do nothing but beat at the bottom? A nose
of buff would not last always, sir, especially if it came in to
th'camp once.

WARD

But Sordido, how shall we do to make her laugh, that I may see   75
what teeth she has? For I'll not bate her a tooth, nor take a black
one into th'bargain.

SORDIDO

Why, do but you fall in talk with her, you cannot choose but
one time or other make her laugh, sir.

WARD

It shall go hard, but I will. [*To her*] Pray what qualities have   80
you beside singing and dancing? Can you play at shittlecock,
forsooth?

ISABELLA

Ay, and at stool-ball too, sir; I have great luck at it.

---

65   *good hearing* good to hear
66   *does her eyes stand well?* are her eyes well-placed?
69   *last* shape (the cobbler's 'last' stretches a shoe to its correct shape)
69–74 *last . . . once* This dialogue on the shape of her nose again alludes to venereal
       disease: one symptom was the collapse of the nose's structure.
73   *buff* strong leather (used for military uniforms), hence tough
74   *camp* military camp. A 'camp-follower' = whore; a 'camp' was associated with
       venereal disease, which would destroy even a 'nose of buff'.
76   *bate* accept less than the full number
83   *stool-ball* a game resembling cricket, in which the wicket was a stool; one player
       defended it from a ball thrown by another. Like the games of 'shittlecock' (l. 81;
       cf. II.ii.79 s.d.n.) and tip-cat ('trap', l. 87; cf. I.ii.87 s.d.n.), the game of stool-ball
       becomes a metaphor for sexual intercourse, reflected in the bawdy dialogue in
       ll. 83–9. The excretory pun is also picked up in this phrase.

WARD

Why, can you catch a ball well?

ISABELLA

I have catched two in my lap at one game. 85

WARD

What, have you, woman? I must have you learn
To play at trap too, then y'are full and whole.

ISABELLA

Anything that you please to bring me up to
I shall take pains to practise.

WARD

[*Aside to* SORDIDO] 'Twill not do, Sordido, we shall never get 90
her mouth opened wide enough.

SORDIDO

No, sir? That's strange! Then here's a trick for your learning.
He yawns[; ISABELLA *yawns also, but covers her mouth*]
Look now, look now; quick, quick there!

WARD

Pox of that scurvy, mannerly trick with handkerchief;
It hindered me a little, but I am satisfied. 95
When a fair woman gapes and stops her mouth so,
It shows like a cloth-stopple in a cream-pot.
I have fair hope of her teeth now, Sordido.

SORDIDO

Why, then y'have all well, sir; for aught I see
She's right and straight enough, now as she stands. 100
They'll commonly lie crooked, that's no matter.
Wise gamesters never find fault with that, let 'em lie still so.

WARD

I'd fain mark how she goes, and then I have all. For of all creatures I cannot abide a splay-footed woman, she's an unlucky
thing to meet in a morning; her heels keep together so, as if she 105

87–8   *full and whole . . . bring me up to* with sexual connotation
97   *cloth-stopple* stopper of cloth
101   *lie crooked* They are not 'straight' when they lie (sexually) down; they tell crooked lies.
102   *gamesters* sexual sportsmen
      gamesters never ed. (Gamesters / Never O)
103   *goes* walks
104   *splay-footed* feet turned out while walking (supposedly a sign to know a witch by)

were beginning an Irish dance still, and the wriggling of her
bum, playing the tune to't. But I have bethought a cleanly shift
to find it: dab down as you see me, and peep of one side when
her back's toward you; I'll show you the way.

SORDIDO

And you shall find me apt enough to peeping,   110
I have been one of them has seen mad sights
Under your scaffolds.

WARD [*To* ISABELLA]   Will it please you walk, forsooth,
A turn or two by yourself? You are so pleasing to me,
I take delight to view you on both sides.

ISABELLA

I shall be glad to fetch a walk to your love, sir;   115
'Twill get affection a good stomach, sir.
[*Aside*] Which I had need have, to fall to such coarse victuals.
    [*She walks about while they duck down to look up her dress*]

WARD

Now go thy ways for a clean-treading wench,
As ever man in modesty peeped under.

SORDIDO

I see the sweetest sight to please my master!   120
Never went Frenchman righter upon ropes
Than she on Florentine rushes.

WARD [*To* ISABELLA]   'Tis enough, forsooth.

ISABELLA

And how do you like me now, sir?

WARD   'Faith, so well,
I never mean to part with thee, sweetheart,
Under some sixteen children, and all boys.   125

106   *Irish dance* begun with one heel touching the other foot's instep, as described
       here
       still always
106–7 *the ... the* ed. (he ... the O)
107   *cleanly shift* neat trick
108   *dab down* duck down
112   *scaffolds* raised areas for spectators
116   *stomach* i.e. sexual appetite
118   *clean-treading* straight-walking; also, 'tread' = sexual intercourse
121   *Frenchman . . . ropes* walking on a tightrope, especially by visiting French per-
       formers. Cf. Jonson's *Epicoene:* 'the Frenchman that walks upon ropes' (II.ii.52–3).
122   *rushes* used as a floor-covering
122–4 *well, / I* ed. (well, I O)

357

ISABELLA
> You'll be at simple pains, if you prove kind,
> And breed 'em all in your teeth.

WARD   Nay, by my faith,
> What serves your belly for? 'Twould make my cheeks
> Look like blown bagpipes.

Enter GUARDIANO

GUARDIANO   How now, ward and nephew,
> Gentlewoman and niece! Speak, is it so or not?   130

WARD
> 'Tis so, we are both agreed, sir.

GUARDIANO   In to your kindred, then;
> There's friends, and wine, and music, waits to welcome you.

WARD
> Then I'll be drunk for joy.

SORDIDO   And I for company,
> I cannot break my nose in a better action.

                                    Exeunt

---

126   *simple pains* great pains; the pains appropriate to a fool (= 'simple')
         kind in your natural character
127   *teeth* A sympathetic toothache was believed to be a common psychosomatic illness
         in a husband whose wife was pregnant.
127–8   *faith, / What* ed. (Faith, what O)
128–9   *cheeks / Look* ed. (cheeks look O)
134   *break . . . action* i.e. suffer in a better cause

ACT IV, SCENE i

Enter BIANCA *attended by two* LADIES

BIANCA
How goes your watches, ladies? What's o'clock now?

1 LADY
By mine, full nine.

2 LADY   By mine, a quarter past.

1 LADY
I set mine by St Mark's.

2 LADY   St Antony's, they say,
Goes truer.

1 LADY   That's but your opinion, madam,
Because you love a gentleman o'th'name.   5

2 LADY
He's a true gentleman, then.

1 LADY   So may he be
That comes to me tonight, for aught you know.

BIANCA
I'll end this strife straight. I set mine by the sun;
I love to set by th'best, one shall not then
Be troubled to set often.

2 LADY   You do wisely in't.   10

BIANCA
If I should set my watch as some girls do
By ev'ry clock i'th'town, 'twould nev'r go true;
And too much turning of the dial's point,
Or tampering with the spring, might in small time

1–18   This dialogue about clocks is also a debate about sexual fidelity. Watches, like
       women, were notoriously unreliable, according to this misogynist analogy, but
       Bianca claims an ironic constancy because she sets her watch 'by the sun' (l. 8), i.e.
       the Duke. The equation woman = clock occurs in several plays of the period –
       Dekker's *The Honest Whore, Part II* (III.i), Jonson's *Epicoene* (IV.ii) and Middleton's
       A Mad World, My Masters (IV.i), among others. Cf. Shakespeare's *Love's Labour's
       Lost*: 'A woman, that is like a German clock, / Still a-repairing, ever out of frame, /
       And never going aright' (III.i.188–90).

   3   *St Mark's* church in Florence. Cf. I.iii.85n.

 3–4   *say, / Goes* ed. (say goes O)

13–14   *dial's point . . . spring* i.e. male and female genitals

Spoil the whole work too. Here it wants of nine now.   15

1 LADY

It does indeed, forsooth; mine's nearest truth yet.

2 LADY

Yet I have found her lying with an advocate, which showed
Like two false clocks together in one parish.

BIANCA

So now I thank you, ladies, I desire
A while to be alone.

1 LADY   And I am nobody,   20
Methinks, unless I have one or other with me.
'Faith, my desire and hers will nev'r be sisters.

                                        Exit LADIES

BIANCA

How strangely woman's fortune comes about!
This was the farthest way to come to me,
All would have judged, that knew me born in Venice   25
And there with many jealous eyes brought up,
That never thought they had me sure enough
But when they were upon me; yet my hap
To meet it here, so far off from my birthplace,
My friends or kindred. 'Tis not good, in sadness,   30
To keep a maid so strict in her young days;
Restraint breeds wandering thoughts, as many fasting days
A great desire to see flesh stirring again.
I'll nev'r use any girl of mine so strictly;
Howev'r they're kept, their fortunes find 'em out –   35
I see't in me. If they be got in court,
I'll never forbid 'em the country, nor the court,
Though they be born i'th'country. They will come to't,
And fetch their falls a thousand mile about,

---

17   *advocate* An advocate 'lies' professionally; hence both are 'false'.
24   *the farthest way* i.e. the most unlikely fate
30   *in sadness* seriously
31–4 *keep . . . strictly* a conventional idea. Cf. Webster's *The White Devil*: 'women are
      more willingly and more gloriously chaste, when they are least restrained of their
      liberty' (I.ii.90–1).
32–3 *fasting . . . stirring* After 1608, laws prohibiting the eating of meat during Lent were
      more strictly enforced; 'stirring' and 'flesh' also have sexual connotations.
36   *got* begotten
39   *fetch . . . about* go a thousand miles out of their way to fall into sin

Where one would little think on't.   40

Enter LEANTIO

LEANTIO

  [*Aside*] I long to see how my despiser looks,

  Now she's come here to court. These are her lodgings;

  She's simply now advanced. I took her out

  Of no such window, I remember, first;

  That was a great deal lower, and less carved.   45

BIANCA

  [*Aside*] How now? What silkworm's this, i'th'name of pride?

  What, is it he?

LEANTIO   A bow i'th'ham to your greatness;

  You must have now three legs, I take it, must you not?

BIANCA

  Then I must take another, I shall want else

  The service I should have; you have but two there.   50

LEANTIO

  Y'are richly placed.

BIANCA   Methinks y'are wondrous brave, sir.

LEANTIO

  A sumptuous lodging!

BIANCA   Y'ave an excellent suit there.

LEANTIO

  A chair of velvet!

BIANCA   Is your cloak lined through, sir?

LEANTIO

  Y'are very stately here.

BIANCA   'Faith, something proud, sir.

LEANTIO

  Stay, stay, let's see your cloth-of-silver slippers.   55

---

40 s.d. As Bianca's reaction at l. 46 indicates, Leantio enters richly dressed.

43 *simply* absolutely

46 *silkworm* dressed in silk, i.e. a fancy dresser

48–50 *three legs ... service* three bows; but with sexual insinuation 'leg' = penis. The bawdy
     dialogue continues with 'service' = deference; sexual satisfaction.

49 *want* lack

51 *brave* well-dressed

53 *lined through* with a lining throughout (a sign of wealth)

55 *cloth-of-silver* cloth with silver threads interwoven (another sign of ostentatious
     wealth)

BIANCA

Who's your shoemaker? H'as made you a neat boot.

LEANTIO

Will you have a pair? The Duke will lend you spurs.

BIANCA

Yes, when I ride.

LEANTIO   'Tis a brave life you lead.

BIANCA

I could nev'r see you in such good clothes
In my time.

LEANTIO   In your time?

BIANCA   Sure, I think, sir,   60
We both thrive best asunder.

LEANTIO   Y'are a whore!

BIANCA

Fear nothing, sir.

LEANTIO   An impudent, spiteful strumpet!

BIANCA

Oh sir, you give me thanks for your captainship;
I thought you had forgot all your good manners.

LEANTIO

And to spite thee as much, look there, there read!   65

                                      [*Gives her a letter*]

Vex, gnaw! Thou shalt find there I am not love-starved.
The world was never yet so cold or pitiless
But there was ever still more charity found out
Than at one proud fool's door; and 'twere hard, 'faith,
If I could not pass that. Read to thy shame, there;   70
A cheerful and a beauteous benefactor too,
As ev'r erected the good works of love.

BIANCA   Lady Livia!

[*Aside*] Is't possible? Her worship was my pandress.
She dote, and send and give, and all to him!

---

57   *pair? The* ed. (pair, / The O)
57–8 *lend . . . ride* lend you assistance. Bianca also takes up the sexual connotation in her
      response in l. 58, where 'ride' = ride a horse; have sexual intercourse.
59   *you in* ed. (you / In O)
59–60 *clothes / In* ed. (clothes in O)
70   *pass that* pass by; surpass
72   as ever established charitable acts; as ever sexually aroused one

Why, here's a bawd plagued home.
[*To him*]   Y'are simply happy, sir,   75
Yet I'll not envy you.

LEANTIO   No, court-saint, not thou!
You keep some friend of a new fashion;
There's no harm in your devil, he's a suckling,
But he will breed teeth shortly, will he not?

BIANCA
Take heed you play not then too long with him.   80

LEANTIO
Yes, and the great one too. I shall find time
To play a hot religious bout with some of you,
And perhaps drive you and your course of sins
To their eternal kennels. I speak softly now –
'Tis manners in a noble woman's lodgings,   85
And I well know all my degrees of duty –
But come I to your everlasting parting once,
Thunder shall seem soft music to that tempest.

BIANCA
'Twas said last week there would be change of weather,
When the moon hung so, and belike you heard it.   90

LEANTIO
Why, here's sin made, and nev'r a conscience put to't;
A monster with all forehead and no eyes!
Why do I talk to thee of sense or virtue,
That art as dark as death? And as much madness
To set light before thee, as to lead blind folks   95
To see the monuments, which they may smell as soon
As they behold; marry, oft-times their heads
For want of light may feel the hardness of 'em.
So shall thy blind pride my revenge and anger,

75   *bawd plagued home* punished with the same 'plague' (of love) she has caused others
      to suffer
      simply absolutely
77   *friend* lover. See II.i.153n.
79   *breed teeth* cut his teeth, i.e. the Duke will soon show his teeth
81   *great one* the Duke; or perhaps the Devil
83   *course* pack (of dogs); flow
86   *know* ed. (knew O)
90   *moon hung* perhaps a reference to the crescent or horned (= cuckold) moon
91   *put to't* troubled
92   *forehead* front; impudence
96   *monuments* an unwitting allusion to the scene of Bianca's fall

That canst not see it now; and it may fall   100
At such an hour when thou least seest of all;
So to an ignorance darker than thy womb,
I leave thy perjured soul. A plague will come!   *Exit*

BIANCA
Get you gone first, and then I fear no greater,
Nor thee will I fear long; I'll have this sauciness   105
Soon banished from these lodgings and the rooms
Perfumed well after the corrupt air it leaves.
His breath has made me almost sick, in troth.
A poor base start-up! Life! Because h'as got
Fair clothes by foul means, comes to rail, and show 'em.   110

Enter the DUKE

DUKE
Who's that?
BIANCA   Cry you mercy, sir.
DUKE   Prithee, who's that?
BIANCA
The former thing, my lord, to whom you gave
The captainship; he eats his meat with grudging still.
DUKE
Still!
BIANCA He comes vaunting here of his new love,
And the new clothes she gave him: Lady Livia.   115
Who but she now his mistress?
DUKE   Lady Livia?
Be sure of what you say.
BIANCA   He showed me her name, sir,
In perfumed paper, her vows, her letter,
With an intent to spite me; so his heart said,
And his threats made it good – they were as spiteful   120
As ever malice uttered, and as dangerous,
Should his hand follow the copy.
DUKE   But that must not.
Do not you vex your mind; prithee to bed, go.
All shall be well and quiet.

---

101 *when . . . all* when she can least 'see' sin, i.e. in the 'dark' world of sexual betrayal
114 *vaunting* boasting
122 *Should . . . copy* should he imitate the model in his copybook, i.e. should he follow
     his threats ('malice') with action

BIANCA   I love peace, sir.
DUKE
  And so do all that love; take you no care for't,   125
  It shall be still provided to your hand.

                                          Exit [BIANCA]

  Who's near us there?

Enter MESSENGER

MESSENGER   My lord?
DUKE   Seek out Hippolito,
  Brother to Lady Livia, with all speed.
MESSENGER
  He was the last man I saw, my lord.   *Exit*
DUKE   Make haste.
  He is a blood soon stirred, and as he's quick   130
  To apprehend a wrong, he's bold and sudden
  In bringing forth a ruin. I know likewise
  The reputation of his sister's honour's
  As dear to him as life-blood to his heart;
  Beside, I'll flatter him with a goodness to her   135
  Which I now thought on, but nev'r meant to practise –
  Because I know her base – and that wind drives him.
  The ulcerous reputation feels the poise
  Of lightest wrongs, as sores are vexed with flies.
  He comes.

Enter HIPPOLITO

  Hippolito, welcome.
HIPPOLITO   My loved lord.   140
DUKE
  How does that lusty widow, thy kind sister?
  Is she not sped yet of a second husband?

---

130   *blood soon stirred* a young man easily aroused
131   *sudden* impetuous
132   *ruin* disastrous result
133   *honour's* ed. (honor O)
135   *goodness* benefit
137   *that wind drives him* i.e. the thought of her benefit will urge him on (as wind fills
      the sails of a ship)
138   *poise* weight
142   *sped yet of* yet furnished with
      second husband Actually, it would be her third; cf. I.ii.50.

A bed-fellow she has, I ask not that;
I know she's sped of him.
HIPPOLITO   Of him, my lord?
DUKE
Yes, of a bed-fellow. Is the news so strange to you?   145
HIPPOLITO
I hope 'tis so to all.
DUKE   I wish it were, sir;
But 'tis confessed too fast. Her ignorant pleasures,
Only by lust instructed, have received
Into their services an impudent boaster,
One that does raise his glory from her shame,   150
And tells the midday sun what's done in darkness;
Yet blinded with her appetite, wastes her wealth,
Buys her disgraces at a dearer rate
Than bounteous housekeepers purchase their honour.
Nothing sads me so much, as that in love   155
To thee and to thy blood, I had picked out
A wormy match for her, the great Vincentio,
High in our favour and in all men's thoughts.
HIPPOLITO
Oh thou destruction of all happy fortunes,
Unsated blood! Know you the name, my lord,   160
Of her abuser?
DUKE   One Leantio.
HIPPOLITO
He's a factor!
DUKE   He nev'r made so brave a voyage
By his own talk.
HIPPOLITO   The poor old widow's son!
I humbly take my leave.
DUKE [*Aside*]   I see 'tis done.
[*To him*] Give her good counsel, make her see her error;   165
I know she'll hearken to you.
HIPPOLITO   Yes, my lord,
I make no doubt, as I shall take the course
Which she shall never know till it be acted;

147 *confessed too fast* admitted too openly
152 *wastes* i.e. she wastes
153 *dearer* higher, greater
156 *blood* family
160 *blood* sexual appetite

And when she wakes to honour, then she'll thank me for't.
I'll imitate the pities of old surgeons   170
To this lost limb, who ere they show their art
Cast one asleep, then cut the diseased part.
So out of love to her I pity most,
She shall not feel him going till he's lost;
Then she'll commend the cure.   *Exit*

DUKE   The great cure's past.   175
I count this done already; his wrath's sure,
And speaks an injury deep. Farewell, Leantio;
This place will never hear thee murmur more.

     Enter LORD CARDINAL *attended* [*by* SERVANTS]

Our noble brother, welcome!
CARDINAL   Set those lights down.
Depart till you be called.
                        [*Exeunt* SERVANTS]
DUKE [*Aside*]   There's serious business   180
Fixed in his look; nay, it inclines a little
To the dark colour of a discontentment.
[*To him*] Brother, what is't commands your eye so powerfully?
Speak, you seem lost.
CARDINAL   The thing I look on seems so
To my eyes, lost for ever.
DUKE   You look on me.   185
CARDINAL
What a grief 'tis to a religious feeling
To think a man should have a friend so goodly,
So wise, so noble, nay, a duke, a brother,
And all this certainly damned?
DUKE   How!
CARDINAL   'Tis no wonder,
If your great sin can do't. Dare you look up   190
For thinking of a vengeance? Dare you sleep,
For fear of never waking, but to death?
And dedicate unto a strumpet's love
The strength of your affections, zeal and health?
Here you stand now; can you assure your pleasures   195
You shall once more enjoy her, but once more?

170   *old surgeons* reference to early uses of anaesthesia during surgery
184   *lost* i.e. lost in thought

Alas, you cannot; what a misery 'tis, then,
To be more certain of eternal death
Than of a next embrace! Nay, shall I show you
How more unfortunate you stand in sin,   200
Than the low private man? All his offences,
Like enclosed grounds, keep but about himself,
And seldom stretch beyond his own soul's bounds;
And when a man grows miserable, 'tis some comfort
When he's no further charged than with himself;   205
'Tis a sweet ease to wretchedness. But, great man,
Ev'ry sin thou commit'st shows like a flame
Upon a mountain; 'tis seen far about,
And with a big wind made of popular breath
The sparkles fly through cities. Here one takes,   210
Another catches there, and in short time
Waste all to cinders. But remember still,
What burnt the valleys, first came from the hill.
Ev'ry offence draws his particular pain,
But 'tis example proves the great man's bane.   215
The sins of mean men lie like scattered parcels
Of an unperfect bill; but when such fall,
Then comes example, and that sums up all.
And this your reason grants: if men of good lives,
Who by their virtuous actions stir up others   220
To noble and religious imitation,
Receive the greater glory after death –
As sin must needs confess – what may they feel
In height of torments and in weight of vengeance,
Not only they themselves not doing well,   225
But sets a light up to show men to Hell?

DUKE

If you have done, I have. No more, sweet brother.

CARDINAL

I know time spent in goodness is too tedious;

201   *low* ed. (love O)
202   *enclosed grounds* fenced-off land
205   *charged* burdened
209   *popular breath* the words or gossip of common people
214   *draws* brings with it, produces
215   *example* i.e. being an example
215–18   *great man . . . all* i.e. the sins of common men are like isolated items of an
          incomplete bill, but when 'great' men fall (or die), their sins are gathered together
          under the heading of 'example', and all such are then so judged

This had not been a moment's space in lust, now.
How dare you venture on eternal pain   230
That cannot bear a minute's reprehension?
Methinks you should endure to hear that talked of
Which you so strive to suffer. Oh my brother!
What were you, if you were taken now?
My heart weeps blood to think on't; 'tis a work   235
Of infinite mercy you can never merit
That yet you are not death-struck, no, not yet.
I dare not stay you long, for fear you should not
Have time enough allowed you to repent in.
There's but this wall betwixt you and destruction   240
When y'are at strongest, and but poor thin clay.
Think upon't, brother. Can you come so near it
For a fair strumpet's love, and fall into
A torment that knows neither end nor bottom
For beauty, but the deepness of a skin,   245
And that not of their own neither? Is she a thing
Whom sickness dare not visit, or age look on,
Or death resist? Does the worm shun her grave?
If not – as your soul knows it – why should lust
Bring man to lasting pain, for rotten dust?   250

DUKE

Brother of spotless honour, let me weep
The first of my repentance in thy bosom,
And show the blest fruits of a thankful spirit;
And if I e'er keep woman more unlawfully,
May I want penitence at my greatest need –   255
And wise men know there is no barren place
Threatens more famine, than a dearth in grace.

CARDINAL

Why, here's a conversion is at this time, brother,
Sung for a hymn in Heaven; and at this instant

---

231   *reprehension* rebuke
234   *taken* i.e. taken by death
238   *stay* delay
240–1 *wall . . . day* conventional metaphors for the frailty of the body
246   *not of their own* i.e. produced by cosmetics
255   *want* lack
258–9 *conversion . . . Heaven* Cf. Luke 15:10: 'There is joy in the presence of the angels of
       God over one sinner that repenteth'.

The powers of darkness groan, makes all Hell sorry. 260
First, I praise Heaven; then in my work I glory.
Who's there attends without?

Enter SERVANTS

SERVANT   My lord.

CARDINAL
   Take up those lights; there was a thicker darkness
   When they came first. The peace of a fair soul
   Keep with my noble brother.

Exit [LORD] CARDINAL [*and* SERVANTS]

DUKE   Joys be with you, sir. 265
   She lies alone tonight for't, and must still,
   Though it be hard to conquer; but I have vowed
   Never to know her as a strumpet more,
   And I must save my oath. If fury fail not,
   Her husband dies tonight, or at the most 270
   Lives not to see the morning spent tomorrow;
   Then will I make her lawfully mine own,
   Without this sin and horror. Now I'm chidden
   For what I shall enjoy then unforbidden,
   And I'll not freeze in stoves; 'tis but a while, 275
   Live like a hopeful bridegroom, chaste from flesh;
   And pleasure then will seem new, fair and fresh.   *Exit*

ACT IV, SCENE ii

Enter HIPPOLITO

HIPPOLITO
   The morning so far wasted, yet his baseness
   So impudent? See if the very sun do not blush at him!
   Dare he do thus much, and know me alive!
   Put case one must be vicious, as I know myself

267   *it* his desire
269   *save my oath* keep my word
275   *freeze in stoves* freeze in rooms where there is heat ('stoves' = rooms heated by hot
     air)

Monstrously guilty, there's a blind time made for't;   5
He might use only that, 'twere conscionable.
Art, silence, closeness, subtlety, and darkness
Are fit for such a business. But there's no pity
To be bestowed on an apparent sinner,
An impudent daylight lecher! The great zeal   10
I bear to her advancement in this match
With Lord Vincentio, as the Duke has wrought it,
To the perpetual honour of our house,
Puts fire into my blood, to purge the air
Of this corruption, fear it spread too far,   15
And poison the whole hopes of this fair fortune.
I love her good so dearly, that no brother
Shall venture farther for a sister's glory
Than I for her preferment.

Enter LEANTIO *and a* PAGE

LEANTIO   Once again
I'll see that glist'ring whore shines like a serpent,   20
Now the court sun's upon her. Page!
PAGE   Anon, sir!
LEANTIO
I'll go in state too; see the coach be ready.

[*Exit* PAGE]

I'll hurry away presently.
HIPPOLITO   Yes, you shall hurry,
And the devil after you; take that at setting forth!

[*Strikes* LEANTIO]

Now, and you'll draw, we are upon equal terms, sir.   25
Thou took'st advantage of my name in honour

4   *Put case* assuming
      vicious i.e. full of vice
6   *conscionable* scrupulous
7   *Art* artifice, cunning
      closeness secrecy
9   *apparent* open, obvious
15   *fear* for fear
20   *glist'ring . . . serpent* She is 'glist'ring' and linked with the serpent (= devil) because
      she is in the 'court sun's' glare, and her new status and rich clothing reflect its light
      as a serpent's skin the sun.
22   LEANTIO This speech ascription comes before l. 23 in O.
24   *at setting forth* to begin with
25   *and* if

371

Upon my sister; I nev'r saw the stroke
Come, till I found my reputation bleeding;
And therefore count it I no sin to valour
To serve thy lust so. Now we are of even hand,   30
Take your best course against me. You must die.

LEANTIO

How close sticks envy to man's happiness!
When I was poor and little cared for life,
I had no such means offered me to die,
No man's wrath minded me.   [*Draws his sword*]
                   Slave, I turn this to thee,   35
To call thee to account for a wound lately
Of a base stamp upon me.

HIPPOLITO   'Twas most fit
For a base mettle. Come and fetch one now
More noble, then, for I will use thee fairer
Than thou hast done thine own soul or our honour;   40
And there I think 'tis for thee.

            [*They fight and* LEANTIO *falls*]

[VOICES] WITHIN   Help, help, oh part 'em!

LEANTIO

False wife! I feel now th'hast prayed heartily for me.
Rise, strumpet, by my fall, thy lust may reign now;
My heart-string and the marriage-knot that tied thee
Breaks both together.   [*Dies*]

HIPPOLITO   There I heard the sound on't,   45
And never liked string better.

         Enter GUARDIANO, LIVIA, ISABELLA,
             WARD, *and* SORDIDO

LIVIA   'Tis my brother!
Are you hurt, sir?

HIPPOLITO   Not anything.

LIVIA   Blessed fortune!
Shift for thyself; what is he thou hast killed?

---

30   *of even hand* in an equal position
37   *base stamp* base nature; false impression on face of a coin
38   *base mettle* base disposition; base metal (linked to coin metaphor in previous line)
40   *own* ed. (*not in* O)
44   *heart-string* nerve or tendon supposed to sustain heart
46   *string* i.e. string of musical instrument
48   *Shift far thyself i.e.* make your own escape

HIPPOLITO
Our honour's enemy.

GUARDIANO   Know you this man, lady?

LIVIA
Leantio? My love's joy?
[*To* HIPPOLITO]   Wounds stick upon thee   50
As deadly as thy sins! Art thou not hurt?
The devil take that fortune. And he dead!
Drop plagues into thy bowels without voice,
Secret and fearful. [*To others*] Run for officers!
Let him be apprehended with all speed,   55
For fear he scape away; lay hands on him!
We cannot be too sure, 'tis wilful murder!
You do Heaven's vengeance and the law just service;
You know him not as I do: he's a villain,
As monstrous as a prodigy, and as dreadful.   60

HIPPOLITO
Will you but entertain a noble patience
Till you but hear the reason, worthy sister!

LIVIA
The reason! That's a jest Hell falls a-laughing at!
Is there a reason found for the destruction
Of our more lawful loves? And was there none   65
To kill the black lust 'twixt thy niece and thee
That has kept close so long?

GUARDIANO   How's that, good madam?

LIVIA
Too true, sir, there she stands, let her deny't;
The deed cries shortly in the midwife's arms,
Unless the parents' sins strike it still-born.   70
And if you be not deaf and ignorant,
You'll hear strange notes ere long.
[*To* ISABELLA]   Look upon me, wench!
'Twas I betrayed thy honour subtly to him
Under a false tale; it lights upon me now.
His arm has paid me home upon thy breast,   75

---

53 *without voice* silently, without warning
60 *prodigy* unnatural marvel
67 *close* secret
71 *ignorant* wilfully disregarding
72 *strange* new, unfamiliar
74–5 *it . . . breast* i.e. my treachery has been returned upon me

My sweet, beloved Leantio!

GUARDIANO   Was my judgement

And care in choice so dev'lishly abused,

So beyond shamefully? All the world will grin at me!

WARD

Oh Sordido, Sordido, I'm damned, I'm damned!

SORDIDO

Damned! Why, sir?

WARD   One of the wicked; dost not see't?   80

A cuckold, a plain reprobate cuckold!

SORDIDO

Nay, and you be damned for that, be of good cheer, sir, y'have
gallant company of all professions; I'll have a wife next Sunday
too, because I'll along with you myself.

WARD

That will be some comfort yet.   85

LIVIA

[*To* GUARDIANO] You, sir, that bear your load of injuries

As I of sorrows, lend me your grieved strength

To this sad burthen who, in life, wore actions

Flames were not nimbler. We will talk of things

May have the luck to break our hearts together.   90

GUARDIANO

I'll list to nothing but revenge and anger,

Whose counsels I will follow.

                         Exeunt LIVIA *and* GUARDIANO

                           [*carrying* LEANTIO'*s body*]

SORDIDO   A wife, quoth'a!

Here's a sweet plum-tree of your guardianer's grafting!

80–1   *see't? / A* ed. (see't, a O)

82–4   arranged as verse in O

   83   *Sunday* when wives will be well-dressed and apparently virtuous, yet actually flirtatious with others. Proverbial misogyny: 'Who will have a handsome wife let him choose her upon Saturday and not upon Sunday' (Tilley, W 378).

88–9   *wore . . . nimbler* i.e. was characterized by actions more energetic ('nimbler') than fire

   91   *list* listen

   92   *quoth'a* said he

   93   *plum-tree* i.e. female genitals

          guardianer's a gardener's grafting of two unlike plants together; the guardian's marrying of two unlike people

          grafting ed. (graffing O)

WARD

Nay, there's a worse name belongs to this fruit yet, and you
could hit on't, a more open one. For he that marries a whore   95
looks like a fellow bound all his lifetime to a medlar-tree; and
that's good stuff, 'tis no sooner ripe but it looks rotten – and so
do some queans at nineteen. A pox on't, I thought there was
some knavery abroach, for something stirred in her belly the
first night I lay with her.   100

SORDIDO

What, what, sir!

WARD

This is she brought up so courtly! Can sing, and dance, and
tumble too, methinks. I'll never marry wife again that has so
many qualities.

SORDIDO

Indeed they are seldom good, master. For likely when they are   105
taught so many, they will have one trick more of their own
finding out. Well, give me a wench but with one good quality,
to lie with none but her husband, and that's bringing-up
enough for any woman breathing.

WARD

This was the fault when she was tendered to me; you never   110
looked to this.

SORDIDO

Alas, how would you have me see through a great farthingale,
sir! I cannot peep through a millstone, or in the going, to see
what's done i'th'bottom.

94–8   *worse . . . queans* not a'plum-tree'but another kind of' fruit' (= female genitals). The
'more open one' is the 'medlar', a small pulpy apple, nearly 'rotten' as soon as it is
'ripe'; because of these characteristics, reminiscent of the symptoms of venereal
disease, the medlar was frequently associated with the degenerate sexuality of
'queans' (whores). The 'open one' also alludes to the dialect name for the medlar,
'open-arse'; see *Romeo and Juliet* II.i.39.

103   *tumble* do acrobatics; have sexual intercourse

104   *qualities* skills, accomplishments. Some writers of the time argued that (over-)
educated women were untrustworthy.

112   *farthingale* a framework of hoops, worn about the waist, which extended a
woman's dress

113   *peep . . . millstone* i.e. see acutely, resolve difficulties; proverbial (Tilley, M 965)
going walking (i.e. while she's walking)

114   *i'th'bottom* at the bottom; at her genitals

WARD

Her father praised her breast, sh'ad the voice, forsooth; I mar-   115
velled she sung so small indeed, being no maid. Now I perceive
there's a young chorister in her belly – this breeds a singing in
my head, I'm sure.

SORDIDO

'Tis but the tune of your wives' cinquepace, danced in a
featherbed. 'Faith, go lie down, master – but take heed your   120
horns do not make holes in the pillowberes. [*Aside*] I would
not batter brows with him for a hogshead of angels; he would
prick my skull as full of holes as a scrivener's sand-box.

Exeunt WARD *and* SORDIDO

ISABELLA

[*Aside*] Was ever maid so cruelly beguiled
To the confusion of life, soul, and honour.   125
All of one woman's murdering! I'd fain bring
Her name no nearer to my blood than woman,
And 'tis too much of that. Oh shame and horror!
In that small distance from yon man to me
lies sin enough to make a whole world perish.   130
[*To him*] 'Tis time we parted, sir, and left the sight
Of one another; nothing can be worse
To hurt repentance, for our very eyes
Are far more poisonous to religion
Than basilisks to them. If any goodness   135
Rest in you, hope of comforts, fear of judgements,
My request is, I nev'r may see you more;
And so I turn me from you everlastingly,
So is my hope to miss you. But for her,

115–18   arranged as verse in O
116–17   *small . . . chorister* i.e. he was surprised she sang so softly (perhaps also at a treble pitch)
          because she was no young girl. He now claims it was the unborn baby's voice.
117–18   *singing in my head* alleged symptom of cuckoldry
    119   *cinquepace* galliard (a lively French dance)
    121   *horns* cuckold's horns
           pillowberes pillowcases
    122   *hogshead of angels* barrel of gold coins (an 'angel' coin had a picture of St Michael
           on one side)
    123   *scrivener's sand-box* perforated box filled with sand, used for blotting ink
    125   *confusion* ruin
    127   *blood* kinship
    135   *basilisks* mythical reptiles (part cock, part serpent), able to kill by their glance
    139   *miss you* i.e. to avoid meeting him 'everlastingly', in Hell

That durst so dally with a sin so dangerous,   140
And lay a snare so spitefully for my youth,
If the least means but favour my revenge,
That I may practise the like cruel cunning
Upon her life, as she has on mine honour,
I'll act it without pity.

HIPPOLITO   Here's a care   145
Of reputation and a sister's fortune
Sweetly rewarded by her. Would a silence,
As great as that which keeps among the graves,
Had everlastingly chained up her tongue;
My love to her has made mine miserable.   150

        Enter GUARDIANO *and* LIVIA [*who talk aside*]

GUARDIANO
If you can but dissemble your heart's griefs now,
Be but a woman so far.

LIVIA   Peace! I'll strive, sir.

GUARDIANO
As I can wear my injuries in a smile,
Here's an occasion offered, that gives anger
Both liberty and safety to perform   155
Things worth the fire it holds, without the fear
Of danger or of law; for mischiefs acted
Under the privilege of a marriage-triumph
At the Duke's hasty nuptials will be thought
Things merely accidental; all's by chance,   160
Not got of their own natures.

LIVIA   I conceive you, sir,
Even to a longing for performance on't;
And here behold some fruits.

        [*Kneels before* HIPPOLITO *and* ISABELLA]
              Forgive me both.
What I am now, returned to sense and judgement,
Is not the same rage and distraction   165
Presented lately to you; that rude form

156–8   *fear . . . marriage-triumph* i.e. the law would be suspended ('privilege' = legal immunity) during the 'marriage-triumph', the masque performed for the marriage. As Middleton notes in *The Revenger's Tragedy*: 'A masque is treason's licence: that build upon – / 'Tis murder's best face, when a vizard's on!' (V.i.177–8).

160   *all's* all as if

161–3   *got . . . conceive . . . longing . . . fruits* These words also refer to conception and pregnancy.

377

Is gone for ever. I am now myself,
That speaks all peace and friendship; and these tears
Are the true springs of hearty, penitent sorrow
For those foul wrongs which my forgetful fury   170
Slandered your virtues with. This gentleman
Is well resolved now.

GUARDIANO   I was never otherways.
I knew, alas, 'twas but your anger spake it,
And I nev'r thought on't more.

HIPPOLITO   Pray rise, good sister.

ISABELLA
[*Aside*] Here's ev'n as sweet amends made for a wrong now   175
As one that gives a wound, and pays the surgeon;
All the smart's nothing, the great loss of blood,
Or time of hindrance. Well, I had a mother,
I can dissemble too. [*To* LIVIA] What wrongs have slipped
Through anger's ignorance, aunt, my heart forgives.   180

GUARDIANO
Why thus tuneful now!

HIPPOLITO   And what I did, sister,
Was all for honour's cause, which time to come
Will approve to you.

LIVIA   Being awaked to goodness,
I understand so much, sir, and praise now
The fortune of your arm, and of your safety;   185
For by his death y'have rid me of a sin
As costly as ev'r woman doted on.
T'has pleased the Duke so well, too, that – behold, sir –
H'as sent you here your pardon,

                              [*Gives him a letter*]
                    which I kissed
With most affectionate comfort; when 'twas brought,   190
Then was my fit just past; it came so well, methought,
To glad my heart.

HIPPOLITO   I see his grace thinks on me.

---

172   *resolved* satisfied, informed
178   *hindrance* incapacity
181   *thus* Many editors emend to 'this is', supplying the supposedly missing verb; but
      Guardiano's line could be either an exclamation or a suspicious question, since O
      frequently uses question-marks and exclamation-marks interchangeably.
183   *approve* prove, demonstrate

LIVIA

    There's no talk now but of the preparation
    For the great marriage.

HIPPOLITO   Does he marry her, then?

LIVIA

    With all speed, suddenly, as fast as cost   195
    Can be laid on with many thousand hands.
    This gentleman and I had once a purpose
    To have honoured the first marriage of the duke
    With an invention of his own; 'twas ready,
    The pains well past, most of the charge bestowed on't;   200
    Then came the death of your good mother, niece,
    And turned the glory of it all to black.
    'Tis a device would fit these times so well, too,
    Art's treasury not better. If you'll join,
    It shall be done, the cost shall all be mine.   205

HIPPOLITO

    Y'have my voice first, 'twill well approve my thankfulness
    For the Duke's love and favour.

LIVIA   What say you, niece?

ISABELLA

    I am content to make one.

GUARDIANO   The plot's full, then;
    Your pages, madam, will make shift for cupids.

LIVIA

    That will they, sir.

GUARDIANO   You'll play your old part still.   210

LIVIA

    What, is't good? Troth, I have ev'n forgot it.

GUARDIANO

    Why, Juno Pronuba, the marriage-goddess.

---

    199   *invention* literary composition
             his own Guardiano's
    200   *pains* effort
             charge bestowed cost paid out
    206   *voice* support
    208   *make one* play a part
             plot's full the cast is complete; the revenge plot is ready
    209   *make shift for* improvise as
    212   *Juno Pronuba* Juno watched over the arrangement of marriages – a highly ironic
             role for Livia to be playing.

LIVIA

'Tis right, indeed.

GUARDIANO [*To* ISABELLA] And you shall play the nymph
That offers sacrifice to appease her wrath.

ISABELLA

Sacrifice, good sir?

LIVIA   Must I be appeased, then?   215

GUARDIANO

That's as you list yourself, as you see cause.

LIVIA

Methinks 'twould show the more state in her deity
To be incensed.

ISABELLA   'Twould, but my sacrifice
Shall take a course to appease you, or I'll fail in't,
[*Aside*] And teach a sinful bawd to play a goddess.   220

GUARDIANO

For our parts, we'll not be ambitious, sir;
Please you walk in and see the project drawn,
Then take your choice.

HIPPOLITO   I weigh not, so I have one.   *Exit*

LIVIA

[*Aside*] How much ado have I to restrain fury
From breaking into curses! Oh how painful 'tis   225
To keep great sorrow smothered! Sure I think
'Tis harder to dissemble grief than love.
Leantio, here the weight of thy loss lies,
Which nothing but destruction can suffice.

                                                  Exeunt

216   *list* choose
217–18   *more . . . incensed* i.e. she would seem more stately if she were angry. Mulryne also
         suggests an unwitting pun on incense (part of the 'sacrifice', l. 215), since Livia
         will be killed by poisoned incense.
222   *project drawn* the plan of the masque written out
223   *weigh* care
224   s.d. Many editions send everyone except Livia off the stage at this point, but
         Holdsworth (p. 90) offers a convincing argument that Hippolito's solitary exit in
         O suggests his new isolation.

ACT IV, SCENE iii

Hoboys

Enter in great state the DUKE *and* BIANCA, *richly attired,*
with LORDS, CARDINALS, LADIES, *and other* ATTENDANTS;
they pass solemnly over. Enter LORD CARDINAL *in a rage,*
seeming to break off the ceremony

CARDINAL

Cease, cease! Religious honours done to sin
Disparage virtue's reverence, and will pull
Heaven's thunder upon Florence; holy ceremonies
Were made for sacred uses, not for sinful.
Are these the fruits of your repentance, brother? 5
Better it had been you had never sorrowed
Than to abuse the benefit, and return
To worse than where sin left you.
Vowed you then never to keep strumpet more,
And are you now so swift in your desires 10
To knit your honours and your life fast to her?
Is not sin sure enough to wretched man
But he must bind himself in chains to't? Worse!
Must marriage, that immaculate robe of honour,
That renders virtue glorious, fair, and fruitful 15
To her great Master, be now made the garment
Of leprosy and foulness? Is this penitence,
To sanctify hot lust? What is it otherways
Than worship done to devils? Is this the best
Amends that sin can make after her riots? 20
As if a drunkard, to appease Heaven's wrath,
Should offer up his surfeit for a sacrifice!
If that be comely, then lust's offerings are

0   s.d. 1 *Hoboys* oboes
0   s.d. 4 *they pass . . . over* They enter the playhouse yard, ascend and cross over the
      stage, and then return to the yard to exit (cf. the opening stage directions to *The
      Revenger's Tragedy*); the Cardinal apparently halts the procession while it is still on
      stage.
17   *leprosy* often associated with syphilis. Cf. II.ii.425.
22   *surfeit* over-indulgence; vomit
23   *comely* decent

On wedlock's sacred altar.
DUKE   Here y'are bitter
  Without cause, brother. What I vowed, I keep   25
  As safe as you your conscience, and this needs not.
  I taste more wrath in't than I do religion,
  And envy more than goodness. The path now
  I tread is honest, leads to lawful love,
  Which virtue in her strictness would not check.   30
  I vowed no more to keep a sensual woman:
  'Tis done; I mean to make a lawful wife of her.
CARDINAL
  He that taught you that craft,
  Call him not master long, he will undo you.
  Grow not too cunning for your soul, good brother.   35
  Is it enough to use adulterous thefts,
  And then take sanctuary in marriage?
  I grant, so long as an offender keeps
  Close in a privileged temple, his life's safe;
  But if he ever venture to come out,   40
  And so be taken, then he surely dies for't.
  So now y'are safe; but when you leave this body,
  Man's only privileged temple upon earth,
  In which the guilty soul takes sanctuary,
  Then you'll perceive what wrongs chaste vows endure,   45
  When lust usurps the bed that should be pure.
BIANCA
  Sir, I have read you over all this while
  In silence, and I find great knowledge in you,
  And severe learning; yet 'mongst all your virtues
  I see not charity written, which some call   50
  The first-born of religion, and I wonder
  I cannot see't in yours. Believe it, sir,
  There is no virtue can be sooner missed
  Or later welcomed; it begins the rest,

26   *this needs not* this reproach is unnecessary
31   *keep a sensual woman* woman kept for sensual purposes
33   *He* i.e. the Devil
42–3 *body ... temple* In the Bible (I Corinthians 3:16), the body is the temple of the Holy
        Spirit – but it is not there a place in which a 'guilty soul' could take 'sanctuary' (l. 44).
47   *read you over* closely observed you
51–5 *first-born ... begins ... order* Cf. I Corinthians 13:13: 'And now abideth faith, hope,
        charity, these three; but the greatest of these is charity'.

And sets 'em all in order. Heaven and angels 55
Take great delight in a converted sinner;
Why should you, then, a servant and professor,
Differ so much from them? If ev'ry woman
That commits evil should be therefore kept
Back in desires of goodness, how should virtue 60
Be known and honoured? From a man that's blind
To take a burning taper, 'tis no wrong,
He never misses it; but to take light
From one that sees, that's injury and spite.
Pray, whether is religion better served, 65
When lives that are licentious are made honest,
Than when they still run through a sinful blood?
'Tis nothing virtue's temples to deface;
But build the ruins, there's a work of grace.

DUKE

I kiss thee for that spirit; thou hast praised thy wit 70
A modest way. On, on there!

Hoboys

CARDINAL   Lust is bold,
And will have vengeance speak, ere't be controlled.

Exeunt

57   *professor* one who professes knowledge (here, one who professes to be a Christian)
67   *Than* or
      blood desire
69   *build the ruins* i.e. restore Bianca's virtue by marrying her
72   *controlled* put down, checked

ACT V, SCENE i

Enter GUARDIANO *and* WARD

GUARDIANO
Speak, hast thou any sense of thy abuse?
Dost thou know what wrong's done thee?

WARD   I were an ass else.
I cannot wash my face, but I am feeling on't.

GUARDIANO
Here, take this galtrop, then; convey it secretly
Into the place I showed you. Look you, sir,   5
This is the trap-door to't.

WARD
I know't of old, uncle, since the last triumph; here rose up a
devil with one eye, I remember, with a company of fireworks
at's tail.

GUARDIANO
Prithee leave squibbing now, mark me and fail not; but when   10
thou hear'st me give a stamp, down with't. The villain's caught
then.

WARD
If I miss you, hang me; I love to catch a villain, and your stamp
shall go current, I warrant you. But how shall I rise up and let
him down too, all at one hole? That will be a horrible puzzle.   15
You know I have a part in't, I play Slander.

GUARDIANO
True, but never make you ready for't.

---

3   *feeling on't* i.e. feeling the cuckold's horns
4   *galtrop* The caltrop or 'galtrop' was a weapon made with four spikes, so that one
     always stands upright; used primarily against cavalry.
6   *trap-door* a standard feature of the Elizabethan/Jacobean stage
7   *triumph* pageant
8   *devil . . . fireworks* The stage-devil, usually a comic figure, was often accompanied
     by fireworks.
10 *squibbing* foolish talk; also pun on 'squib' (= firecracker)
13 *miss you* miss your signal; but also ironic foreshadowing
13-14 *stamp . . . current* The stamp of your foot will be understood as valid; also pun on
     'stamp' = design impressed on coin.
14–15 *rise up . . . let him down . . . at one hole* all with sexual connotations

384

WARD

No? My clothes are bought and all, and a foul fiend's head with
a long contumelious tongue i'th'chaps on't, a very fit shape for
Slander i'th'out-parishes.   20

GUARDIANO

It shall not come so far, thou understand'st it not.

WARD

Oh, oh!

GUARDIANO

He shall lie deep enough ere that time, and stick first upon
those.

WARD

Now I conceive you, guardianer.   25

GUARDIANO

Away, list to the privy stamp, that's all thy part.

WARD

Stamp my horns in a mortar if I miss you, and give the powder
in white wine to sick cuckolds – a very present remedy for the
headache.   *Exit*

GUARDIANO

If this should any way miscarry now –   30
As, if the fool be nimble enough, 'tis certain –
The pages that present the swift-winged Cupids
Are taught to hit him with their shafts of love,
Fitting his part, which I have cunningly poisoned.
He cannot 'scape my fury; and those ills   35
Will be laid all on fortune, not our wills.
That's all the sport on't! For who will imagine
That at the celebration of this night
Any mischance that haps can flow from spite?   *Exit*

---

19   *contumelious* offensive
     chaps jaws
20   *out-parishes* parishes outside the boundaries of the City of London, where popular
     dramatic performances were legally tolerated. Morality-characters such as Slander
     might appear in such older plays.
23   *time, and* ed. (time, / And O)
24   *those* referring to the sharp points of the caltrop
26   *privy* secret
27–9 *Stamp . . . headache* The Ward proposes a medical remedy for cuckoldom (the
     'headache' of the horns), by mixing powdered 'horns' with white wine (a common
     base for mixing medicines).
32   *present* act

385

ACT V, SCENE ii

Flourish. Enter above DUKE, BIANCA, LORD CARDINAL,
FABRITIO, *and other* CARDINALS, LORDS *and* LADIES *in state*

DUKE

    Now our fair duchess, your delight shall witness
    How y'are beloved and honoured: all the glories
    Bestowed upon the gladness of this night
    Are done for your bright sake.

BIANCA   I am the more

    In debt, my lord, to loves and courtesies   5
    That offer up themselves so bounteously
    To do me honoured grace, without my merit.

DUKE

    A goodness set in greatness! How it sparkles
    Afar off like pure diamonds set in gold!
    How perfect my desires were, might I witness   10
    But a fair noble peace 'twixt your two spirits!
    The reconcilement would be more sweet to me
    Than longer life to him that fears to die.
    [*To* LORD CARDINAL] Good Sir!

CARDINAL   I profess peace, and am content.

DUKE

    I'll see the seal upon't, and then 'tis firm.   15

CARDINAL

    You shall have all you wish. [*Kisses* BIANCA]

DUKE   I have all indeed now.

BIANCA

    [*Aside*] But I have made surer work; this shall not blind me.
    He that begins so early to reprove,
    Quickly rid him or look for little love.
    Beware a brother's envy; he's next heir too.   20

  0   s.d. *Flourish* i.e. of trumpets
  7   *grace . . . merit* A specifically Protestant theological point – quite ironic coming
      from Bianca at this point, but the rhetorics of courtesy and religion are cynically
      deployed throughout the play.
 10 *perfect* complete
 15 *seal* Documents were sealed with wax and impressed with a coat of arms or other
      insignia.
 19 *rid* get rid of

Cardinal, you die this night, the plot's laid surely:
In time of sports death may steal in securely;
Then 'tis least thought on.
For he that's most religious, holy friend,
Does not at all hours think upon his end;   25
He has his times of frailty, and his thoughts
Their transportations too, through flesh and blood,
For all his zeal, his learning, and his light,
As well as we poor souls that sin by night.

> [FABRITIO *gives the* DUKE *a paper*]

DUKE
  What's this, Fabritio?
FABRITIO   Marry, my lord, the model   30
  Of what's presented.
DUKE   Oh we thank their loves;
  Sweet duchess, take your seat, list to the argument.
  Reads

> There is a nymph that haunts the woods and springs,
> In love with two at once, and they with her.
> Equal it runs; but to decide these things,   35
> The cause to mighty Juno they refer,
> She being the marriage-goddess. The two lovers,
> They offer sighs; the nymph a sacrifice;
> All to please Juno, who by signs discovers
> How the event shall be; so that strife dies.   40
> Then springs a second; for the man refused
> Grows discontent, and out of love abused
> He raises Slander up, like a black fiend,
> To disgrace th'other, which pays him i'th'end.

BIANCA
  In troth, my lord, a pretty, pleasing argument,   45
  And fits th'occasion well: Envy and Slander
  Are things soon raised against two faithful lovers;
  But comfort is, they are not long unrewarded.

22–3   *securely; / Then* ed. (securely; then O)
  27   *transportations* transports, raptures
  29   *we poor souls* ed. (we, poor soul, O)
  30   *model* outline, plan
  32   *argument* plot summary
  39   *discovers* reveals
  40   *event* outcome
  44   *pays him* brings an appropriate revenge on him

Music

DUKE

This music shows they're upon entrance now.

BIANCA

[*Aside*] Then enter all my wishes!   50

Enter HYMEN *in yellow,* GANYMEDE *in a blue robe powdered
with stars, and* HEBE *in a white robe with golden stars,
with covered cups in their hands. They dance a short dance,
then bowing to the* DUKE, *&c.* HYMEN *speaks*

HYMEN

[*Giving* BIANCA *a cup*] «To thee, fair bride, Hymen offers up
Of nuptial joys this the celestial cup.
Taste it, and thou shalt ever find
Love in thy bed, peace in thy mind.»

BIANCA

We'll taste you, sure, 'twere pity to disgrace   55
So pretty a beginning.

DUKE   'Twas spoke nobly.

GANYMEDE

«Two cups of nectar have we begged from Jove;
Hebe give that to innocence, I this to love.

[HEBE *gives a cup to the* LORD CARDINAL, GANYMEDE
one to the DUKE; *both drink*]

Take heed of stumbling more, look to your way;
Remember still the Via Lactea.»   60

HEBE

«Well, Ganymede, you have more faults, though not so known;
I spilled one cup, but you have filched many a one.»

50   s.d. 1 HYMEN the god of marriage, traditionally represented in yellow robes
      s.d. 1–2 GANYMEDE cupbearer to Zeus (Jove). The 'stars' indicate that Zeus stellified
      him.
      s.d. 2–3 HEBE daughter of Zeus, once cupbearer to Zeus
58   s.d. The Yale copy of O has this manuscript annotation here: 'To the Duke the
      wrong cup by mistake'.
59   *stumbling more* Mulryne identifies the source as William Fulke, *A goodly gallerye* . . .
      (1563): '*Hebe*, one which was *Iupiter's* Cupbearer, on a tyme stombled at a starre,
      and shedde the wyne or mylke, that was in the cuppe, which colloured that part of
      heaven to this daye, wherfore she was pout out of her office' (E6v); he has also
      found this myth in E.K.'s gloss on l. 195 of the November Eclogue in Spenser's
      Shepherd's Calendar.
60   *Via Lactea* the Milky Way

HYMEN

«No more, forbear for Hymen's sake;
In love we met, and so let's parting take.»

Exeunt [HYMEN, GANYMEDE, *and* HEBE]

DUKE

But soft! Here's no such persons in the argument   65
As these three, Hymen, Hebe, Ganymede.
The actors that this model here discovers
Are only four, Juno, a nymph, two lovers.

BIANCA

This is some antemasque belike, my lord,
To entertain time. [*Aside*] Now my peace is perfect.   70
[*To* DUKE] Let sports come on apace; now is their time, my lord.

Music

Hark you, you hear from 'em!

DUKE   The nymph indeed!

Enter two dressed like nymphs, bearing two tapers lighted;
then ISABELLA *dressed with flowers and garlands, bearing*
a censer with fire in it; they set the censer and tapers on JUNO's
altar with much reverence; this ditty being sung in parts

Ditty
Juno, nuptial-goddess,
Thou that rul'st o'er coupled bodies,
Tiest man to woman, never to forsake her,   75
Thou only powerful marriage-maker,
Pity this amazed affection;
I love both, and both love me;
Nor know I where to give rejection,

64   *parting take* ed. (part O). A rhyme with 'sake' seems called for here.
65   *argument* The Duke comments throughout the scene on the discrepancies between
     the 'argument' (ll. 32, 65) or 'plot' (l. 129) of the masque which he is reading and
     the action before him.
69   *antemasque* a brief, often comic, interlude before the masque proper; here, just
     Bianca's cover story
70   *perfect* complete
72   s.d. 4 *in parts* sung separately, not in unison
73–4 *goddess, / Thou* ed. (Goddess, thou O)
75   *Tiest* ed. (Ty'st O)
75–6 *her, / Thou* ed. (her, thou O)
77   *amazed* perplexed, bewildered
77–8 *affection; / I* ed. (affection; I O)
79–80 *rejection, / My* ed. (rejection, my O)

My heart likes so equally, 80
Till thou set'st right my peace of life,
And with thy power conclude this strife.

ISABELLA

[*To* NYMPHS] «Now with my thanks depart you to the springs,
I to these wells of love.

[*Exeunt the two* NYMPHS]
Thou sacred goddess,
And queen of nuptials, daughter to great Saturn, 85
Sister and wife to Jove, imperial Juno,
Pity this passionate conflict in my breast,
This tedious war 'twixt two affections;
Crown one with victory, and my heart's at peace.»

Enter HIPPOLITO *and* GUARDIANO, *like shepherds*

HIPPOLITO

«Make me that happy man, thou mighty goddess.» 90

GUARDIANO

«But I live most in hope, if truest love
Merit the greatest comfort.»

ISABELLA   «I love both
With such an even and fair affection,
I know not which to speak for, which to wish for,
Till thou, great arbitress 'twixt lovers' hearts, 95
By thy auspicious grace, design the man;
Which pity I implore.»

BOTH [HIPPOLITO *and* GUARDIANO]
«We all implore it.»

ISABELLA

«And after sighs, contrition's truest odours,

LIVIA *descends like* JUNO
[*attended by* CUPIDS *with bows*]

---

83   *springs* where the nymphs live (cf. l. 33)
89   *one* ed. (me O)
96   *design* designate, point out
98   s.d. LIVIA *descends* Livia is lowered from the canopy overhead (the 'heavens'), a
     spectacular and highly popular stage effect utilized in many plays, including
     Jonson's *Masque of Hymenaei*, where Juno is lowered, and in Shakespeare's
     Cymbeline, where 'Jupiter descends in thunder and lightning, sitting upon an eagle'
     (V.iv.92 s.d.).

I offer to thy powerful deity,
This precious incense, may it ascend peacefully.»   100

[Poisoned smoke rises]

[Aside] And if it keep true touch, my good aunt Juno,
'Twill try your immortality ere't be long;
I fear you'll never get so nigh Heaven again,
When you're once down.
LIVIA   « Though you and your affections
Seem all as dark to our illustrious brightness   105
As night's inheritance, Hell, we pity you,
And your requests are granted. You ask signs;
They shall be given you, we'll be gracious to you.
He of those twain which we determine for you,
Love's arrows shall wound twice; the later wound   110
Betokens love in age: for so are all
Whose love continues firmly all their lifetime
Twice wounded at their marriage, else affection
Dies when youth ends.» *[Aside]* This savour overcomes me.
[As JUNO*]* «Now for a sign of wealth and golden days,   115
Bright-eyed prosperity which all couples love,
Ay, and makes love, take that!

[Throws flaming gold upon ISABELLA, *who falls dead]*

                        Our brother Jove
Never denies us of his burning treasure,
T'express bounty.»
DUKE   She falls down upon't;
What's the conceit of that?
FABRITIO   As over-joyed, belike.   120
Too much prosperity overjoys us all,
And she has her lapful, it seems, my lord.

---

101   *keep true touch* prove trustworthy (from the testing of gold or silver with a 'touch-
        stone')

105   *to* compared to

114   *savour* ed. (favour O); the odour of the poisoned incense

117   s.d. This stage direction derives from a manuscript annotation in the Yale copy of O.
        The allusion is to Jove's violation ('his burning treasure', l. 118) of Danae as a
        shower of gold; Isabella, like Danae, is overcome by a 'lapful' (l. 122) of 'too much
        prosperity' l. 121). Juno's description in Jonson's *Masque of Hymenaei* is similar:
        'Above her the *region of fire*, with a continual motion, was seen to whirl circularly'.

391

DUKE
This swerves a little from the argument, though.
Look you, my lords!
GUARDIANO
[*Aside*] All's fast; now comes my part to toll him hither;   125
Then, with a stamp given, he's dispatched as cunningly.
HIPPOLITO
Stark dead! Oh treachery! Cruelly made away! How's that?

[HIPPOLITO *angrily stamps on the floor upon discovering*
ISABELLA'*s body;* GUARDIANO *falls through the trap-door*]

FABRITIO
Look, there's one of the lovers dropped away too.
DUKE
Why sure, this plot's drawn false, here's no such thing.
LIVIA
Oh I am sick to th'death, let me down quickly;   130

[*She is lowered to the ground*]

This fume is deadly. Oh 't has poisoned me!
My subtlety is sped, her art has quitted me;
My own ambition pulls me down to ruin.   [*Dies*]
HIPPOLITO
Nay, then I kiss thy cold lips, and applaud
This thy revenge in death.
FABRITIO   Look, Juno's down too.   135

CUPIDS *shoot* [*at* HIPPOLITO]

What makes she there? Her pride should keep aloft.
She was wont to scorn the earth in other shows.
Methinks her peacocks' feathers are much pulled.

---

123   *argument* plot summary
125   *fast* i.e. secure, as planned
       toll him hither entice him to the trap-door; ring his death-knell
127   s.d. This stage direction is speculative; clearly, something goes wrong with Guar-
       diano's plan, and he falls through his own trap. It may be that he himself stamps
       on the floor unwittingly, as most editions of the play suggest; or that he stamps on
       the floor when Hippolito is above the trap, nothing happens, and he goes to test
       the trap himself, with fatal consequences. I am following here G. B. Shand's useful
       suggestion, also adopted by Loughrey and Taylor.
132   *quitted me* requited me, paid me back
138   *peacocks' feathers* Peacocks were sacred to Juno, according to Ovid.

HIPPOLITO

    Oh death runs through my blood in a wild flame too!

    Plague of those Cupids! Some lay hold on 'em.   140

    Let 'em not 'scape, they have spoiled me; the shaft's deadly.

DUKE

    I have lost myself in this quite.

HIPPOLITO

    My great lords, we are all confounded.

DUKE   How?

HIPPOLITO

    [*Points to* ISABELLA] Dead; and I worse.

FABRITIO   Dead? My girl dead? I hope

    My sister Juno has not served me so.   145

HIPPOLITO

    Lust and forgetfulness has been amongst us,

    And we are brought to nothing. Some blest charity

    Lend me the speeding pity of his sword

    To quench this fire in blood. Leantio's death

    Has brought all this upon us – now I taste it –   150

    And made us lay plots to confound each other.

    The event so proves it, and man's understanding

    Is riper at his fall than all his lifetime.

    She, in a madness for her lover's death,

    Revealed a fearful lust in our near bloods,   155

    For which I am punished dreadfully and unlooked for;

    Proved her own ruin too: vengeance met vengeance,

    Like a set match, as if the plagues of sin

    Had been agreed to meet here all together.

    But how her fawning partner fell, I reach not,   160

    Unless caught by some springe of his own setting –

    For on my pain, he never dreamed of dying;

    The plot was all his own, and he had cunning

    Enough to save himself. But 'tis the property

141   *spoiled* destroyed

144   *I worse* because the poison's pain is agonizing; because he also committed incest

152   *event* outcome

158   *Like a set match* as if by agreement   *plagues* ed. (plague O)

159   *all together* ed. (altogether O)

160   *reach* understand

161   *springe* trap, snare

164   *property* quality, tendency

Of guilty deeds to draw your wise men downward.   165
Therefore the wonder ceases. Oh this torment!

DUKE

Our guard below there!

Enter a LORD *with a* GUARD

LORD   My lord.

HIPPOLITO   Run and meet death then,
And cut off time and pain.

[Runs on a GUARD*'s halbert; dies]*

LORD   Behold my lord,
H'as run his breast upon a weapon's point.

DUKE

Upon the first night of our nuptial honours   170
Destruction play her triumph, and great mischiefs
Mask in expected pleasures! 'Tis prodigious!
They're things most fearfully ominous: I like 'em not.
Remove these ruined bodies from our eyes.

[The bodies are taken away]

BIANCA

[*Aside*] Not yet, no change? When falls he to the earth?   175

LORD

Please but your excellence to peruse that paper,
Which is a brief confession from the heart
Of him that fell first, ere his soul departed;
And there the darkness of these deeds speaks plainly.
'Tis the full scope, the manner, and intent;   180
His ward, that ignorantly let him down,
Fear put to present flight at the voice of him.

BIANCA

[*Aside*] Nor yet?

---

168   s.d. *Runs . . . dies* This stage direction derives from a manuscript annotation in the
Yale copy of O.
halbert not a sword, but a weapon with an axelike blade and a steel spike mounted
on the end of a long shaft
168–9 *lord, / H'as* ed. (Lord, h'as O)
171   *triumph* pageant
172   *Mask in* wear a mask as
prodigious ill-omened
178   *him* refers to Guardiano
181   *ignorantly* unintentionally, unwittingly
182   *present* immediate

DUKE [*To* LORD CARDINAL]
        Read, read; for I am lost in sight and strength.

CARDINAL
  My noble brother!

BIANCA   Oh the curse of wretchedness!
  My deadly hand is fall'n upon my lord.   185
  Destruction take me to thee, give me way;
  The pains and plagues of a lost soul upon him
  That hinders me a moment!

DUKE
  My heart swells bigger yet; help here, break't ope,
  My breast flies open next.   [*Dies*]

BIANCA   Oh with the poison   190
  That was prepared for thee, thee, Cardinal!
  'Twas meant for thee.

CARDINAL   Poor prince!

BIANCA   Accursed error!
  Give me thy last breath, thou infected bosom,
  And wrap two spirits in one poisoned vapour.
               [*Kisses the* DUKE*'s lips*]
  Thus, thus, reward thy murderer, and turn death   195
  Into a parting kiss. My soul stands ready at my lips,
  Ev'n vexed to stay one minute after thee.

CARDINAL
  The greatest sorrow and astonishment
  That ever struck the general peace of Florence
  Dwells in this hour.

BIANCA   So my desires are satisfied,   200
  I feel death's power within me!
  Thou hast prevailed in something, cursed poison,
  Though thy chief force was spent in my lord's bosom.
  But my deformity in spirit's more foul;
  A blemished face best fits a leprous soul.   205
  What make I here? These are all strangers to me,
  Not known but by their malice, now th'art gone,
  Nor do I seek their pities.

189–90 It was widely believed that as the moment of death approached, the body's blood
        supply rushed to the heart, making it swell and seem (to the victim) about to burst.
   205 *blemished . . . soul* Even the small amount of poison she has taken from the Duke's
        lips (ll. 195–6) has begun to eat into and deform her face, a suitable outward sign
        of the inner 'leprous soul'.

[She seizes the poisoned cup and drinks from it]

CARDINAL   Oh restrain
  Her ignorant wilful hand!
BIANCA   Now do; 'tis done.
  Leantio, now I feel the breach of marriage   210
  At my heart-breaking! Oh the deadly snares
  That women set for women, without pity
  Either to soul or honour! Learn by me
  To know your foes. In this belief I die:
  Like our own sex, we have no enemy, no enemy!   215
LORD
  See, my lord,
  What shift sh'as made to be her own destruction.
BIANCA
  Pride, greatness, honours, beauty, youth, ambition,
  You must all down together, there's no help for't.
  Yet this gladness is, that I remove,   220
  Tasting the same death in a cup of love.   *[Dies]*
CARDINAL
  Sin, what thou art, these ruins show too piteously.
  Two kings on one throne cannot sit together,
  But one must needs down, for his title's wrong;
  So where lust reigns, that prince cannot reign long.   225

Exeunt

FINIS

---

209 *ignorant* deliberately unknowing
220 *remove* i.e. die

THE
CHANGELING:

As it was Acted (with great Applause)
at the Privat house in D R U R Y ⸴ L A N E,
and *Salisbury Court.*

Written by ⎰ *THOMAS MIDLETON,* ⎱ Gent⸴.
⎰ and ⎱
⎱ *WILLIAM ROWLEY.* ⎰

N ever Printed before.

L O N D O N,
Printed for H U M P H R E Y M O S E L E Y, and are to
be sold at his shop at the sign of the *Princes-Arms*
in St. *Pauls* Church-yard, 1 6 5 3.

Title The word 'changeling' had a range of meanings, nearly all of which seem relevant: the nominal 'changeling' of the play is the pretended fool Antonio, whose disguise provides the opportunity for the 'amazing . . . change' with which he (like his rival, Franciscus) hopes to stun Beatrice into submission (III.iii.118–21); but Antonio's choice of masquerade is a reminder that 'changeling' also meant a 'half-witted person, idiot or imbecile' (*OED* n. 4). This meaning must have derived from what is probably the word's most familiar sense – one metaphorically appropriate to Beatrice's transformation from beautiful virgin to '[deformed] whore' (V.iii.31, 77) – 'a child (usually stupid or ugly) supposed to have been left by fairies in exchange for one stolen' (*OED* n. 3). More simply it referred to 'one given to change, a fickle or inconstant person' (*OED* n. 1) – a sense fitting not only Beatrice, whose 'giddy turning' leads her twice to 'change [her] saint' (I.i.148–9), but Alsemero, whose conversion from fearless traveller to abject lover fills Jasperino with incredulity ('have you changed your orisons?' I.i.34). Finally, a 'changeling' might also be 'a person . . . (surreptitiously) put in exchange for another' (*OED* n. 2) – a sense made apposite by Deflores' adulterous usurpation of Alsemero, and even more conspicuously by Diaphanta's role as Beatrice's physical surrogate on the wedding night. (For other possible applications, see Frost p. 413.)

398

DRAMATIS PERSONAE

[*In the castle*]
VERMANDERO, *father to Beatrice*
TOMAZO DE PIRACQUO, *a noble lord*
ALONZO DE PIRACQUO, *his brother, suitor to Beatrice*
ALSEMERO, *a nobleman, afterwards married to Beatrice*   5
JASPERINO, *his friend*
DEFLORES, *servant to Vermandero*
BEATRICE, *daughter to Vermandero*
DIAPHANTA, *her waiting woman*
[Gentlemen and Gallants   10
Gentlewomen]
Servants

[*In the madhouse*]
ALIBIUS, *a jealous doctor*
LOLLIO, *his man*   15
PEDRO, *friend to Antonio*
ANTONIO, *the changeling*
FRANCISCUS, *the counterfeit madman*

Names Daalder (following William Power, 'Middleton's Way with Names,' *NQ* 205 [1960], 26–9, 56–60, 95–8, 136–40, 175–9) suggests that the names of many of the major characters are meant to be ironically significant, and in the case of DEFLORES a homonymic play on 'deflowers' seems unavoidable. Other possibilities include: BEATRICE = 'she who makes happy', or 'blessed one'; JOANNA = 'the Lord's grace'; ALIBIUS = 'he who is elsewhere'; DIAPHANTA = 'diaphanous' or 'red hot'. TOMAZO, in his scepticism about his brother's death, may recall 'Doubting Thomas' in John 20:25. However, these names (like all those in the main plot) are directly derived from Reynolds' *Triumphs of God's Revenge* – including that of Alibius, which was borrowed from History V, the novella immediately following the story of 'Alsemero and Beatrice-Ioana'. Of course this need not exclude the possibility that Reynolds himself chose the names for their suggestiveness, nor that Middleton and Rowley might have preserved them for the same reason.

6 *friend* Q; but the respectful 'sir' with which Jasperino habitually addresses Alsemero suggests that his role is more that of a superior manservant (albeit a gentleman and confidant whom Alsemero condescends to address as 'friend' – see e.g. I.i.13, 15; and cf. II.i.2)

17 *changeling* idiot, fool (*OED* n. 4; and see below, *Title*). Despite the fact the Q *Dramatis Personae* seems to nominate Antonio as the title-character, there is no reason to suppose that the dramatists were responsible for this list; and it seems unlikely that the play would have been named for such a relatively minor figure. However, although the sub-plot is often cut in modern productions, the part of the pretended fool does appear to have been responsible for much of *The Changeling*'s popular currency in the seventeenth century (see Introduction p. xxxiii), and the popular use of 'Tony' as a synonym for fool seems to have been inspired by Middleton's character (*OED* n[1] 1).

ISABELLA, *wife to Alibius*
Madmen   20
[Fools]

THE SCENE: *Alicant*

22 *The Scene* The action of the main plot is entirely confined to Vermandero's castle in the
    Valencian port of Alicante, except for the opening scene which is imagined as taking
    place outside a church beside the castle gate. The subsidiary action takes place in the
    mad-house supervised by Alibius.

ACT I. [SCENE i.]

Enter ALSEMERO

[ALSEMERO]

'Twas in the temple where I first beheld her,
And now again the same – what omen yet
Follows of that? None but imaginary.
Why should my hopes of fate be timorous?
The place is holy, so is my intent;   5
I love her beauties to the holy purpose,
And that, methinks, admits comparison
With man's first creation – the place blest,
And is his right home back, if he achieve it.
The church hath first begun our interview,   10
And that's the place must join us into one,
So there's beginning and perfection too.

Enter JASPERINO

JASPERINO

O sir, are you here? Come, the wind's fair with you:
You're like to have a swift and pleasant passage.

I.i Author: Rowley (and Middleton?) Q marks act, but not scene divisions; the latter were added by Dyce.

1 *'Twas ... too* With Alsemero's pseudo-pious sophistry, compare Bacon's description of falling in love: 'as if man, made for the contemplation of heaven and all noble objects, should do nothing but kneel before a little idol, and make himself subject, though not of the mouth (as beasts are), yet of the eye, which was given them for higher purposes' (*Of Love*, p. 29). *temple* church

2 *omen* The irony of the positive construction that Alsemero gives to the beginnings of his affair with Beatrice is suggested by the sour admonition which the same episode provokes in Reynolds.

3 *of* ed. (or Q); cf. l. 106

6 *holy purpose* i.e. matrimony

7–9 *that ... it* marriage can be compared to the Garden of Eden, the blessed paradise which was intended as man's true home, and which he can regain through nuptial bliss. On the persistent Fall motif in the play, see Frost, pp. 413–14.

12 *beginning and perfection* The love which began in the church will be perfected there in matrimony; but Alsemero also plays on the idea of man's ultimate salvation as the 'perfection' of what began in Eden.

13–21 *the wind's ... against me* In Reynolds Alsemero's departure is held up by genuinely adverse weather, here the contrary winds are merely a wilfully contrived excuse.

ALSEMERO

    Sure you're deceivèd, friend – 'tis contrary   15

    In my best judgement.

JASPERINO   What, for Malta?

    If you could buy a gale amongst the witches,

    They could not serve you such a lucky penn'orth

    As comes a' God's name.

ALSEMERO   Even now I observed

    The temple's vane to turn full in my face;   20

    I know it is against me.

JASPERINO   Against you?

    Then you know not where you are.

ALSEMERO   Not well indeed.

JASPERINO

    Are you not well, sir?

ALSEMERO   Yes, Jasperino –

    Unless there be some hidden malady

    Within me that I understand not.

JASPERINO   And that   25

    I begin to doubt, sir: I never knew

    Your inclination to travels at a pause

    With any cause to hinder it till now.

    Ashore you were wont to call your servants up,

17–18 *If . . . penn'orth* For this superstition see Webster and Rowley, *A Cure for a Cuckold*, IV.ii.97, on 'The winds that Lapland witches sell to men'; and cf. *Macbeth*, I.iii.11.

18 *penn'orth* pennyworth (as Q); but the word was frequently pronounced and sometimes spelt in the contracted form required by the metre here

19 *a' God's name* in God's name – i.e. in the natural course of events, for nothing (but with an implied contrast between God's work and the devil's)
Even now The metre requires elision here (Ev'n now).

20 *temple's vane* weather-vane on the church tower

21 *it is* ed. ('tis Q). Whoever was responsible for the ms. copy from which Q was printed seems to have had a fondness for colloquial contractions, often preferring them even when the metre requires an uncontracted form.

23 *not well* The trick of repeating a word or phrase and giving it a new meaning is a standard clown's trick and one of which Rowley was particularly fond – see Bawcutt (1958) p. xl.

24 *hidden malady* On the importance of this motif in the play, see Neill, 'Hidden Malady'.

27 *inclination* Dilke (inclinations Q). The awkward double plural, together with *it* in the following line make it likely that Q is a compositor's error. Bruster notes that Middleton was fond of the word, while it does not appear elsewhere in Rowley – one of a number of indications that the former may have been involved in the composition of this scene. In this instance the word is scanned as five syllables: depending on metrical requirements, the *-ion* ending can be treated as either one syllable (as at l. 12) or two (as at ll. 35, 66, 77, 185).

And help to trap your horses for the speed;   30
At sea I have seen you weigh the anchor with 'em,
Hoist sails for fear to lose the foremost breath,
Be in continual prayers for fair winds –
And have you changed your orisons?

ALSEMERO   No, friend,
I keep the same church, same devotion.   35

JASPERINO
Lover I'm sure you're none: the stoic
Was found in you long ago; your mother
Nor best friends, who have set snares of beauty –
Ay, and choice ones too – could never trap you that way.
What might be the cause?

ALSEMERO   Lord, how violent   40
Thou art! I was but meditating of
Somewhat I heard within the temple.

JASPERINO
Is this violence? 'Tis but idleness
Compared with your haste yesterday.

ALSEMERO
I'm all this while a-going, man.   45

Enter SERVANTS

JASPERINO
Backwards, I think, sir. Look, your servants.

1 SERVANT
The seamen call: shall we board your trunks?

ALSEMERO
No, not today.

JASPERINO   'Tis the critical day
It seems, and the sign in Aquarius.

---

30 *help . . . speed* help them harness your horses in order to speed up your departure
34 *orisons* prayers
35 *devotion* 'a veiled reference to Beatrice' (Daalder)
36 *stoic* Stoic moral philosophy, popular in the Renaissance, taught the need to subject all emotions to the absolute control of reason.
48 *critical* In astrology, the *crisis* was a particular conjunction of the heavenly bodies supposed to determine the outcome of a given set of events; in medicine, it referred to the turning point (for better or worse) in an illness.
49 *Aquarius* astrological sign of the Water-carrier, supposedly propitious for sea travel

2 SERVANT [*Aside*]

    We must not to sea today, this smoke will bring forth fire.   50

ALSEMERO

    Keep all on shore. I do not know the end –

    Which needs I must do – of an affair in hand

    Ere I can go to sea.

1 SERVANT   Well, your pleasure.

2 SERVANT [*Aside*]

    Let him e'en take his leisure too: we are safer on land.

Exeunt SERVANTS

Enter BEATRICE, DIAPHANTA, *and* SERVANTS
[ALSEMERO *greets* BEATRICE *with a kiss*]

JASPERINO [*Aside*]

    How now! The laws of the Medes are changed, sure! Salute a   55
    woman? He kisses too – wonderful! Where learnt he this? And
    does it perfectly too! In my conscience, he ne'er rehearsed it
    before. Nay, go on: this will be stranger and better news at
    Valencia than if he had ransomed half Greece from the Turk.

BEATRICE

    You are a scholar, sir.

ALSEMERO   A weak one, lady.   60

BEATRICEsa

    Which of the sciences is this love you speak of?

ALSEMERO

    From your tongue I take it to be music.

BEATRICE

    You are skilful in't, can sing at first sight.

---

50 *this . . . fire* Proverbial cf. Tilley S569 'No smoke without fire'. The seaman's allusion to
    the heat of Alsemero's passion ironically anticipates the fire in which Diaphanta is burnt
    in V.i (Daalder).
54 s.d.2 Q adds 'Joanna' at the end of the s.d., presumably because a scribe or composi-
    tor, finding he had accidentally abbreviated 'Beatrice Joanna' (as the name appeared in
    his copy), assumed that 'Joanna' must refer to a separate character.
55 *laws of the Medes* On the supposedly unbreakable laws of the Medes, see Daniel 6:8.
57 *In my conscience* On my word; To my knowledge (stock phrase)
59 *Greece* Under Turkish rule since 1460.
61 *sciences* branches of knowledge (including arts and humanities). Cf. III.ii.120–5, where
    Antonio proclaims love's superiority to 'all the scrutinous sciences'.
63 *sing . . . sight* sight read (begins the persistent association of eyesight with sexual desire.

ALSEMERO

    And I have showed you all my skill at once;
    I want more words to express me further,   65
    And must be forced to repetition:
    I love you dearly.

BEATRICE   Be better advised, sir:

    Our eyes are sentinels unto our judgements,
    And should give certain judgement what they see;
    But they are rash sometimes, and tell us wonders   70
    Of common things, which when our judgements find,
    They can then check the eyes, and call them blind.

ALSEMERO

    But I am further, lady; yesterday
    Was mine eyes' employment, and hither now
    They brought my judgement, where are both agreed.   75
    Both houses then consenting, 'tis agreed;
    Only there wants the confirmation
    By the hand royal – that is your part, lady.

BEATRICE

    Oh, there's one above me, sir. [*Aside*] For five days past
    To be recalled! Sure mine eyes were mistaken: 80
    This was the man was meant me – that he should come
    So near his time, and miss it!

JASPERINO

    We might have come by the carriers from Valencia, I see, and
    saved all our sea-provision; we are at farthest, sure. Methinks I

68–72 *eyes . . . blind* Cf. III.ii.72–5.

68 *sentinels* Cf. Bacon, 'Of Love', p. 29: 'love can find entrance not only into an open heart, but also into a heart well fortified, if watch be not kept.' The figuration of the human body as a castle was a popular Renaissance trope deriving from medieval allegory – see Neill, 'Hidden Malady'.

74 *employment* Alsemero's pretense of reason is ironically undermined by the unconscious play on 'employ' = copulate.

76–8 *houses . . . royal* Alsemero's conceit imagines his suit as a bill which has been passed by the two houses of parliament, eyesight and judgement, and now awaits the royal signature (i.e. the grant of Beatrice's hand in marriage).

78 *that is* ed. (that's Q)

79 *one above me* A standard formula for God – but in this case referring to her father. Patriarchal theory construed fathers as God's deputies in the domestic realm, just as monarchs were his vice-regents in the larger kingdom.

79–80 *For . . . recalled* If only I could recall the last five days (i.e. the period of her betrothal to Alonzo de Piracquo)

83 *come . . . carriers* used land-transport

84 *we . . . sure* it's clear we're not going to travel any further now

should do something too: I meant to be a venturer in this   85
voyage. Yonder's another vessel, I'll board her – if she be lawful
prize, down goes her top-sail.

Enter DEFLORES

DEFLORES
  Lady, your father –
BEATRICE   Is in health, I hope.
DEFLORES
  Your eye shall instantly instruct you, lady:
  He's coming hitherward.
BEATRICE   What needed then   90
  Your duteous preface? I had rather
  He had come unexpected. You must stall
  A good presence with unnecessary blabbing;
  And how welcome for your part you are,
  I'm sure you know.
DEFLORES   Wilt never mend this scorn,   95
  One side nor other? Must I be enjoined
  To follow still whilst she flies from me? Well,
  Fates do your worst, I'll please my self with sight
  Of her, at all opportunities,
  If but to spite her anger. I know she had   100
  Rather see me dead than living, and yet
  She knows no cause for't but a peevish will.
ALSEMERO
  You seemed displeasèd, lady, on the sudden.

85–7 *venturer . . . sail* Standard tropes of sexual predation. Merchant-venturing and piracy
    were often closely linked in early modern voyaging; lowering one's topsail was a sign of
    surrender.
92 *stall* forestall (i.e. prejudice, damage in advance – *OED* 'forestall' v. 5). It remains
    possible that Dilke's emendation to *stale* is correct: neither Middleton nor Rowley
    elsewhere employs *stall* as a verb, but Middleton has 'stale your friend' in *Wit at Several
    Weapons* (I.i.139).
93 *A good presence* i.e. her father's impressive demeanour. A lord's 'presence' or 'counten-
    ance' included his retinue of servants.
96 *One . . . other* In any way at all
102 *peevish* A variety of senses are probably involved: foolish, mad; spiteful, malignant;
    perverse, headstrong, capricious; ill-tempered, childishly querulous (*OED* n. 1–5).
    will In addition to the modern sense, its meanings included 'desire' and 'sexual appe-
    tite'; sometimes used to refer to the sexual organs themselves.
103 *displeasèd* ed. (displeas'd Q)

BEATRICE

> Your pardon, sir, 'tis my infirmity;
> Nor can I other reason render you   105
> Than his or hers of some particular thing
> They must abandon as a deadly poison,
> Which to a thousand other tastes were wholesome:
> Such to mine eyes is that same fellow there,
> The same that report speaks of the basilisk.   110

ALSEMERO

> This is a frequent frailty in our nature;
> There's scarce a man amongst a thousand sound,
> But hath his imperfection: one distastes
> The scent of roses, which to infinites
> Most pleasing is, and odoriferous;   115
> One oil, the enemy of poison;
> Another wine, the cheerer of the heart
> And lively refresher of the countenance.
> Indeed this fault – if so it be – is general:
> There's scarce a thing but is both loved and loathed;   120
> Myself, I must confess, have the same frailty.

BEATRICE

> And what may be your poison, sir? I'm bold with you.

---

104 *infirmity* 'weakness', but also 'sickness' – cf. Alsemero's identification of love as a disease
    at l. 24
106 *his or hers* this or that person's
    of Dilke (or Q)
    particular personal; peculiar (*OED* a. 31, 7a-b)
106–8 *some . . . wholesome* Cf. 'one man's meat is another man's poison' (*Oxford Dictionary
    of English Proverbs*, p. 522 – though not in Tilley).
109 *fellow* person of low esteem (frequently applied to servants) (*OED* n. 10a, c)
110 *basilisk* fabulous monster, reputedly able to kill with a single glance. Beatrice's instinct-
    ive aversion to Deflores – like his ugliness (II.i.37 ff.) and his servile position (II.i.48–9)
    – is an addition to Reynolds' story.
112 *a thousand sound* a thousand men with [otherwise] perfectly sound constitutions.
    However, since *f* and long *s* (as in Q) were easily confused, it may be that Dilke was
    correct in emending to *found*. Bruster cites Laurentius, quoted in Burton's treatise on
    madness, *The Anatomy of Melancholy* (1621): 'for scarce is there one of a thousand that
    dotes alike' (1.3.2).
113 *distastes* dislikes
114 *infinites* an infinite number of people
115 *odoriferous* fragrant
116–18 *One . . . countenance* Cf. Psalm 104:15: 'wine that maketh glad the heart of man, and
    oil to make his face to shine, and bread which strengtheneth man's heart'.
116 *oil* probably castor oil, a powerful purgative often used in cases of poisoning
118 *lively* invigorating (*OED* adj. 4d)
122 *I'm* ed. (I am Q)

ALSEMERO

What might be your desire perhaps – a cherry.

BEATRICE

I am no enemy to any creature

My memory has, but yon gentleman.   125

ALSEMERO

He does ill to tempt your sight, if he knew it.

BEATRICE

He cannot be ignorant of that, sir:

I have not spared to tell him so; and I want

To help my self, since he's a gentleman

In good respect with my father, and follows him.   130

ALSEMERO

He's out of his place then, now.   [*They talk apart*]

JASPERINO

I am a mad wag, wench.

DIAPHANTA

So methinks; but for your comfort I can tell you we have a
doctor in the city that undertakes the cure of such.

JASPERINO

Tush, I know what physic is best for the state of mine own body.   135

DIAPHANTA

'Tis scarce a well governed state, I believe.

JASPERINO

I could show thee such a thing with an ingredient that we two

---

123 *What* (*And what* Q) Both metre and sense suggest that Dilke was correct in supposing
    Q's *And* was repeated from the previous line.
126 *tempt* make trial of, put to the test (*OED* v. I, 1–2)
    knew it Scanned as a single syllable (*knew't*).
128 *want* lack means
130 *respect* repute, standing
    follows i.e. as a servant; but the simultaneous recognition of Deflores' rank as a gentle-
    man born draws attention to the potential contradiction in his social position
    (cf. II.i.48–9)
131 *place* social rank; domestic office
132 *mad* wild, extravagant in gaiety; sexually infatuated (*OED* adj. 7a; 4a)
    wag mischievous fellow; habitual joker (*OED* n² 1–2)
134 *doctor* i.e. Alibius. Diaphanta pretends to take 'mad' literally.
135 *physic* medicine – here implying sex (Daalder)
136 *well governed state* healthily regulated condition (*OED govern* v. 4, 6), but playing on the
    political sense of the words.
137–8 *thing . . . together* i.e. her vagina filled with their combined sexual juices

would compound together, and if it did not tame the maddest
blood i'th'town for two hours after, I'll ne'er profess physic
again.   140

DIAPHANTA

A little poppy, sir, were good to cause you sleep.

JASPERINO

Poppy? I'll give thee a pop i'th' lips for that first, and begin there
[*Kisses her*]: poppy is one simple indeed, and cuckoo-what-you-
call't another. I'll discover no more now; another time I'll show
thee all.   145

BEATRICE

My father, sir.

Enter VERMANDERO *and* SERVANTS

VERMANDERO   O Joanna, I came to meet thee.
Your devotion's ended?

BEATRICE   For this time, sir.
[*Aside*] I shall change my saint, I fear me: I find
A giddy turning in me. [*Aloud*] Sir, this while
I am beholding to this gentleman   150
Who left his own way to keep me company;
And in discourse I find him much desirous
To see your castle – he hath deserved it, sir,
If ye please to grant it.

VERMANDERO   With all my heart, sir.
Yet there's an article between: I must know   155

---

138 *compound* The bawdy pun on 'pound' is enabled by recollection of the (phallic) mortar-
and-pestle as the usual instrument for compounding substances in an apothecary's
shop.

141 *poppy* opiate

143 *simple* plant or herb employed for medical purposes (*OED* n. 6)

143–4 *cuckoo-what-you-call't* probably Cuckoo-pintle (wild arum), so called after its phallic
shape, a diuretic and purgative used to treat digestive problems; or perhaps Cuckoo-spit
– a name for Lady's Smock or Cuckoo-flower, another diuretic and expectorant, sometimes used in the treatment of madness

144 *discover . . . show* Bawdy *double entendre*.

147 *devotion* act of worship, religious service (*OED* n. 2)

148 *change . . . saint* (1) change from religious to secular worship; (2) change the object of
my adoration (from Piracquo to Alsemero)

149 *giddy* (a) whirling; dizzy (*OED* a. 2c–d); (b) mad (*OED* a. 1a)
turning (a) whirling; vertigo (*OED* n. 1b); (b) conversion, desertion to another side;
change (*OED* n. 10, 11)

Your country. We use not to give survey
Of our chief strengths to strangers; our citadels
Are placed conspicuous to outward view,
On promonts' tops, but within are secrets.

ALSEMERO

A Valencian, sir.

VERMANDERO

          A Valencian? 160
That's native, sir – of what name, I beseech you?

ALSEMERO

Alsemero, sir.

VERMANDERO   Alsemero! Not the son
Of John de Alsemero?

ALSEMERO   The same, sir.

VERMANDERO

My best love bids you welcome.

BEATRICE   He was wont
To call me so, and then he speaks a most 165
Unfeignèd truth.

VERMANDERO   O sir, I knew your father;
We two were in acquaintance long ago
Before our chins were worth Iulan down,
And so continued till the stamp of time
Had coined us into silver. Well, he's gone, 170
A good soldier went with him.

ALSEMERO

You went together in that, sir.

---

156 *survey* Accent on second syllable here.
157 *strengths* strongholds (*OED* n. 10)
159 *promonts* promontories
    within . . . secrets On the trope of secrets in the play, see Neill, 'Hidden Malady'.
160 *Valencian* Accent on third syllable.
161 *native* i.e. to this region
162–3 *Alsemero* Probably scanned as three syllables in l. 162 (Als[e]méro) and four in l. 163
    (Álseméro).
165 *then* i.e. whenever he uses the phrase; in this case he speaks more truly than he knows,
    since Beatrice does indeed welcome Alsemero.
166 *I . . . father* The prior acquaintance of the two men is not part of Reynolds' story.
168 *Iulan* A coinage from *Iulus* Ascanius, the younger son of Aeneas in Virgil's *Aeneid*
    (I, 267), whose name, according to the commentator Servius, derived from a Greek
    word meaning 'the first growth of beard'.
170 *coined . . . silver* turned our hair silver

VERMANDERO

    No, by Saint Jacques, I came behind him.

    Yet I have done somewhat too. An unhappy day

    Swallowed him at last at Gibraltar   175

    In fight with those rebellious Hollanders –

    Was it not so?

ALSEMERO   Whose death I had revenged,

    Or followed him in fate, had not the late league

    Prevented me.

VERMANDERO   Ay, ay, 'twas time to breathe.

    Oh, Joanna, I should ha' told thee news,   180

    I saw Piracquo lately.

BEATRICE [*Aside*]   That's ill news.

VERMANDERO

    He's hot preparing for his day of triumph,

    Thou must be a bride within this sevennight.

ALSEMERO [*Aside*]   Ha!

BEATRICE

    Nay, good sir, be not so violent: with speed

    I cannot render satisfaction   185

    Unto the dear companion of my soul,

    Virginity, whom I thus long have lived with,

    And part with it so rude and suddenly.

    Can such friends divide never to meet again,

    Without a solemn farewell?

---

173 *Jacques* Disyllablic.

175 *Gibraltar* Accent on first and third syllables. The rebellious Dutch won a decisive victory over their former Spanish masters in a naval engagement here on 15 April 1607. The detail is from Reynolds.

178 *late league* The Treaty of the Hague, 9 April 1609, instituted a twelve year truce between the Dutch and Spanish.

179 *Prevented* Forestalled (*OED* v. II, 5)

182 *hot* ardently, urgently (with a suggestion of sexual excitement (*OED* adv. 2; adj. 6c)
his . . . triumph i.e. his wedding day. In sixteenth and seventeenth-century parlance, the weddings and funerals of the great, along with coronations, royal entries and other forms of street pageantry were included in the category of 'triumphs', along with the celebrations of military conquest modelled on the 'triumphs' of Roman generals. Since the wedding of Alonzo and Beatrice has not so far been mentioned, Dilke's emendation of Q *this* to *his* must be correct.

189 *such friends* Ostensibly Beatrice refers to the allegorized companionship between her soul and virginity, but she is also referring to her reluctance to part with Alsemero (*friend* = lover, *OED* n. 4) – just as 'dear companion' (l. 186) at first seems to refer to Alonzo.

| VERMANDERO | Tush, tush! There's a toy. | 190 |

ALSEMERO [*Aside*]

I must now part, and never meet again
With any joy on earth. [*Aloud*] Sir, your pardon,
My affairs call on me.

| VERMANDERO | How, sir? By no means! |

Not changed so soon, I hope? You must see my castle
And her best entertainment ere we part – 195
I shall think myself unkindly usèd else.
Come, come, let's on. I had good hope your stay
Had been a while with us in Alicant;
I might have bid you to my daughter's wedding.

ALSEMERO [*Aside*]

He means to feast me, and poisons me beforehand. 200
[*Aloud*] I should be dearly glad to be there, sir,
Did my occasions suit as I could wish.

BEATRICE

I shall be sorry if you be not there
When it is done, sir – but not so suddenly.

VERMANDERO

I tell you, sir, the gentleman's complete, 205
A courtier and a gallant, enriched
With many fair and noble ornaments:
I would not change him for a son-in-law
For any he in Spain, the proudest he –
And we have great ones, that you know.

| ALSEMERO | He's much | 210 |

Bound to you, sir.

| VERMANDERO | He shall be bound to me, |

---

190 *toy* foolish fancy; trifle (*OED* n. 4, 5); in the context of Beatrice's virginity, a bawdy
significance is also possible (see Williams, *Glossary*, pp. 211–12)
194 *changed* Ironic in view of his daughter's aside at l. 148.
195 *entertainment* The bawdy sense, 'sexual diversion', charges Vermandero's invitation
with unconscious irony.
196 *unkindly usèd* The metre requires elision of the *y* in *unkindly*, while *used* is disyallabic.
202 *occasions* business affairs (*OED* n.¹ 6a)
suit fit my inclinations (*OED* v. 14a)
204 *but not* but I wish it were not
205 *gentleman's complete* Apparently glancing at Henry Peacham's *The Complete Gentleman*
published in the same year that *The Changeling* was first performed (1622), just as
the next line probably remembers the original of all such courtesy books, Baldassare
Castiglione's *The Courtier* (1528; trans Sir Thomas Hoby, 1561).
211 *bound* obliged; Vermandero plays on an alternative sense, 'tied'.

As fast as this tie can hold him, I'll want
My will else.

BEATRICE [*Aside*] I shall want mine if you do it.

VERMANDERO

But come, by the way, I'll tell you more of him:

ALSEMERO [*Aside*]

How shall I dare to venture in his castle,   215
When he discharges murderers at the gate?
But I must on, for back I cannot go.

BEATRICE [*Aside*]

Not this serpent gone yet?   [*Drops a glove*]

VERMANDERO   Look, girl, thy glove's fallen –
Stay, stay – Deflores, help a little.

DEFLORES   Here, lady.   [*Offers the glove*]

BEATRICE

Mischief on your officious forwardness!   220
Who bade you stoop? They touch my hand no more:
[*Removes the other glove*]

There! [*Throws it down*] For t'other's sake I part with this –

212–13 *want my will* fail to achieve what I wish for (and mean to bring about)

213 *mine* Beatrice plays on *will* = (sexual) desire.

214 *by* along

216 *murderers* small cannon (typically deployed to protect the entrance to a castle). Alsemero refers to the deadly effect produced on him by Vermandero's announcement of the impending marriage; however, he may also have in mind the 'killing' effect of Beatrice's eyes – a standard trope of love-poetry, in which the lady's eyes were figured as firing darts or bullets at her lover – thus beginning the progressive association of Vermandero's castle with the body of his daughter (see Neill, 'Hidden Malady', pp. 179–80, 193–4). Ironically Beatrice herself will soon become a literal murderer.

218 *serpent* One of a number of references in the play that associate Beatrice's fall with the Genesis story. Deflores, like his partial model, Iago in Shakespeare's *Othello*, is identified with the Devil, who in the form of a serpent tempted Eve. Cf. III.iii.165, V.iii.67.
s.d. It is unclear whether the dropping of the glove is accidental, or meant as a conscious invitation to Alsemero; but the fact that it occurs during an aside expressing her pathological aversion to Deflores suggests that it may be unconsciously aimed at him – a suggestion supported by the elaborate play with the phallic suggestiveness of fingers in Deflores' soliloquy, as well as in two later scenes (I.ii.27–31; III.iii.26–38, 88).

219 *Deflores . . . little* The command emphasizes the servile role that Deflores, in spite of his gentle birth, is forced to play in Vermandero's household.

222 s.d. As at 218, 219 and 221, the gesture, while not specified in Q, is clearly implicit in the dialogue. Throwing down a glove was a traditional gesture of challenge, and Beatrice may even emphasize this by striking Deflores in the face with it.

Take 'em, and draw thine own skin off with 'em!

Exeunt VERMANDERO, ALSEMERO, JASPERINO, *and* SERVANTS

DEFLORES

Here's a favour come – with a mischief! Now I know
She had rather wear my pelt tanned in a pair   225
Of dancing pumps than I should thrust my fingers
Into her sockets here.   [*Tries to pull the glove onto his hand*]
        I know she hates me,
Yet cannot choose but love her.
No matter: if but to vex her, I'll haunt her still,
Though I get nothing else, I'll have my will.   *Exit*   230

[ACT I. SCENE ii.]

Enter ALIBIUS *and* LOLLIO

ALIBIUS

Lollio, I must trust thee with a secret,
But thou must keep it.

---

223 *draw . . . skin* as a snake might do; but also, as Daalder points out, drawing attention to
  the pustular, pock-marked complexion that so obsesses both Beatrice and Deflores
  himself (II.i.33–45, 53; II.ii.40–1, 72–7, 146)
224 *favour* In the rituals of chivalric or courtly love, gloves were among the most common
  forms of 'favour' offered by ladies to their knightly 'servants', and often worn in tour-
  naments as tokens of their love. In the 1993 BBC version, Bob Hoskins expressed his
  physical infatuation by pressing the glove to his nose and inhaling deeply.
  with a mischief with a vengeance (*OED* n. 9b).
225 *She had* Metre requires elision here.
227 *sockets* i.e. the fingers of the gloves; but *socket* also = vagina (*OED* n. 4a) the obscene
  suggestiveness of Deflores' gesture is underlined by Lollio's similarly indecent word-
  play in the following scene (I.ii.30–1). For a contemporary example of such bawdy
  symbolism see the story (cited in Chakravorty, p. 147) of Prince Henry's refusal to
  accept the glove dropped by Frances Howard, Countess of Essex, at a dance, 'saying
  publicly, he would not have it, it is stretched by another, meaning the Viscount [i.e. her
  lover, Robert Carr, Viscount Rochester].'
230 *get* (1) possess; (2) beget
  will lust; sexual satisfaction
I.ii Author: Rowley. As in much of Rowley's portion of the play, the boundary between verse
  and prose is often uncertain in this scene. Alibius speaks in verse but is given many
  irregular or incomplete lines (e.g. 2, 7, 11, 13, 16, 19); Lollio (as befits his lowly rank)
  generally speaks in prose, but some of his lines seem to fit the verse pattern (e.g. 3, 14,
  17).
  1 and 3, 8, 17 *secret* Continues the motif of secrets from I.i.159. Cf. also II.ii.68, IV.i.25,
  108, IV.ii.111, 139, V.i.6. Lollio characteristically interprets *secret* as = private parts
  (Williams, *Glossary*, p. 271).

LOLLIO

I was ever close to a secret, sir.

ALIBIUS

The diligence that I have found in thee,
The care and industry already past 5
Assures me of thy good continuance.
Lollio, I have a wife.

LOLLIO

Fie sir, 'tis too late to keep her secret: she's known to be married
all the town and country over.

ALIBIUS

Thou goest too fast, my Lollio. That knowledge 10
I allow no man can be barred it;
But there is a knowledge which is nearer,
Deeper, and sweeter, Lollio.

LOLLIO

Well, sir, let us handle that between you and I.

ALIBIUS

'Tis that I go about, man – Lollio, 15
My wife is young.

LOLLIO

So much the worse to be kept secret, sir.

ALIBIUS

Why, now thou meet'st the substance of the point:
I am old, Lollio.

LOLLIO

No, sir, 'tis I am old Lollio. 20

ALIBIUS

Yet why may not this concord and sympathize?
Old trees and young plants often grow together,
Well enough agreeing.

LOLLIO

Ay, sir, but the old trees raise themselves higher and broader
than the young plants. 25

10 *knowledge* i.e. carnal knowledge
14 *handle* With bawdy implication.
17 *worse* (1) harder (the meaning Alibius is meant to assume); (2) less appropriate
21 *this* i.e. this marriage of January and May
   concord agree, be in harmony (*OED* v. 2)
   sympathize have an affinity in nature, harmonize (*OED* v. 2)
24–5 *old . . . plants* i.e. his cuckold's horns would make Alibius seem taller (Daalder)

ALIBIUS

    Shrewd application – there's the fear man:
    I would wear my ring on my own finger;
    Whilst it is borrowed it is none of mine,
    But his that useth it.

LOLLIO

    You must keep it on still, then; if it but lie by, one or other will   30
    be thrusting into't.

ALIBIUS

    Thou conceiv'st me, Lollio: here thy watchful eye
    Must have employment, I cannot always be
    At home.

LOLLIO   I dare swear you can not.

ALIBIUS   I must look out.

LOLLIO

    I know't, you must look out, 'tis every man's case.   35

ALIBIUS

    Here, I do say, must thy employment be –
    To watch her treadings, and in my absence
    Supply my place.

LOLLIO

    I'll do my best, sir; yet surely I cannot see who you should have
    cause to be jealous of.   40

ALIBIUS

    Thy reason for that Lollio? 'Tis a comfortable question.

LOLLIO

    We have but two sorts of people in the house, and both under
    the whip: that's fools and madmen – the one has not wit

---

27 *I . . . finger* The bawdy implication of Alibius' remark (*ring* = vagina – see Williams, *Glossary*, p. 26) is immediately picked up in Lollio's ensuing lines.

32 *Thou conceiv'st me* You get my point

34 *At . . . out* Lollio normally speaks in prose, but here his speech fits the metre, forming an acceptable hexameter with Alibius' lines. Here (and sometimes elsewhere) the layout of Q makes it impossible to be sure whether verse or prose is intended.
    look out leave the house (e.g. on business)

35 *look out* exercise vigilance
    case Lollio puns on *case* = sexual organ (Williams, *Glossary*, p. 66).

37 *treadings* (1) where she goes; (2) acts of copulation (*OED* v. *tread* 8a)

38 *Supply . . . place* Fulfil my office (as head of the household); but Lollio will deliberately misunderstand *place* to mean 'vulva' (Williams, *Glossary*, p. 237)

41 *comfortable* reassuring

42 *house* Holdsworth (p. 269) noting that the word could also mean 'playhouse', suggests that 'a knowing glance outwards should accompany the line' (cf. III.iii.108).

enough to be knaves, and the other not knavery enough to be
fools. 45

ALIBIUS

Ay, those are all my patients, Lollio.
I do profess the cure of either sort –
My trade, my living 'tis, I thrive by it –
But here's the care that mixes with my thrift:
The daily visitants, that come to see 50
My brainsick patients, I would not have
To see my wife. Gallants I do observe
Of quick enticing eyes, rich in habits,
Of stature and proportion very comely –
These are most shrewd temptations, Lollio. 55

LOLLIO

They may be easily answered, sir: if they come to see the fools
and madmen, you and I may serve the turn, and let my mistress
alone – she's of neither sort.

ALIBIUS

'Tis a good ward, indeed. Come they to see
Our madmen or our fools, let 'em see no more 60
Than what they come for; by that consequent
They must not see her: I'm sure she's no fool.

LOLLIO

And I'm sure she's no madman.

---

47 *cure* A conveniently ambiguous term: (1) care, charge (*OED* n. 3); (2) medical treatment (*OED* n. 5a); (3) restoration to health (*OED* n. 6a).

49 *care* anxiety

50 *daily visitants* Madmen are several times represented on the stage as being a source of
entertainment (see e.g. *Northward Ho*, IV.iii.27–36; *Duchess of Malfi*, IV.ii.61–114) It is
generally assumed that this was the practice at Bethlehem Hospital, the London madhouse familiarly known as 'Bedlam' on which Alibius' asylum appears to be modelled;
Carol Thomas Neely, however, has argued that visiting Bedlam for amusement was a
stage convention, and that it was not until the eighteenth century that the madhouse
(partly as a result of its representations in the theatre) became a place of entertainment –
see *Distracted Subjects: Madness and Gender in Shakespeare and Early Modern Culture*
(Ithaca, 2004), Chap. 6, 'Bedlam in History and Drama.'

53 *habits* clothes

54 *comely* handsome

55 *shrewd* wicked, depraved (*OED* a. 1a); dangerous (*OED* n. 2); grievous (*OED* n. 6b);
cunning (*OED* a. 13a)

57 *serve the turn* Daalder suggests a play on the bawdy sense ('provide sexual service' –
see Williams, *Glossary*, pp. 273–4).

59 *ward* defence (*OED* n.² 8); method of keeping watch (*OED* n.² 1)

61 *by . . . consequent* consequently

63 *madman* With a play on the gendered sense of 'man'.

ALIBIUS

Hold that buckler fast, Lollio: my trust
Is on thee, and I account it firm and strong.   65
What hour is't, Lollio?

LOLLIO

Towards belly-hour, sir.

ALIBIUS

Dinner time? Thou mean'st twelve o'clock?

LOLLIO

Yes, sir; for every part has his hour: we wake at six and look
about us, that's eye-hour; at seven we should pray, that's knee-   70
hour; at eight walk, that's leg-hour; at nine gather flowers, and
pluck a rose, that's nose-hour; at ten we drink, that's mouth-
hour; at eleven lay about us for victuals, that's hand-hour; at
twelve go to dinner, that's belly-hour.

ALIBIUS

Profoundly, Lollio! It will be long   75
Ere all thy scholars learn this lesson, and
I did look to have a new one entered – stay,
I think my expectation is come home.

Enter PEDRO, *and* ANTONIO *like an idiot*

PEDRO

Save you, sir. My business speaks it self:
This sight takes off the labour of my tongue.   80

ALIBIUS

Ay, ay, sir;
'Tis plain enough, you mean him for my patient.

64 *buckler* shield
72 *pluck a rose* urinate
77 *new one* i.e. a new patient
78 *is . . . home* has been fulfilled
    s.d. *like an idiot* The frontispiece to Francis Kirkman's collection of drolls, *The Wits*
    (1672), includes amongst its representations of popular stage characters a figure cap-
    tioned 'Changeling', wearing a long-skirted gown and a tall pointed cap, with what
    appears to be a child's primer dangling from his right hand; this is generally taken to be
    Antonio, and may provide a guide to the original costuming.

PEDRO

And, if your pains prove but commodious, to give but some
little strength to his sick and weak part of nature in him. [*Gives
him money*] These are but patterns to show you of the whole
pieces that will follow to you, beside the charge of diet, washing,   85
and other necessaries fully defrayed.

ALIBIUS

Believe it, sir, there shall no care be wanting.

LOLLIO

Sir, an officer in this place may deserve something: the trouble
will pass through my hands.   90

PEDRO

'Tis fit something should come to your hands then, sir.

                                              [*Gives him money*]

LOLLIO

Yes, sir, 'tis I must keep him sweet, and read to him. What is his
name?

PEDRO

His name is Antonio – marry, we use but half to him, only Tony.

LOLLIO

Tony, Tony, 'tis enough, and a very good name for a fool. What's   95
your name, Tony?

ANTONIO

He he he! Well, I thank you cousin, he he he!

83–7 *And . . . defrayed* Q prints this passage as verse; and, since most of Pedro's lines,
including his other big speech at ll. 100–8, are in verse, it is arguable that Rowley
intended to write syllabics here. However the lines are almost impossible to speak as
verse.

83 *commodious* beneficial

85 *patterns* samples

86 *pieces* gold coins (*OED* n. 13 b–c)

86–91 *the charge . . . hands then* Neely (*Distracted Subjects*, pp. 194–5, 199 n.25) suggests
that Alibius was intended as a satirical portrait of Helkiah Crooke, the notoriously
corrupt master of Bethlehem from 1619–33, and this episode may allude to his scandalous extortion of fees and donations. Middleton and Rowley may have been familiar with
Crooke's anatomical treatise, *Mikrocosmographia* (see V.ii.153).

92 *sweet* clean and sweet-smelling

95 *Tony . . . fool* OED suggests that the common use of Tony to mean 'fool' (or, as a
verb, 'to make a fool [of someone]'), may actually derive from *The Changeling*, since no
other examples are recorded before the 1650s; however Lollio's 'a very good name for a
fool' suggests that the term was already in common use (unless some now lost satiric
allusion was intended).

LOLLIO

    Good boy! Hold up your head. He can laugh: I perceive by that
    he is no beast.

PEDRO

    Well, sir, if you can raise him but to any height,   100
    Any degree of wit – might he attain
    (As I might say) to creep but on all four
    Towards the chair of wit, or walk on crutches –
    'Twould add an honour to your worthy pains,
    And a great family might pray for you,   105
    To which he should be heir, had he discretion
    To claim and guide his own. Assure you sir,
    He is a gentleman.

LOLLIO

    Nay, there's nobody doubted that, at first sight I knew him for a
    gentleman – he looks no other yet.   110

PEDRO

    Let him have good attendance and sweet lodging.

LOLLIO

    As good as my mistress lies in, sir; and, as you allow us time
    and means, we can raise him to the higher degree of
    discretion.

PEDRO

    Nay, there shall no cost want, sir.   115

LOLLIO

    He will hardly be stretched up to the wit of a magnifico.

PEDRO

    Oh no, that's not to be expected, far shorter will be enough.

LOLLIO

    I'll warrant you I'll make him fit to bear office in five weeks: I'll
    undertake to wind him up to the wit of constable.

---

  99 *no beast* The idea that laughter is one of the traits that distinguishes men from beasts
     goes back to Aristotle, *De Partibus Animalium* III, 10.
  108 *He . . . gentleman* Compare Deflores' insistence on his own gentle birth at II.i.49.
  109–10 *at first . . . other* Given Antonio's appearance '*like an idiot*' this is clearly meant
     satirically; but it may also suggest that Lollio has seen through his disguise.
  111 *have . . . attendance* be well looked after
     sweet lodging clean quarters – but Daalder suggests a bawdy *double entendre*
  112 *As . . . in* Perhaps implying that Lollio already guesses Antonio's designs.
  116 *magnifico* Originally a Venetian magnate – hence any person of distinction and authority.
  118 *I'll . . . I'll* ed. (Ile warrant you Q; Bawcutt: I'll warrant you I; Williams: I warrant you I'll)
  118–19 Like Dogberry in *Much Ado About Nothing*, constables were presented on the stage
     as notoriously stupid.

PEDRO

If it be lower than that it might serve turn. 120

LOLLIO

No, fie, to level him with a headborough, beadle, or
watchman were but little better than he is; constable,
I'll able him. If he do come to be a justice afterwards, let
him thank the keeper. Or I'll go further with you: say I do
bring him up to my own pitch, say I make him as wise as 125
my self?

PEDRO

Why there I would have it.

LOLLIO

Well, go to, either I'll be as arrant a fool as he, or he shall be as
wise as I, and then I think 'twill serve his turn.

PEDRO

Nay, I do like thy wit passing well. 130

LOLLIO

Yes, you may; yet if I had not been a fool, I had had more wit
than I have too. Remember what state you find me in.

PEDRO

I will, and so leave you. Your best cares I beseech you. *Exit*

ALIBIUS

Take you none with you, leave 'em all with us.

ANTONIO

Oh, my cousin's gone! Cousin, cousin, oh! 135

LOLLIO

Peace, peace, Tony! You must not cry child – you must be
whipped if you do. Your cousin is here still: I am your cousin,
Tony.

---

121 *headborough, beadle, watchman* parish officers ranked successively below the constable.
123 *able him* make him fit for
justice Like constables, justices of the peace were frequently satirized for their stupidity
(see e.g. Shallow and Silence in 2 *Henry IV*, and Greedy in Massinger's *A New Way to Pay
Old Debts*; and cf. IV.i.125–6).
128 *arrant* absolute, complete; but the Q spelling 'errant' suggests that the meaning 'erring'
or 'confused' is also present
129 *serve . . . turn* be adequate for his purposes (perhaps with a bawdy innuendo)
130 *wit* Includes both 'intelligence' and 'good sense'.
passing exceptionally
132 *Remember . . . in* Another appeal for money.
135 *cousin* Need not imply kinship – often simply used as a term of intimacy and affection
(*OED* n. 5).

ANTONIO

He, he! Then I'll not cry, if thou be'st my cousin. He, he, he! 140

LOLLIO

I were best try his wit a little, that I may know what form to place him in.

ALIBIUS

Ay, do, Lollio, do.

LOLLIO

I must ask him easy questions at first. – Tony, how many true fingers has a tailor on his right hand? 145

ANTONIO

As many as on his left, cousin.

LOLLIO

Good; and how many on both?

ANTONIO

Two less than a deuce, cousin.

LOLLIO

Very well answered! I come to you again, cousin Tony: how many fools goes to a wise man? 150

ANTONIO

Forty in a day sometimes, cousin.

LOLLIO

Forty in a day? How prove you that?

ANTONIO

All that fall out amongst themselves, and go to a lawyer to be made friends.

LOLLIO

A parlous fool, he must sit in the fourth form at least, I perceive 155
that. I come again, Tony: how many knaves make an honest man?

---

141 *try* test
   form school class
144–5 *true fingers* (1) fingers excluding thumbs; (2) honest fingers – tailors were proverbially dishonest
148 *deuce* pair
150 *goes to* make up; Antonio chooses to understand Lollio as meaning 'visit'. The use of a singular verb with a plural subject is not uncommon in the period (cf. l. 189 and II.ii.10).
153–4 *All ... friends* Then, as now, jokes at the expense of lawyers were commonplace. Cf. Tilley L130: 'Lawyers's houses are built on the heads of fools'.
155 *parlous* dangerously cunning (originally a contracted form of 'perilous')

ANTONIO

I know not that cousin.

LOLLIO

No, the question is too hard for you. I'll tell you, cousin – there's three knaves may make an honest man: a sergeant, a jailor, and a beadle; the sergeant catches him, the jailor holds him, and the beadle lashes him; and, if he be not honest then, the hangman must cure him.   160

ANTONIO

Ha ha ha! That's fine sport cousin!

ALIBIUS

This was too deep a question for the fool, Lollio.   165

LOLLIO

Yes, this might have served yourself, though I say't. Once more, and you shall go play, Tony.

ANTONIO

Ay, play at push-pin cousin. Ha he!

LOLLIO

So thou shalt: say how many fools are here –

ANTONIO

Two, cousin – thou and I.   170

LOLLIO

Nay, you're too forward there. Tony, mark my question: how many fools and knaves are here? A fool before a knave, a fool behind a knave, between every two fools a knave, how many fools, how many knaves?

ANTONIO

I never learnt so far, cousin.   175

ALIBIUS

Thou putt'st too hard questions to him, Lollio.

---

160 *sergeant* court officer charged with arresting offenders and executing legal orders (*OED* n. 4a)
161 *beadle* (here) court officer charged with enforcing discipline
165 *deep* (1) profound; (2) crafty
166 *this . . . yourself* this would have done for someone as intelligent as you (but with the implication that his joke is also well suited to a crafty knave like Alibius)
168 *push-pin* popular children's game (but with obscene innuendo – see Williams, *Dictionary*, p. 1120)
171 *forward* prompt, eager (*OED* n. 6a); presumptuous (*OED* n. 8)
172 *before* (1) in front of; (2) in preference to; (3) before revealing himself as
173 *behind* (1) to the rear of; (2) following (i.e. serving)
between . . . knave (1) a knave stands between each pair of fools; (2) of any two fools, one is likely to be a knave

LOLLIO

I'll make him understand it easily. – Cousin, stand there.

ANTONIO

Ay, cousin.

LOLLIO

Master, stand you next the fool.

ALIBIUS Well, Lollio.   180

LOLLIO

Here's my place. Mark now, Tony: there a fool before a knave.

ANTONIO

That's I cousin.

LOLLIO

Here's a fool behind a knave, that's I; and between us two fools
there is a knave, that's my master: 'tis but we three, that's all.

ANTONIO

We three, we three, cousin.   185

                                                        MADMEN *within*

FIRST MADMAN *(Within)*

Put's head i' th' pillory, the bread's too little.

SECOND MADMAN *(Within)*

Fly, fly, and he catches the swallow.

THIRD MADMAN *(Within)*

Give her more onion, or the devil put the rope about her crag.

181–4 *Here's . . . master* 'The others of course are really the knaves who are trying to make a
  fool of Alibius' (Bawcutt)
184 *We three* Cf. *Twelfth Night*, II.ii.16–7; alluding to the stock image of two idiots over the
  caption 'We three, loggerheads be' – the third being the viewer himself (in this case,
  Alibius).
185 s.d. In the original staging the shrieks and howls of the inmates will have issued from
  the so-called 'discovery space', until the Madmen finally burst onto the stage in III.ii. In
  a play much concerned with dark 'secrets' and hidden sickness, their off-stage presence
  develops a symbolic resonance – one emphasised in Richard Eyre's 1988 National
  Theatre production, in which the entire performance was framed by a kind of false
  proscenium made of spiral staircases and scaffolding around which the denizens of the
  madhouse clung in grotesque postures: this was, in effect, the 'hell' that 'circumscribes'
  the characters in the final scene (V.iii.164).
186 *the . . . little* there's not enough bread
187 *Fly . . . swallow* Alluding to a proverbial impossibility: 'Fly and you will catch the
  swallow' (Tilley S1024); but given that the other Madmen's speeches register hunger,
  probably punning on *swallow*, as Daalder suggests.
188 *rope* (1) hangman's rope; (2) rope of onions
  crag neck

LOLLIO

You may hear what time of day it is, the chimes of Bedlam goes.

ALIBIUS

Peace, peace, or the wire comes!   190

THIRD MADMAN *(Within)*

Cat-whore, cat-whore! Her Parmesan, her Parmesan!

ALIBIUS Peace, I say! – Their hour's come: they must be fed, Lollio.

LOLLIO

There's no hope of recovery of that Welsh madman was undone
by a mouse that spoiled him a parmesan – lost his wits for't.

ALIBIUS

Go to your charge, Lollio; I'll to mine.   195

LOLLIO

Go you to your madmen's ward, let me alone with your fools.

ALIBIUS

And remember my last charge, Lollio.   *Exit*

LOLLIO

Of which your patients do you think I am? Come, Tony, you
must amongst your school-fellows now: there's pretty scholars
amongst 'em, I can tell you; there's some of 'em at *stultus, stulta,*   200
stultum.

ANTONIO

I would see the madmen, cousin, if they would not bite me.

LOLLIO

No, they shall not bite thee, Tony.

ANTONIO

They bite when they are at dinner, do they not coz?

LOLLIO

They bite at dinner indeed, Tony. Well, I hope to get credit by   205
thee; I like thee the best of all the scholars that ever I brought
up, and thou shalt prove a wise man, or I'll prove a fool my self.

                                                        Exeunt

189 *chimes of Bedlam* cries of the mad
190 *wire* whip made of wire
191 *Cat-whore . . . Parmesan* Spoken by the 'Welsh madman'. The Welsh were proverbially
    fond of cheese; and the speaker is abusing his cat for failing to prevent the theft of his
    Parmesan by a mouse (see l. 194) – *her* being stage-Welsh for 'my'.
194 *spoiled him* despoiled him of
197 *last charge* i.e. to keep a close watch on Alibius' wife
200 *amongst* go amongst, join
201 *at . . . stultum* i.e. they have reached only as far the second declension in their Latin
    grammars; fittingly, the noun they are declining means 'stupid'.
207 *prove* (1) become; (2) turn out to have been (all along)

ACT II. [SCENE i.]

Enter BEATRICE *and* JASPERINO *severally*

BEATRICE

O Sir, I'm ready now for that fair service,
Which makes the name of friend sit glorious on you.
Good angels and this conduct be your guide –   [*Gives a paper*]
Fitness of time and place is there set down, sir.

JASPERINO

The joy I shall return rewards my service.   *Exit*   5

BEATRICE

How wise is Alsemero in his friend!
It is a sign he makes his choice with judgement.
Then I appear in nothing more approved
Than making choice of him;
For 'tis a principle, he that can choose   10
That bosom well who of his thoughts partakes,
Proves most discreet in every choice he makes.
Methinks I love now with the eyes of judgement,
And see the way to merit, clearly see it.
A true deserver like a diamond sparkles –   15
In darkness you may see him, that's in absence,
Which is the greatest darkness falls on love;
Yet is he best discernèd then
With intellectual eyesight. What's Piracquo

II.i Author: Middleton

1–2 *service . . . friend* For Jasperino's role as both servant and friend, see *Dramatis Personae* above; but Daalder is probably right to suppose that, since Beatrice is thinking of Vermandero, *service* also carries an erotic suggestion.

 3 *conduct* document conferring privilege of entry (not in *OED* – presumably an abbreviation of 'safe-conduct', n. 2).

 5 *return* take back (to Alsemero).

10–12 *For . . . makes* Presumably on the grounds that a true friend (as theorists of friendship had insisted from classical times) is a 'second self'.

11 *bosom* intimate friend

13–19 *Methinks . . . eyesight* Beatrice's conviction that her love is the product of insight rather than the notoriously unreliable impressions of the eye is undercut by the repeated emphasis upon her obsession with outward appearances.

15–16 *A . . . him* For the idea that diamonds were luminous, see *Titus Andronicus*, II.iii.226–30; and cf. III.i.30–1.

18 *discernèd* ed. (discern'd Q)

My father spends his breath for? And his blessing   20
Is only mine as I regard his name,
Else it goes from me, and turns head against me,
Transformed into a curse. Some speedy way
Must be remembered – he's so forward too,
So urgent that way, scarce allows me breath   25
To speak to my new comforts.

Enter DEFLORES

DEFLORES [*Aside*]   Yonder's she.
Whatever ails me, now alate especially
I can as well be hanged as refrain seeing her;
Some twenty times a day – nay not so little –
Do I force errands, frame ways and excuses   30
To come into her sight; and I have small reason for't,
And less encouragement, for she baits me still
Every time worse than other, does profess herself
The cruellest enemy to my face in town,
At no hand can abide the sight of me,   35
As if danger, or ill luck hung in my looks.
I must confess my face is bad enough,
But I know far worse has better fortune –

20–1 *his* i.e. Vermandero's
20–3 *blessing . . . curse* Just as, in the formal rite of blessing, a father became the conduit of God's grace, so his curse was the most terrible thing a child could experience.
21 *as . . . name* in so far as I respect his honour (by obeying his wishes)
22 *turns . . . me* rounds on me with all its power (*OED turn* v. 57; *head* n. 29, 57a)
23–4 *Some . . . remembered* i.e. some way of disposing of Alonzo – but at this point Beatrice cannot quite bring herself to say it.
24–5 *he's . . . way* Ambiguous – 'forward' sounds like a complaint against Alonzo's over-zealous suit, but it may (as Daalder supposes) simply refer to Vermandero's eager determination to conclude the match.
26 *my new comforts* i.e. her affair with Alsemero. But note Deflores' entrance (Daalder).
s.d. Though this speech, like ll. 76–88, takes the form of a soliloquy, it is in fact an extended aside. The aside was typically employed for ironic and often comic effect, but a number of the key scenes in Middleton's part of the play (e.g. II.ii, III.iii, IV.i) make extensive use of the device, including such extended passages of reflection, to emphasize the isolation of the characters as they brood over inward secrets.
27 *alate* of late (*OED* adv. *arch.*).
28 *refrain* Stress on first syllable.
32 *baits* bites and tears as dogs attack a chained animal (*OED* v.¹ 3) – cf. ll. 80–1; but perhaps (as Daalder suggests) with a subdued pun on *baits* = tempts (*OED* v.¹ 11)
35 *At no hand* Under no circumstances; On no account
36 *danger* Cf. l. 90.

And not endured alone, but doted on –
And yet such pick-hatched faces, chins like witches,   40
Here and there five hairs, whispering in a corner
As if they grew in fear one of another,
Wrinkles like troughs, where swine-deformity swills
The tears of perjury that lie there like wash
Fallen from the slimy and dishonest eye –   45
Yet such a one plucked sweets without restraint,
And has the grace of beauty to his sweet.
Though my hard fate has thrust me out to servitude,
I tumbled into th' world a gentleman –
She turns her blessed eye upon me now,   50
And I'll endure all storms before I part with't.

BEATRICE [*Aside*]

Again!
This ominous, ill-faced fellow more disturbs me
Than all my other passions.

DEFLORES [*Aside*]   Now't begins again:
I'll stand this storm of hail though the stones pelt me.   55

---

40 *pick-hatched* Bruster conj. (pickhaird Q); cant term for a brothel – deriving from the 'hatch' or half-door, defended with 'picks' (or spikes) commonly used in the London stews (*OED* picked-hatch) – here presumably indicating a face pock-marked as though from syphilis. Bruster's own text prints *pig-haired* (= bristly), a contemptuous term found in Middleton's *A Trick to Catch the Old One* (IV.iv.298–9). Editors who retain Q take *pick-haired* to mean 'covered in spiky hairs' – i.e. 'bristly', or perhaps 'sparsely bearded'.

44 *wash* (1) watery discharge; (2) pig-swill (*OED* n. 9; 11a)

46 *sweets* pleasures (*OED* n. 3a)

47 *grace of beauty* Deflores may be thinking of the classical Three Graces – thus the 'grace of beauty' would be the goddess of beauty herself; but 'grace' (or 'mercy') was what the courtly lover, imitating the language of religion, sought from his mistress (cf. l. 63).
sweet sweetheart (*OED* n. 4). In the popular character-book, *Sir Thomas Ouerbury: His Wife*, we are told of '*A Serving-man*' that 'His inheritance is the Chamber-mayd, but [he] often purchaseth his Master's daughter, by reason of opportunity' (1618 edition, Sig. E1v).

48–9 *Though ... gentleman* In fact many gentlemen were employed as upper servants in great households, but Deflores' disdain for service as a form of degrading 'servitude' echoes the complaints of contemporary pamphleteers, such as 'I.M.' in *A Health to the Gentlemanly profession of Servingmen: or, The Servingmans Comfort* (1598), who argued that changing conditions of employment were rendering domestic service no longer suitable for persons of gentle birth.

52–3 *Again ... me* Q prints this as one line, but its dash after 'Again' – like that after 'So' (l. 76) – may indicate that the word is extra-metrical.

53 *ominous* Cf. I.i.2.

BEATRICE

Thy business? What's thy business?

DEFLORES [*Aside*]   Soft and fair!

I cannot part so soon now.

BEATRICE [*Aside*]   The villain's fixed. –

[*Aloud*] Thou standing toad-pool.

DEFLORES [*Aside*]   The shower falls amain now.

BEATRICE

Who sent thee? What's thy errand? Leave my sight.

DEFLORES

My lord your father charged me to deliver   60

A message to you.

BEATRICE   What, another since?

Do't and be hanged, then! Let me be rid of thee.

DEFLORES

True service merits mercy.

BEATRICE   What's thy message?

DEFLORES

Let beauty settle but in patience,

You shall hear all.

BEATRICE   A dallying, trifling torment!   65

DEFLORES

Signor Alonzo de Piracquo, lady,

Sole brother to Tomazo de Piracquo –

---

56 *Soft and fair* Directed at himself – cf. Tilley S601: 'Soft and fair goes far'; and Proverbs 15:1 'A soft answer turneth away wrath'.

57 *fixed* (1) immoveable; (2) transfixed (i.e. by the sight of her)

58 *standing toad-pool* stagnant water in which poisonous toads were generated (cf. *Othello* IV.ii.62–3: 'a cistern for foul toads / To knot and gender in') *amain* with full force

59–61 *thee ... you* The social distance between Beatrice and Deflores is registered by the way that Beatrice uses the singular pronouns (*thee, thou, thy*) customarily used in addressing servants, children and social inferiors, while Deflores employs the more respectful plural forms (*you, your*). Cf. also II.ii.72, III.iii.168–70.

63 *True ... mercy* Begins a series of equivocations, elaborated in II.ii and III.iii, on the meanings of service. Delivering messages belongs to Deflores' function as a household servant, but by using the term *mercy* he seeks to cast himself in the role of a courtly lover offering a more exalted kind of *service* to the lady of the castle. The lady's grant of 'mercy' often involved a 'favour' such as Deflores claims at I.i.224. Cf. also l. 48.

65 *dallying* (1) idly chattering, time wasting (*OED* v. 1, 4); (2) playing mockingly (*OED* v. 3); (3) amorously playful
trifling (1) mocking, deceitful (*OED* v.); (2) frivolously time-wasting. Gordon Williams (*Dictionary*, p. 1422) notes that the verb *trifle* was 'used with the sense of coit from c. 1560.'

BEATRICE
  Slave, when wilt make an end?
DEFLORES [*Aside*]   Too soon I shall.
BEATRICE
  What all this while of him?
DEFLORES   The said Alonzo,
  With the foresaid Tomazo –
BEATRICE   Yet again!   70
DEFLORES
  Is new alighted.
BEATRICE   Vengeance strike the news!
  Thou thing most loathed, what cause was there in this
  To bring thee to my sight?
DEFLORES   My lord your father
  Charged me to seek you out.
BEATRICE   Is there no other
  To send his errand by?
DEFLORES   It seems 'tis my luck   75
  To be i'th' way still.
BEATRICE   Get thee from me.
DEFLORES [*Aside*]   So!
  Why, am not I an ass to devise ways
  Thus to be railed at? I must see her still;
  I shall have a mad qualm within this hour again –
  I know't, and, like a common Garden-bull,   80
  I do but take breath to be lugged again.
  What this may bode I know not; I'll despair the less
  Because there's daily precedents of bad faces
  Beloved beyond all reason: these foul chops
  May come into favour one day 'mongst his fellows.   85
  Wrangling has proved the mistress of good pastime;

---

68 *Slave* While the regime of service in early modern England did not include literal slavery, 'slave' persisted as term expressing extreme social contempt.

77 *devise* Accent on first syllable.

78 *still* all the time

79 *qualm* bout of sickness – like Alsemero's at I.i.24 Deflores' desire is figured as an illness; and cf. Beatrice's fits of trembling below (l. 91)

80 *common Garden-bull* i.e one of the bulls kept for baiting at Paris Garden, near the theatres in Southwark

81 *lugged* worried, baited (as by dogs)

84 *chops* Literally 'jaws' – here a metonym for the face.

85 *his fellows* other faces as deformed as mine

As children cry themselves asleep, I ha' seen
Women have chid themselves a-bed to men.   *Exit*

BEATRICE

I never see this fellow, but I think
Of some harm towards me, danger's in my mind still,   90
I scarce leave trembling of an hour after.
The next good mood I find my father in,
I'll get him quite discarded – Oh, I was
Lost in this small disturbance and forgot
Affliction's fiercer torrent that now comes   95
To bear down all my comforts.

Enter VERMANDERO, ALONZO, TOMAZO

VERMANDERO   You're both welcome;
But an especial one belongs to you, sir,
To whose most noble name our love presents
The addition of a son, our son Alonzo.

ALONZO

The treasury of honour cannot bring forth   100
A title I should more rejoice in, sir.

VERMANDERO

You have improved it well. Daughter, prepare:
The day will steal upon thee suddenly.

BEATRICE [*Aside*]

Howe'er, I will be sure to keep the night,
If it should come so near me.

                    [BEATRICE *and* VERMANDERO *talk apart*]

---

91 *of* for
  hour Scanned as two syllables.
98 *our* Vermandero makes use of the royal plural on this formal occasion, no doubt
  because in confirming the betrothal he speaks for his entire lineage.
99 *addition . . . son* title of my son, together with the marks of honour belonging to that
  dignity (cf. *King Lear* I.i.136: 'the name and all th'addition to a king')
100 *treasury of honour* the entire store of noble titles
102 *improved it well* amply augmented the honour belonging to that title (*OED improve*
  v.² 4a)
104 *keep the night* preserve the night for myself. Beatrice plays on Vermandero's 'steal' to
  suggest that the wedding will involve a kind of theft (of her virginity), and implies that
  she will not allow the marriage to be consummated – an ironic anticipation (as Daalder
  points out) of what will actually happen on the night of her wedding to Alsemero.
105 *If . . . near* (1) If that day should actually come; (2) If it should affect me so intimately
  (*OED near* adv.² 16b)

TOMAZO	Alonzo.	
ALONZO	Brother?	105

TOMAZO

In troth I see small welcome in her eye.

ALONZO

Fie, you are too severe a censurer
Of love in all points – there's no bringing on you:
If lovers should mark every thing a fault,
Affection would be like an ill-set book,   110
Whose faults might prove as big as half the volume.

BEATRICE

That's all I do entreat.

VERMANDERO   It is but reasonable,
I'll see what my son says to't. – Son Alonzo,
Here's a motion made but to reprieve
A maidenhead three days longer; the request   115
Is not far out of reason, for indeed
The former time is pinching.

ALONZO   Though my joys
Be set back so much time as I could wish
They had been forward, yet, since she desires it,
The time is set as pleasing as before;   120
I find no gladness wanting.

VERMANDERO   May I ever
Meet it in that point still. You're nobly welcome, sirs.

                Exeunt VERMANDERO *and* BEATRICE

TOMAZO

So. Did you mark the dullness of her parting now?

ALONZO

What dullness? Thou art so exceptious still.

---

108 *all points* every respect
    bringing on you (1) advancing your attitude, educating you; (2) exciting you sexually. Q
    has no punctuation after *you*, and Frost suggests that the meaning might therefore be 'I
    cannot make you realise that . . .'; but the syntax seems strained, and Dilke was surely
    right to suppose an error by the compositor.
110 *ill-set* badly type-set
114 *motion* application (as to a court) (*OED* n. 8b)
117 *pinching* pressing; troublesome (*OED* v. 7)
121 *wanting* lacking
121–2 *May . . . still* May I always satisfy your wish for happiness in such matters (*OED satisfy*
    v. 7)
123 *dullness* gloomy lack of interest (*OED* n. 3)
124 *exceptious* disposed to find fault

TOMAZO

    Why let it go, then: I am but a fool   125
    To mark your harms so heedfully.

ALONZO   Where's the oversight?

TOMAZO

    Come, your faith's cozened in her, strongly cozened:
    Unsettle your affection with all speed
    Wisdom can bring it to – your peace is ruined else.
    Think what a torment 'tis to marry one   130
    Whose heart is leapt into another's bosom:
    If ever pleasure she receive from thee,
    It comes not in thy name, or of thy gift –
    She lies but with another in thine arms,
    He the half-father unto all thy children   135
    In the conception; if he get 'em not,
    She helps to get 'em for him in this passion;
    And how dangerous
    And shameful her restraint may go in time to,
    It is not to be thought on without sufferings.   140

ALONZO

    You speak as if she loved some other, then.

TOMAZO

    Do you apprehend so slowly?

ALONZO   Nay, and that
    Be your fear only, I am safe enough:
    Preserve your friendship and your counsel brother
    For times of more distress; I should depart   145
    An enemy, a dangerous, deadly one
    To any but thyself that should but think
    She knew the meaning of inconstancy,
    Much less the use and practice. Yet we're friends:

---

126 *To . . . heedfully* To be so much on the lookout for things that may harm you
     Where's the oversight? What have I overlooked?
127 *cozened* deceived, cheated
137 *in this passion* ed. (in his passions Q; Bruster, *conj.* Sampson: in his absence) i.e. the state
    of sexual arousal produced by the fantasy that she lies in her lover's embrace
138–9 *And . . . to* 'and what dangerous and shameful consequences will eventually result
    from restraining her' (Frost)
142 *and* if
149 *Yet* (1) Nevertheless; (2) Still (with the implication that if Tomazo persists it will destroy
    their friendship)
    we're Q *corr.* (w'are; we are Q *uncorr.*)

Pray let no more be urged, I can endure 150
Much, till I meet an injury to her;
Then I am not myself. Farewell, sweet brother –
How much we're bound to heaven to depart lovingly! *Exit*

TOMAZO
Why here is love's tame madness, thus a man
Quickly steals into his vexation. *Exit* 155

[ACT II. SCENE ii.]

Enter DIAPHANTA *and* ALSEMERO

DIAPHANTA
The place is my charge; you have kept your hour,
And the reward of a just meeting bless you!
I hear my lady coming. Complete gentleman!
I dare not be too busy with my praises,
They're dangerous things to deal with. *Exit*

ALSEMERO   This goes well: 5
These women are their ladies' cabinets,

153 *bound* obligated
154 *love's tame madness* picking up the theme of love-sickness and linking it to the sub-plot
   (cf. e.g. IV.iii.1–4). The idea that love constituted a form of madness is elaborated at
   great length in the section on love melancholy in Robert Burton's *Anatomy of Melancholy* (1621).
155 *vexation* Scanned as four syllables.
II.ii Author: Middleton
 1 *charge* responsibility
 3 *Complete gentleman* Perfect gentleman – as at I.i.205, the phrase probably alludes to
   Henry Peacham's conduct book, *The Complete Gentleman*, published in the year of *The
   Changeling*'s first performance.
4–5 *I . . . with* i.e. if Diaphanta is too effusive in her praise of Alsemero, Beatrice may
   become jealous
6–7 *These . . . 'em* In *Gerardo*, Isdaura's waiting maid, Julia, is described as 'Secretary to
   my most hidden thoughts' (sig. H5); compare also the character of '*A Chamber-maide*' in
   Overbury's *Wife*: 'She is her mistresses she Secretary, and keepes the box of her teeth, her
   haire, & her painting very priuate' (1618 edition, sig. G7v).
 6 *women* waiting-women
   their ed. (the Q)
   cabinets either (a) a small, private room (in which costly paintings and other treasures
   were often kept), or (b) a chest for jewels and other precious possessions; figuratively (c)
   a secret receptacle (*OED* n. 4–6). In *Othello*, the waiting-woman Emilia is similarly
   described by Othello as 'A closet, lock and key of villainous secrets' (4.1.22).

Things of most precious trust are locked into 'em.

Enter BEATRICE

BEATRICE

I have within mine eye all my desires:
Requests that holy prayers ascend heaven for,
And brings 'em down to furnish our defects,   10
Come not more sweet to our necessities
Than thou unto my wishes.
ALSEMERO   We're so like
In our expressions, lady, that unless I borrow
The same words, I shall never find their equals.

BEATRICE

How happy were this meeting, this embrace,   15
If it were free from envy! This poor kiss
It has an enemy, a hateful one,
That wishes poison to't. How well were I now
If there were none such name known as Piracquo,
Nor no such tie as the command of parents!   20
I should be but too much blessed.
ALSEMERO   One good service
Would strike off both your fears, and I'll go near it too,
Since you are so distressed: remove the cause,
The command ceases; so there's two fears blown out
With one and the same blast.
BEATRICE   Pray let me find you, sir.   25
What might that service be so strangely happy?

---

7 *locked* ed. (lock Q)

10 *brings 'em down* i.e. the prayers succeed in bringing the things requested back to earth. For the irregular grammar here, see I.ii.150.
furnish our defects supply us with what we lack, make up for our deficiencies

11 *our necessities* what we need

17–18 *an enemy . . . to't* i.e. Alonso, who would wish their kiss poisoned, if he knew of it; ironically, as we learn at l. 57, their entire rendezvous is being watched by an even more dangerous enemy, Deflores – the 'poison' that Beatrice is destined to 'kiss' (see V.iii.67).

21 *service* As ll. 27–8 show, it is chivalric 'service' that Alsemero has in mind.

23–4 *remove . . . ceases* A paraphrase of the scholastic tag, *ablata causa, tollitur effectus* ('the cause removed, the effect ceases').

25 *blast* puff of breath
find understand

26 *happy* fortunate

435

ALSEMERO

The honourablest piece about man – valour.
I'll send a challenge to Piracquo instantly.

BEATRICE

How? Call you that extinguishing of fear
When 'tis the only way to keep it flaming? 30
Are not you ventured in the action,
That's all my joys and comforts? Pray no more, sir.
Say you prevailed, you're danger's and not mine then:
The law would claim you from me, or obscurity
Be made the grave to bury you alive. 35
I'm glad these thoughts come forth – O keep not one
Of this condition, sir! Here was a course
Found to bring sorrow on her way to death:
The tears would ne'er ha' dried till dust had choked 'em.
Blood-guiltiness becomes a fouler visage, 40
And now I think on one – [*Aside*] I was to blame,
I ha' marred so good a market with my scorn:
'T had been done questionless. The ugliest creature
Creation framed for some use, yet to see
I could not mark so much where it should be. 45

ALSEMERO

Lady!

BEATRICE [*Aside*]Why men of art make much of poison,
Keep one to expel another. Where was my art?

ALSEMERO

Lady, you hear not me.

BEATRICE   I do especially, sir.

27 *about* ed. ('bout Q – another instance of unnecessary colloquial contraction)
31 *ventured* put at risk
32 *That's* Who are
33 *you're* ed. (your Q)
34–5 *The law . . . alive* either you'd fall victim to the law or you'd have to go into hiding
36–7 *one . . . condition* one thought of this kind
38 *to bring . . . death* to make me die of grief
41 s.d. Most eds. begin the aside at the beginning of the line, but Q's dash after *one* suggests that the first part of the line is spoken aloud and that *I think on one* probably means 'I am thinking about [how to find] one' rather than 'I have one in mind'.
42 *marred . . . market* Semi-proverbial (cf. Tilley M672: 'He has made a good market').
43 *done questionless* (1) 'there is no doubt it would have been done by now;' (2) 'done with no questions asked'
46 *make . . . poison* turn to poison to good account (*OED* v.[1] 18d)
47 *Keep . . . another* A standard nostrum of early modern medicine, enshrined in the proverb 'one poison expels [drives out] another' (Tilley P477).

The present times are not so sure of our side
As those hereafter may be: we must use 'em then   50
As thrifty folks their wealth, sparingly now,
Till the time opens.

ALSEMERO   You teach wisdom, lady.

BEATRICE [*Calling*]
Within there, Diaphanta!

Enter DIAPHANTA

DIAPHANTA   Do you call, madam?

BEATRICE
Perfect your service, and conduct this gentleman
The private way you brought him.

DIAPHANTA   I shall, madam.   55

ALSEMERO
My love's as firm as love e'er built upon.

                    Exeunt DIAPHANTA *and* ALSEMERO

Enter DEFLORES

DEFLORES [*Aside*]
I have watched this meeting, and do wonder much
What shall become of t'other; I'm sure both
Cannot be served unless she transgress. Happily
Then I'll put in for one; for if a woman   60

49 *not . . . side* favourable to our cause
52 *time opens* future unfolds
54 *service* Ricks (p. 299) suggests an ironic *double entendre* – Diaphanta will 'serve' Alsmero in a way she does not yet imagine.
55 *private way* Perhaps another ironic *double entendre* (Ricks).
56 *My . . . upon* My love for you is as unshakeable as any on which a mistress ever rested her hopes
57 *I have watched* Possibly an indication that an earlier stage direction has been lost: Deflores was perhaps meant to appear 'above', like Lollio in the parallel episode at III.ii.170 ff., to spy on the lovers – as he did in the 1978 Royal Shakespeare Company production.
58 *t'other* Alonzo
59 *served* sexually satisfied
   Happily Perhaps
60 *put . . . one* apply for a share (with sexual innuendo – cf. IV.iii.34)

Fly from one point, from him she makes a husband,
She spreads and mounts then like arithmetic –
One, ten, a hundred, a thousand, ten thousand –
Proves in time sutler to an army royal.
Now do I look to be most richly railed at,   65
Yet I must see her.

BEATRICE [*Aside*]   Why, put case I loathed him
As much as youth and beauty hates a sepulchre,
Must I needs show it? Cannot I keep that secret,
And serve my turn upon him? See he's here –
[*Aloud*] Deflores.

DEFLORES [*Aside*]   Ha! I shall run mad with joy: 70
She called me fairly by my name, Deflores,
And neither 'rogue' nor 'rascal'.

BEATRICE   What ha' you done
To your face alate? You've met with some good physician;
You've pruned yourself, methinks: you were not wont
To look so amorously.

DEFLORES   Not I.   75
[*Aside*] 'Tis the same physnomy to a hair and pimple
Which she called scurvy scarce an hour ago:
How is this?

BEATRICE   Come hither – nearer, man.

DEFLORES [*Aside*]
I'm up to the chin in heaven.

BEATRICE   Turn, let me see –

61–2 *Fly . . . mounts* 'De Flores uses the language of falconry . . . with [a] sexual suggestion' (Bawcutt 1998).

61 *point* position; with a quibble on *point* = penis (Williams, *Glossary*, p. 241)

64 *sutler* supplier of provisions; 'if a woman, sometimes a prostitute' (Bawcutt (1998))
army royal grand army (*OED royal* a. 10b)

66 *put case* suppose

68 *secret* Cf. I.ii.1–8.

69 *serve . . . him* make use of him for my own purposes; but with an unconscious sexual innuendo (cf. I.ii.57)

72 *you* Beatrice's flattering approach is marked by her switch to the respectful plural pronoun.

74 *pruned* preened, decked out (*OED* v.[1] 1–2)

75 *look so amorously* (1) look so lovable, desirable (*OED amorous* a. II); (2) gaze so fondly, lustfully [at me] (*OED amorous* a. I, 2)

76 *physnomy* physiognomy

77 *scurvy* (1) covered with diseased scabs (*OED* a. 1); (2) worthless, contemptible (*OED* a. 2)

Faugh! 'Tis but the heat of the liver, I perceiv't; 80
I thought it had been worse.

DEFLORES [*Aside*]   Her fingers touched me –
She smells all amber!

BEATRICE
I'll make a water for you shall cleanse this
Within a fortnight.

DEFLORES   With your own hands, lady?

BEATRICE
Yes, mine own, sir: in a work of cure 85
I'll trust no other.

DEFLORES [*Aside*] 'Tis half an act of pleasure
To hear her talk thus to me.

BEATRICE   When we're used
To a hard face, 'tis not so unpleasing,
It mends still in opinion, hourly mends –
I see it by experience.

DEFLORES [*Aside*] I was blest 90
To light upon this minute, I'll make use on't.

BEATRICE
Hardness becomes the visage of a man well,
It argues service, resolution, manhood,
If cause were of employment.

DEFLORES   'Twould be soon seen,
If e'er your ladyship had cause to use it. 95
I would but wish the honour of a service
So happy as that mounts to.

---

80 *Faugh!* The exclamation is extra-metrical.
 heat of the liver In Galenic medicine the liver was the seat of love and the passions; an overheated liver could produce excess of desire, but might also result in physical symptoms.
81 *fingers* Already eroticised by Deflores' play with Beatrice's glove at I.i.224–7.
82 *amber* ambergris – an ingredient of costly perfumes. The detail shows how Deflores' erotic excitement is directly linked to Beatrice's rank and wealth.
83 *water* medicinal tincture (*OED* n. 16a); however, Deflores' response at ll. 86–7 suggests that he chooses to understand it as meaning 'semen' (Williams, *Glossary*, p. 332).
94 *employment* Like *service* capable of a sexual interpretation.
95 *use* With the additional sense 'employ sexually'.
96 *honour of a service* Deflores emphasises the chivalric sense of *service*; but *honour* also = virginity (and hence vagina – Williams, *Glossary*, pp. 161–2).
97 *mounts* bawdy *double entendre*

BEATRICE   We shall try you –
  Oh, my Deflores!

DEFLORES   How's that?
  [*Aside*] She calls me hers already, 'my Deflores'! –
  [*Aloud*] You were about to sigh out somewhat, madam.   100

BEATRICE
  No, was I? I forgot – Oh!

DEFLORES   There 'tis again,
  The very fellow on't.

BEATRICE   You are too quick, sir.

DEFLORES
  There's no excuse for't now I heard it twice, madam:
  That sigh would fain have utterance, take pity on't,
  And lend it a free word – 'las how it labours   105
  For liberty, I hear the murmur yet
  Beat at your bosom.

BEATRICE   Would creation –

DEFLORES
  Ay, well said, that's it!

BEATRICE   Had formed me man!

DEFLORES
  Nay, that's not it.

BEATRICE   Oh, 'tis the soul of freedom!
  I should not then be forced to marry one   110
  I hate beyond all depths; I should have power
  Then to oppose my loathings – nay, remove 'em
  For ever from my sight.

DEFLORES   O blest occasion!
  Without change to your sex, you have your wishes:
  Claim so much man in me.

---

97 *try* put to the test (*OED* v. 7a; with unconscious sexual innuendo – see Williams, *Dictionary*, p. 1430: *try* = 'have sexual experience of')

102 *on't* of it
   quick Perhaps with an unconscious play on *quick* n. = sexual centre (see Williams, *Dictionary*, p. 1129).

103 *for't now I* This edition (for't, now I Q; for't now; I Dilke and most eds).
   now I heard given that I have now heard

107 *creation* Four syllables, stress on final syllable.

112–13 *remove . . . sight* Beatrice's euphemism for murder takes her obsession with eyesight and appearance to its logical extreme.

113 *occasion* opportunity (*OED* n. 1a)

BEATRICE   In thee, Deflores?   115
    There's small cause for that.
DEFLORES   Put it not from me:
    It's a service that I kneel for to you.   [*Kneels*]
BEATRICE
    You are too violent to mean faithfully,
    There's horror in my service, blood and danger:
    Can those be things to sue for?
DEFLORES   If you knew   120
    How sweet it were to me to be employed
    In any act of yours, you would say then
    I failed, and used not reverence enough
    When I receive the charge on't.
BEATRICE [*Aside*]   This is much methinks;
    Belike his wants are greedy, and to such   125
    Gold tastes like angels' food. – [*Aloud*] Rise.
DEFLORES
    I'll have the work first.
BEATRICE [*Aside*]   Possible his need
    Is strong upon him – [*Gives him money*] there's to
      encourage thee:
    As thou art forward and thy service dangerous,
    Thy reward shall be precious.
DEFLORES   That I have thought on;   130
    I have assured myself of that beforehand,
    And know it will be precious – the thought ravishes.
BEATRICE
    Then take him to thy fury.

---

117 *It's . . . you* Deflores adopts the supplicant posture of a knight seeking acceptance as his lady's 'servant' (cf. also Antonio's offer of himself as Isabella's 'servant' at III.ii.117, and Alsemero's offer of 'service' to Beatrice at II.ii.21).

118 *too . . . faithfully* too passionate to mean what you say

122 *act* (1) action; (2) sexual congress (Williams, *Glossary*, p. 24)

124 *the charge on't* your instructions for it

126 *angels' food* manna (see Psalm 78:24–5)

129 *forward* eager (to carry out my will), bold (*OED* a. 6a, c)

131 *myself of that* Q *corr.* (myselfe that Q *uncorr.*)

132 *ravishes* enraptures; but the sexual sense ('rapes'), which Beatrice does not hear, emphasizes the gap between the two kinds of 'reward' they envisage.

133 *Then . . . fury* In the 1993 BBC version Beatrice joined the kneeling Deflores on this line, as though mimicking the ritual of marriage vows – which she appeared to seal with the kiss she gave Deflores at l. 147, after her contemptuous aside about 'his dog-face'.

DEFLORES   I thirst for him.

BEATRICE

Alonzo de Piracquo.

DEFLORES   His end's upon him:

He shall be seen no more.

BEATRICE   How lovely now   135

Dost thou appear to me! Never was man

Dearlier rewarded.

DEFLORES   I do think of that.

BEATRICE

Be wondrous careful in the execution.

DEFLORES

Why, are not both our lives upon the cast?

BEATRICE

Then I throw all my fears upon thy service.   140

DEFLORES

They ne'er shall rise to hurt you.   [*Rises*]

BEATRICE   When the deed's done,

I'll furnish thee with all things for thy flight:

Thou may'st live bravely in another country.

DEFLORES

Ay, ay, we'll talk of that hereafter.

BEATRICE [*Aside*]   I shall rid

Myself of two inveterate loathings at one time: 145

Piracquo and his dog-face.   *Exit*

DEFLORES   O my blood!

Methinks I feel her in mine arms already,

Her wanton fingers combing out this beard,

---

133 *thirst* Cf. Deflores' metaphors of sexual desire as thirst for 'blood' of a different kind (III.iii.107–8; V.iii.170–1; and below l. 146).

135 *He . . . more* Deflores cleverly exploits Beatrice's self-deceiving euphemism at ll. 112–13. *lovely* Not only 'beautiful', but also 'lovable' and 'amorous' (*OED* a. 1–3).

137 *Dearlier* (1) More richly; (2) Lovingly; (3) At greater cost (*OED* a. 2a, 3, 4a, 5a, 6a)

139 *upon the cast* dependent on the throw of this dice

141 s.d. Most eds. insert this s.d. at l. 135, but the visual pun created by the sight of Deflores rising even as he speaks of Beatrice's 'rising fears' is entirely in accord with Middleton's ironic technique.

143 *bravely* splendidly, ostentatiously (*OED* adv. 2)

146 *his dog-face* Beatrice imagines Deflores as one of those monstrous dog-headed humans (*cynopheli*) described by Pliny and his medieval successors, including the fabled Sir John Mandeville; Bawcutt (1958) suggests that Beatrice may be coining a mock-title for Deflores, 'His Dog-Face' (on the model of His Lordship). *blood* sexual desire

And, being pleased, praising this bad face.
Hunger and pleasure, they'll commend sometimes   150
Slovenly dishes, and feed heartily on 'em –
Nay, which is stranger, refuse daintier for 'em.
Some women are odd feeders – I'm too loud:
Here comes the man goes supperless to bed,
Yet shall not rise tomorrow to his dinner.   155

Enter ALONZO

ALONZO
Deflores.
DEFLORES   My kind, honourable lord?
ALONZO
I am glad I've met with thee.
DEFLORES   Sir.
ALONZO   Thou canst show me
The full strength of the castle?
DEFLORES   That I can, sir.
ALONZO
I much desire it.
DEFLORES   And if the ways and straits
Of some of the passages be not too tedious for you,   160
I will assure you, worth your time and sight, my lord.
ALONZO
Pooh! That shall be no hindrance.
DEFLORES   I'm your servant, then.
'Tis now near dinner time; 'gainst your lordship's rising
I'll have the keys about me.
ALONZO   Thanks, kind Deflores.

---

151 *Slovenly* Nasty, disgusting (*OED* a. 3)
154–5 *supperless . . . rise . . . dinner* Extends the sexual metaphor from ll. 150–3.
159 *ways* doorways, gateways (*OED* n. 1f)
   straits narrow places (*OED* n. 1a; and cf. a. 3a)
160 *tedious* irksome (*OED* a. 2)
163 *'gainst . . . rising* i.e. until such time as you rise from the table
164 *keys* For the symbolic significance of these instruments in Deflores' 'work of secrecy'
   (III.i.27), cf. the key with which Beatrice opens Alsemero's closet to discover '*The Book
   of Experiment / Called Secrets in Nature*' (IV.i.18–25), and the 'key of [the] wardrobe'
   which Isabella obtains from Lollio in order to penetrate the secret of Antonio's and
   Franciscus' disguise (IV.iii.44).

DEFLORES

    He's safely thrust upon me beyond hopes.   *Exeunt*   165

      In the act-time DEFLORES *hides a naked rapier*

ACT III. [SCENE i.]

      Enter ALONZO *and* DEFLORES

DEFLORES

    Yes, here are all the keys: I was afraid, my lord,

    I'd wanted for the postern – this is it.

    I've all, I've all, my lord – this for the sconce.

ALONZO

    'Tis a most spacious and impregnable fort.

DEFLORES

    You'll tell me more, my lord. This descent   5

    Is somewhat narrow, we shall never pass

    Well with our weapons, they'll but trouble us.

                           [Takes off his sword]

ALONZO

    Thou sayest true.

DEFLORES   Pray let me help your lordship.

                  [Takes off ALONZO's *sword]*

---

165 *safely* securely, without any risk (to me) – ironic

    s.d. *act-time* Unlike outdoor playhouses, such as the Globe, where the action was continuous, the so-called 'private' theatres, including the Cockpit and Salisbury Court, allowed for intervals between the acts, during which music was customarily played.

    s.d. DEFLORES . . . *rapier* An altogether unusual stage-direction, since the interval between acts is a kind of non-time from which the characters are conventionally excluded: Deflores' exploitation of it becomes a way of representing his unfettered access to the castle's innermost 'secrets'.

III.i Author: Middleton.

  2 *postern* rear door or gate

  3 *sconce* small fort designed to defend a castle gate (*OED* n.³ 1). Holdsworth, 'Notes on *The Changeling*,' *N&Q* ns. 234 (1989) 344–6, suggests a pun on *sconce* n.² = jocular term for the head, and argues that 'this must mean that he intends to club Alonzo with one of the large, heavy keys he is carrying, the very one he is now showing his victim'; Bruster inserts stage directions to this effect at III.i.24 ff.

  5 *tell me more* 'have more to say, be even more impressed [when you have seen more]' – with an ironic innuendo

ALONZO

'Tis done. Thanks, kind Deflores.

DEFLORES   Here are hooks, my lord,

To hang such things on purpose.

ALONZO   Lead, I'll follow thee.   10

Exeunt at one door and enter at the other

DEFLORES

All this is nothing; you shall see anon

A place you little dream on.

ALONZO   I am glad

I have this leisure; all your master's house

Imagine I ha' taken a gondola.

DEFLORES

All but myself, sir, [*Aside*] which makes up my safety.   15

[*Aloud*] My lord, I'll place you at a casement here

Will show you the full strength of all the castle.

Look, spend your eye a while upon that object.

ALONZO

Here's rich variety, Deflores.

DEFLORES   Yes, sir.

ALONZO

Goodly munition.

DEFLORES   Ay, there's ordnance, sir –   20

No bastard metal – will ring you a peal like bells

At great men's funerals. Keep your eye straight, my lord,

Take special notice of that sconce before you:

There you may dwell awhile.   [*Takes up the rapier*]

---

9 *lord* Scanned as two syllables here.

10 s.d. This helps the actors to mime the narrow, winding descent. Most editions begin a separate scene at this point, but since the s.d. indicates that the action is effectively continuous, there seems no point in doing so.

12 *A place . . . on* i.e. the grave

16 *casement* Corruption of *casemate* (*OED casement* n. 4) which is the word in Reynolds: 'A vaulted chamber built in the thickness of the ramparts of a fortress, with embrasures for the defence of the place' (*OED casemate* n. 1).

20 *munition* fortification

21 *bastard metal* corrupt alloy

peal (1) changes rung on a set of bells; (2) discharge of cannons, esp. in salute (*OED* n. 2, 3)

22 *great men's funerals* a by-word for hypocritical behaviour (see Webster, *White Devil*, V.ii.296–7)

24 *dwell* (1) fix your attention; (2) remain when dead

445

ALONZO   I am upon't.

DEFLORES

And so am I.   [*Stabs him*]

ALONZO   Deflores! O Deflores,   25

Whose malice hast thou put on?

DEFLORES   Do you question

A work of secrecy? I must silence you.   [*Stabs him*]

ALONZO

Oh, oh, oh!

DEFLORES   I must silence you.   [*Kills him*]

So, here's an undertaking well accomplished.

This vault serves to good use now – Ha! what's that   30

Threw sparkles in my eye? – Oh, 'tis a diamond

He wears upon his finger. It was well found:

This will approve the work. What, so fast on?

Not part in death? I'll take a speedy course then:

Finger and all shall off. So, now I'll clear   35

The passages from all suspect or fear.   *Exit with the body*

[ACT III. SCENE ii.]

Enter ISABELLA *and* LOLLIO

ISABELLA

Why, sirrah? Whence have you commission

To fetter the doors against me? If you

Keep me in a cage, pray whistle to me,

Let me be doing something.

---

24 *I . . . upon't* I can see it. Deflores' reply twists the phrase to mean 'I have found my target'.
30 *vault* Presumably represented by the curtained 'discovery space' at the rear of the stage.
31 *sparkles . . . diamond* Uncanny echo of II.i.15.
33 *approve* serve as proof of
34 *Not . . . death* An ironic recollection of the marriage vow 'till death us do part' – cf. III.iii.37–8.
III.ii Author: Rowley
  1 *sirrah* term of address expressing authority, reprimand or contempt

LOLLIO

> You shall be doing, if it please you: I'll whistle to you, if you'll   5
> pipe after.

ISABELLA

> Is it your master's pleasure or your own
> To keep me in this pinfold?

LOLLIO

> 'Tis for my master's pleasure, lest, being taken in another man's
> corn, you might be pounded in another place.   10

ISABELLA

> 'Tis very well, and he'll prove very wise.

LOLLIO

> He says you have company enough in the house, if you please to
> be sociable, of all sorts of people.

ISABELLA

> Of all sorts? Why here's none but fools and madmen.

LOLLIO

> Very well – and where will you find any other, if you should go   15
> abroad? There's my master and I to boot too.

ISABELLA

> Of either sort one – a madman and a fool.

LOLLIO

> I would even participate of both then, if I were as you: I know
> you're half mad already; be half foolish too.

ISABELLA

> You're a brave, saucy rascal! Come on, sir,   20
> Afford me then the pleasure of your bedlam:
> You were commending once today to me

---

5 *doing* fornicating

5–6 *I'll . . . after* Daalder suggests that Lollio plays on the proverbial expression 'to dance after someone's pipe' (*Oxford Dictionary of English Proverbs*, p. 166); the proverb is not in Tilley, but is recorded in *OED* (v. 1 e) from 1562.

6 *pipe* obscene *double entendre* (*pipe* = penis; Williams, *Glossary*, p. 236)

8 *pinfold* pound for stray livestock; place of confinement. Daalder suggests a play on *pin* = penis (Williams, *Glossary*, pp. 235–6).

10 *pounded* (1) held in a pound; (2) pounded with a (phallic) pestle
   another place obscene innuendo

16 *abroad* into the world at large
   to boot as well

18 *participate* partake (i.e. sexually)

20 *brave* bold (in a pejorative sense)
   saucy insolent; lascivious (*OED* a. 2a–b)

21 *bedlam* See above, I.ii.50.

22 *once* earlier

Your last come lunatic – what a proper
Body there was without brains to guide it,
And what a pitiful delight appeared   25
In that defect, as if your wisdom had found
A mirth in madness; pray sir, let me partake,
If there be such a pleasure.

LOLLIO

If I do not show you the handsomest, discreetest madman – one
that I may call the understanding madman – then say I am a   30
fool.

ISABELLA

Well, a match: I will say so.

LOLLIO

When you have a taste of the madman, you shall (if you please)
see Fools' College o' th'other side. I seldom lock there: 'tis but
shooting a bolt or two, and you are amongst 'em.   *Exit*   35

    Enters presently [drawing FRANCISCUS *after him]*

Come on, sir; let me see how handsomely you'll behave yourself
now.

FRANCISCUS

How sweetly she looks! Oh, but there's a wrinkle in her brow as
deep as philosophy. Anacreon, drink to my mistress' health, I'll
pledge it. Stay, stay, there's a spider in the cup – no, 'tis but a   40
grape-stone; swallow it, fear nothing, poet; so, so, lift higher.

23 *last come* most recently arrived
    proper handsome (*OED* a. 9)
26 *In . . . defect* i.e in your description of it
32 *a match* it's a deal
34 *o' th'other side* ed. (o'th' side Q)
35 *shooting a bolt* undoing a bolt – with a play both on the proverb 'A fool's bolt is soon
    shot' (Tilley, F515) and on the obscene meanings of 'bolt' and 'shoot'
36 *handsomely* decently (*OED* adv. 5)
39 *Anacreon* Greek poet who celebrated the pleasures of wine (probably addressed to
    Lollio)
40 *spider . . . cup* According to folk-belief, since spiders were venomous, they could poison a
    drink, and to swallow one could be fatal (cf. *Winter's Tale*, II.i.39–45).
41 *grape-stone* Pliny (*Natural History* VII, vii) records the legend that Anacreon choked
    to death on a grapeseed.

ISABELLA

    Alack, alack, 'tis too full of pity

    To be laughed at. How fell he mad? Canst thou tell?

LOLLIO

    For love, mistress. He was a pretty poet too, and that set him

    forwards first; the Muses then forsook him, he ran mad for a   45

    chambermaid – yet she was but a dwarf neither.

FRANCISCUS

    Hail, bright Titania!

    Why standst thou idle on these flowery banks?

    Oberon is dancing with his Dryades;

    I'll gather daisies, primrose, violets,   50

    And bind them in a verse of poesy.   [*Approaches* ISABELLA]

LOLLIO

    Not too near – you see your danger.

                         [*Threatens* FRANCISCUS *with a whip*]

FRANCISCUS

    O hold thy hand, great Diomed!

    Thou feedst thy horses well, they shall obey thee;

    [*Drops onto all fours*] Get up, Bucephalus kneels.   [*Kneels*]   55

LOLLIO

    You see how I awe my flock: a shepherd has not his dog at more

    obedience.

42–3 *Alack . . . tell* l. 42 is one syllable short, l. 43 one syllable too long. Dilke may have been right to read 'it is' for *'tis*, and *canst thou tell* may similarly be a mistake for 'canst tell'; but the scansion in these sub-plot scenes of mingled verse and prose is often unusually rough.

44–5 *set . . . forwards* started him off. Poetic inspiration (like love) was sometimes thought of as a kind of divine madness, the *furor poeticus* – cf. *A Midsummer Night's Dream*, V.i.12–20.

47, 49 *Titania, Oberon* 'Oberon' was the traditional name for the fairy king, but the conjunction with 'Titania', the name given to Oberon's consort in *A Midsummer Night's Dream*, suggests that Franciscus is probably remembering Shakespeare's comedy.

49 *Dryades* wood-nymphs. Lollio implies that Isabella's husband is entertaining himself with other women.

50 *daisies . . . violets* Daalder notes the symbolism of these flowers (freshness, excellence, and chastity).

51 *poesy* (1) poetry; (2) posy of flowers (*OED* n. 1, 4)

53 *Diomed* Diomedes, King of the Bistonians in Thrace, who fed his horses on human flesh; Hercules tamed these savage steeds by feeding them Diomedes' own corpse.

55 *Get up* Mount

    Bucephalus the mighty charger of Alexander the Great, which only the king himself could ride

    s.d. *'Kneels'* Repeats Deflores' gesture at II.ii.117.

ISABELLA

His conscience is unquiet; sure that was
The cause of this. A proper gentleman!

FRANCISCUS

Come hither, Aesculapius, hide the poison.   60

LOLLIO

Well, 'tis hid.   [*Puts away the whip.* FRANCISCUS *rises*]

FRANCISCUS

Didst thou never hear of one Tiresias,
A famous poet?

LOLLIO

Yes, that kept tame wild geese.

FRANCISCUS

That's he, I am the man.   65

LOLLIO

No!

FRANCISCUS

Yes, but make no words on't: I was a man
Seven years ago.

LOLLIO

A stripling, I think you might.

FRANCISCUS

Now I'm a woman, all feminine.   70

LOLLIO

I would I might see that.

FRANCISCUS

Juno struck me blind.

LOLLIO

I'll ne'er believe that; for a woman they say, has an eye more
than a man.

59 *proper* (1) handsome; (2) complete, thorough (*OED* a. 9, 7)
60 *Aesculapius* Greek god of medicine
    poison i.e. the whip, but picking up the image from l. 40.
61 *hid* A visual parallel with Deflores' concealment of the rapier at the beginning of Act III
    may be intended here.
62–3 *Tiresias . . . poet* Not a poet, but a blind prophet from Thebes.
64 *wild geese* prostitutes (see Williams, *Dictionary*, pp. 143–4)
67–70 *I was . . . woman* Tiresias spent seven years as a woman, before changing back into a
    man.
69 *might* might have been
72 *Juno . . . blind* When Tiresias revealed that women derived more pleasure from sex
    than men, the marriage goddess, Juno, punished him with blindness.
73–4 *eye . . . man* i.e. between her legs – an ironic gloss on Beatrice's 'eyes of judgement'
    (II.i.13)

FRANCISCUS

    I say she struck me blind.   75

LOLLIO

    And Luna made you mad: you have two trades to beg with.

FRANCISCUS

    Luna is now big-bellied, and there's room

    For both of us to ride with Hecate;

    I'll drag thee up into her silver sphere,

    And there we'll kick the dog and beat the bush   80

    That barks against the witches of the night;

    The swift lycanthropi that walks the round,

    We'll tear their wolvish skins, and save the sheep.

LOLLIO

    Is't come to this? Nay, then my poison comes forth again.

    [*Shows the whip*] Mad slave indeed – abuse your keeper!   85

ISABELLA

    I prithee, hence with him, now he grows dangerous.

FRANCISCUS [*Sings*]

    Sweet love, pity me:

    Give me leave to lie with thee.

LOLLIO

    No, I'll see you wiser first: to your own kennel.

FRANCISCUS

    No noise, she sleeps; draw all the curtains round,   90

---

76 *Luna* The moon goddess. Not only was the moon credited with the power to drive people 'lunatic', but, as the planet of change, it was supposed to exercise particular influence upon women, because of their monthly cycles – rendering them especially liable to fickleness, change, and emotional instability (cf. V.iii.196 ff.). Lollio implies Tiresias'/ Franciscus' time as a woman made him unusually vulnerable to the malign influence of the moon.

    two trades i.e. blindness and madness

    beg beg with

77 *big-bellied* Franciscus' conceit is that the full moon is pregnant.

78 *Hecate* Greek goddess of witchcraft, frequently identified with the moon goddess Diana/ Artemis, and hence often used as a synonym for the moon itself

80 *dog . . . bush* conventional properties of the man-in-the-moon (see *A Midsummer Night's Dream*, V.i.251–3). The bawdy implication is that Franciscus himself means to be the man in *her* moon.

80–1 *bush / That barks* Franciscus' confused syntax is perhaps encouraged by a pun on *barks*.

82 *lycanthropi* sufferers from lycanthropia who (like Duke Ferdinand in *The Duchess of Malfi*) imagine themselves transformed into wolves. Q prints a comma rather than a semi-colon after *night*, and it may be that *lycanthropi* are being imagined as witches of a sort.

90–2 *No . . . mouse-hole* Noting the rhymes on 'sleeps/creeps', 'round/sound', 'soul/hole', Bruster suggests that these lines may have been intended as a continuation of Antonio's song, forming a lyric with alternating long and short lines.

Let no soft sound molest the pretty soul
But love, and love creeps in at a mouse-hole.

LOLLIO

I would you would get into your hole.

Exit FRANCISCUS

Now, mistress, I will bring you another sort: you shall be fooled
another while – [*Calls*] Tony, come hither, Tony!   95

Enter ANTONIO

Look who's yonder, Tony.

ANTONIO

Cousin, is it not my aunt?

LOLLIO

Yes, 'tis one of 'em, Tony.

ANTONIO

He, he! how do you, uncle?

LOLLIO

Fear him not mistress, 'tis a gentle nidget: you may play with   100
him as safely with him as with his bauble.

ISABELLA

How long hast thou been a fool?

ANTONIO

Ever since I came hither, cousin.

ISABELLA

Cousin? I'm none of thy cousins, fool.

LOLLIO

O mistress, fools have always so much wit as to claim their   105
kindred.

---

92 *mouse-hole* obscene ('mouse' being a term of affection for women)
95 s.d. ed. (*after* 'yonder, Tony' Q)
97 *aunt* (also) prostitute (Williams, *Glossary*, p. 31)
99 *uncle* Daalder suggests this may have the cant meaning of 'procurer' – a conjecture
made more plausible by the fact that, in *Troilus and Cressida*, Cressida is pimped by
Pandarus, whom she repeatedly addresses as 'uncle'.
100 *nidget* colloquial contraction of 'an idiot'
    play copulate (Williams, *Glossary*, p. 238)
101 *bauble* (1) fool's baton (usually with a carved fool's head at its tip); (2) penis (Williams,
Glossary, pp. 36–7)
103 *cousin* Isabella probably interprets *cousin* as a euphemism for 'lover'.

MADMAN (*Within*)

Bounce, bounce! He falls, he falls!

ISABELLA

Hark you – your scholars in the upper room
Are out of order.

LOLLIO

Must I come amongst you there? Keep you the fool, mistress. I'll   110
go up and play left-handed Orlando amongst the madmen.

Exit

ISABELLA

Well, sir.

ANTONIO

'Tis opportuneful now, sweet lady! Nay,
Cast no amazing eye upon this change.

ISABELLA

Ha!   115

ANTONIO

This shape of folly shrouds your dearest love,
The truest servant to your powerful beauties,
Whose magic had this force thus to transform me.

ISABELLA

You are a fine fool indeed.

ANTONIO   Oh, 'tis not strange:
Love has an intellect that runs through all   120
The scrutinous sciences; and, like
A cunning poet, catches a quantity
Of every knowledge, yet brings all home

---

107 *bounce* the noise made by an explosion, the explosion itself (*OED* n.[1] 2), often (as probably here) representing gunfire (cf. *King John*, II.i.462; *2 Henry IV*, III.ii.280)
    falls i.e from a shot or explosion; but here with a sexual innuendo

108 *upper room* Perhaps includes a satiric glance at the audience, since 'room' was the contemporary term for a theatre 'box' (see Holdsworth, *Casebook*, p. 269).

111 *left-handed Orlando* clumsy imitation (*OED left-handed* a. 2) of the hero of Ariosto's epic *Orlando Furioso*

113–14 *'Tis . . . change* Antonio's abandonment of his fool persona is signified by his shift to a slightly pompous style of blank verse. His reference to this 'change' acts as reminder of his own role as the nominal 'changeling' of the title (see also l. 118).

114 *amazing* full of amazement; but Antonio may also be referring to the power of her eye to throw a lover into confusion and bewilderment. Literally speaking, to be 'amazed' is to be trapped in a maze or labyrinth – a recurrent motif in *The Changeling* (cf. III.iii.71; IV.iii.98–100; V.iii.148).

121 *scrutinous* searching
    sciences branches of learning

122 *cunning* skilful

Into one mystery, into one secret
That he proceeds in.

ISABELLA   You're a parlous fool.   125

ANTONIO
No danger in me: I bring nought but Love
And his soft wounding shafts to strike you with –
Try but one arrow; if it hurt you,
I'll stand you twenty back in recompence.   [*Kisses her*]

ISABELLA
A forward fool, too!

ANTONIO   This was Love's teaching: 130
A thousand ways he fashioned out my way,
And this I found the safest and the nearest
To tread the galaxia to my star.

ISABELLA
Profound withal! Certain you dreamed of this –
Love never taught it waking.

ANTONIO   Take no acquaintance   135
Of these outward follies; there is within
A gentleman that loves you.

ISABELLA   When I see him,
I'll speak with him; so in the meantime
Keep your habit, it becomes you well enough.
As you are a gentleman, I'll not discover you –   140
That's all the favour that you must expect.
When you are weary, you may leave the school,
For all this while you have but played the fool.

Enter LOLLIO

---

124 *mystery* religious truth known by revelation (hence part of the religious language of
courtly love); hidden or secret thing (*OED* n. 2, 5a). Cf. also IV.i.25, 38. For the bawdy
sense of *mystery* and *secret*, see Williams, *Glossary*, pp. 212, 271, and above I.ii.1.
125 *proceeds* advances in a course of study (as to a university degree)
parlous (1) dangerously cunning; (a) awful, extraordinary (*OED* a. 2)
126 *Love* i.e. Cupid /Amor
127–8 *soft . . . arrow* Antonio exploits the phallic suggestiveness of Cupid's arrows.
129 *stand* give
130 *forward* (1) presumptuous; (2) lustful – see Ricks (pp. 298–300)
131 *he* ed. (she Q)
132 *the nearest* ed. (nearest Q)
133 *tread* The bawdy sense ('copulate') is probably hinted at.
galaxia i.e the Milky Way
136 *outward . . . within* Continues the motif of secrets within (cf. I.i.159).
discover expose

ANTONIO [*Seeing him*]

    And must again. – He he! I thank you, cousin,

    I'll be your valentine tomorrow morning.   145

LOLLIO

    How do you like the fool, mistress?

ISABELLA

    Passing well, sir.

LOLLIO

    Is he not witty, pretty well for a fool?

ISABELLA

    If he hold on as he begins, he is like

    To come to something!   150

LOLLIO

    Ay, thank a good tutor: you may put him to't; he begins to
answer pretty hard questions. – Tony, how many is five times
six?

ANTONIO

    Five times six, is six times five.

LOLLIO

    What arithmetician could have answered better? How many is   155
one hundred and seven?

ANTONIO

    One hundred and seven, is seven hundred and one, cousin.

LOLLIO

    This is no wit to speak on: will you be rid of the fool now?

ISABELLA

    By no means, let him stay a little.

MADMAN (*Within*)

    Catch there, catch the last couple in hell!   160

LOLLIO

    Again! Must I come amongst you? Would my master were come
home! I am not able to govern both these wards together.   *Exit*

---

145 *valentine ... morning* Perhaps influenced by a song that the mad Ophelia sings in
Hamlet (IV.v.48–66).

147 *Passing* Exceedingly

150 *come to something* With a bawdy *double entendre* (Williams, *Glossary*, pp. 75, 306–7).

151 *put him to't ... hard* Bawdy *double entendre* (*put to* = insert penis; see Williams, *Glossary*,
p. 251).

160 *Catch ... hell* Cry from the popular game known as 'Barley-brake', referred to by
Deflores at V.iii.162–4. The game was played by couples holding hands: one couple were
confined to a circle, known as 'hell', and would try to catch the other couples as they ran
through it; those caught would have to replace the couple in hell, and the game continued until every pair had served its term there.

ANTONIO

Why should a minute of love's hour be lost?

ISABELLA

Fie, out again! I had rather you kept

Your other posture; you become not your tongue,   165

When you speak from your clothes.

ANTONIO   How can he freeze

Lives near so sweet a warmth? Shall I alone

Walk through the orchard of the Hesperides

And cowardly not dare to pull an apple?

This with the red cheeks I must venture for.   [*Kisses her*]   170

Enter LOLLIO *above*

ISABELLA

Take heed, there's giants keep 'em.

LOLLIO [*Aside*]

How now fool, are you good at that? Have you read Lipsius?

He's past *Ars Amandi*; I believe I must put harder questions to

him, I perceive that –

ISABELLA

You are bold – without fear, too.

ANTONIO   What should I fear,   175

Having all joys about me? Do you but smile,

164 *out* out of your role
166 *you . . . clothes* you talk unbecomingly when you speak in a way that does not match
     your fool's costume
167 *Lives* That lives
168 *orchard of the Hesperides* At the rim of the Western world, this orchard, tended by the
     nymphs of the evening (Hesperides), bore golden apples that were guarded by a
     ferocious dragon. Hercules' penultimate task was to pluck three of its apples.
170 s.d.2 Lollio enters to spy on Isabella, as Deflores has previously done on Beatrice-Joanna
     in II.ii. In both scenes the treacherous servant plans to use his discoveries to blackmail
     erotic favours from his mistress. For the possibility that the original staging may have
     given visual emphasis to the parallel, see II.ii.57.
171 *giants keep 'em* A mocking reference to Alibius and Lollio as keepers of the madhouse;
     Isabella's substitution of giants for the dragon of the original myth may be an indication
     that she has caught sight of Lollio above.
172 *Lipsius* renaissance scholar and populariser of neo-Stoic moral philosophy; but included
     here for the pun on 'lips'
173 *Ars Amandi* Ovid's much imitated poem *The Art of Love* was the most popular erotic
     manual of the day.
176 *but smile* ed. (smile Q) – Lollio's otherwise completely accurate repetition of this speech
     at ll. 217–24 suggests that the compositor accidentally omitted 'but' from a line he
     already had difficulty accommodating.

And Love shall play the wanton on your lip,
Meet and retire, retire and meet again;
Look you but cheerfully, and in your eyes
I shall behold mine own deformity,   180
And dress my self up fairer; I know this shape
Becomes me not, but in those bright mirrors
I shall array me handsomely.

LOLLIO   Cuckoo, cuckoo –   *Exit*

[*Enter*] MADMEN *above, some as birds, others as beasts,* [*uttering*
fearful cries]

ANTONIO
What are these?
ISABELLA   Of fear enough to part us,
Yet are they but our schools of lunatics,   185
That act their fantasies in any shapes
Suiting their present thoughts: if sad, they cry;
If mirth be their conceit, they laugh again;
Sometimes they imitate the beasts and birds,
Singing, or howling, braying, barking – all   190
As their wild fancies prompt 'em.

Enter LOLLIO.

ANTONIO   These are no fears.
ISABELLA
But here's a large one, my man.
ANTONIO
Ha he! That's fine sport indeed, cousin.
LOLLIO [*Aside*]
I would my master were come home! 'Tis too much for one

---

178 *Meet and retire* Kissing is imagined as a kind of playful combat, orchestrated by Cupid.
179–80 *in ... deformity* Compare the way in which Deflores is forced to contemplate his
    own 'deformity' in Beatrice's eyes (see e.g. II.i.26–51).
183 *cuckoo* Suggesting that Alibius is about to be cuckolded ('cuckold' derives from
    'cuckoo').
    s.d. Appearing as though in response to Lollio's cry of 'cuckoo', the madmen's
    grotesquerie appears like a quasi-allegorical representation of the bestial passions
    hidden beneath the surface of the play-world, just as their madness mirrors the love-
    madness that possesses so many of the play's superficially sane characters.

shepherd to govern two of these flocks; nor can I believe that   195
one churchman can instruct two benefices at once: there will be
some incurable mad of the one side, and very fools on the other.
– [*Aloud*] Come, Tony.

ANTONIO
Prithee, cousin, let me stay here still.

LOLLIO
No, you must to your book, now you have played sufficiently.   200

ISABELLA
Your fool is grown wondrous witty.

LOLLIO
Well, I'll say nothing; but I do not think but he will put you
down one of these days.

Exeunt LOLLIO *and* ANTONIO

ISABELLA
Here the restrainèd current might make breach,
Spite of the watchful bankers. Would a woman stray,   205
She need not gad abroad to seek her sin –
It would be brought home one ways or other:
The needle's point will to the fixèd north,
Such drawing Arctics women's beauties are.

Enter LOLLIO

LOLLIO
How dost thou, sweet rogue?   210

ISABELLA
How now?

LOLLIO
Come, there are degrees – one fool may be better than another.

ISABELLA
What's the matter?

---

196 *one churchman . . . at once* The corrupt practice of drawing income from more than one
living at a time was widely denounced in the period.
202–3 *put you down* (1) beat or surpass you (*OED* v. 42 e–f); (2) subdue you sexually
(Williams, *Glossary*, pp. 250–1)
205 *bankers* builders of protective banks and dikes (*OED* n.³ 2)
208 *needle's point* Phallic *double-entendre*.

LOLLIO

    Nay, if thou giv'st thy mind to fools'-flesh, have at thee!

                            [Tries to kiss her]

ISABELLA

    You bold slave, you!   215

LOLLIO

    I could follow now as t'other fool did:

    'What should I fear,

    Having all joys about me? Do you but smile,

    And Love shall play the wanton on your lip,

    Meet and retire, retire and meet again;   220

    Look you but cheerfully, and in your eyes

    I shall behold my own deformity,

    And dress my self up fairer; I know this shape

    Becomes me not –'

    And so as it follows; but is not this the more foolish way? Come,   225

    sweet rogue: kiss me, my little Lacedemonian. Let me feel how

    thy pulses beat. Thou hast a thing about thee would do a man

    pleasure, I'll lay my hand on't.   *[Grabs indecently at her]*

ISABELLA

    Sirrah, no more! I see you have discovered

    This love's knight-errant, who hath made adventure   230

    For purchase of my love. Be silent, mute –

    Mute as a statue – or his injunction

    For me enjoying shall be to cut thy throat:

    I'll do it, though for no other purpose;

    And be sure he'll not refuse it.   235

LOLLIO

    My share, that's all! I'll have my fool's part with you.

ISABELLA

    No more – your master!

Enter ALIBIUS

226 *Lacedemonian* Spartan – i.e. 'whore' (by analogy with Helen of Troy, the adulterous former Queen of Sparta; and perhaps involving, as Sampson suggests, a play on 'laced mutton' – a cant term for a prostitute).

227 *thing* i.e. her sex

228 s.d. This edition (*not in* Q)

230 *knight-errant . . . purchase* The bathetic descent from the 'adventure' of knight-errantry (associated with courtly love) to the merchant venturing of 'purchase' is significant.

236 *part* (1) share; (2) role; (3) sexual organ (Williams, *Glossary*, p. 247) – cf. the fool's 'bauble' (above, l. 101)

ALIBIUS   Sweet, how dost thou?

ISABELLA

Your bounden servant, sir.

ALIBIUS   Fie, fie, sweetheart,

No more of that!

ISABELLA   You were best lock me up.

ALIBIUS

In my arms and bosom, my sweet Isabella,   240
I'll lock thee up most nearly. Lollio,
We have employment, we have task in hand.
At noble Vermandero's, our castle-captain,
There is a nuptial to be solemnized –
Beatrice Joanna, his fair daughter, bride –   245
For which the gentleman hath bespoke our pains:
A mixture of our madmen and our fools,
To finish, as it were, and make the fag
Of all the revels, the third night from the first;
Only an unexpected passage-over   250
To make a frightful pleasure, that is all –
But not the all I aim at: could we so act it,
To teach it in a wild, distracted measure,
Though out of form and figure, breaking Time's head,
It were no matter, 'twould be healed again   255
In one age or other, if not in this.
This, this, Lollio! [*Shows him money*]
                     There's a good reward begun,
And will beget a bounty, be it known.

LOLLIO

This is easy, sir, I'll warrant you – you have about you fools and

---

238 *bounden* (1) under obligation for favours received; (2) tied with the bonds of matrimony; (3) made fast in bonds or prison (*OED* ppl. a. 4, 2c, 2a)
241 *nearly* (1) intimately; (2) narrowly, under close surveillance (*OED* adv. 2, 1a)
248 *fag* fag-end (*OED* n.² 2)
250–1 *unexpected . . . pleasure* the madmen will give the guests a delightful frisson of alarm by suddenly rushing through the festivities
253 *measure* dance
254 *out . . . figure* ignoring all the customary patterns of the dance
    breaking . . . head Alibius's conceit imagines a dance so extravagantly out of time as to break the head of Father Time himself.
257–8 This passage (like much of Alibius' excited speech) has caused commentators some difficulty; but it makes best sense to assume that *This, this* refers to the first part of their reward, an advance payment from Vermandero, which Alibius flourishes as an earnest of the even greater *bounty* (l. 258) that will follow, if they succeed.

madmen that can dance very well; and 'tis no wonder: your best   260
dancers are not the wisest men – the reason is, with often
jumping they jolt their brains down into their feet, that their
wits lie more in their heels than in their heads.

ALIBIUS

Honest Lollio, thou giv'st me a good reason,
And a comfort in it.

ISABELLA   You've a fine trade on't: 265
Madmen and fools are a staple commodity!

ALIBIUS

O wife, we must eat, wear clothes, and live:
Just at the lawyers' haven we arrive,
By madmen and by fools we both do thrive.

                                    Exeunt

[ACT III. SCENE iii.]

Enter VERMANDERO, ALSEMERO, JASPERINO, *and* BEATRICE

VERMANDERO

Valencia speaks so nobly of you, sir,
I wish I had a daughter now for you.

ALSEMERO

The fellow of this creature were a partner
For a king's love.

VERMANDERO   I had her fellow once, sir;
But heaven has married her to joys eternal,   5
'Twere sin to wish her in this vale again.
Come, sir, your friend and you shall see the pleasures
Which my health chiefly joys in.

ALSEMERO

I hear the beauty of this seat largely.

268–9 *Just . . . thrive* Asylum keepers and lawyers both grow rich by exploiting the same
    victims, because only a fool or a madman would put his faith in lawyers (or the law).
III.iii Author: Middleton
  6 *vale* i.e. the world (as in the proverbial 'vale of tears')
  9 *largely* [proclaimed] generally, in the world at large (*OED* adv. 4)

VERMANDERO

It falls much short of that.

Exeunt, except for BEATRICE

BEATRICE   So, here's one step   10
Into my father's favour – time will fix him.
I have got him now the liberty of the house.
So wisdom by degrees works out her freedom:
And if that eye be darkened that offends me –
I wait but that eclipse – this gentleman   15
Shall soon shine glorious in my father's liking
Through the refulgent virtue of my love.

Enter DEFLORES

DEFLORES

My thoughts are at a banquet for the deed;
I feel no weight in't, 'tis but light and cheap
For the sweet recompense, that I set down for't.   20

BEATRICE

Deflores?

DEFLORES   Lady?

BEATRICE   Thy looks promise cheerfully.

DEFLORES

All things are answerable: time, circumstance,
Your wishes and my service.

BEATRICE   Is it done, then?

DEFLORES

Piracquo is no more.

BEATRICE

My joys start at mine eyes; our sweet'st delights   25
Are evermore born weeping.

---

11 *fix him* install him permanently (*OED* v. 8c)
14 *eye . . . offends* Cf. Matthew 18:9, Mark 9:47: 'And if thine eye offend thee, pluck it out'; the ironic implication is that the true offence lies in her own eye.
14–15 *darkened . . . eclipse* Beatrice refers to the moment when the light of life is extinguished in Alonzo; but her conceit also depends on the old idea of the sun as the 'eye of heaven'.
17 *refulgent* radiantly reflecting
virtue (1) power, (superhuman) influence; (2) moral goodness (*OED* n. 1–2)
19 *weight* i.e. of sin
20 *For* Compared with

DEFLORES   I've a token for you.

BEATRICE

For me?

DEFLORES But it was sent somewhat unwillingly –

                                        [*Shows the finger*]

I could not get the ring without the finger.

BEATRICE

Bless me! What hast thou done?

DEFLORES   Why, is that more

Than killing the whole man? I cut his heart-strings!   30

A greedy hand thrust in a dish at court

In a mistake hath had as much as this.

BEATRICE

'Tis the first token my father made me send him.

DEFLORES

And I made him send it back again

For his last token; I was loath to leave it   35

And I'm sure dead men have no use of jewels –

He was as loath to part with't, for it stuck

As if the flesh and it were both one substance.

BEATRICE

At the stag's fall the keeper has his fees –

'Tis soon applied: all dead men's fees are yours, sir,   40

I pray bury the finger, but the stone

You may make use on shortly – the true value

(Take't of my truth) is near three hundred ducats.

31–2 *A greedy . . . this* A recognised peril of contemporary banqueting tables, when diners helped themselves from communal dishes with the aid of sharp knives: a similar episode, involving the poet Thomas Randolph, is recounted in William Heminges' satiric 'Elegy on Randolph's Finger' (1632).

31 *thrust . . . dish* Suspecting a bawdy *double entendre* in *dish* (= 'woman as sexual object' – see *Anthony and Cleopatra*, II.vii.125), Daalder sees *thrust* as underlining the phallic suggestiveness of the finger.

36 *jewels* also = 'maidenheads'

38 *As . . . substance* Echoing the biblical notion (repeated in the Anglican marriage service) that man and wife 'shall be one flesh' (Genesis 2:21–4; Matthew 19:6), the ring serves as a reminder that the bond between Alonzo and Beatrice is theoretically unbreakable, since for most purposes a formal betrothal was granted the full moral force of matrimony.

39 *At . . . fees* A warden or 'keeper' could claim the skin, head, and other parts of any deer killed in his killed in his game-park.

40 *applied* i.e. the proverb-like remark can be readily applied to Deflores' situation.

43 *three hundred ducats* i.e. about 135 pounds (a gold ducat was worth about nine shillings) – a gentleman could live modestly on 100 pounds per annum

DEFLORES

    'Twill hardly buy a capcase for one's conscience, though,

    To keep it from the worm, as fine as 'tis.   45

    Well, being my fees, I'll take it –

    Great men have taught me that, or else my merit

    Would scorn the way on't.

BEATRICE   It might justly, sir.

    Why thou mistak'st, Deflores: 'tis not given

    In state of recompence.

DEFLORES   No? I hope so, lady: 50

    You should soon witness my contempt to't then.

BEATRICE

    Prithee, thou look'st as if thou wert offended.

DEFLORES

    That were strange, lady: 'tis not possible

    My service should draw such a cause from you.

    Offended? Could you think so? That were much   55

    For one of my performance, and so warm

    Yet in my service.

BEATRICE

    'Twere misery in me to give you cause, sir.

DEFLORES

    I know so much, it were so – misery

    In her most sharp condition.

BEATRICE   'Tis resolved then.   60

    Look you, sir, here's three thousand golden florins:

    I have not meanly thought upon thy merit.

44 *capcase* travelling case, casket, or chest
45 *worm* the gnawings of remorse. Frost suggests a further allusion to the sufferings of hell –
   'where their worm dieth not, and the fire is never quenched' (Mark 9:46, 48) – described
   in the same passage echoed at l. 15 above.
50 *state* way
53–7 *'tis . . . service* In *Gerardo*, the lecherous Biscayner similarly prefaces his sexual conquest of Isdaura by demanding gratitude for 'my good deeds and service' (sig. H4).
   Deflores' language, though ostensibly referring to his murder of Alonzo, is full of sexual
   innuendo (*performance . . . warm . . . service*).
54 *cause* accusation (*OED* n. 9)
56 *warm* energetic, ardent (*OED* a. 10a)
58 *'Twere . . . me* It would make me miserable
   misery miserliness
61 *three . . . florins* about three hundred pounds (a florin was worth about two shillings)

DEFLORES

What, salary? Now you move me!

BEATRICE   How, Deflores?

DEFLORES

Do you place me in the rank of verminous fellows

To destroy things for wages? Offer gold?   65

The life blood of man! Is any thing

Valued too precious for my recompence?

BEATRICE

I understand thee not.

DEFLORES   I could ha' hired

A journeyman in murder at this rate,

And mine own conscience might have slept at ease,   70

And have had the work brought home.

BEATRICE [*Aside*]   I'm in a labyrinth:

What will content him? I would fain be rid of him.

[*Aloud*] I'll double the sum, sir.

DEFLORES   You take a course

To double my vexation, that's the good you do.

BEATRICE [*Aside*]

Bless me! I am now in worse plight than I was;   75

I know not what will please him. [*Aloud*] For my fear's sake,

---

63 *salary* financial reward (*OED* n. 2)
  move enrage (*OED* n. 9b)
64–5 *Do ... wages* The degradation of feudal service (seen as dependent on reciprocal bonds of obligation) into a mere wage-relationship is a recurrent theme amongst early modern writers on service, such as 'I.M.', who deplore how the old 'kind usage and friendly familiarity', which made domestic service in a great household a suitable calling for a gentleman, has been replaced by the humiliation of 'reward only with bare wages' (pp. 147–58).
64 *rank* In the context of *verminous* (= infested with parasites) a play on *rank* = evil-smelling is likely.
69 *journeyman* 'one who, having served his apprenticeship to a handicraft or trade, is qualified to work at it for days' wages . . . as the servant or employee of another' *OED* n. 1) – in the mouth of the gentleman-born, Deflores, the term is charged with intense social contempt.
70 *slept at ease* ed. (*not in* Q). Most editors accept this conjecture, since the Q line is obviously incomplete.
71 *brought home* either (i) 'delivered to me by someone who had already carried it out' (Daalder); or (ii) 'brought to its intended conclusion' (*OED home* adv. 4a); or perhaps (iii) 'have got someone else to carry out the job in a forcible manner' – cf. l. 87 (Bawcutt 1998)
  labyrinth Sounded as two syllables here ('lab'rinth'). The audience are probably expected to remember the original *labyrinth* of ancient Crete, at whose centre lurked the hideous Minotaur, monstrous offspring of Queen Pasiphae's adultery with a bull, which brought death to anyone penetrating the maze (cf. III.ii.114; IV.iii.97–100; V.iii.148).

I prithee make away with all speed possible;
And if thou be'st so modest not to name
The sum that will content thee, paper blushes not –
Send thy demand in writing, it shall follow thee;   80
But prithee take thy flight.
DEFLORES   You must fly too then.
BEATRICE
  I?
DEFLORES I'll not stir a foot else.
BEATRICE   What's your meaning?
DEFLORES
  Why are not you as guilty, in (I'm sure)
  As deep as I? And we should stick together.
  Come, your fears counsel you but ill: my absence   85
  Would draw suspect upon you instantly;
  There were no rescue for you.
BEATRICE   He speaks home.
DEFLORES
  Nor is it fit we two, engaged so jointly,
  Should part and live asunder.   [*Tries to kiss her*]
BEATRICE   How now, sir?
  This shows not well.
DEFLORES   What makes your lip so strange?   90
  This must not be betwixt us.
BEATRICE [*Aside*]   The man talks wildly.
DEFLORES
  Come kiss me with a zeal now.
BEATRICE [*Aside*]   Heaven, I doubt him!
DEFLORES
  I will not stand so long to beg 'em shortly.
BEATRICE
  Take heed, Deflores, of forgetfulness:
  'Twill soon betray us.

---

84 *stick* Significantly, the same verb used to describe the bond between ring and finger
   (l. 37).
86 *suspect* Accent on second syllable.
87 *speaks home* addresses the very heart of the matter (*OED* adv. 5a)
88 *engaged so jointly* so mutually committed to this business (*OED engage* v. 13); but quib-
   bling on *engaged* and *joint*, as a reminder of the bond symbolised by ring and finger
90 *strange* like that of a stranger
92 *doubt* dread
94 *forgetfulness* i.e. of your rank and station

DEFLORES   Take you heed first!   95
    Faith, you're grown much forgetful, you're to blame in't.
BEATRICE
    He's bold, and I am blamed for't.
DEFLORES   I have eased you
    Of your trouble – think on't: I'm in pain,
    And must be eased of you; 'tis a charity.
    Justice invites your blood to understand me.   100
BEATRICE
    I dare not.
DEFLORES   Quickly.
BEATRICE   Oh, I never shall!
    Speak it yet further off, that I may lose
    What has been spoken, and no sound remain on't.
    I would not hear so much offence again
    For such another deed.
DEFLORES   Soft, lady, soft –   105
    The last is not yet paid for! Oh, this act
    Has put me into spirit; I was as greedy on't
    As the parched earth of moisture when the clouds weep.
    Did you not mark, I wrought my self into't –
    Nay, sued and kneeled for't? Why was all that pains took?   110
    You see I have thrown contempt upon your gold:
    Not that I want it not, for I do piteously –
    In order I will come unto't, and make use on't –
    But 'twas not held so precious to begin with,
    For I place wealth after the heels of pleasure;   115
    And were I not resolved in my belief

---

96 *forgetful* i.e. of your obligations to me (and of the situation in which the crime has placed you)

97 *eased* (1) relieved from pain; (2) purged (*OED* v. 1a; 1c) – compare the dying Beatrice's metaphor at V.iii.150–3. In *Gerardo* the Biscayner similarly presses his affections on Isdaura by presenting his desire as a 'torment . . . mischief and sickness' for which only she can serve as 'the antidote and wholesome physician' (sig. H4–H4v).

100 *your blood* (1) your aristocratic nature; (2) your desire; (3) your bloody disposition; (4) the blood with which your crime has stained you

105 *Soft* Exclamation to enjoin silence or deprecate haste (*OED* adv. 8a).

107 *spirit* (1) courage (*OED* n. 13a); (2) sexual desire – sometimes used as a euphemism for the penis, or for semen (Williams, *Glossary*, pp. 284–5)

107–8 *I . . . moisture* Cf. II.ii.133.

112 *it not* ed. (it Q). The emendation is required by both sense and metre.

That thy virginity were perfect in thee,
I should but take my recompense with grudging,
As if I had but half my hopes I agreed for.

BEATRICE

Why 'tis impossible thou canst be so wicked,   120
Or shelter such a cunning cruelty,
To make his death the murderer of my honour.
Thy language is so bold and vicious,
I cannot see which way I can forgive it
With any modesty.

DEFLORES   Push! You forget yourself: 125
A woman dipped in blood, and talk of modesty?

BEATRICE

O misery of sin! Would I had been bound
Perpetually unto my living hate
In that Piracquo, than to hear these words.
Think but upon the distance that creation   130
Set 'twixt thy blood and mine, and keep thee there.

DEFLORES

Look but into your conscience, read me there –
'Tis a true book, you'll find me there your equal.
Push! Fly not to your birth, but settle you
In what the act has made you, you're no more now;   135
You must forget your parentage to me –
You're the deed's creature: by that name
You lost your first condition; and I challenge you,
As peace and innocency has turned you out
And made you one with me.

BEATRICE   With thee, foul villain?   140

DEFLORES

Yes, my fair murd'ress; do you urge me?
Though thou writ'st 'maid', thou whore in thy affection,

136 *to me* when talking to me; as far as I am concerned
137 *creature* (1) creation (like the fallen Eve, Beatrice has lost her innocent 'first condition'
     and been, in effect, created anew); (2) puppet, slave (*OED* n. 1a; 5)
138 *challenge you* assert my title to you
140 *one with me* i.e. Beatrice has become 'one flesh' with Deflores (elucidating the new
     symbolism of the finger and ring)
     foul (1) wicked, guilty; (2) physically loathsome, ugly (*OED* a. 7a–b; 1a)
141 *urge* provoke to anger (*OED* v. 7b)
142 *whore . . . heart* Cf. Matthew 5:28.

'Twas changed from thy first love – and that's a kind
Of whoredom in thy heart – and he's changed now
To bring thy second on, thy Alsemero,   145
Whom (by all sweets that ever darkness tasted!)
If I enjoy thee not, thou ne'er enjoy'st:
I'll blast the hopes and joys of marriage,
I'll confess all – my life I rate at nothing.

BEATRICE

Deflores –

DEFLORES   I shall rest from all love's plagues then,   150
I live in pain now: that flame-shooting eye
Will burn my heart to cinders.

BEATRICE   O sir, hear me!

DEFLORES

She that in life and love refuses me,
In death and shame my partner she shall be.

BEATRICE

Stay, hear me once for all! [*Kneels*] I make thee master   155
Of all the wealth I have in gold and jewels:
Let me go poor unto my bed with honour,
And I am rich in all things.

DEFLORES   Let this silence thee,
The wealth of all Valencia shall not buy
My pleasure from me.   160
Can you weep Fate from its determined purpose?
So soon may you weep me.

143–5 *'Twas . . . Alsemero* Cf. V.iii.197–8.
143 *first love* In contrast to Reynolds, Middleton and Rowley never suggest that Piracquo
    was simply foisted on Beatrice by her father.
144 *changed* i.e. by death
146 *sweets* sexual pleasures
149 *confess* Stress on first syllable.
150 *love's* ed. (lovers Q)
151 *flame-shooting* This edition (shooting Q; Dyce: love-shooting; Craik: fire-shooting). The
    line is metrically deficient and some addition is also needed to clarify the sense. The
    idea of darts or flames being discharged from the mistress' eyes is a common trope in
    Renaissance love-poetry (cf. I.i.216).
155 s.d. *Kneels* Deflores' 'Come, rise' at l. 166 makes it clear that Beatrice kneels at some
    point in this closing dialogue – by echoing Deflores' kneeling at II.ii.117, the gesture
    expresses the reversed power-relationship between them. In the 1993 BBC production,
    Deflores knelt with her on 'Let this silence thee'.
155 *master* A loaded word, in the context of Deflores' servile position in the household.
161 *determined* (1) resolute; (2) pre-ordained, predestined (*OED* ppl. a. 7a; 4)
162 *you* ed. (*not in* Q)

BEATRICE   Vengeance begins:
  Murder, I see, is followed by more sins.
  Was my creation in the womb so cursed,
  It must engender with a viper first?   165
DEFLORES
  Come, rise, and shroud your blushes in my bosom.

                                                  [*Raises her*]

  Silence is one of pleasure's best receipts:
  Thy peace is wrought for ever in this yielding.
  'Las, how the turtle pants! Thou'lt love anon
  What thou so fear'st and faint'st to venture on.   170

                                           Exeunt

ACT IV. [SCENE i.]

[*Dumb show*]

Enter GENTLEMEN, VERMANDERO *meeting them with action of
wonderment at the flight of* PIRACQUO. *Enter* ALSEMERO, *with*
JASPERINO *and* GALLANTS; VERMANDERO *points to him, the*
GENTLEMEN *seeming to applaud the choice.*
[*Exeunt in procession* VERMANDERO,] ALSEMERO, JASPERINO,
and GENTLEMEN. [*Enter*] BEATRICE *the Bride following* [*them*

---

165 *viper* Cf. I.i.218.
167 *receipts* (1) recipes – or drugs compounded from a recipe; (2) things received, payments
    (*OED* n. 1–2; 3)
168–70 *Thy . . . thou* Deflores' sudden switch from the respectful 'you' marks a turning-
    point in the play: here the singular pronoun expresses intimacy, but also registers the
    reversal of power-relations between mistress and servant as a consequence of his 'mas-
    ter-sin' (V.iii.199); in the 1993 BBC version Beatrice kissed Deflores on 'Thou'lt love
    anon . . .'.
168 *peace* Perhaps emphasising Beatrice's newly subordinate position by playing on the
    quietus est that marked a master's formal discharge of a servant from duty.
169 *'Las . . . on* Middleton may intend an ironic echo of the Epithalamium in Ben Jonson's,
    marriage masque, *Hymenaei*, written to celebrate Frances Howard's first wedding:
    'Shrink not, soft virgin, you will love / Anon what you so fear to prove' – see Lisa
    Hopkins, 'Beguiling the Master of the Mystery,' *MRDE* 9 (1997), 149–61 (154–5).
    turtle turtle-dove (a symbol of love)
    pants For panting as an expression of orgasmic excitement, see Williams, *Glossary*, p.
    121 (citing *Othello*, II.i.81, and *Anthony and Cleopatra*, IV.ix.16).
IV.i Author: Middleton

across the stage] in great state, accompanied with DIAPHANTA,
ISABELLA, *and other* GENTLEWOMEN. [*Enter*] DEFLORES *after all,*
smiling at the accident; ALONZO's *Ghost appears to* DEFLORES *in*
the midst of his smile, startles him, showing him the hand whose
finger he had cut off. They pass over in great solemnity [and
exeunt].

Enter BEATRICE

BEATRICE

This fellow has undone me endlessly:
Never was bride so fearfully distressed.
The more I think upon th'ensuing night,
And whom I am to cope with in embraces –
One that's ennobled both in blood and mind,   5
So clear in understanding (that's my plague now),
Before whose judgement will my fault appear
Like malefactors' crimes before tribunals,
(There is no hiding on't) – the more I dive
Into my own distress. How a wise man   10
Stands for a great calamity! There's no venturing
Into his bed, what course soe'er I light upon,
Without my shame, which may grow up to danger:
He cannot but in justice strangle me
As I lie by him, as a cheater use me.   15
'Tis a precious craft to play with a false die
Before a cunning gamester: here's his closet,

---

  1 *fellow* (1) person of humble station, servant; (2) accomplice (*OED* n. 10a; 1b)
    undone (1) destroyed; (2) ruined by seducing (*OED* v. 8a; 8d)
    endlessly eternally
  2 *fearfully distressed* terribly tormented; tormented by fear
  4 *cope with* have to do with (*OED* v. 5); encounter sexually (Williams, *Glossary*, p. 81)
  5 *that's* ed. (both Q)
 11 *Stands for* Can be reckoned as (*OED* v. 71 f)
 16 *precious* Ironic (= 'worthless', *OED* a. 4b).
    die dice (original singular form)
 17 *Before* Under the attention of
    closet small private room or study; or, a private repository of valuables (*OED* n. 1a, c; 3a).
    For the closet as a place of secrets, see Angel Day, *The English Secretary* (1586), ii. 103
    (cited in *OED*) 'We do call the most secret place in the house appropriate unto our own
    private studies . . . a Closet.' Because in early modern households the closet was one of
    the few rooms likely to be locked, in allegorized descriptions of the human body it was
    frequently used to figure the privacies of the heart.

The key left in't, and he abroad i'th' park –
Sure, 'twas forgot; I'll be so bold as look in't.
Bless me! A right physician's closet 'tis,   20
Set round with vials, every one her mark too.
Sure he does practise physic for his own use,
Which may be safely called your great man's wisdom.
What manuscript lies here? '*The Book of Experiment,*
Called Secrets in Nature' – so 'tis, 'tis so: 25
'How to know whether a woman be with child or no' –
I hope I am not yet – if he should try though!
Let me see: folio forty-five – here 'tis,
The leaf tucked down upon't, the place suspicious:
'If you would know whether a woman be with child or   30
not, give her two spoonfuls of the white water in Glass C' –
Where's that Glass C? Oh, yonder I see't now –
'and if she be with child, she sleeps full twelve hours after, if not,
not.'
None of that water comes into my belly: 35
I'll know you from a hundred; I could break you now
Or turn you into milk, and so beguile
The master of the mystery, but I'll look to you.
Ha! That which is next, is ten times worse:
'How to know whether a woman be a maid, or not.'   40
If that should be applied, what would become of me?
Belike he has a strong faith of my purity,
That never yet made proof; but this he calls
'A merry sleight, but true experiment' –
The author 'Antonius Mizaldus':   45

21 *every one her mark* each duly labelled (*OED mark* n. 11a)
22 *physic* medicine
23 *Which ... wisdom* Because great men are vulnerable to attempts on their lives, especially through poisoning
24–5 *The ... Nature* The title translates that of a work by the French scholar Antonius Mizaldus (1520–78), *De Arcanis Naturae*. However, the tests discovered by Beatrice do not appear in that book – though similar ones are described in his *Centuriae IX. Memorabilium*. The fact that Mizaldus is mentioned by name in the passage quoted at ll. 44 ff. suggests that this is a manuscript compilation put together by Alsemero himself.
35 *water* Cf. II.ii.83.
38 *master of the mystery* Apparently echoing Jonson's *Alchemist*, 4.1.122, where Sir Epicure Mammon, relishing the prospect of success in his alchemical project, declares himself 'master of the mastery'.
    mystery (1) highly technical practice in a trade or art; (2) secret (*OED* n. 8; 5a)
    look to watch out for
43 *That ... proof* Who has never put it to the test

'Give the party you suspect the quantity of a spoonful
of the water in the glass M, which upon her that is a maid
makes three several effects: 'twill make her incontinently
gape, then fall into a sudden sneezing, last into a violent
laughing – else dull, heavy and lumpish.'   50
Where had I been?
I fear it, yet 'tis seven hours to bedtime.

Enter DIAPHANTA

DIAPHANTA
Cuds, madam, are you here?
BEATRICE [*Aside*]   Seeing that wench now,
A trick comes in my mind: 'tis a nice piece
Gold cannot purchase; [*Aloud*] I come hither, wench,   55
To look my lord.
DIAPHANTA [*Aside*] Would I had such a cause
To look him too. [*Aloud*] Why, he's i' th' park, madam.
BEATRICE
There let him be.
DIAPHANTA   Ay, madam, let him compass
Whole parks and forests, as great rangers do,
At roosting-time a little lodge can hold 'em.   60
Earth-conquering Alexander, that thought the world
Too narrow for him, in the end had but his pit-hole.

46–50 *Give ... lumpish* Although the Alsemero's virginity test may appear absurd to
    modern eyes, it is not so different from some of those seriously propounded in con-
    temporary medical treatises (see Dale J. Randall, 'Some Observations on the Theme of
    Chastity in *The Changeling*', *ELR* 14 (1984), 347–66).
48 *several* different
    incontinently immediately
50 *lumpish* stupidly lethargic
51 *Where ... been* What would have become of me (if I had not found out)
53 *Cuds* Contraction of 'God save me'.
54 *nice* scrupulous (*OED* a. 7d)
    piece woman (Williams, *Glossary*, p. 234)
56 *look* seek (*OED* v. 6d)
59 *parks and forests* With sexual innuendo (for *park* = 'woman as sexual landscape', see
    Williams, *Glossary*, p. 228).
    ranger (1) forest officer, gamekeeper; (2) rover, rake (*OED* n. 2a; 1a)
60 *roosting-time* bedtime
61–2 *Earth ... pit-hole* For another example of this trope, which can be traced back to
    Juvenal, *Satire* X, 168–72, see *Hamlet*, V.i.192 ff.
62 *pit-hole* (1) grave; (2) vagina (see Williams, *Glossary*, pp. 159, 237).

BEATRICE

I fear thou art not modest, Diaphanta.

DIAPHANTA

Your thoughts are so unwilling to be known, madam;
'Tis ever the bride's fashion towards bedtime   65
To set light by her joys, as if she owed 'em not.

BEATRICE

Her joys? Her fears thou wouldst say.

DIAPHANTA   Fear of what?

BEATRICE

Art thou a maid, and talkst so to a maid?
You leave a blushing business behind,
Beshrew your heart for't!

DIAPHANTA   Do you mean good sooth, madam?   70

BEATRICE

Well, if I'd thought upon the fear at first,
Man should have been unknown.

DIAPHANTA   Is't possible?

BEATRICE

I will give a thousand ducats to that woman
Would try what my fear were, and tell me true
Tomorrow, when she gets from't: as she likes,   75
I might perhaps be drawn to't.

DIAPHANTA   Are you in earnest?

BEATRICE

Do you get the woman, then challenge me,
And see if I'll fly from't; but I must tell you
This by the way: she must be a true maid,
Else there's no trial, my fears are not hers else.   80

DIAPHANTA

Nay, she that I would put into your hands, madam
Shall be a maid.

66 *owed* owned
68 *maid* virgin
70 *Beshrew* A plague on
   mean . . . sooth really mean what you say
72 *Man . . . unknown* (1) I never would have had anything to do with men; (2) I would have
   avoided carnal knowledge
75 *when . . . from't* when it's all over
   as she likes depending on how much she enjoyed it
77 *Do you get* Imperative.
78 *fly from't* renege on my promise

BEATRICE   You know I should be shamed else,
  Because she lies for me.
DIAPHANTA   'Tis a strange humour!
  But are you serious still? Would you resign
  Your first night's pleasure, and give money too?   85
BEATRICE
  As willingly as live; alas, the gold
  Is but a by-bet to wedge in the honour.
DIAPHANTA [*Aside*]
  I do not know how the world goes abroad
  For faith or honesty; there's both required in this.
  [*Aloud*] Madam, what say you to me? And stray no further: 90
  I've a good mind in troth to earn your money.
BEATRICE
  You're too quick, I fear, to be a maid.
DIAPHANTA
  How? Not a maid? Nay, then you urge me, madam!
  Your honourable self is not a truer
  With all your fears upon you –
BEATRICE [*Aside*]   Bad enough, then.   95
DIAPHANTA
  Than I with all my lightsome joys about me.
BEATRICE
  I'm glad to hear't: then you dare put your honesty
  Upon an easy trial.
DIAPHANTA   Easy? – Anything.
BEATRICE
  I'll come to you straight.   [*Goes to the closet*]

---

83 *lies* (1) deceives; (2) lies with a man
   humour mood, caprice (*OED* n. 5, 6a)
86–7 *alas ... honour* Most eds. treat this as an aside, but there is no reason why Beatrice
   should not further encourage Diaphanta by adding honour to gold and pleasure as
   motives for sleeping with her master.
87 *by-bet* side-bet (*OED*, citing only this example)
   wedge in secure
88–89 *how ... honesty* how much good faith and truthfulness is to be found in the world
   nowadays. But *honesty* also carries the senses 'honour, reputation', and (ironically)
   'female chastity' (*OED* 1c, 3b).
92 *quick* (1) quick to respond; (2) alive [sexually]; (3) pregnant (*OED* a. 21a; 2a; 4b)
93 *urge* Cf. III.iii.141.
96 *lightsome* light-hearted

DIAPHANTA [*Aside*]   She will not search me? Will she?
   Like the forewoman of a female jury?   100
BEATRICE [*Aside*]
   Glass M. Ay, this is it. [*Aloud*] Look, Diaphanta,
   You take no worse than I do.   [*Drinks*]
DIAPHANTA   And in so doing,
   I will not question what 'tis, but take it.   [*Drinks*]
BEATRICE [*Aside*]
   Now if the experiment be true, 'twill praise itself,
   And give me noble ease. [*Diaphanta gapes*] – Begins already: 105
   There's the first symptom; and what haste it makes
   To fall into the second, [*Diaphanta sneezes*] there by this time!
   Most admirable secret! On the contrary,
   It stirs not me a whit, which most concerns it.
DIAPHANTA
   Ha ha ha!
BEATRICE [*Aside*] Just in all things and in order   110
   As if 'twere circumscribed; one accident
   Gives way unto another.
DIAPHANTA   Ha ha ha!
BEATRICE
   How now wench?
DIAPHANTA   Ha ha ha! I am so – so light
   At heart! Ha ha ha! So pleasurable!
   But one swig more, sweet madam?
BEATRICE   Ay, tomorrow;   115
   We shall have time to sit by't.
DIAPHANTA   Now I'm sad again.

99–100 *She ... jury* Alluding to the notorious divorce action of 1613 in which Frances
   Howard, Countess of Essex, having been examined by a panel of noblewomen and
   matrons, secured a divorce on the grounds of non-consummation, and was freed to
   marry her lover, Robert Carr, Earl of Somerset, King James' favourite. The pair were
   subsequently imprisoned for complicity in the murder of Carr's client, Sir Thomas
   Overbury, who had opposed the match. Interest in the case seems to have been reignited
   by the pair's release from prison in January 1622, shortly before this play was licensed.
104 *praise* demonstrate its value
109 *which ... it* (although that is) the very thing it is specifically designed to do
110 *Just* By the book
111 *circumscribed* confined to the prescribed sequence
   accident symptom (*OED* n. 3)
116 *sit by't* 'sit and enjoy its effects at leisure' (Bawcutt 1998)

BEATRICE

It lays itself so gently too. Come, wench –
Most honest Diaphanta I dare call thee now.

DIAPHANTA

Pray tell me, madam, what trick call you this?

BEATRICE

I'll tell thee all hereafter; we must study   120
The carriage of this business:

DIAPHANTA   I shall carry't well,
Because I love the burden.

BEATRICE   About midnight
You must not fail to steal forth gently,
That I may use the place.

DIAPHANTA   Oh, fear not, madam,
I shall be cool by that time. [*Aside*] The bride's place,   125
And with a thousand ducats! I'm for a justice now –
I bring a portion with me, I scorn small fools.

Exeunt

[ACT IV. SCENE ii.]

Enter VERMANDERO *and* SERVANT

VERMANDERO

I tell thee, knave, mine honour is in question,
A thing till now free from suspicion,
Nor ever was there cause. Who of my gentlemen
Are absent? Tell me and truly, how many, and who?

SERVANT

Antonio, sir, and Franciscus.   5

VERMANDERO

When did they leave the castle?

117 *lays itself* subsides (*OED* v. 3a)
121 *The carriage of* how to carry out
121–2 *carry't . . . burden* Bawdy *double entendre.*
124 *use* resort to (*OED* v. 17a)
126–7 *I'm . . . fools* now that I have a dowry, I need not bother with petty fools, I can look to
    marry a great one – like a justice of the peace (cf. I.ii.123).
IV.ii Author: Rowley 1–16; Middleton 17–150

SERVANT

Some ten days since, sir – the one intending to Briamata,
th'other for Valencia.

VERMANDERO

The time accuses 'em: a charge of murder
Is brought within my castle gate – Piracquo's murder;   10
I dare not answer faithfully their absence.
A strict command of apprehension
Shall pursue 'em suddenly, and either wipe
The stain off clear, or openly discover it.
Provide me wingèd warrants for the purpose.   15
See, I am set on again.

Exit SERVANT

Enter TOMAZO

TOMAZO

I claim a brother of you.

VERMANDERO   You're too hot,
Seek him not here.

TOMAZO   Yes, 'mongst your dearest bloods!
If my peace find no fairer satisfaction,
This is the place must yield account for him,   20
For here I left him, and the hasty tie
Of this snatched marriage, gives strong testimony
Of his most certain ruin.

VERMANDERO   Certain falsehood!
This is the place indeed: his breach of faith
Has too much marred both my abusèd love –   25
The honourable love I reserved for him –
And mocked my daughter's joy. The prepared morning
Blushed at his infidelity; he left
Contempt and scorn to throw upon those friends
Whose belief hurt 'em. Oh, 'twas most ignoble   30

---

7 *Briamata* the name of Vermandero's country house in Reynolds
11 *answer* be accountable for (*OED* v. 1b)
14 *discover* Cf. III.ii.140.
16 *set on* harried (by Tomazo)
17 *hot* passionate, angry
18 *bloods* kindred (*OED* n. 10a)
26, 27 *reserved, prepared* Stress on first syllable.
30 *belief* i.e. in Alonzo's good faith

To take his flight so unexpectedly,
And throw such public wrongs on those that loved him!

TOMAZO

Then this is all your answer.

VERMANDERO   'Tis too fair
For one of his alliance; and I warn you
That this place no more see you.   *Exit*

Enter DEFLORES

TOMAZO   The best is,   35
There is more ground to meet a man's revenge on. –
Honest Deflores!

DEFLORES   That's my name indeed.
Saw you the bride? Good sweet sir, which way took she?

TOMAZO

I have blest mine eyes from seeing such a false one.

DEFLORES [*Aside*]

I'd fain get off: this man's not for my company;   40
I smell his brother's blood when I come near him.

TOMAZO

Come hither, kind and true one; I remember
My brother loved thee well.

DEFLORES   O purely, dear sir!
[*Aside*] Methinks I am now again a-killing on him,
He brings it so fresh to me.

TOMAZO   Thou canst guess, sirrah –   45
An honest friend has an instinct of jealousy –
At some foul guilty person?

DEFLORES

'Las, sir, I am so charitable, I think none
Worse then my self – you did not see the bride then?

TOMAZO

I prithee name her not! Is she not wicked?   50

34 *alliance* kinsmen
36 *There . . . on* There are other ways for a man to achieve revenge
37 *Honest Deflores* A reminder that the character of Deflores is partly modelled on that of
    another disloyal servant, whose sobriquet of 'Honest Iago' belies his real nature as a
    hypocrite and diabolical tempter.
43 *purely* absolutely, entirely (*OED* adv. 2b)
46 *An honest* ed. (One honest Q)

DEFLORES

No, no, a pretty, easy, round-packed sinner,
As your most ladies are – else you might think
I flattered her – but sir, at no hand wicked,
Till they're so old their chins and noses meet,
And they salute witches. – I am called, I think, sir.   55
[*Aside*] His company even o'erlays my conscience.   *Exit*

TOMAZO

That Deflores has a wondrous honest heart –
He'll bring it out in time, I'm assured on't.
Oh, here's the glorious master of the day's joy;
'Twill not be long till he and I do reckon.   60

Enter ALSEMERO

Sir!

ALSEMERO You are most welcome.

TOMAZO   You may call that word back:
I do not think I am, nor wish to be.

ALSEMERO

'Tis strange you found the way to this house, then.

TOMAZO

Would I'd ne'er known the cause! I'm none of those, sir,
That come to give you joy, and swill your wine;   65
'Tis a more precious liquor that must lay
The fiery thirst I bring.

ALSEMERO   Your words and you
Appear to me great strangers.

TOMAZO   Time and our swords
May make us more acquainted. This the business:

---

51 *round-packed sinner* i.e. one 'firm in her curves and solid with sin' (Frost)
54 *chins and noses* ed. (sins and vices Q)
55 *salute* greet, kiss; begin an acquaintance with (*OED* v. 2a, e; 4) – as themselves looking like witches
56 *o'erlays* distresses, weighs down (*OED* v. 2a–b)
58 *bring it out* either (i) 'show his honest heart', or (ii) 'discover the truth about Alonzo's disappearance'
59 *glorious* vainglorious (*OED* a. 1a)
60 *'Twill* ed. (I will Q)
   reckon settle our accounts – i.e. come to blows (*OED* v. 11a)
60–1 *reckon. / Sir!* ed. (reckon sir. Q)
   s.d. After 'sir' Q.
66 *lay* appease (*OED* v¹ 3a)

I should have had a brother in your place –   70
How treachery and malice have disposed of him,
I'm bound to enquire of him which holds his right,
Which never could come fairly.

ALSEMERO   You must look
To answer for that word, sir.

TOMAZO   Fear you not:
I'll have it ready drawn at our next meeting.   75
Keep your day solemn. Farewell, I disturb it not;
I'll bear the smart with patience for a time.   *Exit*

ALSEMERO
'Tis somewhat ominous this: a quarrel entered
Upon this day. My innocence relieves me,

Enter JASPERINO

I should be wondrous sad else. – Jasperino,   80
I have news to tell thee, strange news.

JASPERINO   I ha' some too,
I think as strange as yours. Would I might keep
Mine, so my faith and friendship might be kept in't!
Faith sir, dispense a little with my zeal,
And let it cool in this.

ALSEMERO   This puts me on,   85
And blames thee for thy slowness.

JASPERINO   All may prove nothing,
Only a friendly fear that leapt from me, sir.

---

70 *have had* ed. (have Q)
72 *holds his right* possesses what is rightfully his (i.e. Beatrice)
73 *come fairly* come about by lawful means (*OED fairly* adv. 4b)
75 *have . . . drawn* (1) have my answer already drawn up; (2) have my sword drawn and at the ready
76 *Keep . . . solemn* Observe your wedding day with proper ceremony and reverence (*OED keep* v. 12, *solemn* a. 1)
77 *smart* pain, suffering (*OED* n. 1–2)
83 *so . . . in't* provided that I could preserve my faith and friendship to you by keeping it back
85 *let . . . this* allow some cooling in the warmth of my zeal to serve you, so far as passing on this news is concerned
   puts me on urges me onward (*OED* v. 47h)

ALSEMERO

No question it may prove nothing; let's partake it, though.

JASPERINO

'Twas Diaphanta's chance – for to that wench
I pretend honest love, and she deserves it –   90
To leave me in a back part of the house,
A place we chose for private conference;
She was no sooner gone, but instantly
I heard your bride's voice in the next room to me;
And, lending more attention, found Deflores   95
Louder then she.

ALSEMERO   Deflores? Thou art out now.

JASPERINO

You'll tell me more anon.

ALSEMERO   Still I'll prevent thee:
The very sight of him is poison to her.

JASPERINO

That made me stagger too, but Diaphanta
At her return confirmed it.

ALSEMERO   Diaphanta!   100

JASPERINO

Then fell we both to listen, and words passed
Like those that challenge interest in a woman.

ALSEMERO

Peace, quench thy zeal – 'tis dangerous to thy bosom.

JASPERINO

Then truth is full of peril.

ALSEMERO   Such truths are.
Oh, were she the sole glory of the earth,   105
Had eyes that could shoot fire into kings' breasts,

---

88 *No . . . though* Provided the first *it* is elided ('question't') this line forms a rough but
   acceptable hexameter.
90 *pretend* profess (*OED* v. 3)
   honest honourable
96 *out* wide of the mark, mistaken
97 *prevent* forestall (*OED* v. 5)
102 *challenge* lay claim to (*OED* v. 5)
   interest right, title (*OED* n. 1). Daalder reads this passage to mean that the exchange
   between Deflores and Beatrice excited *Diaphanta's* interest (especially after her promise
   to act as Beatrice's substitute on the wedding night); but Jasperino's 'like those that . . .'
   makes it plain that an act of interpretation is involved: the eavesdroppers have heard
   words that sound as if the servant were asserting a physical claim over his mistress.

And touched, she sleeps not here! Yet I have time,
Though night be near, to be resolved hereof;
And prithee do not weigh me by my passions.
JASPERINO
I never weighed friend so.
ALSEMERO   Done charitably.   110
That key will lead thee to a pretty secret
By a Chaldean taught me – and I've spent
My study upon some. Bring from my closet
A glass inscribed there with the letter M;
And question not my purpose.
JASPERINO   It shall be done, sir.   115
ALSEMERO
How can this hang together? Not an hour since,
Her woman came pleading her lady's fears,
Delivered her for the most timorous virgin
That ever shrunk at man's name, and so modest,
She charged her weep out her request to me,   120
That she might come obscurely to my bosom.

Enter BEATRICE

BEATRICE [*Aside*]
All things go well: my woman's preparing yonder
For her sweet voyage, which grieves me to lose;
Necessity compels it; I lose all else.
ALSEMERO [*Aside*]
Push! Modesty's shrine is set in yonder forehead.   125
I cannot be too sure, though. [*Aloud*] My Joanna!
BEATRICE
Sir, I was bold to weep a message to you –
Pardon my modest fears.

---

107 *And touched* And if she has had sexual contact with someone (*OED* v. 2a)
111 *pretty* ingenious; admirable (*OED* a. 2b; 3)
112 *Chaldean* seer, soothsayer (after the people described in Daniel 2:2–12, famous for such
   practices)
   spent Bruster (*not in* Q; Bawcutt: made)
118 *Delivered her for* Described her as (*OED* v. 11a)
121 *obscurely* in the dark (cf. *OED obscure* a. 2)

ALSEMERO [*Aside*]   The dove's not meeker.
  She's abused questionless.

Enter JASPERINO

                 [*Aloud*] Oh, are you come, sir?
BEATRICE [*Aside*]
  The glass, upon my life! I see the letter.   130
JASPERINO
  Sir, this is M.
ALSEMERO   'Tis it.
BEATRICE [*Aside*]   I am suspected.
ALSEMERO
  How fitly our bride comes to partake with us!
BEATRICE
  What is't, my lord?
ALSEMERO   No hurt.
BEATRICE   Sir, pardon me –
  I seldom taste of any composition.
ALSEMERO
  But this, upon my warrant, you shall venture on.   135
                            [*Gives her the glass*]
BEATRICE
  I fear 'twill make me ill.
ALSEMERO   Heaven forbid that.
BEATRICE [*Aside*]
  I'm put now to my cunning: th'effects I know,
  If I can now but feign 'em handsomely.   [*Drinks*]
ALSEMERO [*To* JASPERINO]
  It has that secret virtue it ne'er missed, sir,
  Upon a virgin.   [BEATRICE *gapes, then sneezes*]
JASPERINO [*To* ALSEMERO] Treble qualitied!   140

---

129 *abused* maligned, libelled (*OED* v. 7)
    s.d. *Enter* JASPERINO (*after . . . come, sir?* Q)
134 *composition* substance composed of a mixture of ingredients (*OED* n. 20a)
135 *upon my warrant* I swear
138 *handsomely* skilfully (*OED* adv. 3)
139 *secret* kept from the knowledge of the uninitiated (*OED* a. 1e)
    virtue power, efficacy (*OED* n. 11a)
140 *Treble qualitied* Referring to the three symptoms Beatrice exhibits.

ALSEMERO [*To* JASPERINO]

  By all that's virtuous, it takes there, proceeds!

JASPERINO [*To* ALSEMERO]

  This is the strangest trick to know a maid by.

BEATRICE

  Ha ha ha!

  You have given me joy of heart to drink, my lord.

ALSEMERO

  No, thou hast given me such joy of heart,   145

  That never can be blasted.

BEATRICE   What's the matter sir?

ALSEMERO [*To* JASPERINO]

  See now, 'tis settled in a melancholy

  Keeps both the time and method. [*To* BEATRICE] My Joanna,

  Chaste as the breath of heaven, or morning's womb

  That brings the day forth, thus my love encloses thee!   150

                              [*Embraces her*]

                              Exeunt

[ACT IV. SCENE iii.]

Enter ISABELLA *and* LOLLIO

ISABELLA

  O heaven! Is this the waxing moon?

  Does love turn fool, run mad, and all at once?

  Sirrah, here's a madman, akin to the fool too,

  A lunatic lover.

141 *virtuous* Playing on the efficacious *virtue* of the drug and its proof of Beatrice's moral *virtue*.
     takes is having the intended result (*OED* v. 11c)
     proceeds takes effect (*OED* v. 5)
146 *blasted* blighted (*OED* v. 8)
148 *Keeps* ed. (keep Q)
     Keeps . . . method Follows both the [prescribed] timing and sequence
IV.iii Author: Rowley
   1 *waxing* ed. (waiting Q). It is difficult to make sense of Q *waiting*, and in some hands *x* could easily be misread as *it*. Since lunatics were thought to be governed by the moon (*luna*), madness could be expected to increase as it moved towards the full.
   2 *at* ed. (*not in* Q)

LOLLIO

No, no! Not he I brought the letter from? 5

ISABELLA

Compare his inside with his out, and tell me.

[*Gives him the letter*]

LOLLIO

The out's mad, I'm sure of that, I had a taste on't.

[*Reads*] 'To the bright Andromeda, chief chambermaid to the Knight of the Sun, at the sign of Scorpio, in the middle region, sent by the bellows-mender of Æolus. Pay the post.' 10

This is stark madness.

ISABELLA [*Takes the letter*]

Now mark the inside.

[*Reads*] 'Sweet lady, having now cast off this counterfeit cover of a madman, I appear to your best judgement a true and faithful lover of your beauty.' 15

LOLLIO

He is mad still.

ISABELLA

'If any fault you find, chide those perfections in you which have made me imperfect: 'tis the same sun that causeth to grow, and enforceth to wither –'

LOLLIO

O rogue! 20

6 *Compare ... out* (1) Compare the contents of the letter with what is written on its outside; (2) Compare his inner self with his outward guise

8–10 *To ... Aeolus* A deliberate jumble of astrological and mythical material, laced with bawdy *double entendre*.

8 *bright Andromeda* Both the brilliant constellation and the beautiful heroine of classical myth (= Isabella) whom Perseus rescued from the dragon (= Alibius).

8–9 *chambermaid ... Sun* A mock-astrological description of the relationship between the constellation Andromeda and the Sun, but also recalling the character of 'A Chamber-Mayde' in Overbury's *Wife*, whose lascivious behaviour is encouraged by her passion for chivalric romance; in particular 'She ... is so carried away with *The Mirror of Knighthood*, she is many times resolved to run out of herself, and become a lady errant' (sig. G8) – the reference is to a popular Spanish romance translated and published in nine parts between 1578 and 1601 – one of whose heroes is the Knight of the Sun. Cf. also *chamber* = vagina (Williams, *Glossary*, p. 67).

9 *sign of Scorpio* (1) the name of the inn where Andromeda is imagined to be lodging; (2) the astrological sign supposed to govern the private parts

middle region (1) fifth to eighth months of the astrological year; (2) private parts

10 *Aeolus* god of the winds – hence linked by bawdy association with *the middle region*. Daalder suggests *bellows* = phallus.

post messenger (*OED* n.^{2} 2a)

18 *imperfect* Referring to his degrading disguise as a madman.

18–19 *'tis ... wither* Cf. Tilley, S980: 'The same sun softens wax and hardens clay.'

ISABELLA

'– shapes and trans-shapes, destroys and builds again. I come in
winter to you dismantled of my proper ornaments: by the sweet
splendour of your cheerful smiles, I spring and live a lover.'

LOLLIO

Mad rascal still!

ISABELLA

'Tread him not under foot, that shall appear an honour to your   25
bounties. I remain, mad till I speak with you from whom I
expect my cure, yours all, or one beside himself, Franciscus.'

LOLLIO

You are like to have a fine time on't: my master and I may give
over our professions – I do not think but you can cure fools and
madmen faster then we, with little pains too.   30

ISABELLA

Very likely.

LOLLIO

One thing I must tell you, mistress: you perceive that I am privy
to your skill; if I find you minister once and set up the trade, I
put in for my thirds – I shall be mad or fool else.

ISABELLA

The first place is thine – believe it, Lollio –   35
If I do fall –

LOLLIO   I fall upon you.

ISABELLA   So.

LOLLIO

Well, I stand to my venture.

ISABELLA

But thy counsel now: how shall I deal with 'em?

---

22 *dismantled ... ornaments* stripped of the garments and trappings appropriate to one
   of my rank
25–6 *that ... bounties* whose love will bring honour to you if you treat him generously
33 *skill* (1) in curing fools and madmen; (2) in erotic matters
   minister ... trade (1) treat one patient and set yourself up as a practitioner; (2)
   commit adultery and become a whore
33–4 *I ... thirds* Note the echo of Deflores' 'I'll put in for one' (II.ii.60).
   thirds share (financial and sexual). 'Thirds' were the third share of captures or of certain
   fines due to the crown; also the third part of a husband's estate due to his widow (*OED* n.
   3; 2).
37 *stand to* stand by (with bawdy *double entendre*)
   venture commercial enterprise, speculation (*OED* n. 4a)

LOLLIO

Why, do you mean to deal with 'em?

ISABELLA

Nay, the fair understanding – how to use 'em.   40

LOLLIO

Abuse 'em! That's the way to mad the fool, and make a fool of
the madman, and then you use 'em kindly.

ISABELLA

'Tis easy – I'll practise. Do thou observe it.

The key of thy wardrobe?

LOLLIO

There – fit yourself for 'em, and I'll fit 'em both for you.   45

                                                  [Gives her the key]

ISABELLA

Take thou no further notice than the outside.   *Exit*

LOLLIO

Not an inch, I'll put you to the inside.

Enter ALIBIUS

ALIBIUS

Lollio, art there? Will all be perfect, think'st thou?

Tomorrow night, as if to close up the solemnity,

Vermandero expects us.   50

LOLLIO

I mistrust the madmen most; the fools will do well enough: I
have taken pains with them.

ALIBIUS

Tush, they cannot miss! The more absurdity,

39 *Why* ed. (We Q)

   deal Lollio deliberately misunderstands her to mean 'copulate' (Williams, *Glossary*,
   p. 92).

40 *the fair understanding* understand my words in the decent sense I intended. Ironically *use*
   could also mean 'employ sexually' (Williams, *Glossary*, pp. 320–21).

41 *Abuse* (1) Maltreat; (2) Deceive; (3) Ravish, Defile sexually (*OED* v. 5; 4; 6)

42 *kindly* (1) considerately; (2) as creatures of their kind deserve

43 *practise* plot, employ an artifice or stratagem (*OED* v. 9)

44–7 *The key . . . inside* Compare Beatrice's opening of the closet with Alsemero's key in IV.i
   – the 'wardrobe' like the 'closet' will presumably have been represented either by the
   discovery space at the rear of the Phoenix stage or by the same stage-door.

45 *fit* (1) make ready; (2) prepare for copulation (Williams, *Glossary*, p. 127)

47 *put . . . inside* 'I'll allow you intimate access to your lovers' (Bawcutt 1998); but see also
   Williams, *Glossary*, p. 251: *put to* 'of phallic insertion'

49 *solemnity* i.e. the wedding celebration

The more commends it, so no rough behaviours
Affright the ladies – they are nice things, thou know'st.   55

LOLLIO

You need not fear, sir: so long as we are there with our
commanding pizzles, they'll be as tame as the ladies themselves.

ALIBIUS

I will see them once more rehearse before they go.

LOLLIO

I was about it, sir. Look you to the madmen's morris, and let me
alone with the other. There is one or two that I mistrust their   60
fooling: I'll instruct them, and then they shall rehearse the
whole measure.

ALIBIUS

Do so – I'll see the music prepared. But, Lollio,
By the way, how does my wife brook her restraint?
Does she not grudge at it?   65

LOLLIO

So, so – she takes some pleasure in the house, she would abroad
else. You must allow her a little more length, she's kept too
short.

ALIBIUS

She shall along to Vermandero's with us:
That will serve her for a month's liberty.   70

LOLLIO

What's that on your face, sir?

ALIBIUS   Where, Lollio, I see nothing.

LOLLIO

Cry you mercy, sir, 'tis your nose; it showed like the trunk of a
young elephant.

---

55 *nice* delicate; coy, shy; fastidious, refined (*OED* a. 4c; 5a; 7a)
57 *pizzles* whips made from dried bull-penises
59 *morris* morris-dance – grotesque dance usually representing characters from the
Robin Hood story
60 *the other* i.e. the fools' performance
62 *measure* dance – usually of a grave and stately kind (*OED* n. 20a)
64 *brook* tolerate, endure
65 *grudge* grumble
66 *pleasure* With sexual *double entendre.*
67 *allow . . . length* give her more rope – but (cf. *short*, l. 68) with an obscene reference to
the length of a penis (see Williams, *Dictionary*, p. 800).
70 *month's* Disyllabic, as the Q spelling *moneths* indicates.
72–3 *nose . . . elephant* Lollio implies that Alibius is easily led by the nose; but a phallic joke
may also be involved.

ALIBIUS

Away, rascal! I'll prepare the music, Lollio.   *Exit*

LOLLIO

Do, sir; and I'll dance the whilst. [*Calls*] Tony! Where art thou,   75
Tony?

Enter ANTONIO

ANTONIO

Here, cousin, where art thou?

LOLLIO

Come, Tony, the footmanship I taught you.

ANTONIO

I had rather ride, cousin.

LOLLIO

Ay, a whip take you! But I'll keep you out. Vault in, look you,   80
Tony: fa, la, la, la, la.   [*Dances*]

ANTONIO   Fa, la, la, la, la.   [*Dances*]

LOLLIO

There, an honour.   [*Bows*]

ANTONIO

Is this an honour, coz?   [*Bows*]

LOLLIO

Yes, and it please your worship.

ANTONIO

Does honour bend in the hams, coz?   85

LOLLIO

Marry does it: as low as worship, squireship – nay, yeomanry
itself sometimes; from whence it first stiffened, there rises a
caper.

---

78 *footmanship* skill in dancing (cf. *OED* n. 1)
79 *ride* Bawdy *double entendre*.
82 *honour* bow (*OED* n. 5b)
83 *coz* cousin (cf. I.ii.135)
84 *and* if
85 *bend in the hams* (1) bow, make obeisance; (2) show the bent posture of someone
   suffering from venereal disease (Williams, *Glossary*: 'ham', p. 150)
86 *Marry* Abbreviation of 'By Mary'.
87 *from . . . stiffened* If honour can bend, Lollio suggests, it must first have stiffened (with
   pride) as it rose from the mere yeomanry into the honourable ranks of the lesser gentry
   (*worship, squireship*); a quibble on phallic erection is also involved.
   rises ed. (rise Q)
88 *caper* (1) leap; (2) fantastical proceeding, freak (*OED* n. 1a)

ANTONIO

    Caper after an honour, coz?

LOLLIO

    Very proper: for honour is but a caper, rises as fast and high, has   90
    a knee or two, and falls to th'ground again. You can remember
    your figure, Tony?   *Exit*

ANTONIO

    Yes, cousin, when I see thy figure, I can remember mine.

Enter ISABELLA [*like a madwoman*]

ISABELLA

    Hey, how he treads the air! Shough, shough, t'other way – he
    burns his wings else. Here's wax enough below, Icarus – more   95
    than will be cancelled these eighteen moons.

                                          [ANTONIO *falls*]

    He's down, he's down! What a terrible fall he had!
    Stand up, thou son of Cretan Daedalus,
    And let us tread the lower labyrinth;
    I'll bring thee to the clew.   [*Pulls him*]   100

ANTONIO

    Prithee, coz, let me alone.

90–1 *has a knee* Cf. 'makes a knee' = bows.

92 *figure* (1) set of dance movements; (2) appearance (*OED* n. 16; 1c)

94–100 Q prints this entire passage as verse, but its lineation corresponds to no discernible metrical pattern. Editors have made several attempts to re-line the whole speech, but none is entirely satisfactory. Lines 94 and 98–100 make reasonably good iambic verse, but the rest of the speech is clearly prose. The oscillation between metre and prose rhythms, which is also apparent in some of Antonio's and Franciscus' speeches, is a way of representing the disordered quality of mad utterance.

94 *he* ed. (she Q)

    Shough Exclamation still used by beaters when driving game birds towards the guns – an obsolete, slightly gutteral form of 'shoo' (*OED*).

94–9 *he burns . . . labyrinth* Referring to the myth of the labyrinth built by King Minos of Crete. Daedalus, the architect of this maze, was imprisoned there with his son, Icarus, but engineered their escape with the aid of artificial wings; Icarus, however, flew too close to the sun, melting the wax with which his wings were attached, and plunged to his death in the Icarian Sea (cf. III.ii.114; III.iii.71; V.iii.148).

95–6 *more . . . moons* more than will be used up in sealing eighteen months' worth of legal documents

99 *tread . . . labyrinth* Obscene *double entendre* (see Williams, *Glossary*: 'tread' = copulate, p. 313).

100 *clew* the ball of thread, given to Theseus by Minos's daughter, Ariadne, which enabled the hero to escape from the labyrinth after he had slain the monstrous Minotaur

ISABELLA   Art thou not drowned?
    About thy head I saw a heap of clouds
    Wrapped like a Turkish turban, on thy back
    A crook'd chameleon-coloured rainbow hung
    Like a tiara down unto thy hams.   105
    Let me suck out those billows in thy belly,   [*Bends over him*]
    Hark how they roar and rumble in the straits!
    Bless thee from the pirates!

ANTONIO
    Pox upon you, let me alone!   [*Rises*]

ISABELLA
    Why shouldst thou mount so high as Mercury,   110
    Unless thou hadst reversion of his place?
    Stay in the moon with me, Endymion,
    And we will rule these wild rebellious waves,
    That would have drowned my love.

ANTONIO
    I'll kick thee if again thou touch me,   115
    Thou wild, unshapen antic; I am no fool,
    You bedlam.

ISABELLA   But you are, as sure as I am, mad.
    Have I put on this habit of a frantic,
    With love as full of fury, to beguile
    The nimble eye of watchful jealousy,   120
    And am I thus rewarded?   [*Reveals herself*]

ANTONIO
    Ha! Dearest beauty!

ISABELLA
    No, I have no beauty now,

---

105 *tiara* raised head-dress or turban worn by Persians and other Eastern peoples (*OED* n. 1), here with a long tail-piece at the back
106 *suck . . . belly* 'Probably . . . an indecent advance under the guise of an insane allusion to the myth' (Frost).
107 *straits* (streets Q)
110 *Mercury* winged messenger of the Gods
111 *reversion of his place* entitlement to succeed him in his office
112 *Endymion* beautiful youth with whom the moon-goddess fell in love
113 *rule . . . waves* The moon-goddess controlled the tides.
116 *antic* grotesque performer, clown (*OED* n. 4)
117 *bedlam* lunatic (after Bethlehem Hospital, see above I.ii.50)
118 *frantic* frenzied person, lunatic
122 *Ha . . . beauty* Metrically amphibious, forming a loose pentameter line with either or both of ll. 121 and 123.

Nor never had, but what was in my garments.
You a quick-sighted lover? Come not near me!   125
Keep your caparisons, you're aptly clad;
I came a feigner to return stark mad.   *Exit*

Enter LOLLIO

ANTONIO

Stay, or I shall change condition,
And become as you are.

LOLLIO

Why Tony, whither now? Why, fool?   130

ANTONIO

Whose fool, usher of idiots? You coxcomb,
I have fooled too much.

LOLLIO

You were best be mad another while then.

ANTONIO

So I am, stark mad; I have cause enough,
And I could throw the full effects on thee,   135
And beat thee like a Fury.

LOLLIO

Do not, do not! I shall not forbear the gentleman under the
fool, if you do. Alas, I saw through your fox-skin before now!
Come, I can give you comfort: my mistress loves you, and there
is as arrant a mad-man i' th' house as you are a fool – your rival,   140
whom she loves not. If, after the masque, we can rid her of him,
you earn her love, she says, and the fool shall ride her.

ANTONIO

May I believe thee?

LOLLIO

Yes, or you may choose whether you will or no.

ANTONIO

She's eased of him, I have a good quarrel on't.   145

126 *caparisons* trappings
131 *usher* door-keeper; assistant schoolmaster (*OED* n. 1; 4)
    coxcomb fool – after the cap, decorated with a cock's comb worn by jesters (*OED* n. 3)
136 *Fury* In classical mythology, one of the three avenging spirits sent from the underworld
    to punish crimes; generally, a tormenting spirit.
137 *forbear* spare
142 *ride her* Obscene word-play on 'rid her' (l. 141).
145 *eased* relieved (cf. III.iii.99)

LOLLIO

Well, keep your old station yet, and be quiet.

ANTONIO

Tell her I will deserve her love.   [*Exit*]

LOLLIO

And you are like to have your desire.

Enter FRANCISCUS

FRANCISCUS [*Sings*]

'Down, down, down a-down a-down'; and then with a
    horse-trick

To kick Latona's forehead, and break her bowstring.   150

LOLLIO

This is t'other counterfeit – I'll put him out of his humour
[*Takes out letter and reads*]: 'Sweet Lady, having now cast off
this counterfeit cover of a mad-man, I appear to your
best judgement a true and faithful lover of your beauty.'
This is pretty well for a madman.   155

FRANCISCUS

Ha! What's that?

LOLLIO

'Chide those perfections in you which made me imperfect.'

FRANCISCUS

I am discovered to the fool.

LOLLIO

I hope to discover the fool in you, e're I have done with you.
'Yours all, or one beside himself, Franciscus.' This madman will   160
mend sure.

FRANCISCUS

What do you read, sirrah?

---

146 *old station* existing position (as a fool)
149 *Down . . . a-down* Daalder suggests a deliberate echo of Ophelia's mad song in *Hamlet*
    (IV.v.167).
    horse-trick Cf. 'horse-play' and 'trick' = feat of dexterity (*OED* n. 5a) – so probably an
    extravagant dance-leap; but the bawdy sense of 'trick' = sexual act (Williams, *Glossary*,
    p. 313) suggests that the familiar horse/whores pun is also involved (cf. *Anthony and
    Cleopatra*, I.v.21).
150 *Latona* mother of the goddess Diana, but here apparently confused with Diana herself,
    typically depicted as a hunter with a bow
152 *off* ed. (*not in* Q; but cf. l. 13)
158 *discovered* exposed, revealed

LOLLIO

Your destiny, sir: you'll be hanged for this trick, and another that I know.

FRANCISCUS

Art thou of counsel with thy mistress?   165

LOLLIO

Next her apron-strings.

FRANCISCUS

Give me thy hand.

LOLLIO

Stay, let me put yours in my pocket first [*Puts away the letter*]: your hand is true, is it not? It will not pick? I partly fear it, because I think it does lie.   170

FRANCISCUS

Not in a syllable.

LOLLIO

So, if you love my mistress so well as you have handled the matter here, you are like to be cured of your madness.

FRANCISCUS

And none but she can cure it.

LOLLIO

Well, I'll give you over then, and she shall cast your water next.   175

FRANCISCUS

Take for thy pains past.   [*Gives him money*]

LOLLIO

I shall deserve more, sir, I hope. My mistress loves you, but must have some proof of your love to her.

FRANCISCUS

There I meet my wishes.

LOLLIO

That will not serve, you must meet her enemy and yours.   180

FRANCISCUS

He's dead already.

---

163 *another* i.e. his 'whore's-trick' with Isabella (l. 149)
168 *yours* your hand(writing) – i.e. the letter
169 *hand is true* (1) your handwriting is correct; (2) what you have written is truthful; (3) your hand is honest (*OED* a. 4a–b; 3d; 2)
pick steal (*OED* v. 9a)
175 *give you over* abandon you
cast your water diagnose your condition with a urine sample
180 *meet* fight a duel with (*OED* v. 3a)

LOLLIO

Will you tell me that, and I parted but now with him?

FRANCISCUS

Show me the man!

LOLLIO

Ay, that's a right course now: see him before you kill him in any
case; and yet it needs not go so far neither – 'tis but a fool that   185
haunts the house and my mistress in the shape of an idiot: bang
but his fool's coat well-favouredly, and 'tis well.

FRANCISCUS

Soundly, soundly!

LOLLIO

Only reserve him till the masque be past; and if you find him
not now in the dance yourself, I'll show you. In, in! My   190
master!   [Dances]

FRANCISCUS

He handles him like a feather. Hey!   [Exit dancing]

Enter ALIBIUS

ALIBIUS

Well said! In a readiness, Lollio?

LOLLIO

Yes, sir.

ALIBIUS

Away then, and guide them in, Lollio;   195
Entreat your mistress to see this sight.
Hark, is there not one incurable fool
That might be begged? I have friends.

LOLLIO

I have him for you – one that shall deserve it too.   [Exit]

182 *and* given that
187 *well-favouredly* thoroughly
189 *Only . . . you* The fact the promised face-off between Antonio and Franciscus, like the
masque of madmen itself, never takes place suggests either that there was a change of
plan on the part of the dramatists, or (as some scholars have suggested) that a scene has
been cut from the surviving text.
192 *him* himself
193 *Well said* Well done
197–8 *fool . . . begged* In cases where an heir was legally declared a congenital idiot, his estate
passed to the management of the crown; anyone who wished to enjoy its revenue could
'beg a fool' – i.e. apply through the Court of Wards to be made his guardian.

ALIBIUS

Good boy, Lollio.   200

> [*Enter* ISABELLA, *and* LOLLIO *ushering in the*
> MADMEN *and* FOOLS.]
> *The* MADMEN *and* FOOLS *dance*

'Tis perfect! Well, fit but once these strains,
We shall have coin and credit for our pains.

Exeunt

ACT V. [SCENE i.]

Enter BEATRICE. *A clock strikes one*

BEATRICE

One struck, and yet she lies by't! O my fears!
This strumpet serves her own ends, 'tis apparent now,
Devours the pleasure with a greedy appetite,
And never minds my honour or my peace,
Makes havoc of my right; but she pays dearly for't –   5
No trusting of her life with such a secret,
That cannot rule her blood to keep her promise.
Beside, I have some suspicion of her faith to me,
Because I was suspected of my lord,

---

201 *fit . . . strains* only fit the music (to the wild dance)

V.i Author: Middleton

1–6 *One . . . secret* In *Gerardo*, the maid Julia, similarly substituting for her mistress on her wedding night, is guilty of the same careless indulgence: 'she belike either wearied, or taken with the sweet of so much pleasure, contrary to the order I had given her, fell asleep, and now I knew not which in me was most, my jealousy or fear, and my rage increased the more, when (hearing the clock strike three) I saw so little memory in her of my danger.' Isdaura, 'taking her to be too shallow a vessel for my secrets,' then resolves to kill her (H5–H5v).

1 *lies by't* continues in sin (*OED* v. 3a); Daalder suggests an indecent play on *lie* and *it* (= sexual act; Williams, *Glossary*, p. 172).

2 *serves . . . ends* A play on sexual 'service' and on 'end' = genital area (Williams, *Glossary*, pp. 273–4, 113–14) is unavoidable here.

7 *blood* lustful desires

9 *of* by

And it must come from her. – Hark, by my horrors,   10
Another clock strikes two!   [*Clock*] *strike*[*s*] *two*

Enter DEFLORES.

DEFLORES   Psst! Where are you?
BEATRICE
Deflores!
DEFLORES   Ay – is she not come from him yet?
BEATRICE
As I am a living soul not.
DEFLORES   Sure the devil
Hath sowed his itch within her! Who'd trust
A waiting-woman?   15
BEATRICE
I must trust somebody.
DEFLORES
Push! They are termagants;
Especially when they fall upon their masters
And have their ladies' first-fruits, they're mad whelps,
You cannot stave 'em off from game royal. Then   20
You are so harsh and hardy, ask no counsel –
And I could have helped you to a 'pothecary's daughter
Would have fallen off before eleven, and thanked you too.
BEATRICE
O me! Not yet? This whore forgets herself.

14 *itch* sexual urge (Williams, *Glossary*, p. 172)
16 *I . . . somebody* Metrically amphibious.
17 *termagants* viragos
18 *fall upon* attack (with sexual innuendo – see Williams, *Dictionary*, p. 460)
19 *first-fruits* Ironically, given its bawdy meaning here, the phrase is biblical and referred
   originally to the harvest offerings required by God (see e.g. Exodus 23:16, Leviticus
   23:10; Numbers 28:26); but St Paul employs it as a figure for Christ's sacrifice as 'the first
   fruits of them that sleep' (1 Corinthians 15:20); significantly, in view of the extended play
   on 'falling' and 'rising' in this passage of dialogue, St Paul is discussing the resurrection
   of Christ and the rising of the dead.
20 *stave . . . royal* keep them from worrying game which belongs exclusively to the monarch;
   but 'game' also = wantonness (Williams, *Glossary*, p. 137), so that *game royal* could mean
   something like 'extravagant sexual indulgence'
21 *harsh* rough, rude – perhaps here 'headstrong'
   hardy foolhardy (*OED* a. 2)
22 *a 'pothecary's* Dyce (a Apothecaries Q; an apothecary's Dilke)
23 *thanked* ed. (thank Q)

DEFLORES

    The rascal fares so well – look, you're undone,   25
    The day-star by this hand! See Phosphorus plain yonder.

BEATRICE

    Advise me how to fall upon some ruin;
    There is no counsel safe else.

DEFLORES   Peace! I ha't now,

    For we must force a rising, there's no remedy.

BEATRICE

    How? Take heed of that.

DEFLORES   Tush! Be you quiet,   30

    Or else give over all.

BEATRICE   Prithee, I ha' done then.

DEFLORES

    This is my reach: I'll set some part a-fire
    Of Diaphanta's chamber.

BEATRICE   How? Fire, sir?

    That may endanger the whole house.

DEFLORES

    You talk of danger when your fame's on fire?   35

BEATRICE

    That's true, do what thou wilt now.

DEFLORES   Push! I aim

    At a most rich success, strikes all dead sure:
    The chimney being a-fire, and some light parcels
    Of the least danger in her chamber only,
    If Diaphanta should be met by chance then,   40
    Far from her lodging – which is now suspicious –
    It would be thought her fears and affrights then,

---

26 *Phosphorus* ed. (Bosphorus Q); the morning star – ironically, as Frost points out, *Lucifer* in Latin; see also Isaiah 14:12 ff. 'How art thou fallen from heaven, O day star, son of the morning . . .' – here, however, Lucifer rises.

27 *how* ed. (now Q)

    fall upon have recourse to (*OED* v. 70d)

    ruin (1) downfall (*OED* n. 6a) – but with *fall* picking up the reference to Lucifer at l. 26; (2) dishonour, loss of virginity (*OED* n. 6b)

29 *force a rising* drive everyone out of bed – but with a sardonic play on the fall/resurrection motif (cf. ll. 18, 23, 26, 27)

32 *reach* scheme (*OED* n. 2a)

37 *strikes . . . sure* will make everything safe and secure (but with an ironic quibble on 'strikes . . . dead')

38–9 *light . . . danger* inconsiderable bits and pieces unlikely to cause a major fire

41 *is now* would otherwise be

Drove her to seek for succour; if not seen
Or met at all – as that's the likeliest –
For her own shame she'll hasten towards her lodging.   45
I will be ready with a piece high-charged,
As 'twere to cleanse the chimney – there 'tis proper,
But she shall be the mark.

BEATRICE   I'm forced to love thee now,
'Cause thou provid'st so carefully for my honour.

DEFLORES

'Slid! It concerns the safety of us both,   50
Our pleasure and continuance.

BEATRICE   One word now:
Prithee, how for the servants?

DEFLORES   I'll dispatch them,
Some one way, some another in the hurry,
For buckets, hooks, ladders. Fear not you:
The deed shall find its time, and I've thought since   55
Upon a safe conveyance for the body too.
How this fire purifies wit! Watch you your minute.

BEATRICE

Fear keeps my soul upon't, I cannot stray from't.

Enter ALONZO's *ghost*

DEFLORES

Ha! What art thou that tak'st away the light
'Twixt that star and me? I dread thee not: 60
'Twas but a mist of conscience – all's clear again.   *Exit*

BEATRICE

Who's that, Deflores? Bless me! It slides by.   [*Exit ghost*]

---

46 *piece* gun
   high-charged with a double loading of powder and shot
47 *there . . . proper* it would be appropriate for that purpose
   proper ed. (proper now Q); *now* probably picked up by eye-skip from l. 48
50 *'Slid* Contraction of 'By God's (eye)lid'.
56 *conveyance* riddance (*OED* n. 3)
57 *How . . . wit* Fire was an instrument of purification, used both in alchemical experiment, and (more mundanely) to cleanse foul air: Deflores' remark is itself witty, his conceit being that the very idea of the fire he will light has served to purify his wit (intelligence, ingenuity) – familiarly imagined in metaphors of fire and sparks. In terms of humoral psycho-physiology, heat would nourish wit, whilst the cold and damp of melancholy would dull it.
60 *that star* i.e. Phosphorus/Lucifer

Some ill thing haunts the house, 't has left behind it
A shivering sweat upon me – I'm afraid now.
This night hath been so tedious. Oh, this strumpet!   65
Had she a thousand lives, he should not leave her
Till he had destroyed the last –   [*Clock strikes three*]
                    List! O my terrors,
  Three struck by St Sebastian's!
[VOICES] *Within*   Fire, fire, fire!
BEATRICE
  Already! How rare is that man's speed!
  How heartily he serves me! His face loathes one,   70
  But look upon his care, who would not love him?
  The east is not more beauteous than his service.
[VOICES] *Within*
  Fire, fire, fire!

> *Enter* DEFLORES [*with*] *servants.* [*They*] *pass
> over* [*the stage. A bell rings*].

DEFLORES
  Away! Dispatch! Hooks, buckets, ladders! That's well said!
  The fire bell rings, the chimney works, my charge   75
  The piece is ready.   *Exit*

> *Enter* DIAPHANTA

BEATRICE   Here's a man worth loving! –
                   [*Sees* DIAPHANTA]

---

65 *tedious* long and wearisome; painful; slow (*OED* a. 1; 2; 4)

67 s.d. ed. ('*Struck 3 a clock*' *after* St Sebastian's Q)

69 *rare* exceptional; remarkably good (*OED* a. 5a; 6a)

70 *loathes* excites loathing in (*OED* v. 3)

72 *east ... beauteous* The beauty of sunrise is traditionally charged with a Christian symbolism that contrasts ironically with the rising of Deflores' Phosphorus/Lucifer (l. 26).
    service The bawdy sense is unmistakeable here, although Beatrice is hardly conscious of it.

73 s.d.2 This edition (*Enter Deflores servants: passe over, ring a Bell* Q)

74, 90 *well said* Cf. IV.iii.193.

75 *my charge* the task entrusted to me – with a play on 'charge' = powder and shot for his 'piece'

Oh, you're a jewel!

DIAPHANTA   Pardon frailty, madam:
In troth I was so well, I ev'n forgot myself.

BEATRICE
Y'have made trim work!

DIAPHANTA   What?

BEATRICE   Hie quickly to your chamber;
Your reward follows you.

DIAPHANTA   I never made   80
So sweet a bargain.   *Exit*

Enter ALSEMERO

ALSEMERO   O my dear Joanna,
Alas, art thou risen too? I was coming,
My absolute treasure.

BEATRICE   When I missed you,
I could not choose but follow.

ALSEMERO   Th'art all sweetness!
The fire is not so dangerous.

BEATRICE   Think you so, sir?   85

ALSEMERO
I prithee, tremble not. Believe me, 'tis not.

Enter VERMANDERO, JASPERINO.

VERMANDERO
O bless my house and me!

ALSEMERO   My lord your father.

Enter DEFLORES *with a piece*

VERMANDERO
Knave, whither goes that piece?

DEFLORES
To scour the chimney.   *Exit*

VERMANDERO
Oh, well said, well said!   90
That fellow's good on all occasions.

80 *reward* i.e. death
89 *To . . . chimney* Metrically amphibious.

BEATRICE

A wondrous necessary man, my lord.

VERMANDERO

He hath a ready wit, he's worth 'em all, sir.

Dog at a house on fire – I ha' seen him singed ere now.

The piece goes off

Ha! There he goes!

BEATRICE [*Aside*]   'Tis done.

ALSEMERO   Come, sweet, to bed now;   95

Alas, thou wilt get cold.

BEATRICE   Alas, the fear keeps that out.

My heart will find no quiet till I hear

How Diaphanta, my poor woman, fares –

It is her chamber, sir, her lodging chamber.

VERMANDERO

How should the fire come there?   100

BEATRICE

As good a soul as ever lady countenanced,

But in her chamber negligent and heavy.

She 'scaped a mine twice.

VERMANDERO   Twice?

BEATRICE   Strangely twice, sir.

VERMANDERO

Those sleepy sluts are dangerous in a house,

And they be ne'er so good.

Enter DEFLORES [*with the body of* DIAPHANTA]

DEFLORES   O poor virginity,   105

Thou hast paid dearly for't!

---

94 *Dog at* i.e. he's a dog at – expert in dealing with (*OED* n. 17i)
  on ed. (of Q)
  s.d. ed. (*after* goes Q)
101 *countenanced* favoured, gave patronage to (*OED* v. 5)
102 *heavy* stupid; clumsy, sluggish (*OED* a. 18; 19)
103 *mine* undermining stratagem, blowing up (*OED* n. 3). Beatrice claims that Diaphanta's carelessness has twice come close to involving her in a fatal accident.
105 *And* Even, if
  s.d. *with ... DIAPHANTA* ed. (*not in* Q). Although some editors have disputed this emendation, it is difficult to know what else 'that' and 'thing' (ll. 106–7) can refer to.
105–6 *poor ... for't* you have paid a high price for preserving your wretched and unremunerative virginity

VERMANDERO   Bless us! What's that?

DEFLORES

A thing you all knew once – Diaphanta's burnt.

BEATRICE

My woman, oh my woman!

DEFLORES   Now the flames

Are greedy of her – burnt, burnt, burnt to death, sir!

BEATRICE

O my presaging soul!

ALSEMERO   Not a tear more,   110

I charge you by the last embrace I gave you

In bed before this raised us.

BEATRICE   Now you tie me:

Were it my sister now she gets no more.

Enter SERVANT

VERMANDERO

How now?

SERVANT

All danger's past; you may now take your rests, my lords, the fire   115

is thoroughly quenched. Ah, poor gentlewoman, how soon was

she stifled!

BEATRICE

Deflores, what is left of her inter,

And we as mourners all will follow her;

I will entreat that honour to my servant,   120

Ev'n of my lord himself.

ALSEMERO   Command it, sweetness.

BEATRICE

Which of you spied the fire first?

DEFLORES   'Twas I, madam.

BEATRICE

And took such pains in't too? A double goodness!

'Twere well he were rewarded.

VERMANDERO   He shall be –

Deflores, call upon me.

113 *no more* i.e. tears
s.d. ed. (*after* How now? Q)

504

ALSEMERO   And upon me, sir.   125

                                          Exeunt

DEFLORES
   Rewarded? Precious! Here's a trick beyond me!
   I see in all bouts both of sport and wit,
   Always a woman strives for the last hit.   *Exit*

[ACT V. SCENE ii.]

Enter TOMAZO

TOMAZO
   I cannot taste the benefits of life
   With the same relish I was wont to do.
   Man I grow weary of, and hold his fellowship
   A treacherous bloody friendship; and because
   I am ignorant in whom my wrath should settle,   5
   I must think all men villains, and the next
   I meet, whoe'er he be, the murderer
   Of my most worthy brother – ha! What's he?

Enter DEFLORES, *passes over the stage*

   Oh, the fellow that some call honest Deflores!
   But methinks honesty was hard bestead   10
   To come there for a lodging, as if a queen
   Should make her palace of a pest-house.
   I find a contrariety in nature
   Betwixt that face and me: the least occasion

---

126 *Precious* Abbreviation of 'By God's precious body', but a relatively mild oath in the
   abbreviated form. In the context of 'rewarded' a quibble on the pecuniary sense is
   unavoidable.
127 *sport* (1) fencing; (2) fornication (Williams, *Glossary*, p. 285)
128 *hit* (1) strike in fencing; (2) act of coition (Williams, *Glossary*, p. 158)
V.ii Author: Middleton
  10 *hard bestead* hard put to it (*OED* p. ppl. 5)
  12 *pest-house* plague hospital

Would give me game upon him; yet he's so foul   15
One would scarce touch him with a sword he loved
And made account of; so most deadly venomous,
He would go near to poison any weapon
That should draw blood on him – one must resolve
Never to use that sword again in fight,   20
In way of honest manhood, that strikes him;
Some river must devour it, 'twere not fit
That any man should find it. – What again?

Enter DEFLORES

He walks a-purpose by, sure to choke me up,
To infect my blood.
DEFLORES   My worthy noble lord!   25
TOMAZO
Dost offer to come near and breathe upon me?

                                        [*Strikes him*]

DEFLORES
A blow!   [*Draws his sword*]
TOMAZO   Yea, are you so prepared?   [*Draws*]
I'll rather like a soldier die by th'sword
Than like a politician by thy poison.   [*Advances on him*]
DEFLORES
Hold, my lord, as you are honourable.   30
TOMAZO
All slaves that kill by poison are still cowards!
DEFLORES [*Aside*]
I cannot strike: I see his brother's wounds
Fresh bleeding in his eye, as in a crystal.
[*Aloud*] I will not question this, I know you're noble:

---

15 *give me game* Meaning unclear; Schelling's suggestion, 'cause me to fight with him', has been favoured by most editors, but the passage may be corrupt.
16 *him* ed. (*not in* Q)
   he 'i.e. one' (Daalder)
22 *devour it* ed. (devour't Q)
29 *politician* crafty schemer, practiser of machiavellian 'policy' (*OED* n. 1)
31 *still* always
33 *Fresh bleeding* Probably alluding, as Bawcutt suggests, to the belief that a corpse would bleed again in its murderer's presence.
   crystal piece of rock-crystal used by seers in magical art (*OED* n. 4)

I take my injury with thanks given, sir,   35
Like a wise lawyer, and as a favour
Will wear it for the worthy hand that gave it.
[*Aside*] Why this from him, that yesterday appeared
So strangely loving to me?
Oh, but instinct is of a subtler strain;   40
Guilt must not walk so near his lodge again –
He came near me now!   *Exit*

TOMAZO

All league with mankind I renounce forever,
Till I find this murderer. Not so much
As common courtesy, but I'll lock up: 45
For in the state of ignorance I live in,
A brother may salute his brother's murderer,
And wish good speed to th'villain in a greeting.

                    Enter VERMANDERO, ALIBIUS and ISABELLA

VERMANDERO

Noble Piracquo!
TOMAZO   Pray keep on your way, sir;
I've nothing to say to you.
VERMANDERO   Comforts bless you, sir.   50
TOMAZO

I have forsworn compliment; in troth I have, sir.
As you are merely man, I have not left
A good wish for you, nor any here.
VERMANDERO

Unless you be so far in love with grief
You will not part from't upon any terms,   55
We bring that news will make a welcome for us.

35–7 *I . . . gave it* Deflores presumably means that a prudent lawyer will pretend to take a
    humiliating blow as a token of honour rather than expose himself to the physical and
    legal dangers of a duel.
42 *came near* touched me to the quick, affected me deeply (*OED near* adv. 12b, 16b);
    'almost found me out' (Bawcutt 1998)
45 *lock up* suppress
48 *speed* luck, success
51 *compliment* courtesies of speech
55 *You will* That you will
56 *news will* news that will

TOMAZO
What news can that be?

VERMANDERO   Throw no scornful smile
Upon the zeal I bring you; 'tis worth more, sir.
Two of the chiefest men I kept about me,
I hide not from the law, or your just vengeance.

TOMAZO   Ha!   60

VERMANDERO
To give your peace more ample satisfaction,
Thank these discoverers.

TOMAZO   If you bring that calm,
Name but the manner I shall ask forgiveness in
For that contemptuous smile upon you;
I'll perfect it with reverence that belongs   65
Unto a sacred altar.   [*Kneels*]

VERMANDERO   Good sir, rise!
Why now you overdo as much o' this hand,
As you fell short o' t'other. Speak, Alibius.

ALIBIUS
'Twas my wife's fortune – as she is most lucky
At a discovery – to find out lately   70
Within our hospital of fools and madmen,
Two counterfeits slipped into these disguises:
Their names, Franciscus and Antonio.

VERMANDERO
Both mine, sir, and I ask no favour for 'em.

ALIBIUS
Now that which draws suspicion to their habits: 75
The time of their disguisings agrees justly
With the day of the murder.

TOMAZO   O blest revelation!

VERMANDERO
Nay more, nay more, sir – I'll not spare mine own
In way of justice – they both feigned a journey

---

65 *perfect* Accent on first syllable.
72 *these disguises* i.e. of fool and madman – though Daalder suggests that Alibius may be
carrying the actual disguises as evidence.

To Briamata, and so wrought out their leaves,   80
My love was so abused in't.

TOMAZO   Time's too precious
To run in waste now; you have brought a peace
The riches of five kingdoms could not purchase.
Be my most happy conduct, I thirst for 'em:
Like subtle lightning will I wind about 'em,   85
And melt their marrow in 'em.

                                              Exeunt

[ACT V. SCENE iii.]

Enter ALSEMERO *and* JASPERINO

JASPERINO

Your confidence, I'm sure, is now of proof:
The prospect from the garden has showed
Enough for deep suspicion.

ALSEMERO   The black mask
That so continually was worn upon't
Condemns the face for ugly ere't be seen –   5
Her despite to him, and so seeming bottomless.

JASPERINO

Touch it home then: 'tis not a shallow probe

---

80 *Briamata* Treated as three syllables (as the Q spelling *Bramata* may indicate). At
    IV.ii.7–8 the Servant informed Vermandero that one had pretended to travel to Valencia.
    leaves permission to depart
84 *conduct* guide (*OED* n. 3)
85 *Like . . . 'em* A figure for secret murder, based on the belief that lightning could melt
    the marrow without damaging the skin; Bawcutt (1958) compares Chapman's *Bussy
    D'Ambois*: 'A politician must like lightning melt / The very marrow, and not taint the
    skin' (IV.ii.188–9).
V.iii Author: Rowley (and Middleton?)
 1 *of proof* (1) armoured, impenetrable; (2) shown to be founded on truth (*OED* n. 10a–b,
    a. 1a; n. 1a)
2–3 *prospect . . . suspicion* The detail derives from *Gerardo* (sig. H1v); but here 'garden'
    inevitably picks up the resonances of the play's recurrent Fall motif.
 2 *garden* If spoken with a rolled *r* this word becomes (as Daalder suggests) effectively
    trisyllabic, making the line a regular pentameter.
 3 *black mask* i.e. her treacherous show of scorn (*despite*, l. 6) for Deflores. However,
    Bawcutt (1998) suggests that Beatrice, like other ladies of fashion may actually have worn
    a black mask to protect her complexion from the sun.
 7 *Touch . . . home* Probe deeply (*OED* v. 2d)

Can search this ulcer soundly; I fear you'll find it
Full of corruption. – 'Tis fit I leave you:
She meets you opportunely from that walk;   10
She took the back door at his parting with her.   *Exit*

ALSEMERO

Did my fate wait for this unhappy stroke
At my first sight of woman? – She is here.

Enter BEATRICE

BEATRICE

Alsemero!

ALSEMERO   How do you?

BEATRICE   How do I?

Alas, sir! How do you? You look not well.   15

ALSEMERO

You read me well enough, I am not well.

BEATRICE

Not well, sir? Is't in my power to better you?

ALSEMERO

Yes.

BEATRICE Nay, then you're cured again.

ALSEMERO

Pray resolve me one question, lady.

BEATRICE

If I can.   20

ALSEMERO

None can so sure. Are you honest?

BEATRICE

Ha ha ha! That's a broad question, my lord.

---

10 *that walk* Jasperino gestures at one of the stage doors, imagined as being the entrace to
a garden 'walk'.

12–13 *Did . . . woman* Cf. I.i.1–12.

13 *She is* ed. (She's Q)

15 *sir* ed. (*not in* Q). Not only is the Q line one syllable short, but Craik's emendation
ensures that the proper stress will fall on the first *you*.

15–18 *You . . . cured* Returns to the motif of love as a sickness and Alsemero's 'hidden
malady' (I.i.23–5).

20 *If I can* Metrically amphibious.

21 *honest* (1) truthful; (2) honourable, chaste

22 *broad* (1) capable of too broad an interpretation (to be easily answered); (2) indecent
(*OED* a. 10; 6c)

ALSEMERO

But that's not a modest answer, my lady:
Do you laugh? My doubts are strong upon me.

BEATRICE

'Tis innocence that smiles, and no rough brow   25
Can take away the dimple in her cheek.
Say I should strain a tear to fill the vault,
Which would you give the better faith to?

ALSEMERO

'Twere but hypocrisy of a sadder colour,
But the same stuff. Neither your smiles nor tears   30
Shall move or flatter me from my belief:
You are a whore.

BEATRICE   What a horrid sound it hath!
It blasts a beauty to deformity;
Upon what face soever that breath falls,
It strikes it ugly. Oh, you have ruined   35
What you can ne'er repair again!

ALSEMERO

I'll all demolish and seek out truth within you,
If there be any left. Let your sweet tongue
Prevent your heart's rifling – there I'll ransack
And tear out my suspicion.

BEATRICE   You may, sir –   40
'Tis an easy passage. Yet, if you please,
Show me the ground whereon you lost your love:

---

27 *strain . . . vault* weep enough to fill the heavens with water
29 *sadder* (1) more melancholy; (2) more sombre (*OED sad* a. 5; 8)
30 *stuff* cloth
32 *whore . . . hath* Recalling Desdemona's shocked reaction to her husband's use of the same
   word (*Othello*, IV.ii.160).
   horrid full of horror, abominable (*OED* a. 2)
33 *blasts* blights, withers; brings infamy upon (*OED* v. 8 a–b)
37–9 *demolish, rifling, ransack* Alsemero develops the architectural metaphor latent in
   Beatrice's *ruined* and *repair*, picking up the play's recurrent identification of her body
   with the structure of the castle itself – see I.i.68, 216.
38–9 *Let . . . rifling* Let your honeyed tongue [do its best to] stop me plundering the secrets
   of your heart
41 *easy passage* easy way into my heart (carrying on the architectural metaphor); the
   audience are probably meant to hear an unconscious play on *easy* = sexually compliant
   (Williams, *Glossary*, p. 109)
41–2 *passage. Yet . . . / Show* ed. (passage, yet if you please. / Show Q)
42 *ground* grounds

My spotless virtue may but tread on that
Before I perish.

ALSEMERO   Unanswerable –

A ground you cannot stand on, you fall down   45
Beneath all grace and goodness, when you set
Your ticklish heel on't. There was a visor
O'er that cunning face, and that became you;
Now Impudence in triumph rides upon't.
How comes this tender reconcilement else   50
'Twixt you and your despite, your rancorous loathing,
Deflores? He that your eye was sore at sight of,
He's now become your arms' supporter, your
Lips' saint.

BEATRICE   Is there the cause?

ALSEMERO   Worse: your lust's devil,

Your adultery.

BEATRICE   Would any but yourself say that,   55
'Twould turn him to a villain.

ALSEMERO   It was witnessed
By the counsel of your bosom, Diaphanta.

BEATRICE

Is your witness dead then?

ALSEMERO   'Tis to be feared
It was the wages of her knowledge: poor soul,
She lived not long after the discovery.   60

BEATRICE

Then hear a story of not much less horror
Than this your false suspicion is beguiled with:

43 *My . . . that* so that my spotless virtue may only [have the chance to] trample on it
47 *ticklish* (1) unsteady; (2) lecherous (Williams, *Glossary*: 'tickle', p. 308)
48 *became* (1) was becoming; (2) suited you because you were a hypocrite
49 *Impudence* Shamelessness
   Impudence . . . upon't An allegorical construction – Alsemero imagines Impudence riding her chariot in a street pageant like those Triumphs of Fame, Fortune, Love, and Death popularised by Petrarch and widely illustrated in Renaissance art.
51 *your despite* one whom you despised
53 *arms' supporter* (1) the lover who supports your arm; (2) the heraldic figure who supports your coat of arms
53–4 *your . . . saint* 'that adored person to whom your lips pay devotion' (Frost) – i.e. by kissing. Cf. I.i.148.
54 *there* that
55 *Your adultery* i.e. the object of your adulterous passion
56 *It was* ed. ('Twas Q)

To your bed's scandal, I stand up innocence,
Which even the guilt of one black other deed,
Will stand for proof of – your love has made me   65
A cruel murd'ress.

ALSEMERO   Ha!

BEATRICE   A bloody one.
I have kissed poison for't, stroked a serpent:
That thing of hate – worthy in my esteem,
Of no better employment, and him most worthy
To be so employed – I caused to murder   70
That innocent Piracquo, having no
Better means than that worst, to assure
Yourself to me.

ALSEMERO   Oh, the place itself e'er since
Has crying been for vengeance, the temple
Where blood and beauty first unlawfully   75
Fired their devotion, and quenched the right one –
'Twas in my fears at first; 'twill have it now.
Oh, thou art all deformed!

BEATRICE   Forget not, sir,
It for your sake was done: shall greater dangers
Make the less welcome?

ALSEMERO   Oh, thou shouldst have gone   80

---

63 *To . . . scandal* In reply to the scandal attaching to your marriage bed
    I . . . innocence A slightly obscure turn of phrase, though the broad sense is clear: perhaps 'I stand here defiantly [as the very incarnation of] innocence'; Bawcutt interprets 'I stand up (set up, put forward) my innocence', but *OED* does not allow for a transitive use of the verb before the nineteenth century; Williams suggests that 'innocence' may have resulted from a misreading of 'innocent'.
65 *your love* my love for you
67 *stroked a serpent* The identification of Deflores as a *serpent* picks up the Fall motif; but the unconsciously erotic connotations of 'stroked' inevitably bring out the phallic suggestiveness of the metaphor (see Williams, *Glossary: serpent*, p. 273; *snake*, p. 280; *worm*, pp. 344–5).
74–6 *temple . . . devotion* Cf. I.i.1–2.
75 *blood* (1) Beatrice's aristocratic blood; (2) Alsemero's desire
76 *right one* i.e. devotion to God
77 *'Twas . . . first* Cf. I.i.2–4.
    it i.e vengeance
78 *thou . . . deformed* Ironically Alsemero now recognises in Beatrice's the 'deformity' she once abhorred in Deflores (see e.g. II.i.43, 53; II.ii.40, 43).
79–80 *shall . . . welcome* Rather gnomic: Black suggests 'shall the greater dangers I have dared for you make my welcome less?'; but Beatrice seems to mean something more like 'shall greater dangers (i.e. those attendant on the murder) make lesser ones (i.e. those that would follow from my adultery) seem preferable?'

A thousand leagues about to have avoided
This dangerous bridge of blood – here we are lost.

BEATRICE

Remember, I am true unto your bed.

ALSEMERO

The bed itself's a charnel, the sheets shrouds
For murdered carcasses – it must ask pause   85
What I must do in this; meantime you shall
Be my prisoner only, enter my closet.

             Exit BEATRICE. [ALSEMERO *locks her in the closet*]

I'll be your keeper yet. Oh, in what part
Of this sad story shall I first begin?

Enter DEFLORES

               – Ha!
This same fellow has put me in – Deflores!   90

DEFLORES

Noble Alsemero!

ALSEMERO   I can tell you
News, sir: my wife has her commended to you.

DEFLORES

That's news indeed, my lord! I think she would
Commend me to the gallows if she could,
She ever loved me so well, I thank her.   95

ALSEMERO

What's this blood upon your band, Deflores?

DEFLORES

Blood? No, sure, 'twas washed since.

---

82 *bridge of blood* i.e. Piracquo's murder as the action that enabled Alsemero and Beatrice
    to unite in marriage
84 *charnel* place for storing the bones of the dead; cemetery
85–6 *pause/What* pause (to consider) what
88 *keeper* (1) custodian, warder (cf. Alibius and Lollio); (2) one who keeps a mistress
    (*OED* v. 1a; 4 – the latter sense is not recorded before 1676, but would be easily derived
    from *keep* v. 20b)
    yet still
89 s.d. This edition (*after* l. 90 Q).
90 *put me in* intervened in my deliberations (and thereby given me a clue as to what I
    should do) (*OED* v. 45 h); *me* is probably an ethic dative.
96 *band* collar or ruff (*OED* n. 4a); Daalder suggests 'cuff' as a more likely alternative, but
    OED offers no clear example of this (*OED* n. 3)

ALSEMERO
    Since when, man?
DEFLORES   Since t'other day I got a knock
    In a sword-and-dagger school – I think 'tis out.
ALSEMERO
    Yes, 'tis almost out, but 'tis perceived though.   100
    I had forgot my message: this it is,
    What price goes murder?
DEFLORES   How sir?
ALSEMERO   I ask you, sir.
    My wife's behindhand with you, she tells me,
    For a brave bloody blow you gave for her sake
    Upon Piracquo.
DEFLORES   Upon? 'Twas quite through him, sure!   105
    Has she confessed it?
ALSEMERO   As sure as death to both of you,
    And much more than that.
DEFLORES   It could not be much more –
    'Twas but one thing, and that is she's a whore.
ALSEMERO
    It could not choose but follow. O cunning devils,
    How should blind men know you from fair-faced saints?   110
BEATRICE (*Within*)
    He lies! The villain does belie me!
DEFLORES
    Let me go to her, sir.
ALSEMERO   Nay, you shall to her! –
    Peace, crying crocodile, your sounds are heard!
    Take your prey to you – get you into her, sir.
               Exit DEFLORES. [ALSEMERO *locks him in the closet*]

    I'll be your pander now: rehearse again   115
    Your scene of lust, that you may be perfect

---

98 *Since when, man* Metrically amphibious.
103 *behindhand . . . you* in arrears with her debt to you (*OED: behindhand* a. 1)
108 *that is she's* Bruster (that she's Q; Dyce: that she is)
109 *It* ed. (I Q)
113 *crying crocodile* According to the lore deriving from medieval bestiaries, crocodiles wept hypocritical tears before devouring their prey.

When you shall come to act it to the black audience
Where howls and gnashings shall be music to you.
Clip your adul'tress freely – 'tis the pilot
Will guide you to the Mare Mortuum,   120
Where you shall sink to fathoms bottomless.

Enter VERMANDERO, ALIBIUS, ISABELLA, TOMAZO, FRANCISCUS,
and ANTONIO

VERMANDERO

O Alsemero, I have a wonder for you.

ALSEMERO

No sir, 'tis I – I have a wonder for you.

VERMANDERO

I have suspicion near as proof itself
For Piracquo's murder.

ALSEMERO   Sir, I have proof   125
Beyond suspicion, for Piracquo's murder.

VERMANDERO

Beseech you hear me. These two
                              [*Points at* ANTONIO *and* FRANCISCUS]
                              have been disguised
E'er since the deed was done.

ALSEMERO   I have two other
That were more close disguised than your two could be,
E'er since the deed was done.   130

VERMANDERO

You'll hear me! These mine own servants –

---

117 *black audience* i.e. of devils in hell; given that Alsemero is looking forward to their final
   judgement, *audience* may contain the secondary sense 'judicial hearing' (*OED* n. 3).
118 *howls and gnashing* Recalls the 'weeping [or "wailing"] and gnashing of teeth' to which
   the damned are condemned in the gospels (see e.g. Matthew 8:12, 13:42, 22:13, 24:51,
   25:30; Luke 13:23).
119 *Clip* Embrace (*OED* v.¹1a)
   'tis May refer to Beatrice herself (Daalder) or to their embrace.
120 *Mare Mortuum* the Dead Sea – here punningly imagined as a place of the dead, and so as
   an entrance to hell (much as the River Styx marked the final threshold of the classical
   underworld).
121 *bottomless* Because the Dead Sea was rumoured to be bottomless, Rowley associates it
   with the 'bottomless pit' of hell.

ALSEMERO

Hear me! Those nearer than your servants,

That shall acquit them and prove them guiltless.

FRANCISCUS

That may be done with easy truth, sir.

TOMAZO

How is my cause bandied through your delays!   135

'Tis urgent in blood, and calls for haste;

Give me a brother alive or dead –

Alive, a wife with him; if dead, for both

A recompense for murder and adultery.

BEATRICE (*Within*)

Oh, oh, oh!

ALSEMERO   Hark! 'Tis coming to you.   140

DEFLORES (*Within*)

Nay, I'll along for company.

BEATRICE (*Within*)   Oh, oh!

VERMANDERO

What horrid sounds are these?

ALSEMERO   Come forth, you twins

Of mischief.

Enter DEFLORES *bringing in* BEATRICE [*both wounded*]

135 *bandied* tossed aside (*OED* v. 2)
136 *urgent in blood* (1) pressing for prompt action through its effect on my blood (i.e. stirring up my passion); (2) urgent because of the blood that has been spilt. Dilke proposed 'urgent in my blood' – as it happens, a characteristically Middletonian locution (see Bruster, p. 9); however the line can be made to scan satisfactorily if the *r* in *urgent* is rolled.
137 *alive or dead* Bruster (p. 9) notes the occurrence of 'Dead or alive' in Middleton's share of *A Fair Quarrel* (II.i.121) – another indication of his possible involvement in this scene.
139 *adultery* Since betrothal was normally regarded as binding both in law and in the sight of God, Tomazo (who cannot yet know of her affair with Deflores) regards Beatrice's marriage to Alsemero as adulterous.
140–1 *oh* Beatrice's cries '*Within*', together with the offstage howls of the madmen (I.ii.185–91; III.ii.107, 160) and cries of 'fire' (V.i.68, 73) – like Deflores' 'work of secrecy' and Alonzo's concealed corpse – give theatrical reality to the idea of dangerous secrets hidden 'within' Vermandero's castle (I.i.159). Noting that Beatrice's cries echo those of Alonzo at III.i.28, and conjecturing that 'Alonzo is murdered in the same space that is later used to represent Alsemero's closet', Barker and Nicol suggest that 'the parallel . . . may be intended to emphasise the idea that Beatrice's murder is her punishment for Alonzo's death' (p. 12). Playing on the old idea of orgasm as erotic 'death', a number of productions, including the 1993 BBC version, have made Beatrice's shrieks sound disturbingly like groans of ecstasy.
140 *'Tis coming* i.e. the 'recompense' Tomazo has demanded

DEFLORES   Here we are; if you have any more
    To say to us, speak quickly, I shall not
    Give you the hearing else – I am so stout yet,   145
    And so, I think, that broken rib of mankind.

VERMANDERO
    An host of enemies entered my citadel
    Could not amaze like this. Joanna! Beatrice! Joanna!

BEATRICE
    O come not near me, sir, I shall defile you:
    I am that of your blood was taken from you   150
    For your better health; look no more upon't,
    But cast it to the ground regardlessly,
    Let the common sewer take it from distinction.
    Beneath the stars, upon yon meteor   [*Points at* DEFLORES]
    Ever hung my fate, 'mongst things corruptible,   155
    I ne'er could pluck it from him; my loathing
    Was prophet to the rest, but ne'er believed:
    Mine honour fell with him, and now my life.
    Alsemero, I am a stranger to your bed,
    Your bed was cozened on the nuptial night,   160
    For which your false bride died.

---

145 *I . . . yet* I am still strong enough (to listen)

146 *broken rib* Picks up the Fall motif – Eve having been created from Adam's rib (Genesis 2:21–3).

148 *amaze* Cf. III.ii.114; III.iii.71; IV.iii.98.

149 *O . . . me* Note the echo of Isabella at IV.iii.125.

150–1 *I . . . health* Blood-letting was perhaps the most common treatment in the regime of purgation by which early modern medicine sought to regulate the humoral balance of the body. *Blood* here includes both the 'blood' of aristocratic lineage, and the 'blood' of diseased passion; visually, it is linked to the actual blood coming from Beatrice's wound, and so to the bloodshed for which it is recompense.

153 *Let . . . distinction* The familiar analogy between castle and body underlies this figure – cf. the figure of purgation in Helkiah Crooke's anatomical treatise *Mikrocosmographia* (1618): 'the milt and the reins [bowels] do purge and cleanse the princely palace, and thrust, as it were, out of the kitchen, down the sink, all the filth and garbage' (p. 13).

154–5 *Beneath . . . corruptible* In the old concentric Ptolemaic universe, while the stars were thought to be 'fixed' in their spheres, eternal and unchanging, everything in the sublunary sphere was subject to mutability, corruption, and decay.

154 *meteor* By contrast with the 'fixed stars', the violent mobility of meteors and comets, 'shooting stars' that seemed to defy the sublime order of the other heavenly bodies, made them phenomena of ill omen. The figure is particularly appropriate to Deflores as an ambitious servant, conspicuously 'out of his place' (I.i.131).

155 *hung* ed. (hang Q)

160 *cozened* cheated. Daalder suggests a quibble on *cousin* = strumpet (*OED* n. 6); but *OED* gives no example of this usage before 1700.

ALSEMERO   Diaphanta!

DEFLORES

Yes, and the while I coupled with your mate
At barley-break – now we are left in hell.

VERMANDERO

We are all there, it circumscribes us here.

DEFLORES

I loved this woman in spite of her heart;   165
Her love I earned out of Piracquo's murder.

TOMAZO

Ha! My brother's murderer!

DEFLORES   Yes, and her honour's prize
Was my reward – I thank life for nothing
But that pleasure; it was so sweet to me
That I have drunk up all, left none behind   170
For any man to pledge me.

VERMANDERO   Horrid villain!
Keep life in him for further tortures.

DEFLORES

No, I can prevent you: here's my penknife still;
It is but one thread more [*Stabs himself*] – and now 'tis cut.
Make haste, Joanna, by that token to thee –   175
Canst not forget! – so lately put in mind:
I would not go to leave thee far behind.   *Dies*

BEATRICE

Forgive me, Alsemero, all forgive!
'Tis time to die, when 'tis a shame to live.   *Dies*

162–3 *I . . . hell* Cf. III.ii.160.

164 *circumscribes* Cf. Marlowe's *Dr Faustus* (ed. Roma Gill, 2nd ed.) 'Hell hath no limits, nor is circumscribed / In one self place; for where we are is hell' (v.121–2).
us ed. (*not in* Q)

167 *honour's prize* capture of her honour (*OED: prize* n.³ 1); but the familiar sense of 'reward, trophy' is probably also present

171 *pledge me* drink a toast to me (*OED* v. 5). As Chakravorty (p. 161) points out, Deflores' line is adapted from Thomas Deloney's *The Gentle Craft*, where St Hugh, forced by a tyrant to drink the poisoned blood of St Winnifred, toasts the shoemakers: 'I drink to you all . . . but I cannot spare you one drop to pledge me.'

173 *prevent* forestall

175 *token* i.e. the wound he gave himself in the closet as a proof of his willingness to join her in death

VERMANDERO

Oh, my name is entered now in that record, 180
Where till this fatal hour 'twas never read.

ALSEMERO

Let it be blotted out, let your heart lose it,
And it can never look you in the face,
Nor tell a tale behind the back of life
To your dishonour; justice hath so right 185
The guilty hit, that innocence is quit
By proclamation, and may joy again.
[*To* TOMAZO] Sir, you are sensible of what truth hath done:
'Tis the best comfort that your grief can find.

TOMAZO

Sir, I am satisfied: my injuries 190
Lie dead before me, I can exact no more,
Unless my soul were loose, and could o'ertake
Those black fugitives that are fled from thence
To take a second vengeance; but there are wraths
Deeper then mine, 'tis to be feared, about 'em. 195

ALSEMERO

What an opacous body had that moon
That last changed on us! Here's beauty changed
To ugly whoredom; here servant obedience
To a master sin, imperious murder.
I, a supposed husband, changed embraces 200
With wantonness – but that was paid before;

---

180 *my name* Both Vermandero's family name and his personal honour are compromised by
    Beatrice's crime.
    that record 'the heavenly record which lists criminal actions' (Frost) – or perhaps some
    imagined roll of dishonour (Daalder). Accent on second syllable of *record*.
182 *it* i.e. Beatrice's name
185 *so right* (1) in accordance with justice or righteousness; (2) with such precision (*OED*
    adv. 12; 5, 14, and cf. a. 4b 'right blow')
186 *quit* acquitted – obsolete past participle of 'quit' = acquit (*OED* v. 2b)
187 *proclamation* manifestation (*OED* n. 4) – i.e. because the guilty have been struck down
    by heavenly justice
188–9 *Sir . . . find* Although, as Daalder points out, these lines could be meant for Verman-
    dero, they are more likely to be addressed to Tomazo, who appears to respond to them; *Sir*
    suggests a change of addressee, and its courteous tone is echoed by Tomazo (l. 190).
188 *sensible* conscious
196 *opacous* darkened, lying in (ominous) shadow (*OED* a. 1)
198–9 *servant . . . murder* Alsemero's language underlines the social subversiveness of
    Deflores' crime, in which murder is compounded by an assault on legitimate rank and
    authority.
201 *wantonness . . . before* i.e. Diaphanta, who has already paid for her offence with her life

[*To* TOMAZO] Your change is come too, from an ignorant wrath
To knowing friendship. Are there any more on's?

ANTONIO

Yes, sir, I was changed too, from a little ass as I was to a great
fool as I am; and had like to ha' been changed to the gallows but   205
that you know my innocence always excuses me.

FRANCISCUS

I was changed from a little wit to be stark mad,
Almost for the same purpose.

ISABELLA [*To* ALIBIUS]   Your change is still behind,
But deserve best your transformation:
You are a jealous coxcomb – keep schools of folly,   210
And teach your scholars how to break your own head.

ALIBIUS

I see all apparent wife, and will change now
Into a better husband, and never keep scholars
That shall be wiser than myself.

ALSEMERO

Sir, you have yet a son's duty living –   215
Please you, accept it; let that your sorrow,
As it goes from your eye, go from your heart:
Man and his sorrow at the grave must part.

EPILOGUE

ALSEMERO

All we can do to comfort one another,
To stay a brother's sorrow for a brother,   220
To dry a child from the kind father's eyes
Is to no purpose, it rather multiplies:

---

206 *innocence* A play on the common use of 'innocent' to mean 'half-wit' or 'imbecile' (*OED* n. 3b)
208 *behind* to come (*OED* adv. 4)
211 *break . . . head* i.e. with cuckold's horns
215 *you . . . living* you can still count on my duty as your living son
220 *stay* appease, allay; comfort (*OED* v.¹ 28; v.²1b)
221 *kind* (1) behaving as a father naturally should; (2) loving (*OED* a. 1c; 6)
222 *multiplies* increases the grief

Your only smiles have power to cause re-live
The dead again, or in their rooms to give
Brother a new brother, father a child –   225
If these appear, all griefs are reconciled.

Exeunt OMNES

FINIS

223 *Your only smiles* Your smiles alone (addressed to the audience)
224 *rooms* place

NOTES ON THE TEXTS

The Roaring Girl
ed. Elizabeth Cook

The following note is largely the work of Andor Gomme, my predecessor in this series as editor of *The Roaring Girl*. I have checked his text against two copies of the first quarto of the play and made some silent corrections. In the few instances where my editorial decisions have involved a substantive variation from Gomme's text I have recorded this in the notes with my initials.

E[lizabeth].C[ook].

The Roaring Girl was published by Thomas Archer in 1611 in the only early edition known; Archer did not enter it in the Stationers' Register.[1] Ten copies of the first quarto are known to have survived and are listed in Bowers's textual edition of the play.[2] The present text was prepared from a photographic reproduction of that in the Dyce Collection at the Victoria and Albert Museum, collated with one of two copies in the British Museum (Ashley 1159) and one in the Bodleian Library (Malone 246[1]). I have also used the text prepared by Professor Bowers, which notes all press-variants within the available copies of the quarto, as well as others noted below.

Most of these variants represent the correction of literals and minor amendments of punctuation which are of no significance. Substantive changes occur only in signature I (1^V and 4^r & ^{V}), i.e. IV.ii.48ff. and 219ff. The second of these involved resetting of type loosened when a forme was unlocked for a correction, but no verbal variants; those which occur in the first have no authority. A summary of the evidence of proof-correction is given in the textual introduction to Bowers's edition, which should be consulted for detailed information on variant-readings and accidentals, few of which are recorded in the notes to the present edition. All the few major cruces in the play are discussed briefly in the notes; the only one worth mentioning here is that which was responsible for the alterations at IV.ii.48 and 53. All copies of Q agree in having two consecutive speeches with the same prefix, the second occurrence of which is as the catchword at the bottom of a page. An attempt was apparently made during printing to correct this anomaly, but abandoned, though not without alterations working their way in.

1. R. C. Bald's view ('The Chronology of Middleton's Plays', *Modern Language Review* 32 (1937), p. 37), that the 'book concerning Mall Cutpurse' entered in the Stationers' Register by Ambrose Garland on 18 February 1612 may be *The Roaring Girl*, is really guesswork.
2. See Fredson Bowers, ed., *The Dramatic Works of Thomas Middleton*, Cambridge, 1953-61; IV vols, III, 9, and W. W. Greg, *A Bibliography of the English Printed Drama to the Restoration*, London, 1939–50, p. 298.

The quarto was evidently printed from a carefully prepared manuscript, which Bowers and Price[3] believe to be Dekker's work, though it contains a number of contractions characteristic of Middleton. The transcription was either a fair copy made for the actors or derived from the prompt book – as might be suggested by the comprehensive but somewhat inconsistently worded and occasionally mis-aligned stage directions. Punctuation is variable and occasionally capricious, though generally – as in most of Middleton – light, with extensive use of commas where we might use heavier stops, which were indeed liberally provided by nineteenth-century editors. I have tried to preserve this lightness which seems appropriate for the racy conversational idiom in which so much of the play is written, while bringing some consistency to such matters as capitalisation and the use of question-marks (commonly omitted from Q, and where present often anticip-ating the end of the sentence). Some order has likewise been brought into com-mon constructions which have, like the spelling, all been modernised, so that we read 'I'm' for 'Ime' or 'I'me', 'I'll' for 'Ile', 'You'd' for 'Youlde' and so on. I have kept 'Y'are' where it appears in the copy-text, for it implies a different pronunciation from 'You're', which in this edition where necessary replaces 'Your'. I have also made some attempt to relineate a few passages in which what seemed to me manifestly verse is printed as prose or, occasionally, vice versa. This is a task which must be approached with great caution, for Middleton's verse in particular is highly irregular, containing many lines of greater or less than normal length. Moreover, he moves easily from verse to a strongly rhythmical prose. and some passages are in a mixture of the two: any attempt at wholesale regularisation of the verse is therefore to be avoided; nevertheless, it is clear that some of the irregularities are the result of compositorial endeavours to save or lose space, and it is misplaced piety to retain these. Asides are frequent, though rarely noted as such in Q: I have identified them where it seemed possible that readers might be misled, and have also supplied a few missing stage directions. There are no act and scene divisions in Q: this edition follows those established by Dyce, except that I agree with Bowers in dividing Act I into two scenes.

Since the first quarto, *The Roaring Girl* has appeared in Dodsley's *Select Collec-tion of Old Plays* (1780), in Sir Walter Scott's *Ancient British Drama* (1810), vol. II, and, edited by J. P. Collier, in the third edition of Dodsley (1825). It was included in vol. II of Dyce's *Works of Thomas Middleton* (1840), the first to establish a canon. Bullen's edition of the *Works* (1885), in which *The Roaring Girl* appears in vol. IV, is based closely on Dyce; and Havelock Ellis's selection in the old Mermaid series (1887: *Roaring Girl* in vol. II) is virtually a reprint of parts of Bullen. A facsimile of one of the British Museum copies was issued by J. S. Farmer for the Tudor Facsimile Texts (1914). The full textual edition of Fredson Bowers appeared in 1958 in vol. III of *The Dramatic Works of Thomas Dekker*. Most recently it was edited by Paul A. Mulholland in 1987 for the Revels Plays.

---

3. George R. Price, 'The Manuscript and Quarto of *The Roaring Girl*, *The Library*, fifth series 11 (1956), 182–3.

A Chaste Maid in Cheapside

ed. Alan Brissenden

The Lord Chamberlain, Sir Henry Herbert, licensed the play for publication on 8 April 1630 and it was printed in quarto in the same year, probably by the brothers Thomas and Richard Cotes. This is the only known early edition; twenty copies are accessible and the present text has been prepared from a collation of the copy in the State Library of South Australia and photographic reproductions of those in the Library of Congress and the Henry E. Huntington, Folger and Harvard University libraries. (The State Library of South Australia lacks sig. K4; the Harvard copy is lacking the K gathering and the lower part of sig. 14). A Xerox print of the Huntington copy was used as the working text.

The few variants which occur in no way affect the meaning, but indicate that corrections were made as the play was going through the press. Pages 50, 51, 54 and 55 (sigs. H1v, H2r, H3v and H4r) are incorrectly numbered 36, 33, 40 and 37 in the Folger and Library of Congress copies, for example, while the Harvard, Huntington and State Library of South Australia copies are paginated correctly, indicating that they were printed later in the run.

Over two centuries elapsed before the play appeared again, edited by Alexander Dyce (*The Works of Thomas Middleton*, vol. iv, London, 1840), A. H. Bullen (*The Works of Thomas Middleton*, vol. v, London, 1885–86), which is virtually a reprint of Dyce's, and Havelock Ellis (*Thomas Middleton*, vol. I, London, 1887) for the earlier Mermaid series, based on a collation of those of Dyce and Bullen. Inconsistent in their modernisation, cavalier in their treatment of the verse, and laborious in their punctuation, these nineteenth-century editions at least made this play, and many others, accessible to the student and the general reader. The 1968 New Mermaid was the first twentieth-century edition; this was followed by others, the most important R. B. Parker's for the Revels series, with a richly informative introduction and wonderfully detailed, if sometimes over-imaginative, notes.

The quarto seems to have been printed from a carefully prepared manuscript; it has few of the contractions and punctuation peculiar to Middleton's own hand[4] and except in one place it does not appear to be very close to the prompt book. The one instance is the long direction for the entry of the lovers' funeral (V.iv). The list of characters, the careful act divisions and the general tidiness of the text argue for the preparation of a scribal copy especially for the printing house. Both Parker and Charles Barber in his Fountainwell Drama Texts edition (Edinburgh, 1969) agree that the copy text for the printer was most likely a scribal copy of Middleton's autograph manuscript which had passed through the censor's hands but not been prepared for the playhouse; Parker also thinks that it was not prepared for the printing house.

Punctuation in the quarto relies much on the comma and on capitalisation. There are relatively few full stops. The effect gained is one of lively conversational speech. While this kind of punctuation works well when the lines are spoken aloud,

4. See Middleton, *A Game at Chesse*, ed. R. C. Bald (Cambridge, 1929), pp. 34, 171–3.

and so argues for a close relation to a dramatic text, it can offer some difficulty when read on the page. I have tried to preserve the original vitality by punctuating lightly, and while the quarto consistently uses a vocative capital (e.g. 'How is't with you Sir?'; V.i.36), I have decapitalised but not inserted a vocative comma except where its absence would impair the sense. Also in the interests of pace I have retained the contractions and elisions which occur throughout the play. Names are normalized and speech prefixes expanded, oaths are regularized without an apostrophe ('Foot', not ' 'Foot') and all lines of verse begin with capitals.

The quarto has no scene divisions but gives Latin headings for the acts, from *Actus Primus* to *Actus Quintus*; these become Act I, Act II and so on. Editorial stage directions and other additions are enclosed in square brackets, *Ex*[*eunt*] indicating that the quarto has *Exit* used inappropriately. While Middleton's characters address the audience on many occasions, to keep the text as unencumbered as possible editorial insertion of *Aside* has been kept to a minimum. The reader or actor can quickly work out to whom a speech or part of a speech is to be directed.

Women Beware Women

ed. William C Carroll

The earliest known text of *Women Beware Women* is the octavo printed for Humphrey Moseley in 1657: 'TWO NEW PLAYES. / VIZ. More DISSEMBLERS / besides WOMEN. / WOMEN beware / WOMEN. / WRITTEN / By *Tho. Middleton, Gent.*' Mulryne lists twenty-one surviving copies of this octavo, and he has collated twenty of them. No significant variants have been reported. The present text is based on the Huntington Library copy; the Folger, Harvard and Yale copies have also been consulted. I have also profited from consultation of the recent Revels (1975), Cambridge (1978) and Penguin (1988) editions of the play, and of course from Roma Gill's edition of the play (1968) for this series.

Moseley's edition presents an exceptionally clean text. It is likely that the manuscript used in printing was either a scribal transcript of the author's manuscript, or (much less likely) in Middleton's own hand, with perhaps a few annotations by a theatrical book-keeper. For this edition, the spelling has been modernised, some contractions expanded and the punctuation considerably lightened. The play is remarkable for its many asides; they have been marked in the text where there is little doubt of their occurrence. The text presents some difficulties in its erratic intermingling of prose and verse spoken by the Ward and by Sordido; this edition follows, with minor exceptions, the display indicated in the octavo. Thus, there are sometimes prose to verse shifts within a single speech. The justifications for retaining such a display are, first, that the Moseley text is otherwise so meticulous; and second, that the awkward intermixing is a specific rhetorical device to help characterise these low characters. Unless there is strong reason otherwise, the octavo has been followed in such matters as contractions (thus O's 'nev'r' rather than 'ne'er').

Additions or emendations to the text are either indicated in the notes, or indicated by square brackets [ ]. Stage directions present a particular problem here, as they are relatively full but not always clear earlier in the text, and virtually absent during the confusing final scene; all supplementary directions are given in square brackets.

The previous modern editions listed above have done substantial and important work in providing accurate annotation of the text, and I have consulted all of them in preparing this annotation; in addition to adding many of my own notes, I have attempted simply to gloss many words which seem to me now somewhat arcane to the general reader, in the hope of making the play as readable as possible.

The Changeling
ed. Michael Neill

There exists only one seventeenth-century edition of *The Changeling* – a quarto printed early in 1653 by Thomas Newcombe for the bookseller, Humphrey Moseley. The printer can be identified from the ornament on Sig. B1; while the publisher is named on the title-page attached to thirteen of the surviving copies. Somewhat mysteriously, however, the imprint on the four remaining copies omits any reference to the publisher or his shop. Various explanations have been offered for this omission, but the reason for it remains obscure: Joost Daalder, arguing that Puritan hostility to the theatres in the interregnum meant that 'even the printing of a new play could get one into trouble', speculates that Moseley commissioned a new title-page in order to avoid such unwelcome attention. There is, however, little evidence to support this hypothesis, and Douglas Bruster's more mundane conjecture that Moseley's address was deleted simply in order to facilitate sale by other booksellers seems more plausible. Indeed the fact that enough sheets survived from the original print-run to enable Moseley's widow to republish his edition with a fresh title-page in 1668 suggests that, having seriously overestimated his likely sales, Moseley might have had good reason to widen his market by wholesaling some copies to other retailers.

An editor's task is necessarily simplified by the fact Moseley's edition constitutes the only surviving early text of Middleton and Rowley's play; but it is also complicated by the fact that this edition appeared over thirty years after the play was first performed, more than a quarter of a century after the deaths of the authors. This means that the play appeared without the benefit of any input from the dramatists themselves or from the company which had once owned it. We also have no means of knowing the source and nature of the manuscript that Moseley supplied to Newcomb, though it probably came from reliable sources. A bookseller and publisher with marked royalist connections, Moseley did much to satisfy the continuing interest in drama during the interregnum years, from the outbreak of Civil War in 1642 to the Restoration of Charles II in 1660, when the

London theatres were closed. He produced work by Shakespeare, Webster and Fletcher, among others; and, in the same year in which he published *The Changeling*, secured his claims over fourteen other plays (including three more by Middleton) with a block entry on the Stationers' Register. In all likelihood Moseley acquired his rights to *The Changeling* – along with those for *The Spanish Gypsy* (1623), published later in the same year – from the financially embarrassed theatrical entrepreneur, William Beeston, the former owner of the Cockpit, where these two plays had originally been staged under the management of his father, Christopher. The Lord Chamberlain had confirmed both plays as William's 'propriety' in 1639. However, the fact that *The Spanish Gypsy*, which scholars nowadays credit principally to Dekker and Ford, appeared over the names of Middleton and Rowley alone, suggests that Moseley's connection with Beeston, who must surely have known the real authors, was not a close one.

Moseley's copy, perhaps acquired from Beeston along with the publication rights, does not appear to have been an authorial manuscript, since scholars are agreed that Q lacks many of the authorial spellings and linguistic habits peculiar to its two dramatists – though Rowley's fondness for ' 'um' as an abbreviation for 'them', for example, is as marked in the scenes usually attributed to him as ' 'em' in the scenes given to Middleton. But, if the manuscript supplied to Newcomb was non-authorial, what was its origin? In his 1958 Revels edition, N. W. Bawcutt, adducing the clear marking of entries and exits, as well as one or two theatrical-sounding stage directions, conjectured that 'the source of the printed text was probably a transcript from a theatrical prompt-copy' (Revels, p. xvi). While the term 'prompt-copy' may itself be misleading – as recent theatre historians, aware of the physical difficulties of successful prompting in early modern playhouses have argued – it is clear that acting companies will have needed a working copy of the play-text in addition to the precious 'allowed copy' submitted for the approval of the Master of the Revels, and the individual 'parts' distributed to the actors. However, in the case of *The Changeling*, the evidence for the text's theatrical origins is rather slender – and Bawcutt himself seems to have abandoned his claim by the time he produced his facsimile edition fifteen years later. As Bruster and others have noted, Q's entrances are often marked late[5] – after a speaker has registered the entrant's presence on the stage – whereas in manuscripts marked up for playhouse use it was usual to mark an entrance early, so that the book-keeper could alert the actor in good time. Furthermore, Q's stage directions are generally sparser than we might expect from a theatrical manuscript; and, while some – notably the unique '*In the act–time* DEFLORES *hides a naked rapier*' at the beginning of Act III – must have been composed by someone with the material conditions of performance in a private theatre clearly in mind, there is no reason why that should not have been Middleton, whose experience in writing for these houses stretched back nearly twenty years to his work with the boy companies at the beginning of the century.

5. See Douglas Bruster, ed. *The Changeling*, in *Companion*, p. 1095; Bawcutt (1973), p. 2.

Another commonly recognised clue to a text's playhouse origins is evidence of cutting; and some scholars have been attracted by the possibility, first advanced by E. H. C. Oliphant, that two scenes may have been excised from the sub-plot in the text that has come down to us: on the one hand the characters of Antonio and Franciscus, the pretended fool and madman, are not only allowed to remain unnamed in the spoken text, but are introduced in a somewhat abrupt fashion, without any attempt to prepare the audience for their appearance in the madhouse; on the other hand, the wild dance of fools and madmen, meant to be performed by Alibius' inmates as part of Beatrice's wedding revels, never eventuates – even though it has promised to be the spectacular climax of the sub-plot.[6] If the dramatists were originally careful to fill these apparent gaps, then any excision must presumably have occurred as a result of theatrical cutting. However, even those, like Roger Holdsworth, who are attracted by Oliphant's thesis, admit that such carelessness about motivation and the naming of characters is relatively common in the period: Vermandero himself – as Bruster (p. 1095) points out – remains anonymous for more than half the play, until Alibius names him in III.iii. As far as the 'madmen's morris' is concerned, it has, of course, been commissioned to wind up the wedding festivities on 'the third night from the first' (III.ii.249): this must be the night signalled by the arrival of Alibius and Isabella at the castle in the final scene (V.iii.121) just before the public indictment of Beatrice and Deflores; so the time–scheme actually allows no opportunity for it to be performed, except via the rehearsal at the end of Act IV – though it is conceivable, I think, that this antimasque may have been repeated after the epilogue in imitation of those 'jigs' that traditionally rounded off performances in the outdoor theatres.

Moseley's text seems to have been printed with reasonable care by the standards of the time – though, in accordance with usual printing-house practice, it was proofed only in the course of printing, and then in a somewhat unsystematic way, with corrections made only to the outer formes of the B, D and G gatherings. Most of these involve nothing more than obvious misprints – although there are two instances in which the proof-reader seems to have borne in mind the demands of sense and/or metre (II.i.149; II.ii.131). Apart from a number of surviving misprints and occasional missing words, the main deficiencies of the Q text are in its treatment of the verse: there are numerous examples of mislineation (especially where two half-lines, or a line and a half have been crammed into a single line), verse is several times set as prose, and in a few instances prose is mistakenly set as verse. Such errors are particularly common in the scenes attributed to Middleton and seem, more often than not, to derive from the dramatist's manuscript habits, though sometimes the compositor may have been compelled to save space as a result of poor casting off. Where other kinds of lineation problem arise it is often difficult to be sure whether they result from faulty transcription by a scribe or compositor, or simply from the author's habits

---

6. This omission seemed serious to Tony Richardson, who chose to stage the masque in his 1961 Royal Court production, making it the occasion for exposing the imposture of Antonio and Franciscus.

of composition. Rowley's madhouse scenes present particular difficulties, since they frequently involve dialogue in which some characters speak in verse while their interlocutors reply in prose: theatrical convention dictated that verse was normally used to mark the speech of characters of higher rank, while prose was assigned to their inferiors; but prose could also be used (as in *Hamlet,* for example) to signal the falling away from decorum entailed by madness. In *The Changeling* the result is that Alibius and Isabella speak almost entirely in verse; their servant Lollio is predictably a prose speaker; the pretended fool, Antonio, employs prose when in disguise, but reverts to verse when speaking *in propria persona*; while the pretended madman, Franciscus, mixes prose and verse in his imposture, but, like his rival, is naturally a speaker of verse. In the mixed dialogue that results, however, it is sometimes hard to be sure whether some of Isabella's lines, for example, are to be treated as incomplete verse or as prose, or whether (influenced by her interlocutors) she sometimes sinks to prose (see e.g. III.ii.42–3) – as she seems to do when herself feigning madness (see e.g. IV.iii.94–6); by the same token it is equally hard to know whether the iambic beat apparent in some of Lollio's lines is purely accidental, or whether, influenced by Isabella or Alibius, he occasionally rises to verse (see e.g. I.ii.17, 34). In addition to this, Rowley (who did not have a particularly subtle ear for the music of iambic verse) sometimes produces lines of such disconcerting metrical awkwardness that, if they are verse at all, can only be accounted for as crude syllables (see e.g. I.ii.83–7). Middleton, by contrast, was a genuinely innovative dramatic poet, who treats the verse form with considerable freedom, not only making extensive use of feminine endings and hexameters, but sometimes composing lines that might be a syllable or two short (e.g. III.iii.137), or include one or more extra-metrical syllables (e.g. III.iii.139), without ever losing the rhythmic pulse. To complicate matters further, the Q text is marked by a fondness for contractions that sometimes overrides the requirements of metre – thus, for example, Q prints ' 'tis' at I.i.21 where the metre appears to require 'it is', just as it prints 'that's' for 'that is' at I.i.78,' 'bout' for 'about' at II.ii.27, and ' 'Twas' for 'It was' at V.iii.56: it is possible that such seeming aberrations reflect the habits of whoever was responsible for the manuscript copy, but they may simply reveal the strength of the dramatists' shared predilection for idiomatic speech. The combined effect of all these metrical uncertainties was to license nineteenth-century editors like Dilke and Dyce to iron out perceived irregularities in the verse; a modern editor, however, must proceed more circumspectly, listening with particular care for Middleton's characteristically spiky rhythms, before deciding whether or not to emend the text.